GW01368746

The Performance of Christian and Pagan Storyworlds

MEDIEVAL IDENTITIES: SOCIO-CULTURAL SPACES

*Editorial Board under the auspices of the
Centre for Medieval Studies, University of Hull*

Adrian P. Tudor, *University of Hull*
Anu Mänd, *Tallinna Ülikool (Tallinn University)*
Lesley A. Coote, *University of Hull*
Ildar H. Garipzanov, *Universitetet i Oslo*
Sophie Cassagnes-Brouquet, *Université de Toulouse-II-Le Mirail*
Catherine Emerson, *National University of Ireland, Galway*

VOLUME 3

The Performance of Christian and Pagan Storyworlds

Non-Canonical Chapters of the History of Nordic Medieval Literature

Edited by

Lars Boje Mortensen and
Tuomas M. S. Lehtonen,
with Alexandra Bergholm

BREPOLS

British Library Cataloguing in Publication Data

The performance of Christian and pagan storyworlds : non-canonical chapters of the history of Nordic medieval literature. -- (Medieval identities ; 3)
 1. Scandinavian literature--History and criticism.
 2. Oral tradition--Scandinavia--History--To 1500.
 3. Rhetoric, Medieval--Scandinavia.
 4. Latin literature, Medieval and modern--Scandinavia--History and criticism.
 5. Christianity and literature--Scandinavia--History--To 1500.
 6. Literature and society--Scandinavia--History--To 1500.
 7. Literature and folklore--Scandinavia--History--To 1500.
 8. Folklore--Performance--Scandinavia--History--To 1500.
I. Series
II. Mortensen, Lars Boje editor of compilation.
III. Lehtonen, Tuomas M. S. editor of compilation.
IV. Bergholm, Alexandra editor of compilation.
839.5'09-dc23

ISBN-13: 9782503542362

© 2013, Brepols Publishers n.v., Turnhout, Belgium

All rights reserved. No part of this publication may be reproduced, stored in a retrieval system, or transmitted, in any form or by any means, electronic, mechanical, photocopying, recording, or otherwise, without the prior permission of the publisher.

D/2013/0095/106
ISBN: 978-2-503-54236-2
e-ISBN: 978-2-503-54261-4
Printed in the E.U. on acid-free paper

Contents

Illustrations	vii
Acknowledgements	ix
Introduction: What Is Nordic Medieval Literature? LARS BOJE MORTENSEN and TUOMAS M. S. LEHTONEN	1

Part I. The Impact of Latin Song, Book, and Service

The Word of God and the Stories of Saints: Medieval Liturgy and its Reception in Norway ÅSLAUG OMMUNDSEN	45
The Arrival and Development of Latin Literacy on the Edge of Europe: The Case of Medieval Finland TUOMAS HEIKKILÄ	67
Spoken, Written, and Performed in Latin and Vernacular Cultures from the Middle Ages to the Early Seventeenth Century: *Ramus virens oliuarum* TUOMAS M. S. LEHTONEN	109

Part II. Christian Discourse Framing Pagan Stories

Zoroaster, Saturn, and Óðinn: The Loss of Language and the Rise of Idolatry JONAS WELLENDORF	143
Edda and 'Oral Christianity': Apocryphal Leaves of the Early Medieval Storyworld of the North HENRIK JANSON	171

Ethnocultural Knowledge and Mythical Models: The Making of
St Olaf, the God of Thunder, and St Elijah during the First Centuries
of the Christian Era in the Scandinavian and Baltic Regions
    LAURI HARVILAHTI   199

Part III. Educating and Disciplining the Community

The Performative Texts of the Stave Church Homily
    AIDAN CONTI   223

The Performative Non-Canonicity of the Canonical:
Íslendingasǫgur and their Traditional Referentiality
    SLAVICA RANKOVIĆ   247

Provider of Prosperity: The Image of St Anne
in Finnish and Karelian Folklore
    IRMA-RIITTA JÄRVINEN   273

(Re)Performing the Past: Crusading, History Writing,
and Rituals in the Chronicle of Henry of Livonia
    LINDA KALJUNDI   295

Part IV. Oral Poetics through the Social Spectrum

Two Medieval Ballads on Betrayal and Deception:
Interpreting the Story of the First Christian Bishop in Finland
through the Story of Judas Iscariot
    PERTTI ANTTONEN   341

Female Mourning Songs and Other Lost Oral Poetry
in Pre-Christian Nordic Culture
    ELSE MUNDAL   367

'She was fulfilled, she was filled by it...':
A Karelian Popular Song of St Mary and the Conception of Christ
    SENNI TIMONEN   389

Index   433

Illustrations

Figures

Figure 1, p. 49. One leaf from a breviary written in England, containing a part of Nicholas's legend. Oslo, Riksarkivet, MS Lat. fragm. 1023, fol. 1^r. Early twelfth century.

Figure 2, p. 54. A fragment from a liturgical manuscript containing parts of Nicholas's highly popular sequence *Congaudentes exultemus*. Oslo, Riksarkivet, Lat. fragm. 471, fol. 1^r. Around or just before 1200.

Figure 3, p. 58. Part of the *Passio Olavi* divided into liturgical lessons, in one 'leaf' from a lectionary written in Norway. Oslo, Riksarkivet. *c.* 1200.

Figure 4, p. 61. Fragment containing St Olaf's sequence *Lux illuxit*. Oslo, Riksarkivet, Lat. fragm. 932, fragm. 932, fol. 1^v. Thirteenth century.

Figure 5, p. 75. An English missal. Helsinki, Kansalliskirjasto, F.m. I.21, fol. 1^r. Eleventh century.

Figure 6, p. 92. Two graduals written in the Bridgettine monastery of Naantali. Helsinki, Kansalliskirjasto, F.m. II.118, fol. 1^v, and Helsinki, Kansalliskirjasto, F.m. II.120, fol. 1^v. Fifteenth century.

Figure 7, p. 96. Charter in Swedish of the easternmost town of the Swedish realm, Viborg, which received its town rights in 1403. Helsinki, Kansallisarkisto, Pergamentti-kokoelma 6. 1403.

Figure 8, p. 99. *Habent sua fata libelli*: A copy of Vincent of Beauvais's *Speculum historiale*, originating from the cathedral library of Troyes. Helsinki, Kansalliskirjasto, MS F.m. V.Var.26, fol. 16^r. Late thirteenth century.

Figure 9, p. 182. The Gosforth stone.

Figure 10, p. 182. The Altuna stone.

Figure 11, p. 225. Drawing of Urnes stave church in Sogn.

Figure 12, p. 276. Wooden sculpture of St Anne with Mary in the Church of Urjala, Finland. Helsinki, Suomen kansallismuseo. Fifteenth century.

Figure 13, p. 277. Birchwood sculpture, carved in Finland, representing St Anne, Mary, and Jesus. Lokalahti Church, Finland. *c.* 1500.

Figure 14, p. 401. Icon representing the Annunciation. Originally from Valamo Monastery, Ladoga Karelia, now held in Kuopio, Suomen Ortodoksinen Kirkkomuseo. Seventeenth century.

Graphs

Graph 1, p. 82. The number of extant localized and dated remains of manuscripts in the *fragmenta membranea* collection of the National Library of Finland by date.

Graph 2, p. 90. The relative proportions (%) of the manuscripts localized to certain areas of the total number of datable and localizable fragments of codices from the period in question.

Graph 3, p. 95. The number and language of pre-1400 charters written in Finland.

Maps

Map 1, p. 4. Scandinavia and the Baltic Sea Region. Kingdoms and most important dioceses, *c.* 1300–1600.

Map 2, p. 397. Map of historical provinces comprising Orthodox Karelia and Ingria.

Acknowledgements

The life of a scholar would be solitary, poor, nasty, brutish, and short without the help of generous individuals and institutions. Indeed without a supportive scholarly community the whole pursuit of knowledge would be impossible and pointless. This book is a part of the research done within the framework of the Nordic Centre of Medieval Studies (NCMS, 2005–10), a Nordic centre of excellence, funded by the Joint Committee for Nordic Research Councils for the Humanities and the Social Sciences (NOS-HS), managed by the Centre of Medieval Studies (CMS) at the University of Bergen, and comprising four nodes at the universities of Bergen, Gothenburg, and Southern Denmark in Odense, and the Finnish Literature Society in Helsinki. We are very grateful to NOS-HS and to the entire NCMS for the financial, institutional, and intellectual support that has created exceptional and excellent conditions for our work. Additionally, in the last phase the project 'Oral and Literary Culture in the Medieval and Early Modern Baltic Sea Region: Cultural Transfer, Linguistic Registers, and Communicative Networks' funded by the Academy of Finland (no. 137906) gave its support to finalize our work.

We are deeply indebted to the director of the NCMS, Professor Sverre Bagge at the CMS, University of Bergen, and to the other team leaders: Professor Torstein Jørgensen, University of Bergen; Associate Professor Kurt Villads Jensen, University of Southern Denmark, Odense; and Professor Thomas Lindkvist, University of Gothenburg. For fruitful discussions and exchange of ideas we would also like to thank Professor Veikko Anttonen, University of Turku, and Associate Professor Leif Søndergaard, University of Southern Denmark in Odense. Furthermore we have received thoughtful comments by the members of the scientific advisory board of the NCMS: Professor Marianna Kalinke, University of Illinois; Professor Patrick J. Geary, UCLA; and Professor Hans-Werner Goetz, University of Hamburg. Intellectual endeavour is never feasible without an efficient administration. We owe our gratitude for smooth operations to the head of administration Kirsten Moen and Professor Leidulf Melve at the CMS, University of Bergen, and for everlasting good humour and efficiency to project manager Ilona Pikkanen at the Finnish Literature Society, Helsinki. It has been a long journey we made together. As editors we are of course indebted to our engaged members of the 'Culture Team' of NCMS who have written this book and to our diligent co-editor Alexandra Bergholm who contributed significantly in the later phase, and much beyond the call of duty. Without such a lively and challenging *compagnie de route* we would never had experienced such intellectual pleasures nor achieved much.

Our research team has consisted of scholars located in various academic institutions throughout the Nordic countries. The work would not have been possible without the hospitality of several institutions where we have had our gatherings. It is a pleasure to thank the Institutum Romanum Finlandiae at Villa Lante in Rome, the Institut finlandais in Paris, the Instituto Iberoamericano de Finlandia in Madrid, as well as the Universities of Helsinki, Tartu, and Jyväskylä for welcoming us and allowing us to benefit from their premises, services, and inspiring atmosphere. Our warmest thanks also go to Tine Dam Bendtsen who compiled the index at very short notice.

Finally we are grateful that our book was accepted by Brepols to be included in their prestigious series MISCS. We owe our thanks to the anonymous reviewers and the editorial board for their comments and corrections. We would especially like to thank Dr Simon Forde and editorial assistant Els Schröder for their patient guidance.

The editors, December 2011

Introduction: What Is Nordic Medieval Literature?

Lars Boje Mortensen and Tuomas M. S. Lehtonen

Scope

The present collection offers a number of inroads into Nordic medieval literature. You will not, however, find chapters on skaldic poetry, Saxo Grammaticus, kings' sagas, *The King's Mirror*, the *Visions* of Birgitta, Swedish and Danish *Rhyme Chronicles*, the classical Scandinavian ballad, or the Kalevalaic heroic epic; with two exceptions (the *Edda* and the genre of the sagas of Icelanders) the acknowledged masterpieces of Nordic medieval literature have been passed over. This is partly due to excellent treatment elsewhere, but also expressive of our conviction that Nordic medieval literary history has been somewhat distorted by its placement on strong national and disciplinary trajectories and that important literary fields have thus fallen out of focus.

What we offer here are only some alternative glimpses of Nordic literary life, not a series of chapters that make up a new master narrative. We will point to groups of texts that are overlooked in the traditional narrative and capitalize on the performative turn in cultural studies.[1] A special focus will be on the smaller forms of literature and those with a connection to rituals and ritualized

---

[1] For instance, Foley, *Traditional Oral Epic*; Green, *Medieval Listening and Reading*; Holsinger, 'Analytical Survey'; Burke, *What Is Cultural History?*; Stacey, *Dark Speech*.

Lars Boje Mortensen, University of Southern Denmark and University of Bergen, Professor, labo@hist.sdu.dk

Tuomas M. S. Lehtonen, Finnish Literature Society, Secretary General, Adjunct Professor, tuomas.lehtonen@finlit.fi

speech.² Although small, many of them, like songs and sermons, were in fact crucial in shaping local and new Christian identities. We also want to focus on the reproductive aspect of literature and not solely on those texts that a later age has deemed original compositions, because we are convinced that marked speech in a ritual context was at the root of many literary forms which are barely visible today. As indicated in the volume title, the emergence and maintenance of storyworlds — crucial for identities at all levels — owes everything to (more or less formalized) performances.³ The studies collected here do not in any way offer a survey of Nordic storyworlds — that is a much larger task. But they all explore different aspects of verbal performances as a primary vehicle for storyworlds. On a general level the present book also argues for the primacy of the Christian storyworld(s) over the pagan (hence the order in the title):⁴ the pagan concepts, figures, and stories we encounter in these studies are without exception embedded in a Christian discourse;⁵ to understand how that discourse emerged, spread, was maintained, and developed is therefore a key concern here.

The emphasis lies on three languages: Latin, Old Norse, and Finnish.⁶ The presence of Finnish may come as a surprise for some, but since the eastern Baltic also became part of Latin Europe, and as the Latin culture of Finland (and Estonia) is coming more into focus (cf. Heikkilä and Kaljundi below), the inclusion of Finland seems natural in this context. An extension of the timeframe into the early modern age is also used in some chapters to throw light on medieval phenomena which have mainly or solely been documented later (like the ballad and Kalevalaic epic in some previous surveys).⁷

---

² For an energetic attempt to 're-embody' literature that has suffered all too long from 'disembodied' readings, and for the concept of 'ritualized speech', see Habinek, *The World of Roman Song*.

³ For the concept of 'storyworld' and a brilliant application of it in a historical study, see Wiseman, *The Myths of Rome*; in a medieval context, see Tyler, 'The *Vita Ædwardi*'; Tyler, 'Trojans in Anglo-Saxon England'.

⁴ The concept of 'paganism' was hotly debated and challenged in the preparatory workshops of the contributors. In some fields, like classical studies and large parts of medieval history, it is perceived as a neutral term descriptive of all kinds of pre-Christian practices and beliefs; in other fields, such as comparative religion and anthropology, it is avoided as being pejorative. The editors adhere to the former usage, and although it is unfortunate that the term is not neutral for all, we feel that it directly addresses a long tradition of medieval historical and literary scholarship and that good alternatives are not available.

⁵ Compare Guðrún Nordal, *Tools of Literacy*.

⁶ That medieval Danish and Swedish only appear very occasionally in these studies is not programmatic.

⁷ The implications of this procedure are different, depending on the material, and are

Orally circulated compositions on saints and the Virgin Mary form such an opening from later material (Anttonen, Timonen, Järvinen). The role of Latin liturgy in the development of literary activity in the whole region needs to be much better analysed on the basis of recent fragment research, but here we try to chart some of the material and recent research (Ommundsen, Heikkilä). Other Latin writings (chronicles, songs) attest to the pervasive presence of Latin throughout the period and area (Kaljundi, Lehtonen). The encounters between paganism and Christianity are treated through texts that have rarely, if ever, been discussed in a common Nordic literary context (Harvilahti, Kaljundi). Finally a number of contributions deal with Old Norse literature — either with an overlooked and non-canonical genre (Mundal), with an apocryphal version of the introduction to the *Edda* (Wellendorf), with the performance and circulation of one of the canonical genres (Ranković), or with the significance of the Latin learning behind homiletic and mythological composition in the vernacular (Conti, Janson).

In this way there is a general emphasis on 'lived' literature, performativity, and social and religious identities attached to, or mainly documented through, certain smaller literary forms or specimens. At the same time we want to foreground the widespread use of Latin and the interface between Latin and the vernacular. With these 'non-canonical chapters' we wish to open up new directions for the writing of a possible future history of Nordic medieval literature, in which this undergrowth of texts lying in the borderlands between song, spoken and written, and between Latin and the vernaculars across the entire linguistic spectrum is allowed to play a role.

Another way to reconfigure the vernacular/Latin divide is to use the time-honoured dichotomy between 'great and little tradition', developed in the 1950s by the American anthropologist Robert Redfield. His insistence on the 'little community', primarily as a designation of a dominant form of peasant social life and its similar workings throughout the world, is also highly relevant for medieval societies. The peasant communities were small unities, closed around themselves, but not culturally isolated; they were permeable to the civilizational influences of the greater world, mainly through their contacts with (and dependence on) the militarized and travelling elite and the markets/ towns and, not least, through the parish church. In our context this means that Nordic communities of peasants were engulfed in Latin Christian civilization in the centuries *c.* 1000–1300 by applying bits and pieces of this great tradition to their own little traditions (of which we know next to nothing in most

discussed in each of the relevant studies.

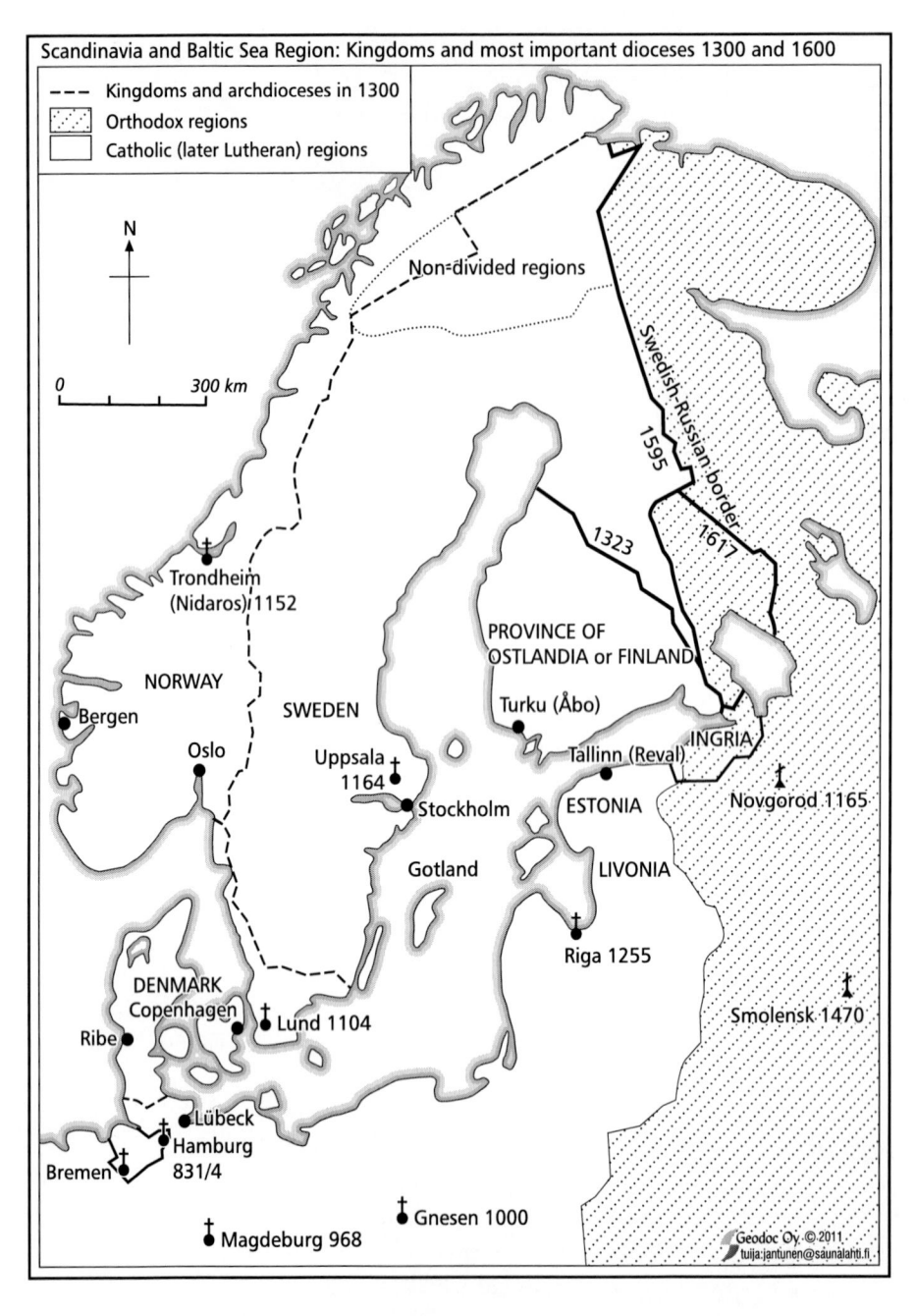

Map 1. Scandinavia and the Baltic Sea Region. Kingdoms and most important dioceses, c. 1300–1600. © Geodoc Oy, tuija.jantunen@saunalahti.fi.

cases). Seen in this way — from the peasants' point of view — the great tradition and the wider world could turn up in Latin liturgy as well as in vernacular preaching, and in heroic stories of chieftains of old who turned to Christian ways (as in the sagas of Icelanders). Almost all the Nordic writing we have from the Middle Ages represents the great tradition, the elite championing new ideals and new storyworlds. But that does not mean that the little traditions did not shape new variants of that storyworld and new oral poetics that could feed back into the great tradition in its local representation — documenting this is simply much more difficult than it was for an anthropologist working with contemporary peasant societies in the middle of the twentieth century.[8]

Space and Speech

Let us first try to define the broader frame within which each of the following chapters maps out a little piece of territory. Is there really any inherent unity in the subject with respect to chronology, geography, and literary languages?

In a recent posthumously published book by Preben Meulengracht Sørensen two reasons are given for a common treatment of 'Nordic medieval literature'.[9] One is medieval linguistic unity — people understood each other from Reykjavik to Ribe, from Bergen to Uppsala, from Lofoten to Lund. However, as Sørensen notes, this did not automatically create a common literary forum — the Icelanders' sagas, for example, are not known to have spread to Denmark or Sweden. Another reason is the history of reception: from the seventeenth century on Old Norse literature was gradually turned into an important part of Nordic identity — compare the Danish term 'oldnordisk' and the Swedish 'fornnordisk'. Sørensen is aware that in his construction, Nordic medieval literature is first and foremost a literature composed and transmitted by Icelanders. The two reasons are certainly valid as such. However, it could be objected that both points count for more when one concentrates the account largely on the golden age of Old Norse literature, that is, before c. 1300, when the linguistic unity was more pronounced, and on the concerns with the pagan past in that literature which became such a powerful attraction for nineteenth-century ideas of a common Nordic (and Germanic) pre-Christian cultural identity.

---

[8] Redfield, *The Little Community*; Redfield, *Peasant Society and Culture*. Especially relevant in this literary connection is Chapter 3 of *Peasant Society and Culture*: 'The Social Organization of Tradition'.

[9] Meulengracht Sørensen, *Kapitler af Nordens litteratur*, pp. 14–15.

Before trying to widen the frame it would be good to heed the caveat mentioned by Meulengracht Sørensen: linguistic unity or mutual intelligibility does not necessarily imply a common literary space of reception and reproduction. This is not a particular flaw of regional histories of literature, as it can be levelled with equal force against the premodern chapters of any mainstream national history of literature. Notker Labeo's translations of Latin classics into German around 1000 and the Anglo-Saxon epic *Beowulf* (tenth century) are fascinating specimens of real literary life and towering works in modern national narratives but were virtually unread in the Middle Ages. Even popular authors from the period just before or around 1200, such as Chrétien de Troyes and Wolfram von Eschenbach, were mainly known in certain trend-setting courts and through specific aristocratic and learned networks — popular, but certainly not performed and read throughout the entire French or German realm (in either political or linguistic terms). It is only through modern educational mobilization and romantic ideas about language and people that medieval works of literature can function as canonical identity markers for a nation.

While we cannot expect a transparent literary 'marketplace' for the Nordic region, common processes were still at work that gave the vast area a cultural coherence. The geographical space from which our sample analyses derive covers all the way from present-day Finland, Estonia, and Latvia to Norway and Iceland. In many ways we are actually dealing with two separate cultural spaces: the lands around the North Sea and those around the Baltic Sea. From the early period (ninth to eleventh centuries) the archiepiscopal see of Hamburg-Bremen looked to both spaces for their missionary activity, with success, however, only from the eleventh century. The ecclesiastical history by Adam of Bremen (*c.* 1070) can claim to be the first piece of Nordic literature inasmuch as his account is the first in writing that speaks consistently with a 'native' voice: he is the mouthpiece of an institution which had missionary responsibility for the entire North (and moreover he reproduces information directly from the Danish king Sven Estridsen). With the establishment of the archiepiscopal see at Lund in 1104, a new centre was founded which also faced towards both the North and the Baltic Seas, conveniently located as it was close to Øresund. When the Archsees of Trondheim (1153) and Uppsala (1164) were founded the North received the main ecclesiastical structure that was to last up to the Reformation: one centre for the North Sea realm, one for the Baltic, and one which lay at the intersection and still had prerogatives in certain matters (the Archbishop of Lund enjoyed the status of primas).

The development and diffusion of ecclesiastical institutions from the eleventh to the thirteenth century to some degree worked separately in the two spaces (and of course in many smaller spaces on the local level): in the North Sea realm with a predominant English influence; in Denmark, Sweden, and the Baltic area mainly based on German models for scribal culture and ecclesiastical organization. But the division was not watertight, and both cultural scenes were open to direct inspirations from French and Italian ecclesiastical and university culture in the twelfth and thirteenth centuries. Perhaps most important in this context was the relatively high degree of common exegetical and liturgical practices, the inventory of important saints, the level of local learning and education (and absence of universities until 1477 (Uppsala) and 1479 (København)), the same waves of monastic movements (Benedictine, Augustinian canons, Cistercian, mendicant, Bridgettine),[10] and similar distances to the European centres of learning and to the Holy See, all of which made for a certain uniformity of ecclesiastical culture in the two spaces. These features were gradually shared with the Baltic areas which were contested territory for mission between Danish, German, Polish, and Russian authorities. In the present collection we include material dealing with Estonia and Livonia as examples of discourses on mission and paganism on the borders of the Nordic world.

Let us briefly mention another factor which made for a certain integration of the two spaces and also had importance for literary life. From the thirteenth century the three kingdoms of Norway, Denmark, and Sweden (each with their own archdiocese) emerged as decisive political units in increasing competition. Their rivalry and shifting alliances became more and more formalized, not least in the period of Nordic Unions (1319–1520). Though this development fostered certain national sentiments (according to some scholars)[11] and an increasing nationalization of ecclesiastical resources and culture (culminating in the Reformation), it also made for a deeper integration of the highest echelons of society and thus of shared culture.[12]

A final factor which enhanced cultural traffic between the two spaces was the pace of urban development in the thirteenth century. On one level this meant that a class of merchants and craftsmen enjoyed some interregional

---

[10] Though the Finnish coast entered Latin Europe too late for the first three.

[11] The widespread claim that national sentiments (if not nationalism) is an invention of the eighteenth and nineteenth centuries has met with criticism in later years. The nation is a medieval concept, and the beginnings of a coupling of language and people can be discerned from the Hundred Years' War, and equally from the fourteenth century in Denmark and Sweden. See Kersken, *Geschichtsschreibung im Europa der 'nationes'*; Hastings, *The Construction of Nationhood*; Leegaard Knudsen, *Saxostudier og rigshistorie på Valdemar Atterdags tid*.

[12] Helle, 'Growing Inter-Scandinavian Entanglement'; Olesen, 'Inter-Scandinavian Relations'.

and international integration — previously a privilege of the warrior elite and their close relatives in the ecclesiastical elite. Apart from the three kingdoms, the Hanseatic League became the key player in the region's urbanization and organization of trade. The main town, Lübeck, lay at the optimal intersection between the Baltic and the North Sea, and from there its network of other Hanseatic towns and offices in other important centres spread from Brugge to Tallinn and from Bergen to Köln.

The importance of the German-dominated trading culture from the thirteenth to the sixteenth century leads us to the question of linguistic unity and diversity in the Nordic space. This space itself — in line with the above — is not defined by language groups nor by modern states, but by religious affiliation and political domination. It includes areas Christianized and administered by one of the three kingdoms and archbishoprics. Depending on the exact period this definition is open for various territorial adjustments, but in the thirteenth and fourteenth centuries it would have excluded the northernmost territories dominated by the non-sedentary Saami and have included most of coastal and southern Finland, coastal Estonia and Livonia, Iceland (and the Faroes, Orkney, Shetland, and the southern tip of Greenland), and of course present-day Sweden, Norway, and Denmark, although with somewhat different internal and external borders.[13]

Linguistically the major part of the region (where some sort of Scandinavian was spoken) became characterized by the consistent presence of two international languages which left deep imprints on local speech and writing: Latin and Low German. This trilingual situation resembled the one found in the lands east of the Empire where High German also acted as an important third written and spoken language.[14] The difference from the East Central European scenario was that Low German and the Scandinavian languages were so closely related that communication between German and Scandinavian speakers was the order of the day in many towns. This was possible due to a wide overlap of vocabulary and of phonology (for instance correspondence in part of the vowel system — *hus* in Scandinavian and Low German, *haus* in High German). In addition to merchant communication, the Danish and Swedish aristocracy also mingled substantially with their peers in Northern Germany, especially in the

---

[13] Krötzl, *Pilger, Mirakel und Alltag*, pp. 36–37, gives a similar definition of the Nordic realm for his investigation of pilgrimage in the region (except for Estonia and Livonia).

[14] Vizkelety, 'Die deutsche Sprache und das deutsche Schrifttum'; Hlaváček, 'Dreisprachigkeit im Bereich der Böhmischen Krone'.

fourteenth century — and Low German would often have been their first or second language. The result of all these exchanges was that the Scandinavian languages (except Icelandic and Faroese) imported or adapted a significant percentage of their present vocabulary from Low German during the late Middle Ages and furthermore were recognizably influenced by word formation, phonology, and syntax.[15] As a lingua franca and as a common source for change, Low German thus became an integrating cultural force in large areas of both sea spaces.

Although Latin and Low German entered into the eastern and northern shores of the Baltic Sea too, the linguistic situation was radically different from the Scandinavian scene. A Baltic Finnic language group, that is, Estonian, Finnish, Karelian, Izhor, and Livvian, and others, formed a non-Indo-European pocket between Germanic (including Scandinavian), Slavonic, and Baltic peoples. These languages had been influenced by both Germanic and Slavonic languages over several centuries or, according to a mainstream linguistic hypothesis, even over several millennia. It seems that Baltic Finnic languages also exerted a strong influence on one of the Indo-European languages, namely Latvian.

Without almost any written sources earlier than the age of the Reformation, the linguistic evidence can be dated only on a relative scale. However, there are some features which can be loosely dated as medieval. In Estonian and in Finnish some Christian keywords like 'priest' (*pappi*), 'Bible' (Fi. *Raamattu*; E. 'book', *raamat*) and 'cross' (Fi. *risti*, E. *rist*) are Eastern Slavonic loanwords (although *Raamattu* is ultimately derived from Greek *grammata*, letters or writings). Thus, it seems that some of the earliest Christian contacts took place in a Slavonic context. German words (in Estonian) and Swedish words (in Finnish) dominated the linguistic exchange in the latter part of the Middle Ages. In the case of Finnish the linguistic world can be sketched as fourfold:

— Written Latin in the ecclesiastical and administrative world; spoken Latin limited to sacred ceremonies and the scholarly environment.

— Written and spoken Low German dominating commerce and some cultural and social exchange, and also featuring in some cases as an administrative language (in addition to a profusion of written documents some toponyms in Finland seem to be German loans).

---

[15] Braunmüller, 'Der Einfluss des Mittelniederdeutschen'; Winge, *Dänische Deutsche – deutsche Dänen*.

— Spoken and written Swedish as administrative, legal, and sometimes commercial language but also strongly present as the native tongue of peasant colonizers of the Finnish coast and archipelago.

— Spoken Finnish which also produced a strong oral poetic idiom that evidently enjoyed a certain mythical and sacred status.

Thus, the hierarchical relations between, on the one hand, Latin and different vernaculars and, on the other hand, oral and written languages were manifold and complex. Furthermore, Karelia forms its own case. The region was situated between the spheres of Western or Catholic and Eastern or Orthodox churches, and between the secular realms of Sweden and Novgorod (and later the Grand Duchy of Moscow). This contested borderland was religiously and politically divided so that its southernmost parts in the Karelian Isthmus were under Swedish rule and belonged to the diocese of Turku (Sw. Åbo) while the northern parts (Ladoga Karelia and Archangel or White Sea Karelia) were under Novgorodian rule and followed the Greek-Orthodox rite. Izhors (Ingrians) at the base of the Gulf of Finland (the region around present-day St Petersburg) remained under the Novgorodians throughout the Middle Ages. The Orthodox parts of Karelia also became a haven for the Kalevala-metre poetic idiom, and it was there that Finnish and Karelian oral poetry was not only preserved but developed further. In Karelia Church Slavonic held a similar position to Latin in the West, although the Eastern Church never established a sacred linguistic hierarchy similar to that of its Western counterpart. Nevertheless, Slavonic was the cultic and literate language, although written Karelian is documented as early as in the thirteenth century among the Novgorodian birch-bark letters (otherwise in Russian).[16]

Surveys of Nordic Medieval Literature

Issues of chronology and possible outlines of the development of Nordic literature cannot be dealt with without entering into definitions of 'literature'. Before sketching our conceptual frame for supplementing and widening 'Nordic medieval literature' both thematically and geographically, it will be useful to look at the scope and the underlying assumptions in some recent attempts to survey the field.

---

[16] Lind, 'Scandinavian Nemtsy and Repaganized Russians'; Haavio, 'Tuohikirje no. 292'.

It seems to be the case that the impetus to write a common literary history of the Nordic countries comes mainly from outside the region itself. It is the bird's-eye view of the region in which literary histories of each Nordic country have shown little interest.

Let us begin with an interesting exception to the rule that only foreign projects plan a unified literary narrative for the Nordic countries. The two volumes edited by Mogens Brøndsted in 1972 offer a survey in the Scandinavian languages of Nordic literature for the benefit of readers from other Nordic countries. The post-medieval chapters are divided in the usual manner between the five modern countries, but the medieval section is an admirable essay of about a hundred pages by the Swedish Old Norse scholar Peter Hallberg in which he surveys the Nordic countries, including Finland, in a unified narrative.[17]

Hallberg divides his contribution into three chronological sections, 'Forntid' (antiquity), 'den äldre medeltid' (the older Middle Ages) from about 1100 to 1300, and 'den yngre medeltid' (the younger Middle Ages) from 1300 to 1500. This is a sound and well-proven chronology also known from a number of national literary narratives. In the first section he duly treats runes and Eddic and skaldic poetry; in the second, laws, translations, historical writing, family sagas, and other Old Norse literature. In the final part he mainly focuses on the ballad common to Norway, Denmark, and Sweden, but supplements with brief accounts of the *Kalevala*, Birgitta's *Visions*, *Rhyme Chronicles*, and more. At the beginning of the second section he notes that it is really only with the coming of the book to the North around 1100 that we can properly speak of literature[18] — but he does not take this problematization of the key concept any further. In connection with the first wave of Latin books and their use, translation, adaptation, and conceptual impact in the Nordic realm he states that this enormous process can hardly be overestimated, but that it will be passed over in his treatment — except for a few brief examples. As far as we can see, this is the only instance where Hallberg raises the question of representativity in his survey of the traditional medieval canon.

In general, Hallberg is to be praised for a clear and useful essay involving a serious effort of merging the usual national narratives, but of course its age does shine through. His recurrent use of the dichotomy religious/profane has not aged well and strikes the reader today as artificial. What he means is ecclesiastical and secular (whether courtly or popular); 'profane' as the opposite

---

[17] Hallberg, 'I: Forntid', 'II: Den äldre medeltid', 'III: Den yngre medeltid'.
[18] Hallberg, 'I: Forntid', p. 51.

of religious (meaning ecclesiastical) was also in use until fairly recently in the study of early Christian literature in order to characterize the non-Christian literature of antiquity. But with the recent emphasis on the ritual side of Roman and Greek pagan literature, it becomes increasingly meaningless to lump all non-Christian writings together as 'profane'. Hallberg for instance treats *The King's Mirror* as profane, even though it deals with the right order of the world, the king's place in it, the idea of good manners, etc. — all within a highly religious view of the world. Finally it should be mentioned that he is, of course, aware of the problems in discussing the ballad as well as the *Kalevala*[19] in the medieval section — and perhaps one would emphasize those caveats more today, even though the two latest histories of Danish literature do include the ballad before the limit of *c.* 1500.[20]

The next example is more typical in that it comes from a German history of world literature. The chapter by Preben Meulengracht Sørensen of about thirty dense pages in *Propyläen Geschichte der Literatur* from 1981 is also basically divided into three periods: antiquity, twelfth and thirteenth centuries, and the late Middle Ages from around 1300 to 1500.[21] The latter receives a rather short shrift, and again much space is taken up by runes and Eddic and skaldic poetry before the introduction of writing. What is new in Sørensen's treatment — and this is no doubt due to the diffusion of orality/literacy studies in the 1970s — is the section on 'Kirche, Königtum und Schriftkultur' and the section on the 'useful' literature of the twelfth century which he places before the extensive section on the sagas of the thirteenth century. This gives Sørensen an opportunity to deal in more detail with the impact of both imported and locally composed Latin books of the twelfth century, the importance of which Hallberg recognized but deliberately left out. Sørensen does not give much space to Latin literature, but he does accomplish a striking juxtaposition of Ari's Book

---

[19] The *Kalevala* was composed by Elias Lönnrot, a Finnish collector of folk poetry, in the 1830s and 1840s on the basis of oral poetry mostly collected outside the borders of the Grand Duchy of Finland (and present-day Finland), primarily from Archangel (or White Sea) Karelia and to a lesser extent from Ingria next to St Petersburg, both Finnic areas bordering on Russia. It was published first in 1835 and in an enlarged edition in 1849. It has given the generic name to the Finnish and Karelian vernacular oral idiom, the so-called Kalevala metre characterized by alliterative trochaic metre without rhymes. The earliest written pieces of Kalevalaic poetry were recorded in the late sixteenth and seventeenth centuries.

[20] Kaspersen and others, *Dansk litteraturhistorie*; Mortensen and Schack, *Dansk litteraturs historie*.

[21] Meulengracht Sørensen, 'Die skandinavischen Sprachen'.

of Icelanders (in Old Norse) and the Legend of St Canute (in Latin) written in Denmark by the English monk Ælnoth. Both works are from the 1120s and stand at the emergence of each country's national literature.[22] Sørensen thus takes the genre of saints' legends seriously and to some degree allows for a dynamic role played by Latin (both in practice ignored by Hallberg). Indeed, he even says that the composition of the anonymous forerunner of Ælnoth who wrote a brief legend of St Canute around 1100 is the oldest literary work — in a real sense — written in the Nordic countries ('im eigentlichen Sinne literarische Werk').[23] Finland is absent from Propyläen's *Mittelalterliche Welt* — but, astonishingly, so is the entire Slavonic and Byzantine world.

An essay of similar length to Sørensen's, but occasioned by a somewhat different context, was co-authored in 2003 by two Old Norse philologists, Lars Lönnroth and Véstein Ólason, and a Latinist, Anders Piltz. The occasion was the first volume of the *New Cambridge History of Scandinavia*. Here Nordic medieval literature has already been embedded in a Scandinavian context, but in an otherwise completely historical volume. The emphasis is canonical in the thorough description of the highlights of Old Norse literature (Finland is absent, although included in the concept of the volume). The unavoidable Latin works by Saxo and Birgitta are briefly treated, and the most important scholastic contributions by Danish and Swedish intellectuals from the thirteenth and fourteenth centuries are mentioned. What is peculiar is the lack of clear chronology. Although ballads are treated towards the end and the volume includes a final single page on the late Middle Ages, we are pulled back and forth through the Middle Ages in a somewhat confusing manner. This is both due to a lack of integration between the Latin paragraphs and the main vernacular storyline, but can also, we suspect, derive from the authors' view regarding the exceptionality of Icelandic literature. The difference between the dominance of the vernacular in western Scandinavia, especially Iceland, and Latin in eastern Scandinavia can, according to the authors, to some extent be explained by the fact that in Iceland the 'Church' became integrated into the secular power structure, whereas in Denmark and Sweden 'there was always a very wide gap between the (native) culture of the people and the (foreign) culture of the clerics'.[24]

---

[22] Ælnoth's work has recently been backdated to *c.* 1113; see Gelting, 'Two Early Twelfth-Century Views of Denmark's Christian Past'.

[23] Meulengracht Sørensen, 'Die skandinavischen Sprachen', p. 292.

[24] Lönnroth and others, 'Literature', p. 490.

With just a brief look at the careers and family affiliations of the great intellectuals of the twelfth to fourteenth centuries in Denmark and Sweden, we find this a very hard claim to swallow. Be that as it may, this conviction leads the authors to minimize the importance of the arrival of the Latin book in the late eleventh and early twelfth centuries, because the written literature in western Scandinavia is mainly seen as a continuation of traditional oral culture. In contrast, the strong Latin culture of Denmark and Sweden is supposed to have eliminated all previous oral traditions. This model and its general lack of emphasis on the book revolution of the twelfth century represents, in our view at least, a reversal to a more traditional and national paradigm before the literacy turn.

Our final specimen is much more modern, and the author is acutely aware of the importance of media, manuscript transmission, *Verschriftlichung*, etc. We are referring to the medieval chapter in the impressive one-volume *Skandinavische Literaturgeschichte* edited by the Scandinavist Jürg Glauser, in which he himself, being also an Old Norse scholar, has written the first fifty pages on the Middle Ages.[25] The scope of the book is partly new because it includes not only Finland, but also the literatures of Greenland, the Saami, and the Faroese, not usually treated in Nordic surveys. (This, however, has no impact on the medieval chapter because Finland is not discussed there.) Other welcome novelties in the medieval section are the application of concepts like 'cultural memory' (*kulturelles Gedächtnis*), and 'spaces of memory' (*Erinnerungsräume*) applied for instance in the discussion of the Icelanders' sagas, and a re-evaluation of the late medieval period of Old Norse literature. The later genres and the creative work of transmission and adaptation in fourteenth- and fifteenth-century Iceland are allotted more space and weight than usual. Another benefit of Glauser's approach lies in the implicit reflection on representativity.

The editor underlines that the book is not intended as a handbook in which one finds basic information about all important works of each period. This partly excuses the original structure of the medieval chapter, which is even less chronological than in the Cambridge volume. To give just one example: Saxo is treated before the runes, because his reflections on the runes are used as an introduction. It is not fair to criticize Glauser for his ordering or for what he leaves out, as his chapter is professedly impressionistic; he is aware that all literary history is canonizing,[26] but he is also emphatically saying that his his-

---

[25] Glauser, *Skandinavische Literaturgeschichte*.
[26] Glauser, 'Vorwort', p. xvii.

tory is merely a supplement to others. The result of his priorities, however, is that he reproduces a pattern created by his predecessors by not engaging at any length with the vast Latin record. He stresses that the volume cannot be used as a handbook, but that the emphasis is instead on an exposé of phenomena which are regarded as 'important and interesting'.[27] This leads to the exclusion of Nordic literature in non-Nordic languages, such as Latin and German (and modern immigrant literature),[28] implying, indirectly, that Latin and German in the Middle Ages and in the early modern period are unimportant and uninteresting. Again, any delimitation is also practical, but his choice shows the need for other studies, like the present one, which tackle the multilingual situation more head-on.

Glauser's predicament is no different from most European literary histories in which you can hardly find one happily merged narrative of Latin and vernacular literary history — due to the large disciplinary divide. Admittedly, in practice Glauser cannot quite be confined within his own limits. In the medieval chapter he ventures the following definition of 'altnordische Literatur':[29] literature composed in Scandinavian Northern Europe in the period *c.* 800–1500 in Old Nordic language (*altnordische Sprache*) which was taken down in writing from the eleventh century on. But then he adds that depending on the point of departure and procedure ('je nach Ausgangspunkt und Vorgehensweise'), Latin literature — which (it is acknowledged) especially in Denmark and Sweden amounts to the greatest part of medieval literature — is to be considered Old Nordic literature (*altnordische Literatur*), a definition which opens the way for a fine, though brief, treatment of some saints' legends, Saxo, the scholastics, and Birgitta.

We will not discuss Meulengracht Sørensen's recent (unfinished and posthumously edited) book referred to above, although it must have been planned as a comprehensive history of Nordic literature. It keeps within the same chronological scheme as his 1981 essay, but it deals almost exclusively with Old Norse literature from Iceland with the expected canonical works. There are signs that he wanted to integrate Latin saints' lives as he had sketched earlier, but the book we have is a very readable account of Old Norse literature — in spite of its title.

---

[27] 'Vielmehr liegt der Akzent dieser Literaturgeschichte auf der diskursiven Erörterung ausgewählter, allerdings als wichtig und interessant': Glauser, 'Vorwort', p. xv.

[28] 'Bereiche, die aus diesen Gründen gar nicht oder nur ansatzweise behandelt werden, sind etwa die in Fremden Sprachen (Lateinisch, Deutsch etc.)': Glauser, 'Vorwort', p. xv.

[29] Glauser, 'Mittelalter', p. 4.

Apart from the difficulties of defining the Nordic space and the exclusion or inclusion of the Finnish and Baltic areas dealt with above, it is possible to discern at least three problematic points in the recent attempts to narrativize Nordic medieval history in one integrated text.

1. Common to all the surveys is the feature that Latin literature, if not completely absent, is only present in an instrumental way.[30] Whenever it can be used as an illustration or an elaboration to a narrative already built on Old Norse literature, it may be mentioned — but for the most part it is usually ignored. The upshot of such a procedure amounts to what social scientists term 'sampling on the dependent variable': this here implies that the cultural role projected onto a certain literature is strengthened by referring only to those specimens whose importance is being stressed. This ultimately reflects a didactic situation in which Old Norse literature is taught as a discipline on all levels — inside and outside of Scandinavia — and each major work needs a literary historical guidance and elucidation of the supposed developmental lines between those works. Nordic Medieval Latin, on the other hand, has never been part of the regular curricular activity at any level, but only an appendix to Classical Latin, and has in practice only existed as a research field. So while the situation is easily explicable, it is perhaps not equally defendable: what if Latin literature in the Nordic countries is not only a handy add-on unit in case of special interest? What if, for instance, Latin saints' lives during the twelfth century were a major dynamic force in the evolution of vernacular literature, including in Iceland and Norway?[31] And what if the active engagement with the so-called 'useful' foreign Latin literature during the revolutionary twelfth century played a similar catalyst role?

In a recent website on Nordic Medieval Latin literature, about fifty authors and as many important anonymous works from all five modern Nordic countries

---

[30] A recent Finnish-Swedish literary history presents a significant exception to this rule: see Wrede and Knapas, *Finlands svenska litteraturhistoria*. It includes not only medieval but also early Medieval Latin (although not German) literature; compare also Lehtonen, 'Latinet och folkspråken'; Lehtonen, 'Piae Cantiones'. The exception is at least partly due to the still continuing bilingual situation in Finland (Finnish, Swedish), but also to the conscious choice by the editors to present a multilingual view. A somewhat similar programme can be found in the Finnish equivalent Varpio and Huhtala, *Suomen kirjallisuuden historia*, although since the early 1960s Latin and Swedish literature have been seen as an integral part of the national literature.

[31] As initially suggested by Turville-Petre, *Origins of Icelandic Literature*. Compare Mortensen, 'Den formative dialog mellem latinsk og folkesproglig litteratur'. For similar arguments against the 'nativist' representation of Old Irish literature, see McCone, *Pagan Past and Christian Present*.

are described.[32] Thus, even from a quantitative point of view it is difficult to overlook Latin literature, but the crucial issue here is to raise suspicion about the interaction between Latin and the vernacular and whether it can tell us something about general literary development from the eleventh to fifteenth century in the entire northern periphery.

2. This leads to a second point. The canon represented in existing surveys seems impenetrable to important foreign works circulating in the Nordic region — except when they have been translated or paraphrased in writing in the local vernacular. This is in line with modern literary history which is not directly concerned with what people read, discuss, and learn from, but only with what is produced by their countrymen in their own language. Perhaps this is the only practical approach to modern national literatures, but it may be inadequate in explaining how a new storyworld developed in the North between the eleventh and fifteenth centuries. Again saints' lives, miracles, classical, biblical, and apocryphal stories would have been of paramount importance in creating an entirely new reservoir of literary content and form. Finally, liturgical performance needs to be placed at the centre of literary life — as a recent critic has put it: 'the study of medieval vernacular literatures will need to reckon much more comprehensively than it yet has with the liturgy, site of the most enduring, expansive, elaborate, widespread and influential cultures of performance in the pre-modern West'.[33]

3. Our third and last point concerns representativity. The increased awareness of the impact of writing and the introduction of the book has highlighted the precarious transmission of a number of key texts which to some degree are orally derived. They were not taken down in writing through a 'natural' or negligible process, but in specific textual and social circumstances, and with a considerable selective and editorial mechanism at work.[34] In other words, when drawing a map of real medieval literary life we should be more humble before we make inferences from the canonical literary forms and matters known to us. Even on the level of what has been composed in writing (in Latin and in the vernacular) the issue of representativity is rarely discussed. This is positivism at its most basic flaw, particularly in regard to the reconstruction of pre-

---

[32] Borgehammar and others, *Nordic Medieval Literature in Latin*.

[33] Holsinger, 'Analytical Survey', p. 292.

[34] Again, for a similar reasoning within the field of early Irish literature, see McCone, *Pagan Past and Christian Present*. The 'nativists' have to disregard the monastic interests and contexts in which pagan stories and lore were selected, reinterpreted, and stored within Christian writing.

modern cultural phenomena: we admit to having only a few scraps of evidence, but will talk endlessly about them and the connections we can draw between them because it is 'unscientific' (to stay within a positivist epistemology) to talk about what we do not have. The extremely limited survival of key texts should alert us to the nature of our map and the lines drawn on it, but it rarely seems to do so, because, again, the writing of literary history is chiefly governed by a didactical urge to explain the canon present in *our* classroom rather than to admit the haphazard nature of its transmission.

All three points circle around the definition of 'literature': From which elements should we choose to construct a narrative? How far should we go to ignore or, alternatively, to describe the white spots for which we have only, at best, very circumstantial evidence? We think that the circumscription of the topic should be made in two complementary moves: one guided by book history (from the 'literary' end of the spectrum) and one by performed texts as agents for social identities (*identitätsstiftend*) (from the oral side). These two ways of defining literature are interlocking and overlapping. Although the second definition includes an infinitely larger portion of 'textual life', priority in description should still be given to the introduction and spread of the book, because its impact from top to bottom in the social fabric became a historical frame for 'lived' literature while the reverse is not the case.

The Impact of the Book — The Codification of Wisdom

Following this line of argument an overview of Nordic literary discourse in the Middle Ages should rightly start with the arrival, diffusion, and development of book culture beginning in the second half of the eleventh century. Literature in this narrow sense means texts copied in parchment books.[35] Such texts could be argumentative, narrative, lyrical, didactic, etc. They were copied, adapted, or translated from texts in other books, or they were freshly composed for a new local book or taken down in writing from the performances of orally composed texts. Even if we adopt a much more generous concept of literature (see below) it would still be natural to base a historical understanding of literature on the

---

[35] Runes are consequently not dealt with here as literature, although runic inscriptions are highly important as linguistic and historical documents. Rune stones were mainly erected in present-day Sweden (fewer in Denmark and Norway), roughly in the century preceding the advent of book culture (*c.* 950–1100), chiefly as Christian commemorations. With very few exceptions, they do not reflect any oral poetics (or written literature for that matter).

much firmer ground of books, especially since the earlier oral forms known to us are all preserved in books. We may be able to extrapolate many non-book literary forms from written texts, but such extrapolation should be undertaken only after an appreciation of the impact of book culture, both in terms of medieval literary life itself and of its transmission to us (cf. above on representativity).

From a modern perspective, the delimitation of literature as written texts in books is rather generous in itself. The implication is that we should take into account all older texts copied in Nordic books, including a number of more 'technical' or 'practical' texts such as law collections, grammars, and herbals. Both categories do in fact figure in most national literary histories (if the given texts are in the vernacular). Armed with this definition, let us have a brief look at the spread of book culture in the Nordic regions. When, where, and how were books made, what where their chief contents, and how were they used?

The decades around 1070 increasingly stand out as the crucial period for the establishment of a book culture in the North. It has long been known that the earliest locally produced books in Denmark were made from Saxon models around that time in Lund, and that the beginning of Old Norse writing in books in Iceland around 1100 presupposed a local familiarity with Latin books and script.[36] But recent research on Norwegian and Swedish parchment fragments has shown that books were both being imported and even produced locally before 1100 (or at least in the beginning of the twelfth century) in these areas as well.[37]

The key to this development is the reorganization and expansion of the episcopal structure in the involved areas.[38] The interest in books, and hence the beginnings of literature in a strict sense, certainly came about through episcopal concerns for the adaptation and spread of a correct form of Roman rite throughout the dioceses. In order to enact the rituals in a valid way, books became necessary on a grand scale from the twelfth century on. Fragment

---

[36] On the beginnings of Danish book production, see Petersen, *Living Words and Luminous Pictures*.

[37] For Swedish fragment research and references to early books, see Abukhanfusa, *Mutilated Books*; Brunius, *Medieval Book Fragments in Sweden*; Gullick, 'Preliminary Observations on Romanesque Manuscript Fragments'. For Norwegian, see Karlsen, 'Katalogisering av latinske membranfragmenter som forskningsprojekt'; Karlsen, 'Liturgiske bøker i Norge'; Ommundsen, *The Beginnings of Nordic Scribal Culture*; Ommundsen, 'Books, Scribes and Sequences in Medieval Norway'; Åslaug Ommundsen, this volume. For surveys of the Finnish fragments, see Tuomas Heikkilä in the present volume with further references.

[38] Compare the surveys by Gelting, 'The Kingdom of Denmark'; Bagge and Nordeide, 'The Kingdom of Norway'; Blomkvist, Brink, and Lindkvist, 'The Kingdom of Sweden'.

research again helps us gain a concrete idea of how dominating the ordinary liturgical books were in the Nordic countries throughout the Middle Ages — a fact that is often neglected in general literary history both due to a lack of interest in the diffusion of international texts and due to the very poor survival rate of complete codices.[39] In Sweden three quarters of around six thousand codices from which fragments exist today were ordinary Latin liturgical books.[40] The Christianization and partial conquest of the Finnish, Estonian, and Livonian areas during the twelfth and thirteenth centuries meant that a fairly uniform book culture centred around ecclesiastical rituals and organized mainly through bishoprics had penetrated the entire Nordic region in the two centuries spanning from *c.* 1070 to *c.* 1270.

During the twelfth and thirteenth centuries a local scribal culture emerged in episcopal, and to some degree in monastic, environments. Vernacular types of books and texts were developed from the Latin — beginning with texts at the margin of the liturgy (local saints were added to the international pantheon and their stories divulged in both Latin and the vernacular), and local laws were mainly written down in the vernacular.[41] Not only was a book culture firmly established, with canonical literary forms such as legends, histories, romances, and family sagas having made their mark, but the entire elite culture was changed through a literate rationality that effectively took root during the period from *c.* 1150 (when a variety of local writings are visible to us) to *c.* 1300 (when we have books and texts from the entire Nordic realm and in all three Scandinavian vernaculars).

We will not go into the whole array of rational techniques in trading, law, administration, calculation, measuring, book-keeping, archiving, teaching, scholastic inquiry, etc. that were dependent (directly or indirectly) on the literacy of the book,[42] as so convincingly described in Alexander Murray's classic work *Reason and Society in the Middle Ages* (1978). In the context of literature it will suffice to give three brief examples of how continental learning was

---

[39] The much more destructive character of the Nordic Reformations in comparison to those in Germany and England would need a study in itself. Compare Abukhanfusa and others, *Helgerånet*; Petersen, *Living Words and Luminous Pictures*, pp. 16–17.

[40] Brunius, 'Medieval Manuscript Fragments in the National Archives', pp. 11–12, based this figure on the existing fragments in Stockholm, the survival of which does not conform to a perfect random sample, but rather favours certain medieval book types. The real percentage of liturgical books was probably higher.

[41] Compare Mortensen, 'Den formative dialog mellem latinsk og folkesproglig litteratur'.

[42] And for which the previously existing literacy of runic inscriptions is irrelevant.

imported and put into use in the Nordic region. In the late eleventh and early twelfth centuries the connection to Saxon learned schools dominated, and we have some strong evidence that members of the Icelandic and Danish elite studied there. From the mid-twelfth century, however, attention shifted to northern France, and of course in the thirteenth century to the University of Paris. The import and update of learning was again kept up mainly by canons and bishops, but with important new input and contacts established through Cistercian and mendicant institutions in the North.

One example of the transmission of written knowledge and literate habits is supplied by the Danish nobleman and Archbishop Anders Sunesen (d. 1228). He studied arts and theology in Paris and law in Bologna in the 1180s (and taught for a period in Paris as well), was used for diplomatic and administrative tasks as chancellor to the king, and became Archbishop of Lund in 1202. He was a key figure as primas for the entire Nordic region, as a participant in the Fourth Lateran Council (1215), and as ecclesiastical head of the subjugation and Christianization of Estonia during the years 1206 to 1222 (cf. Kaljundi's chapter below). He stands out in a literary context because of his administrative letters, his Latin rephrasing of Scanian law (the vernacular literalization of which occurred around the same time), and his long theological didactic poem *Hexaëmeron* which reflected the latest teachings in Paris. In addition we possess a list of books he bequeathed to the chapter of Lund. Again, biblical exegesis (and liturgy), theology, and canonical law dominate. We even possess a remarkable testimony of how Sunesen put his specialist knowledge to use, namely in Henry of Livonia's *Chronicle* (x. 13): As spiritual head of the Crusade, he was travelling in the Baltic and was forced to spend the winter of 1206/07 in Riga. He set up a school for the local clergy and initiated them in the higher theology. It is rare that we catch a glimpse of this type of exclusive learning trickling down to the local level. If the local priests and missionaries did not understand everything, they at least received important confirmation of the fact that their practices rested on the best of grounds — that their superior was in line with the highest standards of divine understanding. Anders Sunesen embodies the literate mentality into which the Nordic elites branched their activities and invested their prestige during the later twelfth century, bringing back from the learned centres top competence within theology and law, international networks, and authoritative reference books. All these strengths were put to use, if not directly on a practical level, then at least as powerful symbols of authority.[43]

---

[43] On Anders and his learning, see Sunesøn, *Hexaemeron*, ed. by Ebbesen and Mortensen, I, 19–47 (Introduction); Ebbesen, 'The Danes, Science, Scholarship, and Books'. For the social

Another example is the English-born Bishop Thomas of Finland (d. 1248) who was first a canon of Uppsala and later acted as a missionary bishop in Finland. Information about him is extremely scarce; however, he was active among recently baptized people even though his diocese had not yet been fully organized according to canonical standards. He seems to have been a highly learned clergyman, but he was demoted from his episcopal status because he had mutilated someone. He passed his last years in internal exile at a Dominican house in Visby in Gotland. In his will he donated a manuscript of Hugh of St Cher's commentary to Petrus Comestor's *Historia scholastica* to the Dominicans of Sigtuna in Sweden. The manuscript is based on Hugh's lectures at Paris in the mid-1230s, and it exemplifies the speed of the diffusion of books and book culture at that time in a distant North still in the midst of the Christianization process and emergent ecclesiastical organization. An even more striking piece of information, however, is found in the last folio of the manuscript: a list of fifty-eight manuscript volumes containing mostly theological and biblical texts with commentaries by Anselm of Laon, Petrus Cantor, Hugh of St Cher, and Stephen Langton, among others. A Finnish medievalist and manuscript scholar, Anja-Inkeri Lehtinen, has interpreted this list as a book order. Bishop Thomas seems to have been very keen to introduce the Catholic 'great tradition' (Redfield) to his illiterate Finnish congregation.[44]

The parallel to Anders and Thomas in the Norwegian archdiocese was the local nobleman Øystein Erlendsson (archbishop 1161–88), a towering figure of the organization, learning, and even political drama of his age. Like his colleagues he had international experience and networks, studying in France, and later assisting at Bury St Edmunds during his brief exile in England. We know that he was involved in shaping both the ideology and the documents of the kingdom and the archdiocese in a very formative phase. He organized the extension of the Cathedral in Trondheim and the adaptation of parts of the liturgy, wrote part of the official legend of St Olaf, was the dedicatee of a Latin chronicle on the Norwegian kings, left his imprint on ecclesiastical law collections, etc. Like Anders and Thomas he also exemplifies a mechanism of cultural exchange between centre and periphery: with the right networking relations to northern France, some parts of the cultural transfer are surprisingly modern; in

---

mechanisms of bringing back learning from abroad in this context, see Mortensen, 'Philosophical Learning'; Mortensen, 'The Nordic Archbishoprics as Literary Centres'.

[44] Lehtinen, 'Kirjoja ja kirjastoja keskiajan Suomessa'; Lehtinen, 'The Apopeciae of the Manuscripts of Hugh of St. Cher's Works'; Lehtinen, 'From Fragments into Codices'.

Øystein's case the Trondheim diocese can be seen to be fairly advanced in parts of the liturgical song.[45]

The change within two or three generations to literate habits, the metamorphosis of a part of the Northern elite into highly educated intellectuals, and the resulting shift in legal, administrative, theological, and literary discourse from the concrete to the abstract — and from a society where elite wisdom ('the encyclopaedia of society' or the 'great tradition') was orally guaranteed to one in which there was a final resort to book knowledge in all important matters — can perhaps better be appreciated if compared to Eric Havelock's description of how the Greek enlightenment came about through the 'Platonic revolution'.[46] Even if Havelock today is grouped among the pioneers of the 'technology view' of literacy (with too little recognition of the interaction and overlapping of written and oral modes),[47] his description of the literate revolution in Greece during the period between *c.* 450–350 BCE is still intriguing and worth considering in connection with other societies' transition towards a codification of wisdom, and to a learned and literary discourse dependent on books.

One of Havelock's important discoveries is the long 'incubation' period after the invention of the Greek alphabet (*c.* 700 BCE) before a truly literate revolution took place, roughly in the century from Herodotus (*c.* 450 BCE) to Plato (427–347). A number of poetical works (including Homer) had been taken down in writing, perhaps in the seventh or at least in the sixth century, and the Greek enlightenment had even produced its first philosophical texts during the sixth century. But Havelock insists that since most, if not all, of these texts were in verse, they only represented a basically oral encyclopaedia in a new medium, the proper technology of which was metrical memorization and composition. The breakthrough of the written word and its power not only to reorganize knowledge, but to bring human understanding to a new level of abstraction, is expressed most forcefully and symptomatically by Plato. It is in this context that Plato's almost hysterical enmity towards 'the poets' should be seen (for which no adequate explanation had been offered before Havelock). The poets were to be expelled from Plato's ideal city and should have no influence on the

---

[45] For a survey, see Bagge, 'Den heroiske tid', who underlines the important coordinating role assumed by Archbishop Øystein; for the musical record, see the collection Kruckenberg and Haug, *The Sequences of Nidaros*; for his role in literature, see Mortensen and Mundal, 'Erkebispesetet i Nidaros'.

[46] Havelock, *Preface to Plato*; Havelock, *The Muse Learns to Write*.

[47] See Melve, *Med ordet som våpen*.

education of the young. The entire traditional encyclopaedia (Homer, Hesiod, etc.) with its emphasis on the very concrete custom laws (*nomos*) and folk ways (*ethos*)[48] must be replaced, Plato urges, by real knowledge of abstract entities, strict definitions, and methods of arguing, etc. — the entire intellectual habitus that we (and the Middle Ages) find in a systematic university education.

In a later chapter on 'the special theory of Greek orality', Havelock lists five theses to explain the uniqueness of the Greek case, of which three are relevant in our context:[49]

— the society was politically and socially autonomous both in its oral and literate periods, and consequently possessed a firm consciousness of its own identity;

— at the point where this language came to be transcribed, the invention necessary for the purpose was supplied by the speakers of the language within the society itself;

— the application of the invention to transcribe anything and everything that might be both spoken and preservable continued to be controlled by Greek speakers.

Although the differences from the Nordic situation *c*. 1100–1300 become striking while looking at these points, there are also similarities. The period between *c*. 800–1100 CE in the North can be likened to the period between the introduction of the alphabet in Greece *c*. 700 BCE and the late fifth- and early fourth-century literate mentality. After a long period with a partial knowledge of alphabetization (runes) and the existence of books (missionaries) came the breakthrough in the twelfth century when local elites began to participate in and encourage education that was based on books. This education, like the one advocated by Plato, massively replaced previous (and to a large extent unknown) forms of the transmission of the *nomos* and *ethos* in Nordic societies. Although the proper university education was to be sought abroad, the local guarantors were at the highest level of training and enjoyed a social position that allowed this knowledge to spread.[50] The North also produced original philosophers, but the main impact of knowledge from books came in the fields

---

[48] Havelock's translation from a passage of Hesiod; these very concrete translations are intended to contrast with the technical sense into which these terms developed (codified law and ethics).

[49] Havelock, *The Muse Learns to Write*, pp. 86–87.

[50] Compare Mortensen, 'Philosophical Learning'.

of liturgy, theology, and canon law, so crucial for upholding and teaching the *nomos* and *ethos* of a Christian society.

Another similarity is the absence of any imperial power defining or pushing through this shift. A number of groups in the Nordic area were certainly dominated by elites coming from other parts of the Nordic realm, but by and large the acquisition of new norms and models of behaviour which, in the last resort, were based on texts in books, was a voluntary affair. This did not directly make for a clear, common identity throughout the enormous realm, and there were no Panhellenic festivals to promote such a cultural coherence. However, as sketched above, the three kingdoms and the three archiepiscopal sees enjoyed a fair amount of cultural interaction, as well as common sources of inspiration.

The striking difference to the Greek situation, which distinctively made the North into a cultural periphery, is the fact that in order to gain this new coveted education, members of the elite had to learn foreign languages, first and foremost Latin, but in many cases French and German as well. Moreover, they had to accept a wide body of wisdom as a fait accompli (although it was being quickly refashioned and widened in the twelfth and thirteenth centuries). The secondary invention of vernacular alphabetic writing (for books) was of course controlled by native speakers, but it is important to note that even in the case of the most prolific written vernacular (Old Norse), most books in circulation throughout the Middle Ages conveyed learned and literary material and forms that were directly or indirectly inspired by the cultural centres (liturgy, historiography, saints' lives, laws, romances, etc.).

Books not only brought a new level of abstract knowledge — an enlightenment if you like — and a radically new way to ground the *nomos* and the *ethos* of society (considered valid by the mass of non-literate people as well), but also stimulated the (oral and literate) spread and constitution of a new Christian storyworld. The diffusion and retelling of key biblical and saints' stories must have been the glue with which a new Christian identity was kept together — and which became the productive meeting point between the great tradition and the little traditions.

How did Christian narratives spread across the social spectrum? The starting point would naturally be the highest elite, the royal families and magnates who had frequent contact with Christian elites abroad. These contacts had, for that matter, been cultivated for centuries, and we can hardly deny that a number of Christian narratives were known — if only rarely accepted in all their implications — among the members of the elite all the way back to the eighth and ninth centuries. This elite can perhaps be defined as those aristocrats who were internationally integrated to some degree (and one should probably include some of their retinue and traders who were equally mobile and internationalized). This international integration deepened in the eleventh and twelfth centuries, and the foreign elites they met tended to partake in ecclesiastical institutions. But this in itself is only one factor which can explain the new momentum for the wide acceptance of Christian discourse.

The turning point in this diffusion came when the more numerous layer below the highest elite — the local elites who were not integrated internationally — began investing in churches during the late eleventh and twelfth centuries, much like a petty peripheral Hellenistic magnate deciding to make a point of his cultural identity by financing a temple or a theatre. (It is normally assumed in all Nordic countries that the majority of these stone churches were initially financed privately and run by local farmers of good means.) This very visible adherence to the Christian cult must in itself have been the result of an intense imitation, negotiation, and competition between the internationalized high elite and the local elites. In this process the exchange of Christian narratives must have been one important element. One could hardly build a church without being able to summarize the key narratives of Christianity and those of the dedicatee saints. By vouching for the relevance of the stories of Mary, Peter, Nicholas, Lawrence, etc. on their own soil, the small magnates or rich farmers placed themselves as local representatives of the universally or internationally acclaimed holy.[51] With churches in a non-urban landscape and with a social, cultic, and financial investment from a critical number of the local elites, the integration of the masses into Christian beliefs, rituals, and stories was inevitable. The episcopal administration of the liturgy and its practice in the parish churches during the twelfth and the thirteenth centuries (in some areas) can be seen as the key channel for a Christian storyworld.

Christianization and adaptation to the written word and literate culture took place differently in various Nordic regions. All areas including Scandinavia, Finland, and the Baltic countries had received Christian influences for centuries, but regulated ecclesiastical organization was established between 970 and 1270. In Denmark, Norway, Iceland, and Sweden it was the local elites who took the decisive steps towards conversion, and the new religion was adopted as a part of the thorough socio-cultural change resulting in new political structures (monarchy), legislation (written law), and administration based on the written word. Even though cultural influences were adopted from the Christian West there was never a political or military conquest, and

---

[51] Compare Mortensen, 'Writing and Speaking of St Olaf', with further references.

colonization (mainly German) occurred as a spread of new commercial networks and related urbanization (Hansa).

In this sense the eastern Baltic Sea region was radically different, although the most recent scholarship has come to the conclusion that the cultural, social, and political shift was not as sharp as the earlier mainstream interpretation saw it.[52] Nevertheless, Estonia and Livonia, as well as Finland (and the provinces of Tavastia and Karelia that were later included in it) were conquered by linguistically, culturally, and politically different groups, that is, by Danes, Germans, and Swedes (and the Karelians in the East by Novgorodians). The Livonian and Estonian conquest is better documented and seems to have been much more violent than what took place in the northern shores of the Gulf of Finland. In Estonia and Livonia this meant an aristocratic and urban German colonization with the establishment of linguistic and social borders (*Undeutsch* and *Deutsch*), whereas in Finland the strong Swedish peasant colonization in the southern and south-western coastal regions resulted in a linguistic, but not a social, political, or cultural border. In medieval Karelia Novgorodians, and later Muscovites, practised political and religious overlordship, but colonization remained practically non-existent.

We can thus outline three variations of Christianization, namely adaptation (Scandinavia), conquest and colonization by relatively similar groups with linguistic differences (Finland and Karelia conquered by the Swedes and Novgorodians respectively), and conquest by a relatively different social, cultural, and linguistic order (Estonia and Livonia conquered by Danes and Germans respectively). These form the background for the different literary and oral cultures. In the fringes of Scandinavia it led to the literate blossoming of local traditions (Old Norse poetry in Iceland), whereas in the peripheries of the Baltic Finnic regions oral poetry survived in various forms up to the nineteenth and twentieth centuries.

Performed Texts and Social Identities

In thinking about the oral spread of Christian stories we have to a certain extent already transgressed the narrow codex-fixated concept of literature. But at the same time we hope it has become clear that all the supposedly oral or orally derived 'literary' forms we know of were reported in a world where books had

---

[52] Compare Lehtonen, 'Préliminaires: colonisation et culture écrite'; Lehtonen, 'Conquête et construction de l'histoire sacrée'.

conquered the position of 'the last resort'. Therefore the much broader definition of literature should take the above scenario into account — the minor oral forms, for example, did not circulate in a space of their own, and regardless of the reminiscences of a long past pagan world of texts they might evoke (such as skaldic and Eddic poetry according to the standard account), all our known texts have been selected by Christian compilers with specific interests in mind (cf. Janson in this volume).

In the broad outline, Nordic literature in this sense could be any kind of marked speech from lullabies through incantations, legal formulas, sermons, etc., often performed in a ritual context; in brief all sorts of oral poetics created by ordinary people or by professionals. The essential period to cover would still be from *c.* 1100 up to the Reformation, and the literary matter need not be of indigenous origin or in the vernacular language. The geographical and chronological delimitation is only pertinent for the performance (of which scribal reproduction is a small subset): when and where did it take place? Of course much less than one percent of such 'literature' is known, but perhaps enough to at least describe some typical performance settings and story matter.

All performances and oral poetics ultimately further a collective identity. In the words of Havelock: 'Oral verse was the instrument of a cultural indoctrination, the ultimate purpose of which was the preservation of group identity',[53] and a little later:

> In sum then, Plato's conception of poetry [...] was basically correct. Poetry was not 'literature' but a political and social necessity. It was not an art form, nor a creation of the private imagination, but an encyclopedia maintained by co-operative effort.[54]

Although this is Havelock's description of characteristics of the oral mode, it is also helpful when considering textual performances in a book culture such as that of the Nordic Middle Ages. The question is, then, which social identities can we discern in the textual specimens discussed in the present volume, and how do they relate to medieval performances (and to the survival of their traces to our date)?

It has been argued that, roughly speaking, the elites and the common people ('masses') in premodern societies never shared cultural identities, even if they happened to share language(s) and respect for the same gods. In general the common people were despised by the elites, who in fact respected and shared

---

[53] Havelock, *Preface to Plato*, p. 100.
[54] Havelock, *Preface to Plato*, p. 125.

culture to a much larger degree with elites of other languages and localities.[55] But Christianity and Islam can be said to have tilted this structure towards a more common understanding of cultural identity between the social layers, as both creeds force or strongly favour universal participation among their own peoples and a sharp sense of a boundary separating them from the other faith (and from pagans). The idea of universal participation, and ultimately universal redemption or punishment, certainly made for at least an abstract sense of commonality. This has nothing to do with any democratization of culture because privileged access and closeness to the divine was still completely dominated by the elite (cf. recruiting to monasteries, bishoprics, and higher education). However premodern medieval Christianity and Islam remained, the agenda of a cross-social Christian identity became important — also in terms of the identities strengthened by literary discourse.

As already explained, no strong common Nordic identity exists in any medieval texts (except some vague statements regarding geographical and cultural unity in the sagas and Saxo, and a political agenda in some Union texts), but numerous group identities are expressed on all levels: the three kingdoms and archbishoprics, the monastic orders, the dioceses, the retinue around a local chieftain or a rich landholder, the merchant guilds, and even on lower level units, such as the little communities of peasants.

Although the chapters below all deal with the performance of stories and the shaping of storyworlds, and most of them deal with aspects of the interface between Latin and the vernacular, between Christian and pagan, and between the great and the little tradition, the main emphasis in the articles also places them into four clusters — the four subheadings into which the book is divided:

    I.   The impact of Latin song, book, and service;

    II. Christian discourse framing pagan stories;

    III. Educating and disciplining the community;

    IV. Oral poetics through the social spectrum.

I. The first heading comprises the contributions by Åslaug Ommundsen, Tuomas Heikkilä, and Tuomas M. S. Lehtonen, all of whom focus on the impact of Latin books and the performance primarily associated with them, that of the divine service.

---

[55] Mann, *The Sources of Social Power*, I; Crone, *Pre-Industrial Societies*.

Ommundsen's introduction to the Roman rite and its books in Norway is of fundamental importance for the present volume, as it opens up the process that introduced a new storyworld to the North and underlines the performance (music, keywords, context) in a very illustrative manner. One of her important contributions is to point to the mechanisms that partly bridged the gap between Latinate and unlearned, between elite and peasants. Christianity was clearly for everyone — although at the same time direct access to the 'great tradition' was equally elitist. Her article also underlines the attractive sides of the Latin liturgy (uncommon in Protestant scholarship) — both the acoustic and narrative delights. The dialectic between the introduction of local saints and the circulation of the basic storylines of other saints (here St Nicholas) is another important theme that figures in several of the other contributions as well. Finally, Ommundsen's article reveals the potential of the recent blossoming of scholarship in liturgical fragments in Sweden, Norway, and Finland during the last decade.

The books used and copied in Latin Christendom's north-eastern corner, present-day Finland, were comparatively few and mainly contained copies of liturgical texts as described in Tuomas Heikkilä's chapter. In the twelfth and thirteenth centuries the surviving evidence points to a literate culture that was part and parcel of the archdiocese of Uppsala to which it had been added (as the bishopric Turku (Åbo)). The primary target group for these books was the clergy who mainly originated from mainland Sweden; the ties with Uppsala and Linköping seem to have been particularly strong. Of course, the presence of books and trained personnel at the episcopal see and in the growing number of parish churches in the area had an impact on the structures of authority and on the status of the written word. In contrast to other Nordic regions no traces of other previous writing systems like runes exist, and we are therefore dealing with an interesting 'pure' case in which writing in sacred books was primary in all respects; charters and other kinds of administrative or practical writing was also a later phenomenon (beginning in the later thirteenth century). In the fourteenth and fifteenth centuries, as stressed by Heikkilä, not only was the Swedish connection strengthened through the establishment of a Bridgettine monastery, but the more international network of the Dominicans in particular had already made its presence felt in the diocesan liturgy and book production by the late thirteenth century. Moreover, in a typical pattern, after *c.* 1350 the relative rise of vernacular writing (in charters and other contexts) was spectacular. At that time both the German tradesmen and the mainly Swedish-speaking residents of Turku began writing in their vernacular languages. The written culture of the diocese of Turku, not least the town itself, thus faced across the sea ever tighter networks, ecclesiastical, royal, and mercantile. The establishment and growth of this centre became highly important in later Swedish-Finnish culture, but in the Middle Ages itself, not much evidence exists of literate or cultural influence beyond the diocese.

Latin and vernacular marked speech lived side by side. In the Finnish-speaking area the Christian tradition strongly influenced vernacular oral poetic forms such as incantations and charms, Kalevalaic poetry on local and international saints, and wider vernacular mediations of Christian teaching. Tuomas M. S. Lehtonen studies an example of the translation of a Latin hymn into the Finnish vernacular relating the missionary expedition of Bishop Henry of Finland and King Eric Jedvardsson. The Latin poem *Ramus virens oliuarum* (The Green Branch of the Olive Tree), composed perhaps in the early fourteenth century by a canon, later Bishop of Turku, Ragvaldus (printed in 1582), was published in a Finnish translation by a local parish priest Hemmingius de Masco in 1616. Strikingly the translation follows a slightly twisted form of Kalevalaic vernacular oral poetics usually avoided by the reformed Lutheran clergy. On the basis of other remnants of some other nearly contemporary examples of Kalevalaic poetry it seems that Hemmingius was applying well-known traditional formulae. Written, chanted, and performed Latin Christian traditions lived side by side with syncretistic vernacular oral traditions. Christian and pre-Christian poetic registers and storyworlds intermingled. These forms of marked and ritualized speech carried a sacral imprint which, later after the Lutheran reformation, was demonized as 'pagan' regardless of whether the content was really pagan or Catholic.

II. After this focus on the basis of a Nordic Christian culture and of the Latin framing of vernacular forms, the next cluster deals with examples of how pre-Christian (or contemporary non-Christian) figures, stories, and practices surface in Christian writings.

In his analysis of a non-canonical version of the prologue to the highly canonical prose *Edda* (usually attributed to Snorri Sturluson), Jonas Wellendorf directs our attention to the disputed status of pagan deities. The longer and learned version has usually been disregarded as an uninteresting interpolation into the original work of Snorri, but Wellendorf rightly emphasizes that we are here dealing with a serious medieval reading and understanding of the pagan past, probably made in a Benedictine monastery in Iceland before *c.* 1350. The cultural identity expressed in the text can perhaps be characterized as a sharper (more monastic?) interpretation of the erroneous beliefs of the Icelandic past. But the amount of Latin learning put into this effort must also be seen as symptomatic of the importance of the pagan world as present in narrative verbal art

— and of the anxieties it created. At any rate, the case illustrates that there was more than one 'canonical' solution to the problem of preserving pagan stories within a Christian framework.

Next, in a new reading of Thor's fishing expedition as told in Snorri's *Edda* (in which the Midgard serpent is caught), Henrik Janson draws attention to its quite clear model in Latin Christian literature. This relationship has either been forgotten or significantly underplayed in mainstream *Edda* scholarship. Janson emphasizes that both the narrative framing by Snorri and the motif borrowing from a Christian storyworld should have a wider impact on the way we think about pagan mythology in its canonical Eddic representation. The tendency in much scholarship of especially literary and religious historians to accept certain (or most) parts of the mythology as a coherent indigenous pagan (and sometimes even Indo-European) system bears witness to very resilient romanticist traditions of research which neglect the fact that Snorri and his contemporaries were living in a world where Christian stories had been dominant for centuries. In the present context we can also note that the Icelandic thirteenth-century audience for Snorri's *Edda* — probably a quite restricted elite one — was equally steeped in an orally transmitted Christian storyworld.

Lauri Harvilahti traces a geographical as well as a social trajectory when discussing St Olaf's legacy in Finland. Moving from the high political or elite level, with texts such as Snorri's *Heimskringla* and the Swedish *Rhyme Chronicle*, to the lower-level 'ethnocultural knowledge' encoded in rituals and oral poetics, he exemplifies the adaptability and flexibility of the tradition and, one could say, of the interface between the larger and the small world. The cult of St Olaf was imported to Finland probably as early as the twelfth century and flourished in ecclesiastical life. In the same centuries Olaf (and Elijah) served as thunder or weather deities, similar to the pagan Ukko, and were venerated and invoked, among other things, against drought by peasant communities around the Gulf of Finland (in present-day Finland, Russia, Estonia, and Latvia). Thus a clear continuity of the functions of pagan deities and Christian saints can be surmised, pointing to yet another type of Christian framing of pagan elements. In terms of literature one can also note that Harvilahti moves from the canonical to the non-canonical. The rich undergrowth of oral poetics, here exemplified in Finnish and Latvian, shows that saints, introduced originally by the ecclesiastical elite, were taken seriously as forces directly relevant to the concerns of peasants and formed part of their 'ethnocultural' poetics, and in this way also had a literary life outside the liturgy.

III. The adoption and consolidation of new norms and the storyworld that accompanied them required persuasion — sometimes as a top-down rhetoric (and occasionally violent), sometimes as a more civilized peer-to-peer process. Preaching would have underlined the importance of proper behaviour and church attendance as enabling reconciliation between man and God. The social setting of the Old Norse Stave Church homily (on the dedication of a church) from around 1200 analysed by Aidan Conti turns out to be at least twofold. As a written performance in various specific text collections it is made by and for the very few literate priests who could reuse elements or entire texts and text collections. On a more obvious level, although the homily addresses itself to a congregation, it should not be taken as a literal transcript, but rather as an indication of a type of performance. Inconsistencies in the mode of address also point to the fact that adaptations to specific preaching situations were taken for granted. The Latin learning behind the vernacular text again links the large and the small world (both for the preachers and for the typical audience) and guarantees the norms to be inculcated. In literary terms, as Conti argues, this, and other sermons, 'bridges oral and written, Latin and vernacular, authorial and anonymous' and 'although not frequently considered canonical literature by belletristic standards, represents par excellence medieval literary production'.

In her contribution on selected Icelandic family sagas, Slavica Ranković draws attention to the wider fluid text, storyworld, or tradition if you like, which is of paramount importance for a modern understanding of the performativity of the sagas. By using the concept of traditional referentiality (Foley), Ranković points to this wider oral dimension of the written sagas (whether read aloud, retold, etc.). That dimension is mostly lost to us, but not completely. Through comparative considerations and specific names and motifs which must have triggered certain responses beyond the purely intratextual or intertextual, she points to the flexibility of the tradition and its interest in influencing, rather than just reflecting, social norms in thirteenth- and fourteenth-century Iceland. The norms inherent in the stories thus had the potential of regulating and civilizing behaviour among peers. Although the storyworld of the classical family sagas may have been a more closed system of references, names, and motifs, Ranković's analysis is also relevant for other storyworlds in Iceland (like that of saints) and, in principle, for the whole Nordic region of 'agrarian' oral poetics: the enormous potential in professional or semi-professional storytelling must have allowed for many more layers of both sheer entertainment and moral instruction than what we are able to grasp through our written literature. But the rich Icelandic material gives us better glimpses than most other medieval storytelling we know of in the North.

In her article on the popular memory of the mother of Mary, St Anne, Irma-Riitta Järvinen explains some surprising transformations from late medieval motifs to nineteenth- and twentieth-century folklore — and yet a certain continuity in Anne's role as healer and provider of riches. The spread of the cult of St Anne from the late fourteenth century in urban centres in Northern Europe also affected the Finnish coastal area in the pre-Reformation period as can be seen in sculptures, paintings, and altar dedications. Late medieval Anne was originally a merchant, urban phenomenon, stressing family values, marital prosperity, and ideals of parenthood. As the mild-mannered head of the family she passed on knowledge (teaching Mary to read) as well as protection and wealth. By analysing proverbs and charms from the late folklore record, Järvinen shows that Anne was both associated with peasant women's work before Christmas (with a December date for her memorial) and conceived as a spirit of the woods in Karelia (following the Eastern Church's September date) where she could secure good hunting results. Although little evidence exists between the sixteenth century and the nineteenth century, these different roles at least suggest some remarkable adaptations from urban to rural life and from an educational role to a 'supervisor' of the goods of the land and the woods.

The extraordinary (Latin) *Chronicle* by Henry of Livonia is the subject of Linda Kaljundi's article. Henry addressed himself primarily to the northern German clerical elite who had followed German merchants and crusaders in a daring expansion to the north and east around 1200. His eye-witness chronicle was written from the point of view of the small community established in a hostile country in Riga as a report to a papal legate as well as a local memory of the Riga church. Kaljundi reads the text as a performance in itself, as an act of writing and speaking the mind of the German Christians in this outpost, thereby defining their mission in a historical perspective, equating their adventures and setbacks with biblical events. On another level Kaljundi underlines the potential of Henry's chronicle to elucidate the rituals and the symbolic and linguistic performativity of the missionary activities themselves — and indeed their mirror image in pagan rituals and performances. This reading occurs in dialogue with recent theoretical discussion about rituals and performance in and through medieval texts in general. Henry's chronicle thereby appears as a remarkable piece of identity making on the frontier (in contrast not only to pagans, but also to the Danish, Swedish, and Russian mission in adjacent areas). The chronicle is usually not taken into account in a broader Nordic context, because it is 'German' and in Latin, but it certainly belongs in the Baltic literary space. Furthermore, its representation of crusading, frontier society, and threatening paganism, while being extreme, may entail lessons for students of other Nordic areas. The inculcation and propagation of Christian norms was, also in the North, linked to violence, military domination, and colonization — and in Henry's case self-professedly so.

IV. Several of the above papers touch upon textual expressions of high and low social identities (e.g. Harvilahti), and the last cluster of articles focuses more specifically on the (mostly oral) poetics shaped and consumed by the lower strata of society.

In Pertti Anttonen's contribution we are presented with a non-ecclesiastical variant of the story of Finland's martyr, Bishop Henry, and his supposed murderer called Lalli (certain evidence for the name is found only in the early modern transmission). In exploring this vernacular narrative — attested in writing only in the early seventeenth century, but with sufficient medieval iconographic material to vouch for wide circulation of the motifs before the Reformation — Anttonen deals with formal, didactic-psychological, social, and performative aspects. Reference is made to the debate over the origin and diffusion of the late medieval ballad (mainly rural or urban setting?) and to the wide appeal of the short and dramatic form. An apocryphal version of the story of Judas (exemplified through an early English ballad) highlights the popular attraction to the psychology of the traitor, the possibility of a woman behind his evil behaviour, and his guilt and death. On all these counts Anttonen is able to suggest an extraecclesiastical setting as the social framework for inventing and maintaining these alternative twists to the stories. In the case of the late medieval song (dates have been suggested between *c.* 1275 and *c.* 1450) about Henry and Lalli, a rural Finnish setting seems to be obvious, but it is important in this context to underline the imports that lay in the background as models: the biblical story, of course, but also the Norwegian story of the martyrdom of St Olaf. The interplay between ancient biblical, more recent Nordic, and local myth-making within and outside of the Church is thus richly illustrated in this material.

Else Mundal presents us with two forms of improvised oral poetics in Old Norse — so non-canonical and improvised that it is in fact difficult to ascertain their existence. Through a few written fragments, allusions in other texts, and terminological analysis, she makes the case that female mourning songs (at funeral rites) and obscene verses recited at harvest or other fertility festivities, for instance, were living oral genres in western Scandinavia well into Christian times. In looking at these genres she also highlights female agency in Old Norse oral poetics (women were probably also present at the fertility parlour games). Mundal's contribution also beautifully underlines the point made above about canonicity and representativity: not only were many medieval poetic forms not designed to be transmitted in writing, they were in fact not even created to be memorized. Only the social and ritual context and a certain register of vocabulary, content, and length identified them to their contemporary users. They can be seen as examples of poetic forms 'from below' inasmuch as they hardly depended on professional singers/storytellers.

Finally, another intriguing analysis of (mainly) female songs in the early modern and modern period — with a medieval pedigree or at least some very probable parallels — is undertaken by Senni Timonen. In Karelia and Ingria, which lay in the border region between Roman and Orthodox rites, a number of versions of a song about Mary picking berries has been preserved in the folklore record of the nineteenth and twentieth centuries. They reflect in different ways the social reality of women picking berries in late summer — either as part of a farming culture (Ingria) or of a more mixed economy of hunting, farming, and forestry (Karelia). The highly original imagery, although with some interesting parallels to southern Slavic material, depicts the Virgin Mary becoming pregnant with the Saviour by eating a berry. The sometimes explicit allusions to sexuality and fertility form part of the imagery — a daring appropriation of the figure of Mary. Although these songs are attested only from the seventeenth century on, they can still help us imagine some of the syncretistic medieval voices from below.

* * *

It is our hope that the present collection can further both interdisciplinary and interregional studies of Northern literary culture in the Middle Ages. We also hope to have convinced at least some readers that for future syntheses there is a difficult, but necessary, balance to strike between constructing an alternative master narrative and giving in to a series of fragmented images. It is difficult to predict where a solution may lie, but the studies presented here could, when taken together, contribute towards making a strictly national or disciplinary narrative less credible.

Works Cited

Primary Sources

Sunesøn, Anders, *Andreae Sunonis filii Hexaemeron*, ed. by Sten Ebbesen and Lars Boje Mortensen, Corpus philosophorum Danicorum medii aevi, 11, 2 vols (København: Gad, 1985–88)

Secondary Works

Abukhanfusa, Kerstin, *Mutilated Books: Wondrous Leaves from Swedish Bibliographical History* (Stockholm: Riksarkivet, 2004)

Abukhanfusa, Kerstin, and others, eds, *Helgerånet: från mässböcker till munkepärmar* (Stockholm: Riksarkivet, 1993)

Bagge, Sverre, 'Den heroiske tid — kirkereform og kirkekamp 1153–1214', in *Ecclesia Nidrosiensis 1153–1537: søkelys på Nidaroskirkens og Nidarosprovinsens historie*, ed. by Steinar Imsen (Trondheim: Tapir, 2003), pp. 51–80

Bagge, Sverre, and Sæbjørg Walaker Nordeide, 'The Kingdom of Norway', in *Christianization and the Rise of Christian Monarchy: Scandinavia, Central Europe and Rus' c. 900–1200*, ed. by Nora Berend (Cambridge: Cambridge University Press, 2007), pp. 121–66

Blomkvist, Nils, Stefan Brink, and Thomas Lindkvist, 'The Kingdom of Sweden', in *Christianization and the Rise of Christian Monarchy: Scandinavia, Central Europe and Rus' c. 900–1200*, ed. by Nora Berend (Cambridge: Cambridge University Press, 2007), pp. 167–213

Borgehammar, Stephan, and others, eds., *Nordic Medieval Literature in Latin: A Website of Authors and Anonymous Works c. 1100–1530* (Universitetet i Bergen) <https://wikihost.uib.no/medieval> (2012)

Braunmüller, Kurt, 'Der Einfluss des Mittelniederdeutschen auf die altskandinavischen Sprachen in neuer Sicht', *Niederdeutsches Jahrbuch: Jahrbuch des Vereins für niederdeutsche Sprachforschung*, 117 (1994), 93–108

Brunius, Jan, 'Medieval Manuscript Fragments in the National Archives: A Survey', in *Medieval Book Fragments in Sweden: An International Seminar in Stockholm, 13–16 November 2003*, ed. by Jan Brunius (Stockholm: Riksarkivet, 2005), pp. 9–17

——, ed., *Medieval Book Fragments in Sweden: An International Seminar in Stockholm, 13–16 November 2003* (Stockholm: Kungliga Vitterhets Historie och Antikvitets Akademien, 2005)

Burke, Peter, *What Is Cultural History?* (Cambridge: Polity, 2004)

Crone, Patricia, *Pre-industrial Societies* (Oxford: Oneworld, 2003)

Ebbesen, Sten, 'The Danes, Science, Scholarship, and Books in the Middle Ages', in *Living Words and Luminous Pictures: Medieval Book Culture in Denmark*, ed. by Erik Petersen (København: Kongelige Bibliotek, 1999), pp. 119–26

Foley, John Miles, *Traditional Oral Epic: The Odyssey, Beowulf, and the Serbo-Croatian Return Song* (Berkeley: University of California Press, 1990)

Gelting, Michael, 'The Kingdom of Denmark', in *Christianization and the Rise of Christian Monarchy: Scandinavia, Central Europe and Rus' c. 900–1200*, ed. by Nora Berend (Cambridge: Cambridge University Press, 2007), pp. 73–120

——, 'Two Early Twelfth-Century Views of Denmark's Christian Past: Ailnoth and the Anonymous of Roskilde', in *Historical Narratives and Christian Identity on a European Periphery: Early History Writing in Northern, East-Central, and Eastern Europe (c. 1070–1200)*, ed. by Ildar H. Garipzanov, Medieval Texts and Cultures of Northern Europe, 26 (Turnhout: Brepols, 2011), pp. 33–55

Glauser, Jörg, 'Mittelalter (800–1500)', in *Skandinavische Literaturgeschichte*, ed. by Jörg Glauser (Stuttgart: Metzler, 2006), pp. 1–50

——, 'Vorwort', in *Skandinavische Literaturgeschichte*, ed. by Jörg Glauser (Stuttgart: Metzler, 2006), pp. ix–xviii

——, ed., *Skandinavische Literaturgeschichte* (Stuttgart: Metzler, 2006)

Green, Dennis H., *Medieval Listening and Reading: The Primary Reception of German Literature 800–1300* (Cambridge: Cambridge University Press, 1994)

Gullick, Michael, 'Preliminary Observations on Romanesque Manuscript Fragments of English, Norman and Swedish Origin in the Riksarkivet (Stockholm)', in *Medieval Book Fragments in Sweden: An International Seminar in Stockholm, 13–16 November 2003*, ed. by Jan Brunius (Stockholm: Kungliga Vitterhets Historie och Antikvitets Akademien, 2005), pp. 31–82

Guðrún Nordal, *Tools of Literacy: The Role of Skaldic Verse in Icelandic Textual Culture of the Twelfth and Thirteenth Centuries* (Toronto: University of Toronto Press, 2001)

Haavio, Martti, 'Tuohikirje no. 292: vanha suomalaisen muinaisuskonnon lähde', *Virittäjä* (1964), 1–17

Habinek, Thomas, *The World of Roman Song: From Ritualized Speech to Social Order* (Baltimore: Johns Hopkins University Press, 2005)

Hallberg, Peter, 'I: Forntid', in *Nordens litteratur*, ed. by Mogens Brøndsted, 2 vols (København: Gyldendal, 1972), I: *Før 1860*, pp. 13–47

——, 'II: Den äldre medeltid', in *Nordens litteratur*, ed. by Mogens Brøndsted, 2 vols (København: Gyldendal, 1972), I: *Før 1860*, pp. 51–91

——, 'III: Den yngre medeltid', in *Nordens litteratur*, ed. by Mogens Brøndsted, 2 vols (København: Gyldendal, 1972), I: *Før 1860*, pp. 95–128

Hastings, Adrian, *The Construction of Nationhood: Ethnicity, Religion and Nationalism* (Cambridge: Cambridge University Press, 1997)

Havelock, Eric, *The Muse Learns to Write: Reflections on Orality and Literacy from Antiquity to the Present* (New Haven: Yale University Press, 1986)

——, *Preface to Plato* (Oxford: Oxford University Press, 1963)

Helle, Knut, 'Growing Inter-Scandinavian Entanglement', in *The Cambridge History of Scandinavia*, I: *Prehistory to 1520*, ed. by Knut Helle (Cambridge: Cambridge University Press, 2003), pp. 411–20

Hlaváček, Ivan, 'Dreisprachigkeit im Bereich der Böhmischen Krone: zum Phänomen der Sprachbenutzung im böhmischen diplomatischen Material bis zur hussitischen Revolution', in *The Development of Literate Mentalities in East Central Europe*, ed. by

Anna Adamska and Marco Mostert, Utrecht Studies in Medieval Literacy, 9 (Turnhout: Brepols, 2004), pp. 289–310

Holsinger, Bruce W., 'Analytical Survey 6: Medieval Literature and Cultures of Performance', in *New Medieval Literatures*, VI, ed. by David Lawton, Rita Copeland, and Wendy Scase (Oxford: Oxford University Press, 2003), pp. 271–311

Karlsen, Espen, 'Katalogisering av latinske membranfragmenter som forskningsprojekt: Del 2', in *Arkivverkets forskningsseminar, Gardemoen 2003*, Riksarkivaren, Rapporter og Retningslinjer, 16 (Oslo: Riksarkivet, 2003), pp. 58–88

——, 'Liturgiske bøker i Norge inntil år 1300 — import og egenproduksjon', in *Den kirkehistoriske utfordring*, ed. by Steinar Imsen (Trondheim: Tapir, 2005), pp. 147–70

Kaspersen, Søren, and others, eds, *Dansk litteraturhistorie*, I: *Fra runer til ridderdigtning o. 800–1480* (København: Gyldendal, 1984)

Kersken, Norbert, *Geschichtsschreibung im Europa der 'nationes': Nationalgeschichtliche Gesamtdarstellungen im Mittelalter* (Köln: Böhlau, 1995)

Krötzl, Christian, *Pilger, Mirakel und Alltag: Formen des Verhaltens im skandinavischen Mittelalter* (Helsinki: Suomen Historiallinen Seura, 1994)

Kruckenberg, Lori, and Andreas Haug, eds, *The Sequences of Nidaros: A Nordic Repertory and its European Context* (Trondheim: Tapir, 2006)

Leegaard Knudsen, Anders, *Saxostudier og rigshistorie på Valdemar Atterdags tid* (København: Museum Tusculanum, 1994)

Lehtinen, Anja-Inkeri, 'The Apopeciae of the Manuscripts of Hugh of St. Cher's Works', *Medioevo: rivista di storia della filosofia medievale*, 25 (1999–2000), 1–167

——, 'From Fragments into Codices: On Reconstitution of Theological and Philosophical Works', in *Medieval Book Fragments in Sweden: An International Seminar in Stockholm, 13–16 November 2003*, ed. by Jan Brunius (Stockholm: Kungliga Vitterhets Historie och Antikvitets Akademien, 2005), pp. 109–31

——, 'Kirjoja ja kirjastoja keskiajan Suomessa', in *Kirja Suomessa*, ed. by Esko Häkli (Helsinki: Helsingin yliopiston kirjasto, 1997), pp. 15–30

Lehtonen, Tuomas M. S., 'Conquête et construction de l'histoire sacrée en Finlande', in *Les Élites nordiques et l'Europe occidentale (XIIe-XVe siècle)*, ed. by Tuomas M. S. Lehtonen and Élisabeth Mornet, Histoire ancienne et médiévale, 94 (Paris: Publications de la Sorbonne, 2007), pp. 169–88

——, 'Latinet och folkspråken', in *Finlands svenska litteraturhistoria. Första delen: 1400–1900*, ed. by Johan Wrede and Rainer Knapas (Helsinki: Svenska litteratursällskapet, 1999), pp. 26–40

——, 'Piae Cantiones', in *Finlands svenska litteraturhistoria. Första delen: 1400–1900*, ed. by Johan Wrede and Rainer Knapas (Helsinki: Svenska litteratursällskapet, 1999), pp. 40–50

——, 'Préliminaires: colonisation et culture écrite; les sources du pouvoir des élites au nord de la mer Baltique', in *Les Élites nordiques et l'Europe occidentale (XIIe-XVe siècle)*, ed. by Tuomas M. S. Lehtonen and Élisabeth Mornet, Histoire ancienne et médiévale, 94 (Paris: Publications de la Sorbonne, 2007), pp. 11–19

Lind, John, 'Scandinavian Nemtsy and Repaganized Russians: The Expansion of the Latin West during the Baltic Crusades and its Confessional Repercussions', in *The Crusades and the Military Orders: Expanding the Frontiers of Medieval Christianity*, ed. by Zsolt Hunyadi and József Laszlovszky (Budapest: Central European University Press, 2001), pp. 481–97

Lönnroth, Lars, and others, 'Literature', in *The Cambridge History of Scandinavia*, I: *Prehistory to 1520*, ed. by Knut Helle (Cambridge: Cambridge University Press, 2003), pp. 487–520

Mann, Michael, *The Sources of Social Power*, 2 vols (Cambridge: Cambridge University Press, 1986–93)

McCone, Kim, *Pagan Past and Christian Present in Early Irish Literature*, Maynooth Monographs, 3 (Maynooth: Department of Old Irish, 1990)

Melve, Leidulf, *Med ordet som våpen: Tale og skrift i vestleg historie* (Oslo: Norske Samlaget, 2001)

Meulengracht Sørensen, Preben, *Kapitler af Nordens litteratur i oldtid og middelalder* (Aarhus: Aarhus Universitetsforlag, 2006), pp. 14–15

——, 'Die skandinavischen Sprachen und Literaturen', in *Propyläen Geschichte der Literatur*, ed. by Erika Wischer, 6 vols (Berlin: Propyläen, 1981), II: *Die mittelalterliche Welt 600–1400*, pp. 280–309

Mortensen, Klaus P., and May Schack, eds, *Dansk litteraturs historie*, 5 vols (København: Gyldendal, 2006–09)

Mortensen, Lars Boje, 'Den formative dialog mellem latinsk og folkesproglig litteratur ca 600–1250: Udkast til en dynamisk model', in *Reykholt som makt- og lærdomssenter i den islandske og nordiske kontekst*, ed. by Else Mundal (Reykholt: Snorrastofa, 2005), pp. 229–71

——, 'The Nordic Archbishoprics as Literary Centres around 1200', in *Archbishop Absalon of Lund and his World*, ed. by Karsten Friis-Jensen and Inge Skovgaard-Petersen (Roskilde: Roskilde Museum, 2000), pp. 133–57

——, 'Philosophical Learning on the Edges of Latin Christendom: Some Late Twelfth-Century Examples from Scandinavia, Poland, and Palestine', in *Medieval Analyses in Language and Cognition: Acts of the Symposium 'The København School of Medieval Philosophy', January 10–13, 1996*, ed. by Sten Ebbesen and Russell L. Friedman (København: Kongelige Danske Videnskabernes Selskab, 1999), pp. 301–13

——, 'Writing and Speaking of St Olaf: National and Social Integration', in *Saints and their Lives on the Periphery: Veneration of Saints in Scandinavia and Eastern Europe (c. 1000–1200)*, ed. by Haki Antonsson and Ildar H. Garipzanov, Cursor Mundi, 9 (Turnhout: Brepols, 2010), pp. 207–18

Mortensen, Lars Boje, and Else Mundal, 'Erkebispesetet i Nidaros — arnestad og verkstad for Olavslitteraturen', in *Ecclesia Nidrosiensis 1153–1537: søkelys på Nidaroskirkens og Nidarosprovinsens historie*, ed. by Steinar Imsen (Trondheim: Tapir, 2003), pp. 353–84

Murray, Alexander, *Reason and Society in the Middle Ages* (Oxford: Clarendon Press, 1978)

Olesen, Jens E., 'Inter-Scandinavian Relations', in *The Cambridge History of Scandinavia*, I: *Prehistory to 1520*, ed. by Knut Helle (Cambridge: Cambridge University Press, 2003), pp. 710–70

Ommundsen, Åslaug, 'Books, Scribes and Sequences in Medieval Norway', 2 vols (unpublished doctoral thesis, Universitetet i Bergen, 2007)

——, ed., *The Beginnings of Nordic Scribal Culture, ca 1050–1300: Report from a Workshop on Parchment Fragments, Bergen 28–30 October 2005* (Bergen: Centre for Medieval Studies, 2006)

Petersen, Erik, ed., *Living Words and Luminous Pictures: Medieval Book Culture in Denmark* (København: Kongelige Bibliotek, 1999)

Redfield, Robert, *The Little Community: Viewpoints for the Study of a Human Whole*, Gottesman Lectures (Uppsala University), 5 (Uppsala: Almqvist and Wiksells, 1955)

——, *Peasant Society and Culture: An Anthropological Approach to Civilization* (Chicago: University of Chicago Press, 1956)

Stacey, Robin Chapman, *Dark Speech: The Performance of Law in Early Ireland* (Philadelphia: University of Pennsylvania Press, 2007)

Turville-Petre, Gabriel, *Origins of Icelandic Literature* (Oxford: Clarendon Press, 1953)

Tyler, Elizabeth M., 'Trojans in Anglo-Saxon England: Precedent without Descent', in *Troy and the European Imagination*, ed. by Elizabeth Archibald and James Clark (forthcoming)

——, 'The *Vita Ædwardi*: The Politics of Poetry at Wilton Abbey', *Anglo-Norman Studies*, 31 (2009), 135–56

Varpio, Yrjö, and Liisi Huhtala, eds, *Suomen kirjallisuuden historia*, I (Helsinki: Suomalaisen Kirjallisuuden Seura, 1999)

Vizkelety, András, 'Die deutsche Sprache und das deutsche Schrifttum im ungarischen Mittelalter', in *The Development of Literate Mentalities in East Central Europe*, ed. by Anna Adamska and Marco Mostert, Utrecht Studies in Medieval Literacy, 9 (Turnhout: Brepols, 2004), pp. 277–87

Winge, Vibeke, *Dänische Deutsche – deutsche Dänen: Geschichte der deutschen Sprache in Dänemark 1300–1800 mit einem Ausblick auf das 19. Jahrhundert* (Heidelberg: Winter, 1992)

Wiseman, T. P., *The Myths of Rome* (Exeter: University of Exeter Press, 2004)

Wrede, Johan, and Rainer Knapas, eds, *Finlands svenska litteraturhistoria*, I: *1400–1900* (Helsinki: Svenska litteratursällskapet i Finland, 1999)

Part I

The Impact of Latin Song, Book, and Service

The Word of God and the Stories of Saints: Medieval Liturgy and its Reception in Norway

Åslaug Ommundsen

From Performance to Dead Letters

Several generations ago one of Norway's most prominent literary figures, Sigrid Undset, remarked that it was curious how people in general were so unaware of what we owe the medieval Church and early Latin literacy for the rise of vernacular literature.[1] While the general awareness of the importance of Latin may not have grown considerably since Undset's time, in modern research it is becoming increasingly clear that not only Latin literacy in general, but Latin liturgy in particular has played an important role in the development of the local literature of Europe's northern periphery.

The liturgy of the medieval Church consisted of a huge corpus of texts and music which was introduced to the North along with Christianity in the eleventh and twelfth centuries. Early liturgical book fragments kept in the National Archives in Oslo constitute important sources for the adoption and later adaptation of the Christian liturgy. While the literary activity of the eleventh century consists of the copying of liturgical books, in the twelfth century there is an increased consciousness regarding the liturgical texts and their role in defining a local Christian identity. This is most clearly seen in the second half of the twelfth century, after the establishment of the archdiocese of Nidaros (1152/53), which spread across the Norwegian mainland and the islands in

---

[1] Undset, *Norske helgener*, pp. 58–60, 67.

the West. The desire for higher ecclesiastical independence and a more defined self-image resulted not only in the entire archdiocese of Nidaros making a programme for a uniform liturgy,[2] but also in the production of the first locally composed Latin texts. Among the first texts were the miracles and the *passio* of St Olaf the king and martyr, patron saint of Nidaros (d. 29 July 1030), and the histories of the Norwegian kings. As shown by Lars Boje Mortensen in his comparative study, the Norwegian literary development follows a pattern similar to that of Denmark and Hungary, where the stories pertaining to the royal primary saints, the figures most important for a local Christian identity, are those first told in local literary compositions.[3] One important purpose for the *Passio Olavi* was liturgical, and passages from the text were performed on Olaf's feast day, 29 July, in songs and lessons.

A philologist's perspective on a medieval liturgical text — be it a *lectio*, hymn, or sequence — is often that of the 'silent reader'. The knowledge about the texts' natural arena — the medieval Mass or Divine Office — is often too theoretical to influence our modern readings and interpretations, and we tend to ignore that the purpose of the liturgical texts was to serve as instruction for the performance of a religious ritual. A Christian Mass can still be experienced today, but it is a different experience from that of the Middle Ages. The vernacular has taken the place of Latin, and the once very important celebrations of local Scandinavian saints remain only as pieces of text and written music in the fragments of medieval service books. Even when the songs and narratives of the past are performed, as is occasionally the case with the liturgy of the Norwegian patron saint Olaf on 29 July, it is as a remnant and re-enactment of a ritual from the past on a modern stage. The Latin liturgy, and particularly the celebrations of local saints, have, at least to the people in Scandinavia, become religious rituals which are no longer performed, but only preserved in writing, and are thus 'dead letters' in the words of Roy Rappaport.[4]

This article is an attempt to see beyond the 'dead letters' of the Christian liturgy that chance has left us from the Middle Ages, and it tries to catch a glimpse of the ritual itself and its participants. Liturgical texts written for the universal saint Nicholas and the local saint Olaf and performed on their feast days will serve as illustrations of how texts could interact with other texts, and

---

[2] The Nidaros ordinal was begun by Archbishop Øystein Erlendsson (1161–88), who worked on it in the 1170s. It was finished after his death, presumably shortly after 1200; see *Ordo Nidrosiensis ecclesiae*, ed. by Gjerløw.

[3] Mortensen, 'Sanctified Beginnings and Mythopoietic Moments'.

[4] Rappaport, *Ritual and Religion*, p. 135.

how they sometimes seem to reveal an effort to facilitate the reception of a message, even when it was expressed in Latin, a language understood by only a few. Not only the Latin language, but also the performance itself posed challenges for the receiver or participant. The effect of the medieval religious rituals would have been different on different people, and while some might have been trained to understand the meaning of what they saw and heard, many people were not.

Christianity Made Local

The liturgical texts of the Christian Church were not immediately accessible to people on the northern outskirts of the Christian world. The most obvious obstacle was the foreign language the texts were written and performed in: Latin, a language remote from the Scandinavian vernacular. The distance in time and space from the original Roman Church created an odd effect not intended by those who formed the initial ritual, namely that the Latin language, which once served to clarify and transmit the word of God, became a language of foreign sounds and unknown words which further mystified the already complex message of salvation. In a sense the majority of the participants in a Mass did not necessarily have the proper codebook to decipher the message that was being transmitted.

A knowledge of Latin was not widespread in Norway. The true *literati* were a very small part of the population and would have been found primarily among the priests and the men and women of the religious orders. In his discussion of early Norwegian literacy, Sverre Bagge estimates that there were approximately two thousand priests in Norway *c*. 1300 and that the people who could read or write amounted to only a small percentage of the population, possibly only 1 per cent.[5] Only a small minority would have been able to grasp the effort and purpose behind the organization of the liturgical celebration. A larger group, but still small, would have had the ability to understand the larger part of the contents in the liturgical celebrations that occurred from day to day, from feast to feast. Members of the monastic community were active in the celebration and in most cases would have had a relatively high degree of understanding of the texts performed. The cathedral housed people with various levels of education, where some would have known the texts intimately, and a wealthy few

---

[5] Bagge, *Da boken kom til Norge*, p. 19.

among the lay people would have had the necessary grasp of Latin to understand parts of the contents of the Mass. For some, the Latin training was limited to the Psalter, while others may have moved on to higher grammatical training.

A ritual where the participants do not understand the words is by no means meaningless per definition. While conceding that the meaning of ritual might be indefinitely manifold, Rappaport divides the meaning of ritual into three levels, where the semantic meaning is referred to as the 'low order meaning'.[6] Whether the listeners understood all, some, or none of the Latin words of the liturgical texts, the liturgy would have worked on different levels of communication for the various groups in a church. The very presence of a formalized and performed liturgy for a feast or saint would in itself have held a message. The solemnity of the ritual and the unavailability of the spoken words would have made an impression on the spectators.[7] The Latin spoken in local churches gave the religious ritual the air of something veiled, mysterious, and magical, which eventually worked its way into popular magic spells.[8] Even if people were unable to grasp the literal meaning, other levels of meaning were still available to them. When Rappaport discusses a high- or highest-level meaning, it is experiential rather than intellectual, an experience that gives a sense of unity and identity.[9]

The promotion of local saints could make people identify with their church in a more profound way. In addition to St Olaf, who was the *rex perpetuus* of Norway and Nidaros, the smaller dioceses had their own patron saints, often with a local connection. The stories of their lives and miracles were reworked into a shape that made them suitable for lessons at the Night Office, and in some cases also turned into a sequence or other liturgical songs. It is difficult to distinguish a 'trademark' for local liturgy, and for good reasons. Uniqueness would not have been the goal of a composer or organizer of the liturgy of a local saint; quite the opposite. When people in the North saw their own local saints celebrated in the same manner as the saints from the first centuries of Christianity, it would have sent the message that one of their own had qualified for the highest honour in the Church. The formality of the liturgy, and the outspoken presence of the saint in the celebration of Mass, would have effectively thrust a saint from the local realm into universal sainthood. The celebration

---

[6] Rappaport, *Ritual and Religion*, p. 70.
[7] See discussion in Bagge, *Da boken kom til Norge*, pp. 148–49.
[8] Compare Bang, *Norske hexeformularer og magiske opskrifter*.
[9] Rappaport, *Ritual and Religion*, p. 71.

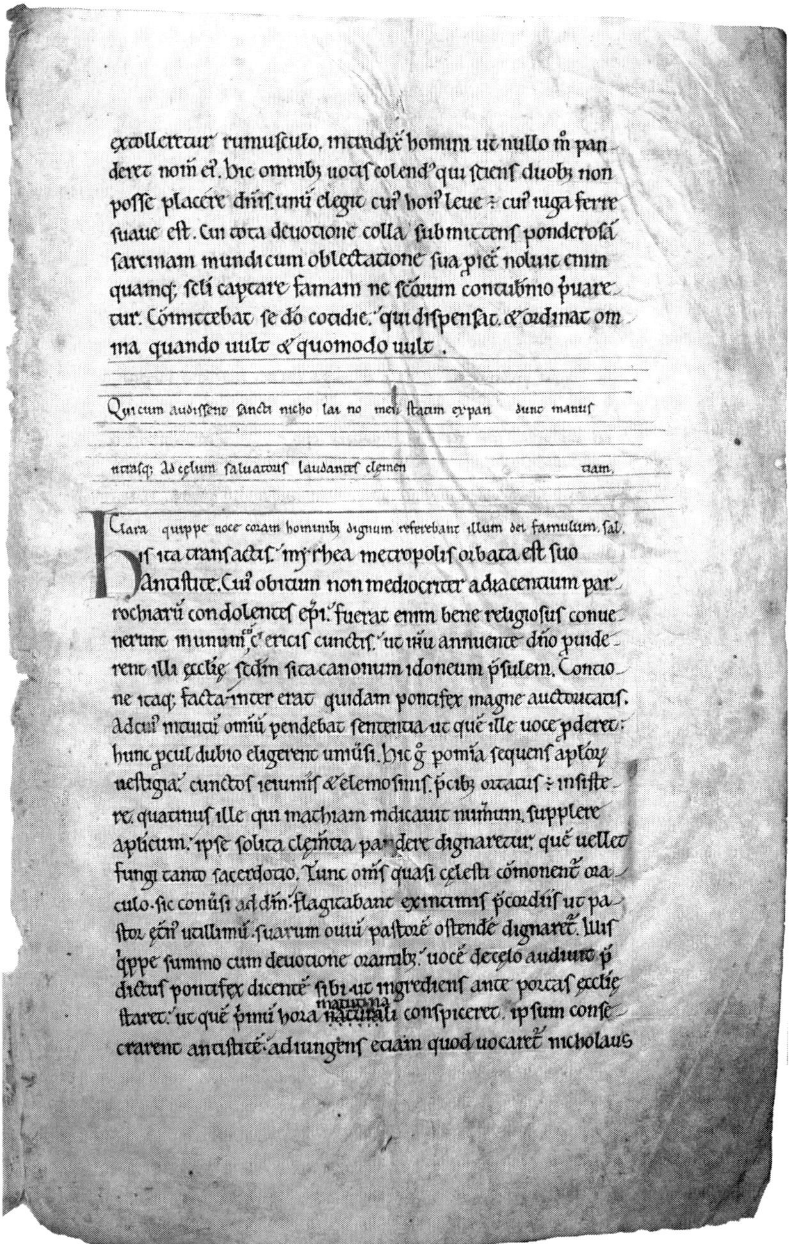

Figure 1. One leaf (30 x 18.5 cm) from a breviary written in England, containing a part of Nicholas's legend. Oslo, Riksarkivet, MS Lat. fragm. 1023, fol. 1ʳ. Early twelfth century. Reproduced with permission.

of St Olaf, for example, as one among other saints in the Church would have indicated that Nidaros was an important part of the Christian world. The local saints supplied a recently converted people with 'their own' special protectors. While the liturgy required the legends of local saints to be told in Latin, the elements of their lives and miracles were conveyed to the people in the form of stories in the vernacular, through pictures, and through everyday conversation, providing them with alternative ways of understanding the message outside of the ritual itself.

Singing the Stories of Saints

One of the characteristics of the Nidaros ordinal was a large and complex repertoire of sequences. The sequence is a particularly interesting liturgical genre due to its form, subject matter, and history. North of the Alps, in the Carolingian era, ways were found to include the local saints and their stories in the liturgical celebrations through other means than simple lessons, and among these was the sequence. At the outset, prose texts suitable for the celebration of the day were composed to fit with the originally textless *iubilus* melodies that followed the Alleluia in the celebration of Mass. In spite of the rather special origin of the sequences as 'texted' melodies, the texts were not, or at least did not remain, a secondary element. The genre developed, moving gradually from prose to verse, and from texted melodies to a more equal text-melody relationship.[10] The composers of sequences collected their subject matter from hagiographic texts, and often referred to specific episodes and miracles which people would have known from a saint's legend. The condense manner in which the narrative elements were treated almost gave them the character of internal codes — the episodes could be recognized through the use of key words, but were not laid out in detail.

The sequences reached the height of their popularity as Christianity reached the northern boundaries of Europe in the eleventh and twelfth centuries. Consequently, the sequences were part of the Christian liturgical 'package' presented to the converted North. The remains of medieval liturgical manuscripts from the Archsee of Nidaros show that not only was the official repertory from *c.* 1200 unusually large,[11] but a large number of sequences other than

[10] For the history and development of the sequence, see, for instance, Kruckenberg, 'Sequenz'.

[11] Compare *Ordo Nidrosiensis ecclesiae*, ed. by Gjerløw, pp. 431–39; Kruckenberg, 'Making a Sequence Repertory'.

those prescribed were also available in the North.[12] The sequence evidently found both promoters and an audience. The large majority of sequences in Nidaros, as in the rest of Scandinavia, were imported. In Nidaros only a few saints are known to have had proper sequences that were presumably local (and in some cases rather late) compositions, namely St Olaf (29 July) and St Hallvard (15 May) on the Norwegian mainland, St Jón of Hólar in Iceland (7 November), and St Magnus of the Orkneys (16 April).

One advantage of the sequence is that it was a way to introduce episodes from hagiographical texts into the Mass where there would otherwise have not been room for them, since the lessons of the Mass, the Epistle, and the Gospel were reserved for biblical texts. The readings from the Latin saints' legends took place at the Night Office (the *matutinus*) where they were heard primarily by priests or members of religious communities. In a sequence, on the other hand, the virtues, good deeds, and miracles of a saint were placed at the centre of the Mass, right between the Epistle and the Gospel reading.

The Medieval Mass

Main elements: Lessons (Epistle and Gospel) and Holy Communion
Main books: Missal (all elements) or Gradual (songs only)

> Introitus
> Kyrie eleison
> Gloria in excelsis
> Oratio collecta
> Epistola (first reading)
> Graduale (responsorial song)
> Alleluia (with verse)
> **Sequentia**
> Evangelium (second reading)
> Credo
>
> Offertorium
> Praefatio ('vere dignum')
> Sanctus – Benedictus
> Canon ('te igitur')
> Oratio super oblata (or secreta)

---

[12] Compare Eggen, *The Sequences of the Archbishopric of Nidaros*. See also the index of sequences in Ommundsen, 'Books, Scribes and Sequences', I, 240–46.

Pater noster
Agnus Dei
Communio (the distribution of bread and wine)
Communio (antiphonal song)
Oratio ad complendum (or Postcommunio)
Ite missa est/Benedicamus

In addition to the lessons, the sequences were surrounded by a mosaic of antiphons, prayers, and other liturgical elements and interacted with these other texts on several levels. Not only was the composer aware of the context for which he was writing, but the other texts would also have been fresh in the ears of his listeners. The intertextual relationships of the sequence would have extended beyond the Mass of the day, and over to the hagiographical texts, as well as other sequence texts. Most sequences had a similar structure, opening with the encouragement to celebrate, followed by a middle section with the core topic of the day, and ending in a prayer for intercession on the participants' behalf. The use of 'sequence words and topics' like joy (*gaudia*), glory (*gloria*), today (*hodie*), and flocks of angels singing *Alleluia* were commonplaces for the sequences. For a sequence to 'work', it had to find the balance between commonplaces — things people expected to hear — and key words referring to the stories unique to a particular saint, making the saint distinguishable, but yet equal to other saints.

The presentation of texts through chant could make the words and sentences more difficult to grasp, even for people with knowledge of Latin. While a lesson was recited or chanted with a simple and predictable melodic line, antiphons or sequences had a complex and often difficult melody, posing greater demands on the performing singer as well as the listener. To understand the meaning of any uttered words, the listeners had to actually hear the words, pick up the sounds, and distinguish the syllables from each other. When a text is conveyed by voice alone, the demand is on the performer to make his words reach the ears of the listeners, which can be challenging in a large, crowded room. During a medieval Mass none of the prescribed texts were plainly spoken, including the lessons, which were recited according to standard melodies. To recite the lessons in the form of a chant added volume to the voice, making it easier for people to hear the text in comparison to a plainly read lesson. Singing or chanting was an efficient way of making the voice carry further, and was also more pleasant to the ear than shouting.

While the melody of a chanted lesson is designed specifically to make the words stand out clearly and define the sentences, the melody of an antiphon is a different matter. In a song with an elaborate melodic line and a melismatic character, the embellishment of the melody can make the words and sentences more difficult to distinguish. In antiphons, often using short lines from the Psalms, the texts were known to those who had a minimum level of education and they would need little aid to recognize the quotation. Regarding the reception of a chanted or sung text, a general principle may be this: the simpler the melody, the easier it is to hear the text. When the melody is complex, the text is more difficult to perceive, unless it is a text previously known.[13]

A sequence, on the other hand, would not have been a generally known text and would therefore have posed a greater challenge to impart its contents. The very form of the sequence facilitates an understanding of the text, as it is a genre with a text and melody that follow each other syllable for syllable. The sequences are difficult to sing with a complex melody that covers a wide range of notes, but the melody never continues alone leaving the text hanging in the air. An example of how an imported sequence could relate the story of a saint is the case of *Congaudentes*, a very popular sequence written for St Nicholas.[14]

Saint Nicholas and Congaudentes

Congaudentes was sung in Nidaros, as in most other parts of Europe, at the Mass of St Nicholas's day on 6 December.[15] From the church province of Nidaros there are fragments from seven different liturgical manuscripts testifying to the use of *Congaudentes*, the oldest of them dateable to the late twelfth century.[16] Seven manuscript witnesses may sound like a low number, but it is in fact relatively high: due to the large amount of Norwegian medieval manuscripts that are lost, only one other sequence has been found in as many as seven different copies in Norway. *Congaudentes* represents the 'transitional style' in sequences, typical for the late eleventh and the early twelfth centuries. It stands out with regard to

---

[13] The same observation is expressed by performers of the twentieth century: 'If you start talking about the leaves, the love, baby, those things, words you've already heard a million times, text doesn't matter because you can take those melismatically and turn them all over the place and people can still follow the contour of the idea. But if you're talking about concepts or using phrases which are unfamiliar, it's hard to get that information across if you're singing elaborate musical lines at the same time' (Zappa, *Classic Albums*).

[14] *Analecta hymnica medii aevi*, ed. by Blume and others, pp. 54, 66.

[15] Compare *Ordo Nidrosiensis ecclesiae*, ed. by Gjerløw, p. 298.

[16] Compare Ommundsen, 'Books, Scribes and Sequences', I, 241.

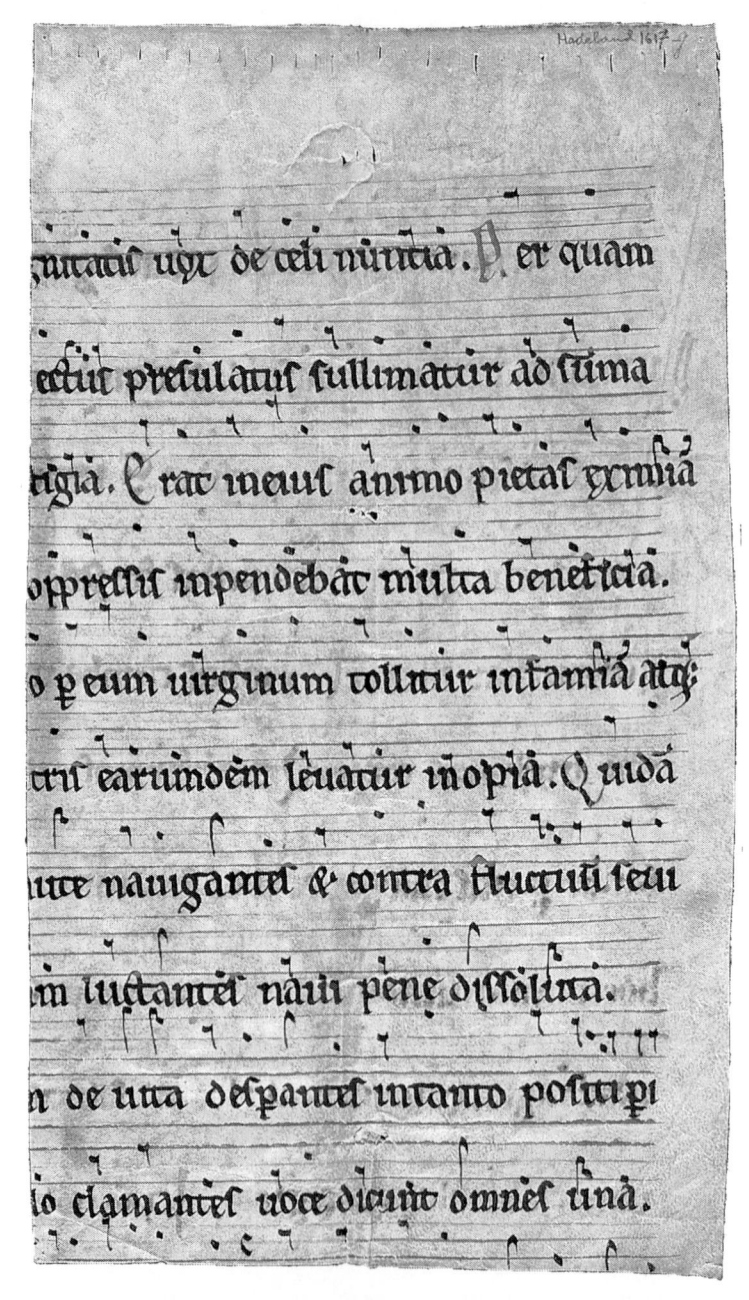

Figure 2. A fragment (22 x 12 cm) from a liturgical manuscript containing parts of Nicholas's highly popular sequence *Congaudentes exultemus*. Oslo, Riksarkivet, Lat. fragm. 471, fol. 1ʳ. Around or just before 1200. Reproduced with permission.

its popularity, since it spread so widely and quickly across Europe.[17] The 'high' number of Norwegian surviving copies of the *Congaudentes* may also be interpreted as a testimony to its appeal. As is common in sequences, it opens with an encouragement to celebrate the feast of the saint with song, in this case the feast of St Nicholas. By the second strophe it has already moved on to the virtues and deeds of Nicholas as laid out in his *vita*. The Latin version of Nicholas's *vita* was written *c*. 880 by John the Deacon and, just like the sequence, spread to most parts of Europe.[18] Among the fragments from manuscripts used in Nidaros during the Middle Ages, at least three fragments hold lessons from St Nicholas's *vita*, all of them extracts from the *vita* by John the Deacon.[19]

The sequence explains how Nicholas kept the fast as early as when we was lying in the cradle ('Qui in cunis adhuc iacens servándo ieiúnia'). This refers to the story in his *vita* that on Wednesday and Friday, the days of fasting, little baby Nicholas would only take milk from his mother's breast once. The sequence continues with the virtues of his youth, recounting his desire for studies and how he was immune to the immoral lifestyle of young people:

>   3a. Aduléscens amplexátur literárum stúdia,
>   3b. Aliénus et immúnis ab omni lascívia.
>
>   [3a. As a young man he embraced the study of books,
>   3b. a stranger to, and immune to, all immorality.]

The word *lascivia* rings of the *vita* of Nicholas: 'et non sicut illa aetas assolet lascivias complexus est mundi' ('and he did not embrace the immorality of this world, like that age usually does').[20] In strophe four we learn how his dignity as bishop was proclaimed by a voice from heaven ('vox de caelo nuntia'). Again the words in the sequence are reminiscent of those in the corresponding paragraph in the *vita* ('vocem de caelo audivit'):[21] The bishop in charge of the election of the Bishop of Myra heard a voice from heaven stating that the first per-

---

[17] *Congaudentes* has been analysed by Lori Kruckenberg with regard to its quick dissemination, its contents, rhyme, rhythm, melody, and transmission; see Kruckenberg, 'The Sequence from 1050–1150', pp. 227–29.

[18] See, for instance, Jones, *Saint Nicholas of Myra, Bari and Manhattan*, p. 45. For an edition of the text, see *Sanctuarium*, ed. by Mombritius, pp. 296–309.

[19] Oslo, Nat. Arch., Lat. fragm. 714; Oslo, Nat. Arch., Lat. fragm. 930; Oslo, Nat. Arch., Lat. fragm. 1023; see *Antiphonarium Nidrosiensis ecclesiae*, ed. by Gjerløw, pp. 48, 273–74, and pl. 14, 79.

[20] *Sanctuarium*, ed. by Mombritius, p. 297.

[21] *Sanctuarium*, ed. by Mombritius, p. 299.

son he saw coming to the church in the morning should be elected bishop. This person turned out to be Nicholas. The hagiographical material in the sequences is treated in a very compressed manner, but for those who know the stories the brief references will be enough.

Strophe five is dedicated to what may be Nicholas's most famous good deed, namely the gold used to rescue a father from surrendering his daughters to prostitution:

> 5b. Auro per eum vírginum tóllitur infámia atque patris earúndem levátur inópia.
>
> [5b. Through gold from him the virgins were saved from disgrace and their father relieved from poverty.]

Fragments from two of the remaining Nidaros manuscripts, both from the twelfth century, happen to tell the story of the three virgins and their father, although only a few sentences are extant.[22] Looking at the full text of the *vita*, it seems clear that the choice of words in the sequence is influenced by it: 'Decrevit omnino ex suis abundantiis earum supplere inopiam: ne puellae nobilibus ortae natalibus lupanari macularentur infamia' ('So he decided to relieve their poverty from his own abundance, so that the girls who were of noble origin should not be stained by the shame of the brothel').[23] Both *inopia* and *infamia* occur in both texts, in addition to the natural occurrences of *pater*, *aurum*, and *virgines* (although not in the quoted passage).

The climax of the sequence appears with a reference to some sailors ('Quidam naute navigantes') on a ship that was nearly falling apart ('navi pene dissoluta'), calling out to Nicholas in desperation. Their prayer is given in direct speech in the seventh strophe:

> 7a. O beáte Nicholáe, nos ad portum maris trahe de mortis angústia!
> 7b. Trahe nos ad portum maris, tu qui tot auxiliáris pietátis grátia!
>
> [7a. 'O blessed Nicholas, bring us to the harbour of the sea from the grasp of death!
> 7b. Bring us to the harbour of the sea, you who aid so many for the sake of your piety!']

As a response to the sailors' desperate prayer Nicholas proclaims that he is by their side ('ecce, quidam dicens, adsum ad vestra presídia'), and immediately he calms the weather:

---

[22] Oslo, Nat. Arch., Lat. fragm. 714 (Norway, late twelfth century); Oslo, Nat. Arch., Lat. fragm. 1023 (England, early twelfth century).

[23] *Sanctuarium*, ed. by Mombritius, pp. 298–99; see Figure 1 above.

8b. Statim aura datur grata et tempéstas fit sedáta, quievérunt mária

[8b. At once comes a welcome breath of air and the storm is settled, the oceans calm.]

The sequence approaches the end with a reference to oil and miracles at Nicholas's tomb in strophe nine, and in strophe ten a prayer that he should come to the aid of those about to suffer shipwreck on the ocean of sins in this world:

10a. Nos qui sumus in hoc mundo vitiórum in profúndo iam passi naufrágia.
10b. Glorióse Nicholáe, ad salútis portum trahe ubi pax et glória.

[10a. We who are in this world are now suffering shipwreck on the ocean of sins.
10b. Glorious Nicholas, pull us to the harbour of the sea where there is peace and glory.]

Nicholas's sequence is used to present a brief and condensed version of the episodes in Nicholas's *vita*, using significant key words that make it easier to identify the story. In strophe five, verse b, the reference to the gold (*aurum*), the virgins (*virgines*), disgrace (*infamia*), the father (*pater*), and his poverty (*inopia*) would have helped the listeners, even those with a very limited knowledge of Latin, to identify the strophe as a reference to the story about St Nicholas and the three virgins, even if they were not able to connect the words syntactically. Since to a large extent the choice of words in the sequence is the same as in the *vita*, the audience's familiarity with the words would have been even stronger, especially for those who, only a few hours before hearing (or performing) the sequence, had heard lessons from Nicholas's *vita* at Matins.

The strophes referring to the miracle of the sailors contain the same type of key words, with reference to the sailors (*naute*), sailing (*navigantes*), and the ship (*navis*). The essential plea to St Nicholas for salvation is repeated three times (while it is not repeated in the *vita*), and it is worth noticing that the words are more or less the same both in 7a ('nos ad portum maris trahe'), 7b ('trahe nos ad portum maris'), and 10b ('ad salutis portum trahe'), although this expression is not found in the *vita*.[24] The use of key words and the repetition of words are devices that may facilitate the comprehension of a performed text, especially if the language is not the mother tongue of the recipients. Thus while intertextual references (for instance from a saint's *vita*) may serve to add to the authority of one particular sequence, a side benefit may also be that it becomes more immediately understandable. One specific response to the demands of textual performance may be the transition from *Variatio delectat* to *Repetitio*

---

[24] *Sanctuarium*, ed. by Mombritius, p. 300.

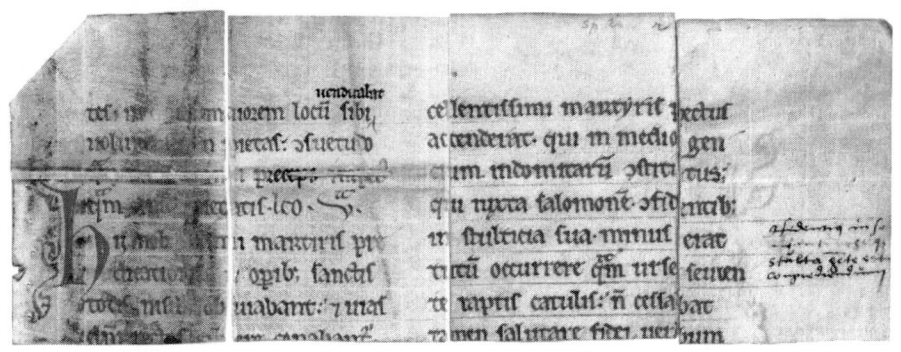

In situ 4A 121 32: 119, 6 C, 1–2ʳ.   Lat. fragm. 537, 34–35ʳ.

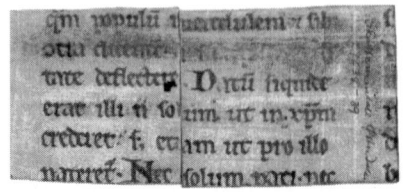

Lat. fragm. 479, 1–2ʳ.

Lat. fragm. 537, 36ʳ.

Figure 3. Part of the *Passio Olavi* divided into liturgical lessons, in one 'leaf' from a lectionary written in Norway; the leaf was presumably *c.* 30 x 22 cm when whole. Oslo, Riksarkivet, *c.* 1200. Reproduced with permission.

delectat. An example is the similarities between St Olaf's *Lux illuxit letabunda* sequence and the sequences of St Victor in Paris.[25] In a local extension of this, St Hallvard's sequence opens with the *Lux illuxit letabunda* incipit, echoing the text and melody of St Olaf's sequence.

[25] Compare Reiss, *Musiken ved den middelalderlige Olavsdyrkelsen*, p. 16.

St Olaf as the Light

Within a few years of his death in 1030, St Olaf of Nidaros had been celebrated with his own Mass and office. In the twelfth century the old office was replaced with a new one, based on the *Passio Olavi*, and the Mass celebration was supplied with a proper sequence, *Lux illuxit*.[26] Both initiatives were probably part of an undertaking to strengthen the image of Nidaros and increase the authority of St Olaf and his cult.[27] The sequence *Lux illuxit* is found on fragments from only three Norwegian medieval manuscripts, which certainly illustrates the immense losses of manuscript material in Norway.[28]

One aspect of liturgical texts in performance is the fact that they appear in context among other texts performed at the same occasion. Much has been written about the sequence of St Olaf and its relationship to other texts and melodies.[29] Still, less attention has been bestowed on the context in which it was performed and its relationship with the texts heard immediately before or after. The sequence *Lux illuxit* may be seen in light of the other textual efforts to promote St Olaf's sainthood in the second half of the twelfth century, first and foremost the office *In regali fastigio*, which textually is closely related to the *Passio Olavi*.[30] The investigation shows that not only did the sequence and the office reflect the same image of St Olaf as king and saint, but it also seems that some of the same rhetorical figures were favoured, namely those repeating similar words — like words from the same root. In this context it is worth considering whether the repeated words and repetitive rhetorical figures were not only due to the tastes of the time, but also connected to the demands of a performance.

---

[26] *Analecta hymnica medii aevi*, ed. by Blume and others, 42, 302.

[27] For the offices of Saint Olaf, see *Antiphonarium Nidrosiensis ecclesiae*, ed. by Gjerløw, pp. 182–86; Iversen, 'Transforming a Viking into a Saint'; Østrem, *The Office of Saint Olaf*. The earliest liturgy for Saint Olaf has only survived in English manuscripts: the Mass celebration in the 'Red Book of Darley' dated to the early 1060s (Cambridge, CCC, MS 422), and the office in the Leofric Collectar, written *c.* 1050–60 (BL, MS Harley 2961).

[28] Ommundsen, 'Books, Scribes and Sequences', I, 243.

[29] For editions of *Lux illuxit*, see Reiss, *Musiken ved den middelalderlige Olavsdyrkelsen*, pp. 12–44, and Eggen, *The Sequences of the Archbishopric of Nidaros*, I, 213–21. Both discussed possible parallels between *Lux illuxit* and sequences from St Victor. For a text edition, see also *Analecta hymnica medii aevi*, ed. by Blume and others, XLII, 302.

[30] Compare Ommundsen, 'A Saint and his Sequence'. Here is also the full text and English translation, as well as a fuller analysis of its formal features.

The eight strophes or verse pairs of the sequence for St Olaf emphasize the following elements:

- str. 1–3: Olaf as the light, and the joyful celebration of the day (parallels most sequences, as well as the opening of the Mass with its introit *Gaudeamus omnes in Domino*);
- str. 4–6: that amidst his royal duties, Olaf longed for Christ, and, unbroken by threats, fear of death, and hard struggle, he saved his people from their erroneous ways, receiving only hatred and hardship in return;
- str. 7: that he had a vision of Christ on the night before the battle;
- str. 8: that Olaf, 'our special protector', should save us from the evils of this world (to pray for intercession or protection was a common way for sequences to end).

The reference to Olaf as the light in the first strophe of *Lux illuxit* should be seen as significant:[31]

> 1a. Lux illuxit letabunda, lux illustris, lux iocunda, lux digna preconio.

> [1a. A joyous light has begun to shine, a bright and cheerful light, a light worthy of praise.]

The emphasis and four-time repetition of *lux* led Reiss to suggest the influence of the Victorine sequences, first and foremost the Pentecost sequence *Lux iocunda, lux insignis*, the Easter sequence *Lux illuxit dominica*, or the sequence for St Vincentius: *Triumphalis lux illuxit*.[32] While these probably influenced the composition of Olaf's *Lux illuxit* (possibly through a direct connection with St Victor in Paris), it is doubtful that the listeners were expected to make the connection, as none of these Victorine sequences were prescribed in the Nidaros ordinal. St Olaf as the light is not particularly emphasized in the office *In regali fastigio*, and it may be more tempting to see the emphasis on the light in connection with *Geisli*, the vernacular poem performed at the establishment of the Archsee of Nidaros in 1152/53, comparing Olaf to a ray of light.[33] Although only a few people in the Middle Ages would have been familiar with the poem *Geisli* itself, they should have been familiar with the *concept* of Olaf

---

[31] Discussed in more detail in Ommundsen, 'A Saint and his Sequence'.

[32] All of which were discussed by Reiss, *Musiken ved den middelalderlige Olavsdyrkelsen*, p. 16.

[33] Einarr Skúlason, *Geisli*, ed. by Chase.

Figure 4. Fragment containing St Olaf's sequence *Lux illuxit*. The fragment comes from a missal in octavo format (*c.* 14 cm wide) written in Norway, presumably in Trondheim. Oslo, Riksarkivet, Lat. fragm. 932, fol. 1ᵛ. Thirteenth century. Reproduced with permission.

as the light shining in the North, established textually primarily through *Geisli* and *Lux illuxit*.

One important aspect of the performed sequence is the melody, and the melody of *Lux illuxit* borrows from several other sequences. As pointed out by Erik Eggen, the first strophe of *Lux illuxit* melodically quotes the transitional sequence *Letabundus exultet*, prescribed in Nidaros for the *Epiphania Domini* (6 January).[34] Whether or not the *letabunda* (joyful) in the first strophe of Olaf's sequence is a direct reference to the *letabundus* in *Letabundus exultet* is not easy to say, but there is no reason why it should not be: the textual reference to Olaf as the light, as part of his *imitatio Christi*, is supported by the fact that the melody points to the Epiphany, the feast celebrating the manifestation of Christ on Earth.

Strophes two and four show what may be seen as direct textual references to the office *In regali fastigio*. The 'felici commercio' (happy trade) in the second strophe of the sequence is also found in the verse of the ninth responsory of Matins in the office (which is not one of the texts taken from *Passio Olavi*).[35]

---

[34] Eggen, *The Sequences of the Archbishopric of Nidaros*, I, 219. For the epiphany, see *Ordo Nidrosiensis ecclesiae*, ed. by Gjerløw, p. 172.

[35] For a broader discussion on the *felici commercio*, see Ommundsen, 'A Saint and his Sequence'.

Furthermore, in strophe four we find a reference to the first responsory of Matins, which has also given the twelfth-century office its title: *In regali fastigio*. The text in the responsory is taken more or less directly from the *Passio Olavi*, with 'rex Olavus' added to the *passio* text ('In regali fastigio constitutus spiritu pauper erat rex Olavus'; 'Although placed in royal dignity King Olaf was poor in spirit'). 'In regali fastigio' is transformed to 'in regni fastigio' in the sequence, which here also includes 'rex Olavus' as part of the lyrics:

> 4a. Inter curas absolutus rex Olavus constitutus in regni fastigio.
>
> [4a. Detached in the midst of his duties, King Olaf was placed in the dignity of kingship.]

What we can conclude from these examples is that *Lux illuxit* was not made in a textual vacuum, and that it reflects other sequences as well as the twelfth-century office *In regali fastigio*.

Missa Sancti Olavi: A Textual Mosaic

The Mass of St Olaf, the immediate context of *Lux illuxit*, received its form not long after his death in 1030, and although the Swedish sources reveal a large diversity,[36] in Norway the Mass seems to have remained more or less unaltered for five hundred years.[37] The prayers and chants of St Olaf's Mass were taken from the commons and were not unique to Olaf.[38] Still, the selection was far from random and emphasized the virtues of kingship. The texts of the gradual (*Posuisti, Domine*, with the verse *Desiderium animae eius*), the offertory (*Posuisti, Domine*), and the communion (*Magna gloria eius*) are all taken from Psalm 20 (21). 3–6 (2–5), which describe the ideal king who is chosen by God and true to Him:

> Desiderium animae eius tribuisti ei et voluntate labiorum eius non fraudasti eum. Quoniam praevenisti eum in benedictionibus dulcedinis posuisti in capit eius coronam de lapide pretioso. Vitam petiit a te et tribuisti ei longitudinem dierum in saeculum et in saeculum saeculi. Magna gloria eius in salutari tuo, gloriam et magnum decorem inpones super eum.

---

[36] Compare Brunius, *Atque Olavi*.

[37] *Ordo Nidrosiensis ecclesiae*, ed. by Gjerløw, p. 124.

[38] For the liturgy of St Olaf in the Nidaros ordinal, see *Ordo Nidrosiensis ecclesiae*, ed. by Gjerløw. For the prayers of the Mass, see Iversen, 'Transforming a Viking into a Saint', p. 405.

[Thou hast given him his heart's desire: and hast not withholden from him the will of his lips. For thou hast prevented him with blessings of sweetness: thou hast set on his head a crown of precious stones. He asked life of thee: and thou hast given him length of days for ever and ever. His glory is great in thy salvation: glory and great beauty shalt thou lay upon him.]

In the case of St Olaf the Epistle is taken from *Liber Sapientiae* (10. 10–14), describing how Wisdom (*Sapientiae*) followed the Just and protected him from his enemies, how she never left his side when he was betrayed, and finally led him to the royal sceptre and empowered him against those who were against him. In the Gospel text from Matthew (16. 24–28), Jesus explains that whoever wants to come after him must take up his cross and follow him:

> Qui enim voluerit animam suam salvam facere perdet eam, qui enim perdiderit animam suam propter me inveniet eam. Quid enim prodest homini si mundum universum lucretur, animae vero suae detrimentum patiatur? aut quam dabit homo commutationem pro anima sua?

> [If any man will come after me, let him deny himself, and take up his cross, and follow me. For he that will save his life, shall lose it: and he that shall lose his life for my sake, shall find it. For what doth it profit a man, if he gain the whole world, and suffer the loss of his own soul? Or what exchange shall a man give for his soul?]

The composer of *Lux illuxit* knew that these texts would be read immediately before or after his song, and thus would have composed the sequence with them in mind, along with other sequences and the hagiographical material. It is therefore almost surprising to see that the words of the sequence do not echo those of the readings. On a conceptual level, however, the sequence and its surrounding texts fit remarkably well. In the central part of the sequence Olaf becomes the king of Psalm 20, blessed by God and crowned, given eternal life and great glory. He is the Just in *Liber Sapientiae* who is followed by Wisdom through his hardships, protected from his enemies, and will be given royal power in the end. He is Christ's follower, as described by Matthew, who has taken up his cross to follow Christ, and has saved his soul because he gave his life for him. A textual reference to the cross is not found in *Lux illuxit*, but a deliberate connection may be found in its melodic references to the Victorine sequence *Laudes crucis*, similarities pointed out by both Reiss and Eggen.[39] *Laudes crucis* was used in Nidaros for the feast of the finding of the cross, the

---

[39] Reiss, *Musiken ved den middelalderlige Olavsdyrkelsen*, p. 52; Eggen, *The Sequences of the Archbishopric of Nidaros*, I, 219.

Inventio crucis (3 May). It is not possible to establish whether or not the composers of the melody of *Lux illuxit* intended to establish recognizable melodic allusions to *Laudes crucis*. Still, the sound of the performed sequence may have reminded people of the important Victorine sequence *Laudes crucis* and the feast of the cross, just before the reading of the Gospel encouraging those who would follow Christ to pick up their cross, which thus would have further emphasized the *imitatio Christi* of St Olaf.

Compared with the specific narrative sequence of Nicholas, the *Congaudentes*, it is striking how Olaf's sequence moves on an abstract level and does not include deeds, events, and miracles, apart from the vision on the night before the battle. Instead of using lists of miracles as raw material for the sequence, the composer blended two major ingredients: the words and style of the sequences of his time and of St Olaf's office *In regali fastigio*, along with the ideas and ideals from the chants and readings of Olaf's Mass.

For the listeners who were not fluent in Latin and who would have had difficulty grasping the concepts of ideal kingship in connection with biblical texts, his sequence still contains some basic textual markers or key words. On that level the references to *Christi martyr, rex Olavus, rex et martyr*, would have left no doubt in their minds that the sequence was in honour of St Olaf alone.

Conclusion

The liturgy of the Christian Church played an important role in the development of literacy in Norway, from the copying of the first books to the production of the first texts. When the people of the twelfth century organized the liturgy of Nidaros, and supplied their missals and breviaries with locally composed liturgy of local saints, they were part of the process of defining a local, Christian identity. Nevertheless, only a few would have considered the liturgical texts as written pieces; the majority would have experienced them as a performance.

Any performance has limitations owing to the situation itself and the level of preparation on the part of the audience. It would be unrealistic to assume that a performed sequence or any other liturgical text, however clear the Latin text and however well trained the singer, would enable even the most learned listener to make a thorough simultaneous interpretation of it. However, if the written text were shaped in such a way that the subject matter could be identified and the important elements recognized, the performed text would serve its purpose and convey a meaning, much as an altar frontal in which one may recognize the motif at first glance, without being able to explain all the details of the picture. When people heard the name of a saint and references to his miracles, it presumably confirmed that the celebrated saint was present in the words sounding within the walls of the church.

Works Cited

Manuscripts and Archival Documents

Cambridge, Corpus Christi College, MS 422
London, British Library, MS Harley 2961
Oslo, National Archives, Lat. fragm. 714
Oslo, National Archives, Lat. fragm. 930
Oslo, National Archives, Lat. fragm. 1023

Primary Sources

Analecta hymnica medii aevi, ed. by Clemens Blume and others, 55 vols (Leipzig: Reisland, 1886–1922)
Antiphonarium Nidrosiensis ecclesiae, ed. by Lilli Gjerløw (Oslo: Universitetsforlaget, 1979)
Einarr Skúlason, *Einarr Skúlason's 'Geisli': A Critical Edition*, ed. by Martin Chase (Toronto: University of Toronto Press, 2005)
Ordo Nidrosiensis ecclesiae, ed. by Lilli Gjerløw (Oslo: Universitetsforlaget, 1968)

Secondary Works

Bagge, Sverre, *Da boken kom til Norge* (Oslo: Aschehoug, 2001)
Bang, Anton Christian, *Norske hexeformularer og magiske opskrifter* (Kristiania: Dybwad, 1901)
Brunius, Jan, *Atque Olavi: Nordiska helgon medeltida mässböcker* (Stockholm: Runica et mediævalia, 2008)
Eggen, Erik, *The Sequences of the Archbishopric of Nidaros*, Bibliotheca Arnamagnæana, 21–22, 2 vols (København: Munksgaard, 1968)
Iversen, Gunilla, 'Transforming a Viking into a Saint: The Divine Office of St. Olaf', in *The Divine Office in the Latin Middle Ages*, ed. by Margot E. Fassler and Rebecca A. Baltzer (Oxford: Oxford University Press, 2000), pp. 401–29
Jones, Charles W., *Saint Nicholas of Myra, Bari and Manhattan: Biography of a Legend* (Chicago: University of Chicago Press, 1978)
Kruckenberg, Lori, 'Making a Sequence Repertory: The Tradition of the Ordo Nidrosiensis Ecclesiae', in *The Sequences of Nidaros: A Nordic Repertory and its European Context*, ed. by Lori Kruckenberg and Andreas Haug (Trondheim: Tapir, 2006), pp. 7–16

——, 'The Sequence from 1050–1150: Study of a Genre in Change' (unpublished doctoral thesis, University of Iowa, 1997)

——, 'Sequenz', in *Die Musik in Geschichte und Gegenwart*, ed. by Ludwig Finscher (Kassel: Bärenreiter, 1998), pp. 1254–86

Mortensen, Lars Boje, 'Sanctified Beginnings and Mythopoietic Moments: The First Wave of Writing on the Past in Norway, Denmark and Hungary, c. 1000–1230', in *The Making of Christian Myths in the Periphery of Latin Christendom (c. 1000–1300)*, ed. by Lars Boje Mortensen (København: Museum Tusculanum, 2006), pp. 247–73

Ommundsen, Åslaug, 'Books, Scribes and Sequences in Medieval Norway', 2 vols (unpublished doctoral thesis, Universitetet i Bergen, 2007)

——, 'A Saint and his Sequence: Singing the Legend of St. Olaf', *Viking and Medieval Scandinavia*, 5 (2009), 151–76

Østrem, Eyolf, *The Office of Saint Olaf: A Study in Chant Transmission* (Uppsala: Acta Universitatis Upsaliensis, 2001)

Rappaport, Roy, *Ritual and Religion in the Making of Humanity* (Cambridge: Cambridge University Press, 1999)

Reiss, Georg, *Musiken ved den middelalderlige Olavsdyrkelsen i Norden* (Kristiania: Dybwad, 1912)

Undset, Sigrid, *Norske helgener* (Oslo: Aschehoug, 1937)

Zappa, Frank, in *Classic Albums: Frank Zappa – Apostrophe/Over-Nite Sensation*, documentary dir. by Matthew Longfellow (Eagle Rock Entertainment/Isis Productions, 2007) [on DVD]

The Arrival and Development of Latin Literacy on the Edge of Europe: The Case of Medieval Finland

Tuomas Heikkilä

Introduction: On the Edge of Literacy

The development of literacy in the central areas of medieval Europe (in Germany, France, England, or Italy, for instance) is nowadays, after decades and even centuries of serious scholarship, rather well known. The introduction of writing and its uses and impacts in European peripheries, in turn, is much less familiar to the scholars of medieval literacy. However, in order to fully understand the significance and the essence of the medieval cultural unity of the *Latinitas* and *Christianitas*, a comparison of the heartlands with the peripheral areas is of utmost importance. Hence, it is relevant to become acquainted with the arrival and development of literacy to the edge of the European periphery — namely medieval Finland[1] — which the written word reached only very belatedly, and to ask how the Christian religion and Latin literacy tied the periphery to a part of Western Europe despite its faraway location. This article aims to outline the development based on the extensive use of primary source material.

The expansion of Latin literacy to the north-easternmost corner of western Christianity and the Latin sphere of culture during the Middle Ages is very poorly known. Yet the conversion and development of literacy in medieval

---

[1] On the detailed overall picture of the written culture in medieval Finland, see Heikkilä, *Kirjallinen kulttuuri keskiajan Suomessa*.

Finland is an interesting case study in the broader European context: the development that took place during the centuries of the high and late Middle Ages in the area of present-day Finland to a large extent dictated the later history of that corner of Europe. Previous international and national scholarship has ignored the study of the development of literacy in this European periphery. As the field of study has lacked the convenient building blocks due to the poor state of basic manuscript research, the scrutiny of the subject would have required the exploration of a substantial number of original, mostly unexplored sources in a very fragmentary state. If Finnish scholars have considered the topic too laborious, it has been much more so to scholars of other nations because of the extra obstacle presented by language. In recent decades international medieval studies has paid a relatively large amount of attention to the expansion of *Latinitas* and *Christianitas* in the course of the Middle Ages from many, often interdisciplinary points of view. However, emphasis has mostly been placed on political and, to a lesser extent, ecclesiastical history. Even though the development of literacy and its implications for culture in general have been studied in a most praiseworthy manner, the geographical focus has not been directed to the ultima Thule. Questions similar to the ones posed in this article have been pondered with a focus on East Central Europe, medieval Poland, Hungary, and Bohemia, for instance. Such studies have emphasized the role of East Central Europe as the eastern periphery of the *Latinitas*.[2] Still, the medieval diocese of Åbo (Finnish *Turku*), covering much of the area of modern Finland, is at least as favourable an example as Poland, Hungary, Bohemia, or Scandinavia, for that matter, since the area was Christianized and the process of *Verschriftlichung* began much later there. This article therefore aims to introduce a new and interesting geographical region to medieval studies concentrating on literacy.

Unlike in the heartlands of Europe, the direct influence of the ancient Roman civilization was not of significance, but Latin culture and the western, Latin interpretation of the Christian faith reached the area after they were already fully developed in their medieval form. As no pre-existent written culture existed, the expansion of Latin literacy to the medieval diocese of Åbo provides a scholar with the opportunity to explore the development of literacy in vitro. What happens when a well-developed literary culture is planted in a place with no writing or previous book culture? What are the processes and consequences of such a procedure?

---

[2] Adamska and Mostert, 'Preface', p. 2.

First, what is meant by literacy? In this article, literacy is both more and less than the ability to read and write. Such ability was not generally achieved in Finland — or anywhere else in Europe during the Middle Ages. Restricting the meaning of literacy only to the ability to read and write would also impede the analysis of reading and writing, books and documents, in their broader social context.[3] Like elsewhere in the Latin sphere of culture, reading and writing reached a central position in many fields of life in medieval Finland: the everyday actions of the Church, administration, and trade could not be performed without the aid of the written word. Thus, writing and reading, literary culture and literacy go hand in glove, and literacy includes much more than just the ability to interpret letters and draw them.[4] Literacy refers to a form of culture in which the written word is an important medium of everyday communication in various fields of society; in a broad sense it denotes the social and cultural phenomena associated with the uses of writing. More than just literacy itself, this article deals with the process of development of literacy that may — for lack of a proper English term — be referred to by the German term *Verschriftlichungsprozeß*, the dynamic 'literalization' of the culture of a certain geographic area.[5]

Even if the development of literacy of the north-easternmost edge of Europe is interesting for the development of the *Latinitas* in general, it is worth underlining that the spread and uses of literacy must in every single case be seen against the given background and context. Although the process of *Verschriftlichung* had many features in common with what is now Finland, Sweden, Scandinavia, East Central Europe, and the heartlands of our continent, equally significant differences were always present as well. As an example, the medieval development of literacy in present-day eastern Finland would be interesting to explore, since the area did not belong to the westward-oriented diocese of Åbo and was right on the edge of the western and eastern Churches. However, as the extant sources are virtually non-existent, many important questions remain unsolved.[6]

---

[3] See Bäuml, 'Varieties and Consequences of Medieval Literacy and Illiteracy', p. 239.

[4] The term was first used to refer only to the ability to read in the 1930s. See Adamson, 'The Extent of Literacy in England', p. 163; Galbraith, 'The Literacy of Medieval English Kings', p. 201. In modern scholarship, the use of the term has broadened and loosened from its original meaning. On the terminology of the subject matter, see Adamska, 'The Study of Medieval Literacy'.

[5] On the problems of terminology, see Mostert, 'New Approaches to Medieval Communication?', esp. p. 29.

[6] For the coexistence of Latin and Orthodox literate cultures, see, for example, Franklin,

The Written Word as the Catalyst of Change

Knowledge of the Christian faith had already been filtered for the medieval inhabitants of the area of present Finland centuries before their actual conversion, and unchallengeable evidence exists for Christian communities in the Åland Islands and the south-western corner of Finland from the beginning of the second millennium, at the very latest.[7]

According to the 'official' medieval tradition, established in the late thirteenth-century *Legenda s. Henrici* written in Åbo, the Christianization of Finland took place in the mid-twelfth century through a crusade of the Swedes led by King Erik and Bishop Henry of Uppsala.[8] Modern scholarship has shown this view to be too formulaic, and even the historicity of Bishop Henry has been questioned. It is of historiographical interest that the Swedish scholars have been inclined to give up the idea of an actual crusade to Finland, whereas their Finnish colleagues have traditionally wanted to adhere to it — thus committing themselves to the over seven-hundred-year-old idea of the legend as a worthy starting point for the history of a 'nation', the Finnish 'big bang', as it were.[9]

Whatever the exact means and date of the conversion of the area, the fact remains that the region of modern-day south-western Finland was drawn to Christianity on a large scale during the twelfth century. The new doctrine was rooted as the central part of local high and folk culture, and the Church structured the society together with the Swedish crown during the following centuries. The mechanism of the Christianization was very similar to that of other areas that converted to Christianity during the Middle Ages. The formal conversion of the earliest stage was followed by a slow, prolonged moulding of society's values, cults, and different ideas into a new, Christian form. The most important instrument in this development was the Latin written culture that carried and mediated the new ideas and values. Already by the time of its Christianization, Finland was surrounded by literary culture in the west as well as in the east: in Sweden, the Latin culture had had an influence for several generations, and in the east, in Rus, the use of writing had taken root even earlier, in the tenth century.[10]

Writing, Society and Culture in Early Rus.

[7] Compare, for example, Purhonen, *Kristinuskon saapumisesta Suomeen*, pp. 45–58.

[8] *Legenda s. Henrici*, ed. by Heikkilä, lectio 2 (pp. 400–02).

[9] On the discussion, see Heikkilä, *Pyhän Henrikin legenda*, pp. 55–73.

[10] See Franklin, *Writing, Society and Culture in Early Rus*, pp. 10, 12–15, 120–27.

Latin literacy and the Christianization that reached Finland in the high Middle Ages have had a wide-ranging significance in Finnish history. The western version of Christian faith, Latin written culture, and the annexation to the Swedish realm were the factors that tied the area to Western Europe culturally as well as politically and ideologically. The region of present Finland has been detached from the Catholic Church for half a millennium, and the political ties to Sweden were cut two centuries ago. The cultural identity built on Latin written culture and its products in the Middle Ages has, however, proven to be more lasting than religious or political observances, and continues to have impact even today. Therefore, the question of the arrival and development of Latin literacy is still highly topical in Finland, and it is surprising how little attention the subject has received in local history writing.

Fragmentary Sources, Methodological Challenges

From the entire medieval period only a handful of traces of literature written in Finland are known. In addition to the above-mentioned *Legenda s. Henrici* (BHL 3818) not more than a few fragments of other works are known: the *Chronicle of the Bishops of Åbo* from the fourteenth century,[11] very laconic Annals of Åbo from the early fifteenth century,[12] as well as a sermon (*Legenda nova*, BHL 3818b)[13] of St Henry from the fifteenth century. In addition to the named works probably written in Åbo there were some efforts to translate Latin ecclesiastical texts into Swedish in the monastery of Naantali (Sw. Nådendal) near the episcopal see.

Regarding whole medieval books, the Finnish collections contain only a very small number — about two dozen — of more or less complete codices that can be judged to have been used in the medieval diocese of Åbo. Moreover, an equivalent amount of additional quires was added to the end of the printed works from the end of the Middle Ages. The contents of the Swedish collections of manuscripts add some codices and fragments of Åbo origin to the overall picture.

---

[11] Only one fragment is known: Uppsala, Uppsala universitetsbibliotek, MS Palmskiöldiana 312, Åbo och Åland, 369–73.

[12] Only one fragmentary *passus* of the text is known (in two exemplars): Uppsala, Uppsala universitetsbibliotek, MS K12a and Stockholm, Kungliga bibliotek, MS A942.

[13] The only surviving manuscript of the homily is Uppsala, Uppsala universitetsbibliotek, MS C292, fols 82^r–85^v.

The main reason for the scarcity of the codices remaining from the edge of medieval Europe is the Reformation of the sixteenth century. As the Latin liturgical books of Roman observance served no purpose for the Reformation, the majority of the medieval manuscripts of Åbo, and those of the other Swedish dioceses, were confiscated by the Crown during the sixteenth century. Although the contents of the books were of no interest in the new situation, their material value remained, and the durable parchment leaves of the manuscripts were soon discovered to be of very practical value as cover wrappings for the tax books of the royal bailiffs. This soon resulted in the dismemberment of thousands of confiscated manuscripts into tens of thousands of *bifolia* or single leaves that were used either locally or in the central administration to protect the tax books. Finally, the cameral books ended up in the archives of the central administration in Stockholm. A major change took place in the early nineteenth century when Sweden lost Finland to Russia and was forced to hand over all the documents concerning Finland to the Finnish archives. As a consequence, the remains of a considerable number of medieval manuscripts were delivered to the National Library of Finland. The major part of the whole collection still remains in the Riksarkivet in Stockholm.

The collection of parchment fragments (*fragmenta membranea*, f.m.) of the National Library of Finland is by far the largest collection of sources providing insight into the medieval literacy of Åbo diocese. It houses about 9200–9300 parchment leaves that originate from about 1400–1500 different manuscripts. Thus, the collection is by far more important for the study of medieval literacy of the diocese than the more or less complete extant codices.

As mentioned above, the shaping of a general view of the literary culture and literacy of medieval Finland as a part of the Swedish realm, Christianity, and the Latin sphere of culture is still in its early stages. Most of the material is literally very fragmentary and has been previously used only by few scholars. Although the cataloguing of the fragments and the reconstruction work of the leaves into incomplete codices has been ongoing since the 1920s and is bound to be finished relatively soon, we still lack an overview and important insights into the forces that formed the collection of sources.

With the lack of in-depth studies of every individual manuscript reconstruction, this article aims to outline the medieval development of literacy based on the dating and localization of the fragments performed during the cataloguing work.[14] As a great part of the fragments have been very hard to localize

---

[14] Haapanen, *Verzeichnis der mittelalterlichen Handschriftenfragmente*; Taitto, *Catalogue of Medieval Manuscript Fragments in the Helsinki University Library*, I. The calendars, manuals,

and are dated rather vaguely, this kind of approach evidently deals with only a part of the whole collection of over nine thousand fragment leaves. Taking into account the very high number of sources, it has not been possible to re-examine and verify the grounds for the localization and dating, with the exception of some single cases. However, the number of fragments (that is, remains of codices) available for this general approach is still so high that the possible flaws, misdatings, and incorrect localizations inevitably present in every catalogue do not lead to a distortion of the overall picture. All in all, the fragment material used in this article is comprised of the remains of 339 reconstructed, located, and dated manuscripts. I am confident that such an amount of original sources allows us to draw firm conclusions about the earliest stages of the arrival of literacy on this edge of medieval Latin Europe.

However, the field of work is very laborious and tricky. Because of the relatively humble tradition of manuscript studies in Finland much of the basic work remains in the field of fragments and codices. To some extent, this can be applied to the Swedish situation as well, in spite of the much stronger traditions and much higher number of manuscript scholars. For instance, the identification of Scandinavian manuscripts on palaeographical grounds is more complicated than in some other areas, since the northern texts often combine features commonly associated palaeographically with England, France, or Germany.[15]

It has proven to be virtually impossible for previous scholarship to distinguish uniquely 'Finnish' or Åbo traits in the palaeographical and codicological features of the medieval manuscripts remaining in modern Finland. Considering the non-existent background in the field of literacy in the newly converted diocese and the obvious fact that the vast majority of books and the know-how to produce them came during the early stages of literacy from Sweden or from outside Scandinavia, this is hardly surprising. Therefore, the most tenable conclusions are normally made on the basis of the contents of the texts. This, however, is not entirely without problems either, since the vast majority of the fragments are liturgical in content, and the early development of the liturgy followed within the missionary bishopric and later diocese of

---

lectionaries, the *hagiographica*, and the previously uncatalogued breviaries, missals, graduals, psalters, etc. are being catalogued currently, and the results of the work have been used in this study. Anja Inkeri Lehtinen has long been preparing a catalogue of the biblical, theological, and juridical fragments. It is not yet possible, however, to use her results. Still, most of the theological and juridical fragments were probably imported to the Åbo diocese.

[15] Ommundsen, 'Books, Scribes and Sequences', passim, esp. I, 92–104; Gullick, 'Preliminary Observations on Romanesque Manuscript Fragments', pp. 58–65.

Åbo is still rather inadequately known. In addition, it is questionable if the churches of the pre-fourteenth-century diocese could have afforded not to use any liturgical manuscript available to them, no matter what kind of liturgical nuances they might have contained. Consequently, there is generally very little evidence available on the use of an imported manuscript within the diocese at the earliest stages of literate culture in Finland. Sometimes the sixteenth- or seventeenth-century cameral notes written on parchment leaves and the existence of the leaves in a Finnish collection are the only clues combining the remains of a certain manuscript with the medieval Åbo diocese. These kinds of hints are often rather uncertain and pose their own methodological problems.

One further aspect exacerbating the study of the variety of books written and used in the medieval bishopric of Åbo is the fact that we (almost) exclusively have remains of parchment manuscripts. Paper manuscripts of pre-reformatory contents were not of importance for the administration and bailiffs seeking to reuse the parchment. In addition, the contents of such paper books were outdated and even dangerous. Consequently, what remains of the paper books is a dozen hand-written manuscripts and a handful of printed works from the last decades of the Middle Ages. This is a great loss, since the presumed broadening of interest in a greater variety of books that took place in Europe occurred at the very same time that paper became common as a material for manuscript books in Scandinavia. Hence, it is probable that the extant parchment fragments only give us a one-sided picture of the variety of books used in Northern Europe.

In spite of all the reservations, a study of all the possible extant written sources from the Middle Ages, and especially the fragments as the most important evidence of the manuscript culture, remains the only way to explore the arrival and development of literacy in the European periphery of the diocese of Åbo. In this way we are able to gain insight into the development of cultural ties and of the different influences within the Latin sphere of written culture.

The Earliest Traces: The Missionary Period

The dissemination and spread of Latin literary works could be very fast in the Middle Ages. The broad networks and the effort of the Western Church to have universal, catholic forms and similar liturgy in every corner of Latin Christendom made it possible to import and export books that could be used for similar purposes in a multitude of contexts. Consequently, the manuscripts that were old-fashioned or even outdated in the major European centres could be circulated to the peripheries, in which the contents of the text could still be of use.

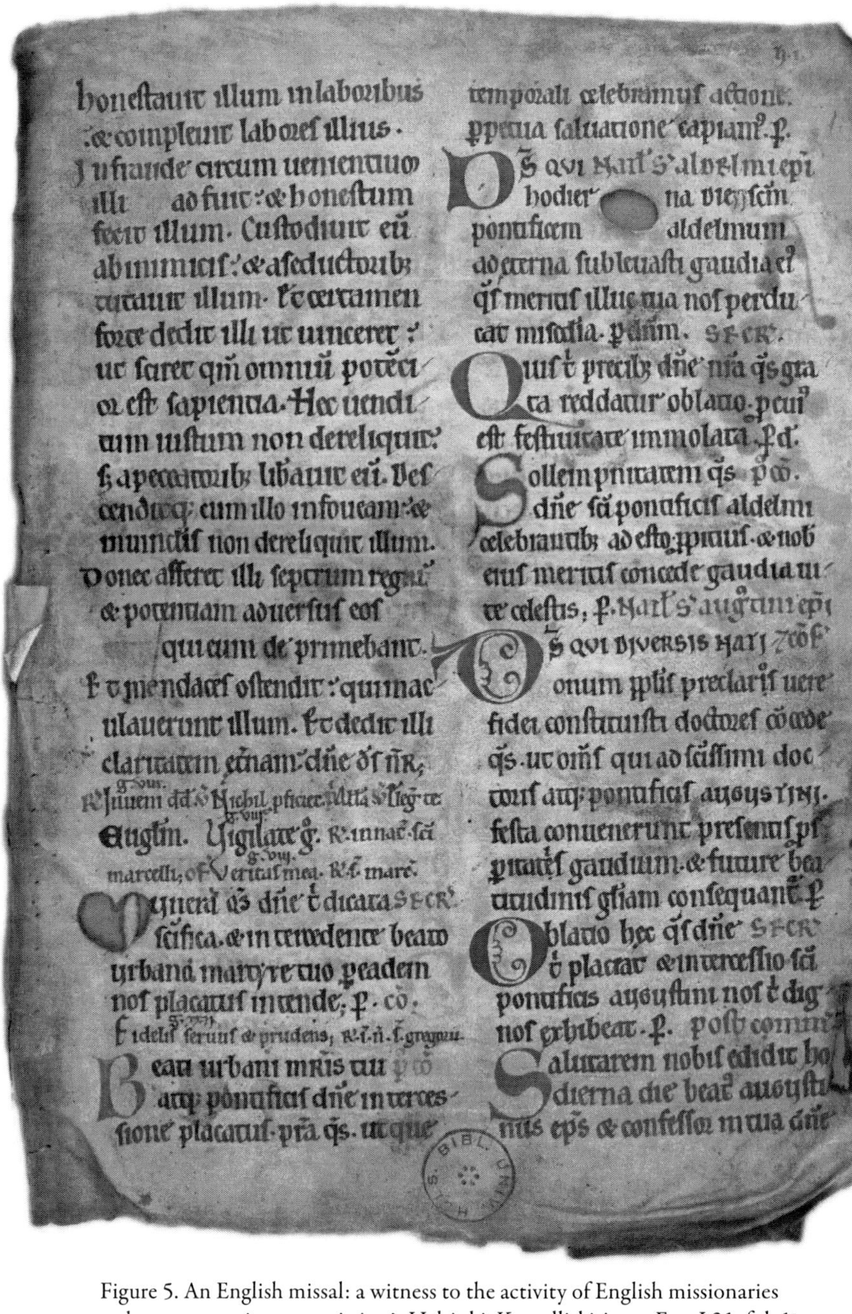

Figure 5. An English missal: a witness to the activity of English missionaries or to later manuscript transmission? Helsinki, Kansalliskirjasto, F.m. I.21, fol. 1^r. Eleventh century. Reproduced with permission.

The missionaries active in Finland surely brought books with them, as Christianity reached the area in the eleventh to thirteenth centuries. It is not clear, however, whether the still extant books and their fragments dating to this period were brought to the ultima Thule by the missionaries or whether they represent a later stage of manuscript import — both the methods and dates of provenance are probably represented in the remaining material. Either way, all the extant manuscripts and their remains from this period are of foreign, that is, non-Swedish, origin: the books written in the twelfth and thirteenth centuries are totally dominated by material of English, French, or German origin.[16] As manuscript production was only taking its first steps in Sweden, the literate influence of more southern parts of Europe in the conversion process of the area of modern-day south-western Finland seems to have been of decisive importance.[17]

The fragments of English origin or with English features dominate in the oldest layer of extant fragments in Finland. This strongly suggests the activity of English preachers and missionaries in the area until the beginning of the thirteenth century.[18] It seems that English books were brought to the missionary area through Sweden to fulfil the needs of preaching and those of the emerging local churches. On the other hand, it is clear that the early Swedish manuscript production received a great deal of influence from England,[19] and therefore the English traits of a manuscript do not necessarily reveal the place of its origin.

All in all, the conception of an early and relatively strong English influence in the field of literacy gained by the study of our rather patchy manuscript material is credible, since we know from other sources that the English contribution to the Christianization of Sweden was substantial. According to

---

[16] English: Helsinki, Kansalliskirjasto, F.m. I.21, I.24, I.30 (?), III.54 (?), IV.1, IV.2 (?), IV.5, IV.10, VII.33, VII.86, MS C IV 10. F.m. VII.24 has English traits, but was probably written in Sweden; French: Helsinki, Kansalliskirjasto, F.m. I.9, I.30 (?), II.10, III.12, III.29 (?), III.54 (?), IV.2 (?), VII.136; German: III.2, III.13, III.14, III.18, III.33 (?), VII.6. See Haapanen, *Verzeichnis der mittelalterlichen Handschriftenfragmente*, I, p. xxxiii.

[17] See Heikkilä, 'Scripta manent'.

[18] Compare Taitto, 'British Saints in the Fragmenta membranea Collection', p. 1.

[19] A possible example: Helsinki, Kansalliskirjasto, F.m. IV.1. I would like to thank Michael Gullick for pointing this out to me in his letter of 16 December 2007; compare Taitto, *Catalogue of Medieval Manuscript Fragments in the Helsinki University Library*, I, 31–33 (no. 1). See Gullick, 'Preliminary Observations on Romanesque Manuscript Fragments', pp. 31–32. Compare, for example, Stockholm, Riksarkivet, Fr. 2070; Abukhanfusa, *Mutilated Books*, p. 21. In general, Nedkvitne, *The Social Consequences of Literacy*, p. 9.

the medieval tradition, the semi-legendary apostle of Finland and Bishop of Uppsala, St Henry, was of English origin,[20] as were his missionary colleagues, Sts Eskil and Sigfrid, the patrons of the Swedish dioceses of Skara and Strängnäs. It is also of interest that the first canonically chosen Bishop of Finland, Thomas (d. 1248), was, from a medieval perspective, an Englishman as well.[21] He had collected a rather extensive library, mostly in Paris,[22] and it is easy to imagine that he was eager to promote the development of literacy in his distant diocese. Through his contacts it would have been easy for him to acquire books from England or France for the needs of the churches in Finland.

Although the time of the strongest English impact seems to have ended during the thirteenth century due to the emerging Nordic book production, it left a lasting legacy for centuries to come. The contents of the texts were affected by English liturgy, and some of the features adopted into the local practices remained in use in the diocese of Åbo until the Reformation.[23] In addition, the import of English manuscripts continued to play a part — albeit rather a modest one — even later in the Middle Ages. This is nicely elucidated by a breviary that was probably written in London in the mid-thirteenth century for the local Dominicans: it was in Scandinavia in the fifteenth century, at the very latest, and was finally used in the diocese of Åbo towards the turn of the fifteenth and sixteenth centuries.[24]

Some manuscripts and fragments that clearly show French features are present among the earliest extant material. Almost all of the earliest monasteries of Sweden were part of the broad network of Cistercians that had spread from France throughout Latin Europe. This network was very eager to diffuse manuscripts, as well, and the manuscripts produced locally commonly show French traits.[25] Consequently, the French appearance of a manuscript does not inevitably speak to its French origin. The Cistercian traits of the fragments

[20] *Legenda s. Henrici*, ed. by Heikkilä, lectio 1 (p. 398).

[21] Juusten, *Chronicon episcoporum Finlandensium*, ed. by Porthan, I, 126; Juusten, *Suomen piispainkronikka*, ed. and trans. by Simo Heininen, p. 41.

[22] The contents of his book collection are known from a repertory that is contained within Uppsala, Uppsala universitetsbibliotek, MS C 134.

[23] Taitto, 'British Saints in the Fragmenta membranea Collection', p. 5. Compare Toy, 'The Fragments Reveal New Evidence'.

[24] Helsinki, Kansalliskirjasto, MS C IV 10; see Maliniemi, 'Englantilaisperäinen 1200-luvun dominikaanibreviarium Suomessa'.

[25] See Gullick, 'Preliminary Observations on Romanesque Manuscript Fragments', pp. 58–59, 65.

remaining in Finland have not yet been analysed, but if such a study were to be undertaken the punctuation of the text would need to be taken into account, since the distinctive use of flex punctuation (*punctus flexus*) is very common in Cistercian manuscripts.[26]

Despite the remaining fragments of French origin that were probably used in Finland during the Middle Ages, there seems to be little reason to believe that they would indicate a major French influence on the Christianization of the area during the high Middle Ages. In fact, many of the remains of manuscripts showing French traits can be explained as the result of Northerners studying at Paris and by cheap, partly outdated manuscripts bought there at a much later time, namely during the fourteenth century.[27] What is more, some manuscripts with 'French' contents may turn out to be of Dominican origin. Thus, many fragments with French features may testify more to the spread of Dominican liturgy than to the wide-scale import of manuscript books from France.

One good example of the many possible interpretations of the oldest layer of extant fragments is a group of manuscripts that have been dated to the eleventh to thirteenth centuries and were probably written in the church province of Cologne in Germany.[28] Do they point to evidence of German missionary activity in the northern Baltic area? The archbishopric of Hamburg-Bremen in particular is known to have had a keen interest in the missionary work on the shores of the Baltic in the high Middle Ages. Or is the group of fragments proof of studies in Germany and the concomitant manuscript import from there at a much later point? The area of Cologne is known to have been of importance later, when the Åbo Dominicans frequented the local *studium*.

The fact that all the manuscripts of the group are breviaries may suggest the use of books during the missionary period, since the contents of a breviary are very comprehensive. As the breviaries were rather compact books containing a concentration of many different liturgical books, it was a good choice if one was to have only a very small number of books in one's use. In actuality, the breviaries were needed for the office of canonical hours rather than the actual Mass. However, in spite of the clear instructions underlining the importance of the office it is probable that the canonical hours were not celebrated in all the

---

[26] A good example is Helsinki, Kansalliskirjasto, F.m. VII.24 that uses a peculiar form of flex punctuation. The manuscript was in all likelihood written in Scandinavia. Cf. Gullick, 'Preliminary Observations on Romanesque Manuscript Fragments', pp. 51, 61–62. I would like to thank Jesse Keskiaho for his observations about the fragment.

[27] See especially Nuorteva, *Suomalaisten ulkomainen opinkäynti*, pp. 53–66.

[28] Helsinki, Kansalliskirjasto, F.m. III.2, III.13, III.14, III.18 and possibly III.33.

churches of the diocese. Hence, even in the heyday of the local church at the end of the Middle Ages, not to mention earlier, the churches of the Åbo diocese that celebrated the office frequently were probably a small minority compared to those that only celebrated Mass. There was probably no point in importing many breviaries after the missionary period, and therefore the contents of the group with clearly German palaeographical traits seem to suggest that the import of the manuscripts had taken place during the missionary period.

All in all, the earliest surviving manuscripts in Finland suggest a situation in which the newly converted area was influenced from many directions. In many cases, the other Swedish dioceses probably acted as intermediaries. It seems plausible that the geographically nearest bishoprics of Uppsala, Linköping, Strängnäs, and Västerås played the most important role. In particular, the liturgical practices of Uppsala and Linköping are known to have affected the Åbo liturgy in the Middle Ages. The ties between those dioceses and Åbo are known to have been close during the last centuries of the Middle Ages, as the south-western parts of the Åbo bishopric had became a natural, central part of the realm.

Foreign manuscripts and literate influences may also have transmitted directly to Finland, possibly from England, but especially from Northern Germany. According to previous scholars, Hamburg-Bremen played a very important part in the Christianization of Sweden and Finland until the early thirteenth century.[29] As far as I can see, the most intensive period of the conversion of Finland took place when the missionaries originating in Germany were met with new rivals from England, and the overall situation was thus more multi-faceted. The same kind of multitude of influences can be seen in the early book production and liturgy of Norway, for instance.[30]

Since the number of extant manuscripts dating from the missionary period is rather low, it is not possible to draw definite conclusions. Still, the multiformity of the remaining sources succeeds in illustrating the different influences that played their part in the earliest stage of Christian Finland. In the light of the manuscripts, the German and English influences that had competed with each other earlier, in the conversion of Sweden, were of upmost significance in the Christianization of Finland as well.

The picture shaped by the extant manuscripts follows a pattern known from other areas that converted to Christendom and were annexed into the Latin

---

[29] See Taitto, 'British Saints in the Fragmenta membranea Collection', p. 2.
[30] Ommundsen, 'Books, Scribes and Sequences', I, 56; see *Antiphonarium Nidrosiensis ecclesiae*, ed. by Gjerløw; *Ordo Nidrosiensis ecclesiae*, ed. by Gjerløw, pp. 85–110.

sphere of written culture in the high Middle Ages. During this first stage of literacy, the use of writing remained rather limited, and orality continued to play a very important role in all spheres of the society. The few needed books were brought from elsewhere, and the local production of manuscripts was practically non-existent.[31] Literacy was centred on books rather than charters of secular administration that did not play an important role within the development of written culture.

At this point, it is obvious that the use of the written word was limited to the needs of the Church and the religion as well as ecclesiastical administration. The number of extant charters written in Finland during this time period is next to non-existent. Still, judging from the later charter material it is clear that the literate communication needed by both the ecclesiastical and temporal administration was completely in the hands of the clergy.

As there was no prior written culture in the area, it is logical that the art of producing and deciphering writing was concentrated in the hands of the incomers. During the earliest stage of literacy in Finland, the written word had, above all, a religious and liturgical function. On the one hand, this magical use of the word had many points in common with the traditional non-written religion of the area and was probably well understood by the neophytes. Later Finnish folklore is filled with examples of motifs borrowed from liturgy to popular magic. On the other hand, the concentration of the new skill of interpreting writing and the Latin language created a new, foreign elite that was in command of the religious sphere.

The Broadening Literacy: Imports and Charters

Books, reading, writing, and literacy as a whole were an advantageous and central instrument for the Church and, somewhat later, for the secular administration of the areas newly drawn to the Latin sphere of culture, and some aspects of literacy were often absorbed surprisingly quickly. Local manuscript production may have begun in Sweden already during the eleventh century, but at the

---

[31] A similar kind of pattern can be seen in the Christianization and *Verschriftlichung* of Bohemia, for instance: the earliest liturgical manuscripts needed by the new local churches were imported from Bavaria and Saxony. See Vezin, 'La Production et la circulation des livres', p. 211. Many of the earliest manuscripts used in Hungary were brought from Germany or Lorraine; see Rado, *Libri liturgici manuscripti bibliothecarum Hungariae*, pp. 230–36. The earliest books needed by the churches in Poland came, to a great extent, from Bavaria and Rhineland. See Gieysztor, 'Symboles de la royauté en Pologne'; Semkowicz, *Paleografia łacińska*, p. 294.

very latest in the latter half of the twelfth century.[32] Thus, books were already being copied in Sweden at the time when the Swedes organized the Christian communities of south-western Finland and annexed the area to Sweden during the Finnish 'missionary period'. In the light of the extant manuscript fragments in Scandinavian collections, this production was already rather extensive by the thirteenth century and increased by the decade. At first, the influences on writing came to Sweden from abroad: the copied exemplars were brought mainly from England, Germany, and France, and the recent manuscript culture was additionally influenced by the monastic and mendicant orders that reached Sweden from the south.[33]

There is a clear trend in the sources of medieval — and other — history: the further back we try to reach, the smaller the absolute and relative amount of extant sources.[34] The coincidences of the destruction or preservation of sources do not in themselves, however, explain the different amount of late medieval manuscripts and those of earlier times. Books really did become more and more common throughout the Middle Ages, especially during the last two centuries of the period. This was a development that took place in Sweden in the very same manner as in the rest of Latin Europe. The eastern part of the realm, the diocese of Åbo, came into literacy belatedly, and, in comparison to other parts of the Swedish kingdom, its process of *Verschriftlichung* dragged behind for centuries. It should be mentioned, however, that the diocese was a rather heterogeneous area in terms of *Verschriftlichung*. Whilst the town of Åbo and its closest surrounding area formed an important part of the Swedish realm by the end of the Middle Ages, literacy arrived in the more peripheral parts of the bishopric only slowly and late.

---

[32] For example, the Bible Bi 81 (in Stockholm), dated to the late twelfth century. It has English traits but was written in Sweden. See Stockholm, Riksarkivet, Fr. 112, 116–21, 124, 130–33, 152–55, 184, 726, 7762, 9034, 9303, 10113, 10770; the three and a half leaves of the reconstructed Helsinki Bible Bi 15 belong originally to the same manuscript. I am indebted to Michael Gullick for pointing this out in his letter of 10 March 2008. Compare Lehtinen, 'From Fragments into Codices', p. 124. According to her, Helsinki Bi 15 is a part of another Bible — not Bi 81 — in the Swedish Riksarkivet. The Stockholm missal Riksarkivet, Fr. 686, 711 was written by the same scribe as Stockholm Bi 81 and Helsinki Bi 15. Along with the Helsinki Bi 15, a *lectionarium officii* f.m. VII.24 (saec. XII ex.) may belong to the material written in Sweden at this early stage.

[33] For general information see, for example, Björkvall, 'Kort översikt över fragmentmaterialet'.

[34] About the Swedish fragment material, see Brunius, 'Landskapshandlingarna i Kammararkivet', p. 23.

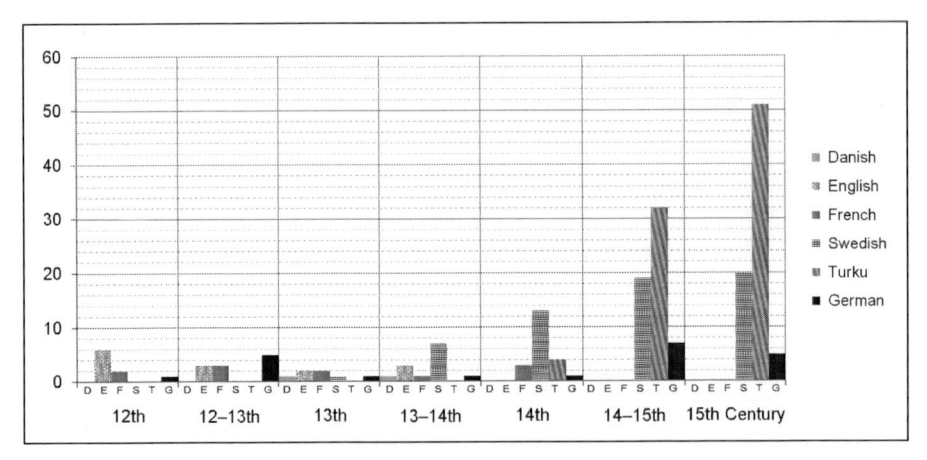

Graph 1. The number of extant localized and dated remains of manuscripts in the *fragmenta membranea* collection of the National Library of Finland by date.

As the number of books produced in Sweden rose, the disparity between the already well-developed western part of the realm and the eastern region that was only in the early stages of its literacy made it natural to import the needed books to the diocese of Åbo from the other Swedish dioceses. This can clearly be seen in the codices and fragments remaining in Finland: whilst foreign influence had had the greatest significance in the literate culture during the missionary period, the manuscripts and influences circulating within the Swedish realm began to play the major role later. The Swedish political and ecclesiastical control of the newly acquired and converted lands grew firmer, and important changes began to take place in the literary culture of the area. All in all, a great amount of manuscripts remain that were probably used in the eastern part of the kingdom during the Middle Ages and that have been dated to the thirteenth and especially fourteenth centuries and considered to be of Swedish origin by previous scholars.[35] The study of all the codices and fragments as a whole shows an important change in the field of literacy during the late thirteenth and early fourteenth centuries. The absolute number and relative importance of the books imported from abroad fell significantly, while at the same time the number of extant manuscripts of Swedish origin grew almost exponentially. Moreover, the overall amount of remaining books and their fragments began to increase.

[35] Compare, for example, Helsinki, Kansalliskirjasto, F.m. I.131, I.199, II.40, III.68, VII.5, VII.21.

Whereas the liturgical books of English, French, or German origin seem to have dominated during the first stage of the process of literacy, that is, the missionary period, the effective organization of the new diocese from the mid-thirteenth to the early fourteenth century was executed with the aid of manuscripts and scribes that originated from elsewhere. Only a very small amount of manuscripts from this time have been identified as likely representing the earliest local book production of Finland, and it is obvious that the young churches of the Åbo bishopric were supplied with the modest amount of manuscripts they needed by means of books imported from other parts of the realm. The amount of parishes and churches within the diocese was very limited well into the late thirteenth century[36] and, hence, the number of required books was fairly small. Because of this, it makes sense for the manuscripts to have been written elsewhere in Sweden and then imported. In principle it would have been possible to move some scribes from other dioceses to Finland and let them work there, but as the books were infinitely easier to transport than all the instruments, tools, and personnel for making manuscript codices, it is plausible that the number of imported books was much higher than the number of those produced locally.

At the high point of the book importation from other dioceses of Sweden, literacy had already gained a broader foothold in the daily life of the Christian population of the bishopric in respect to the missionary period. The spread of Christian faith and culture was an ongoing process within the area well into the sixteenth century, but the late thirteenth and early fourteenth centuries marked a milestone in the development, as the south-western parts of the diocese were being properly organized both ecclesiastically and secularly. Both of these partly overlapping organizations were grounded in the written word. Churchgoers were surrounded by the written *formulae* of God's own words read aloud by the priests. In the secular sphere of the administration of both the Church and the Crown the written, Latin, charters began to play an ever-growing role. Thus, the populace of the central, south-western parts of the Åbo diocese had already been fully drawn into the world of Latin literacy, whereas those living in the outskirts of the bishopric were probably experiencing their first contacts with it. In spite of the very modest absolute dimensions of the written culture, even in the heartlands of the diocese, the absorption of the written word had been rather swift, taking only a few generations. Hence the power and possibilities of reading and writing must have seemed revolutionary. From these revelations about the rewards of literacy, there was but a small step to the rise of local book production.

[36] Compare Palola, 'Yleiskatsaus Suomen keskiaikaisten seurakuntien'.

The number of manuscripts produced in Sweden or with clearly Swedish traits in relation to the total number of extant manuscripts remaining in the collections of the National Library of Finland was at its height in the late thirteenth and fourteenth centuries, after which the books produced locally in the Åbo diocese took the leading role. This reflects the most logical pattern, when we take into account the overall process of the arrival and development of literacy within the area in focus. The different phases — manuscript import from faraway countries, import from the earlier developed parts of the same realm, and finally local book production — correspond to the degree of literacy and manuscript production in the heartlands of Latin literacy, in the areas converted relatively early in the high Middle Ages, and finally those annexed into the Latin sphere of culture among the very latest regions of Europe.

No charters written within the diocese of Åbo survive from the twelfth century, and the number of charters surviving from the thirteenth century is next to non-existent as well.[37] It is plausible that it was in the late thirteenth and early fourteenth centuries that this pragmatic form of literacy in the ecclesiastical and secular administration began to take shape. The extreme scarcity of the early document sources is probably due in large part to the destruction of Åbo by the Novgorodians in 1318.[38] The damages done to the local archives hamper an outline of the earliest stages of this side of written culture, but as the number of charters surviving from the years right after the Novgorodian raid is relatively high, the reasonably widespread use of pragmatic literacy must have begun to make its first real steps in the previous decades. This, in turn, goes well together with what we know of the rapid ecclesiastical organization of the diocese in the late thirteenth century. All in all, the rise of the literate administration conformed very nicely to the endeavours of the bishops of Åbo to develop their diocese.

The development shaped above suggests the major role of the bishop and the cathedral chapter in introducing the wider use of charters within the diocese. This was a natural course of development, since the ability to write and read

---

[37] The material explored is mainly contained within *Finlands medeltidsurkunder*, ed. by Hausen; the charters are also accessible on the internet: <http://extranet.narc.fi/DF/index.htm> [accessed 9 January 2013]. The oldest known charter written in Finland that we know of is *Finlands medeltidsurkunder*, ed. by Hausen, no. 81, a document written for Bishop Thomas in Nousiainen in 1234.

[38] See *Finlands medeltidsurkunder*, ed. by Hausen, nos 387 and 389, which lament the destruction of the written records by the Novgorodians; for example, ibid., no. 387: 'cum omnibus privilegiis et clenodiis quam plurimis ecclesiae Aboensis [et] episcope'.

was concentrated in the hands of the clergymen, who seem to have composed the greater part of the earliest charters written in Finland. The vast majority of the handful of extant documents written in the young bishopric before the early fourteenth century is in Latin, and the language of the Church remains the major language of the charters well into the last quarter of the fourteenth century. Swedish was used alongside Latin throughout the century, but it remained of minor importance until the mid-fourteenth century: from the first quarter of the century no local charters written in Swedish exist whatsoever, and only about seven percent of the surviving charters of the second quarter were written in Swedish; the rest were composed in Latin.

The First Local Literary Efforts

The import of books from France, England, Germany, or other parts of Sweden tied the bishopric of Åbo closely to Latin Europe. The local manuscript production started when the western connection was already self-evident. At this point there had been generations of imported books, and the imported knowledge for making books had already taken root in Finland.

The ecclesiastical organization of the diocese and the building of a secular administration required an ever broader and new culture based on reading and writing, and eventually their needs could not be satisfied only by books and scribes imported from elsewhere. The shaping of a denser network of parishes during the thirteenth century, the establishment of the cathedral chapter in 1276, and the transfer of the episcopal see to Åbo at the end of the century were all milestones in the process, during which local writing grew more and more important. At first, many members of the local clergy probably moved to their parishes from other Swedish dioceses, and the training of the new generations in reading and writing most likely would have taken place by literates of other than Finnish origin. In all probability, the Dominicans and possibly Franciscans as well had a role in this process.

Quite logically, it seems to have been the nearest circle of the Bishop of Åbo and the cathedral chapter that took the decisive role when the diocese's own book production began.[39] The oldest known text certainly composed within the

---

[39] In addition to the *Legenda s. Henrici*, a small number of chartularies written to meet the needs of the cathedral chapter testify to its scribal activities. See, for example, Stockholm, Kungliga biblioteket, MS A57, A942; Uppsala, Uppsala universitetsbibliotek, MS K12a; *Registrum ecclesiae Aboensis eller Åbo domkyrkas Svartbok*, ed. by Pispala; *Registrum ecclesiae Aboensis*, ed. by Jaakkola; *Codex Särkilahti*, ed. by Jaakkola.

diocese is the liturgical legend of the local patron saint, *Legenda s. Henrici* (BHL 3818),[40] that contained a brief *vita* of the saint and a relatively modest collection of eleven of his miracles. The oldest surviving manuscript fragments of the legend date from the early fourteenth century,[41] but the contents of the work suggest that it was written in Åbo between the late 1270s and the early 1290s.[42]

In a broader comparison of the early literary works written in areas drawn relatively late to *Christianitas* and *Latinitas* in the high Middle Ages, one is able to see a pattern in which the very first literary efforts concerned the hagiography of local saints.[43] Whereas in many newly converted areas the local royal or dynastic saints played the most important role in early local hagiography, in Finland it was the alleged missionary bishop who took the central role. Very little is known of the actual practices of Christianizing the area and its annexation to the Swedish realm, but the emphasis on the missionary activities in the earliest forms of local historiographical self-understanding may suggest that the religious aspect really was more important than the political one.

In other areas, such as in Scandinavia and East Central Europe, for instance, the previous local nobility was drawn into the process of Christianization and cultural remoulding by giving it a clear administrative and religious role in the process. The latter aspect was demonstrated by early local hagiography glorifying the deeds of the local nobility in converting the area into the true faith. This aspect, however, is totally ignored in the literary works of newly converted Finland. *Legenda s. Henrici*, on which the later tradition was based, concentrates decidedly on the missionary bishop St Henry. Even though the legend implies that it was the cooperation of both secular and ecclesiastical powers that brought the success of the crusade to Finland, and the current status of the converted region as a part of the Swedish realm is described as self-evident, the secular counterpart of St Henry, the Swedish king St Eric, is only mentioned in passing.[44] No mention is made, however, of the local nobility, whose role in the early process of Christianization thus remains unclear and is only scarcely illuminated by some archaeological finds.

---

[40] *Legenda s. Henrici*, ed. by Heikkilä.

[41] Lund, Universitetsbiblioteket, Fragment 106.

[42] Heikkilä, *Pyhän Henrikin legenda*, pp. 226–46.

[43] Adamska, 'The Introduction of Writing in Central Europe'; Mortensen, 'Sanctified Beginnings and Mythopoietic Moments', p. 269.

[44] In addition, St Eric is represented astonishingly seldom as a subject of ecclesiastical art, as a patron of churches, or in the folklore in the Åbo diocese. All in all, his cult seems to have taken root only after much hesitation in Finland.

One can speculate on the evidently important and thoroughly negative role of the murderer of St Henry in local ecclesiastical art and folklore of the Middle Ages. As early as the late thirteenth-century *Legenda s. Henrici*, the murderer is described in a way that allows us to consider him a part of the local nobility. This is a view eagerly taken up by the previous, nationalistic Finnish historiography.[45] The fact remains that the earliest stage of local literary production in the young bishopric of Åbo refers to the overwhelming role of the Church — and the Swedes — in the Christianization and political reorganization of the area. It is possible that the emphasized interest of the legend in ecclesiastical matters only reflects the low participation of the indigenous elite in the new literate culture and thus the intended audience of the legend.

The emphasis on the missionary bishop rather than the Christianized lay elite of the society differentiates *Legenda s. Henrici* from most of its counterparts in the other newly converted peripheral parts of Europe. Still, the very writing of the legend as well as its contents fit very well into the overall picture in which the earliest Christian generations of a recently Christianized region sought to demonstrate the glory of their first saints in order to establish their status as proper parts of Christendom and the Church, as well as to inspire devotion. Moreover, while the literate inhabitants of the European periphery were, at least to some extent, conscious of their peripheral status within the Latin sphere of culture, hagiography was an apt instrument for making geographical periphery as equally central religiously as in the heartlands of Europe. According to this ideology, it was the actions of God that made a certain place central or peripheral.[46]

In this framework, it was typical that the earliest literary works of a country that had joined Christendom dealt with the history of the conversion and thus with the new local self-understanding. Very good Scandinavian examples describing the laudable activities of local Christian kings are, among others, *Passio s. Olavi* (BHL 6322)[47] and the *Legenda s. Erici* (BHL 2594–95).[48] In Bohemia and Hungary, as well, it was the activities of the local Christian roy-

---

[45] For example Gallén, 'Erik den helige, Finland'; Anthoni, 'Korstågstiden och dess innebörd'; Pirinen, *Suomen kirkon historia*, p. 42; Jokipii, 'Ensimmäinen ristiretki Suomeen ja sen lähin jälkimaine'.

[46] Compare Geary, 'Reflections on Historiography and the Holy', p. 328.

[47] *Passio et miracula beati Olaui*, ed. by Metcalfe. See Mortensen and Mundal, 'Erkebispesetet i Nidaros'.

[48] *Vita et miracula Sancti Erici regis Sueciae*, ed. by Nelson.

alty that gained attention in the earliest literary works: in Bohemia the hagiographical lives of St Ludmila (BHL 5025–31) (d. *c.* 921) and St Wenceslas (BHL 8821–44) (Václav, d. probably 935);[49] in Hungary Sts Stephen (BHL 7918–21) (d. 1038), Emeric (BHL 2528) (d. 1031), and Ladislaus (BHL 4670–71) (d. 1095).[50] In Poland, in turn, the early literary works concentrated on the missionary St Adalbert (d. 997) and the local early hermits.[51] The dedication of the very earliest literary work written in Finland to St Henry fits very well in this overall picture.

A closer examination of the sources used in *Legenda s. Henrici* elucidates the international influences that affected the early stages of the local manuscript production in the Åbo diocese. The composer of the text was, rather self-evidently, well acquainted with the previous hagiography on St Eric, St Henry's secular counterpart. Many passages of the legend show the direct influence of Eric's *vita* (BHL 2594).[52] In addition to using this piece of Swedish hagiography, the legend quotes *Passio s. Olavi* (BHL 6322), a Norwegian hagiographical text that had previously influenced the texts on Eric. Along with the earlier hagiography and the topoi of the genre, the Bible was the source of medieval ecclesiastical texts *non plus ultra*. Therefore, the legend is filled with biblical references, allusions, and quotations.[53] It is worth mentioning that the composer of *Legenda s. Henrici* was probably even familiar with the sermons of St Bernard of Clairvaux; the legend uses metaphors and images that are known from a number of sources but appear together only in Bernard's sermons.

Legenda s. Henrici was by no means a distinctively peripheral product. Its choice and use of sources, its rather high-level Latin, its structure, as well as its contents were all aspects that made it a solid piece of medieval hagiography — a text that could be used both in liturgy and for other pious purposes, and that could be disseminated, read, copied, and understood outside Åbo, Sweden, or Scandinavia. The proliferation of the text to Sweden, Denmark, England, Germany, and elsewhere during the late Middle Ages clearly indicates that the

---

[49] See *Fontes rerum Bohemicarum*, ed. by Emler, I; Bláhová, 'The Function of the Saints'.

[50] See *Scriptores rerum Hungaricarum*, ed. by Szentpétery, II; Veszprémy, 'Royal Saints in Hungarian Chronicles'.

[51] See *Monumenta Poloniae historica*, ed. by Bielowski and others, IV. 1–3 (1962–73); Kersken, 'God and the Saints in Medieval Polish Historiography'.

[52] See the comparison between the texts in Heikkilä, *Pyhän Henrikin legenda*, pp. 190–93.

[53] Heikkilä, *Pyhän Henrikin legenda*, pp. 194–96.

once peripheral and belatedly converted area of Finland had developed into a part of the Latin sphere of culture.[54]

The Rise of Local Book Production

The need for books was by all appearances rather modest in medieval Finland. It has been estimated that a typical parish church in Norway had a maximum of ten liturgical books in its collections.[55] The estimate for Swedish parishes is somewhat lower, from three to eight books.[56] The Norwegian number is obviously much too high to be used in the estimations of the total amount of books in Finland in the Middle Ages, and it is doubtful whether the number of books in the churches of the Åbo diocese would have come close to the Swedish number, either. Still, if we assume for the sake of the argument that all of the roughly one hundred parish churches and the roughly forty chapels that existed in the diocese at the end of the Middle Ages had as many as eight books each, the total number of books for the entire diocese would have been 1100.[57] It should be mentioned that the library of the Swedish monastery of Vadstena alone had more books than the entire Åbo diocese. As suggested above, the total number of over a thousand manuscripts is probably still much too high, and the real figure is possibly less than one thousand.[58] In any case, this shows how limited the need for books really was on the edge of Latin Christendom during the last centuries of the Middle Ages.

In spite of the very limited need for books in medieval Finland, it was natural that their production was moved locally from other parts of Sweden as soon as the development of local literacy allowed it. This seems to have taken place in the fourteenth century, during which the number of local products topped the

---

[54] About the dissemination of the text, see Heikkilä, *Pyhän Henrikin legenda*, pp. 166–69; Roos and Heikkilä, 'Evaluating Methods for Computer-Assisted Stemmatology'; Roos, Heikkilä, and Myllymäki, 'A Compression-Based Method for Stemmatic Analysis'.

[55] Ommundsen, 'Books, Scribes and Sequences', I, 177.

[56] Brunius, 'Medieval Manuscript Fragments in the National Archives', p. 9; Brunius, 'Sockenkyrkornas liturgiska böcker', pp. 457–58; Helander, 'Sockenkyrkans liturgiska profil', p. 195.

[57] Åslaug Ommundsen estimates that the total number of books in Norway was 10,000–12,000; the number of books in Sweden has been estimated to have been about the same or slightly higher than in Norway. See Ommundsen, 'Books, Scribes and Sequences', I, 177.

[58] See Keskiaho, 'Bortom fragmenten'.

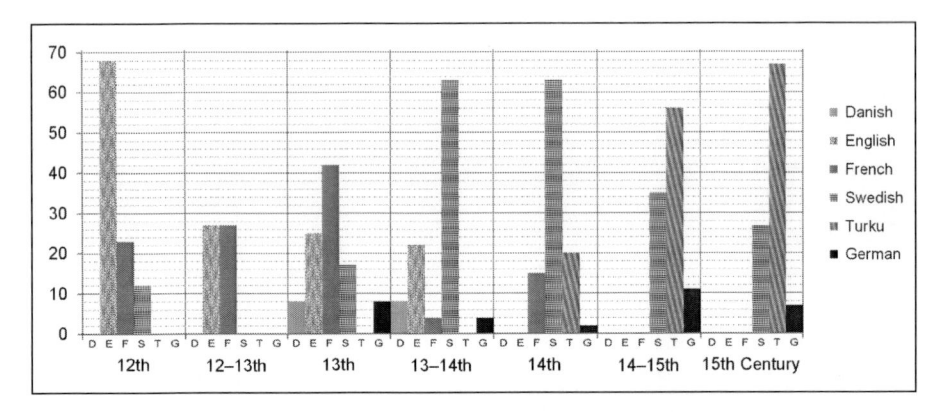

Graph 2. The relative proportions (%) of the manuscripts localized to certain areas of the total number of datable and localizable fragments of codices from the period in question.

amount of Swedish imports. During the rest of the Middle Ages the situation remained clear, and local book production seems to have secured its position.

Taking into account the modest need for books and manuscript imports, the yearly volume of local production in the diocese of Åbo was probably only a handful of books. This kind of volume did not require many well-equipped centres of writing. It is, therefore, more likely that most of the locally produced manuscripts were written as the need arose, and there was no reserve of ready, unused books. In this respect, it is of interest to note the obvious rise of local manuscript production in the first half of the fifteenth century, during which a reorganization of the diocese took place. The reorganization included the forming of many new parishes and building of new churches,[59] which, in turn, resulted in a growing demand for liturgical books.

Of the numerous monastic and religious orders of the Church, only the Dominicans, the Franciscans, and the Bridgettines really transmit their influence to Finland during the Middle Ages. Of the two major mendicant orders, the Dominicans soon won the upper hand in Finland, and the Dominicans and Bridgettines in particular came to be of importance in the book production of the Åbo diocese. The fact that the earliest canonically chosen bishop of the diocese, Thomas, had close ties to the Dominicans and even donated his book collection to the Dominican convent of Sigtuna may suggest very early cooperation

---

[59] Hiekkanen, *Suomen keskiajan kivikirkot*, pp. 24–25; Palola, *Maunu Tavast ja Olavi Maununpoika*, pp. 206–26.

between the order and the bishops of Finland.[60] At any rate, the Dominican influence was so significant in the early formation of Åbo liturgy[61] that it is often difficult, if not impossible, to make a distinction between a genuine Dominican manuscript and a book of secular liturgy with Dominican influences.

The clear dominance of Dominican books over those of the Franciscans begins to appear as early as the fourteenth century and is even more pronounced during the last century of the Middle Ages.[62] The speculations about imported manuscripts of the late Middle Ages aside, the extant books and fragments indicate that whereas the role of the Franciscans in local book production was limited, the Dominicans — by all appearances, and especially at the old convent of St Olaf in Åbo — succeeded in having a major role in producing books for the needs of the diocese. This was surely augmented by the favourable location of the convent in the cathedral town, the very early presence of the order in the diocese, and the Dominican traits of the local liturgy.

As an example of the Dominican production of liturgical books for the needs of the diocese and its parish churches, a group of four missals may be mentioned.[63] They were probably written in the convent of St Olaf in the early decades of the fifteenth century and testify to the writing potential of the convent. Although the four books were mainly written by only one scribe, some of their fragments show the participation of as many as three scribes on one book, plus the later comments and corrections by the readers. A convent with at least three scribes, possibly working at the same time, was, by local standards, already a significant centre of writing. Still, the convent of St Olaf should probably not be seen as a stable *scriptorium* but rather as a literate workshop, a place

---

[60] Unlike in many other areas, the coexistence of the Dominicans and the secular clergy was, from all appearances, amicable from very early on. See Gallén, *La Province de Dacie de l'ordre des frères precheurs*, p. 101.

[61] The Dominican liturgy was officially considered to be the basis of the liturgy of the diocese from the time of Bishop Benedictus (1321–38). It is plausible, however, that the Dominican influence was very strong even before this.

[62] See e.g. Helsinki, Kansalliskirjasto, F.m. I.115, I.199, I.278, I.283, I.285, I.288, I.291, I.308, I.329, III.113, III.150, III.186, IV.27, IV.31, IV.32, IV.35, IV.45, IV.46, IV.51, VII.1. Compare Haapanen, *Verzeichnis der mittelalterlichen Handschriftenfragmente*, I, p. xxxiv.

[63] The remains of the manuscripts can be reconstructed from the fragment collections of the Finnish National Library and the Swedish National Archives: (a) Helsinki, Kansalliskirjasto, F.m. I.278; Stockholm, Riksarkivet, Fr 8639, Fr 9101 (altogether 19 leaves); (b) Helsinki, Kansalliskirjasto, F.m. I.283; Stockholm, Riksarkivet, Fr 7971, Fr 8187, Fr 8322, Fr 10897 (61 leaves); (c) Helsinki, Kansalliskirjasto, F.m. I.288; Stockholm, Riksarkivet, Fr 8342 (10 leaves); (d) Helsinki, Kansalliskirjasto, F.m. I.291; Stockholm, Riksarkivet, Fr 8691 (12 leaves).

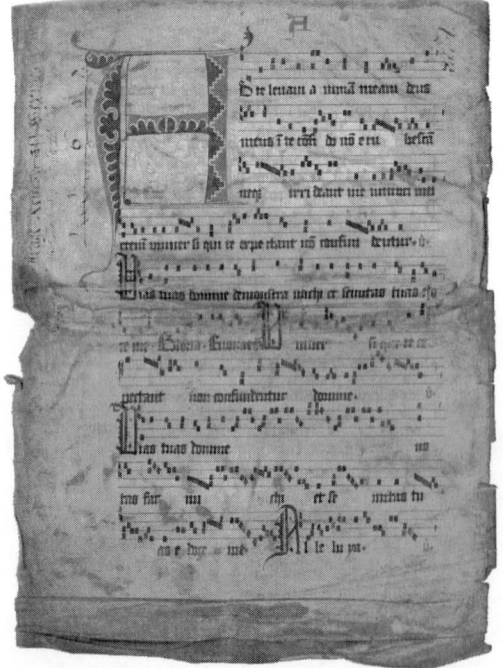

Figure 6. Two graduals written in the Bridgettine monastery of Naantali; both apparently copied from the same exemplar. Helsinki, Kansalliskirjasto, F.m. II.118, fol. 1ᵛ (above), and Helsinki, Kansalliskirjasto, F.m. II.120, fol. 1ᵛ (below). Fifteenth century. Reproduced with permission.

where those with knowledge of writing could come together when needed. The convent — and the whole cathedral city, for that matter — seem to have been rather modest as a writing and literate milieu. The writing practices of the Dominican workshop seem by all appearances to have been rather liberal: The *missalia* show a knowledge of example books, but the example was not followed very faithfully. Neither do the books show a certain house-style of writing, which points to the lack of a uniform education in writing — it was more likely a matter of using and combining the skills of scribes and literates who had received their education elsewhere. The heterogeneity of the manuscripts produced by the same group of people points to such a modest amount of needed books that it had not yet been necessary to harmonize the different stages of the production. Still, one should not pay too much attention to the shortcomings of the scriptorial practices in the context of early fifteenth-century Finland. It suffices to know that the Dominican convent of St Olaf was, at least occasionally, able to produce books even for the needs of the parishes.[64]

The monastic orders reached the Åbo bishopric as the Bridgettine monastery *Vallis gratiae* was established in Naantali (Sw. Nådendal) in the early 1440s. It was to remain the only monastery in Finland throughout the Middle Ages, and thus Finnish historians have been eager to associate every possible kind of significance to this status. At least in the field of cultural history the high reputation of the monastery is justified, as reading and writing were traditionally important aspects of Bridgettine life, and the Naantali monastery really was the only and thus the best example of monastic literacy within the diocese. The literary culture of the monastery is still surprisingly unknown, and the differentiation between extant manuscript fragments written and used in the Bridgettine monastery of Vadstena in the diocese of Linköping and those of Naantali poses problems to the shaping of the monastery's own manuscript production and library. In any case, the Bridgettine monastery at Naantali was a part of a broad international network, through which ideas, books, texts, and literate skills were transmitted swiftly.

Naantali was certainly one of the centres of literacy in the late medieval diocese of Åbo. It was alone in possessing a scriptorium of its own that aspired to a distinguishable house style in writing and producing manuscripts, as can clearly be seen in a group of extant fragments that were written by three to

---

[64] On the group of fragments and the writing in St Olaf, see Heikkilä, 'I ett medeltida *scriptorium* i Åbo'. On another group of manuscripts written in the Åbo diocese, see Tahkokallio, 'Texter från ett scriptorium i Åbo'.

seven different scribes in the latter half of the fifteenth and in the beginning of the sixteenth century.[65] All in all, the different manuscripts and fragments definitely or probably written in Naantali contain writing of dozens of hands.[66] The relatively vivacious writing activity of Naantali probably had very much to do with the influences from the Vadstena monastery, since the literate contacts between this *non plus ultra* of the written culture of the Swedish realm and the newly established Naantali are known to have been very close.[67] The manuscripts and fragments of certain Naantali origin show a rather wide variety of different liturgical books: *gradualia*, breviaries, antiphonaries, etc. In addition to this relatively uniform group of fragments and books, there are about two dozen other manuscripts, the origin of which may possibly be traced to Naantali.[68] The monastery was also the writing milieu of the earliest local author known by name, Jöns Budde, who wrote in the third quarter of the fifteenth century. His manuscripts have a special place among the surviving books of the monastery. His main activities included writing charters, copying books, and translating Latin texts into the vernacular Swedish.[69]

The vernacular texts were an interesting new trait in the literacy of the diocese of Åbo, a trait that could probably not have emerged anywhere else than

---

[65] Walta, 'Kirjallisuus, kirjat ja kirjoittaminen Naantalin luostarissa', pp. 104–05 and passim; I would like to thank Jesse Keskiaho for the use of the manuscript of his article on the subject before it was published (Keskiaho, 'En grupp handskrifter från slutet av 1400-talet'). The remains of the identified books produced in Naantali are scattered throughout several archives and libraries: (a) Helsinki, Kansalliskirjasto, F.m. II.90; (b) Helsinki, Kansalliskirjasto, F.m. II.117 — Stockholm, Riksarkivet, Fr. 10367; (c) Helsinki, Kansalliskirjasto, F.m. II.118 — Stockholm, Riksarkivet, Fr. 28359; (d) Helsinki, Kansalliskirjasto, F.m. II.120 — Åbo, Maakuntamuseo, uncatalogued fragment leaf b; (e) Helsinki, Kansalliskirjasto, F.m. II.121; (f) Helsinki, Kansalliskirjasto, F.m. IV.138; (g) Helsinki, Kansalliskirjasto, F.m. IV.156 — Stockholm, Riksarkivet, Fr. 8994, Fr. 10407, Fr. 20274; (h) Helsinki, Kansalliskirjasto, F.m. IV.157 — Åbo, Maakuntamuseo, uncatalogued fragment leaf c — Stockholm, Riksarkivet, Fr. 1385, Fr. 10370, Fr. 10406, Fr. 20275; (i) Helsinki, Kansalliskirjasto, F.m. IV.160 — Stockholm, Riksarkivet, Fr. 20340; (j) Helsinki, Kansalliskirjasto, F.m. IV.170 — Stockholm, Riksarkivet, Fr. 10437; (k) Helsinki, Kansalliskirjasto, F.m. IV.173; (l) Helsinki, Kansalliskirjasto, F.m. VII.132 (= III.180?); (m) Helsinki, Kansalliskirjasto, Ms. A° II 55; (n) possibly Stockholm, Riksarkivet, Fr. 2859; (o) possibly Stockholm, Riksarkivet, Fr. 7856.

[66] Walta, 'Kirjallisuus, kirjat ja kirjoittaminen', pp. 104–06.

[67] See *Finlands medeltidsurkunder*, ed. by Hausen, nos 6652, 6852; Lamberg, *Jöns Budde*, pp. 13, 377–78.

[68] For a complete list of remaining Naantali manuscripts and fragments, see Walta, 'Kirjallisuus, kirjat ja kirjoittaminen Naantalin luostarissa'.

[69] On Jöns Budde, see Lamberg, *Jöns Budde*.

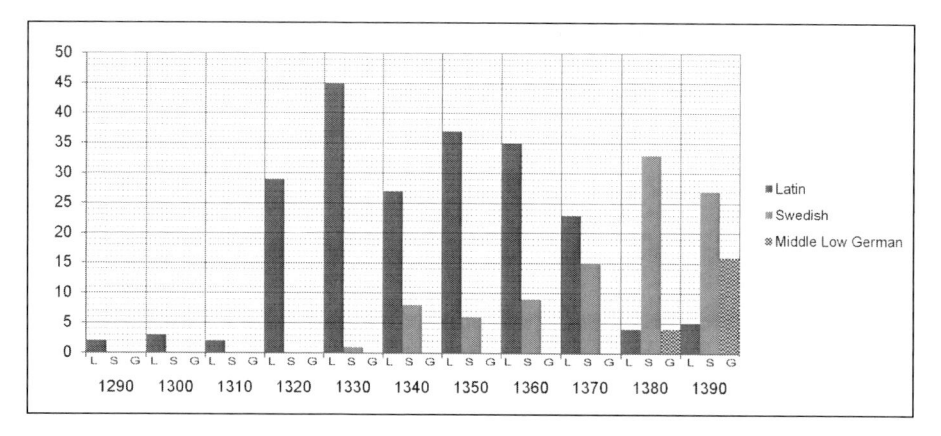

Graph 3. The number and language of pre-1400 charters written in Finland.

in a monastic context. The literacy and the reading public of the diocese were so modest that it is difficult to imagine a real public for a number of vernacular books outside the walls of a monastic community. The scarcity of the remains of manuscripts written in the vernacular — Swedish and German — obviously reflects the low number of such books that was needed in Finland in the Middle Ages. In any case, it is interesting to note how the vernacular reached the book production in Finland only generations after becoming the dominating language of the charters written within the diocese. This may be seen as one of the consequences of the differences between the audiences, the uses, and the very raison d'être of the sacral, that is, liturgical and ecclesiastical, and pragmatic literacy.

In the latter half of the fourteenth century, a rather quick change seems to have taken place regarding the balance between Latin and the vernacular in the pragmatic literacy of the charters. During the second and last third of the century, the share of the Swedish charters rose rapidly. In the third quarter of the century it rose to 22 per cent of the total — the rest were still in Latin. But by the last quarter the general situation changed drastically: the majority of charters were written in the vernacular, 70 per cent in Swedish and 20 per cent in German. The share of Latin documents fell during a few decades from an overwhelming majority to a small minority of 10 per cent. Whilst Latin was used for all kinds of documents in all spheres of society in the early fourteenth century, its use was reduced to ecclesiastical circles by the end of the century, and even clerics used Swedish in many of their documents.

The swift increase in the amount of charters written in Swedish was connected with the new legislation of King Magnus Eriksson in the mid-fourteenth

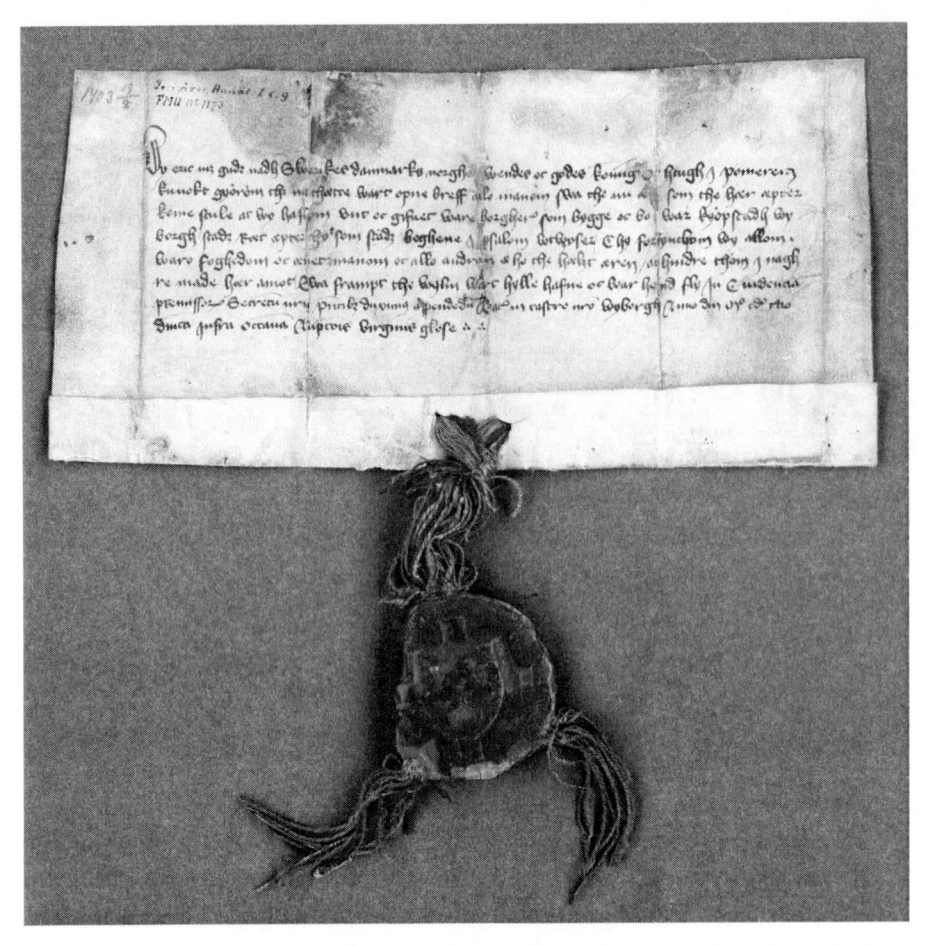

Figure 7. Charter in Swedish of the easternmost town of the Swedish realm, Viborg, which received its town rights in 1403. Helsinki, Kansallisarkisto, Pergamentti-kokoelma 6. 1403. Reproduced with permission.

century, according to which the documents of legal importance, such as different contracts and court decisions, were to be written in the vernacular.[70] Consequently, Latin ceased to be the 'official' language of the secular administration around the 1340s and 1350s.[71] However, in comparison to the other dioceses within the Swedish realm, the decrease in the use of Latin as the lan-

---

[70] Compare Nedkvitne, *The Social Consequences of Literacy*, pp. 89, 99; Söderberg and Larsson, *Nordisk medeltidsliteracy*, pp. 106–08.

[71] Nedkvitne, *The Social Consequences of Literacy*, p. 11; Larsson, *Svenska medeltidsbrev*.

guage of the charters is much more remarkable in the diocese of Turku.[72] This was probably due to the scarcity of ecclesiastical institutions within the diocese; by the mid-fourteenth century there were no monasteries anywhere in Finland and just one or two mendicant convents.

The swift change of the late fourteenth century certainly reflects the arrival at a new stage of literacy in Finland at that time. The new dominance of the vernacular testifies to new needs and new possibilities for literacy. The growing importance of trade and its developing procedures necessitated the use of literacy, reading, and writing in the vernacular. The enhanced organization of secular government also had its particular needs. All in all, literacy sought and found new, everyday uses and reached new social groups. Even if the ecclesiastics still controlled the manuscript production proper, they no longer had a monopoly over the written word. While it is probable that there were no professional scribes in book production in Finland, there were certainly clerks who wrote charters and kept accounts as a profession.[73] These tasks were performed in the vernacular, that is, in Swedish and German. The use of Latin remained more and more for clerics and for the production of books.

Foreign Imports of the Late Middle Ages

Even if the rise in local book production in the fourteenth century reduced the need for imported manuscripts, a considerable number of books were still brought from abroad. The study of the development of literacy in other peripheries of Latin Europe in the Middle Ages has shown that the emergence of local manuscript production coincided with a growth in the variation of different genres written, read, and collected. When the immediate needs of the parishes for books were fulfilled, the literates did not content themselves with liturgical books, but rather wanted to acquaint themselves with books of canon law or theology, for instance.[74] It is plausible that the local production in the diocese of Åbo concentrated on a variety of liturgical books, and the interest in other literary genres still had to be satisfied, mainly with imports. The years abroad at foreign universities provided a welcome opportunity to many clerics of the

---

[72] Compare the numbers given in Graph 3 with for example Larsson, *Svenska medeltidsbrev*, pp. 200, 254.

[73] Salminen, 'Unknown Hands, Trusted Men'.

[74] See Adamska, 'The Introduction of Writing in Central Europe', pp. 176–77 with further literature.

diocese for acquiring fascinating books of philosophical, juridical, or other contents, and this method of importing manuscripts seems to have been of great significance.[75] This is also implied by the contents of the book donations made to the Cathedral of Åbo during the Middle Ages; they consisted mainly of books of high theology or canon law,[76] obviously books that the library of the cathedral lacked in general. The cataloguing work of fragments of these kinds of books in Finnish collections has been ongoing for decades, but the results are not yet available in their entirety. However, the preliminary findings seem to confirm the hypothesis that they are mainly of foreign origin.

The manuscripts of English origin of the late Middle Ages are next to non-existent in the Finnish collections. However, a fair amount of fragments of French manuscripts from the fourteenth century exist in the same collections — possibly simply because of this 'university import'. The importance of the English and French books was, however, probably on the wane. This, in turn, was due to a number of reasons: the constant rise of local production, the Great Schism, in which Scandinavia and France were on opposite sides, and the popularity of German universities over the more traditional University of Paris in the fifteenth century may all have played their part.

German influence did not wane simultaneously with the English and French import of books during the fourteenth and fifteenth centuries. In fact, the number of manuscripts written in Germany or with German influence grew towards the end of the Middle Ages. However, the amount is still rather limited, and one should be careful not to draw conclusions that are too rash based on the extant fragments. Nonetheless, the rising importance of German connections can be seen in other fields of culture at the very same time. To name just one example, the import of altarpieces and statues of saints from Germany to the diocese of Åbo multiplies during the fifteenth century.[77] Emphasizing German connections was natural because of the ever-growing importance

---

[75] A fine example is the library of Törnerus Andreae, who had acquired a collection of some thirty books while studying in Prague. Compare Uppsala, Uppsala universitetsbibliotek, MSS C 199; C 272; C 453; Maliniemi, 'Muistoja praagilaisesta vaikutuksesta'.

[76] The largest known donations were those of Bishop Thomas of Finland (Uppsala, Uppsala universitetsbibliotek, MS C 134; *Finlands medeltidsurkunder*, ed. by Hausen, no. 92), Bishop Hemming of Åbo (ibid., no. 647; *Registrum ecclesiae Aboensis*, ed. by Jaakkola, p. 158), and schoolmaster Henricus Tempil (*Finlands medeltidsurkunder*, ed. by Hausen, no. 649; *Registrum ecclesiae Aboensis*, ed. by Jaakkola, p. 160). See Lehtinen, 'Kirjoja ja kirjastoja keskiajan Suomessa', pp. 16–22.

[77] See Bonsdorff, *Kunstproduktion und Kunstverbreitung*.

Figure 8. *Habent sua fata libelli*: A copy of Vincent of Beauvais's *Speculum historiale*, originating from the cathedral library of Troyes, ended up being used in the diocese of Åbo. Helsinki, Kansalliskirjasto, MS F.m. V.Var.26, fol. 16[r]. Late thirteenth century. Reproduced with permission.

of the Hanseatic League, and because the majority of burghers in Åbo, for instance, were of German origin and had close ties to the previous homeland of their families.

The natural connections between the diocese of Åbo and Germany were beneficial when the diocese became interested in printed books for its own use in the end of the Middle Ages. In the 1480s, the diocese of Åbo appears to have bought a considerable number of manuscripts of a Dominican breviary printed by Anton Koberger in Nuremberg in 1485 in order to circulate the copies to the parishes and thereby unify the liturgical practices.[78] Soon, however, there was a need for the diocese's own missal, *Missale Aboense*, that was printed as a modified edition of a Dominican missal by Bartholomaeus Ghotan in Lübeck in 1488.[79] Another printed work commissioned by the diocese of Åbo was a manual, printed in Halberstadt in 1522.[80] Although there had been printers active in Sweden since the late fifteenth century, it was natural for the Bishop of Åbo to commission the works in Germany: the ties to the German centres were close and old, and Germany represented the epicentre of printing at the time.

The Development of Literacy in a European Periphery

The best way to form a general overview of the arrival and development of literacy in the north-easternmost periphery of western *Christianitas* and *Latinitas* is to explore the extant written sources as widely as possible. The picture thus outlined reveals three different stages in the development.

There was no previous written culture in the area, and the introduction of literacy to medieval Finland took place slowly from the eleventh century onwards. It was obviously closely tied to Christianity from early on, and the development accelerated significantly in the twelfth century, as the area of present south-western Finland became the object of a more or less organized and rather intensive missionary activity. The earliest books and their extant remains in the Finnish collections date from the twelfth century. The remaining codices and fragments are very limited in number but reveal the clear domination of

---

[78] Heikkilä, *Pyhän Henrikin legenda*, p. 84; Maliniemi, *Zur Kenntnis des Breviarium Aboense Cod. Holm. 56*, p. 16.

[79] *Missale Aboense*, ed. by Parvio.

[80] *Manuale seu exequiale*. In spite of the place of printing, the contents of the manual follow faithfully those of the Uppsala manual, printed in 1487. See Parvio, 'Manuale Aboense 1522', pp. 140, 171.

foreign written material at the earliest stage of literacy. The books of English origin or with English traits dominate, but even French, Swedish, and German material is present among the earliest sources.

The second stage of literacy is marked by the distinctive rise of Swedish manuscripts in Finland in the late thirteenth and fourteenth centuries, and by the introduction of the use of charters in both the ecclesiastical and secular sphere. Most of the books needed east of the Gulf of Bothnia were probably imported from other parts of Sweden. The development was related to the increasingly organized ecclesiastical and secular administration of the area, its ever closer ties to the motherland Sweden, and the rise of manuscript production in Sweden in general. The import of manuscripts from other parts of Sweden continued until the end of the Middle Ages, but it was of greatest significance during the late thirteenth and fourteenth centuries. By the end of the thirteenth century the area converted a few generations earlier had become an integral part of the Swedish realm as the bishopric of Åbo. The growth of the uses of literacy in ecclesiastical, political, and social life can be observed, for instance, in the growing use of Latin charters from the early fourteenth century onwards.

Genuine local book production began in the diocese of Åbo during the fourteenth century. Although the need for books remained rather limited within the scarcely populated country, at least three modest centres of writing seem to have emerged: the close circle of the local cathedral chapter, the convent of St Olaf in Åbo, and the Bridgettine monastery of Naantali. It must be stressed, however, that the number of manuscripts needed for and produced in the diocese of Åbo remained by all accounts very limited even in comparison to other Swedish dioceses. Still, the emergence of the local production was an eloquent sign of a new stage in the development of literacy: the skills for making books had been adopted in the degree necessary for the local context, and the number of locally produced manuscripts soon exceeded that of the Swedish imports during the latter half of the fourteenth century, after which local books dominated the literate scene. After the fourteenth century, literacy had reached the point in which reading and writing were considered as the normal means of communication in many fields of society. Again, the new understanding is mirrored in the extant charters, which became more and more practical in nature and began to satisfy an ever more diversified variety of needs. Whereas Latin had earlier dominated as the language of the charters, the number of documents written in Swedish and German rose significantly after the mid-fourteenth century, and from the last quarter of the century onwards the vast majority of the charters were written in Swedish. This kind of secularization and 'pragmaticization' of literacy was, however, never reached in the field of book production of the Middle Ages, which remained sacral in nature and in ecclesiastical hands.

A pattern similar to that outlined above has also been noticed in other areas annexed to the Latin sphere of culture during the high Middle Ages.[81] It is interesting, however, to see that the relative pace of development was somewhat faster in Finland, which was brought to the sphere of written culture later than other areas of North or East Central Europe. By the fifteenth century, the diocese of Åbo had already, mutatis mutandis, reached the very same level of literacy as most of Latin Europe and was able to communicate with them almost *inter pares*, so to speak. On the other hand, the number of books and charters needed and used in the Åbo diocese was relatively small in comparison to almost any other area within western Christendom.

The growth of literacy did not occur in a cultural vacuum. In spite of the lack of previous literate culture on the north-eastern shores of the Baltic, the Latin written word had to replace, or rather find its place among, the earlier non-literate forms of communication. Even at the end of the Middle Ages, only a portion of society actively participated in the literate culture, while the majority still lived in a secondary oral culture. The people knew some of the ways in which writing worked, but did not use writing themselves, since they found the traditional oral ways of communicating sufficient to their needs.[82] They took part in the literacy only passively or orally, for example via spells and charms that used material borrowed from written texts. Thus, 'literacy' and 'illiteracy' coexisted in different — and partially overlapping — social spheres.

A social group can be considered to have a literate mentality, and to live in a culture of literacy, when the members of the group take it as a matter of course that certain acts are written down, when they see and understand the motivation behind the action, and when they use the accumulated knowledge actively. This mentality was obviously reached early in ecclesiastical circles, and not very much later within the secular administration. All in all, the *Verschriftlichung* of the newly Christianized and organized bishopric of Åbo took place in close interaction with authority, the exercise of both ecclesiastical or religious and secular power.

---

[81] Compare Adamska, 'The Introduction of Writing in Central Europe', p. 168.

[82] Compare Ong, *Orality and Literacy*, pp. 136–37; Goody, *The Logic of Writing and the Organization of Society*; Green, 'Orality and Reading'.

The rise of pragmatic literacy, that is, the use of reading and writing in daily life, so central in the development of broad literate mentalities, was, in turn, absorbed only more slowly. Even by the end of the Middle Ages, books and charters, reading and writing, were only a distant part of the lives of the majority, even if they were of some consequence to a major part of the society. The traditional non-literate means of communication had not lost their importance. Therefore, it would be fruitful in future scholarship to study the arrival and development of literacy in the European periphery, taking the questions of folklore, oral tradition, and oral culture closely into account.

Works Cited

Primary Sources

Antiphonarium Nidrosiensis ecclesiae, ed. by Lilli Gjerløw (Oslo: Universitetsforlaget, 1979)
Codex Särkilahti, ed. by Jalmari Jaakkola, Codices medii aevi Finlandiae, 2 (Helsinki: Societas Finlandae historica, 1952)
Finlands medeltidsurkunder, ed. by Reinhold Hausen, 8 vols (Helsinki: [Statsarkiv], 1910–35)
Fontes rerum Bohemicarum, ed. by Josef Emler, 4 vols (Prague: Spolek historický v Praze, 1873–84)
Juusten, Paulus, *M. Pauli Juusten Chronicon episcoporum Finlandensium, annotationibus et apparatu monumentorum illustratum*, Henrici Gabrielis Porthan, Opera selecta, 1–2, 2 vols (Helsinki: Finska litteratursällskapet, 1859–62)
——, *Suomen piispainkronikka*, ed. and trans. by Simo Heininen, Suomalaisen Kirjallisuuden Seuran toimituksia, 476 (Helsinki: Suomalaisen Kirjallisuuden Seura, 1988)
Legenda s. Henrici, in *Pyhän Henrikin legenda*, ed. by Tuomas Heikkilä, Suomalaisen Kirjallisuuden Seuran toimituksia, 1039 (Helsinki: Suomalaisen Kirjallisuuden Seura, 2005), pp. 398–419
Manuale seu exequiale secundum ritum ac consuetudinem alme ecclesie Aboensis (Halberstadt: Stuchs, 1522)
Missale Aboense: secundum ordinem fratrum praedicatorum, ed. by Martti Parvio (Porvoo: Werner Söderström, 1988)
Monumenta Poloniae historica, new ser., ed. by August Bielowski and others, 12 vols to date (Warszawa: Polska Akademia Umiejętności, 1960–)
Ordo Nidrosiensis ecclesiae, ed. by Lilli Gjerløw (Oslo: Universitetsforlaget, 1968)
Passio et miracula beati Olaui, ed. by Frederick Metcalfe (Oxford: Clarendon Press, 1881)
Registrum ecclesiae Aboensis, ed. by Jalmari Jaakkola, Codices medii aevi Finlandiae, 1 (Helsinki: Societas Finlandae Historica, 1952)
Registrum ecclesiae Aboensis eller Åbo domkyrkas Svartbok, ed. by Elisa Pispala, trans. by Jüri Kokkonen (Helsinki: Kansallisarkisto, 1996)
Scriptores rerum Hungaricarum, ed. by E. Szentpétery, 2 vols (Budapest: Academia litterarum Hungarica, 1937–38)
Vita et miracula Sancti Erici regis Sueciae, ed. by Axel Nelson (København: Munksgaard, 1944)

Secondary Works

Abukhanfusa, Kerstin, *Mutilated Books: Wondrous Leaves from Swedish Bibliographical History* (Stockholm: Riksarkivet, 2004)
Adamska, Anna, 'The Introduction of Writing in Central Europe (Poland, Hungary and Bohemia)', in *New Approaches to Medieval Communication*, ed. by Marco Mostert, Utrecht Studies in Medieval Literacy, 1 (Turnhout: Brepols, 1999), pp. 165–90

——, 'The Study of Medieval Literacy: Old Sources, New Ideas', in *The Development of Literate Mentalities in East Central Europe*, ed. by Anna Adamska and Marco Mostert, Utrecht Studies in Medieval Literacy, 9 (Turnhout: Brepols, 2004), pp. 13–47

Adamska, Anna, and Marco Mostert, 'Preface', in *The Development of Literate Mentalities in East Central Europe*, ed. by Anna Adamska and Marco Mostert, Utrecht Studies in Medieval Literacy, 9 (Turnhout: Brepols, 2004), pp. 1–4

Adamson, J. W., 'The Extent of Literacy in England in the Fifteenth and Sixteenth Centuries', *The Library*, 19 (1930), 162–93

Anthoni, Eric, 'Korstågstiden och dess innebörd', in *Kring korstågen till Finland: ett urval uppsatser tillägnat Jarl Gallén på hans sextioårsdag den 23 maj 1968*, ed. by Kaj Mikander ([Helsinki]: [Kirjavälitys], 1968), pp. 155–72

Bäuml, Franz, 'Varieties and Consequences of Medieval Literacy and Illiteracy', *Speculum*, 55 (1980), 237–65

Björkvall, Gunilla, 'Kort översikt över fragmentmaterialet med tonvikt på den tidigare perioden 1150–1250 och sekvenserna', *Kungliga Vitterhets Historie och Antikvitets Akademiens årsbok* (2002), 139–45

Bláhová, Marie, 'The Function of the Saints in Early Bohemian Historical Writing', in *The Making of Christian Myths in the Periphery of Latin Christendom (c. 1000–1300)*, ed. by Lars Boje Mortensen (København: Museum Tusculanum, 2006), pp. 83–119

Bonsdorff, Jan von, *Kunstproduktion und Kunstverbreitung im Ostseeraum des Spätmittelalters*, Finska fornminnesföreningens årsskrift, 99 (Helsinki: Finska fornminnesföreningen, 1993)

Brunius, Jan, 'Landskapshandlingarna i Kammararkivet: från kammarens register till databas', *Arkiv, samhälle och forskning* (2000), 7–27

——, 'Medieval Manuscript Fragments in the National Archives: A Survey', in *Medieval Book Fragments in Sweden: An International Seminar in Stockholm, 13–16 November 2003*, ed. by Jan Brunius (Stockholm: Riksarkivet, 2005), pp. 9–17

——, 'Sockenkyrkornas liturgiska böcker: studier i pergamentsomslagen i Riksarkivet', in *Kyrka och socken i medeltidens Sverige*, ed. by Olle Ferm, Studier till det medeltida Sverige, 5 (Stockholm: Riksantikvarieämbetet, 1991), pp. 457–72

Franklin, Simon, *Writing, Society and Culture in Early Rus, c. 950–1300* (Cambridge: Cambridge University Press, 2002)

Galbraith, Vivian Hunter, 'The Literacy of Medieval English Kings', *Proceedings of the British Academy*, 21 (1935), 201–38

Gallén, Jarl, 'Erik den helige, Finland', in *Kulturhistoriskt lexikon för nordisk medeltid: från vikingatid till reformationstid*, ed. by Ingvar Andersson and others, 22 vols (Helsinki: Akademiska bokhandeln, 1956–78), IV: *Epistolarium–Frälsebonde*, ed. by Gunvor Kerkkonen (1959), p. 16

——, *La Province de Dacie de l'ordre des frères precheurs*, I: *Histoire générale jusqu'au grand schisme* (Helsinki: Söderström, 1946)

Geary, Patrick, 'Reflections on Historiography and the Holy: Center and Periphery', in *The Making of Christian Myths in the Periphery of Latin Christendom (c. 1000–1300)*, ed. by Lars Boje Mortensen (København: Museum Tusculanum, 2006), pp. 323–29

Gieysztor, Aleksander, 'Symboles de la royauté en Pologne: un groupe des manuscrits du XIe et du début du XIIe s', *Comptes rendus de l'Academie des inscriptions et belles-lettres* (1990), 132–33

Goody, Jack, *The Logic of Writing and the Organization of Society* (Cambridge: Cambridge University Press, 1986)

Green, Dennis H., 'Orality and Reading: The State of Research in Medieval Studies', *Speculum*, 65 (1990), 271–75

Gullick, Michael, 'Preliminary Observations on Romanesque Manuscript Fragments of English, Norman and Swedish Origin in the Riksarkivet (Stockholm)', in *Medieval Book Fragments in Sweden: An International Seminar in Stockholm, 13–16 November 2003*, ed. by Jan Brunius (Stockholm: Riksarkivet, 2005), pp. 31–82

Haapanen, Toivo, *Verzeichnis der mittelalterlichen Handschriftenfragmente in der Universitätsbibliothek zu Helsingfors*, Helsingin yliopiston kirjaston julkaisuja, 4, 7, 16, 3 vols (Helsinki: Helsingfors universitetsbibliotek, 1922–32)

Heikkilä, Tuomas, 'I ett medeltida *scriptorium* i Åbo', *Historiskt tidskrift för Finland* (2008), 253–84

——, *Pyhän Henrikin legenda*, Suomalaisen Kirjallisuuden Seuran toimituksia, 1039 (Helsinki: Suomalaisen Kirjallisuuden Seura, 2005)

——, 'Scripta manent — On the Role of Manuscript Studies in Shaping Early Missionary History of Finland', in *Maasta, kivestä ja hengestä – Earth, Stone and Spirit: Markus Hiekkanen Festschrift*, ed. by Hanna-Maria Pellinen (Helsinki: Suomen kirkkohistoriallinen seura, 2009), pp. 26–35

——, ed., *Kirjallinen kulttuuri keskiajan Suomessa* (Helsinki: Suomalaisen Kirjallisuuden Seura, 2010)

Helander, Sven, 'Sockenkyrkans liturgiska profil', in *Kyrka och socken i medeltidens Sverige*, ed. by Olle Ferm, Studier till det medeltida Sverige, 5 (Stockholm: Riksantikvarieämbetet, 1991), pp. 189–230

Hiekkanen, Markus, *Suomen keskiajan kivikirkot*, Suomalaisen Kirjallisuuden Seuran toimituksia, 1117 (Helsinki: Suomalaisen Kirjallisuuden Seura, 2007)

Jokipii, Mauno, 'Ensimmäinen ristiretki Suomeen ja sen lähin jälkimaine', in *Muinainen Kalanti ja sen naapurit*, ed. by Veijo Kaitanen and others (Helsinki: Suomalaisen Kirjallisuuden Seura, 2003), pp. 300–411

Kersken, Norbert, 'God and the Saints in Medieval Polish Historiography', in *The Making of Christian Myths in the Periphery of Latin Christendom (c. 1000–1300)*, ed. by Lars Boje Mortensen (København: Museum Tusculanum, 2006), pp. 153–94

Keskiaho, Jesse, 'Bortom fragmenten: handskriftsproduktion och boklig kultur i det medeltida Åbo stift', *Historiskt tidskrift för Finland* (2008), 209–52

——, 'En grupp handskrifter från slutet av 1400-talet — från Nådendals scriptorium?', *Historiskt tidskrift för Finland* (2008), 318–50

Lamberg, Marko, *Jöns Budde: birgittalaisveli ja hänen teoksensa*, Suomalaisen Kirjallisuuden Seuran toimituksia, 1115 (Helsinki: Suomalaisen Kirjallisuuden Seura, 2007)

Larsson, Inger, *Svenska medeltidsbrev: om framväxten av ett offentligt skriftbruk inom administration, förvaltning och rättsordning* (Stockholm: Norstedts, 2003)

Lehtinen, Anja-Inkeri, 'From Fragments into Codices: On Reconstitution of Theological and Philosophical Works', in *Medieval Book Fragments in Sweden: An International Seminar in Stockholm, 13–16 November 2003*, ed. by Jan Brunius (Stockholm: Kungliga Vitterhets Historie och Antikvitets Akademien, 2005)

——, 'Kirjoja ja kirjastoja keskiajan Suomessa', in *Kirja Suomessa*, ed. by Esko Häkli (Helsinki: Helsingin yliopiston kirjasto, 1997), pp. 15–30

Maliniemi, Aarno, 'Englantilaisperäinen 1200-luvun dominikaanibreviarium Suomessa', *Historiallinen arkisto*, 50 (1944), 378–87

——, 'Muistoja praagilaisesta vaikutuksesta Suomen ja Ruotsin kirjalliseen kulttuuriin keskiajalla', *Suomen museo*, 33 (1926), 58–71

——, *Zur Kenntnis des Breviarium Aboense Cod. Holm. 56*, Documenta historica, edidit Academia scientiarum Fennica, 9 (Helsinki: Academia scientiarum Fennica, 1957)

Mortensen, Lars Boje, and Else Mundal, 'Erkebispesetet i Nidaros — arnestad og verkstad for Olavslitteraturen', in *Ecclesia Nidrosiensis 1153–1537: søkelys på Nidaroskirkens og Nidarosprovinsens historie*, ed. by Steinar Imsen (Trondheim: Tapir, 2003), pp. 353–84

——, 'Sanctified Beginnings and Mythopoietic Moments: The First Wave of Writing on the Past in Norway, Denmark and Hungary, *c.* 1000–1230', in *The Making of Christian Myths in the Periphery of Latin Christendom (c. 1000–1300)*, ed. by Lars Boje Mortensen (København: Museum Tusculanum, 2006), pp. 247–73

Mostert, Marco, 'New Approaches to Medieval Communication?', in *New Approaches to Medieval Communication*, ed. by Marco Mostert, Utrecht Studies in Medieval Literacy, 1 (Turnhout: Brepols, 1999), pp. 15–37

Nedkvitne, Arnved, *The Social Consequences of Literacy in Medieval Scandinavia*, Utrecht Studies in Medieval Literacy, 11 (Turnhout: Brepols, 2004)

Nuorteva, Jussi, *Suomalaisten ulkomainen opinkäynti ennen Turun akatemian perustamista 1640*, Bibliotheca historica, 27 (Helsinki: Suomalaisen Kirjallisuuden Seura, 1997), pp. 53–66

Ommundsen, Åslaug, 'Books, Scribes and Sequences in Medieval Norway', 2 vols (unpublished doctoral thesis, Universitetet i Bergen, 2007)

Ong, Walter J., *Orality and Literacy: The Technologizing of the Word* (London: Methuen, 1982)

Palola, Ari-Pekka, *Maunu Tavast ja Olavi Maununpoika: Turun piispat 1412–1460*, Suomen Kirkkohistoriallisen Seuran toimituksia, 178 (Helsinki: Suomen kirkkohistoriallinen seura, 1997), pp. 206–26

——, 'Yleiskatsaus Suomen keskiaikaisten seurakuntien perustamis-ajankohdista', *Faravid*, 18–19 (1996), 67–104

Parvio, Martti, 'Manuale Aboense 1522', in *Manuale seu exequiale Aboense 1522*, ed. by Martti Parvio, Suomen Kirkkohistoriallisen Seuran toimituksia, 115 (Helsinki: Suomen kirkkohistoriallinen seura, 1980), pp. 133–77

Pirinen, Kauko, *Suomen kirkon historia*, I: *Keskiaika ja uskonpuhdistuksen aika* (Porvoo: Werner Söderström, 1991)

Purhonen, Paula, *Kristinuskon saapumisesta Suomeen: uskontoarkeologinen tutkimus*, Suomen Muinaismuistoyhdistyksen aikakauskirja, 106 (Helsinki: Suomen Muinaismuistoyhdistys, 1998)

Rado, Polikarp, *Libri liturgici manuscripti bibliothecarum Hungariae et limitropharum regionum* (Budapest: Akadémiai Kiadó, 1973)

Roos, Teemu, and Tuomas Heikkilä, 'Evaluating Methods for Computer-Assisted Stemmatology using Artificial Benchmark Data-Sets', *Literary and Linguistic Computing* (2009) <http://llc.oxfordjournals.org/cgi/content/abstract/fqp002> [accessed 12 June 2012]

Roos, Teemu, Tuomas Heikkilä, and Petri Myllymäki, 'A Compression-Based Method for Stemmatic Analysis' (2006) <http://www.cs.helsinki.fi/u/ttonteri/pub/ecai06full.pdf> [accessed 12 June 2012]

Salminen, Tapio, 'Unknown Hands, Trusted Men: Professional Writing in Finnish Medieval Town Administration', in *Reclaiming the City*, ed. by Marjaana Niemi and Ville Vuolanto, Studia Fennica historica, 6 (Helsinki: Suomalaisen Kirjallisuuden Seura, 2003), pp. 99–120

Semkowicz, Władysław, *Paleografia łacińska* (Krakow: Nakł. Polskiej Akademii Umiejętności, 1951)

Söderberg, Barbro, and Inger Larsson, *Nordisk medeltidsliteracy i ett disglossiskt och digrafiskt perspektiv* (Stockholm: Stockholms universitet, 1993)

Tahkokallio, Jaakko, 'Texter från ett scriptorium i Åbo från mitten av 1400-talet?', *Historiskt tidskrift för Finland* (2008), 285–317

Taitto, Ilkka, 'British Saints in the Fragmenta membranea Collection at the Helsinki University Library', in *Ex insula lux: Manuscripts and Hagiographical Material Connected with Medieval England* (Helsinki: Helsinki University Library, 2001), pp. 1–11

——, *Catalogue of Medieval Manuscript Fragments in the Helsinki University Library; Fragmenta membranea*, IV: *Antiphonaria*, Helsingin yliopiston kirjaston julkaisuja, 67–68, 2 vols (Helsinki: Helsinki University Library, 2001), I: *Text* (2001)

Toy, John, 'The Fragments Reveal New Evidence of the Cult of English Saints in Sweden', in *Medieval Book Fragments in Sweden: An International Seminar in Stockholm, 13–16 November 2003*, ed. by Jan Brunius (Stockholm: Riksarkivet, 2005), pp. 99–108

Veszprémy, László, 'Royal Saints in Hungarian Chronicles, Legends and Liturgy', in *The Making of Christian Myths in the Periphery of Latin Christendom (c. 1000–1300)*, ed. by Lars Boje Mortensen (København: Museum Tusculanum, 2006), pp. 217–45

Vezin, Jean, 'La Production et la circulation des livres dans l'Europe du xe siècle', in *Gerbert l'Européen: actes du colloque d'Aurillac 4–7 juin 1996*, ed. by Nicole Charbonnel and Jean-Eric Iung (Clermont-Ferrand: Société des lettres, sciences et arts 'La Haut-Auvergne', 1997), pp. 205–18

Walta, Ville, 'Kirjallisuus, kirjat ja kirjoittaminen Naantalin luostarissa (1438–1591)' (unpublished master's thesis, University of Helsinki, 2008)

Spoken, Written, and Performed in Latin and Vernacular Cultures from the Middle Ages to the Early Seventeenth Century: *Ramus virens oliuarum*

Tuomas M. S. Lehtonen*

The Early Modern Scene:
Latin and Traditional Vernacular Side Currents

In 1582 a student from Nyland (Uusimaa), Finland, Theodoricus Petri (*c.* 1560–*c.* 1617), or Dijderijk Pehrsson Ruutha, as he signed his name in Swedish, gave a collection called *Piae Cantiones* to Augustin Ferber's press in Greifswald. This octavo-size book contained 199 pages with seventy-four Latin pious songs and their musical notation. It seems that the collection reached some popularity within the Swedish realm. In 1625 Theodoricus's relatives from the town of Viipuri (Sw. Wiborg) in Karelian Isthmus were behind the second larger edition printed in Rostock. Later on, in the seventeenth and eighteenth centuries, there were several reprints with or without musi-

---

* I am indebted to Lauri Harvilahti, Irma-Riitta Järvinen, Kati Kallio, and Senni Timonen for their knowledgeable and generous comments, references, and corrections. Furthermore, I am grateful to Alexandra Bergholm who pointed out some flaws in thought and language. I would like to also thank the participants of the research seminar at the Finnish Literature Society and the culture team members of the NCMS for their comments. I am, of course, solely responsible for all the remaining flaws.

Tuomas M. S. Lehtonen, Finnish Literature Society, Secretary General, Adjunct Professor, tuomas.lehtonen@finlit.fi

cal notes.[1] The popularity of the collection is demonstrated by the fact that by 1616 it was translated by the vicar of Masku parish, Hemmingius Henrici (Hollo) (*c.* 1550–1619). A partial Swedish translation was made roughly at same time by Sigfrid Aronus Forsius (*c.* 1560–1624), who was also born in Finland (and returned there in his later life after working in Uppsala and Stockholm). Swedish and Finnish Lutheran hymnals bear traces of the influence of these Latin — and mostly medieval Catholic — songs.[2]

The use of common hymns as part of the religious service was essentially a reformed Lutheran idea. The Catholic Mass was full of singing, recital, and ritual performance, but the role of the illiterate and uneducated congregation as participants in the common religious service was essentially changed by the Reformation. Thus Lutheran reformers considered the creation of vernacular hymnals extremely urgent.[3] During the sixteenth and seventeenth centuries several vernacular, that is, Swedish and Finnish hymnals, were produced.[4] Religious singing in the vernacular was a central device for Lutheran teaching and a new medium between literate and oral cultures. Because hymns were written, their content, form, and length was fixed, while oral poetry varied rather freely.[5] Many scholars have also emphasized the fact that the hymns were not written according to the traditional Finnish poetical metre and alliterative structure (without rhymes) but with rhymed metres of German origin. This has sometimes been interpreted as an active denial of the vernacular, so-called Kalevala

---

[1] *Piae Cantiones ecclesiasticae [...] 1582*, ed. by Marvia; *Cantiones piae et antiquae* (1625); Dreves, 'Vorwort', pp. 11–14; Lagerborg, 'Vår äldsta konstdiktning'; Norlind, *Latinska skolsånger i Sverige och Finland*; Maliniemi, 'Suomen keskiaikainen kirjallisuus'; Maliniemi, 'Finland som bevarare av P. C. -sångerna'; Mäkinen, *Die aus frühen bömischen Quellen*; Mäkinen, *Piae Cantiones*; Bohlin, 'Piae Cantiones'; Bohlin, 'Tobias Norlind'; Lehtonen, 'Piae Cantiones'; Lehtonen, *Hopeamarkkojen evankeliumi*, pp. 140–58.

[2] Hemmingius de Masco, *Vanhain Suomen maan Piispain ja Kircon Esimiesten*; Lagerborg, 'Vår äldsta konstdiktning', pp. 74–84; Norlind, *Latinska skolsånger i Sverige och Finland*, pp. 1–45, 65–84, 151–87; Kurvinen, *Suomen virsirunouden alkuvaiheet v:een 1640*, pp. 384–409; Bohlin, 'Tobias Norlind'; Lehtonen, 'Piae Cantiones'.

[3] Kurvinen, *Suomen virsirunouden alkuvaiheet v:een 1640*, pp. 58–67; Suomi, 'Suomenkielinen lyriikka ennen vuotta 1640'; see also Pirinen, *Suomen kirkon historia*.

[4] Kurvinen, *Suomen virsirunouden alkuvaiheet v:een 1640*; see also Lagerborg, 'Vår äldsta konstdiktning'; Lempiäinen, 'Ensimmäinen suomalainen virsikirja'.

[5] On the nature of oral poetry, see Siikala, *Mythic Images and Shamanism*; see also Zumthor, *Introduction à la poésie orale*; Zumthor, *La Lettre et la voix*; Zumthor, *La Poésie et la voix*; Finnegan, *Literacy and Orality*; Foley, *The Theory of Oral Composition*.

metre for its pagan origins and thus as something that clergymen and teachers should uproot.[6] It is true that the use of traditional Finnish poetic forms outside the oral cultural sphere remained an exception.[7] Even though we have very limited information regarding medieval and early modern vernacular musical performances (except Lutheran hymns), we have enough evidence from later traditions to assume that there were significant differences between the registers of Catholic tradition, reformed hymnal chant, and traditional vernacular musical performances.[8]

The medieval Latin forms seem to have survived alongside the newly introduced Lutheran literature through the sixteenth and seventeenth centuries and even later, not necessarily as a mainstream feature, but nevertheless as something rather integral even inside the walls of the Lutheran church — or perhaps especially inside them. Furthermore, there are several indicators that folk piety turned into pure Lutheran creed only gradually during the centuries to come. A profusion of traditional oral poetry referring to saints like St Olaf and others also exists, not to mention features which seem to denote Catholic beliefs and practices but which are evidently more open to various interpretations.[9] In the sixteenth and the early seventeenth centuries the Lutheran teaching had an official position, but in the learned Latin world a Catholic or medieval side current persisted and, diametrically, the vernacular oral world preserved its syncretistic features from Catholic and pre-Christian practices and beliefs. *Piae Cantiones* and its Finnish translation present such side currents. Paradoxically, it seems that through these side currents elements of the learned elite culture met with traditional vernacular culture in a strange mixture of ingredients from both the written and spoken spheres.

---

[6] Suomi, 'Suomenkielinen lyriikka ennen vuotta 1640', pp. 247, 251–52; Viinamäki, 'Hemminki Maskulainen — virsirunoilija'; Sarajas, *Suomen kansanrunouden tuntemus*, pp. 24–47; on the metrical and formal features of early Finnish hymns, see Kurvinen, *Suomen virsirunouden alkuvaiheet v:een 1640*, pp. 77–81.

[7] Compare Sarajas, *Suomen kansanrunouden tuntemus*; Suomi, 'Suomenkielinen lyriikka ennen vuotta 1640'; Leino, *Language and Metre*, pp. 16–19.

[8] Kurvinen, *Suomen virsirunouden alkuvaiheet v:een 1640*, pp. 58–81; Mäkinen, *Die aus frühen bömischen Quellen*; Pajamo, *Lehti puusta variseepi: suomalainen koululauluperinne*, p. 11; Laitinen, 'Runolaulu'.

[9] Kurvinen, *Suomen virsirunouden alkuvaiheet v:een 1640*, pp. 58–59; Kuusi, 'Keskiajan kalevalainen runous'; Siikala, 'Myytit, riitit ja tietäjän toimet', pp. 185–86.

Medieval Latin and Vernacular Poetic Idiom: Spoken and Written

The *Piae Cantiones* collection contains mostly medieval poetry and medieval music. Both textual scholars and musicologists have been able to trace the roots of the collection to medieval sources. The oldest poetical and musical layers seem to date back at least to the eleventh century. Some of the musical forms of the collection were definitively old-fashioned in the sixteenth century.[10] The collection also contains texts from some known authors like Philippus Cancellarius (d. 1236), chancellor of Notre Dame of Paris; the Bohemian reformer Jan Hus (1370–1415); the Icelandic bishop Gísli Jónsson (d. before 1549); and Morten Børup (1446–1526), a headmaster from Aarhus, Denmark.[11] It seems that the collector of the songs, perhaps a certain schoolmaster and an author of the earliest Finnish hymnal, Jacobus Petri Finno (*c.* 1540–88), used manuscripts known to him in the diocese of Turku (Sw. Åbo).[12] In his preface Theodoricus

---

[10] Mäkinen, *Die aus frühen bömischen Quellen*; Maliniemi, 'Finland som bevarare av P. C.-sångerna'; Dreves, 'Vorwort', p. 11.

[11] Lagerborg, 'Vår äldsta konstdiktning', pp. 76–77, 85, 90–94; Norlind, *Latinska skolsånger i Sverige och Finland*; Andersén and Mäkinen, *Piae Cantiones*, pp. 124–27; Lehtonen, 'Piae Cantiones', pp. 42–43.

[12] In the preface of the *Piae Cantiones ecclesiasticae [...] 1582*, ed. by Marvia, Theodoricus Petri states: 'Cum vero vsus talium Cantilenarum non sit exiguus: cumque non solum in Scholis, verum etiam alias in Inclyto Regno Sueciae Patria mea carissima passim vsurpentur, eademque insuper opera Magnificorum & illustrium virorum in Ciuitate Aboënsi nuper reuisae & approbatae sint: ego eas, cum propter gloriam DEI, ad quam singuli nostra consilia studia & actiones referre debemus: tum propter vtilitatem Ecclesiae Scholarumque, quae in Patria mea sunt, quibus me totum dedere ijsque omnia mea quasi consecrare debere agnosco, typis elegantibus excudendas curaui' (pp. 9–10). Hemmingius Henrici de Masco, in the preface of his translation in 1616 (frontispiece), gives all credit for the collecting, revising, and publishing of the collection to Jacobus Petri Finno. A few years later some relatives of Theodoricus Petri were active in republishing a new larger edition of the songs, and they wanted to give full credit to their kinsman (*Cantiones piae et antiquae* (1625)). Johannes Schefferus agrees with Hemmingius in his *Svecia litterata* (1680). Since the early nineteenth century, opinions have oscillated between favouring either Jacobus Petri Finno or Theodoricus Petri Rutha as the original compiler, editor, and publisher of the collection (see Lagerborg, 'Vår äldsta konstdiktning', pp. 70–72). Most of the modern scholars believe that both of them had a share in the compilation and editing (for example, Lagerborg, 'Vår äldsta konstdiktning'; Norlind, *Latinska skolsånger i Sverige och Finland*; Maliniemi, 'Suomen keskiaikainen kirjallisuus'; Maliniemi, 'Finland som bevarare av P. C.-sångerna'; Mäkinen, *Piae Cantiones*; Lehtonen, 'Piae Cantiones'; Lehtonen, *Hopeamarkkojen evankeliumi*). Folke Bohlin has argued that Theodoricus Petri was the sole editor since there is nothing in the contents of the collection that supports attribution to Jacobus Petri Finno (see Bohlin, 'Piae cantiones'; Bohlin, 'Tobias Norlind'). Nevertheless, we have Theodoricus's own statement about the revisions made by an illustrious man from the city of Turku (Sw. Åbo)

Petri reports that the songs were used throughout 'the wide realm of Sweden' ('in inclyto regno Sueciae passim usurpatae'). The assumption that a local manuscript tradition existed in the diocese of Turku is based on the fact that both Hemmingius de Masco and the editors of the 1625 edition included some songs that did not appear in the 1582 edition in their collections. Hemmingius also mentions that these songs were widely used in the schools of Finland.[13] Some medieval Catholic references to saints, and especially to the Virgin Mary, were omitted to fit the collection's contents with the Lutheran dogma.[14]

It is remarkable that some of the songs seem to have been originally composed by Nordic authors. In at least seven cases there is an acrostic that may refer to an author or his patron (BIRGERUS, OLAUUS, RAGUUALDUS, JOHANNES, PETRUS, THOMAS, and IACOBUS). The first three names are distinctly Scandinavian, and the other four were all common international names in the Nordic countries. Among the above-mentioned authors were two nearly contemporary Scandinavian figures, Bishop Gísli Jónsson and headmaster Morten Børub.[15] Only one song is directly related to the diocese of Turku, that is, *Ramus virens oliuarum* (The green branch of the olive-tree) which relates how Finns were Christianized in the mid-twelfth century by King Eric of Sweden and by Bishop Henry of Uppsala.

Hemmingius Henrici, vicar of Masku parish near the town and cathedral see of Turku, was an active promoter of the Finnish vernacular. Not only did he translate the *Piae Cantiones* collection, but he also produced a new Finnish hymnal in 1605. His Finnish has been evaluated as much better and more adapted to various poetical needs than that of his predecessor Jacobus Petri Finno, and even more remarkable than that of Mikael Agricola, the great hero

---

and the nearly contemporary attribution by Hemmingius Henrici (supported later by Johannes Schefferus) to Jacobus Petri Finno. Hence, it seems sound to suppose that in fact both Jacobus and Theodoricus had a considerable role in compiling, revising, and editing the collection.

[13] There has been a kind of national contest between a few Finnish and Swedish scholars to prove the collection as either 'Finnish' or 'Swedish'. However, the content thoroughly demonstrates an international Latin tradition from various sources around Europe. See Bohlin, 'Piae Cantiones'; Bohlin, 'Tobias Norlind'; Maliniemi, 'Finland som bevarare av P. C. -sångerna'; compare Lehtonen, 'Piae Cantiones', pp. 42–43; Lehtonen, *Hopeamarkkojen evankeliumi*, pp. 140–43. The only source directly referring to the collecting process is Hemmingius Henrici's preface (1616) where he claims that the songs were from the diocese of Turku. It is a bit farfetched to assume that either Jabobus Petri or Theodoricus Petri would have needed or could have carried out a wide-range collection process to compile a Latin hymnal containing seventy-four songs.

[14] Lagerborg, 'Vår äldsta konstdiktning', pp. 85–87.

[15] Bohlin, 'Piae Cantiones'; Lehtonen, 'Piae Cantiones', p. 42.

of the Lutheran Reformation and creator of the Finnish literate idiom.[16] The main reason for this praise is that Hemmingius was the very first literate person to widely use the features of the so-called Kalevala metre in some of his translations.[17] Here the evaluation of his literary value is not needed, but what is of primary importance is the fact that he used the traditional oral idiom.

Hemmingius not only knew the traditional idiom, but he also took parts of the vernacular tradition that were related to Bishop Henry into his translations. As such, we have here an interesting case — and one of the earliest existing in Finland — of the interface of the oral and written, as well as of the vernacular and Latin. It is symptomatic that this instance takes place in the context of the medieval, Latin, and Catholic tradition. Does it mean that what we have here is a late example of a much more common, but not recorded phenomenon? Strictly speaking, it does not seem reasonable to suppose that the Reformation period was favourable for preserving the Catholic tradition both in Latin and in the vernacular. Whatever the better hypothesis may be, it is a fact that the oldest occurrences of traditional Finnish poetical idiom were related to medieval Catholic heritage.[18]

Other examples of the traditional Finnish poetic idiom are found mostly in charms and incantations that have survived occasionally in the margins of account books and more frequently in judicial documents that are usually related to accusations of witchcraft.[19] More relevant are the mentions of the vernacular poem called 'Ballad of the Death of Bishop Henry' (*Piispa Henrikin surmavirsi*, also known as 'The Song of the Slaying of Bishop Henry'). During the seventeenth century the existence of a vernacular tradition relating the deeds, martyrdom, and miracles of St Henry seems to have been rather well known to various authors and academic writers interested in local antiquities and folklore.[20] Sometime in the late seventeenth century, perhaps in the

---

[16] Suomi, 'Suomenkielinen lyriikka ennen vuotta 1640', pp. 253–58; see also Laitinen, 'Barokki tunteen ja järjen dialogina'; Viinamäki, 'Hemminki Maskulainen — virsirunoilija'.

[17] Sarajas, *Suomen kansanrunouden tuntemus*, pp. 14–47, 40–41; Suomi, 'Suomenkielinen lyriikka ennen vuotta 1640'; Laitinen, 'Barokki tunteen ja järjen dialogina', Viinamäki, 'Hemminki Maskulainen — virsirunoilija'.

[18] Rapola, 'Vanhan runon kuvastelua'; Sarajas, *Suomen kansanrunouden tuntemus*.

[19] Kaivola-Bregenhøj, 'Ruton sanat, vanhin suomalainen loitsumuistiinpano'; Siikala, *Mythic Images and Shamanism*, pp. 71–92, passim; see also Kuusi, 'Keskiajan kalevalainen runous', pp. 273–92; Heikkinen, *Paholaisen liittolaiset*; Nenonen, *Noituus, taikuus ja noitavainot Ala-Satakunnan*; Nenonen, *Synnin palkka on kuolema*.

[20] *Suomen kansan vanhat runot*, ed. by Toivonen, no. 990 (pp. 124–25); Haavio, *Piispa*

1680s, the supposedly oldest manuscript containing 'The Ballad of the Death of Bishop Henry' was produced. Since then, variants of the same story have been reported in various parts of western Finland.[21]

The supposedly earliest manuscript of the song is preserved at the Folklore Archives of the Finnish Literature Society where it has been kept since it was found in 1852 in Toholampi, Eastern Bothnia by Th. Reinius.[22] There are only clues about the earlier provenance of the manuscript. It is rather striking that no one has paid any attention to the material features of the manuscript except the handwriting, which is thought to be from the late seventeenth century. The manuscript quite evidently imitates printed books from the same period with its *locus sigilli* and other typographical features.[23] In fact, the page size of the manuscript is very close to the octavo-form used for early hymnals, academic prints, and everyday literature.[24] In addition, the handwriting is not typical of the late seventeenth century but seems to imitate the printed text from the same period.[25]

The contents of the vernacular song have instead received permanent attention since its earliest recordings; I have also dealt with it in another context myself.[26] Three features are of particular relevance for the present discussion. The first is that its contents represent a medieval and Catholic tradition — it is rather improbable that such a vernacular story about a Catholic saint would have been created while the most rigorous Lutheran orthodoxy and anti-Catholicism prevailed in late seventeenth-century Sweden (and its eastern provinces in present-day Finland). Secondly, the vernacular tradition related to St Henry was rather well known in western Finland, both among the populace

---

Henrik ja Lalli, pp. 14–28; Sarajas, *Suomen kansanrunouden tuntemus*, pp. 17–28, passim; see also Heikkilä, *Pyhän Henrikin legenda*, pp. 38–42; Lehtonen, 'Conquête et construction de l'histoire sacrée'.

[21] *Piispa Henrikin surmavirsi*, ed. by Vento; *Suomen kansan vanhat runot*, ed. by Toivonen, no. 990 (pp. 124–25); Haavio, *Piispa Henrik ja Lalli*, pp. 14–28; Lehtonen, 'Conquête et construction de l'histoire sacrée'.

[22] *Suomen kansan vanhat runot*, ed. by Toivonen, no. 990 (pp. 124–25).

[23] For this observation I am indebted to Marek Tamm who noticed the fact while visiting the Folklore Archives of the Finnish Literature Society in the spring of 2007.

[24] Compare Perälä, 'Typografinen aineisto ja sen tutkimus'; Laine, *Vanhimman suomalaisen kirjallisuuden käsikirja*.

[25] I am indebted to Tuija Laine for this observation.

[26] Lehtonen, 'Conquête et construction de l'histoire sacrée'.

as well as among the learned clergy.[27] Thirdly, when the song was committed to writing it was made in a manner that imitated authoritative printed books like hymnals, law books, prayer books, and academic prints. Whoever did this was well aware of the meaning, value, and authoritative status of the text. He (or less likely she) even wanted to elevate its standing not only by writing it down, but also by giving it a form that secured its value.

'The Ballad of the Death of Bishop Henry' is the earliest surviving, more or less complete narrative poem recorded representing the Finnish vernacular tradition. Thus, it seems fairly evident that this kind of medieval Christian tradition, however Catholic, was at least appreciated by some among the ordinary semi-literate or illiterate populace as well as among the learned and literate elite. The fact that this piece of oral tradition was considered valuable enough to be written down emphasizes its special status. Again, the interface of the oral and written takes place in relation to a medieval Catholic tradition, and this time, in relation to its vernacular form. The fact is even more striking because the vernacular tradition was elevated to the same level as the Latin tradition, as is the case with *Legenda s. Henrici* from the late thirteenth century, or *Catalogus et successio ordinaria episcoporum Finlandensium* (partly based on medieval manuscript tradition but completed by Bishop Paulus Juusten in 1565, although not printed until the late eighteenth century).[28]

Ramus virens oliuarum: Textual History and Dating

The *Piae Cantiones* collection is divided under nine headings: songs about the Nativity and Passion, songs for Pentecost, songs about Trinity and the Eucharist, songs for prayer, songs about the fragility and misery of the human condition, songs about school life, songs about concord, historical songs, and songs about springtime.[29] *Ramus virens oliuarum* is among the historical songs,

---

[27] *Suomen kansan vanhat runot*, ed. by Toivonen, no. 990 (pp. 124–25); Haavio, *Piispa Henrik ja Lalli*, pp. 14–28; Sarajas, *Suomen kansanrunouden tuntemus*, pp. 17–28, passim; see also Heikkilä, *Pyhän Henrikin legenda*, pp. 38–42; Lehtonen, 'Conquête et construction de l'histoire sacrée'.

[28] Heininen, 'Einleitung'; Heininen, *Suomalaisen historiankirjoituksen synty*; Heikkilä, *Pyhän Henrikin legenda*; Lehtonen, 'Conquête et construction de l'histoire sacrée'; Lehtonen, 'La *Respublica christianorum* et ses ennemis'.

[29] *Piae Cantiones ecclesiasticae [...] 1582*, ed. by Marvia; see Lagerborg, 'Vår äldsta konstdiktning'; Norlind, *Latinska skolsånger i Sverige och Finland*; Maliniemi, 'Suomen keskiaikainen kirjallisuus'; Maliniemi, 'Finland som bevarare av P. C. -sångerna'; Mäkinen, *Die aus frühen bömischen Quellen*; Mäkinen, *Piae Cantiones*; Bohlin, 'Piae Cantiones'; Lehtonen, 'Piae Cantiones'.

Historicae cantiones. The other two songs under the same heading deal with biblical history: the first relates the story of Zaccheus (Luke 19. 2–8), and the second is built on the parable of Jesus about the king who invites everyone to his feast but only a few arrive (Luke 14. 16–24). I have argued elsewhere that the heading 'historical' should be taken seriously;[30] however, 'historical' is not used in the sense of referring to just any historical narrative but to salvation history, which is the common denominator for all three songs. Zaccheus in the tree, the parable of the king's feast, and *Ramus virens*, a story about the arrival of Christianity to Finland, all represent cases in which people are offered the possibility of saving their souls.

As I mentioned above, *Ramus virens* has two specific features among the songs of *Piae Cantiones*: first, it belongs to a small group of songs having an acrostic which might denote its possible author (or the author's patron): RAGUUALDUS. Secondly, it is definitively the only song in the collection that refers to Finland. In fact, it is the only one in the 1582 edition that has any historical and local coordinates apart from the references to biblical times and places. Actually, Theodoricus Petri's foreword notwithstanding, this is the only actual reference to Finland in the 1582 edition.[31] And, finally, the song itself deals with the single most important historical event in Finland — that is, the arrival of Christianity — from the Christian point of view.[32]

It would be fascinating if we were able to find other variants of the same song, but at least to date there has not been any trace of an earlier manuscript tradition for *Ramus virens* or the totality of the *Piae Cantiones*. Two bishops called Ragvaldus are found in Finnish medieval sources. Most scholars have been tempted to identify our Ragvaldus with the early fourteenth-century canon and later bishop of Turku Cathedral.[33] The acrostic is the only indication

---

[30] Lehtonen, 'Conquête et construction de l'histoire sacrée'.

[31] There is one song (no. 15 *In dulci iubilo*) with macaronic strophes that uses Swedish, which can, of course, be understood as a sort of reference to its local adherence; see *Piae Cantiones ecclesiasticae [...] 1582*, ed. by Marvia, pp. 34–35; Lehtonen, 'Latinet och folkspråken', pp. 26–27; Lehtonen, 'Piae Cantiones', pp. 42–43.

[32] Paulus Juusten has similar emphasis; see Juusten, *Catalogus et ordinaria successio episcoporum*, ed. by Heininen; Lehtonen, 'La *Republica christianorum* et ses ennemis'.

[33] Dreves, 'Cantiones Suecicae', pp. 153–54; Lagerborg, 'Vår äldsta konstdiktning', pp. 85–91; see also Maliniemi, 'Suomen keskiaikainen kirjallisuus'; Lehtonen, 'Piae Cantiones', p. 43; Juusten, *Catalogus et ordinaria successio episcoporum*, ed. by Heininen, pp. 53, 55; Lagerborg, 'Vår äldsta konstdiktning', pp. 86–87, 90–91. The earlier Bishop of Turku, Ragvaldus I (1258–66), is a more unlikely candidate for authorship due to the fact that even the

of the song's author. It is formed by the initials of the first ten strophes; the last strophe starts with the word Christus — should we read the initial C as denoting *canonicus*?[34]

Bishop Ragvaldus is known from several sources, but the information they provide is rather scarce and laconic. He was consecrated as a bishop in 1309 and passed away in 1321. Paulus Juusten tells us that he was born in the Åland Islands and built the Bishop's Castle in Kuusisto some twenty kilometres from his cathedral in Turku (Sw. Kustö, Lat. Cuusto, which was attacked and burnt by the Novgorodians in 1319 and rebuilt several times since then).[35] If we assume that the song was composed while he was still a canon at the cathedral chapter, that would give us an *ante quem* dating of 1309.

There is also some circumstantial evidence for the dating of *Ramus virens*. The song celebrates St Eric, king of Sweden, and St Henry, bishop of Uppsala, and their trip to Finland to establish Christianity. The cult of St Eric became established in the diocese of Uppsala in the latter part of the thirteenth century.[36] St Henry's liturgy and legend were also composed sometime between the 1270s and 1290s.[37] In his *Catalogus et successio ordinaria episcoporum Finlandensium*, Paulus Juusten relates that the new Cathedral of Turku was consecrated in the year 1300 and the relics of St Henry were moved to the cathedral.[38] There have been some doubts as to how reliable Juusten's account is. He completed his work in 1565, but he used an older manuscript tradition that has partly survived. Thus, it is fairly plausible that what is related in *Catalogus* about the events around the year 1300 was taken from a source that, if not contemporary, is at least from the fourteenth century.[39]

Legenda s. Henrici is considered to have been written at least a two decades later. See Heikkilä, *Pyhän Henrikin legenda*; Lehtonen, 'Conquête et construction de l'histoire sacrée'.

[34] Guido Maria Dreves argues that the last strophe has been changed from its original form '*Praesul* or *Pater nobis Deum oret*' (Dreves, 'Cantiones Suecicae', p. 154), which, of course, means that there would not have been a 'C' in the acrostic. However, '*praesul*' would make even more sense in this context. One should obviously be rather cautious and not over-interpret acrostics.

[35] Juusten, *Catalogus et ordinaria successio episcoporum*, ed. by Heininen, p. 55; see also Heininen, *Suomalaisen historiankirjoituksen synty*, p. 56.

[36] Lehtonen, 'Conquête et construction de l'histoire sacrée', pp. 171–77.

[37] Heikkilä, *Pyhän Henrikin legenda*, pp. 226–35; Lehtonen, 'Conquête et construction de l'histoire sacrée', p. 171.

[38] Juusten, *Catalogus et ordinaria successio episcoporum*, ed. by Heininen, p. 54; see also Heininen, *Suomalaisen historiankirjoituksen synty*, p. 55.

[39] Heininen, 'Einleitung', pp. 18–19; Heininen, *Suomalaisen historiankirjoituksen synty*, pp. 32–57.

Therefore, we may suppose that *Ramus virens* was also composed to support the spread and establishment of the cult of the patron saint for the diocese of Turku. This said, we still have only circumstantial evidence for the dating of the song. It may have also been composed later, for example, in the mid-fifteenth century when Bishop Magnus Olai (Tavast, bishop of Turku 1412–50) was strongly promoting the cult of St Henry.[40]

The Deluge before Us: Typological Sacred History and Intertextuality

Ramus virens is intertextually supported by different master narratives. First, there is the story of the deluge which binds the baptizing of Finns to typological biblical history. Secondly, it obviously refers to the legends and liturgies of both St Eric and St Henry. The actual storyline is a brief version of their efforts to bring Christianity to Finland. Only the very core points of these stories are referred to in the song, but the audience was, of course, aware of the broader storyline behind it. The references carry an echo of more general topoi and patterns of hagiographic literature to support the basic message. Individual lines carry multiple biblical allusions that refer to the New Testament in particular.

> RAmus virens oliuarum per columbiam panditur:
> Binum genus animarum arca Noë clauditur.
> Ergo plebs Finnonica Gaude de hoc dono,
> Quòd facta es Catholica Verbi Dei sono.
>
> Apex montis abscondatur, aquae vis dùm tollitur,
> Nubis sordes expurgatur, signum rei ponitur.
> Ergo plebs &c.
>
> Grande mirum, pietatis arca dùm saluatur:
> At tunc cunctis animatis ira Dei datur. Ergo &c.
>
> Velut nostro demonstratur doctori Finlandiae,
> Fides Christi dùm fundatur, linquenti terram Angliae.
>
> Vpsalensem praesulatum Regno rex Sueciae,
> Per Ericum sublimatú, pro cultu fiduciae. Erg:&c.

---

[40] See Juusten, *Catalogus et ordinaria successio episcoporum*, ed. by Heininen, p. 60; Edgren, 'Pyhä Henrik'; Palola, *Maunu Tavast ja Olavi Maununpoika*, pp. 242–44; Heikkilä, *Pyhän Henrikin legenda*, pp. 80–81.

Ardor strinxit caritatis corda Patronorum,
Via ducti veritatis, sorte supernorum. Ergo &c.

Laeti petunt Finnorum terram peruenire,
Cultum pellunt Daemonum, palmam reperire. Erg.

Doctor mirae sanctitatis ponens se periculis,
Formam verae pietatis turbis dans incredulis. Erg:

Versus partes Rex Ericus tendens domicilij,
Sanctus praesul hic Henricus comes fit exilij. Ergo.

Subit poenas patienter palmam per martyrij,
Adest lictor vehementer potú dans exitij. Erg:&c.

Christus nobis Patrem oret, pacem seruans patriae,
Laudis turba quem decoret, firma fide variè.
Ergo plebs Finnonica gaude &c.

[The green branch of the olive tree is brought by a dove:
The animals are shut in Noah's ark in pairs.
Hence the Finnish people rejoice for this gift,
that you are made Catholic by the sound of God's word.

The peak of the mountain is hidden when the power of the waters rises,
Low clouds are cleaned, and the sign of God is given.
Hence the Finnish people &c.

As a grand miracle, the ark of piety is saved:
but then the wrath of God is turned against all living things.
Hence &c.

Similarly the teacher of Finland sets an example for us,
he leaves the land of England to establish faith in Christ.

The prelate of Uppsala comes from the realm of the King of Sweden,
with sublime Eric to cultivate the fidelity.
Hence &c.

Ardour binds by cords of charity the Patrons,
the way is directed by truth to heavenly share.
Hence &c.

Happily they rush to get to the land of Finns,
they crush the cult of demons to receive the palm,
Hence &c.

With miraculous sanctity the teacher puts himself in danger,
and gives the form of real piety for the incredulous crowd.
Hence &c.

King Eric turns to his home country,
St Bishop Henry remains in exile.
Hence &c.

He patiently suffers punishment for the palm of martyrdom,
the headsman comes vehemently and gives the drink of death.

Christ prays our Father to serve peace for the fatherland,
Praise embellishes a crowd, firm faith everyone
Hence Finnish people rejoice &c.][41]

Ramus virens begins with a direct and powerful image of the end of the deluge, which triggers a vast intertextual process equating sacred biblical history to the worldly history of Finns. They have a place in the divine plan, perfectly in line with the medieval theology of history and a typological reading of the Bible. A dove bringing a branch of the olive tree anticipates the baptism of Christ. The poem attaches itself to the Christian master narrative of the Old Testament, anticipating the New Testament, and thus following the mainstream of medieval theology. As the Old Testament already foretold the advent of Christ, the baptism of Christ carries a promise of the salvation of humankind, including an almost unknown tribe of the Finns living in the uttermost north-eastern periphery of Western Christendom.

The song consists of three parts. First is the short description of the deluge and Noah's ark (strophes 1–3). Noah's ark reaches the top of the mountain, the force of waters disappears, and the clouds are dispersed. As a great miracle, the ark is saved, and the wrath of God is over. The second and third strophes refer shortly to the end of the deluge. The deluge and its end are equated with the victory of Christianity over paganism as this miracle was demonstrated by the teacher of Finland (in the fourth strophe).

The poem then moves on from the biblical typology to local events by relating the story of the expedition of Sts Henry and Eric to Finland. Bishop Henry and King Eric are bound to each other by fidelity (*pro cultu fiduciae*); ardent love (*caritas*) leads them to the road of truth (compare John 14. 6; II Peter 7. 2; Book

---

[41] *Piae Cantiones ecclesiasticae [...] 1582*, ed. by Marvia, pp. 195–96. I have followed the emendations by Guido Maria Dreves (Dreves, 'Cantiones Suecicae') and Rolf Lagerborg (Lagerborg, 'Vår äldsta konstdiktning'). English translation by Tuomas M. S. Lehtonen.

of Wisdom 5. 6; Ecclesiasticus 34. 22). In the seventh strophe they go to the land of the Finns to abolish the cult of demons. The short allusion made here to the liturgy of St Henry, in which Eric and Henry reach the palm of victory, is, of course, intertextually referring to the palm of victory Jesus Christ receives in the New Testament (compare Matthew 26. 67; John 12. 13, 15. 2, 4–6; Book of Revelation 7. 9). The teacher of Finland (*doctor Finlandiae*, i.e. Henry) puts himself in danger while teaching the 'form of true piety to the incredulous masses' ('Formam verae pietatis turbis dans incredulis'). King Eric returns home but Bishop Henry stays in exile where he receives his glorious martyrdom.

The third interpretative part is formed by the refrain and the eleventh strophe, which urge the Finns to rejoice for the gift of God and tell us that Christ beseeches his Father to bring peace for *patria* while the praise of God adorns the crowd. The refrain gives a deeper theological and metaphysical meaning to the historical events related by the storyline: 'Hence, Finnish people, rejoice for this gift, that you are made universal Catholics by the sound of God's word' ('Ergo plebs Finnonica Gaude de hoc dono, Quod facta es Catholica Verbi Dei sono'). The key biblical expression here is *verbum Dei sono – verbum Dei*, a phrase that is found most often in the New Testament.[42] Two instances seem to be relevant here. In the Acts of Apostles 11. 7 we are told about the dissemination of Christian faith: 'et verbum Dei crescebat et multiplicabatur numerus discipulorum in Hierusalem valde multa etiam turba sacerdotum obediebat fidei' (in the Douay-Rheims Bible: 'And the word of God increased; and the number of the disciples multiplied in Jerusalem greatly; and a great company of the priests were obedient to the faith'). Later, in St Paul's epistle for the Ephesians (24. 17), appear the words: 'et galeam salutis adsumite et gladium spiritus quod est verbum Dei' ('And take the helmet of salvation, and the sword of the Spirit, which is the word of God'). The allusion becomes even more relevant when the song moves to the actual historical event of the mission of Sts Eric and Henry in Finland — it is there that the multiplying of disciples could be seen, but the helmet of salvation and the sword of the Spirit were also needed (and perhaps even some more tangible instruments for personal protection and for convincing the heathens).

There is always a danger of overinterpreting the intertextual elements, since the medieval writer or listener obviously had neither databases nor printed concordances at hand. On the other hand, these kinds of biblical motifs or

---

[42] According to the *ARTFL Project Multilingual Bibles Database*, it occurs thirty-nine times in *Vulgata*. Two of these appear in the Old Testament, two in the Apocrypha and thirty-five in the New Testament (especially in Acts 13, Luke 5, and six times in the letters of St Paul).

formulae naturally resonated the general biblical or sacred register in addition to reminding one of the missionary task of spreading the Christian faith. It is not necessary to identify the exact biblical context, but rather to understand the allusive bridge that joins the song with its authoritative and sacred subtexts.[43] In this instance, *Vulgata* was undoubtedly the main subtext at hand. Although the text is in Latin, we may assume that the audience and the singers (who were also part of the audience of the actual message of the poem) all shared at least a basic knowledge of these master narratives and subtexts. The poem is, however, original in its biblical typology when it equates the deluge with paganism.

It may also be noted that the poem pays only passing attention to the murder of St Henry, which thus seems to have had only minor importance. It is of course needed for Henry to reach martyrdom and sainthood, but otherwise the event itself is only implied in the line '*Subit poenas patienter palmam per martyrij | Adest lictor vehementer potum dans exitij*' ('*He patiently suffers punishment for the palm of martyrdom*, the headsman comes vehemently and gives the drink of death'). This emphasizes the saintliness of Henry. The Latin legend of St Henry is somewhat more explicit but it is only in the vernacular tradition where the murder and the events leading to it are more widely elaborated.[44]

In sum, the song alludes to a well-known story with strong biblical and theological overtones. It interprets local history within the framework of universal Christian history. Its audience must have been learned clerics and students who were well informed of the master narratives and subtexts needed to understand the song's message. It naturally provides a grand perspective for local history. The language of the poem is laden with biblical expressions. We can be quite certain that some of them were recognized and understood as allusions, for instance the dove bringing the olive branch, which alludes both to Noah's ark and to the baptism of Christ and serves as an emblem of the Holy Spirit. Other allusions may have passed unnoticed but were nevertheless recognized more generally as biblical expressions.[45]

Ramus virens plays with its vocal, aural, and textual features. It was meant to be sung, but some of its features, such as the acrostic, were apparent only to the reader who had a manuscript or printed version available. We may assume that

---

[43] On medieval intertextuality, see Lehtonen, *Fortuna, Money, and the Sublunar World*; Lehtonen, *Hopeamarkkojen evankeliumi*.

[44] See Lehtonen, 'Conquête et construction de l'histoire sacrée'.

[45] About biblical intertextuality in Medieval Latin secular poetry, see Lehtonen, *Fortuna, Money, and the Sublunar World* (esp. the chapter on *Evangelium secundum marcas argenti*).

most of the intertextual allusions were also evident to those who performed or heard the text. It is evident that everyone who had received a basic education in Latin and Christian theology had been educated not only by textual and written means, but mostly by refined mnemotechnics and oral-aural methods.[46]

The Healing Dove and Lalli the Evil Pagan: Formulae and Immanent Tradition

While the original Latin *Ramus virens* is a product of a highly literate culture, its translation by Hemmingius clearly works in a different way. He opens central biblical references and explains the allegorical equation between the deluge and the state of paganism. On the other hand, he refers in various ways to the oral tradition, which brings to mind what American folklorist and classical scholar John Miles Foley has called the 'immanent tradition' and 'traditional referentiality', and what Finnish folklorist Lotte Tarkka has dealt with as an intertextual system within a locally closed traditional and oral community.[47]

RAMUS VIRENS OLIUARUM

ELävist custan laiist pari /
Noen arckin annettin /
Cuin coco maan piiri ymbäri /
Vedhell caick upotettin.
Jloidze siis Suomen maa /
Tähdhen laupjan lahjan:
Etts Christin canssan yhteyn said /
Cautt Herran sanan saarnan.
  Sangen suuri ihme ilmas:
Arcki vesajos varjellan /
Cuin muoll caick eläväd mailmas
Yppovat vihan alla. Jloidze.
  Oljupuun oxan vihoitavan
Toi mettinen merkixi:
Vedhen voiman vähendyvän /
Jo vihan leppynexi. Jloidze.

---

[46] Compare Carruthers, *The Book of Memory*; Green, *Medieval Listening and Reading*; Lehtonen, *Fortuna, Money, and the Sublunar World*; Coleman, *Public Reading and the Reading Public*.

[47] Foley, *Immanent Art*; Tarkka, 'Intertextuality, Rhetorics and Interpretation of Oral Poetry'; Tarkka, *Rajarahvaan laulu*.

Jumal sitt armon liiton teke /
Taevan Caaren merkixi pane:
Mailmat ei upotta käke
Vedhen paisumall enä. Jloidze.
  Muinen upoxis pimeyn all /
Macais surkja Suomen maa:
Asui sitt armon Auringo jäll
Paistaman pacanan maall. Jloidze.
  Niin cuin Christin usco kylvettin
Ensinä Suomen saaren /
Cautta pyhän Piispan Henrichin /
Tullen Englandin äärest. Jloidze.
  Erich Kungingan cudzumahan /
Riensi Ruodziin saarnaman /
Uscoo Upsalon levittämän /
Piispautta pitämän. Jloidze.
  Sytyi rackaus sydhämihin
Kuningan ja Päämiesten /
Totuun tietä viedhyd hyvin /
Auun annoll ylhäidzen. Jloidze.
  Suomen sotaan sitt hangidzevat /
Pacanoihin pyrkivät /
Pirun palveljoita polkevat /
Velhod ylidzvoittavat. Jloidze.
  Pyhä mies oikja opettaja /
Annoi idzens vaarahan:
Oikjan uscon opin tavan /
Eteen pannein pacanain. Jlo.
  Ruotziin riensi Kuningas Erich /
Jäll valdans vallidseman.
Jäi tännä pyhä Piispa Henrich /
Pacanoit opettaman. Jloidze.
  Jollen pahoin palcan maxoi /
Lalli paha pacana.
Pyhän Piispan murhalda tapoi /
Vuodhatt veren viattoman. J.
  Christe anna raoha Ruodzin maall
Sun sanas pitä saisim
Samad molemad suo suomen maall.
Ett uscosas pysyisim. Jloidze.

[A pair of each animal species /
Was put in Noah's Ark /

When everything around the circle of earth /
Was sunken under waters.
Rejoice thus land of Finland /
For this merciful gift:
That you were given a contact with Christ /
Through the Lord's word and sermon.
  Such a grand miracle in the world:
The Ark is guarding its protégées /
When in the rest of the world all living creatures
are sinking under wrath. Rejoice.
  A green branch from an olive tree
A dove brought as a sign:
The power of waters is diminishing /
The wrath is over. Rejoice.
  God is making a covenant of grace /
And gives as a sign the rainbow:
He does not want the world to be sunken
By the deluge anymore. Rejoice.
  In ancient times the pitiful land of Finland
Was laying sunken into darkness:
The sun of grace rose again
to shine on the pagan land. Rejoice.
  As the Christian faith was sown
First on the island of Finland /
Through St Bishop Henry /
Who came from distant England. Rejoice.
  Invited by King Eric, /
he hurried to preach in Sweden /
to spread the faith in Uppsala /
and to keep the episcopate. Rejoice.
  The love tended to hearts
the King's and Lord's /
way of truth was well followed /
With the help of the highly born. Rejoice.
  They prepare themselves for war in Finland /
To the pagans they strive /
To trample on the servants of devil /
To win over the wizards. Rejoice.
  Holy man, righteous teacher /
Put himself in danger:
For the righteous faith and habit /
he put forth for pagans. Rejoice.
  King Eric hurried back to Sweden /

>   To reign over his realm.
>   Here remained St Henry /
>   To teach the pagans. Rejoice.
>   For whom badly paid /
>   Lalli evil pagan
>   By murdering he killed Holy Bishop
>   And spilled the innocent blood. Rejoice.
>   Christ give peace to the land of Sweden
>   That we might hold on to your word
>   Give them both also for the land of Finland
>   That we may remain in your faith. Rejoice.][48]

Hemmingius's solutions in his translation are interesting. It seems that he tried to modify the Latin metric structure into Finnish, thus enabling the use of the original melody from the *Piae Cantiones*.[49] However, he did so in a highly original way that set him apart from predecessors and contemporaries such as Mikael Agricola and Jacobus Petri Finno. Hemmingius used elements of the vernacular Finnish poetic tradition instead of Germanizing or Latinizing his Finnish, which was the standard solution among his peers and actually remained in the mainstream for literate poetics up to the present time with only some individual Kalevala-metre exceptions.[50] Hemmingius reorganized the original song and added some lines and one whole strophe to make his translation understandable for an audience not as used to biblical, liturgical, and hagiographic allusions as an audience fluent in Latin was assumed to be. Occasionally he also used alliteration (*arckin annettin*, *cuin coco*, *laupjan lahjan*, *Christin canssan*, *sanan saarnan*, etc.) typical for the vernacular poetic idiom. He combined features from Kalevala-metre oral poetry with new literate features like rhyme and iambic or *Knittel* metre, which were introduced into Finnish hymn poetry by Mikael Agricola and especially by Jacobus Petri Finno.[51]

---

[48] Hemmingius de Masco, *Vanhain Suomen maan Piispain ja Kircon Esimiesten*, pp. 115–18. Transliteration by Senni Timonen and Tuomas M. S. Lehtonen (see also <http://kaino.kotus.fi/korpus/vks/meta/virret/hem1616_rdf.xml>) [accessed 30 November 2009]). English translation by Tuomas M. S. Lehtonen.

[49] I am indebted to Kati Kallio for her help in metric analysis of both the Latin and Finnish versions.

[50] Kurvinen, *Suomen virsirunouden alkuvaiheet v:een 1640*; Suomi, 'Suomenkielinen lyriikka ennen vuotta 1640'; on Finnish metrical systems, see Leino, *Language and Metre*.

[51] Compare Finno, *Virsikirja*, ed. by Lempiäinen; Suomi, 'Suomenkielinen lyriikka ennen vuotta 1640', pp. 247, 251–52; Viinamäki, 'Hemminki Maskulainen — virsirunoilija'; Sarajas,

Hemmingius opens his version with a scene from Noah's ark. The three first strophes of the Latin original are put in a new order: the animals fill Noah's ark, the world is sunk in water, the miracle of the ark is lauded, and finally, the branch from the olive tree is brought by a dove. The waters start to diminish and the wrath of God is over — a rainbow is given as a sign that the deluge has ended. Here Hemmingius adds an explanation, a strophe not found in the Latin original: in ancient times Finland was sunk in darkness, but then the sun of grace shone on the pagan land. While the Latin original trusts that its audience understands the biblical typology and the allegory of the deluge, Hemmingius explains it. From here on the translation stays rather faithful to the original with some remarkable exceptions, the most meaningful of which is the penultimate strophe dealing with the murder of St Henry and the naming of the murderer, for the first time ever in printed sources, as Lalli.[52]

The biblical key figure of the Latin original is *columba*, a dove, which brings the branch from the olive tree, represents the Holy Ghost and baptism, and as such forms the typological bridge from the Old to the New Testament, from the deluge to its end, and from paganism to Christianity. Hemmingius translates this key figure with the Western Finnish word *mettinen*, which in older Finnish means a dove. *Mettinen* is also a mythical healing bird in Finnish folklore. In Eastern Finnish it is often mixed with *mehiläinen*, that is, a bee. In some cases this dove or bee, or simply a mythical bird, was represented together with the Virgin Mary.[53] Thus, Hemmingius actually combines, either consciously or unconsciously, both biblical and vernacular beliefs in his translation. We cannot say with any certainty how he himself or his audience understood the healing features of *mettinen*, but it is not farfetched to assume that 'the immanent tradition' was at work when he adapted alliterative features of the vernacular poetic idiom (*toi mettinen merkixi*) and simultaneously used a powerful figure known both in biblical and in local vernacular tradition as a carrier of transcendental healing abilities.

Suomen kansanrunouden tuntemus, pp. 24–47; on the metrical and formal features of early Finnish hymns, see Kurvinen, *Suomen virsirunouden alkuvaiheet v:een 1640*, pp. 77–81.

[52] Haavio, *Piispa Henrik ja Lalli*, p. 154; Hemmingius's mention of the name may also be the earliest written mention of it in general. However, a Swedish translation of the *Ramus virens* survives in a manuscript by Sigfrid Aronus Forsius that is dated roughly to 1615 (Lagerborg, 'Vår äldsta konstdiktning', pp. 77–78; see also Sarajas, *Suomen kansanrunouden tuntemus*).

[53] Ganander, *Mythologia Fennica*, pp. 56–57; Kulonen, *Suomen sanojen alkuperä*, II, 163–64; Haavio, 'Vanhojen runojemme maailmankäsityksestä'. I am indebted to Senni Timonen for this observation.

As a translator Hemmingius seems to be sensitive to his vernacular audience's abilities to understand his texts. He gives explanations, reorganizes line structures, uses common well-known expressions, adds new strophes, and combines features (both metric and symbolic) from local folklore with Christian elite culture.

The most striking example of this is when he introduces the murderer of St Henry by the name Lalli. The Latin original remains rather lapidarian while reporting the bishop's murder ('Subit poenas patienter palmam per martyrij, | Adest lictor vehementer potum dans exitij'; 'He renders himself patiently to revenge for the palm of martyr | the headsman comes vehemently and gives him the drink of death'). The emphasis in the Latin is on St Henry's martyrdom, while Hemmingius stresses the fact that he was murdered by a named individual ('Jollen pahoin palcan maxoi | Lalli paha pacana. | Pyhän Piispan murhalda tappoi | Vuodhatt veren viattoman'; 'For whom badly paid | Lalli the evil pagan. | By murdering he killed the Holy Bishop | and spilled the innocent blood'). *Jollen pahoin palcan maxoi* (for whom badly paid) and *paha pakana* (evil pagan) are common alliterative *formulae* found in other poetic contexts, for example in the nineteenth-century Archangel Karelia.[54] There is no doubt that here Hemmingius incorporates established tradition and traditional *formulae*. Lalli, the evil-doer, is widely known by name in the vernacular tradition recorded later in the seventeenth, eighteenth, and nineteenth centuries about the slaying of Bishop Henry, but he does not appear in any Latin texts before the early seventeenth century on Bishop Henry and his violent death. Hemmingius's contemporary and Swedish translator of *Piae Cantiones*, Sigfrid Aronus Forsius, mentions Lalli in his manuscript from 1615.[55] It seems that in the vernacular tradition an anonymous evil-doer did not satisfy the audience's needs and so the murderer became an individual — and in some cases a much more vivid person than the undisputed hero, Bishop Henry.[56]

---

[54] Eighty-two occasions are recorded in the *Suomen kansan vanhat runot* Database for *paha pakana* from the late eighteenth to early twentieth century, mostly from eastern Finland and Russian Karelia. *Pahoin palcan maxoi* is known from a poem called *Viron orja ja isäntä* (The slave of Estonia and his master), recorded in the late nineteenth century in Eastern Karelia; see the *Suomen kansan vanhat runot* Database.

[55] Haavio, *Piispa Henrik ja Lalli*, p. 54; Sarajas, *Suomen kansanrunouden tuntemus*, pp. 21–25.

[56] Lehtonen, 'Conquête et construction de l'histoire sacrée', pp. 181–86; see also Anttonen, 'Transformations of a Murder Narrative; Anttonen, 'A Catholic Martyr and Protestant Heritage'.

Here again Hemmingius adapts the universal, abstract, and allusive Latin into the local, concrete, and literal vernacular. This does not mean that his version does not contain as many other intertextual and immanent meaningful elements, quite the contrary; he seems to master the vernacular tradition not in a poetically pure form, but in using its resonances for his own purposes.

A Writing Lesson in Medieval Finland: Reflections on Orality, Aurality, and Literacy

Ramus virens oliuarum and its Finnish translation give a glimpse of the interface of literate Latin culture and vernacular oral tradition. It is a remarkable fact that the earliest written examples of oral tradition are related to Catholic tradition rather than to pre-Christian storyworlds. All of the supposedly 'pagan' folklore appears later in the sources. Even the imagery of incantations and exorcisms tends to be syncretistic or Christian.[57] It seems that the vernacular oral culture had been vividly infused by Catholic Christianity, and with the new spread of literacy promoted by the Reformation, it paradoxically became recorded in script. However, we may speculate that several cultural, ideological, and religious clashes were also taking place.

Most of the Finnish Kalevala-metre folklore was either collected from Orthodox Karelia, which was never part of the same cultural, religious, and political entity as western Finland, or from the eastern parts of Finland in close connection with Karelian culture. Based on linguistic evidence, the spread of the so-called Kalevala-metre poetry among nearly all Baltic Finnic peoples around the Baltic Sea region, and some rare occurrences of the Kalevala-metre poetry in western parts of Finland, the standard hypothesis argues that the Finnic vernacular poetic idiom as well as its mythical motifs and heroes were common to almost all Baltic Finnic languages and traditions. According to this argument the process of literacy, Swedish and German influences, and above all, Christian indoctrination caused the vernacular idiom to almost disappear from the wealthier and more populated parts of western Finland. In sum, as the main population turned its back on the traditional oral poetic idiom, it was preserved in thinly populated fringes which did not share the economic, religious, and political developments of the more central regions.[58]

---

[57] See Kuusi, 'Keskiajan kalevalainen runous', pp. 273–92; Kaivola-Bregenhøj, 'Ruton sanat, vanhin suomalainen loitsumuistiinpano'; Siikala, *Mythic Images and Shamanism*, p. 323; Siikala, 'Myytit, riitit ja tietäjän toimet', pp. 176–86.

[58] See, for example, Siikala, *Mythic Images and Shamanism*, pp. 18–22.

The very idea of the developed cultural centres and undeveloped peripheries has been strongly criticized.[59] In addition, the so-called 'historico-geographical method' in folklore studies has lost its credibility among scholars. Nevertheless, the most basic hypothesis about the 'Finnic tradition' shared by all the members of the 'Finnic linguistic community' has remained unchallenged. The emphasis laid on Kalevala-metre poetry has turned from reconstructing 'the original versions' or 'locating the place of origin' to a contextual study of the poetry as it was used and understood by the communities or individuals who still practised it in the nineteenth and twentieth centuries.[60]

For a student of the Middle Ages and the early modern times a challenge remains: what can we assume about the vernacular tradition from much later evidence, or, as in the case dealt with here, from scattered and random evidence? We certainly know traditional oral poetry exists that clearly preserves remnants from the Catholic period even though it was, for the most part, recorded much later in the nineteenth century. From this evidence we can conclude that Latin written, aural, chanted, and performed traditions lived side by side with syncretistic oral traditions, allowing Christian and pre-Christian storyworlds to intermingle. Perhaps even more relevant were the highly skilled ways in which the vernacular and oral culture adapted any suitable materials from the ecclesiastical elite culture (compare the Finnish formula for charlatan magic, *hokkuspokkus*, which is derived from the Latin Eucharistic sentence *hoc est corpus meus*).[61]

It is tempting to move a little bit further in speculating about the understanding of different linguistic features and poetic registers. In the late Middle Ages there were four languages used regularly in Finland: Latin as a sacred ecclesiastical and to some extent administrative language; Swedish as an administrative, legal, and to some extent commercial language; Low German as the dominant commercial language; and Finnish as a local tongue. Latin was highly literate and it bore the highest status because of its learned and sacred use.[62] In addition, in the late Middle Ages Swedish and Low German were literate languages while Finnish remained practically an unwritten oral tongue.

---

[59] Tarkka, *Rajarahvaan laulu*, pp. 374–77.

[60] See, for example, Siikala, *Mythic Images and Shamanism*, pp. 18–42.

[61] Compare Kuusi, 'Keskiajan kalevalainen runous'; Siikala, 'Myytit, riitit ja tietäjän toimet'; see also incantations using Christian *formulae*, Kaivola-Bregenhøj, 'Ruton sanat, vanhin suomalainen loitsumuistiinpano'.

[62] This can also be observed in some of the songs of *Piae Cantiones*; see Lehtonen, 'Piae Cantiones'; Lehtonen, 'Conquête et construction de l'histoire sacrée'.

Paradoxically, it may be that both Latin and Finnish had strong religious and sacred connotations. The former is, of course, evident, but the latter claim gains support from the fact that later, in the sixteenth and seventeenth centuries, several Finnish incantations mixed Catholic elements with folk beliefs. Furthermore, Hemmingius's translation of *Ramus virens* and the anonymous 'Ballad of the Death of Bishop Henry' seem to associate traditional Finnish poetic idiom with sacred topics. It could be asked, at least hypothetically, whether Latin and the Finnish Kalevala-metre idiom were both interpreted as the carriers of sacredness — and whether they both clashed with the new Lutheran use of the vernacular language.

It has been repeatedly argued that it was due to Lutheran religious indoctrination that traditional vernacular poetry lost ground rather early in southwestern parts of Finland. Scholars have assumed that Lutheran clergymen attacked not only traditional beliefs, whether pagan or Catholic, but that they also fought against the oral poetic form itself.[63] In this context Hemmingius has been seen as a liberal-minded exception. We might also assume that Hemmingius associated Kalevalaic features with the older Catholic tradition, and that he consciously or unconsciously shared the feeling that the Kalevala-metre poetic register carried certain archaic and sacred connotations.

The Reformation not only changed the religious practices and the position of the ecclesiastical elite. It also led to a deep change in cultural, linguistic, and vernacular practices. The medieval ecclesiastical elite formed a professional class of the written word. Lay literacy was, of course, spreading among secular administrators and the merchant class in Low German and Swedish usage. However, the Finnish vernacular remained oral. The religious Catholic heritage was adopted among the populace through vernacular legends and adaptations of hagiographic storyworlds. We may speculate about the role of mendicant orders like the Dominicans (established in Finland by 1249) and the Franciscans (established in Finland in 1403). It is plausible that the Bridgettine order (established in Finland in 1441) also had some influence — the earliest

---

[63] Suomi, 'Suomenkielinen lyriikka ennen vuotta 1640', pp. 251–52; see also Sarajas, *Suomen kansanrunouden tuntemus*; Kuusi, 'Keskiajan kalevalainen runous'. I have not found especially strong evidence for this claim from sixteenth-century sources. Remarks about impious folksongs can be found, but it is difficult to find anything about the poetic form itself. The almost sole contemporary source for this interpretation has been Jacobus Petri Finno's foreword to his Finnish hymnal where he identifies rhymed metre as the one practised in Christian countries (Finno, *Virsikirja*, ed. by Lempiäinen, pp. 174–75). Whether he is attacking 'paganism' or vernacular Catholic poetic tradition is unclear.

writer known through his own texts in Finland was the Bridgettine monk Jöns Budde (c. 1435–c. 1495) who translated various religious texts into his native Swedish.[64] We also know that some of the basic Christian texts like *credo* and *Pater noster* had been probably translated into Finnish.[65]

We may confidently assume that written, aural, chanted, and performed Christian traditions in Latin lived side by side with syncretistic oral traditions. Christian and pre-Christian storyworlds intermingled with each other, as can be seen from incantations and vernacular poetry on Catholic saints. During the Reformation the Finnish vernacular was turned into a literary language. Furthermore, it gained a new sacral status as the language of liturgical celebrations, prayers, hymns, and sermons. Jacobus Petri Finno states in his oft-quoted preface to the first Finnish hymnal in 1583: 'wastan perkelen mieldä ia Pauin kieldö edhes panit' ('This is proposed against the devil's will and the pope's language').[66] Latin did not lose its status among the learned elite, but its sacred nature was contested. The vernacular tradition posed other problems for the reformers: it was a carrier of folk beliefs and the syncretistic fusion of Catholic tradition. Moreover, it seems that both poetic and musical registers were considered as being strongly attached to these contents. With the exception of Hemmingius's songs, all other contemporary Lutheran religious poetry avoided the vernacular poetic idiom.

Traditionally this has been interpreted as a part of Lutheran indoctrination, but we might ask whether the reformers in fact targeted two simultaneous competitive linguistic, poetic, and musical registers: Catholic Latinity and the vernacular religion. Lutheran hymns sung by the congregation were a novelty that was considered a central tool for religious education. There are some passages (like another mentioned by Jacobus Petri Finno) that hint at the competition between the vernacular song tradition and the new reformed practice.[67]

The Lutheran reformers attacked both vernacular and Catholic traditions. Yet we must bear in mind that they did not necessarily make a clear distinction

---

[64] Lamberg, *Jöns Budde*; see also Lehtonen, 'Latinet och folkspråken'.

[65] We have circumstantial evidence that both the *Pater noster* and *credo* existed in Finnish. The former was first printed by the German Sebastian Münster in his *Cosmographey* in 1555. The version seems to be independent from the Reformation translations from the same time. We may furthermore speculate about the vernacular sermons, mystery plays, and the influence of ecclesiastical mural paintings.

[66] Finno, *Virsikirja*, ed. by Lempiäinen, pp. 174–75.

[67] Finno, *Virsikirja*, ed. by Lempiäinen, pp. 173–75; see also Lagerborg, 'Vår äldsta konstdiktning'; Suomi, 'Suomenkielinen lyriikka ennen vuotta 1640'.

between 'pagan' and 'Catholic' practices: the latter were also blamed for idolatry and magic. Christianity had to be purified of both of these. Thus the label 'pagan' was used on all religious practices and beliefs regarded as 'un-Christian'. There was an ongoing clash of belief systems ('pagan' pre-Christian or syncretistic beliefs and practices: incantations, charms, pre-Christian cosmological mythology; Catholic traditions: saints, hagiographic storyworlds, pictures, statues, and magical elements of Catholic practices), as well as a clash of languages and poetics (the new vernacular rhymed metrics in religious use in contrast to the traditional trochaic and alliterative Kalevala metre). The exceptionality of Hemmingius lies in the fact that he seems to side-step these clashes. By translating a Catholic song collection into Finnish and ably using traits of the traditional poetic idiom, he also reveals to us a rich world of vernacular adaptations from a Catholic heritage.

Works Cited

Primary Sources

ARTFL Project Multilingual Bibles Database, <http://www.lib.uchicago.edu/efts/ARTFL/public/bibles/vulgate.search.html> [accessed 30 November 2009]

Cantiones piae et antiquae, veterum episcoporum & pastorum in inclyto regno Sveciae (Rostock: [n.pub.], 1625)

Finno, Jacobus Petri, *Jaakko Finnon Virsikirja: näköispainos ensimmäisestä Suomalaisesta virsikirjasta sekä uudelleen ladottu laitos alkuperäisestä tekstistä ja sitä täydentävistä käsikirjoituksista*, ed. by Pentti Lempiäinen (Helsinki: Suomalaisen Kirjallisuuden Seura, 1988)

Ganander, Christfrid, *Mythologia Fennica eller förklaring öfver De nomina propria deastrorum, idolorum, locorum, virorum &c* (Helsinki: Suomalaisen Kirjallisuuden Seura, 1984)

Hemmingius de Masco, *Vanhain Suomen maan Piispain ja Kircon Esimiesten Latinan kielised laulud* (Stockholm: Meurer, 1616)

Juusten, Paulus, *Catalogus et ordinaria successio episcoporum*, ed. by Simo Heininen, Suomen Kirkkohistoriallisen Seuran toimituksia, 147 (Helsinki: Suomen kirkkohistoriallinen seura, 1988)

Piae Cantiones ecclesiasticae et scholarum veterum episcoporum 1582, Theodoricus Petri (Rutha), Nylandensis, ed. by Einari Marvia, Documenta musicae Fennicae, 10 (Helsinki: Fazer, 1967)

Piispa Henrikin surmavirsi: Suomalaisen Kirjallisuuden Seuran kansanrunousarkiston vanhin käsikirjoitus – The Ballad of the Death of Bishop Henry: The Oldest Manuscript in the Folklore Archives of the Finnish Literature Society, ed. by Urpo Vento (Helsinki: Suomalaisen Kirjallisuuden Seura, 1999)

Suomen kansan vanhat runot, ed. by Aukusti Robert Niemi and others, 34 vols (Helsinki: Suomalaisen Kirjallisuuden Seura, 1908–48, 1997), VIII: *Varsinais-Suomen runot*, ed. by Yrjö Henrik Toivonen (1932)

Suomen kansan vanhat runot Database, <http://dbgw.finlit.fi/skvr/> [accessed 30 November 2009]

Secondary Works

Andersén, Harald, and Timo Mäkinen, *Piae Cantiones: vanhoja kirkko- ja koululauluja* (Helsinki: Fazer, 1967)

Anttonen, Pertti, 'A Catholic Martyr and Protestant Heritage: A Contested Site of Religiosity and its Representation in Modern Finland', in *Creating Diversities: Folklore, Religion and the Politics of Heritage*, ed. by Anna-Leena Siikala and others, Studia Fennica folkloristica, 14 (Helsinki: Suomalaisen Kirjallisuuden Seura, 2004), pp. 190–221

——, 'Transformations of a Murder Narrative: A Case in the Politics of History and Heroization', *Norveg: Journal of Norwegian Folkore*, 40 (1997), 3–28

Bohlin, Folke, 'Piae Cantiones', in *Kulturhistoriskt lexikon för nordisk medeltid: från vikingatid till reformationstid*, ed. by Ingvar Andersson and others, 22 vols (Helsinki: Akademiska bokhandeln, 1956–78), XIII: *Ormer–regnbue*, ed. by John Granlund (1968), pp. 267–73

——, 'Tobias Norlind — en kort biografi', in *Om Tobias Norlind, en pionjär i musikforskning*, ed. by Folke Bohlin (Lund: Tobias Norlind samfundet för musikforskning, 2004), pp. 7–12

Carruthers, Mary, *The Book of Memory: A Study of Memory in Medieval Culture*, Cambridge Studies in Medieval Culture, 10 (Cambridge: Cambridge University Press, 1996)

Coleman, Janet, *Public Reading and the Reading Public in Late Medieval England and France* (Cambridge: Cambridge University Press, 2005)

Dreves, Guido Maria, 'Cantiones Suecicae', in *Cantiones et muteti*, III: *Cantiones variae, Bohemicae, Suecicae*, ed. by Guido M. Dreves, Analecta hymnica medii aevi, 45b (Leipzig: Reisland, 1904), pp. 127–79

——, 'Vorwort', in *Cantiones et muteti*, III: *Cantiones variae, Bohemicae, Suecicae*, ed. by Guido M. Dreves, Analecta hymnica medii aevi, 45b (Leipzig: Reisland, 1904), pp. 5–14

Edgren, Helena, 'Pyhä Henrik', in *Pyhän Henrikin sarkofagi*, ed. by Helena Edgren and Kirsti Melanko (Helsinki: Museovirasto, 1996), pp. 38–48

Finnegan, Ruth, *Literacy and Orality: Studies in the Technology of Communication* (Oxford: Blackwell, 1988)

Foley, John Miles, *Immanent Art: From Structure to Meaning in Traditional Epic* (Bloomington: Indiana University Press, 1991)

——, *The Theory of Oral Composition: History and Methodology* (Bloomington: Indiana University Press, 1988)

Green, Dennis H., *Medieval Listening and Reading: The Primary Reception of German Literature* (Cambridge: Cambridge University Press, 2005)

Haavio, Martti, *Piispa Henrik ja Lalli: Piispa Henrikin surmavirren historiaa* (Porvoo: Werner Söderström, 1948)

——, 'Vanhojen runojemme maailmankäsityksestä', *Kalevalaseuran vuosikirja*, 8 (1928), 195–231

Heikkilä, Tuomas, *Pyhän Henrikin legenda*, Suomalaisen Kirjallisuuden Seuran toimituksia, 1039 (Helsinki: Suomalaisen Kirjallisuuden Seura, 2005)

Heikkinen, Antero, *Paholaisen liittolaiset: noita ja magiakäsityksiä ja – oikeudenkäyntejä Suomessa 1600-luvun jälkipuoliskolla (n. 1640–1712)*, Historiallisia tutkimuksia, 78 (Helsinki: Suomen Historiallinen Seura, 1969)

Heininen, Simo, 'Einleitung', in Paulus Juusten, *Catalogus et ordinaria successio episcoporum Finlandensium*, ed. by Simo Heininen, Suomen Kirkkohistoriallisen Seuran toimituksia, 147 (Helsinki: Suomen kirkkohistoriallinen seura, 1988), pp. 9–46

——, *Suomalaisen historiankirjoituksen synty: tutkimus Paavali Juustenin piispainkronikasta*, Suomen Kirkkohistoriallisen Seuran toimituksia, 147 (Helsinki: Suomen kirkkohistoriallinen seura, 1989)

Kaivola-Bregenhøj, Annikki, 'Ruton sanat, vanhin suomalainen loitsumuistiinpano', in *Lännen maita ja Karjalan kyliä*, ed. by Saima-Liisa Laatunen, Kalevalaseuran vuosikirja, 58 (Helsinki: Suomalaisen Kirjallisuuden Seura, 1978), pp. 199-213

Kulonen, Ulla-Maija, ed., *Suomen sanojen alkuperä: etymologinen sanakirja*, Suomalaisen Kirjallisuuden Seuran toimituksia, 556, Kotimaisten kielten tutkimuskeskuksen julkaisuja, 62, 3 vols (Helsinki: Suomalaisen Kirjallisuuden Seura, 1992-2000)

Kurvinen, Pietari Joonas Immanuel, *Suomen virsirunouden alkuvaiheet v:een 1640* (Helsinki: Suomalaisen Kirjallisuuden Seura, 1929)

Kuusi, Matti, 'Keskiajan kalevalainen runous', in *Suomen kirjallisuus*, ed. by Matti Kuusi and others, 8 vols (Helsinki: Suomalaisen Kirjallisuuden Seura, 1963-70), I: *Kirjoittamaton kirjallisuus*, ed. by Matti Kuusi, pp. 273-397

Lagerborg, Rolf, 'Vår äldsta konstdiktning', *Skrifter utgifna af Svenska litteratursällskapet i Finland*, 78 (1907), 57-111

Laine, Tuija, ed., *Vanhimman suomalaisen kirjallisuuden käsikirja*, Suomalaisen Kirjallisuuden Seuran Toimituksia, 686 (Helsinki: Suomalaisen Kirjallisuuden Seura, 1997)

Laitinen, Heikki, 'Barokki tunteen ja järjen dialogina', in *Runosta runoon: suomalaisen runon yhteyksiä länsimaiseen kirjallisuuteen antiikista nykyaikaan*, ed. by Sakari Katajamäki and Johanna Pentikäinen (Helsinki: Werner Söderström, 2004), pp. 110-28

——, 'Runolaulu', in *Suomen musiikin historia*, ed. by Liisa Aroheimo-Marvia and others, 8 vols (Helsinki: Werner Söderström, 1995-2006), VIII: *Kansanmusiikki*, ed. by Anneli Asplund, pp. 14-79

Lamberg, Marko, *Jöns Budde: birgittalaisveli ja hänen teoksensa*, Suomalaisen Kirjallisuuden Seuran toimituksia, 1115 (Helsinki: Suomalaisen Kirjallisuuden Seura, 2007)

Lehtonen, Tuomas M. S., 'Conquête et construction de l'histoire sacrée en Finlande', in *Les Élites Nordiques et l'Europe occidentale (XIIe-XVe siècle)*, ed. by Tuomas M. S. Lehtonen and Élisabeth Mornet, Histoire ancienne et médiévale, 94 (Paris: Publications de la Sorbonne, 2007), pp. 169-88

——, *Fortuna, Money, and the Sublunar World: Twelfth-Century Ethical Poetics and the Satirical Poetry of the Carmina Burana*, Bibliotheca historica, 9 (Helsinki: Suomen Historiallinen Seura, 1995)

——, *Hopeamarkkojen evankeliumi: kirjoituksia sydänkeskiajan kulttuurihistoriasta* (Helsinki: Werner Söderström, 2000)

——, 'Latinet och folkspråken', in *Finlands svenska litteraturhistoria*, I: *Åren 1400-1900*, ed. by Johan Wrede and Rainer Knapas (Helsinki: Svenska litteratursällskapet i Finland, 1999), pp. 26-40

——, 'Piae Cantiones', in *Finlands svenska litteraturhistoria*, I: *Åren 1400-1900*, ed. by Johan Wrede and Rainer Knapas (Helsinki: Svenska litteratursällskapet i Finland, 1999), pp. 40-50

——, 'La *Republica christianorum* et ses ennemis dans la diocèse de Turku: Paulus Juusten et son *Catalogus et ordinaria successio episcoporum finlandensium*', in *Itinéraires du savoir de l'Italie à la Scandinavie (X^e-XVIe siècle): études offertes à Élisabeth Mornet*, ed. by Corinne Péneau (Paris: Publications de la Sorbonne, 2009), pp. 299-318

Leino, Pentti, *Language and Metre: Metrics and the Metrical System of Finnish*, Studia Fennica, 31 (Helsinki: Suomalaisen Kirjallisuuden Seura, 1986)

Lempiäinen, Pentti, 'Ensimmäinen suomalainen virsikirja', in *Jacobus Petri Finno, Jaakko Finnon Virsikirja: Näköispainos ensimmäisestä suomalaisesta virsikirjasta sekä uudelleen ladottu laitos alkuperäisestä tekstistä ja sitä täydentävistä käsikirjoituksista*, ed. by Pentti Lempiäinen (Helsinki: Suomalaisen Kirjallisuuden Seura, 1988), pp. 358–61

Mäkinen, Timo, *Die aus frühen bömischen Quellen überlieferten 'Piae cantiones' Melodie*, Studia historica Jyväskylaensia, 2 (Pieksämäki: Jyväskylän yliopisto, 1964)

——, *Piae Cantiones sävelmien lähdetutkimuksia*, Acta musicologica fennica, 1 (Helsinki: Suomen musiikkitieteellinen seura, 1968)

Maliniemi, Aarno, 'Finland som bevarare av P. C. -sångernaa', in *Kulturhistoriskt lexikon för nordisk medeltid: från vikingatid till reformationstid*, ed. by Ingvar Andersson and others, 22 vols (Helsinki: Akademiska bokhandeln, 1956–78), XIII: *Ormer–regnbue*, ed. by John Granlund (1968), pp. 273–74

——, 'Suomen keskiaikainen kirjallisuus', in *Suomen kirjallisuus*, ed. by Matti Kuusi and others, 8 vols (Helsinki: Suomalaisen Kirjallisuuden Seura, 1963–70), II: *Ruotsin ajan kirjallisuus*, ed. by Martti Rapola (1963), pp. 7–68

Nenonen, Marko, *Noituus, taikuus ja noitavainot Ala-Satakunnan, Pohjois-Pohjanmaan, ja Viipurin Karjalan maaseudulla 1620–1700*, Historiallisia tutkimuksia, 165 (Helsinki: Suomen Historiallinen Seura, 1992)

——, *Synnin palkka on kuolema: suomalaiset noidat 1500–1700-luvulla* (Helsinki: Otava, 1994)

Norlind, Tobias, *Latinska skolsånger i Sverige och Finland*, Lunds universitets årsskrift Avd. 1: Teologi, juridik och humanistiska ämnen, 5.2 (Lund: Håkan Ohlssons boktryckeri, 1909)

Pajamo, Reijo, *Lehti puusta variseepi: suomalainen koululauluperinne* (Porvoo: Werner Söderström, 1999)

Palola, Ari-Pekka, *Maunu Tavast ja Olavi Maununpoika: Turun piispat 1412–1460*, Suomen Kirkkohistoriallisen Seuran toimituksia, 178 (Helsinki: Suomen kirkkohistoriallinen seura, 1997)

Perälä, Anna, 'Typografinen aineisto ja sen tutkimus', in *Kirjahistoria: johdatus vanhan kirjan tutkimukseen*, ed. by Tuija Laine, Suomalaisen Kirjallisuuden Seuran toimituksia, 647 (Helsinki: Suomalaisen Kirjallisuuden Seura, 1996), pp. 73–128

Pirinen, Kauko, *Suomen kirkon historia*, I: *Keskiaika ja uskonpuhdistuksen aika* (Porvoo: Werner Söderström, 1991)

Rapola, Martti, 'Vanhan runon kuvastelua parissa 1500-luvun suomalaisessa virressä', *Kalevalaseuran vuosikirja*, 14 (1934), 149–69

Sarajas, Annamari, *Suomen kansanrunouden tuntemus 1500–1700-lukujen kirjallisuudessa* (Helsinki: Werner Söderström, 1956)

Siikala, Anna-Leena, *Mythic Images and Shamanism: A Perspective on Kalevala Poetry*, Folklore Fellow Communications, 280 (Helsinki: Suomalainen Tiedeakatemia, 2002)

——, 'Myytit, riitit ja tietäjän toimet', in *Savo ja sen kansa*, ed. by Matti Räsänen and Riitta Räsänen, Suomalaisen Kirjallisuuden Seuran toimituksia, 1192 (Helsinki: Suomalaisen Kirjallisuuden Seura, 2008), pp. 109–86

Suomi, Vilho, 'Suomenkielinen lyriikka ennen vuotta 1640', in *Suomen kirjallisuus*, ed. by Matti Kuusi and others, 8 vols (Helsinki: Suomalaisen Kirjallisuuden Seura, 1963–70), II: *Ruotsin ajan kirjallisuus*, ed. by Martti Rapola (1963), pp. 245–62

Tarkka, Lotte, 'Intertextuality, Rhetorics and Interpretation of Oral Poetry: The Case of Archived Orality', in *Nordic Frontiers*, ed. by Pertti J. Anttonen and Reimund Kvideland, Nordic Institute of Folklore Publications, 27 (Turku: Nordic Institute of Folklore, 1993), pp. 165–93

——, *Rajarahvaan laulu: Tutkimus Vuokkiniemen kalevalamittaisesta runokulttuurista 1821–1921*, Suomalaisen Kirjallisuuden Seuran toimituksia, 1033 (Helsinki: Suomalaisen Kirjallisuuden Seura, 2005)

Viinamäki, Anna, with Raija Miikkulainen, 'Hemminki Maskulainen — virsirunoilija' (Helsinki: Kotimaisten kielten tutkimuskeskus, 2005), <http://scripta.kotus.fi/www/artikkelit/maskulainen/> [accessed 13 June 2012]

Zumthor, Paul, *Introduction à la poésie orale*, Collection poétique (Paris: Seuil, 1983)

——, *La Lettre et la voix: de la 'littérature' médiévale*, Collection poétique (Paris: Seuil, 1987)

——, *La Poésie et la voix dans la civilisation médiévale: essais et conférences* (Paris: Presses Universitaires de France, 1989)

Part II

Christian Discourse Framing Pagan Stories

Zoroaster, Saturn, and Óðinn: The Loss of Language and the Rise of Idolatry

Jonas Wellendorf

Work

The prose *Edda* is universally considered one of the highlights of Old Norse literature.[1] This treatise on poetics and mythology consists in its present incarnation of four parts that are unequal in length and general appeal. The Icelandic chieftain Snorri Sturluson (d. 1241) is usually credited as its author. The prose *Edda* is our main repository of Old Norse myths about the pre-Christian gods and cosmology, and the most important source for the comprehension of Old Norse skaldic poetry. The prominent position of the prose *Edda* is reflected by the volume of scholarly literature devoted to this work. The prose *Edda* is thus a central part of the canon of Old Norse literature.

Nevertheless, the laws and workings of medieval literature are not the same as those governing more recent literature, and it might be useful to ask what the prose *Edda* actually is. Here the theoretical distinction between a work as an abstract entity and its potential of being realized in differing texts is useful. This division is often more visible when dealing with medieval literature preserved

---

* My thanks go to Karl G. Johansson, University of Oslo, for his comments.

[1] The *Younger Edda*, the *Prose Edda*, and *Snorra Edda* are all different names of the same work. These titles are used to distinguish this work from the other *Edda*, the *Older Edda*, which is also known as the *Poetic Edda* and *Sæmundar Edda*. None of these terms is entirely felicitous, but in order to avoid additional confusion the designation 'prose *Edda*' has been chosen here.

Jonas Wellendorf, University of California, Berkeley, Assistant Professor, wellendorf@berkeley.ed

in handwritten codices than with post-medieval literature preserved in printed books, since a medieval work of literature, when preserved in more than one manuscript, is represented by differing texts in the different manuscripts. These texts or textual witnesses to the work diverge from each other in various ways. Such divergences may range from accidentals on a graphemic or orthographic level and details of punctuation on one end of the scale, to the addition, deletion, or rearrangement of substantial amounts of text on the other. But these differing texts may all be said to represent the same work. An analogy to this situation might be sought in the difference between the unchanging platonic ideas and the changing objects that are reflections of these ideas. Only one work was stable and unchangeable in theory and by definition, though not in practice, and that was the word of God preserved in the Bible. As a result of this one could refer to a Bible or a gospel book as *textus*, 'the text', in Latin or as *texti* in Old Norse.[2]

This distinction between the work as an abstract entity and its concrete realizations in distinct texts might have been somewhat foreign to medieval man. This can be seen, for instance, in the Old Norse word *bók*, 'book', which points both to a concrete object we can hold in our hands, a codex, and the abstract entity behind its concrete realization, the work. An example of this dual meaning can be found in the initial rubric of the Uppsala manuscript (**U**) of the prose *Edda*:

> Bók þessi heitir Edda. Hana hefir saman setta Snorri Sturluson eptir þeim hætti sem hér er skipat. Er fyrst frá ásum ok Ymi. Þar næst Skáldskaparmál ok heiti margra hluta. Síðast Háttatal er Snorri hefir ort um Hákon konung ok Skúla hertoga.
>
> [This book is called *Edda*. Snorri Sturluson has compiled it according to the way in which it is arranged here. First is told about the Æsir and Ymir, next is Skáldskaparmál and the poetic names for many things, and lastly Háttatal, which Snorri has composed about King Hákon and Earl Skúli.][3]

In this paragraph the codex itself is named *Edda* and so is its content which, although presented in precisely this codex, might be found elsewhere as well.

---

[2] However, in the Middle Ages people would not have encountered the Bible in the form of the single volume we find on bookshelves today, and the parts that were used in the liturgy, the Psalter and the Gospels, would have been much more widely disseminated. On the meaning of the word *text* and its closest relatives in the Middle Ages, see Ziolkowski, 'Texts and Textuality, Medieval and Modern'.

[3] Snorri Sturluson, *Snorre Sturlasons Edda: Uppsala-handskriften DG 11*, ed. by Grape, Kallstenius, and Thorell, ii, 1 (hereafter **U**). Translation Clunies Ross, *Skáldskaparmál*, p. 10. Unnormalized quotations have been silently normalized.

Thus, behind the concrete manifest *bók* lies another immaterial *bók*, which is the abstract entity we call 'the work'.

In the case of the prose *Edda* this entity is usually considered to consist of four parts:

1. A prologue which will be discussed below.
2. *Gylfaginning*, 'The tricking of Gylfi', takes the form of a dialogue between a legendary king Gylfi of Sweden and three hypostases of Óðinn and provides information on the traditional mythological Old Norse views on cosmogony, cosmology, and eschatology. Furthermore it offers a retelling of a number of myths.
3. *Skáldskaparmál*, 'The diction of poetry', gives an overview of the kinds of poetic circumlocutions that are used in Old Norse poetry, and also presents some myths.
4. *Háttatál*, 'The enumeration of metres', is an Old Norse *clavis metrica* in the form of a long poem in praise of the Norwegian king Hákon Hákonarson (d. 1263) and Earl Skúli (d. 1240), interspersed with prose comments on metre and stylistics.

In order to fit the four sections of the work with the three sections mentioned in the rubric of **U** some students of the *Edda* see the prologue and *Gylfaginning* as a single unit.[4]

Common belief holds that the traditional Icelandic art of poetry was in danger of extinction in the early thirteenth century because the extensive mythological knowledge needed to compose and understand the verses of the skálds was soon to be forgotten. Therefore, Snorri wrote the *Edda* in order to preserve this knowledge and pass it on to future generations of poets. In a discursive section of the prose *Edda* we read the following about the intent behind the work:

> En þetta er nú at segja ungum skáldum þeim er girnask at nema mál skáldskapar ok heyja sér orðfjǫlda með fornum heitum eða girnask þeir at kunna skilja þat sem hulit er kveðit þá skili hann þessa bók til fróðleiks ok skemtanar. En ekki er at gleyma eða ósanna svá þessar frásagnir at taka ór skáldskapnum fornar kenningar þær er hǫfuðskáldin hafa sér líka látit. En eigi skulu kristnir menn trúa á heiðin goð, ok eigi á sannendi þessa sagna annan veg en svá sem hér finnsk í upphafi bókar

---

[4] This amalgamation of the first two sections is supported by the fact that only one of the relevant manuscripts clearly marks a break between the prologue and *Gylfaginning* with a larger than usual initial letter at the beginning of the section; see Snorri Sturluson, *Edda Snorra Sturlusonar: Codex Wormianus*, ed. by Finnur Jónsson (hereafter **W**). In the other manuscripts no visual markers are used to signify that there is an important break between the prologue and *Gylfaginning*.

er sagt er frá atburðum þeim er mannfolkit villtisk frá réttri trú. Ok þá næst frá Tyrkjum hvern veg Asíamenn þeir er æsir eru kallaðir, fǫlsuðu frásagnir frá þeim tíðendum er gerðusk í Tróju til þess at landfolkit skyldi trúa þá goð vera.

[But these things have now to be told to young poets who desire to learn the language of poetry and to furnish themselves with a wide vocabulary using traditional terms; or else they desire to be able to understand what is expressed obscurely. Then let such a one take this book as scholarly inquiry and entertainment. But these stories are not to be consigned to oblivion or demonstrated to be false, so as to deprive poetry of ancient kennings which major poets have been happy to use. Yet Christian people must not believe in heathen gods, nor in the truth of this account in any other way than that in which it is presented at the beginning of this book, where it is told what happened when mankind went astray from the true faith, and after that about the Turks, how the people of Asia, known as Æsir, distorted the accounts of the events that took place in Troy so that people of the country would believe that they were gods.][5]

The intention of the prose *Edda*, as it is formulated in the work itself, is thus twofold: firstly to furnish the would-be *skáld* with the mythological and stylistic knowledge necessary to compose and understand skaldic poetry and, secondly, to unfold the background of this special poetic style. Only the second of these aspects will be discussed here.

The prologue to the prose *Edda*, *Gylfaginning*, and *Ynglinga saga* — the saga that introduces the voluminous chronicle of Norwegian history known as *Heimskringla*, usually ascribed to Snorri as is the prose *Edda* — tells how Óðinn and his following of Æsir came to the North where they managed to convince the local populace that they were gods, and came to be venerated as such. Óðinn and the Æsir are described as culture heroes bringing law to the North, even though, from a medieval Christian point of view, they also introduced falsehood, in particular in the form of the worship of false gods and idolatry. They were able to do so because of their extraordinary, and in some respects superhuman, skills. *Ynglinga saga* draws particular attention to Óðinn's manner of speaking:

Ǫnnur var sú at hann talaði svá snjallt ok slétt, at ǫllum, er á heyrðu, þótti þat eina satt. Mælti hann allt hendingum, svá sem nú er þat kveðit, er skáldskapr heitir. Hann ok hofgoðar hans heita ljóðasmiðir, því at sú íþrótt hófsk af þeim í Norðrlǫndum.

[For another matter, he spoke so well and so smoothly that all who heard him believed all he said was true. All he spoke was in rimes, as is now the case in what is

---

[5] **W**, p. 55. Translation from Snorri Sturluson, *Edda*, trans. by Faulkes, pp. 64–65.

called skaldship. He and his temple priests are called songsmiths, because that art began with them in the northern lands.][6]

According to *Ynglinga saga* Óðinn brought the art of poetry to the North. But this poetry cannot be appreciated or understood without a proper knowledge of the stories that are used as the basis of the complicated system of synonyms and noun paraphrases (*kenningar* and *heiti*) that constitute a major part of the Old Norse poetic diction. The part of the prose *Edda* known as *Gylfaginning* tells how Óðinn, disguised as a sort of trinity, imparted this knowledge to the local Swedish population, represented by King Gylfi. Óðinn told Gylfi stories about the Trojan War but he (and the Æsir) managed to trick the locals into believing that the stories about Troy were in fact stories about themselves, and in order to make this all the more convincing they adopted the names of the Trojans:

> Asíamenn þeir er Æsir eru kallaðir fǫlsuðu frásagnir frá þeim tíðendum er gerðusk í Tróju til þess at landfolkit skyldi trúa þau goð vera. Priamus konungr í Tróju var hǫfðingi yfir ǫllum her Tyrkja, ok hans synir váru tignastir af ǫllum her hans. Sá salr inn ágæti er Æsir kǫlluðu Brímis sal eða bjǫrsal, þat var hǫll Priamus konungs. En þat er þeir gera langa frásǫgn af ragnarǫkk(r) þat er Trójumanna orrosta. Þar (er) svá sagt at Ǫku-Þórr egndi uxahǫfði ok dró at borði miðgarðsorm. En ormrinn hjalp svá lífinu at hann søkktisk í hafit. Eptir þeim dómum er þetta sagt er Ektor drap Volocronte ágætan kappa at ásjánda inum mikla Akille ok teygði hann svá at sér með hǫfði ins drepna þess er þeir jǫfnuðu til uxans þess er Ǫku-Þórr braut hǫfuðit. En er Akilles var dreginn í þetta ófóri með sínu kappi, þá var honum sú ein lífshjǫlpin at flýja undan banvænu hǫggi Ektoris ok þó sárr.
>
> [the people of Asia, known as Æsir, distorted the accounts of the events that took place in Troy so that the people of the country would believe that they were gods. King Priam in Troy was a great ruler over all the host of Turks, and his sons were the highest in rank over his whole host. That magnificent hall that the Æsir called Brimir's hall or beer-hall, was King Priam's hall. And whereas they give a long account of Ragnarok, this is the Trojan war. The story goes that Oku-Thor used an ox-head as bait and pulled the Midgard serpent up to the gunwale, but the serpent survived by sinking into the sea. This story is based on the one about how Hector killed the splendid Volucrontes while the great Achilles was looking on, and this lured Achilles towards him with the head of the slain man whom they saw as corresponding to the ox from which Thor had taken the head. And when Achilles had been drawn into this dangerous situation by his impetuosity, then the only way for him to save his life was to run away from Hector's deadly stroke, wounded though he was.][7]

---

[6] Snorri Sturluson, *Heimskringla*, ed. by Bjarni Aðalbjarnarson, I, 17. Translation from Snorri Sturluson, *Heimskringla: History of the Kings of Norway*, trans. by Hollander, p. 10.

[7] **W**, pp. 55–56. Translation Snorri Sturluson, *Edda*, trans. by Faulkes, p. 65.

The Óðinn that came to the North was the twentieth descendant of King Priamus of Troy, who was called Óðinn as well. Thus the Asians fooled the ancient Scandinavians into believing that they were in fact the Trojans of the Trojan War. The stories they told about this war were told obliquely in the guise of myth and not as history. This means, for instance, that Hector's killing of Volucrontes and the ensuing battle with Achilles (which ended in a draw) was told as the story of the fishing expedition of Þórr.[8]

The Æsir who came to the North were not identical with the ancient Trojans/Asians but they were their descendants and they still used their language. When they taught the art of poetry to the Scandinavians it was the language of the Trojans they taught them. A knowledge of the stories of Troy, as the younger Óðinn uniquely narrates them, is thus presented as a prerequisite for an understanding of the way of speaking that eventually became poetry for the northerners. It is this essential knowledge that Óðinn imparts to Gylfi. Since Gylfi later recounted what he had seen and heard, this knowledge spread orally until it finally, we must surmise, ended up in written form in the work that is now called the prose *Edda*.[9]

Texts

In his influential critique of philology Bernard Cerquiglini underscores that variance is a primary characteristic of medieval vernacular literature, and that philologists and text editors, in their eagerness to pin down the most original and, chronologically speaking, primary form of a work, have neglected precisely this aspect.[10] Whether editors have attempted to reconstruct a hypotheti-

---

[8] The character Volucrontes is identified with the ox that Þórr slays and uses as bait in the myth about his attempt to catch the Midgard serpent. Achilles is identified with the Midgard serpent and Hector with Þórr. A character named Volucrontes otherwise appears only in the version of *Trojumanna saga* β that can be found in the manuscript *Hauksbók*; *Trojumanna saga*, ed. by Louis-Jensen, p. 179. Faulkes suggests that this name is a mistake for Polypoetes; see Faulkes, 'Descent from the Gods' p. 122. Compare Dares Phrygius, *De excidio Troiae historia*, ed. by Meister, p. 30: 'Hector Polypoetem ducem fortissimum occidit dumque eum spoliare coepit, Achilles supervenit' ('Hector killed Polypoetes, a most strong commander, and when he was about to plunder his body, Achilles came up to him') ... and then they fight.

[9] A strictly utilitarian view of the purpose of the *Edda* is, however, faulty since many of the stories related in *Gylfaginning* are simply entertaining stories in their own right and their relevance for the understanding of Old Norse poetic diction is sometimes questionable as well.

[10] Cerquiglini, *In Praise of the Variant*, trans. by Wing. On the variance of vernacular medieval literature, see also Bumke, 'Der unfeste Text'.

cal archetype-text or have been content with printing a select 'best text' from a single manuscript, the variance inherent in the medieval tradition has been relegated to the critical apparatus printed in small type at the bottom of the page. In this way one of the main features of medieval vernacular literature is rendered much less conspicuous. Despite the somewhat sweeping nature of some of Cerquiglini's statements, the prose *Edda* is a case in point. The manuscript tradition of this work, in particular in the section labelled *Skáldskaparmál*, shows that it did not achieve a stable form in the Middle Ages, but was repeatedly revised, reordered, and reshaped. This variance has continued in the post-medieval period as well.

The prose *Edda* can thus be characterized as an unstable or fluid work. Its unstable nature is immediately apparent from the differences between the four manuscripts that are usually seen as the physical representations of the work and as the carriers of its texts. These are the four manuscripts that Anthony Faulkes in the introduction to his edition of the prologue and *Gylfaginning* characterizes as having 'independent textual value', namely **U**, **R**, **W**, and **T**.[11] 'Independent textual value' in this context means that these are the manuscripts that editors have considered useful when attempting to reconstruct an archetype of the texts.[12] Of these four manuscripts, the text of **R** is usually considered the best, and this is the text commonly used as the basis for modern scholarly as well as popular editions, even though readings from the other manuscripts are included to a greater or lesser extent as well.[13]

---

[11] Snorri Sturluson, *Edda*, trans. by Faulkes, p. xxix. **U**: Uppsala, Uppsala universitetsbibliotek, MS DG 11, *c.* 1300–25, **R**: Reykjavík, Stofnun Árna Magnússonar í íslenskum fræðum, MS GKS 2367 4°, *c.* 1300–50, **W**: København, Den arnamagnæanske håndskriftssamling, MS AM 242 fol., *c.* 1350, **T**: Utrecht, Bibliotheek der Rijksuniversiteit, Trajectinus 1374, *c.* 1595. The datings are from the Index volume of Degnbol and others, *Ordbog over det norrøne prosasprog*. Johansson dates **W** slightly later (1340–70); see Johansson, *Studier i Codex Wormianus*, p. 18. There are other manuscripts as well, but these four texts are those that contain what is considered to be the whole work (more or less).

[12] By only considering the texts with 'independent textual value', however, the variation in the manuscript tradition becomes artificially enlarged because the *codices descriptorum*, manuscripts derived directly from preserved manuscripts with independent value, are then neglected even though, as 'dependent' manuscripts and texts, they could point to the stability of a tradition instead of its instability. An example of this would be the unedited København, Den arnamagnæanske håndskriftssamling, MS AM 756 4° (*c.* 1400–1500), containing part of *Gylfaginning* and *Skáldskaparmál*, that is characterized by its great similarity with **W**. See Snorri Sturluson, *Edda Snorra Sturlusonar*, ed. by Arnamagnæanske Kommision, III, pp. lxxviii–lxxx; Snorri Sturluson, *Edda*, ed. by Finnur Jónsson, p. xvii.

[13] The edition by Faulkes stays much closer to the text of **R** than does the edition of Finnur

These four texts preserve all four of the parts that constitute the canonical form of the work, but no manuscript transmits the four parts as a unified and coherent whole. The closely related manuscripts **R** and **T** contain a section with versified lists of poetic synonyms — so-called *þulur* — between sections 3 and 4. In **U**, on the other hand, sections 3 and 4 are separated by a text known as the *Second Grammatical Treatise*, while sections with lists of *skálds* and law speakers and some genealogical material are inserted in the middle of section 3. In **W**, finally, four grammatical treatises and a prologue to these treatises separate sections 3 and 4.[14] All these differences concern the latter two sections of the work. At the beginning, on the other hand, the two first sections are always preserved in conjunction with each other. The connection between the two sections is so close that one would in fact be wary of treating them as separate sections of the work if **W** did not clearly indicate that there is a major break between the two sections, by an extra large initial letter. Furthermore, none of the four manuscripts names the section that is here called 'the prologue'.

Even though the facts rehearsed above are well known to students of Old Norse literature, it is worthwhile to remember that how we encounter the parts of the prose *Edda* in the usual editions is far from how a medieval reader would have met them. This has great consequences for the modern reader who also lacks a presumably essential part of the cultural qualifications that the intended readership of the text necessarily must have had. The following is an attempt to analyse the prologue to the prose *Edda* as it is found in the manuscript **W**. The text of the prose *Edda* was transcribed from **W** by Finnur Jónsson in 1924, and this edition is used throughout the present chapter.[15] **W**, *Codex Wormianus*, was written *c*. 1350 by a very productive professional scribe, probably in one of the Benedictine houses in northern Iceland.[16]

Jónsson, but both editors are faced with the problem that the first page of **R** (containing the beginning of the prologue) is missing. Their solutions differ: Faulkes supplements with text from seventeenth-century manuscripts, while Finnur Jónsson uses **W** and **T** as '*Leittexte*'. See Snorri Sturluson, *Edda: Prologue and Gylfaginning*, ed. by Faulkes.

[14] For a more thorough survey of the manuscripts and their content, see Guðrún Nordal, *Tools of Literacy*, pp. 41–72.

[15] Therefore the quotations on the earlier pages from the prose *Edda* were, as a matter of principle, from **W** as well, even though they might as well have been taken from the editions of Faulkes or Finnur Jónsson. The differences between the texts in these cases are so insignificant that they become lost in translation, and Faulkes's translation, primarily following **R**, could be used without alterations. The text of the entire codex transcribed by Karl G. Johansson can be found in the online Medieval Nordic Text Archive as well: <http://www.menota.org/> [accessed 18 January 2013].

[16] On this manuscript, see Johansson, *Studier i Codex Wormianus*.

Some scholars have disputed Snorri's authorship of the prologue,[17] but if the fluid nature of the text is to be taken seriously, the issue of original or first authorship is of secondary importance.[18] A matter of much greater significance is that the prologue seems to occupy a central position in regards to the interpretation of *Gylfaginning* and the two remaining parts of the work as well, *Skáldskaparmál* in particular.[19]

The text of the prologue in **W** is almost twice as long as the prologue of the *Edda* constructed by Finnur Jónsson in his edition of 1931,[20] and the prologue in **U** is shorter still. Two longer passages and one shorter in **W** are unparalleled in the other manuscripts.[21] These sections are not included in the most commonly read editions[22] and are ignored in most discussions of the prologue. If they are mentioned, they are typically referred to as interpolations and are, as a consequence thereof, considered unimportant.[23] Accordingly, the prologue in the **W**-form is rarely analysed in the otherwise numerous studies that have contributed so significantly to the understanding of the prologue, its intellectual context, and its relation to the remaining parts of the prose *Edda*. The judgement of Nordal that the sections found only in **W** 'offer nothing of interest'[24] has largely been accepted. An exception is Johansson who briefly states that 'the interpolations strengthen the argument of the original prologue'.[25]

---

[17] On the discussion of authorship of the prologue, see most recently Beck, 'Zur Diskussion über den Prolog der Snorra-Edda'.

[18] At any rate, no one would deem it possible to reconstruct Snorri's *ipsissima verba*.

[19] See Clunies Ross, *Skáldskaparmál*.

[20] Snorri Sturluson, *Edda*, ed. by Finnur Jónsson, pp. 1–7.

[21] These sections are, according to Johansson, p. 2, l. 27–p. 3, l. 33; p. 4, l. 18–p. 6, l. 38; and p. 8, ll. 27–30 in the edition of **W** (Johansson, *Studier i Codex Wormianus*, p. 36).

[22] The editions of Faulkes (1988) and Finnur Jónsson (1931). It is, however, included in some older editions such as the old Arnamagnæan edition (Snorri Sturluson, *Edda Snorra Sturlusonar*, ed. by Arnamagnæanske Kommision).

[23] An exception is Boer, who regarded the prologue in **W** as the one closest to the archetype. Boer's view does not seem to have found any supporters. See Boer, 'Studier over Snorra Edda', pp. 185–90.

[24] *Codex Wormianus*, ed. by Sigurður Nordal, p. 15.

[25] Johansson, *Studier i Codex Wormianus*, p. 39: 'interpolationerna [förstärker] den argumentation som redan finns i den ursprungliga prologen'. Strerath-Bolz also devotes two pages to the **W**-form of the prologue in her monograph on the prologue of the prose *Edda*; see Strerath-Bolz, *Kontinuität statt Konfrontation*, pp. 78–79. See also Strerath-Bolz, 'Sprache und Religion in Prolog der *Snorra Edda*', p. 273; Johansson, 'Skriptorier och kompilationer'.

For the present undertaking, the question of whether the prologue as it is found in **W** is a part of the prose *Edda* as Snorri originally conceived it is ignored. The fact is that it is found in one of the manuscripts, and it must have ended up there because someone included it on purpose — be it the scribe of **W**, his commissioner, or one of their predecessors. Since the text of **W** is not otherwise characterized by heavy deviations from the **R** and **T** texts of the prose *Edda* — except that some chapters of section 3 have been left out, seemingly on purpose — these additional parts of **W** become all the more important.

The Story of the Short Version

The prologue does not limit itself to the description of how the Æsir emigrated from Troy and arrived in the North. It begins at the very beginning, when God created heaven and earth, and then moves rapidly through the first five ages of the history of man, that is, from Creation to the birth of Christ. The focus, however, is different from the one usually found in surveys of world (or salvation) history, since the birth of Christ is not mentioned and neither is the expression 'age of the world' used.

The story told in the shorter version of the prologue explains that mankind lost the knowledge of the true God because they would not mention his name. God, however, granted them wisdom so they could understand all earthly things. Therefore, by contemplating the workings of nature with their 'earthly understanding' (*jarðligri skilningu*),[26] they reached the conclusion that the cosmos in its entirety must have been created by one almighty god and is now governed by this same god. But they were ignorant of the name of this god.

This way of reasoning is well attested throughout the Latin tradition and is known as the 'argument of design' for the existence of God.[27] The model for it was provided by the Book of Wisdom (13. 1–9), a work ascribed to Solomon that was considered canonical in the Middle Ages (and before). Naturally, the understanding gained by the heathens without Christian revelation was in some ways faulty, so with their limited understanding they came to the conclusion that all things were made out of some material. This material theory of creation is in direct contrast to the Christian doctrine of creation ex nihilo, but

---

[26] **W**, p. 3.

[27] See the learned expositions by Dronke and Dronke, 'The Prologue of the Prose *Edda*'; Faulkes, 'Pagan Sympathy'. Interestingly, the same argument forms the basis of much of Ibn Tufail's twelfth-century philosophical novel *Hayy ibn Yaqdhan*, the *Philosophus autodidactus*.

the prologue still describes this 'groping towards truth by pagan thinkers'[28] in sympathetic terms and avoids the condemnation that is typical of many medieval writings on the same subject, such as the sermon *On the Origin of Disbelief* that can be found in *Hauksbók*.[29] In its general positive attitude the prologue concords with the Book of Wisdom where it is written that those who begin to worship elements of nature as gods 'are to be criticized the less, and perhaps they err while they seek God and want to find him' ('sed tamen adhuc in his minor est querella et hii enim fortassis errant Deum quaerentes et volentes invenire'; Book of Wisdom 13. 6).

One example of this partly true / partly false understanding in *Gylfaginning* is when Gylfi asks who the best and oldest among the gods is. The answer he is given is Alfǫðr, 'All-father'. This Alfǫðr created heaven and earth, rules everything, created man, and gave him an eternal soul. Everyone who believes in him and is virtuous (*réttsiðaðr*) will live with him after death at a place called Gimlé or Vingólf,[30] even though their bodies decay or are burned to ashes.[31] All this sounds very much like it was taken straight from a theological primer akin to *Elucidarius*, and it probably was. At the same time, as Anne Holtsmark has emphasized, this seeming harmony with *Elucidarius* dissolves when Gylfi asks where the dwelling of this Alfǫðr was before the creation of heaven and earth.[32] He is told that Alfǫðr dwelled with the frost giants (i.e. with demons). With this last addition the orthodox edifice collapses, and any medieval reader would immediately understand that this Alfǫðr is not the true God, who most definitely would not have cohabited with demons. The belief of the heathens is thus in many ways correct, but in some respects terribly distorted as well.

After having described how mankind obtained this imperfect but nonetheless not completely false understanding, the shorter version of the prologue turns to Troy. This famous city is situated near the middle of the earth where one finds 'all beauty and splendour and wealth of earthly produce, gold and

---

[28] Faulkes, 'Pagan Sympathy', p. 305.

[29] *Hauksbók*, ed. by Eiríkur Jónsson and Finnur Jónsson, pp. 156–64.

[30] The etymologies of these names are uncertain. Common interpretations are that Gimlé might mean a place where there is shelter from fire (*gim-hlé*) whereas Vingólf is a hall (*gólf*) where one is reunited with friends (*vin-*).

[31] **W**, pp. 10–11.

[32] Holtsmark, *Studier i Snorres mytologi*, pp. 22–26. Just as the student in *Elucidarius* asks whether God was all by himself ('solitarium vitam duxerit') before Creation; see *Elucidarius*, ed. by Firchow and Grimstad, p. 16.

jewels' ('ǫll fegrð ok prýði ok eign jarðar ávaxtar gull ok gimsteinar').[33] In a similar manner Troy itself is described with great grandeur as being 'built much larger than others [that is, 'other cities'] and with greater skill in many respects using the wealth and resources available there' ('miklu meiri gerr en aðrir ok með meira hagleik á marga lund með kostnaði ok fǫngum').[34] Troy is ruled by Priamus. His son Tror is explicitly equated with Þórr and described in dithyrambic terms: in comparison with other men he is as ivory inlaid in oak and his hair is more beautiful than gold. As a twelve-year-old, he does away with his foster-father, seizes his kingdom (Tracia equated with Þrúðheimr, Þórr's abode in Old Norse mythology) and travels the world. On his travels he defeats all the berserkers and giants, an enormous dragon, and many other animals before he marries a most beautiful woman with hair like gold.

Clearly, this is a very positive description, and Klingenberg has shown how the text deliberately, through the characterization of Tror, seeks to emulate and even surpass the descriptions of Aeneas (who laid the ground for the foundation of Rome) in the *Aeneid*.[35] The descendants of Tror through eighteen generations are then enumerated. The last descendant mentioned is Óðinn, who was 'an outstanding person for wisdom and all kinds of accomplishments' ('ágætr maðr af speki ok allri atgervi').[36] He and his wife possess the gift of prophecy, and this enables him to predict that he will become the most honoured of kings if he travels to the northern part of the world; consequently, Óðinn sets out with a large following. Along the way he conquers a great part of Northern Europe and institutes his sons as rulers in the lands he has subjugated. Everywhere they go the indigenous population perceives them as gods rather than men. Finally, they come to Svíþjóð, Sweden, where King Gylfi offers Óðinn power in his realm because of the peace and prosperity that have followed the Asians. Thus Óðinn settles in Sigtún and builds a new Troy. The local population adopts their language in all the lands where the Asians have settled and now rule.

Embedded in this Asian and Óðinnic language was the understanding, imperfect but nonetheless analogous to the Christian revelation, that man had gained by contemplating the workings of nature. Weber writes about the adoption of the language of the Asians in the North:

---

[33] **W**, p. 4. Translation from Snorri Sturluson, *Edda*, trans. by Faulkes, p. 3.
[34] **W**, p. 4. Translation from Snorri Sturluson, *Edda*, trans. by Faulkes, p. 3.
[35] Klingenberg, 'Trór Þórr (Thor) wie Trōs Aeneas'.
[36] **W**, p. 7. Translation from Snorri Sturluson, *Edda*, trans. by Faulkes, p. 3.

The means of expression, the linguistic ability of naming the elements of Creation which God gave Adam, becomes a store of this analogous knowledge of the heathens and also remains this for Christian descendants that constitute a linguistic continuity of this pagan age even after the babylonian ramification of languages. He [Snorri] finds expression of this knowledge in 'the language of poetry'.[37]

Clunies Ross concludes along the same lines that the prologue demonstrates 'a desire to show how the language of early Icelandic poetry expressed the basic tenets of the pre-Christian Scandinavian religion and represented a serious attempt to understand the basic principles of the cosmos'.[38]

The tale of the shorter prologue is a story about a noble people, possessing as good an understanding of the divine as it is possible to obtain while being restricted to earthly understanding. Perhaps they, as stated in the Book of Wisdom, simply erred while seeking the truth. In addition, it is the story about their migration to the North where they took rule over the Northerners who could see that the Asians were their superiors and that subjugation to their regime would be for their own good. The Asians intermarried with the local population who eventually adopted the language of the Asians. The entire description of the Asians in Troy and their emigration is in this way kept in positive terms.

The Story of the Long Version

In the long version of the prologue, **W**, the situation is changed radically and the sympathetic view is much less prominent. The author of this text does not achieve this by making changes to the text that exists, but by the inclusion of three new passages. The three passages that are peculiar to this version give the prologue an entirely different atmosphere and have significant consequences for the reading of the entire prologue,[39] as I will show in the following.

---

[37] 'Damit aber wird ihr Ausdrucksmittel, das von Gott an Adam verliehene sprachliche Bennenungsvermögen für die Phänomene der Schöpfung, auch über die babylonische Sprachverzweigung hinaus als Speicher dieses analogen Wissens der Heiden wichtig und bleibt dies auch für den in der sprachlichen Kontinuität stehenden christl. Nachfahren dieser heidn. Menchenzeitalter. Er [Snorri] findet diese Wissen ausgedrückt in der "Sprache der Dichtung"': Weber, 'Edda, jüngere', p. 402 (my translation).

[38] Clunies Ross, *Skáldskaparmál*, p. 20. See also Strerath-Bolz, *Kontinuität statt Konfrontation*, pp. 63–65.

[39] And naturally for the understanding of the interrelationship between the prologue and

Reading the long version of the prologue as a fully valid and coherent text in its own right, one finds that it is a story about presumption, conquests, and arrogance that lead to the rise of idolatry and loss of language. Seen in the context of the long prologue, the emigration of the Asians and their settling in the North appears much less like a triumphal procession. The text achieves this by narrating three episodes from the history of mankind that are all modulations on the same themes. The main characters in these three stories are (1) Zoroaster,[40] (2) Saturn, and (3) Óðinn. Many parallels can be found between these three episodes, and one of the messages the text intends to convey to its readers/listeners seems to be that history repeats itself. Consequently, the last episode told, the migration of the Asians to the North, is to be understood in terms of the earlier episodes about Zoroaster and Saturn. There is thus no great difference between the achievements of Óðinn and the Æsir on the one hand and of these two other mythological characters on the other (figures that the prologue sees as inventors of idolatry).[41]

The first section unique to **W** follows immediately upon the exposition of the 'argument of design', and how humans arrived at a sort of understanding without divine revelation. The shorter canonical version of the prologue states:

> En til þess at heldr mætti frá segja eða í minni festa, þá gáfu þeir nǫfn með sjǫlfum sér ok hefir þessi átrúnaðr á marga lund breysk, svá sem þjóðirnar skiptusk ok tungurnar greindusk.
>
> [But so as to be better able to give an account of this and fix it in memory, they then gave a name among themselves to everything, and this religion has changed in many ways as nations became distinct and languages branched.][42]

The knowledge gained by observing nature was enshrined in the names which the heathens gave to the elements of nature, and as the names changed, the beliefs changed accordingly. Thus, although there might have been some elements of truth in the heathen understanding of the universe, these elements were distorted as the languages changed. The shorter version of the prologue does not discuss this further and turns to Troy. **W**, on the other hand, uses this

---

the rest of the work as well, but these larger consequences will not be discussed here.

[40] When he appears in Old Norse writings his name is most often given the form *Zoroastres*. Zoroaster was the name commonly used in medieval Europe for Zarathustra.

[41] Whatever the historical origin of Zarathustra, his incarnation in Western medieval literature is of mythical proportions.

[42] **W**, p. 2. Translation from Snorri Sturluson, *Edda*, trans. by Faulkes, p. 2.

statement as an opportunity to unfold the story of the Tower of Babel and, equally important in this context, the rise of idolatry. In **W** these two events are intimately connected.

Genesis (11. 1–9) tells the myth about the fall of the one human language and the rise of the many different tongues. It is brief and enigmatic, and as all long-lived myths it seems to raise more questions than it answers. It therefore has the ability to be interpreted meaningfully in various contradictory ways simultaneously. The myth has been the point of departure for many medieval and post-medieval reflections on the status of the human language(s) and its/their referentiality and conventional nature.[43]

The story of the Tower of Babel in **W** diverges in interesting ways from the biblical and canonical one found in Genesis. The Bible does not name a single individual as the one who took the initiative to build the tower,[44] but in the mainstream patristic tradition this important role is given to Nimrod, who is the great grandson of Noah through Ham and Cush.[45] In **W** the tower is erected by Zoroaster, who is made to be a descendant of Ham, the son of Noah. Initially this substitution of Nimrod with Zoroaster seems a bit surprising, but there is some precedence for this correspondence. One example can be found in the Pseudo-Clementine *Homiliae*.[46] That it was Zoroaster who built the Tower of Babel is, on the other hand, very rarely spelled out; thus, when Borst, in his monumental *Der Turmbau von Babel*, makes brief reference to the exchange of identity in **W**, he sees it as an example of the carelessness, 'Nachlässigkeit', of the author of the prologue.[47]

Throughout Late Antiquity and the Middle Ages Zoroaster was identified with various descendants of Ham, or even with Ham himself.[48] Since Ham received Africa when Noah in his old age divided the world between his three sons, and the Tower of Babel was situated at the Sennaar plain near Babylon (i.e. in Asia), the Hamites had to move. In **W** their move is motivated by greed and pride. The Hamites conquer the whole of Asia, the land Noah had allotted to the Semites, but the world is not enough for their insatiable pride. Zoroaster

---

[43] A fairly recent survey can be found in Fyler, *Language and the Declining World*.

[44] It rather seems to have been a collective decision ('dixitque alter ad proximum suum [...]', Genesis 11. 3).

[45] See von der Toorn and van der Horst, 'Nimrod before and after the Bible'.

[46] Stausberg, *Faszination Zarathushtra*, p. 442. Further examples are mentioned by von der Toorn and van der Horst, 'Nimrod before and after the Bible', pp. 27–28.

[47] Borst, *Der Turmbau von Babel*, p. 783.

[48] See Stausberg, *Faszination Zarathushtra*, pp. 439–502.

therefore initiates the building of the Tower of Babel in order to subdue the heavens to his rule as well. As is well known, God obstructs the construction of the tower by confusing their tongues. Because of mutual misunderstandings they cannot carry their plan to an end, and the seventy-two giants (*risar*) who were the master builders of Babel leave. This does not put an end to the pride of Zoroaster, who builds the city of Babylon, becomes king, and lets himself be venerated as god under the name Baal or Bel. He had many other names as well, 'and', the text underlines, 'as the names multiplied, the truth was lost' ('En sem nǫfnin fjǫlguðusk, þá týndisk með því sannleikrinn').[49] The prologue states that the error of idolatry arose from Zoroaster, along with the sacrifice to animals, the air, the heavenly bodies, and transitory things. This unbelief spread all over the earth. Only one people retained their knowledge, and that was the Hebrews. In other words, the non-revelatory understanding that mankind had achieved by contemplating the workings of nature with their earthly understanding was all but lost after the division of the tongues and the rise of idolatry.

The text does not convey much additional information on the character of Zoroaster, but the readers are informed that he 'laughed before he cried when he came into the world' ('hann hló fyr en grét er hann kom í verǫldina').[50] One meets the tradition of Zoroaster's laughter at birth elsewhere in Old Norse literature as well,[51] and it can be traced back to Pliny's *Naturalis historia* (VII. 16).[52] In the Old Norse text the laughter of Zoroaster might seem like a positive trait in a character who is otherwise only worthy of blame, but as readers of Augustine's *De civitate Dei* (bk XXI, chap. 14)[53] would have been well aware, this laughter was not a portent of any good. Augustine writes that even though Zoroaster was the inventor of magic, not even magic could help him attain happiness in the present life, since King Ninus had defeated him. One reader of Augustine was Vincent of Beauvais (d. 1264) who in his *Speculum historiale* quotes this very passage from Augustine.[54] Vincent is in turn quoted in translation in the Old Norse text *Stjórn I*:

[49] **W**, p. 3. Translation from Snorri Sturluson, *Edda*, trans. by Faulkes, p. 3.

[50] **W**, p. 3. Translation from Snorri Sturluson, *Edda*, trans. by Faulkes, p. 3.

[51] In *Stjórn I* and in a short late fourteenth-century text edited by Kålund in *Alfræði íslenzk*, I under the title *Heimsaldrar*; see *Stjórn*, ed. by Astås, pp. 153–54; *Alfræði íslenzk*, ed. by Kålund and Beckman, I, 49.

[52] Plinius, *Naturalis historia*, ed. by von Janus and Mayhoff.

[53] Augustine, *De civitate Dei*, ed. by Dombart and Kalb.

[54] Vincent of Beauvais, *Speculum historiale*, I. 101.

> Menn segja at einn saman Zoroastres hafi þat gort at hlæja á sínum burðartíma. Ok eigi bendi sá inn skyrsiligi ok inn herfiligi hlátr nǫkkut gott fyrir, þvíat allt at eins varð hann af Nino Serkjakonungi sigraðr í bardaga ok yfirstiginn.
>
> [People say that alone Zoroaster laughed at the time of his birth. And this portentous and wretched laughter did not augur any good, since he was nevertheless defeated in battle and overcome by Ninus the king of the Assyrians.][55]

Augustine (and Vincent and *Stjórn I*) are here following a tradition that goes back at least to Eusebius (d. 399) where Zoroaster is seen as the king of the Baktrians. According to some traditions Ninus is the son of Bel, whom the **W**-prologue identifies with Zoroaster; according to the patristic tradition Bel is simply another name for Saturnus.[56] This equation lived on in the Middle Ages through its inclusion in Isidore of Seville's *Etymologiae* (8, 11, 23).[57] Thus Zoroaster can be identified with Saturnus, and this correspondence provides a nice bridge to the second episode in the **W** prologue that is not found in the shorter versions.

The story told about Saturnus is in many respects the same as the one told about Zoroaster, even though some details are different. This time the story begins with Saturnus, the king of Crete. He was not born king but became one through his extraordinary skills and strength. He was in many ways superior to his contemporaries — bigger, stronger, better looking, wiser — and in particular had prophetic powers. In addition, he was able to make gold out of ore. His line of descent is not given in the prologue, but in other Old Norse writings his genealogy is traced back to Japheth, the son of Noah who was allotted Europe.[58] He causes the crops to grow abundantly, and for all of these reasons the Cretans (and the Macedonians) begin to worship him as a god. Saturnus claims to rule heaven as well as earth. He builds seventy-two cities in Crete and obtains three sons: Jupiter, Neptunus, and Plutus. Jupiter was the most

---

[55] *Stjórn*, ed. by Aståas, p. 154; 'hlæja' is a variant reading from København, Den arnamagnæanske håndskriftsamling, MS AM 226 fol. The main text of the edition reads 'hlegit'.

[56] See, for example, Jerome's commentary on Isaias (Jerome, *Commentariorum in Isaiam prophetam*, ed. by Migne, col. 450): 'Bel, whom the Greeks call Belus and the Latins Saturnus' ('Bel: quem Graeci Belum, Latini Saturnum vocant').

[57] Isidorus, *Etymologiae*, ed. by Lindsay.

[58] For instance, in the *Langfeðgatal frá Nóa til várra konunga* ('Genealogy from Noah to our kings'), in *Alfræði íslenzk*, ed. by Kålund and Beckman, III, 57–58, where the line of descent is as follows: Nói, Jahpet, Japhans, Zechim, Ciprus, Celíus, Saturnus í Krít, Jupiter, … Óðinn, … etc. all the way down to Haraldr hárfagri. See also Klingenberg, 'Odin und die Seinen', pp. 41–45.

powerful of these and for this reason the **W** prologue identifies him with Þórr ('því er Jupiter settr fyrir Þór').[59]

Another Old Norse variant of this tale is found in a version of *The Saga of the Trojans*, *Trojumanna saga β*. There Saturnus conquers heaven and earth.[60] It is not made clear in **W** that Saturnus acts similarly, but it is more than implied by the fact that he divides his kingdom between his three sons in such a way that Jupiter receives Heaven, Neptunus Earth,[61] and Plutus Hell. Jupiter, however, is not satisfied with the realm he was allotted, so he conquers earth and dethrones and castrates his father Saturnus who has to flee to Italy. In Italy Saturnus acts as a kind of cultural hero and teaches the local populace how to cultivate the land. Finally, he changes his name to Njǫrðr to prevent Jupiter from finding him. This is important because the last and shortest section that is unique to **W** consists of three lines that state that Óðinn, after having settled in Sigtún, changes his name and calls himself Njǫrðr.[62] Thus, the three characters of Zoroaster, Saturnus, and Óðinn not only partake in similar stories, but they are connected through their names and allonyms as well.

From Jupiter and Saturn the story now moves on to Troy and a short version of the exodus of the Asians to the North is told. Here Óðinn does not emigrate because he has foreseen a great future in the northern parts of the world, but instead he is chased away by Pompey, just as Saturn was driven away by Jupiter. The glorious expedition to the North is in this way replaced by a much less heroic getaway.

Themes

As should be clear from the synopsis of the text, a number of parallels between the three episodes exist. I will comment briefly on two of them.

Conquests, Migrations, and the Loss of Language

A number of characters in the prologue migrate because they are dissatisfied with the land they have been allotted. Along the way, they conquer new land and overthrow the previous rulers. Zoroaster and the Hamites are discontent

---

[59] **W**, p. 5.

[60] *Trojumanna saga*, pp. 1–2.

[61] Neptunus is not allotted the sea, as one might expect. I consider this a lapsus rather than a deliberate reinterpretation.

[62] **W**, p. 8.

with their land (Africa), and so they conquer the land of the Semites (Asia) and move there. They attempt in vain to conquer Heaven by building the Tower of Babel. Saturnus is presumably thought to be a Japhetide. He is the King of Crete, but it must be assumed that he makes large conquests because he is able to divide his kingdom between his three sons in such a way that Jupiter receives Heaven, Neptunus the Earth, and Plutus Hell. Saturnus, in other words, succeeded where Zoroaster failed, even without building a tower comparable to that of Babel. But it does not help him in the end, since his own son, Jupiter, overthrows him and conquers (a part of) Earth. Saturnus then has to flee to Italy. Tror conquers the land of his foster-father and increases the size of his realm. Finally Óðinn, a descendant of Tror, has to flee to the North along with a host of Asians. On the way he conquers a large part of Northern Europe and installs his sons as rulers of the different lands. He rules Sigtún in Sweden himself.

Antediluvian man forgot the name of God and consequently was incapable of telling their descendants about God. Thus the knowledge of God was lost. In the postdiluvian period before Babel humans had regained part of their previous knowledge from the argument of design and realized that one god governed the whole universe. This knowledge was gained without the Christian revelation and was in some ways imperfect, but nevertheless described in sympathetic terms in the prologue. The prologue attaches great importance to the act of naming in order to remember. So when this new knowledge is gained, humans embed it in the names they give the elements:[63] 'And in order that one could more easily talk about them and fix them in memory, they then gave names among themselves to all things' ('En til þess at heldr mætti frá segja eða í minni festa þá gáfu þeir nǫfn með sjǫlfum sér').[64]

The element of truth in this naming is secondary to that of the primordial names that Adam gave to the animals in Genesis (1. 19–20) when God led them all before him to see what he would call them, and where Adam called all the animals by 'their names' (*nominibus suis*). Augustine pondered on the nature of this original language, even though the subject did not seem to occupy him to a very high degree: 'Is there any point in trying to find out [what language was spoken before the fall of the tower]?' Augustine asks in *De Genesi ad litteram*. The answer is clearly, as he sees it, 'no', but he does think that it was the same language as the one Adam used when he gave the animals 'their names'.[65] Whatever

---

[63] See Strerath-Bolz, 'Sprache und Religion in Prolog der *Snorra Edda*'.

[64] **W**, p. 2. Translation from Snorri Sturluson, *Edda*, trans. by Faulkes, p. 3.

[65] Augustine, *De Genesi ad litteram*, ed. by Migne, IX. 12. 20 (col. 401): 'Quaecumque autem illa lingua fuerit, quid attinet quaerere? Illa certe tunc loquebatur Adam, et in ea lingua, si

'their names' means it seems clear that the names Adam gave the animals were the correct names, or the names they were supposed to have. According to the story of Genesis mankind lost these names at the dispersal of tongues in Babel, but as we saw, the prologue to the prose *Edda* states that mankind had already lost at least the most important of these primordial names before Babel, when they refused to utter the name of God. In this way, the prologue inserts an extra layer of lost knowledge between the Fall and Babel.

After Babel a great number of different languages came into being, but all of these are three times removed from the original language.[66] The same persons and things are referred to under many different names according to the prologue. Examples of these are given at various places in the text. Thus three of Zoroaster's allonyms are listed: Zoroaster, Bel, and Baal. Of Óðinn's names, Oðinn, Uodenn, and Oðenn[67] are mentioned and Priamus as well, but the narrator of the prologue is uncertain as to whether this last name was given by Óðinn himself out of arrogance, or whether it actually stems from the division of tongues ('[Óðinn] kallaði Priamum hafa heitit Óðin [...] ok hvárt er Óðinn sagði þat til metnaðar við sik eða þat hafi svá verit með skipti tunganna þá hafa þó margir fróði menn haft þat fyrir sannenda sǫgn').[68] Other examples are Munon/Mennon, Tror/Þor, Tracia/Þrúðheimr, Lora/Glora, Athra/Annan, and Frigiða/Frigg.[69]

One consequence of the conquest of Asia by Zoroaster and the Hamites was that most of mankind lost the language in which truthful knowledge was embedded, and in a similar way Óðinn's conquest of the North led to the loss of the original northern, but not pre-confused, tongue. These old and original or more original ante-Babylonian languages are, however, not completely lost, since vestiges of them can be found. In Asia among the Hebrews, who kept the original tongue, and in the North, smaller vestiges of the language spoken

---

adhuc usque permanet, sunt istae voces articulatae, quibus primus homo animalibus terrestribus et volatilibus nomina imposuit.'

[66] Only the Hebrews retain the original language and, presumably, the names with the embedded earthly understanding.

[67] These three names appear to be variations on the same name, but the prologue lists them as different names.

[68] **W**, p. 6.

[69] All these examples are from p. 7 of the edition of **W**. The name Frigiða appears to be derived from Phrygia (Klingenberg, 'Odin und die Seinen', p. 57) and not from the Latin *frigida*. Athra and Annan are identical with the feminine and masculine forms repectively in the accusative singular of the quantor *annarr*, 'other, second'.

before the Asian invasion can be found as well. These are preserved in old place names ('Þeir æsir hafa haft tunguna norðr hingat í heim í Nóreg ok Svíþjóð, í Danmǫrk ok Saxland, ok í Englandi eru forn landsheiti eða staða þau er skilja má at af annarri tungu eru gefin en þessi').[70] But in contradistinction to Hebrew the remains of the original northern tongue are only fragmentary.

The Rise of Belief in False Gods

This theme lies at the very heart of the **W** version of the prologue and sets it most clearly apart from the shorter version. Strerath-Bolz underlines that nowhere does the prologue in the shorter version speak of worshipping the immigrated Asians as gods. They are honoured as god*like*, because of their beauty and extensive knowledge, but only as godlike beings and not as gods.[71] The shorter version of the prologue is thus free of the condemning tendency that permeates so many medieval writings on heathen gods. The **W** text of the prologue, on the other hand, is more explicit concerning the connection between the Asians and the rise of belief in false gods in the North, and is thus more in tune with *Gylfaginning*. Indeed the stories about Zoroaster and Saturnus in **W** are mainly concerned with the rise of beliefs in false gods, since both of them let themselves be worshipped as gods: Saturn in Crete by the Cretans and the Macedonians and Zoroaster in Babylon. By aligning these stories with the story of the emigration of Óðinn and the Asians to the North, a view much less sympathetic towards heathendom than the view scholars have of the shorter version of the prologue is apparent.

How, then, did the belief in false gods arise? A favourite explanation among patristic and medieval authors was that extraordinary humans came to be venerated as gods. This rationalizing historicism is known as euhemerism.[72] The euhemerist explanation was used by early Christian apologists, such as Lactantius (d. *c.* 320). In the first book of his *Divinae institutiones* entitled *De falsa religione* ('On the false religion') he explains at great length how the Greek

---

[70] **W**, p. 9.

[71] Strerath-Bolz, *Kontinuität statt Konfrontation*, pp. 66–68.

[72] The inventor of this method was Euhemeros, who around 300 BC wrote an account of an imaginary journey on the Indian Ocean. During his travels he came to the island of Panchaea where, on a golden monument, one could read that Uranos, Kronos, and Zeus had been great kings who were worshipped as gods after their death. Euhemeros's original novel is lost, but his quotations are preserved by other writers, most importantly Diodorus Siculus (d. *c.* 27 BC), and in a Latin translation by Ennius (d. 169 BC) which is lost as well but quoted by later authorities.

and Roman gods were mere humans, not gods, and he uses Saturnus in particular as an example.[73]

The myth about the Roman god Saturnus is told in many contexts and was well known in the Middle Ages. Even though details often vary between different versions of the myth, some motifs reoccur as well.[74] The most stable motifs seem to be the conflict between father and son (Saturn and Jupiter), the castration, and the Italian rule of Saturnus. One of the other standard motifs is somewhat surprisingly not included in **W**: the myth about how Saturn seeks to devour his own children. One of his sons (Jupiter) escapes this fate because Saturn's wife hides him on Crete. In **W** Saturnus is instead made the king of Crete.[75] In Crete, he let himself be venerated as a god, and even though nothing is said about his veneration in Italy, it can be safely assumed that the author of the prologue thought that he was venerated there as well. Saturnus is a complex figure and is said to have introduced law and order and the art of agriculture into Italy as well. For the Romans, the age of Saturnus's rule was a golden age and he was seen as a bearer of culture, for which he was venerated as a god.[76] To other writers, however, more intent on debunking heathen gods, Saturnus was nothing more than a human being with extraordinary skills at best, a bloodthirsty demon demanding a yearly human sacrifice at worst.[77] Alternatively, as in the long version of the prologue, he was the equal of Zoroaster/Nimrod/Baal, the inventor of magic and idolatry.

The account of the rise of idolatry in Babylon in **W** is in some respects quite far removed from the standard versions. The biblical explanations of the origin of idolatry can be found in the Book of Wisdom (14. 12–21). The Old Norse *Stjórn I* summarizes this explanation as follows:

---

[73] Lactantius, *Divinae institutiones*, ed. by Migne, chaps 11–14.

[74] See the survey in Tinkle, 'Saturn of the Several Faces'.

[75] The tradition that Saturn was the King of Crete is found in the *Hauksbók* homily, *On the Origin of Disbelief* (*Hauksbók*, ed. by Eiríkur Jónsson and Finnur Jónsson, p. 158) as well as in the Old English *De falsis diis* by Ælfric (d. *c.* 1010) from which it seems to be derived. But Saturnus's kingship of Crete does not figure prominently in the material surveyed in Tinkle, 'Saturn of the Several Faces'.

[76] He is presented in this way in many places such as in the beginning of the first book of Paul the Deacon's *Historia Romana* (*c.* 770).

[77] Some mythographers, such as the Third Vatican Mythographer (following Fulgentius) derive his name from *saturandus* 'the one that is to be sated': 'Hic itaque in agricultura magnum impendens exercitum, et per annonae praerogationem ad se populos attrahens, a *saturando* Saturnus meruit appellari' (The Third Vatican Mythographer, *De diis gentium et illorum allegoriis*, ed. by Bode, p. 153).

Þrir hlutir eggjuðu menn í fyrstunni mest framm at dýrka ok stunda upp á þess háttar líkneskju, eptir því sem ritat er in Libro Sapientie. It fyrsta var ástúð ok elskhugi lífandi manna eptir sína vini ok frændr [...]. Annat var ótti ok veinurð við þá konunga sem þat vildu gjarna gera ok fram fara. It þriðja var hagleikr ok vandvirkt smiðanna þeira sem líkneskin ok grófu eða pentuðu, svá at menn lysti at líta þau ok sjá þar upp á.

[At first, three things in particular incited man to worshipping and being occupied with this kind of image according to the Book of Wisdom: The first was the love and affection of living men for their [dead] relatives and friends [...]. The second was fear of and the insincerity [i.e. flattery] towards those kings who wanted to do and continue with that. The third was the skill and solicitude of the artisans who also carved or painted the images in such a way that men were eager to watch them and look up to them.][78]

The compiler of *Stjórn I* saw the events at Babylon as an example of the first explanation of the rise of idolatry and does not connect the rise of idolatry with Zoroaster (who in *Stjórn I* and its sources is identified with Ham) but with Ninus, son of Belus.

When Belus died, *Stjórn I* explains, Ninus had a statue made of him for comfort. He honoured the statue so much that he gave peace and great gifts to all men who sought protection from the statue, no matter what crimes they had committed. Because of this, people began to worship the statue, and many began to make statues of their own relatives in imitation of this. They named all the statues Bel after the first, but since people spoke different languages, some called their statues Beel, others Baal, others Baalim, and yet others Beelphegor or Beelzebub.[79] As can be seen, the first variants of the name are the same as can be found in the **W** text of the prologue, although the dead man who was worshipped is not identified with Zoroaster.

The source used by *Stjórn I* for the story about the rise of idolatry is Vincent of Beauvais's *Speculum historiale* (bk 1, chap. 101). Vincent himself mentions *Historia scholastica* by Petrus Comestor (d. 1178) as his source. These two works, *Speculum historiale* and *Historia scholastica*, were among the most important historical reference works in the latter part of the Middle Ages[80] and

---

[78] *Stjórn*, ed. by Astås, pp. 154–55; 'vandvirkt' is a variant reading from København, Den arnamagnæanske håndskriftssamling, MS AM 226 fol. The main text of the edition reads 'vanvirkt'.

[79] *Stjórn*, ed. by Astås, p. 154.

[80] *Historia scholastica* covered the period from the Beginning until the ascension of Christ, whereas *Speculum historiale* aims at covering the history of the world from the Beginning up to 1244.

are often used as sources in Old Norse writings. When the author of *Stjórn I* follows these two works he must be considered to follow the mainstream of the tradition. The same tradition can be found in *Elucidarius*, supposedly written by Honorius Augustodunensis around 1100.[81] *Elucidarius*'s section on the rise of idolatry was even extrapolated and inserted in the important manuscript *Hauksbók* as a separate section under the rubric: 'Here is told how the sacrifice to idols began'. After having briefly related the story of Ninus and Belus, *Elucidarius* continues:

> En þar námu aðrir eptir ok gerðu líkneski eptir ástvinum sínum, eða eptir inum ríkustu konungum dauðum ok buðu lýðinum at blóta þá svá sem rómaborgarmenn Romulum, krítarmenn Þór eða Óðin.
>
> [But others imitated this and made statues of the beloved friends or of the most powerful kings, when they were dead, and commanded people to sacrifice to them, like the Romans [sacrificed to] Romulus and the Cretans to Þórr or Óðinn.][82]

In this way the rise of idolatry in Babylon and on Crete is connected yet again, and this is a work the author of the longer prologue is very likely to have known well.

Conclusion

In their introduction to *Hauksbók*, Eiríkur Jónsson and Finnur Jónsson specifically refer to the **W** text of the prologue to the prose *Edda*, writing that 'the interpolators of the thirteenth and fourteenth centuries rarely exhibited critical acumen'.[83] By taking a closer look at the longer prologue, however, it has become apparent that this criticism is not entirely just. The author of the long version of the prologue possessed a significant amount of learning and was well capable of transforming and applying this learning in his writings. His account of the rise of idolatry deviates somewhat from the standard accounts, but he seems to deviate on purpose in order to be able to line up the stories of the

---

[81] An Old Norse translation of this work counts among the oldest preserved vernacular writings in Iceland. It is preserved in a number of manuscripts, the oldest (København, Den arnamagnæanske håndskriftssamling, AM 674a, 4to) from *c.* 1150–1200 according to Degnbol and others, *Ordbog over det norrøne prosasprog*.

[82] *Elucidarius*, ed. by Firchow and Grimstad, pp. 111–12.

[83] *Hauksbók*, ed. by Eiríkur Jónsson and Finnur Jónsson, p. cii: 'det 13. og 14. årh.s interpolatorer viser sig sjælden som kritiske hoveder'.

three characters of Zoroaster, Saturnus, and Óðinn as essentially three versions of one and the same story. The shorter version of the prologue might well be permeated by a sympathetic attitude towards the northern mythology as the currently favoured interpretations argue. But the longer version of the prologue does much to undermine this by introducing the Tower of Babel, Zoroaster, and Saturnus as parallels to Troy, Sigtún, and Óðinn.

Works Cited

Primary Sources

Alfræði íslenzk: Islandsk encyklopædisk litteratur, ed. by Kristian Kålund and Natanael Beckman, 3 vols (København: Møller, 1908–18), I: *Cod. mbr. AM. 194, 8vo.*, ed. by Kristian Kålund (1908); III: *Landalýsingar m. fl.*, ed. by Kristian Kålund (1917–18)

Augustine, *De civitate Dei*, ed. by Bernard Dombart and Alphonse Kalb, Corpus Christianorum Series Latina, 47 (Turnhout: Brepols, 1955)

——, *De Genesi ad litteram*, in *Patrologiae cursus completus: series latina*, ed. by Jacques-Paul Migne, 221 vols (Paris: Migne, 1844–64), XXXIV (1845), cols 219–46

Codex Wormianus: MS. no. 242 fol. in the Arnamagnean Collection in the University Library of København, ed. by Sigurður Nordal (København: Munksgaard, 1931)

Dares Phrygius, *De excidio Troiae historia*, ed. by Ferdinand Otto Meister (Leipzig: Teubner, 1873)

Elucidarius, ed. by Evelyn Scherabon Firchow and Kaaren Grimstad (Reykjavík: Stofnun Árna Magnússonar, 1989)

Hauksbók, ed. by Eiríkur Jónsson and Finnur Jónsson, 3 vols (København: Thiel, 1892–96)

Isidorus, *Etymologiae*, ed. by W. N. Lindsay (Oxford: Oxford University Press, 1951)

Jerome, *Commentariorum in Isaiam prophetam libri duodeviginti*, in *Patrologiae cursus completus: series latina*, ed. by Jacques-Paul Migne, 221 vols (Paris: Migne, 1844–64), XXIV (1845)

Lactantius, *Divinae institutiones*, in *Patrologiae cursus completus: series latina*, ed. by Jacques-Paul Migne, 221 vols (Paris: Migne, 1844–64), VI (1844), cols 111–52

Plinius, *Naturalis historiae libri XXXVII*, ed. by Ludwig von Janus and Karl Friedrich Theodor Mayhoff (Stutgardiae: Teubner, 1967)

Snorri Sturluson, *Edda*, ed. by Finnur Jónsson (København: Gyldendal, 1931)

——, *Edda*, trans. by Anthony Faulkes (London: Dent, 1987)

——, *Edda: Prologue and Gylfaginning*, ed. by Anthony Faulkes (London: Clarendon Press, 1982)

——, *Edda Snorra Sturlusonar: Codex Wormianus AM 242, fol.*, ed. by Finnur Jónsson (København: Gyldendal, 1924)

——, *Edda Snorra Sturlusonar: Edda Snorronis Sturlæi*, ed. by Det Arnamagnæanske Kommision, 3 vols (København: Legatus Arnamagnæani, 1848–87)

——, *Heimskringla*, ed. by Bjarni Aðalbjarnarson, Íslensk fornrit, 26–28, 3 vols (Reykjavík: Hið íslenzka fornritafélag, 1941–51)

——, *Heimskringla: History of the Kings of Norway*, trans. by Lee M. Hollander (Austin: University of Texas Press, 1964)

——, *Snorre Sturlasons Edda: Uppsala-handskriften DG 11*, ed. by Anders Grape, Gottfrid Kallstenius, and Olof Thorell, 2 vols (Stockholm: Almqvist & Wiksell, 1962–77)

Stjórn, ed. by Reidar Astås (Oslo: Riksarkivet, 2009)

The Third Vatican Mythographer, *De diis gentium et illorum allegoriis*, ed. by Georg Heinrich Bode, in *Scriptores rerum mythicarum Latini tres Romae nuper reperti*, 2 vols (Celle: Schulze, 1834), I, 152–256

Trojumanna saga, ed. by Jonna Louis-Jensen, Editiones Arnanagmæanæ, A.8 (København: Munksgaard, 1963)

Vincent of Beauvais, *Speculum historiale*, vol. IV of *Speculum quadruplex sive Speculum maius* (Graz: Akademische Druck u. Verlagsanstalt, 1965)

Secondary Works

Beck, Heinrich, 'Zur Diskussion über den Prolog der Snorra-Edda', in *Poetik und Gedächtnis: Festschrift für Heiko Uecker zum 65. Geburtstag*, ed. by Karin Hoff and others (Frankfurt a.M.: Lang, 2004), pp. 145–54

Boer, R. C, 'Studier over Snorra Edda', *Aarbøger for nordisk oldkyndighed og historie*, 14 (1924), 145–272

Borst, Arno, *Der Turmbau von Babel: Geschichte der Meinungen über Ursprung und Vielfalt der Sprachen und Völker*, 4 vols (Stuttgart: Hiersemann, 1957–63)

Bumke, Joachim, 'Der unfeste Text: Überlegungen zur Überlieferungsgeschichte und Textkritik der höfischen Epik im 13. Jahrhundert', in *'Aufführung' und 'Schrift' in Mittelalter und früher Neuzeit*, ed. by Jan-Dirk Müller (Stuttgart: Metzler, 1996), pp. 118–29

Cerquiglini, Bernhard, *In Praise of the Variant: A Critical History of Philology*, trans. by Betsy Wing (Baltimore: Johns Hopkins University Press, 1999)

Clunies Ross, Margaret, *Skáldskaparmál: Snorri Sturluson's ars poetica and Medieval Theories of Language* (Odense: Odense Universitetsforlag, 1987)

Degnbol, Helle, and others, eds, *Ordbog over det norrøne prosasprog*, 3 vols (København: Den Arnamagnæanske Kommision, 1989–2004)

Dronke, Peter, and Ursula Dronke, 'The Prologue of the Prose *Edda*: Explorations of a Latin Background', in *Sjötíu ritgerðir helgaðar Jakobi Benediktssyni*, ed. by Einar G. Pétursson and Jónas Kristjánsson (Reykjavík: Stofnun Árna Magnússonar, 1977), pp. 153–76

Faulkes, Anthony, 'Descent from the Gods', *Mediaeval Scandinavia*, 11 (1978–79), 92–125

——, 'Pagan Sympathy: Attitudes to Heathendom in the Prologue to *Snorra Edda*', in *Edda: A Collection of Essays*, ed. by Robert J. Glendinning and Haraldur Bessason (Winnipeg: University of Manitoba Press, 1983), pp. 283–314

Fyler, John M., *Language and the Declining World in Chaucer, Dante and Jean de Meun* (Cambridge: Cambridge University Press, 2007)

Guðrún Nordal, *Tools of Literacy: The Role of Skaldic Verse in Icelandic Textual Culture of the Twelfth and Thirteenth Centuries* (Toronto: University of Toronto Press, 2001)

Holtsmark, Anne, *Studier i Snorres mytologi* (Oslo: Universitetsforlaget, 1964)

Johansson, Karl G., 'Skriptorier och kompilationer: interpolationerna i Snorra Eddas prolog i Wormsbók', in *Frejas psalter: en psalter i 40 afdelinger til brug for Jonna Louis-Jensen*, ed. by Bergljót S. Kristjánsdóttir and Peter Springborg (København: Arnamagnæanske institut, 1997), pp. 90–96

——, *Studier i Codex Wormianus: skrifttradition och avskriftsverksamhet vid ett isländskt skriptorium under 1300-talet* (Göteborg: Acta universitatis Gothoburgensis, 1997)

Klingenberg, Heinz, 'Odin und die Seinen: Altisländischer Gelehrter Urgeschichte anderer Teil', *Alvíssmál*, 2 (1993), 31–80

——, 'Trór Þórr (Thor) wie Trōs Aeneas: *Snorra Edda* Prolog, Vergil-Rezeption und Altisländische Gelehrte Urgeschichte', *Alvíssmál*, 1 (1992), 17–54

Stausberg, Michael, *Faszination Zarathushtra: Zoroaster und die Europäische Religionsgeschichte der Frühen Neuzeit* (Berlin: de Gruyter, 1998)

Strerath-Bolz, Ulrike, *Kontinuität statt Konfrontation: der Prolog der Snorra Edda und die Gelehrsamkeit des Mittelalters* (Frankfurt a.M.: Lang, 1991)

——, 'Sprache und Religion in Prolog der *Snorra Edda*', in *Snorri Sturluson: Beiträge zu Werk und Rezeption*, ed. by Hans Fix, Ergänzungsbände zum Reallexikon der germanischen Altertumskunde, 18 (Berlin: de Gruyter, 1998), pp. 267–74

Tinkle, Theresa, 'Saturn of the Several Faces: A Survey of Medieval Mythographic Traditions', *Viator*, 18 (1987), 287–307

Toorn, K. von der, and P. W. van der Horst, 'Nimrod before and after the Bible', *Harvard Theological Review*, 83 (1990), 1–29

Weber, Gerd Wolfgang, 'Edda, jüngere', in *Reallexikon der germanischen Altertumskunde*, ed. by Heinrich Beck, Dieter Geuenich, and Heiko Steuer, 2nd edn, 35 vols (Berlin: de Gruyter, 1973–2008), VI: *Donar-þórr–Einbaum* (1986), pp. 394–421

Ziolkowski, Jan, 'Texts and Textuality, Medieval and Modern', in *Der unfeste Text: Perspektiven auf eine literatur- und kulturwissenschaftlichen Leitbegriff*, ed. by Barbara Sabel and André Bucher (Würzburg: Königshausen & Neumann, 2001), pp. 109–31

Edda and 'Oral Christianity': Apocryphal Leaves of the Early Medieval Storyworld of the North

Henrik Janson

Introduction

Until the end of the eleventh century Scandinavia was still to a large extent an unknown and frightening world to the Western Church. From around 1100, however, under the age of the crusading movement, it quickly became a firmly integrated part of Latin Christianity and of the culture of Carolingian heritage. This transformation of Northern Europe in the high Middle Ages received prominent literary expression in Saxo Grammaticus's Latin chronicle, *Gesta Danorum*, from the decades around 1200, and in the explosion of vernacular history writing in Iceland in the first half of the thirteenth century. A central theme in this literature is indeed the integration and conversion of the indigenous culture of the North into the Christianity of the Latin Church. It might even be fair to say that the central assignment for the authors of these texts was to write the northern past into the history of Western Europe and of the Latin Church.

The most original contribution to this project was without doubt Snorri Sturluson's *Edda*, from the 1220s. Snorri tried to make the poetry and the referential system of the Old Norse poetic tradition understandable to young poets in his own time. Since the seventeenth century, however, Snorri's *Edda* has primarily been used as a source for the reconstruction of a pre-Christian

---

Henrik Janson, University of Gothenburg, Associate Professor, henrik.janson@history.gu.se

Scandinavian, Germanic, and even Indo-European past. Together with the so-called *Poetic Edda* — a fairly loose collection of poems, mainly brought together around 1240 — Snorri's *Edda* came to be fundamental for German Romanticism.[1]

Since the publication of Jacob Grimm's *Deutsche Mythologie* in 1835 — the first[2] of its kind in an extensive row of monographs with slightly varying titles on the same subject — the romantic perspective on these sources has held a firm grip on the interpretations of the pre-Christian religion of the Scandinavian North. Grimm's mythology was founded in a fierce scientific battle over the source value of the Eddic material, a battle that had already been fought in 1812 in the once famous clash between the young Grimm brothers and the first professor in history at the University of Berlin, Friedrich Rühs.[3] To the Grimms the *Edda* material, and in particular the Eddic poetry, was a pure expression of the pre-Christian Germanic 'Geist des Volkes', untouched by Christian influences. To Friedrich Rühs it was a product of Christian culture and erudition ('das Werk der Cultur und Erlernungs'), a creation of the Icelandic Middle Ages.[4] As the Grimms and Romanticism won a complete victory in this battle, the dominating opinion to the present day has been that the Eddic material represents a pre-Christian, Old Norse Germanic society and should be interpreted in the context of this society unless otherwise proved, even though from a methodological point of view the opposite position should be demanded, that is, that the Eddic stories represent thirteenth-century Icelandic society unless otherwise proved.

---

[1] For the structure and different versions of the *Edda*, see further Wellendorf's article in the present volume.

[2] This might, of course, be a matter of discussion since N. F. S. Grundtvig had already treated the same subject in monographic form in 1808 and once more in 1832; compare Auken, *Sagas spejl*. However, Grundtvig did not set the standards for the modern scientific genre of monographs in the field, whereas Jacob Grimm's work and method did.

[3] See most recently Fidjestøl, *The Dating of Eddic Poetry*, pp. 30–45.

[4] Rühs, *Die Edda*, p. 99. Compare Meyer, *'Völuspa': eine Untersuchung*, p. 2: 'Niemals sind die Grimms erregter gewesen als in diesem Streit um das Allerheiligste. Das Würdigste in die Welt, die Poesie, die von Anbeginn die Höhe und Tiefe der Natur umfasse und die sich auch in der *Edda* so Eingreifend äussere, schien ihnen von unsauberen schadenfrohen Hände angetastet' (Never were the Grimms more enraged than in this battle over the Holy of Holies. The worthiest in the world, the poetry, that from the very beginning comprised the heights and depths of nature and was also thoroughly expressed in the *Edda*, appeared to them as touched by unclean, malicious hands).

Germanic Volksgeist *or Latin Learning?*

One consequence of the Romantic triumph in the nineteenth century was that the great disputes about Snorri's *Edda* in the twentieth century were not about whether there was an orally transmitted Germanic mythology from the pagan Scandinavian past behind its stories or not, or whether this oral tradition had played any significant part in what Snorri wrote. Instead the main issue was to which extent Snorri, the great recorder of Germanic mythology, had been afflicted in his writing by influences and erudition from his contemporary Latin Christianity.

In 1908 Andreas Heusler demonstrated that quite a vast amount of such learned influence existed in the preserved version of Snorri's *Edda*, but he claimed that almost none of it — especially not the obviously very 'learned' *Prologue* to the work — came from Snorri's hand, but were later extensions and interpolations in his text.[5] This line of argument — a 'cleansing' so to speak of Snorri and his texts from foreign influences — opened for Hans Kuhn's Nazi-era idea that Snorri was really not a Christian at all, but in fact still believed in the old Germanic religion about which he wrote.[6]

In opposition to Kuhn's extreme standpoint, in 1950 Walter Baetke accepted the *Prologue* as Snorri's own work, and argued for a significant amount of Christian theology within Snorri's treatment of the pre-Christian history and religion of the North.[7] In this he was followed by Anne Holtsmark and Gerd Wolfgang Weber, for example, while Ursula and Peter Dronke and Margaret Clunies Ross tried to show that when writing the *Edda* Snorri was deeply influenced by highly modern Neoplatonist, scholastic ideas in his contemporary Christian Europe.[8]

This 'theologisierung der *Edda*', as Klaus von See has entitled it,[9] was indeed a strong trend within the scholarship on Snorri's *Edda* in the second half of the twentieth century, but in a broader perspective it was nonetheless quite a marginal phenomenon with little effect on how most scholars — historians of religion, archaeologists, philologists, and even literary historians — actually used

---

[5] Heusler, *Die gelehrte Urgeschichte im altisländischen Schrifttum*.

[6] Kuhn, 'Das nordgermanische *Heidentum*'.

[7] Baetke, *Die Götterlehre der Snorra-Edda*.

[8] Holtsmark, *Studier i Snorres mytologi*; Dronke and Dronke, 'The Prologue of the Prose *Edda*'; Weber, 'Siðaskipti'; Weber, 'Intellegere historiam'; Clunies Ross, *Skáldskaparmál*.

[9] Von See, *Mythos und Theologie*, p. 17; compare von See, 'Zum Prolog der Snorra *Edda*'.

Snorri's *Edda* as a source for pre-Christian Scandinavian culture and religion. And not even among the *theologisierung* scholars were there any doubts that once the learned elements in Snorri's *Edda* had been picked out, there was a considerable amount of pure pagan culture left to which the Eddic and Scaldic poetry served as testimonies. None of these scholars, therefore, came even close to the position of Friedrich Rühs, that is, denying that Snorri had any significant amount of orally preserved material from the pre-Christian Germanic North at his disposal. So even if Baetke and his followers did indeed open the possibility for Latin learning in Snorri's *Edda*, they still left a significant amount of undiluted Germanic *Volksgeist* behind for the reconstructionists of Old Norse religion and culture to work with.

Latin Learning or Oral Tradition?

Between the world wars one isolated voice in Germany moved against the powerful mainstream. The renowned Germanist Eugen Mogk began to argue early in the 1920s that Snorri did not actually possess much more source material than had been preserved to modern times. According to Mogk, it was evident from 'the purely didactic parts of the Edda' that Snorri's reference material is almost entirely in our possession as well.[10] On this basis Mogk tried to display the impressive amount of creativity that Snorri had shown in shaping a new genre: 'mythological novels' ('novellistsiche Darstellungen mytologischer Stoffe') as Mogk called them. In Reykholt (and Stafaholt) Snorri had, according to Mogk, founded nothing less than a 'Workshop of creative intellectual and literary activity' ('Werkstatt geistiges Schaffens und literarischer Tätigkeit'), and the members of this 'Werkstatt' — a real mythological 'school' — were introduced to Snorri's new 'genre of fictitious story-telling' ('Dichtungsart'), that is, 'the mythological novel' as it is found in the *Edda* and the *Ynglingasaga*.[11] What was not plain fantasy, on the basis of — at best — mythological fragments, was interpretation and very free embellishment of allusions to 'myths' made in skaldic poetry.[12]

---

[10] Mogk, *Novellistische Darstellung mythologischer Stoffe Snorris*, p. 10.

[11] Mogk, *Novellistische Darstellung mythologischer Stoffe Snorris*, pp. 9–11.

[12] Mogk, *Novellistische Darstellung mythologischer Stoffe Snorris*; compare Mogk, 'Die Uberlieferungen von Thors Kampf'; Mogk, *Zur Bewertung der Snorra Edda*.

This very challenging new perspective was drowned, however, in the intellectual world of Germany and Germanic scholarship in the 1930s, though it did trigger Hans Kuhn's extremist position of 1942. But perhaps more surprisingly it did not, as one might have expected, float up to the surface of discussion in the post-war era either, even if it did offer inspiration to Walter Baetke and his *theologisierung* school.[13] The reason for this was probably the authority of Grimm's Romantic perspective on these sources within many disciplines, in combination with the great dominance in the second half of the twentieth century of the French historian of religion Georges Dumézil, through whom the perspectives of the interwar period could be quite acrobatically channelled into the history of Germanic and Old Norse religion.[14]

In recent years there has been an intensified interest in 'oral culture' within Scandinavian studies and the relationship between orality and literacy in Scandinavia, and especially in Iceland. This is part of an international trend enforced by studies such as Michael Clanchy's *From Memory to Written Record* (1979) and Walter Ong's *Orality and Literacy* (1982), but in connection with the literacy of the thirteenth-century Icelandic *Schriftkultur*, the new trend has caused a drift even further away from Mogk. The confrontation — or maybe some would rather prefer amalgamation — of orality and literacy seems surprisingly often to be understood not only as a clash between orality and literacy in the traditional sense, but as a confrontation between pagan orality and Christian literacy. One of the more conscious and elaborated defences for such a position is Gisli Sigurðsson's study *The Medieval Icelandic Saga and Oral Tradition: A Discourse on Method* from 2004.[15]

With reference to the authority Georges Dumézil,[16] Gisli Sigurðsson also brusquely rejects Eugen Mogk as well as Walter Baetke and his follow-

---

[13] Compare Lindow, 'Mythology and Mythography', p. 36: 'These hypotheses now seem exaggerated, but they had the benefit of drawing attention to Snorri's mythography.'

[14] See Janson, 'The Organism Within'.

[15] Sigurðsson's book was first published in Icelandic under the title *Túlkun íslendingasagna í ljósi munnlegrar hefðar: tilgáta um aðferð* by the Árni Magnússon Institute in Reykjavik 2002, and then translated into English and published by the Milman Perry Collection of Oral Literature at Harvard University as the second volume in the series Publications of the Milman Parry Collection of Oral Literature 2004. Consequently it was published, and granted some authority, by two of the leading institutes in the field.

[16] According to Sigurðsson, in 1948 Dumézil had 'demonstrated that various central ideas in Snorri's myths reflect themes going back to common Indo-European mythology' — a view with which Sigurðsson obviously wholeheartedly agrees; see Gísli Sigurðsson, *The Medieval Icelandic Saga and Oral Tradition*, p. 7 n. 9. He fails to mention, however, that Dumézil's

ers.[17] He states quite frankly that there is no 'Latin-based learning' at all in Snorri's *Edda*. Indeed, 'the bulk of the material contained in his [i.e. Snorri's] work and the ideological background holding it together come from a native tradition of learning on poetry and myths that Snorri could hardly have acquired other than from the lips of those who had mastered the tradition'.[18]

That the stories of Snorri's *Edda* came from the lips of those who mastered the tradition and not from the pen of a creative author is a central idea to those scholars who want to use the Eddic literature without paying too much attention to the fact that it was written in the thirteenth century. This makes it possible on the one hand to minimize the role of the 'writers' of the thirteenth century, while enhancing the strength and importance of 'native' oral tradition on the other. Snorri and other thirteenth-century 'writers' are consequently (again) turned into mere tools for 'the domestic tradition'. Accordingly, Latin learning plays no role in Snorri's *Edda* according to Sigurðsson, and neither does in fact Snorri himself. We are thus back in a situation where Snorri is actually reduced to nothing but a folklorist who is carefully gathering and taking down on parchment the 'native tradition' from the pagan Icelandic, Germanic and indeed Indo-European past.

---

methodology and ideological basis (for example, Momigliano, 'Georges Dumézil and the Trifunctional Approach'; Ginzburg, '*Mitologia germanica* e nazismo'; Arvidsson, *Aryan Idols*; Janson, 'The Organism Within') just as the empirical founding of his daring and extremely pretentious model (for example, Page, 'Dumézil Revisited'; Wiseman, *Remus: A Roman Myth*, pp. 18–30), indeed his entire scholarly approach (Belier, *Decayed Gods*), has been under severe criticism for several decades now, and that those who still follow his theories have come to be regarded more or less as a sect unsusceptible to scholarly arguments (von See, *Europa und der Norden im Mittelalter*, p. 144). Renfrew speaks of 'a closed and rather cosy mythological world [...] a golden land [...] rooted neither in time nor in space', which seems to be a modern version of the Grimms' Romantic past for the same groups; see Renfrew, *Archaeology and Language*, p. 286. Wouter W. Belier, who has undertaken the most extensive examination of Dumézil's working methods, concluded, after an extraordinarily thorough analysis, that the theory of a 'tripartite' structure of Indo-European societies might perhaps be of aesthetic value for some, but it has no scholarly validity (Belier, *Decayed Gods*). There are in fact very good reasons today to doubt whether such a thing as a 'common Indo-European mythology' has ever existed, or if it is merely a dream about an ideal origin for the bourgeoisie of the western world in the nineteenth and twentieth centuries (Arvidsson, *Aryan Idols*; compare Lincoln, *Theorizing Myth*). At the very least, the days are certainly gone when the authority of Dumézil's work could be taken for granted.

[17] Startlingly overlooking von See; compare for example von See, *Texte und Thesen*.

[18] Gísli Sigurðsson, *The Medieval Icelandic Saga and Oral Tradition*, p. 9.

As in the days of Frierich Rühs and the Grimms, the central reason for the greatly divergent opinions on Snorri's *Edda* still mainly seems to dwell in the widely diversified pictures of the surrounding thirteenth-century society. From the early Romantic Era to the present day there has been a strong tendency among scholars from different fields to diminish the role of the 'learned' in the thirteenth century and/or to picture a strong and deep heathen tradition in the broader layers of society. In fact since Friedrich Rühs's great defeat under the attack of the Grimms the dominating — indeed for long periods unquestioned — position has been that the *Eddas* contained an ancient pre-Christian 'native tradition' which could form the basis for the reconstruction of pagan Germanic religion.

However, when Sophus Bugge in 1867 definitively proved that *Sæmundr Fróði* had nothing to do with the preserved Eddic material, he suddenly opened up a wide time span between the end of the pagan era in the early eleventh century and the recording of the Eddic poems in the 1230s or 1240s. For at least a hundred years of this period Iceland had been a thoroughly Christian society, fully comparable to any other part of Christian Europe; furthermore, this was an age of extreme religious intolerance — the age of the Crusades when monasteries and churches were built and rebuilt everywhere and when continuous warfare was legitimized in every possible way — not only against Muslims and other pagans, but also against the slightest divergences within Christendom itself. It seems very hard to explain how a broad and deep heathen tradition would have been able to survive in such an intolerant intellectual milieu. On the contrary, there are good reasons to conclude that nothing of the kind existed at the end of the twelfth century.[19]

From a historian's perspective it seems that the focus of the discussion has to shift. The central question is not how learned and Christian Snorri and other literary active Icelanders in the thirteenth century were, but rather how pagan[20] the 'native tradition' was with which they were dealing, and how Snorri and his contemporaries treated this tradition when they put it down on parchment. And, most important of all: Why did they put it down on parchment?

---

[19] See for example Orri Vésteinsson, *The Christianization of Iceland*, p. 62: 'The only thing we know is that Gunnlaugr seems confident that there were no remnants of heathendom in his own time.'

[20] Compare Janson, 'What Made the Pagans Pagans?' (2003); Janson, 'What Made the Pagans Pagans?' (2010).

An Illustrative Example: Thórr's Fishing Expedition

One of the more famous scenes in the Eddic literature is when Thórr, with the giant Hymir or Ymir by his side in a boat, catches the Midgard serpent on the hook and in a ferocious struggle manages, while his feet go through the bottom of the boat, to pull the beast up to the surface where their flashing eyes meet. The story seems to have been widely known in Northern Europe during the early and high Middle Ages. It appears in several sources from different times and places, which makes the story especially suited to illuminating problems related to the religious and cultural context in which we are to interpret the stories of the *Eddas*.

Two more extensive literary accounts of this episode exist: it is told in the part of Snorri's *Edda* called *Gylfaginning*, and it is also treated in a poem called *Hymiskviða* within the so-called *Poetic Edda*. The dating of *Hymiskviða* is not altogether agreed upon among scholars, but good arguments speak in favour of its composition a few years after Snorri had put together his *Edda* in the middle of the 1220s. From a manuscript point of view it can be traced back to a lost source from 1230–40,[21] and there is nothing to indicate that it had existed earlier than this, even if the subject itself, the story of a fishing expedition, did.[22]

In addition to these two sources references to the story are also found in skaldic poetry, attributed to five different poets who are claimed to have lived in the ninth and tenth centuries, that is, allegedly before the Christianization of the North. However, these poems and stanzas are preserved only in Snorri's *Edda*. In other words: our only source for these verses is Snorri, or in fact the preserved manuscripts of his *Edda*, and consequently it is impossible to know exactly how they might have looked in the ninth and tenth centuries.[23]

Modern scholarship is largely in agreement about the religious context of the story of Thórr's fishing expedition. In the 1950s both Georges Dumézil and Franz Rolf Schröder found it to be an ancient Indo-European monster-killing

---

[21] Lindblad, 'Poetiska Eddans förhistoria och skrivskicket i Codex regius'.

[22] Reichardt, 'Hymiskviða: Interpretation, Wortschatz, Alter'; Wolf, 'Sehweisen und Darstellungsfragen in der Gylfaginning', pp. 14–19; Meulengracht Sørensen, 'Thor's Fishing Expedition', p. 260. Compare Janson, 'Snorre, Tors fiskafänge och frågan om den religionshistoriska kontexten', pp. 45–50.

[23] These skaldic stanzas, it should also be noted, only allude to details, or describe pictures of the story, and consequently they give little information about the religious context in which they are to be interpreted.

myth.[24] On this basis Otto Gschwantler, in the memorable year 1968 — in the Festschrift to Otto Höfler nota bene — declared that it was indisputable that the story was 'eine alte Germanische vorstellung'.[25] In an influential study in more recent years, Preben Meulengracht Sørensen identified two different levels in the development of the myth. Originally its 'fundamental meaning' was the preservation of the 'cosmic balance', but later, under the influence of Christianity around the year 1000 AD, it had developed into a more traditional dragon-killing myth.[26]

Consequently, what was Indo-European to Dumézil and Schröder was later a Christian influence to Meulengracht Sørensen. But in spite of this almost diametrical opposition between the two interpretations, these scholars all shared a common understanding in that what appeared on Icelandic parchment in the high Middle Ages was ancient pagan Old Norse, Germanic, or even Indo-European lore. The point at issue was not how the story of Thórr's fishing expedition was to be interpreted, because that was open for discussion. The really controversial point, which in a tacit understanding was turned into a fundamental precondition, was that the 'myth' had been a part of that old pre-Christian world before the year 1000 AD and was to be interpreted in that context.

In his discussion of Thórr's fishing expedition Gisli Sigurðsson concludes that Snorri knew not only the poetry but also the stories themselves as part of a living oral tradition, which was familiar to him and his contemporaries in thirteenth-century Iceland. Indeed, he goes even further than his predecessors and states that Snorri's

> prose retellings can stand as original source every bit as much as the poems he quotes from. […] Before modern scholars start accusing Snorri of 'misunderstanding' or 'misinterpreting' something 'correct' or 'original', we need to examine closely exactly what he and his contemporaries say in their writings and take it as genuine evidence of the tradition as it existed in their times.[27]

Commenting on the whole complex of sources to Thórr's fishing expedition in Northern Europe he states:

> Putting all the evidence together, the story of Þórr's fishing expedition emerges as one of the best known and best attested myths of the Scandinavian heathendom.

---

[24] Dumézil, *Les Dieux des indo-européens*, pp. 24–26; Schröder, 'Das Hymirlied'; compare Schröder, 'Indra, Thor und Herakles'.

[25] Gschwantler, 'Christus, Thor und die Midgardschlange', p. 150.

[26] Meulengracht Sørensen, 'Thor's Fishing Expedition'.

[27] Gísli Sigurðsson, *The Medieval Icelandic Saga and Oral Tradition*, p. 16.

> The sheer variety of the sources that refer to it provide an unambiguous indication that the myth rests on ancient roots and almost certainly, in some form, constituted an element in the belief system of the peoples of the North prior to the arrival of Christianity. It is rare to be able to provide such strong grounds for believing in the existence of a Scandinavian myth as in this instance. The case thus serves to increase our general faith that the extant written sources for Scandinavian heathendom must be in some way linked to a living oral tradition going back to ancient times. This in turn acts as a powerful counter argument to all notions that Snorri and his contemporaries were in the habit of 'making up' their myths themselves.[28]

In other words, according to Sigurðsson the story is a myth from pre-Christian times and can as such be used as a first-hand source for the pre-Christian religion of the North. This is furthermore proof that other stories from thirteenth-century Iceland are valid as well.

However persuasive this reasoning may seem to students of Old Norse religion and culture, a number of criticisms can be levelled against it. Firstly, there are some important studies that are overlooked by Sigurðsson, which reveal quite a different understanding of what Snorri actually does. In the following I will try to illustrate this by looking at the material once more.

King Gylfi Is Deceived

'According to Snorri' is an often used phrase when scholars refer to the stories told in Snorri's *Edda*. However, the conditions are in fact much more complicated than this. The story of Thórr's fishing expedition is found in the part of his *Edda* called *Gylfaginning*, which means 'the tricking of Gylfi'.[29] In this scene in *Gylfaginning* King Gylfi of Sweden comes to the Æsir in Asgard disguised as an old man to find out the reason for their success. The Æsir, led by the magician and prophet Óðinn, however, foresaw his arrival and confront him with an illusory castle and an enormously high hall building over which Gylfi could hardly see. The door slams hard just behind him as he enters the hall, and Gylfi is led to the king of the Æsir, who turns out to be a kind of tripartite character with the strange names 'High', 'Just-as-high', and 'Third'.

---

[28] Gísli Sigurðsson, *The Medieval Icelandic Saga and Oral Tradition*, p. 13.

[29] Guðrun Nordal has emphasized the importance of not seeing Snorri's *Edda* as an all too fixed textual unit, but rather as parts under more or less constant revision; see Guðrun Nordal, *Tools of Literacy*, and also Wellendorf in the present volume. In the case of the *Prologue*, compare Beck, 'Zur Diskussion über den Prolog der Snorra-Edda', and literature cited there.

A dialogue takes place in which Gylfi questions the peculiar tripartite king of the Æsir about the nature of things and about the gods and the powers that rule the world. In the beginning the answers he receives closely resemble fundamental Christian doctrines, but gradually they drift further and further away from Christian teaching. King Gylfi is fed stories, each one stranger than the other, about Óðinn and Thórr, about other gods and goddesses, and about giants and monsters. When the questions begin to reach the end of the world, Gylfi suddenly hears a great noise. Looking around he notices that the hall and the castle are gone, and he finds himself standing alone in an open field: 'then he went off on his way and came back to his kingdom and told of the events he had seen and heard about. And from his account these stories passed from one person to another'.[30]

'According to Snorri', then, it is the king of the Æsir, that is, the historical individual Óðinn, who in the middle of a spectacular illusionary trick introduces the stories about the gods to a king of Sweden who brought them back to Sweden from where they were later transmitted for many generations in the North.

Thórr's Fishing Expedition before Snorri

The earliest place we can identify the story about Thórr's fishing expedition with any certainty, however, is not in Iceland nor in Scandinavia, but in a picture on a stone from the early tenth century in the church of Gosforth in north-western England.[31] The context here is not pagan but Christian. The same is true for another depiction of the story found on the Altuna stone in Uppland.[32] This rune stone, which is a century or so younger than the Gosforth stone, was designed by people who we know were Christians, and the style is typical for other Christian rune stones in eleventh-century Uppland. Accordingly, the motif seems here to have also been chosen because it made sense and was familiar in a Christian context.

But this, in fact, is not very surprising. That the story could be interpreted in a Christian context is well known from literary sources as well.[33] Already in

---

[30] Snorri Sturluson, *Edda*, ed. by Finnur Jónsson, p. 76; translation Snorri Sturluson, *Edda*, trans. by Faulkes, p. 57.

[31] Bailey and Cramp, *Corpus of Anglo-Saxon Stone Sculpture*, pp. 108–09.

[32] *Upplands runinskrifter*, ed. by Wessén and Jansson, no. 1161.

[33] See Gschwantler, 'Christus, Thor und die Midgardschlange'; Marschand, 'Leviathan and the Mousetrap'.

Figure 9. The Gosforth stone.
Copyright Corpus of Anglo-Saxon
Stone Sculpture. Photo: T. Middlemass.
Reproduced by permission.

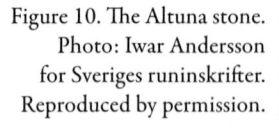

Figure 10. The Altuna stone.
Photo: Iwar Andersson
for Sveriges runinskrifter.
Reproduced by permission.

1882 Karl Gustav Brøndsted had demonstrated that it actually coincided in a remarkable way with a widely spread Christian motif. Around the year 400 AD an allegory began to appear among leading Christian authorities in which God was allegorically depicted as a fisher who captures Leviathan on a fishing hook and pulls him up from the deep. God baited the cross by taking on the flesh and becoming a man. The Devil, who had not otherwise dared to confront God's superior power, saw the man and opened the jaws of death to swallow this descendant of Adam. But the flesh was only the bait. When Leviathan/Satan/Death snatched the bait, the hook of divinity that was hidden in the flesh stung through his jaw. The gates of Hell were broken, and the Devil could be pulled up from the abyss. This allegory was well known in the European Middle Ages. It occurs in the works of Gregory the Great, for example, and Brøndsted was able to show that it was also known in Iceland in the late Middle Ages.[34]

Brøndsted's important study was soon forgotten in Scandinavia — and quite symptomatically it is not even mentioned in Gisli Sigurðsson's treatment of the 'myth'. Thanks to a few, mainly German, scholars, however, his idea did not totally perish, and in 1968 Otto Gschwantler published a substantially expanded variant of it. It had now come to light that the Christian allegory had in fact been much more widespread than even Brøndsted had thought.[35] Indeed, as James W. Marschand later declared, it is one of the most common allegories of the cross in the Middle Ages.[36] It was not only widespread among the leading Christian authors until the twelfth century, as early as in the twelfth century (i.e. before Snorri) it was also known in Iceland. It is indeed to be found in some of the oldest texts preserved from the Icelandic Middle Ages.

In the Old Icelandic translation of the apocryphal Gospel of Nicodemus, called *Niðrstigningarsaga*, probably composed in the early twelfth century, a few rather freely translated passages from the works of Gregory the Great were inserted. One of these reads:

> Sa inn ricasti allvalldr leit þa til Jorsalaborgar oc melte: 'Gilldra su er at Jorsolom er gør verþi miþgarþsormi at skada.' Hann fal þa øngul, þann er horvenn var agni oc eigi sia mate, i ezlino, þvi er i gilldrona var lagit, oc sva vaþinn gat han folget, svat

---

[34] Brøndsted, 'En kirkelig allegori og en nordisk mythe', pp. 21–29.

[35] Gschwantler, 'Christus, Thor und die Midgardschlange', pp. 148–57; compare Janson, 'Snorre, Tors fiskafänge och frågan om den religionshistoriska kontexten', p. 41.

[36] Marschand, 'Leviathan and the Mousetrap', p. 330 with n. 9.

eigi of mate sia. Þa bauþ han nøcquerom dyrlingom sinom at fara fyrer ser oc gøra vart viþ como sina til helvitis.[37]

[That one, the most powerful leader (*inn ricasti allvaldr*), then looked toward Jerusalem and said: 'The trap which is ready at Jerusalem is destined to maim the world-serpent (*miðgarðsormi at skaða*).' He hid the hook inside the bait so that it could not be seen; thus was it laid upon the trap. The fishing line he was also able to hide, so that it could not be seen. Then he requested several of his holy companions to go before him and make known his coming to hell.][38]

In this passage the Midgard serpent appears in a context in which we are not used to finding him. Indeed, it is God himself who refers to the Devil by this name. In the following we are allowed to know how Satan was in fact captured in the trap God had set up for him:

Þa er Satan com ut, þa sa hann englaliþ mikit vera comet til helvitis en gec eigi til fundar viþ ða, oc sneide hann þar hia. Þa bra hann ser i dreca like oc gerðiz þa sva mikill, at hann þotesc liggia mundo umb heimen allan utan. Hann sa þau tiðende at Jorsolom, at Jesus Cristr var þa i andlati, oc for þangat þegar oc ætlaði at slita ondina þegar fra honum. En þa er hann com þar oc hugþez glæpa mundo hann oc hafa með ser, þa beit øngullin godomsens hann, en crossmarkit fell a hann ovan, oc varþ hann þa sva veidr sem fiscr a øngle eða mus under treketi, eða sem melraki i gilldro, epter þvi sem fyrer var spat. Þa for til dominus noster oc bat hann, en qvade till engla sina at varþveita hann.[39]

[Then when Satan came out, he saw that a large force of angels had come to hell, but he did not go to meet them. He turned aside. Then he changed himself into the shape of a dragon and made himself so huge that it seemed he would encircle the entire earth. He saw those events in Jerusalem and that Jesus Christ was near death and went there immediately and intended to tear the soul from him. But when he came there and thought that he would swallow him and carry him away, then the hook of divinity snagged him and the cross fell upon him and he was caught like a fish on a hook or a mouse in a trap or a fox in a snare, as had been foretold. Then our Lord came forward and bound him and told his angels to guard him.][40]

Yet another variant of this tricking of the Devil is found in the Icelandic *Hómíliubók*, a book of sermons from the twelfth century preserved in a manuscript from about 1200. This passage also stems from a text by Gregory the

---

[37] *Heilagra Manna Sögur*, ed. by Unger, II, 4, compare p. 20.
[38] Translation in 'Niðrstigningarsaga', trans. by Aho, p. 153.
[39] *Heilagra Manna Sögur*, ed. by Unger, II, 5, compare p. 10.
[40] Translation in 'Niðrstigningarsaga', trans. by Aho, p. 154.

Great in which the Midgard serpent also appears, but this time in the context of Gregory referring to the biblical text which is the very basis for the allegory of God's fishing expedition, that is, the Book of Job 40–41:

> það sýnde dróttenn, þa es hann mælte viþ enn sæla iób. Mon eige þu draga leviaþan a öngle eþa bora kiþr hans meþ báuge. sia gléypande hvalr merkr gróþgan annskota, þann es svelga vill allt mannkyn ídauþa. Agn es lagt a öngol, en hvas broddr léynesc. þenna orm tók almáttegr goþ a öngle. þa es hann sende son sinn til dáuþa sýnelegan at líkam en o sýnelegan at goþdóme. Diabolus sa agn likams hans, þat es hann beit oc vilde fyrfara. en goþdoms broddr stangaþe hann svasem öngoll. A öngle varþ hann tekenn. þuiat hann beidesc at gripa lícams agn þat es hann sa. en vas goþdóms brodr sa es léyndr vas særðe hann. A ongle varþ hann tekenn, þuiat hann fek scaþa af þui, es hann béit. oc glataþe hann þeim es hann hafþe áþr vellde yver. þuiat hann tréystesc at grípa þann es hann hafþe etke vellde i gegn.[41]

> [This the Lord revealed when he spoke to the blessed Job: 'You cannot draw out Leviathan with a hook or pierce his jaw with a ring.' This voracious whale signifies the greedy Devil who wishes to swallow all mankind in death. The bait is put on the hook and the sharp point is hidden. Almighty God took the serpent with a hook when he sent his son to die, visible in body, but invisible in divinity. The Devil saw the bait of his body which he bit upon and wished to destroy, but the point of divinity snagged him like a hook. He was taken on a hook, because he was enticed to seize the bait of the body, which he saw. But the sharp point of divinity which was hidden wounded him. He was taken on a hook, because he was hurt by that on which he bit. And he lost that over which he previously had power, because he sought to seize the One against Whom he had no power.][42]

After having finished copying this translation of Gregory's text, the same hand returns to the passage and writes *Miðgarðarormr* — and we notice the not yet standardized form of the name — above Leviathan to optimize the effect of the text on the audience of the sermon. Obviously Leviathan in the Book of Job and in Gregory's text did not quite fit the taste of the religious Icelandic language.

We can consequently establish that the ancient story about God's fishing expedition was well known in Iceland in the twelfth century at the latest, and probably earlier.[43] God had, according to this story, taken on the flesh to deceive the Devil, because in the flesh the sharp hook of divinity could be hidden without frightening the Midgard serpent. The fishing line of divinity between the Father

---

[41] *The Icelandic Homily Book*, ed. by de Leeuw van Weenen, fol. 35ᵛ.
[42] Translation Marschand, 'Leviathan and the Mousetrap', pp. 331–32.
[43] Gschwantler, 'Christus, Thor und die Midgardschlange', p. 157.

and the Son was concealed in Christ's human descent from Adam. The Devil was fooled; he swallowed the bait and was caught on the hook, and the cross hit him from above when he snatched away the One who had been nailed upon it.

Snorri, Thórr, and Christ

'According to Snorri' it was, as we have seen, the three-headed king of the Æsir by the name of High, Just-as-high, and Third, who presented the story about Thórr's fishing expedition to the king of the Swedes in the middle of a fabulous illusion act. With supercilious arrogance King Gylfi is informed that this story was not unknown even among the unlearned. According to High, as a young man Thórr had travelled out across Midgard to the giant Hymir. When the giant went on a fishing tour Thórr wanted to come along, but the giant thought Thórr looked too small and weak. Thórr insisted and asked what bait they should have. The giant answered that Thórr could find his own bait. Thórr then went to a herd of cattle that Hymir owned and tore off the head of the biggest ox. He went aboard and rowed so far out that the giant became terrified. Hymir was concerned about the danger of the Midgard serpent, but Thórr continued further out. Snorri then has High continue:

> En þa er Þorr lagþi vpp ararnar, greiddi hann til vað helldr sterkian ok eigi var öngvllinn minni eþa eþa oramligre; þar let Þorr koma a öngvlinn öxa höfvþit ok kastaþi firir borð, ok for öngvllinn til grvnnz, [...] Miðgarðzormr gein ifir oxa höfviþit, en öngvllinn va igominn orminvm, en er orminn kenndi þess, bra hann við sva hart, at baþir hnefar Þors skvllv vt at borþinv. Þa varþ Þorr reiðr ok færþiz iasmegin, spyrndi við fast sva, at hann liop baþvm fotvm gognvm skipit ok spyrndi við grvnni, dro þa orminn vpp at borþi; en þat ma segia, at engi hefir sa sét ogvrligar sionir, er eigi matti sia er Þorr hvesti avgvn áorminn en orminn starþi neþan imot ok blés eitrinv. Þa er sagt at iotvnninn Hymir gerþiz litverpr, favlnaþi ok ræddiz, er hann sa orminn ok þat, er særinn fell vt ok inn of nokqvan, ok iþvi bili, er Þorr greip hamarinn ok færþi alopt, þa famlaþi iotvnnin til agnsaxinv ok hio vað Þors a borþi, en ormin sökþis i isæinn, en Þorr kastaþi hamrinvm eptir honvm, ok segia menn, at han lysti af honvm höfvdit við hronnvnvm en ec hygg hitt vera satt at segia, at Miðgarþzormr lifir enn ok liggr ivmsia.[44]

> [And when Thor had shipped his oars, he got out a line that was pretty strong, and the hook was no smaller or less mighty-looking. On to this hook Thor fastened the ox-head and threw it over board, and the hook went to the bottom. [...] The Midgard serpent stretched its mouth round the ox-head and the hook stuck into the

---

[44] Snorri Sturluson, *Edda*, ed. by Finnur Jónsson, pp. 62–63.

roof of the serpent's mouth. And when the serpent felt this, it jerked away so hard that both Thor's fists banged down on the gunwale. Then Thor got angry and summoned up his As-strength, pushed down so hard that he forced both feet through the boat and braced them against the sea-bed, and then he hauled the serpent up to the gunwale. And one can claim that a person does not know what a horrible sight is who did not get to see how Thor fixed his eyes on the serpent, and the serpent stared back up at him spitting poison. It is said that then the giant Hymir changed colour, went pale, and panicked when he saw the serpent and how the sea flowed out and in over the boat. And just at the moment when Thor was grasping his hammer and lifting it in the air, the giant fumbled at his bait-knife and cut Thor's line from the gunwale, and the serpent sank into the sea. But Thor threw his hammer after it, and they say that he struck off its head by the sea-bed. But I think in fact the contrary is correct to report to you that the Midgard serpent lives still and lies in the encircling sea.][45]

The correspondences between the Christian allegory and High's description of Þórr's fishing expedition are overwhelming, and the Christian implications of the story, as we have seen, were spread throughout the North Sea region, at least since the beginning of the tenth century, that is, many generations before Snorri presented Óðinn fooling King Gylfi. By the twelfth century at the latest the story was also widely known in Iceland. Otto Gschwantler found it likely that the identification[46] of Leviathan as the Midgard serpent in Iceland went even further back in time, and that it had certainly reached deep levels of society, for instance through sermons.[47] When taking all the evidence together one important conclusion can be drawn: When Snorri wrote about Þórr's fishing expedition he must have been well aware of its Christian connotations. In fact it seems quite obvious that it was in a Christian context that the story reached Snorri — and his audience.

So why, then, did Snorri tell such a perverted version of this well-known Christian allegory without giving the slightest hint about its Christian connotations? The answer is, of course, that he did not. It is the quick-change artist Óðinn who, according to the scene Snorri has created, somewhere far back in time told it to King Gylfi of Sweden who then brought it to the North. Gylfi was

---

[45] Translation Snorri Sturluson, *Edda*, trans. by Faulkes, pp. 46–47.

[46] To Gschwantler, that the Midgard serpent had originally been a pre-Christian, Germanic feature was of course beyond discussion, but it is quite reasonable to ask whether a Midgard serpent ever existed before Leviathan.

[47] Gschwantler, 'Christus, Thor und die Midgardschlange', p. 157. Compare Wamers, 'Hammer und Kreuz' and Hägg, 'Med textilier som källmaterial', pp. 135–36.

not capable of understanding its true meaning, and he was tricked into believing that Thórr, who conducted these brave deeds, was a god in the family of the Æsir. The thirteenth-century audience to whom Snorri addressed his work, however, must have immediately seen what the true connotations of the story were, as Óðinn probably also did; or, more correctly: Snorri probably intended his audience to think that when Óðinn deceived Gylfi he also knew what the allegory really was about. Aage Kabell has pointed out that, according to High, the name of the ox that Thórr tore the head off of was *Himinhrjótr*, that is, 'he who flies out of heaven' (or 'he who roars in heaven' or something similar[48]), without any explanation for what on earth this ox had to do with heaven.[49]

King Gylfi did not wonder about that of course — after all he was only a Swede — but to the audience of Snorri's *Edda* the connection must have been clear enough, as it was probably also to Snorri's Óðinn. It seems likely that Snorri's depiction of Óðinn in the form of the trinity was an indication that the king of the Æsir was fully aware of the proper (i.e. Christian) meaning of symbols such as those in the story about Thórr's fishing expedition, and that he was deliberately fooling the poor king of the Swedes by presenting them in a totally erroneous referential system.[50] This fits very nicely with the fact that *Gylfaginning* as a whole seems to play upon its connections to Christian truth, beginning close to it and ending in a totally corrupt world view in an illusory building over which Gylfi could not quite see, and from which he never really came out.[51]

---

[48] Snorri Sturluson, *Edda*, ed. by Finnur Jónsson, p. 62 [R and W]; compare Snorri Sturluson, *Edda Snorra Sturlusonar*, ed. by Arnamagnæanske Kommision, I, 484; Snorri Sturluson, *Edda: Gylfaginning*, ed. by Holtsmark and Jon Helgason, p. 61; Snorri Sturluson, *Edda: Prologue and Gylfaginning*, ed. by Faulkes, p. 44.

[49] Kabell, 'Der Fischfang Thórs', p. 127.

[50] Such a conclusion would have implications for another problem with the preserved versions of Snorri's *Edda*. There are good reasons to think that the parallels to Troy and the Trojan heroes are later interpolations in Snorri's text. This was pointed to earlier by Heusler in 1908, and has in later years been most vividly displayed by Heinrich Beck; see Beck, *Snorri Sturlussons Sicht der paganen Vorzeit*, pp. 1–60 (esp. pp. 49–59), and Beck, 'Ragnarøkr und der Kampf um Troja'; compare von See, *Mythos und Theologie*, p. 46, see also Janson, 'Snorre, Tors fiskafänge och frågan om den religionshistoriska kontexten', pp. 48–50. So far it seems that the criticism against the preserved version of the *Prologue* as a work of Snorri is correct, but this, however, does not mean that Christian theology and history writing did not play a decisive role in Snorri's version of the *Edda*. Compare Wellendorf's reading of the Trojan elements in Snorri's *Edda* in this volume.

[51] Marold, 'Der Dialog in Snorris Gylvaginning', p. 145. Even if Snorri had intended for

It should be kept in mind that in Snorri's comprehension Óðinn was a prophetic man from the middle of the world who had fled to the North when Christianity was about to overtake the Mediterranean region because he could see that he and his Æsir had their future in the North — for some time yet.[52] It is a world historical scenery, and we can notice the literary play — with chronology in this case — so typical for Snorri, when he lets the fake trinity king High, Just-as-high, and Third conclude: 'But Thor threw his hammer after it [i.e. the Midgard serpent], and *they say* (*segia men*) that he struck off its head by the sea-bed. But *I think* (*ec hygg*) in fact the contrary is correct to report to you that the Midgard serpent lives still and lies in the encircling sea.' What had been predicted in Job's book in the Old Testament, and had begun to be fulfilled with the Passion of Christ, was not to be finished before the Gospel had reached the end of the world — in both a temporal and a geographical sense.[53]

The construction might seem a bit complicated, but it is explained by the fact that Snorri's *Edda* is not a history of religion or collection of folklore but a schoolbook for young skalds who were to interpret its stories as he says 'for learning and fun' ('til froþleiks ok skemtvnar').[54] *Gylfaginning* was a pedagogic method to allow young poets to learn the skaldic language by deciphering (*skilia*) the text just as they had to decipher what was obscurely formulated (*hulit qveþit*) in skaldic poetry with its complicated kenning system. As a mas-

Óðinn himself to not understand the sacred meaning of the story, or why the ox had the name he had, he used the name *Himinhrjótr* to indicate to his audience where the story had its proper origin.

[52] Janson, 'Snorre, Tors fiskafänge och frågan om den religionshistoriska kontexten', pp. 48–50.

[53] Compare Hymiskviða's comment (*Norræn fornkvæði*, ed. by Bugge, p. 109): 'for in forna; fold avll saman; savcþiz siþan; sa fiscr i mar' ('the ancient world now totally collapsed; then that fish sank into the see'; my translation). Compare also a short passage on St Peter's denial (i.e. the cut with the bait knife), in the saga of the apostles John and Jacob (*Postola sögur*, ed. by Unger, p. 559), where it is said that Christ at the point of death on the cross came 'heriandi nu til helvitis með afli guðdomsins, knyiandi lokur ok lasa helvitzkra herbuda með hvellum hamri sins almattigs anda, lemiandi diöfulsins höfuð, sem fyrir var heitit i heims upphafi' ('harrying now to Hell with the power of divinity, smashing locks and bolts on the hellish compounds with the thundering hammer of his almighty spirit, crashing the head of the Devil, as it had been foretold in the beginning of the world'; my translation). In a German poem by Frauenlob, from *c.* 1300 AD, the author has St. Mary say: 'Der smid von oberlande; warf sinen hamer in mine schoz' ('The smith from the land above [i.e. God], hurled his hammer into my womb'; my translation), and the hammer in question is nothing less than *verbum Dei*; see Kemper, 'Der smit von oberlande'.

[54] Snorri Sturluson, *Edda*, ed. by Finnur Jónsson, p. 86 (translation mine).

ter of skaldic poetry Snorri was a formidable expert in deciphering such often extremely farfetched allusions, and by writing his *Edda* he could train his disciples in this way of thinking.

But there was also another reason for Snorri to advance the historical construction of *Gylfaginning*; in fact, it solved a great problem for his poetic schoolbook. It was a fundamental chronological precondition for history writing at the time that Scandinavia had been Christianized around the year 1000 AD.[55] However, it was also an unavoidable fact for young poets that the story about the famous fishing expedition occurred in skaldic poetry that was attributed to skalds who were thought to have been active before this year. Consequently, it seems to have been part of the skaldic referential system much earlier than the triumph of Christianity. By presenting Óðinn and the Æsir as bringing the story from the South, and introducing a corrupt version with misdirected connotations in pagan Scandinavia, Snorri could explain how that was possible. Through the delusion caused by Óðinn and the Æsir, Viking Age Scandinavian poets had been able to allude to the allegory of God's fishing expedition even before the arrival of Christianity, which according to the chronology of history writing had been firmly fixed to the time of the famous saint kings around the year 1000 AD. Unlike Snorri's thirteenth-century audience, however, the pagan poets had, according to Snorri's perspective, no means of understanding the true connotations of the story. To them it remained a mystery why the ox had been named *Himinhrjótr*. But Snorri's audience knew.[56]

Conclusion

Among uncountable myths and stories about dragon- and serpent-slaying in Europe there is, as Brøndsted pointed out, no myth that corresponds to the allegory of God's fishing expedition, which, on the other hand, was widespread by the early Middle Ages. There is only one exception: Thórr's fishing expedition in the Eddic literature, in which the correspondence is, as we have seen, so great that it cannot possibly be coincidental. It therefore seems highly unlikely that the story about Thórr's fishing expedition, as we know it from the *Edda*, has an independent origin in pre-Christian Germanic or Indo-European culture, even if such a thing ever existed. On the contrary, there are very good

---

[55] The idea of the year 1000 AD as the great turning point in the North stems from Adam of Bremen; compare Janson, 'Making Enemies'.

[56] Compare Beck, *Snorri Sturlussons Sicht der paganen Vorzeit*, pp. 31–36.

grounds on which to agree with Snorri, Brøndsted, and others in that the Eddic story about Thórr's fishing expedition must have had its origin in Christian allegory.

When writing his *Edda*, and when training young poets in the old skaldic poetry, Snorri Sturluson confronted some quite intricate historical problems, especially when he presented the stories that were necessary for an understanding of the old poets. In spite of the fact that some of these skalds were supposed to have composed their poetry long before St Olaf, they used symbols that seemed to presuppose knowledge of Christian history and Christian ideas. Snorri was consequently forced to explain how this was possible, and that meant in practice that he had to invent a pagan variant of it. This, however, was a task that suited his overly inventive skaldic mind unusually well.

It should be mentioned that the story about the fishing expedition is Christian until it appears in Snorri's *Edda*, where it is suddenly like a skaldic stanza in prose form stripped — by Snorri's Óðinn — of all explicit Christian connotations. The reason can hardly be anything else than a deliberate plan by a conscious author — an unusually conscious author, in fact — who made it a challenge for young poets to *skilia* what was obscurely *qveþit*, that is, to interpret *Gylfaginning* and its stories *til froþleiks ok skemtvnar*, just as they had to decipher the skaldic poetry and its kennings.

Snorri made an impressive work of giving literary form to the transformation of Northern Europe from the ninth to the twelfth centuries, and by redrawing some lines of development as far back as to the establishment of a new royal dynasty in the North with the arrival of Óðinn and the Æsir. Gisli Sigurðsson may well be right in that Snorri was not as influenced by modern scholastic ideas as has been suggested by some scholars, and Snorri might also have had a more ample oral tradition at hand than Eugen Mogk thought. But this does not mean that we 'need to' take what Snorri and his contemporaries say in their writings 'as genuine evidence of the tradition as it existed in their time',[57] at least not if 'genuine evidence' means that the stories, as they were written by Snorri and others, must necessarily have also existed in a pre-Christian Indo-European past, as Sigurðsson and so many other modern scholars seem to imply.[58] If anything, this neglects the results from modern research into

---

[57] Gísli Sigurðsson, *The Medieval Icelandic Saga and Oral Tradition*, p. 16.

[58] Compare for example Gísli Sigurðsson, *The Medieval Icelandic Saga and Oral Tradition*, p. 13: 'the extant written sources for Scandinavian heathendom must in some way be linked to a living oral tradition going back to ancient times'; and p. 7 n. 9: 'various central ideas in Snorri's myths reflect themes going back to common Indo-European mythology'.

oral cultures, because one circumstance that was firmly established by folklorists as early as in the nineteenth century was that orally transmitted materials — stories or 'myths' — do not stop at a linguistic border, and are not restricted to a 'people' — whatever that might be.[59]

In recent years there has indeed been a steadily more popular trend among students of Old Norse literature to see the clash between 'orality' and 'literacy' in High Medieval Iceland as if it were a confrontation between a pagan heritage and a Christian culture. But orality did not necessarily mean 'pagan' in twelfth- and thirteenth-century Iceland. A central aspect that is generally overlooked in this connection is that until around 1200 AD Christianity was, in fact, to a very large extent — it is even fair to say primarily — an oral religion with an advanced orally transmitted mythology that had been spreading through Europe in 'floating' retellings for more than a thousand years. The belief, still generally accepted as a premise, that medieval Icelandic literature can be used as 'genuine evidence' for an ancient oral tradition that has preserved 'a genuine heathen world view (*forestillingsverden*)',[60] be it Old Norse, Germanic or Indo-European — is to be seen as a manifestation of the fact that Romanticism still holds a firm grip around this field of research, and that the 'normal science' established by the Grimm brothers is still normal.[61]

By 1200 AD, after two turbulent centuries, Scandinavia and Iceland had been firmly integrated in the society of the Latin Church, and Romanesque churches, either of stone or wood, had been raised everywhere. This also meant the introduction of a new literary universe and a new Latin *Schriftkultur* into which the Scandinavian history had to be integrated.

According to the new chronology a sharp line was drawn between paganism and Christianity around the year 1000 AD. According to Snorri, therefore, whatever King Gylfi thought he had heard or seen and passed on to following generations, and whatever the skalds of the North had alluded to before this year, it must have been some kind of *vana superstitio*.

Eventually however, it was precisely these stories, stripped as they were of all Christian connotations, that became a virtual goldmine for Romanticist and

---

[59] Krohn, *Skandinavisk Mytologi*, pp. 11–12. Compare Gísli Sigurðsson, *The Medieval Icelandic Saga and Oral Tradition*, p. 13: 'the myth rests on ancient roots and almost certainly, in some form, constituted an element in the belief system of the peoples of the North prior to the arrival of Christianity'.

[60] Meulengracht Sørensen, 'Om Eddadigtenes alder', pp. 224–26; compare Janson, 'Snorre, Tors fiskafänge och frågan om den religionshistoriska kontexten', pp. 45–48.

[61] Compare Fidjestøl, *The Dating of Eddic Poetry*, pp. 48–68.

nationalist scholars of the nineteenth century, scholars eager, like the Grimms, to reconstruct a common pre-Christan organic past for different Germanic 'peoples'. To these scholars it was absolutely essential that what was found in the *Eddas*, and other texts produced by Snorri and his contemporaries, could be used 'as genuine evidence of the tradition as it existed in their times'. It was completely vital that 'myths' like the one about Thórr's fishing expedition represented 'eine alte Germanische vorstellung' or rested 'on ancient roots and almost certainly, in some form, constituted an element in the belief system of the peoples of the North prior to the arrival of Christianity'. After all, without these texts from thirteenth-century Iceland there would not be much of an Old Norse, Germanic mythology.

The oral culture of early thirteenth-century Iceland is, however, extremely unlikely to have preserved 'a genuine heathen world view'. Snorri certainly had a rich oral culture at hand, but that oral culture was an oral Christian culture. This 'oral Christianity' was an ancient and very widely spread storyworld in which God could, for instance, turn up as a fisherman.[62] Much more scholarship is called for in order to better understand how this 'oral Christianity' of the early and high Middle Ages relates to the Eddic literature. If we do not appreciate this by treating Snorri as a conscious author in relation to that oral culture, and as a teacher of young intellectual men,[63] we run the risk of ending up as King Gylfi, who after his confrontation with Óðinn, was left in the middle of nowhere, without understanding anything about the puzzling trickery to which he had been a victim.

[62] Compare Krohn, *Skandinavisk mytologi*, pp. 157–60.
[63] Compare Guðrun Nordal, *Tools of Literacy*; Guðrún Nordal, *Skaldic Versifying and Social Discrimination*. Another important aspect to consider has recently been discussed in Wanner, *Snorri Sturluson and the 'Edda'*.

Works Cited

Primary Sources

Heilagra Manna Sögur, ed. by Carl R. Unger, 2 vols (Christiania: Bentzen, 1877)

The Icelandic Homily Book, Perg. 15 4° in the Royal Library, Stockholm, ed. by A. de Leeuw van Weenen, Íslensk handrit, Series in Quarto, 3 (Reykjavík: Stofnun Árna Magnússonar á Íslandi, 1993)

'Niðrstigningarsaga: An Old Norse Version of Christ's Harrowing of Hell', trans. by Gary Aho, *Scandinavian Studies*, 41 (1969), 151–59

Norrœn fornkvæði: islandsk samling af folkelige oldtidsdigte om Nordens guder og heroer almindelig kaldet Sæmundar Edda hins fróða, ed. by Sophus Bugge (Christiania: Mallings forlagsboghandel, 1867)

Postola sögur: Legendariske fortællinger om apostlernes liv, ed. by Carl R. Unger (Christiania: Bentzen, 1874)

Snorri Sturluson, *Edda*, ed. by Finnur Jónsson (København: Gyldendal, 1931)

——, *Edda: Gylfaginning og Prosafortellingene av Skálskaparmál*, ed. by Anne Holtsmark and Jon Helgason (København: Munksgaard, 1950)

——, *Edda*, trans. by Anthony Faulkes (London: Dent, 1987)

——, *Edda: Prologue and Gylfaginning*, ed. by Anthony Faulkes (London: Clarendon Press, 1982)

——, *Edda Snorra Sturlusonar: Edda Snorronis Sturlæi*, ed. by Den Arnamagnæanske institute, 3 vols (København: Legatus Arnamagnæani, 1848–87)

Upplands runinskrifter, ed. by Elias Wessén and S. B. F. Jansson, Sveriges runinskrifter, 6–9 issued in parts (Stockholm: Almqvist & Wiksell, 1940–78)

Secondary Works

Arvidsson, Stefan, *Aryan Idols: Indo-European Mythology as Ideology and Science* (Chicago: University of Chicago Press, 2006)

Auken, Sune, *Sagas spejl: mytologi, historie og kristendom hos N. F. S. Grundtvig* (København: Gyldendal, 2005)

Baetke, Walter, *Die Götterlehre der Snorra-Edda*, Berichte über die Verhandlung der Sächsischen Akademie der Wissenschaften zu Leipzig, Philologische-historische Klasse, 97.3 (Berlin: Akademieverlag, 1950)

Bailey, Richard, and Rosemary Cramp, eds, *Cumberland, Westmorland and Lancashire North-of-the-Sands*, vol. II of *Corpus of Anglo-Saxon Stone Sculpture*, ed. by Rosemary Cramp and others (Oxford: Oxford University Press, 1988)

Beck, Heinrich, 'Ragnarøkr und der Kampf um Troja (Skáldskaparmál 87,1–88,3)', in *Snorri Sturluson: Beiträge zu Werk und Rezeption*, ed. by Hans Fix, Ergänzungsbände zum Reallexikon der germanischen Altertumskunde, 18 (Berlin: de Gruyter, 1998), pp. 1–8

——, *Snorri Sturlussons Sicht der paganen Vorzeit*, Nachrichten der Akademie der Wissenschaften in Göttingen, 1; Philologisch-historische Klasse, 1 (Göttingen: Vandenhoeck & Ruprecht, 1994), pp. 1–60

——, 'Zur Diskussion über den Prolog der Snorra-Edda', in *Poetik und Gedächtnis: Festschrift für Heiko Uecker zum 65. Geburtstag*, ed. by Karin Hoff and others (Frankfurt a.M.: Lang, 2004), pp. 145–54

Belier, Wouter, *Decayed Gods: Origin and Development of Georges Dumézil's 'idéologie tripartie'* (Leiden: Brill, 1991)

Brøndsted, Karl Gustav, 'En kirkelig allegori og en nordisk mythe', *Historisk Tidsskrift (Norsk)*, 11 (1882), 21–43

Clunies Ross, Margaret, *Skáldskaparmál: Snorri Sturluson's ars poetica and Medieval Theories of Language* (Odense: Odense Universitetsforlag, 1987)

Dronke, Peter, and Ursula Dronke, 'The Prologue of the Prose *Edda*: Explorations of a Latin Background', in *Sjötíu ritgerðir helgaðar Jakobi Benediktssyni*, ed. by Einar G. Pétursson and Jónas Kristjánsson (Reykjavík: Stofnun Árna Magnússonar, 1977), pp. 153–76

Dumézil, Georges, *Les Dieux des indo-européens* (Paris: Presses Universitaires de France, 1952)

Fidjestøl, Bjarne, *The Dating of Eddic Poetry: A Historical Survey and Methodological Investigation*, Bibliotheca Arnamagnæana, 41 (København: Reitzel, 1999), pp. 30–45

Ginzburg, Carlo, '*Mitologia germanica* e nazismo: su un vecchio libro di Georges Dumézil', *Quaderni storici*, 57 (1984), 857–82

Gísli Sigurðsson, *The Medieval Icelandic Saga and Oral Tradition: A Discourse on Method*, Publications of the Milman Parry Collection of Oral Literature, 2 (Cambridge, MA: Harvard University Press, 2004)

Gschwantler, Otto, 'Christus, Thor und die Midgardschlange', in *Festschrift für Otto Höfler zum 65. Geburtstag*, ed by H. Birkhan and O. Gschwantler (Wien: Notring, 1968), pp. 145–68

Guðrún Nordal, *Skaldic Versifying and Social Discrimination in Medieval Iceland*, The Dorothea Coke Memorial Lecture in Northern Studies (London: University College, 2003)

——, *Tools of Literacy: The Role of Skaldic Verse in Icelandic Textual Culture of the Twelfth and Thirteenth Centuries* (Toronto: University of Toronto Press, 2001)

Hägg, Inga, 'Med textilier som källmaterial: Glimtar ur vikingatidens historia', *Saga och Sed*, 2006, 113–45

Heusler, A., *Die gelehrte Urgeschichte im altisländischen Schrifttum*, Abhandlungen der königlich preussischen Akademie der Wissenschaften, Phil.-hist. Klasse, 3 (Berlin: Königlich Akademie der Wissenschaften, 1908)

Holtsmark, Anne, *Studier i Snorres mytologi* (Oslo: Universitetsforlaget, 1964)

Janson, Henrik, 'Making Enemies: Aspects on the Formation of Conflicting Identities in the Southern Baltics around the Year 1000', in *Medieval History Writing and Crusading Ideology*, ed. by Tuomas M. S. Lehtonen and others, Studia Fennica historica, 9 (Helsinki: Finnish Literature Society, 2005), pp. 141–54

——, 'The Organism Within: On the Construction of a Non-Christian Germanic Nature', in *Old Norse Religion in Long-term Perspectives: Origins, Changes and Interactions*, ed. by Anders Andrén, Kristina Jennbert, and Catharina Raudvere, Vägar till Midgård, 8 (Lund: Nordic Academic Press, 2006), pp. 393–98

——, 'Snorre, Tors fiskafänge och frågan om den religionshistoriska kontexten', in *Hedendomen i historiens spegel: bilder av det förkristna Norden*, ed. by C. Raudvere, A. Andrén, and K. Jennbert (Lund: Nordic Academic Press, 2005), pp. 33–55

——, 'What Made the Pagans Pagans?', in *Medieval Christianitas: Different Regions, 'Faces', Approaches*, Mediaevalia Christiana, 3 (Sofia: Voenno izdatelstvo, 2010), pp. 13–30

——, 'What Made the Pagans Pagans?', in *Scandinavia and Christian Europe in the Middle Ages: Papers of the 12th International Saga Conference, Bonn/Germany, 28th July – 2nd August 2003*, ed. by R. Simek and J. Meurer (Bonn: Hausdruckerei der Universität Bonn, 2003), pp. 250–56

Kabell, Aage, 'Der Fischfang Thórs', *Arkiv for nordisk filologi*, 91 (1976), 123–29

Kemper, Tobias A., 'Der smit von oberlande: Zu Frauenlobs Marienleich 11,1 f. und verwandten Stellen', in *Beiträge zur Geschichte der deutschen Sprache und Literatur*, 121 (1999), 201–13

Krohn, Kaarle, *Skandinavisk mytologi* (Helsinki: Schildt, 1922)

Kuhn, Hans, 'Das nordgermanische *Heidentum* in den ersten christlichen Jahrhunderten', *Zeitschrift für deutsches Altertum und deutsche Literatur*, 79 (1942), 133–66

Lincoln, Bruce, *Theorizing Myth: Narrative, Ideology, and Scholarship* (Chicago: University of Chicago Press, 1999)

Lindblad, Gustaf, 'Poetiska Eddans förhistoria och skrivskicket i Codex regius', *Arkiv for nordisk filologi*, 95 (1980), 142–67

Lindow, John, 'Mythology and Mythography', in *Old Norse-Icelandic Literature: A Critical Guide*, ed. by Carol J. Clover and John Lindow (Ithaca: Cornell University Press, 1985), pp. 21–67

Marold, E., 'Der Dialog in Snorris Gylvaginning', in *Snorri Sturluson: Beiträge zu Werk und Rezeption*, ed. by Hans Fix, Ergänzungsbände zum Reallexikon der germanischen Altertumskunde, 18 (Berlin: de Gruyter, 1998), pp. 131–59

Marschand, James M., 'Leviathan and the Mousetrap in the Niðrstigningarsaga', *Scandinavian Studies*, 47 (1975), 328–38

Meulengracht Sørensen, Preben, 'Om Eddadigtenes alder', in *Nordisk Hedendom: et symposium*, ed. by Gro Steinsland and others (Odense: Odense Universitetsforlag, 1991), pp. 217–28

——, 'Thor's Fishing Expedition', in *Words and Objects: Towards a Dialogue Between Archaeology and History of Religion*, ed. by Gro Steinsland (Oslo: Norwegian University Press, 1986), pp. 257–78

Meyer, Elard Hugo, *'Völuspa': eine Untersuchung* (Berlin: Mayer & Müller, 1889)

Mogk, Eugen, *Novellistische Darstellung mythologischer Stoffe Snorris und seiner Schule*, Folklore Fellows Communications, 51 (Helsinki: Suomalainen Tiedeakatemia, 1923)

——, 'Die Uberlieferungen von Thors Kampf mit dem Riesen Geir-röd', in *Festskrift tillägnad Hugo Pipping på hans sextioårsdag den 5 november 1924*, Skrifter utgivna av

Svenska litteratursällskapet i Finland, 175 (Helsinki: Svenska litteratursällskapet i Finland, 1924), pp. 379–88

——, *Zur Bewertung der Snorra Edda als religionsgeschichtliche und mythologische Quelle des nordgermanischen Heidentums: Mit 1. Tafel*, Berichte über die Verhandlung der Sächsischen Akademie der Wissenschaften zu Leipzig, Philologische-historische Klasse, 84.2 (Leipzig: Hirzel, 1932)

Momigliano, Arnoldo, 'Georges Dumézil and the Trifunctional Approach to Roman Civilization', *History and Theory*, 23 (1984), 312–30

Orri Vésteinsson, *The Christianization of Iceland: Priests, Power, and Social Change 1000–1300* (Oxford: Oxford University Press, 2000)

Page, R. I., 'Dumézil Revisited', *Saga-Book of the Viking Society*, 20 (1978–79), 49–69

Reichardt, Konstantin, 'Hymiskviða: Interpretation, Wortschatz, Alter', *Beiträge zur Geschichte der deutschen Sprache und Literatur*, 57 (1933), 130–56

Renfrew, Colin, *Archaeology and Language: The Puzzle of Indo-European Origins* (London: Cape, 1987)

Rühs, Friedrich, *Die Edda: nebst einer Einleitung über nordische Poesie und Mythologie und einem Anhang über die historische Literatur und Isländer von Friedrich Rühs* (Berlin: Realschulbuchhandlung, 1812)

Schröder, Franz Rolf, 'Das Hymirlied: zur Frage verblasster Mythen in der Götterlieder der Edda', *Arkiv for nordisk filologi*, 70 (1955), 1–40

——, 'Indra, Thor und Herakles', *Zeitschrift für deutsche Philologie*, 76 (1957), 1–41

See, Klaus von, *Europa und der Norden im Mittelalter* (Heidelberg: Winter, 1999)

——, *Mythos und Theologie*, Skandinavische Arbeiten, 8 (Heidelberg: Winter, 1988)

——, *Texte und Thesen: Streitfragen der deutschen und skandinavischen Geschichte*, Frankfurter Beiträge zur Germanistik, 38 (Heidelberg: Winter, 2003)

——, 'Zum Prolog der Snorra *Edda*', *Skandinavistik*, 2 (1990), 111–26

Wamers, Egon, 'Hammer und Kreuz: Typologische Aspekte einer nordeuropäischen Amulettsitte aus der Zeit des Glaubenswechsel', in *Rom und Byzanz im Norden: Mission und Glaubenswechsel im Ostseeraum während des 8.–14. Jahrhunderts*, ed. by Michael Müller-Wille, 2 vols (Stuttgart: Steiner, 1997), I, 83–107

Wanner, Kevin J., *Snorri Sturluson and the 'Edda': The Conversion of Cultural Capital in Medieval Scandinavia*, Toronto Old Norse-Icelandic Series, 4 (Toronto: University of Toronto Press, 2008)

Weber, Gerd Wolfgang, 'Intellegere historiam: Typological Perspectives on Nordic Prehistory', in *Tradition og historieskrivning*, ed. by Kirsten Hastrup (Aarhus: Aarhus universitetsforlag, 1987), pp. 95–141

——, 'Siðaskipti: das religionsgeschichtliche Modell Snorri Sturlusonar in Edda und Heimskringla', in *Sagnaskemmtun: Studies in Honour of Herman Paulsson*, ed. by R. Simek, Jónas Kristjánsson, and Hans Bekker-Nielsen (Wien: Böhlau, 1986), pp. 309–29

Wiseman, T. P., *Remus: A Roman Myth* (Cambridge: Cambridge University Press, 1995)

Wolf, Alois, 'Sehweisen und Darstellungsfragen in der Gylfaginning: Thors Fischfang', *Skandinavistik*, 7 (1977), 1–27

Ethnocultural Knowledge and Mythical Models: The Making of St Olaf, the God of Thunder, and St Elijah during the First Centuries of the Christian Era in the Scandinavian and Baltic Regions

Lauri Harvilahti

Introduction

This article attempts to elucidate the contacts between pagan folk beliefs and Christianity in the medieval Scandinavian and Baltic regions with a few textual examples. I use the term *ethnocultural poetics* in order to refer to the knowledge concerning what sorts of words, narratives, myths, and other means of expression typically exist in one's own culture.[1] In this respect, mythical traditions form a part of a culture-bound model of communication, a large semantic network, suited to the expression of different meanings. The variation of individual words, formulas, lines, and line clusters makes up systems of elements that, as Foley mentions, 'stand in relationships to their referents, with those referents being much larger and more complex than those to which the usual modes of textualization have access'.[2] Idioms, registers, and formulas act as a

---

[1] Compare Siikala, 'Kertomus, kerronta, kulttuuri', pp. 106–07; Siikala, 'Variation and Genre as Practice', p. 216; Harvilahti, *The Holy Mountain*, p. 95; Harvilahti, 'Textualising an Oral Epic'.

[2] Foley, *The Singer of Tales*, p. 50.

Lauri Harvilahti, Finnish Literature Society, Director of the Folklore Archive, University of Helsinki, Adjunct Professor, lauri.harvilahti@finlit.fi

metonymic network of associations that are essential for conveying the meaning of the text.[3] The basic elements of cognition, which underlie the processes of traditional performances, rely on the collective tradition of the community, that is, on congruent features of the shared semantic knowledge.

The ethnocultural registers function in oral texts as storage containers for idiomatic means of communication. A number of scholars have used the term 'structure of expectation'[4] or 'horizon of expectation'[5] to refer to the mental processes by which listeners recognize features of registers and genres and other expressive strategies within their own culture. It is thus possible to analyse the specific ethnocultural essence of traditions by making allowance for the narrative registers of the vernacular. In speaking of this, Dell Hymes uses the expression 'co-variation of form and meaning' launched by Roman Jakobson.[6] Without embarking on a deeper analysis of the theory of ethnopoetics, I would go so far as to say that the scholars mentioned above see tradition as springing from archaic models, as a collage produced from memory, but varied according to the context.

According to Mortensen the *mythopoiesis* of Christians and pagans in the early centuries of Christianity were structurally similar and formed a response at the local level to external ideological impulses.[7] During the first centuries of the Christian era this kind of network of meanings involved the strategies of adapting Christian elements to the mythical world view. The tradition related to St Olaf in medieval Finland offers an illustrative example of these strategies.

St Olaf and his Legacy in Finland in the Light of Folk Beliefs

The ninth chapter of Snorri Sturluson's *Óláfs Saga Helga* in *Heimskringla* includes a description of Olaf Haraldsson's visit to Finland in 1008. According to the sagas and other sources Olaf Haraldsson was born in 995. He would thus have been thirteen years old during the raid. The text reads as follows:

> Síðan sigldi hann aptr til Finnlands ok herjaði þar ok gekk á land upp, en lið allt flýði á skóga, ok eyddi byggðina at fé ǫllu. Konungr gekk upp á landit langt ok yfir

---

[3] Foley, *The Singer of Tales*, pp. 65–66; Harvilahti, 'Textualising an Oral Epic'.

[4] Siikala, 'Kertomus, kerronta, kulttuuri', pp. 99–100; van Dijk, *Macrostructures*.

[5] Foley, *The Singer of Tales*, p. 49; Jauss, *Literaturgeschichte als Provokation der Literaturwissenschaft*.

[6] Hymes, *'In Vain I Tried to Tell You'*, p. 8.

[7] Mortensen, 'Sanctified Beginnings and Mythopoietic Moments', p. 269.

skóga nǫkkura. Þar váru fyrir dalbyggðir nǫkkurar. Þar heita Herdalar. Þeir fengu
lítit fé en ekki af mǫnnum. Þá leið á daginn ok snøri konungr ofan aptr til skipa.

En er þeir komu á skóginn þá dreif lið at þeim ǫllum megin ok skaut á þá ok
sóttu at fast. Konungr bað þá hlífa sér ok vega í mót slíkt er þeir mætti við komask.
En þat var óhœgt, því at Finnar létu skóginn hlífa sér. En áðr konungr kvæmi af
skóginum lét hann marga menn ok margir urðu sárir, kom síðan um kveldit til skipa.

Þeir Finnar gerðu um nóttina œðiveðr með fjǫlkynngi ok storm sjávar. En
konungr lét upp taka akkerin ok draga segl ok beittu um nóttina fyrir landit. Mátti
þá enn sem optar meira hamingja konungs en fjǫlkynngi Finna. Fengu þeir beitt
um nóttina fyrir Bálagarðssíðu ok þaðan í hafit út. En herr Finna fór it øfra svá sem
konungr sigldi it ýtra.[8]

[Then he [Olaf] sailed back to Finland and waged war there and went up into the
country, but all the people escaped into the forests and emptied their houses of all
goods. The King went further up inland and through some woods; there were some
valley regions called *Herdalar*. They got a little property, but no men. It was getting
late in the day, so the King returned back to the ships.

But as they came to the woods, people rushed upon them from all directions and
shot at them and attacked them hard. The King asked his men to protect themselves
and fight against them in order to get through. But it was impossible, since the Finns
made the forest shelter them. And before the King got out of the woods he lost
many men, and many were wounded, and then in the evening he came to the ships.

The Finns made in the night a great storm and hard weather by their witchcraft.
But the King ordered to lift up the anchor and raise the sails, and tack off from the
land during the night. And as often, so it was this time that the King's good luck[9]
was stronger than the witchcraft of the Finns. They were able to tack along the
coast of *Bálagarðssíða* during the night and then out to the sea. But the Finnish
warriors followed on the land as the King sailed on the sea.][10]

In medieval sources such as the sagas the population referred to as *Finnar*
would have denoted the Saami rather than the (Baltic) Finns. But what was
the location of Herdalar? Judith Jesch proposes that Herdalar is in Finland,
though she admits that the location is not certain.[11] The looting expedition of
Olaf Haraldsson described in *Heimskringla* and in the skaldic verses has quite
recently appeared in the limelight, since in some parts of Finland the local com-

---

[8] Snorri Sturluson, *Heimskringla*, ed. by Bjarni Aðalbjarnarson, II, 10–11.

[9] See Bagge, *Society and Politics in Snorri Sturluson's 'Heimskringla'*, p. 219 for *hamingja*
('luck') in Snorri's work.

[10] Translation into English by Lauri Harvilahti.

[11] Jesch, *Ships and Men in the Viking Age*, p. 95.

munities have organized festivities for the thousandth anniversary of Olaf's raid. At the end of August 2008 the community of Ingå (Inkoo) organized the premiere of a play dedicated to the Battle of Hirdal, since the place name was interpreted as a parallel to the Herdalar of the Old Norse sources. Hirdal, located in southern Finland, around seventy kilometres west of Helsinki, is not the only place that has been proposed as the scene of this battle. Among other alternatives is Karis (Karjaa), about fifteen kilometres north-west of Hirdal.[12]

The location of Bálagarðssíða, referred to in several other sagas, also remains somewhat uncertain. In *Brennu-Njáls Saga* Þorkell went out one evening to fetch water east of the Bálagarðssíða. There he encountered a monster called *finngálkn* and fought it for a long time before he was able to kill it.[13] According to de Vries, Bálagarðssíða might be a kenning for 'sea', connoted, for example, by the particular meaning of burning the deceased in a ship that was sent to the sea; it might, however, simply mean 'unhealthy coast'.[14] Egilsson refers to Bálagarðssíða only as the south-western coast of Finland, and Salo proposes Karjaa as the probable location.[15] Other (not plausible) explanations include a Wendic place name Belgrad, 'the white town'. One of the most popular explanations for *Bálagarðssíða* is that it refers to the system of signal fires lit along the coast line in order to alarm people to fight enemies.[16]

According to Snorri, Ólaf was sailing back to Finland from Eysýslu, which is the Old Norse name for the island of Saaremaa (Ösel), off the western coast of present-day Estonia. The geographical information and the sequence of events described in the first part (1–56) of *St Olaf's Saga* by Snorri are fairly consistent, in spite of the difficulty with some place names mentioned above. As for the composition of the saga, Bagge notes that the first part (chaps 1 to 56) and the third do not present particular problems, and contain mostly straightforward narrative.[17] Even if the information of the skaldic poetry and the sagas is not historically reliable, Hirdal, situated on the opposite coast north-east of Saaremaa, would be a possible location for the scene of the raid described in Snorri's *Heimskringla*.

---

[12] Salo, *Ajan ammoisen oloista*, pp. 142, 199, 255.

[13] *Brennu-Njáls Saga*, ed. by Einar Ól. Sveinsson, pp. 302–03.

[14] De Vries, *Altnordisches etymologisches Wörterbuch*, pp. 23–24.

[15] Sveinbjörn Egilsson, *Lexicon poeticum antiquae linguae septentrionalis*, p. 38; Salo, *Ajan ammoisen oloista*, p. 255.

[16] See Knuutila, *Soturi, kuningas, pyhimys*, p. 49.

[17] Bagge, *Society and Politics in Snorri Sturluson's 'Heimskringla'*, pp. 34–36.

After Olaf's death on 29 July 1030 in the Battle of Stiklestad (Stiklastaðir), his cult as the patron saint of Norway spread to Sweden and later on further to Finland, and he became the most venerated Scandinavian saint in the Middle Ages. In the Middle Ages it was even believed that he was canonized, an inaccurate assertion that has been repeated even very recently in Finnish scholarship.[18] St Olaf was not canonized until 1888 by Pope Leo XIII. As Krötzl notes, the proclamation of Olaf as a saint by the local Bishop of Nidaros, Grimkell (of English origin), in order to avoid the influence of Hamburg-Bremen and to resist the Danish dominance of Norway, could well have been sufficient for establishing the saint's cult.[19]

The first miracles started to proliferate after Olaf's death. One year and five nights later, as Bishop Grimkell opened the grave, he found Olaf's body incorrupt; Olaf's wounds were healed and the nails and hair had continued to grow. His remains were then translated to St Clement's Church. The cult started to grow in the eleventh century at the local level, but there is no evidence that it had a broad appeal before the twelfth century.[20] In the twelfth century the cult was further promoted by the expansion of the cathedral in the 1130s and 1140s, and by Bishop Eysteinn in 1161–88.[21] The cult of St Olaf gained increasing popularity during the thirteenth century in Scandinavia and Finland.

The cult of pilgrimage made St Olaf, together with Bishop Henry, the most popular among saints in Finland.[22] Haavio regards as certain that the cult of St Olaf began immediately after the first crusade to Finland in the 1150s and claims that the Lemböte Church built in Ahvenanmaa (Åland) as early as around 1100 was named after St Olaf.[23] Haavio does not, however, mention

---

[18] See Timonen, 'Saint Olaf's Cruelty', pp. 285–86; compare Krötzl, *Pilger, Mirakel und Alltag*, pp. 61–64; Krötzl, *Pietarin ja Paavalin nimissä*, pp. 114–15.

[19] Krötzl, *Pilger, Mirakel und Alltag*, pp. 62–63; see also Knuutila, *Soturi, kuningas, pyhimys*, pp. 19–21, 366.

[20] See Mortensen, '*Historia Norwegie* and Sven Aggesen'; compare Lindow, 'St Olaf and the Skalds', pp. 106–08; Jaakkola, *Suomen varhaiskeskiaika*, p. 10. Knuutila notes, however, the liturgical texts from eleventh-century England: *Red Book of Derby* (*The Red Book of Darley*), and the liturgical books donated by Bishop Leofric to the Cathedral of Exeter (*Leofriccollectarium*, *Leofricmissale*, and *Leofricpsalterium*). According to Knuutila, Bishop Grimkel developed the cult of St Olaf in the first half of the eleventh century by using the English cults of royal saints as a model; see Knuutila, *Soturi, kuningas, pyhimys*, pp. 21–23, 366.

[21] See Krötzl, *Pilger, Mirakel und Alltag*, pp. 62–63.

[22] See in detail Tuomas Heikkilä and Pertti Anttonen in this volume.

[23] Haavio, *Suomalainen mytologia*, p. 484.

any source for the dating of the earliest churches of Ahvenanmaa. More recent sources indicate that the (originally wooden) chapel of Lemböte was built towards the end of the twelfth century at the earliest, and the St Olaf Church of Jomala, not mentioned by Haavio, dates from the latter part of the thirteenth century.[24]

According to Mortensen, the Legend of King Olaf (*Passio et miracula beati Olaui*) was most probably written in Nidaros (Trondheim) around 1175, and shorter versions of miracles might have existed even earlier than the 1140s.[25] The legends, miracles, sagas, and skaldic poems formed a large and varied oral and literary tradition on St Olaf. As Mortensen points out, in comparison to the initial wave of writing in Norway, Denmark, and Hungary between the eleventh and thirteenth centuries, the 'local codified mythology' was created in a short period of time on the basis of creative activity (originally by and for the elite) as a number of mythopoetical moments. This kind of local mythology also served the local political aims of the Church and state.[26]

Folk beliefs have often been adapted to new conditions by 'translating' the new religious concepts into the local religious register. This kind of religious inversion is a very common phenomenon with abundant illustrative examples.[27] The strategies of adapting Christian elements to the mythical world view in Northern Europe forms an essential part of crucial ethnocultural processes. In the history of the conversion of the Finns to Christianity, the mythopoetical elements were part of the conscious shaping of the pagan myths.

According to some sources the Dominican priory of Turku named after St Olaf was already established in 1249.[28] Twenty-three churches or chapels were dedicated to St Olaf in Finland between the thirteenth and the mid-sixteenth centuries, and altogether seventy-one church buildings were connected to the veneration of St Olaf.[29] The best known of these are the St Olaf Churches

---

[24] See Hiekkanen, *Suomen keskiajan kivikirkot*, pp. 386–91, 406–07.

[25] Mortensen, 'Sanctified Beginnings and Mythopoietic Moments', p. 257; see also Mortensen and Mundal, 'Erkebispesetet i Nidaros', pp. 363–68; Lindow, 'St Olaf and the Skalds', p. 106; and Krötzl, *Pilger, Mirakel und Alltag*, pp. 62–64.

[26] Mortensen, 'Sanctified Beginnings and Mythopoietic Moments', p. 269; compare Lindow, 'St Olaf and the Skalds', pp. 107–08.

[27] Compare Rowell, *Lithuania Ascending*, pp. 120–21.

[28] Heikkilä in this volume; compare DuBois, 'Sts Sunniva and Henrik', p. 86; Haavio, *Suomalainen mytologia*, p. 484; Smith, 'School Life in Mediæval Finland', p. 85; Knuutila, *Soturi, kuningas, pyhimys*, pp. 175–76, 273.

[29] Knuutila, *Soturi, kuningas, pyhimys*, pp. 404–05.

in Tyrvää, Hattula, Hauho, and more especially, in Ulvila, in the town that carries St Olaf's name from the Middle Ages. In the outer wall of the ruined church of Pälkäne there is a fresco painting that possibly depicts St Olaf, a personage with a nimbus around his head, holding an axe-like object in his hand.[30] In the (historical) provinces of Satakunta and Häme as many as nine medieval churches and chapels with dedications to St Olaf were verifiably built between the thirteenth and fifteenth centuries.[31] The cult of St Olaf most probably spread to Ulvila, on the coast of western Finland, with settlers from Gotland and central Sweden as early as the beginning of the thirteenth century. Because the settlers came from regions in which St Olaf was venerated as the patron of seafarers (as in Gotland), it is natural that religious sites were dedicated to him and that sculptures and other specimens of art depicting St Olaf were obtained mostly from Gotland, and later from Germany. St Olaf also became the patron of good harvests and cattle. After the time of sowing his sculpture was carried around the fields in the Middle Ages, a tradition that continued in some parts of Finland until the nineteenth century. Of utmost interest is the fact that in 1872 the peasants from the Kalvola region refused to give one of the sculptures of the 'Vanha Uoti' 'the Old Olaf' to the National Museum because, according to local legends, to do so might cause death.[32] As Knuutila notes, in the sculptures of the thirteenth and fourteenth centuries the saint was depicted as a miracle-working saint-king in civilian clothing holding an axe in his hand, but later, in the fifteenth and sixteenth centuries, he became, in accordance with the Hanseatic ideals, a warrior king depicted with an axe and holding a dragon under his feet.[33]

St Olaf's Castle (Olavinlinna) in Savonlinna was built in 1475 by Erik Axelsson Tott in order to protect the Savo region against the Russian threat. In 1483 Bishop Magnus Olai Stiernkors (Särkilahti) wrote to Gaute, the archbishop of Nidaros, that St Olaf had won great fame in Finland and was known even in Novgorod.[34] According to Dollinger the church dedicated to St Olaf was established in Novgorod by the Gotlanders, and it was mentioned as early

---

[30] See Edgren, 'Hämeen ja Satakunnan keskiaikaiset kalkkimaalaukset', pp. 97–98.

[31] Knuutila, 'Pyhä Olavi Hämeessä ja Satakunnassa', pp. 144–46.

[32] Knuutila, 'Pyhä Olavi Hämeessä ja Satakunnassa', p. 148.

[33] Knuutila, 'Pyhä Olavi Hämeessä ja Satakunnassa', p. 146; Knuutila, *Soturi, kuningas, pyhimys*, pp. 252–302, 408–09.

[34] Haavio, *Suomalainen mytologia*, p. 484; see also Knuutila, *Soturi, kuningas, pyhimys*, pp. 22, 52, 58–60.

as the 1080s.[35] Jackson recently pointed out in a conference paper that a cult of St Olaf with a number of miracles existed in Novgorod, and a 'Varangian' church of St Olaf was built in Novgorod in the beginning of the twelfth century, but according to Russian chronicles it was destroyed in a fire in 1152: 'eight churches were burnt down, and a ninth, the Varangian one'.[36]

Patron of Sharp-Edged Weapons

The Swedish medieval *Rhyme Chronicle* reports that Finns, defending themselves against the Russian attack in the war of 1495–97 during the time of Sten Sture the Elder, had pictures of St Eric and St Olaf on their banners:

> Ganska lithen var cristna manna makht,
> Thy leeth gudh see syna werdugha kraffth,
> The saaghe och tw baneer paa bergith staa,
> Alla reedha tiil stadz mwren ath gaa
> Alle blanke som en iis,
> Och wille mz gudz makth wynna priis,
> Wisselegha sancti Erikx och sancti Olafs ware the,
> Thz finge Ryzer same daghen at see.
>
> [Very small was the power of the Christian men,
> Then God showed His dignified power to them,
> And they saw two banners staying on the hill,
> All ready to go to the city wall,
> All pale as ice,
> And wanted to win with God's might the price,
> Truly the ones of St Eric and St Olaf were they,
> This the Russians got to see the same day.][37]

In the concluding chapter of his *Suomalainen Mytologia* (Finnish Mythology), Haavio proposes that in the Finnish oral tradition St Olaf became the patron of bladed or sharp-edged weapons because of his popular attribute, the axe, and the miracles related to staunching blood by the saint.[38] Haavio further refers

---

[35] Dollinger, *The German Hansa*, ed. by Ault and Steinberg, p. 7.

[36] Jackson, 'The Church and Cult of St Óláfr'.

[37] *Svenska medeltidens rim-krönikor*, ed. by Klemming, vv. 3847–3854 (p. 133), translated by Lauri Harvilahti. See also Knuutila, *Soturi, kuningas, pyhimys*, p. 394; Suvanto, *Suomen poliittinen asema Sten Sture*; Haavio, *Suomalainen mytologia*, pp. 484–85; Ganander, *Mythologia Fennica*, p. 109.

[38] Haavio, *Suomalainen mytologia*, pp. 482–86. See also Knuutila, *Soturi, kuningas, pyhimys*, pp. 292–94.

to the protocol of the summer assize organized in Kuopio in 1686.[39] The court accused a man called Olof Laurinpoika (Larsson) Tolloin of practising witchcraft. He responded that he could heal wounds caused by iron (i.e. a blade) with an ointment (*smiöria*) and could staunch the bleeding by performing a charm, as the rural juridical chief Caianus witnessed. Tolloin performed a spell (he was not able to read, as was written in the protocol: 'läsande brukar han inte') in front of the court, and it was written down by the scribe.[40] The spell that has been preserved in a more or less recognizable Kalevala metre is as follows:

Rauta Poica Wolaiatar	[The son of iron, Wolaiatar
Poicaisi teki paha,	Your son made a bad wound,
tule työsi tundeman	come to know your deed
Wamaisi parandaman,	to heal your hurt
enen cuin Eijckoisi Pala,	before your grandmother will burn,
Wanhembasi cummene.	Your parents will become heated.][41]

Haavio maintains that the name *Wolaitar* (in other texts *Vuolahinen*, *Vuolahainen*, *Vuolangoinen*) is related to the Saami forms of *Olaf*: *Vuola*, *Vuollo*, *Vuolu*, and thus the saint called upon for help would have been St Olaf. There are other etymologies for words like *Vuolahinen* and *Vuojola*, as well,[42] and these mythological words might be parallels of the *Pohjola* (the North) of the

---

[39] *Suomen kansan vanhat runot*, ed. by Niemi and others, VI. 2, no. 3, and VI. 1, no. 3347. There are also some two million lines of poetry in Kalevala metre in the archives of the Finnish Literature Society, collected mainly in the nineteenth century. About two thirds have been published in the thirty-four-volume *Suomen kansan vanhat runot* 'Ancient Poems of the Finnish People'. All published materials have been available as a digital corpus on the web since 2007 at <http://dbgw.finlit.fi/skvr/> [accessed 5 September 2012].

[40] *Suomen kansan vanhat runot*, ed. by Niemi and others, VI. 2, no. 3: 'Olof Larsson Tolloin af länsmannen Samuel Anderssson producerades, och anklagades hafwa medh Truldoom och Signerie omgånget ifrån den ena Sockn till den andra, Tolloin tillfrågades, om han sådan konst kunde, hwar till han svarade, at han intet annat kan, än see på Såår, som af jern skadt, det leker han medh smiöria, men läsande brukar han intet [...] Länsmannen Caianus intygade, at han för honom berättat hafwer, at han läser på sååret, och enär han läser, så stadnar blodet, detta wille han intet bekänna, omsijden ofwertygade länsmannen honom, at han sådant för honom läset hafwer, hwar till han sedermehra ej nekade, utan läxan upläste, således lydande.'

[41] Translated into English by Lauri Harvilahti. A rough Swedish translation was also given in the original: 'Thet är, Wuolaiatar du som ähr een gudh öfwer Järn, din Son giorde skada, kom nu förbättra din gärning förrän din Moormoder, eller Fader moder brinner, och din Fader eller moder blifwa siudande heet.'

[42] See Siikala, *Mythic Images and Shamanism*, pp. 155, 174.

Finnish mythical Sampo poems. In the light of ethnocultural poetics the same words with variations (such as the examples above) might have been used in a number of meanings forming a large semantic network referring to mythical helpers, both of pagan and Christian origin. In addition to the assumption that he was the patron of sharp weapons, the legacy of St Olaf comprises other traditional genres as well.

Olaf's Sheep

In the liturgical calendar St Olaf's day (29 July) has often been mentioned as *totum duplex* (as for instance in the *Missale Aboense*, 1488), one of the highest feasts, or at least the second highest, that is, *duplex*.[43] The liturgical material, prayers, and other religious acts attached to the feast have, quite naturally, influenced folk religion, ritual practices, and other traditional genres.

The rituals that included sacrificing animals are rather rare in the accounts obtained from Finland. Uno Harva nevertheless assumed that the animals slaughtered as sacrifices to saints, and in particular Olaf's sheep (in Finnish: *Olavin lampaat*), killed on the eve of St Olaf's Day (29 July), and Ilja's oxen, slaughtered on the eve of St Ilja's Day (20 July), were descendants of the former sacrifices to *Ukko*, the god of thunder.[44] Olaf's sheep have been slaughtered in some parts of Estonia as well, on the eve of the commemoration day of St Olaf.[45] The main reason for organizing this ritual was to ensure a good harvest. A Finnish proverb 'Eerikki tähkän antaa, Olavi kakun kantaa' ('Eric gives the spike, Olaf brings the cake') has a Swedish parallel 'När Erik ger ax, ger Olof Kaka'.[46] Hammarstedt mentions that the hard time before the next crop in July was called *Uotin koukku* 'the hook of Olaf',[47] known in Swedish-speaking Finland and in Sweden as *olsmessekroken*. Harva further mentions that St Olaf was identified in Scandinavia with the thunder gods *Thor* and (Finnic) *Ukko*, since the attribute of his martyrdom was an axe that resembled one of

---

[43] Knuutila, 'Pyhä Olavi Hämeessä ja Satakunnassa', p. 146; Knuutila, *Soturi, kuningas, pyhimys*, pp. 342–47; *Missale Aboense*, ed. by Parvio, pp. 9, 493–95.

[44] Harva, *Suomalaisten muinaisusko*, p. 120; compare Knuutila, *Soturi, kuningas, pyhimys*, p. 92.

[45] Harva, *Suomalaisten muinaisusko*, pp. 120–21.

[46] Hammarstedt, 'Olsmessa och Torsbolt', p. 32.

[47] Hammarstedt, 'Olsmessa och Torsbolt', p. 32.

the attributes of the thunder god.[48] Hammarstedt provides us with a detailed description of the feast called *Olafsmessa* or *Olsmessa* and its relation to the sacrifices made in honour of Thor in Swedish and Finnish-Swedish folk tradition.[49] Bing adds an account of ritual feasts that were organized in Norway on St Olaf's commemoration day. According to Bing, the tradition of the *vigilia* and *messa* organized in the Middle Ages on the eve of 29 July in honour of the patron saint Olaf has been carried on in the folk tradition as *Olsok* tradition (< Óláfsvaka) or *Olsmesse* (< Óláfsmessa), in the same manner as other feasts, such as *Syftesok*, *Larsok*, *Barsok*, or *Mikkelsmess*. Bing claims that the tradition is rooted not only in medieval Christianity, but even in earlier wake rituals.[50]

Ukko's Baskets

Harva and Hammarstedt provide us with materials that would indicate the identification of St Olaf with the tradition related to the god of thunder. In some ritual practices St Olaf has taken the role of the former god of thunder (the Finnish *Ukko*), or its Christianized cognate Ilja (St Elijah). As will be seen from examples provided below, St Olaf, among other Christian saints, became incorporated into the ethnocultural poetics.

Mikael Agricola added a list of Finnish pagan gods to his preface of David's psalter (*Dauidin psaltari*, 1551). Agricola commented on the rites organized in early summer in honour of Ukko, referred to as *Ukon wacka* 'Ukko's basket', and how the propagator of reformation expressed his anger because of the heavy drinking of both men and women during this feast:

Ja quin Keuekyluö kyluettin,	[And when the spring sowing was done,
silloin vkon Malia iootijn.	Then they drank from Ukko's bowl.
Sihen haetin vkon wacka	The basket of Ukko was brought there
nin ioopui Pica ette Acka	and the maid and the wife got drunk
Sijtte palio Häpie sielle tehtin	Then many shameful deeds were done
Quin seke cwltin ette nechtin.[51]	As was both heard and seen there.]

According to Haavio, Agricola's brother-in-law Clemet Henrikinpoika Krook (alias Clemet, scriffuare aff Finlandh), who was the bailiff of the Castle of

---

[48] Harva, *Suomalaisten muinaisusko*, p. 121.
[49] Hammarstedt, 'Olsmessa och Torsbolt'; Harva, *Suomalaisten muinaisusko*, p. 121.
[50] Bing, *Olsoktradition*, pp. 13–19; see also Bø, *Heilag Olav i norsk folketradisjon*.
[51] Agricola, *Alcupuhe (Dauidin psaltari)*, p. 213 (my translation).

St Olaf and the Savo province, ordered the local peasants to pay eight pounds of wheat as a fine for drinking from the bowl of Thor.[52] This was expressed in a letter of complaint sent by the peasants of the region to King Gustaf Vasa around 1545: 'än haffue vij almoghen vthgjort 8 pundh huethe för thet [vi] drucko thordhns gilde'. It is assumable that the scribe replaced the Finnish Ukko with Thor in order to make the context understandable for the recipient.

Ilja (St Elijah) has often been used as a counterpart of Ukko, especially in eastern parts of Finland. Hammarstedt gives a detailed comparison of folk beliefs related to Ukko and St Ilja in eastern Finland and Russia, as well as among some other Fenno-Ugric and Slavic peoples.[53] An event related to the tradition of 'Ukko's basket' was noted down by E. Salmelainen at Rautalampi in central Finland in the nineteenth century:

> On a certain day the best sheep in the flock was chosen, slaughtered and cooked. Then small portions of this stew and the household's other supplies were placed in birch-bark baskets and taken to the feast to be held on a ridge sanctified for this purpose called Ukko's hill. There they left the food untouched for the night, along with the ale and spirits, which had to be plentiful. Any food that had not been tasted by Ukko when they came to look in the morning was eaten up by the feasters, but a little of the ale and spirits was poured on Ukko's hill to ensure that the summer would not be too dry.[54]

There are also reports of Ukko's baskets from other parts of Finland. At Kurkijoki, for example, according to Samuli Paulaharju, a feast known as Ukko's basket was held to ward off drought. Various foods were eaten. and they drank ale made from malt prepared specially for the purpose of getting drunk.[55]

Other examples of feasts held in honour of Ukko are the Ingrian *vakkove*. As a result of Orthodox influence they later became established as rites in memory of St Ilja and also St Petro (St Peter). The aim of the ritual was once again to ensure rain. A Kalevala-metric poem from Ingria is called *Iljan virsi*, 'The lay of Ilja':

Iilia pyhä isäntä,	[Ilia, holy Lord,
Pyhä Pedra armolliin,	Holy Pedra, merciful,
Tule meille vierahisse	Come to visit us,
Oluttynnyrin tyvvee,	To the base of the beer barrel,

---

[52] Haavio, *Suomalainen mytologia*, p. 148; see also Mäkelä-Alitalo, 'Krook, Klemetti', p. 473; Arwidsson, *Handlingar till upplysning af Finlands häfder*, p. 309.

[53] Hammarstedt, 'Elias, åskguden'; compare Jaakkola, *Suomen varhaiskeskiaika*, pp. 38–39.

[54] See Haavio, *Suomalainen mytologia*, p. 152.

[55] Harva, *Suomalaisten muinaisusko*, p. 108.

Viinavaatin varjoisee!	To the shadow of the basin of spirits!
Kaikki on saatu,	Everything has been got,
k[aikki] o[n] tuotu	everything has been brought
Pyhän Iilian varaksi,	Owing to the holy Ilia,
Pyhän Pedran kunniaksi.	In honour of Saint Pedra.][56]

Ilja is also mentioned in the charm of the 'Origin of fire', alongside Ukko, the Virgin Mary, the smith hero *Ismaroinen*, and the old sage *Väinämöinen*, as in the following:

Ukko pilves' on väkövä,	[Ukko is strong in the clouds
Maaria tulelle selvä,	Maria knows how to make fire,
Ilia on jyrylle kovempi.	Ilia is harder to peal.
Iski tulta Ismaroinen,	Struck fire Ismaroinen,
Väykähytti Väinämöinen,	Flashed Väinämöinen,
Selvällä meren selällä,	Above the fair sea
Lakialla lainehella.	On the rough waves.][57]

The Baltic Vakka Institution

The Estonian *vakka* institution offers a further example of a similar feast as the Finnish ritual in honour of Ukko or Ilja and is presumably also based on ancient sacrificial rites. The Latvian, Estonian, and Finnish feasts in honour of the god of thunder all seem to have certain things in common: the gathering beforehand of food and drink, the communal participation in the feast, the serving and sacrificing of ale, and the sacrificing of cattle. Such feasts could also be held at the start of the harvest season and, as in Latvia, to ward off some threat, such as an epidemic.

---

[56] *Suomen kansan vanhat runot*, ed. by Niemi and others, III. 2, no. 1569. Soikkola, Uusikylä, Volmari Porkka. Ibid., III, no. 437 (1881–83). 'The lay of Ilia' is sung during the feast of Ilia or at other big feasts in honour of a saint. English translation by Lauri Harvilahti.

[57] *Suomen kansan vanhat runot*, ed. by Niemi and others, III. 3, no. 4357. Soikkola. Länkelä 1006. 58. Translated into English by Lauri Harvilahti. Compare Harva, *Suomalaisten muinaisusko*, pp. 74–75, 90. There is an interesting parallel in the Serbian folk poetry that Slavica Ranković noted to the author (Bergen, 10 June 2008). In Vuk Karadžić's collection *Srpske narodne pjesme* 'Serbian folksongs' (*Srpske narodne pjesme*, ed. by Karadžić, I, no. 231, and II, no. 2), *sveti Ilija* ('St Ilija') or *Gromovik Ilija* ('the Thunder Ilija') occurs in parallel verses with *Ognjena Marija* ('the fiery Marija'). In the former case, in the mythological song *Ženidba mjesečeva* ('The wedding of the Moon'), a number of other saints such as St Peter, St Nicolaus, and St Ioannis are mentioned as well, in a long sequence of parallel verses (compare Senni Timonen in this volume).

The early champions of the Lutheran faith described the worship rites of the Latvians in the seventeenth century as follows:

> Annual feasts and other special occasions are celebrated with joint sacrifices. At dry times of the year they call upon the god *Pērkons* on hills surrounded by forest and sacrifice a black bull calf, a black goat or a black cock. These are slain in the customary manner. The whole congregation gathers for such feasts, during which they pass three times round a fire lit at the site carrying a full vessel of beer. The beer is poured and the god *Pērkons* is requested to send rain.[58]

It is also said that while an epidemic was raging in the early seventeenth century, the Latvians collected money to buy sacrificial animals, each person brought corn with which to brew ale and bake sacrificial loaves, and all enjoyed them together.[59]

The Latvian language has several words that may refer to the Baltic-Finnic *vakka* or basket institution. The Latvian word *vāka* is thought to be of Estonian origin and to signify either the obligation of a peasant to work a prescribed number of days for his master, or the tax paid to the manor, often in the form of grain. However, the words *vāka*, *vāks*, and *vācele* also exist, meaning a bushel or a basket that among other things was used as a measure of grain. In the folksongs these words denote the metaphorical basket of songs that the maiden gathered during her youth, and from which she can pick up the songs while working after getting married:

Kad es biju jauna meita,	[When I was a young maiden,
Man bij dziesmu vācelīte;	I had a bushel of songs;
Kad es gāju tautiņās,	When I went to the people (i.e. got married),
Pa vienai izdaliju.	I picked them up one by one.][60]

The westernmost part of present-day Finland has been historically called *Vakka-Suomi* 'the Basket Finland'. The etymological explanation of this place name usually refers to the export of handmade baskets or bushels from *Vakka-Suomi* to other parts of the Baltic region and Scandinavia,[61] but mythological connotations are not excluded.

---

[58] Brückner, *Starożytna Litwa*, pp. 138–39 (my translation); compare Ivanov and Toporov, 'Perkunas'.

[59] Brückner, *Starożytna Litwa*, pp. 138–39.

[60] <http://www.dainuskapis.lv/meklet/pa-vienai%20izdaliju>, see also Harvilahti, 'Lehmuksen tytär, tammen poika'. Translation from Latvian by Lauri Harvilahti.

[61] Häkkinen, 'Vakka'; Kulonen, 'Vakka'.

The words *vāka*, *vāks*, and *vācele* in Latvian and the Finnish (Ukon) *vakka* might form a network of meanings that has connotations with the homonymic Scandinavian corollary *vaka* to mean, among many other meanings, 'ritual wake'. In his *Chronicle* of Livonia (*Chronica der Provintz Lyfflandt*, 1584), Balthasar Russow tells about the feasts (*Wacken*) organized in the area of present Estonia.[62] The villages were divided into districts that were also called *Wacke*. The feast around St Michael's day that included heavy drinking began after the taxes were collected. According to Korhonen, the tribute and the feasts were arranged by a special official, called *vacka-verden* or *werdige/wardige*, in Estonian *vardia*.[63] The official was responsible for the daily working duties of the peasants, taxation, and organizing the feasts. As Haavio comments, the *vakka* gathering signified multiple things: collecting taxes, organizing a court, and (formerly) holding a ritual sacrificing ceremony. He further notes the connotation of drinking the Ukko's bowl with the Scandinavian ritual toasts that were dedicated (*helga* or *signa full*) to the gods Odin, Thor, and Freyr,[64] and subsequently the toasts (*minni*) dedicated to saints such as St Olaf, St Henry, or, in the eastern part of Europe, St Elijah, that replaced the former pagan ritual toasts.

Conclusion

In all eras the processes of writing and performing (as well as collecting and recording) texts have taken place in changing sociohistoric, cultural, and political settings. For this reason the texts, despite sometimes having a relatively stable content, order, or structure, do not have fixed meanings, but rather constitute a multidimensional and multilevel network of forms of manifestation and interdependences. The different types of discourse, genres, and the pertinent elements of texture enable a suitable choice in the multitude of possible realizations in a given situation.[65] Traditional meanings and mental models ensure that the textualization processes result in something that fits the vernacular

---

[62] See Mänd, *Urban Carnival*, pp. 175–76, and passim; Haavio, *Suomalainen mytologia*, pp. 156–57; Balthasar Russow, *Liivinmaan kronikka*, ed. by Reko, pp. 120–29.

[63] Korhonen, *Vakkalaitos*, pp. 112, 154–58; Haavio, *Suomalainen mytologia*, pp. 156–57.

[64] Haavio, *Suomalainen mytologia*, pp. 158–59; de Vries, *Altgermanische Religionsgeschichte*, p. 292.

[65] See Bauman and Briggs, 'Poetics and Performance as Critical Perspectives'.

culture.[66] Instead of an open sea of orality ('det muntliga havet'), Theodore Andersson discerns from the saga material at least three types of overall options for organizing the narratives.[67] The first is the biographical structure that involves all the kings' sagas and bishops' sagas, and also the so-called outlaw sagas (as for example *Gísla saga* and *Grettis saga*). The second option is a kind of local chronicle based on regional events and historical legends, as in *Eyrbyggja saga* or *Ljósvetninga saga*, and the third is based on feud or conflict, as in *Njáls saga* or *Hrafnkels saga*. These patterns are not, however, pure types or genres, but choices or styles of presentation that oral storytellers also had at their disposal.

In his book dealing with a five-century period (ninth to thirteenth centuries) of Nordic religions during the Viking Age, Thomas DuBois proposes an approach that would take into account the extensive, long-term intercultural contacts and the religious practices that were altered in various ways over the course of time.[68] The interchange of folk religion and Christianity may be regarded as an extensive, long-term process of mutual relations between various religious and ideological currents, and as a constant correlation between oral and literary genres. A genre may come into being, become popular, and sink into oblivion again. The fate of genres is influenced by history, trends in society, and cultural conditions in general. Thus, for example, the incantations and epic poems that flourished in pre-literate peasant culture lost their relevance as a living tradition in the urbanized and literate culture. The lost genres were replaced by new phenomena better suited to changing conditions, although there was a decrease in the genres relying solely on oral transmission. According to Wellendorf, the genre of visions, as in the initial visionary ballad *Draumkvæde* (*Draumkvedet*), became outdated and the ballad genre became open for refashioning in order to fit the new and varying contexts.[69]

Clearly the characteristics of oral poetry vary from one culture to another. As Mundal points out in her article on the variations in the different versions of *Vǫluspa*, the Eddic (and partly also skaldic) stanzas probably changed little in the oral tradition, and the genre is quite close to memorized poetry.[70] On the other hand, the archaic bizarre metaphors of the oldest skaldic poetry (the archaic Old Norse kenning system) were based on different aesthetics than the

---

[66] Harvilahti, *The Holy Mountain*, p. 95.

[67] Andersson, 'From Tradition into Literature in the Sagas', pp. 13–15.

[68] DuBois, *Nordic Religions in the Viking Age*, pp. 29–68, 59–60.

[69] Wellendorf, 'Apocalypse Now?', p. 146.

[70] Mundal, 'Oral or Scribal Variation in *Vǫluspa*', pp. 224–25.

imagery of the Christian skalds. As Birgisson notes, during the transition from pagan to Christian times, and from oral to written, the archaic mentality of the pre-Christian oral culture was changed into the harmonically grounded system of metaphors.[71]

In the examples cited in this article there are many elements that might be called milieu-morphological adaptations (referring to the late professor Lauri Honko).[72] Honko claimed that the variants in a given tradition were based on a tradition-ecological system. The background of tradition was in use and alive at the same time as the performer or writer of a text. During the first centuries of the Christian era in the North (in *c.* 1100–1300), the dominant Christian figures and local saints were interpreted and adapted as part of the foundational stories, myths, and other genres of the collective tradition.[73] This provided a template for new versions of texts: oral performers and annalists drew on their store of motifs within the confines of the traditional rules and their personal competence and the features typical of adaptation to the particular cultural conditions.

---

[71] Birgisson, 'What Have We Lost by Writing?', pp. 163–79.

[72] Honko, 'Rethinking Tradition Ecology', pp. 69–75; Honko, 'Types of Comparison and Forms of Variation', pp. 119–20.

[73] Compare Mortensen, 'Sanctified Beginnings and Mythopoietic Moments', pp. 256–69; Assmann, *Das kulturelle Gedächtnis*, pp. 75–77, and passim.

Works Cited

Primary Sources

Agricola, Mikael, *Alcupuhe (Dauidin psaltari)*, in *Mikael Agricolan teokset*, 4 vols (Porvoo: Werner Söderström, 1987), III: *Käsikiria; Messu eli Herran echtolinen; Se meiden Herran Iesusen Christusen pina; Dauidin psaltari; Weisut ia ennustoxet; Ne prophetat: Haggaj, Sacharia, Maleachi*, pp. 212–14

Balthasar Russow, *Liivinmaan kronikka: 1584*, ed. by Timo Reko (Helsinki: Suomalaisen Kirjallisuuden Seura, 2004)

Brennu-Njáls Saga, ed. by Einar Ól. Sveinsson, Íslenzk fornrit, 12 (Reykjavík: Hið Íslenzka fornritafélag, 1954)

Ganander, Christfrid, *Mythologia Fennica eller förklaring öfver De nomina propria deastrorum, idolorum, locorum, virorum &c* (Helsinki: Suomalaisen Kirjallisuuden Seura, 1984)

Missale Aboense: secundum ordinem fratrum praedicatorum, ed. by Martti Parvio (Porvoo: Werner Söderström, 1988)

Snorri Sturluson, *Heimskringla*, ed. by Bjarni Aðalbjarnarson, Íslensk fornrit, 26–28, 3 vols (Reykjavík: Hið íslenzka fornritafélga, 1941–51)

Srpske narodne pjesme, ed. by Vuk Stefanović Karadžić, 4 vols (Beograd: Prosveta, 1976)

Suomen kansan vanhat runot, ed. by Aukusti Robert Niemi and others, 34 vols (Helsinki: Suomalaisen Kirjallisuuden Seura, 1908–48, 1997)

Svenska medeltidens rim-krönikor: Nya krönikans fortsättningar eller Sture-krönikorna; fortgången af Unions-striderna under Karl Knutsson och Sturarne 1867–68 [1452–1520], ed. by G. E. Klemming, Samlingar utgivna av Svenska fornskriftsällskapet, part 3, 1st ser., Svenska skrifter, 17.3, Efter handskrifter utgifna av G. E. Klemming (Stockholm: Norstedt, 1867–68)

Secondary Works

Andersson, Theodore M., 'From Tradition into Literature in the Sagas', in *Oral Art Forms and their Passage into Writing*, ed. by Else Mundal and Jonas Wellendorf (København: Museum Tusculanum, 2008), pp. 7–18

Arwidsson, Adolf Iwar, *Handlingar till upplysning af Finlands häfder*, 10 vols (Stockholm: Norstedt, 1846–58)

Assmann, Jan, *Das kulturelle Gedächtnis: Schrift, Erinnerung und politische Identität in frühen Hochkulturen* (München: Beck, 1992)

Bagge, Sverre, *Society and Politics in Snorri Sturluson's 'Heimskringla'* (Berkeley: University of California Press, 1991)

Bauman, Richard, and Charles Briggs, 'Poetics and Performance as Critical Perspectives on Language and Social Life', *Annual Review of Anthropology*, 19 (1990), 59–88

Bing, Kristen, *Olsoktradition* (Bergen: Floor, 1919)

Birgisson, Bergsveinn, 'What Have We Lost by Writing? Cognitive Archaisms in Skaldic Poetry', in *Oral Art Forms and their Passage into Writing*, ed. by Else Mundal and Jonas Wellendorf (København: Museum Tusculanum, 2008), pp. 163–84

Bø, Olav, *Heilag Olav i norsk folketradisjon* (Oslo: Norske Samlaget, 1955)

Brückner, Aleksander, *Starożytna Litwa: ludy i bogi, szkice historyczne i mitologiczne, opracował i stępem poprzedził Jan Jaskanis* (Olsztyn: Pojezierze, 1979)

Dijk, Teun A. van, *Macrostructures* (Hillsdale: Erlbaum, 1980)

Dollinger, Philippe, *The German Hansa*, ed. and trans. by D. S. Ault and S. H. Steinberg (London: Macmillan, 1970)

DuBois, Thomas A., *Nordic Religions in the Viking Age* (Philadelphia: University of Pennsylvania Press, 1999)

——, 'Sts Sunniva and Henrik: Scandinavian Martyr Saints in their Hagiographic and National Contexts', in *Sanctity in the North: Saints, Lives and Cults in Medieval Scandinavia*, ed. by Thomas DuBois (Toronto: University of Toronto Press, 2008), pp. 65–99

Edgren, Helena, 'Hämeen ja Satakunnan keskiaikaiset kalkkimaalaukset', in *Ristin ja Olavin kansaa: keskiajan usko ja kirkko Hämeessä ja Satakunnassa*, ed. by Marja-Liisa Linder and others, Tampereen museoiden julkaisuja, 55 (Tampere: Bellaprint, 2000), pp. 81–100

Foley, John Miles, *The Singer of Tales in Performance* (Bloomington: Indiana University Press, 1995)

Haavio, Martti, *Suomalainen mytologia* (Helsinki: Werner Söderström, 1967)

Häkkinen, Kaisa, 'Vakka', in *Nykysuomen etymologinen sanakirja* (Juva: Bookwell, 2004), p. 1437

Hammarstedt, N. E., 'Elias, åskguden: ännu en tillägg till "Olsmessa och Torsbolt"', *Fataburen* (1916), 21–29

——, 'Olsmessa och Torsbolt', *Fataburen* (1915), 32–40

Harva, Uno, *Suomalaisten muinaisusko* (Helsinki: Werner Söderström, 1948)

Harvilahti, Lauri, *Lehmuksen tytär, tammen poika: kokoelma latvialaisia dainoja* (Helsinki: Suomalaisen Kirjallisuuden Seura, 1985)

——, 'Textualising an Oral Epic: A Mission Impossible?', *FF Network for the Folklore Fellows*, 26 (2004), 3–5

Harvilahti, Lauri, in collaboration with Zoja S. Kazagacheva, *The Holy Mountain: Studies on Upper Altay Oral Poetry*, Folklore Fellows Communications, 282 (Helsinki: Academia scientiarum Fennica, 2003)

Hiekkanen, Markus, *Suomen keskiajan kivikirkot*, Suomalaisen Kirjallisuuden Seuran toimituksia, 1117 (Helsinki: Suomalaisen Kirjallisuuden Seura, 2007)

Honko, Lauri, 'Rethinking Tradition Ecology', *Temenos*, 21 (1985), 55–82

——, 'Types of Comparison and Forms of Variation', *Journal of Folklore Research*, 23 (1986), 105–24

Hymes, Dell, *'In Vain I Tried to Tell You': Essays in Native American Ethnopoetics* (Philadelphia: University of Pennsylvania Press, 1981)

Ivanov, V. V., and V. N. Toporov, 'Perkunas', in *Mify narodov mira*, II (Moskva: Sovetskaja èntsiklopedija, 1982), pp. 303–04

Jaakkola, Jalmari, *Suomen varhaiskeskiaika: Kristillisen Suomen synty*, vol. III of *Suomen historia*, ed. by Jalmari Jaakkola and others (Helsinki: Werner Söderström, 1958)

Jackson, Tatjana, 'The Church and Cult of St Óláfr in Novgorod', unpublished paper delivered at the international conference 'Saints and Hagiography across Northern and Eastern Europe (c. 800–1200)', 2–4 June 2008, Bergen

Jauss, Hans Robert, *Literaturgeschichte als Provokation der Literaturwissenschaft* (Konstanz: Universitätsverlag, 1969)

Jesch, Judith, *Ships and Men in the Viking Age: The Vocabulary of the Runic Inscriptions and Scaldic Verse* (Woodbridge: Boydell and Brewer, 2008)

Knuutila, Jyrki, 'Pyhä Olavi Hämeessä ja Satakunnassa', in *Ristin ja Olavin kansaa: keskiajan usko ja kirkko Hämeessä ja Satakunnassa*, ed. by Marja-Liisa Linder and others, Tampereen museoiden julkaisuja, 55 (Tampere: Bellaprint, 2000), pp. 141–49

——, *Soturi, kuningas, pyhimys: Pyhän Olavin kultti osana kristillistymistä Suomessa 1200-luvun alkupuolelta 1500-luvun puoliväliin*, Suomen kirkkohistoriallisen seuran toimituksia, 203 (Jyväskylä: Bookwell, 2010)

Korhonen, Arvi, *Vakkalaitos: Yhteiskuntahistoriallinen tutkimus*, Historiallisia tutkimuksia, 6 (Helsinki: Suomen historiallinen seura, 1923)

Krötzl, Christian, *Pietarin ja Paavalin nimissä: paavit, lähetystyö ja Euroopan muotoutuminen (500–1250)* (Helsinki: Suomalaisen Kirjallisuuden Seura, 2004)

——, *Pilger, Mirakel und Alltag: Formen des Verhaltens im skandinavischen Mittelalter* (Helsinki: Suomen Historiallinen Seura, 1994)

Kulonen, Ulla-Maija, 'Vakka', in *Suomen sanojen alkuperä: etymologinen sanakirja*, ed. by Ulla-Maija Kulomen, Suomalaisen Kirjallisuuden Seuran toimituksia, 556, Kotimaisten kielten tutkimuskeskuksen julkaisuja, 62, 3 vols (Helsinki: Suomalaisen Kirjallisuuden Seura, 1992–2000), III: *R–Ő* (2000), pp. 395–96

Lindow, John, 'St Olaf and the Skalds', in *Sanctity in the North: Saints, Lives and Cults in Medieval Scandinavia*, ed. by Thomas DuBois (Toronto: University of Toronto Press, 2008), pp. 103–27

Mäkelä-Alitalo, Anneli, 'Krook, Klemetti', in *Suomen kansallisbiografia*, ed. by Matti Klinge and others, 11 vols (Helsinki: Suomalaisen Kirjallisuuden Seura, 2003–07), V: *Karl–Lehtokoski* (2005), pp. 471–73

Mänd, Anu, *Urban Carnival: Festive Culture in the Hanseatic Cities of the Eastern Baltic, 1350–1550*, Medieval Texts and Cultures of Northern Europe, 8 (Turnhout: Brepols, 2005)

Mortensen, Lars Boje, '*Historia Norwegie* and Sven Aggesen: Two Pioneers in Comparison', in *Historical Narratives and Christian Identity on a European Periphery: Early History Writing in Northern, East-Central, and Eastern Europe (c. 1070–1200)*, ed. by Ildar H. Garipzanov, Medieval Texts and Cultures of Northern Europe, 26 (Turnhout: Brepols), 2011, pp. 57–70

——, 'Sanctified Beginnings and Mythopoietic Moments: The First Wave of Writing on the Past in Norway, Denmark and Hungary, c. 1000–1230', in *The Making of Christian Myths in the Periphery of Latin Christendom (c. 1000–1300)*, ed. by Lars Boje Mortensen (København: Museum Tusculanum, 2006), pp. 247–73

Mortensen, Lars Boje, and Else Mundal, 'Erkebispesetet i Nidaros — arnestad og verkstad for Olavslitteraturen', in *Ecclesia Nidrosiensis 1153–1537: søkelys på Nidaros-*

kirkens og Nidarosprovinsens historie, ed. by Steinar Imsen (Trondheim: Tapir, 2003), pp. 353–84

Mundal, Else, 'Oral or Scribal Variation in *Vǫluspa*: A Case Study in Old Norse Poetry', in *Oral Art Forms and their Passage into Writing*, ed. by Else Mundal and Jonas Wellendorf (København: Museum Tusculanum, 2008), pp. 209–27

Rowell, S. C., *Lithuania Ascending: A Pagan Empire within Central Europe, 1295–1345* (Cambridge: Cambridge University Press, 1994)

Salo, Unto, *Ajan ammoisen oloista: Satakunnan ja naapurimaakuntien esihistoriaa* (Helsinki: Suomalaisen Kirjallisuuden Seura, 2008)

Siikala, Anna-Leena, 'Kertomus, kerronta, kulttuuri', in *Kieli, kertomus, kulttuuri*, ed. by Tommi Hoikkala (Helsinki: Gaudeamus, 1987), pp. 98–117

——, *Mythic Images and Shamanism: A Perspective on Kalevala Poetry*, Folklore Fellows Communications, 280 (Helsinki: Suomalainen Tiedeakatemia, 2002)

——, 'Variation and Genre as Practice: Strategies for Reproducing Oral History in the Southern Cook Islands', in *Thick Corpus, Organic Variation and Textuality in Oral Tradition*, ed. by Lauri Honko (Helsinki: Finnish Literature Society, 2000), pp. 215–42

Smith, Donald, 'School Life in Mediæval Finland: Mainly in the Town of Viborg', *Transactions of the Royal Historical Society*, 13 (1930), 83–116

Suvanto, Seppo, *Suomen poliittinen asema Sten Sture vanhemman valtakautena vuosina 1483–1497*, Historiallisia tutkimuksia, 38 (Helsinki: Finnish Historical Society, 1952)

Sveinbjörn Egilsson, *Lexicon poeticum antiquae linguae septentrionalis: Ordbok over det norsk-islandske skjaldesprog*, 2nd edn, rev. by Finnur Jónsson (København: Lynge, 1966)

Timonen, Asko, 'Saint Olaf's Cruelty: Violence by the Scandinavian King Interpreted over the Centuries', *Journal of Medieval History*, 22 (1996), 285–96

Vries, Jan de, *Altgermanische Religionsgeschichte*, Grundriss der germanischen Philologie, 12 (Berlin: de Gruyter, 1956)

——, *Altnordisches etymologisches Wörterbuch*, 2nd rev. edn (Leiden: Brill, 2000)

Wellendorf, Jonas, 'Apocalypse Now? The Draumkvæde and Visionary Literature', in *Oral Art Forms and their Passage into Writing*, ed. by Else Mundal and Jonas Wellendorf (København: Museum Tusculanum, 2008), pp. 135–50

Part III

Educating and Disciplining the Community

The Performative Texts of the Stave Church Homily

Aidan Conti

The Stave Church and its Homily

The Norwegian stave churches represent perhaps one of the most identifiable symbols of the Middle Ages in the northern periphery of Europe.[1] Their images and their artwork, especially those examples which can be construed to depict the interaction between pagan and Christian world views, decorate modern tourist mementos and the covers of modern scholarly publications alike.[2] Of these churches, which are believed to have once numbered near the one thousand mark, twenty-eight survive in varying states of preservation, restoration, and recreation, preserved almost uniquely in Norway.[3] Their story offers a fitting reflection and indeed projects a relatively common narrative of a modern Scandinavian nation coming to terms with its medieval past. The churches

---

[1] For a brief introduction and bibliography, see Lidén, 'Stave Church'. Another helpful and somewhat more in depth overview can be found at Jørgen Jensenius's website: <http://www.stavkirke.info/> [accessed 15 January 2013].

[2] Perhaps the most recognizable is the carving, believed to have comprised the portal of an earlier church, now found in the north wall of Urnes stave church; the image of the lion therefrom can be found on the covers of Berend, *Christianization and the Rise of Christian Monarchy*, and the Skaldic Poetry of the Scandinavian Middle Ages series.

[3] There is one stave church in present-day Sweden, suggesting that formerly there may have been more. Additionally, one stave church (originally in Vang) was deconstructed and rebuilt in Germany (present-day Poland).

Aidan Conti, University of Bergen, Associate Professor, aidan.conti@cms.uib.no

proliferated throughout Norway until the plague, introduced near Bergen in 1349, decimated the population and led to a consolidation of parishes. During the following centuries, reformation and changes in liturgical requirements left the churches in varying states of maintenance and repair until approximately 270 remained in 1650. Awareness of the stave churches grew in the nineteenth century following the first publication about them by J. C. Dahl in 1837, and subsequently due to the creation of the Society for the Preservation of Ancient Monuments (Fortidsminneforeningen) in 1844 and the publications of one of its early chairmen Nicolay Nicolaysen. Yet, the church law of 1851, which required seating for three tenths of the congregation (a provision for which the smaller stave churches were ill-suited) threatened the wooden buildings with extinction.[4] If the preservation of the more dilapidated churches owes itself to the Romantic impulses of the nineteenth century, we must acknowledge that much of the more radical restoration was also done in the same spirit.[5]

Given the present-day status of the stave church as Norway's unique contribution to an understanding of the European Middle Ages, it is not surprising that of the works that comprise the corpus of Old Norse sermons, the so-called stave church homily occupies a place of prominence and holds a fair claim to be considered one of the most widely known works found in the earliest monuments of vernacular literary production in Scandinavia. More fittingly referred to as the dedication homily — it is titled *In dedicatione templi sermo* or *Kirkjodagsmal* in manuscript form[6] — the work, which runs about five printed pages, is completely preserved in the Icelandic Homily Book (IHB; Stockholm, Kungliga Bibilioteket, Cod. Holm. Perg. 15 quarto), the Norwegian Homily Book (NHB; København, Det Arnamagnæanske Institut (AM), 619 quarto), and a late medieval miscellany, Reykjavík, Stofnun Árna Magnússonar í íslenskum fræðum

---

[4] For an overview, see Christie, 'Da Fortidsminnesmerkeforeningen reddet stavkirkene'.

[5] Gol (relocated to an open-air museum in Bygdøy, Oslo, now part of the Norsk Folkemuseum), Hopperstad, and Fortun (relocated to Fantoft, Bergen, destroyed by arson in 1992 and rebuilt in 1997) stave churches were all restored based on the model of Borgund stave church, which is considered the best preserved, and in the popular imagination probably the most typical, of the medieval stave churches. Christie, 'Da Fortidsminnesmerkeforeningen reddet stavkirkene', offers a number of before-and-after depictions as well as a number of other pictures from Dahl, *Denkmale einer sehr ausgebildeten Holzbaukunst*. Vang stave church, relocated to Germany (present-day Poland), was rebuilt largely by craftsmen using largely new material who had never seen a stave church; due to its relatively more accessible location it is likely the stave church visited by the largest number of tourists.

[6] Moreover, the homily need not refer specifically to a stave church, but may refer to another wooden edifice; see Bekker-Nielsen, 'The Old Norse Dedication Homily'.

Figure 11. Drawing of Urnes stave church in Sogn from J. C. C. Dahl, *Denkmale einer sehr ausgebildeten Holzbaukunst aus den frühesten Jahrhunderten in den innern Landschaften Norwegens* (1837), which is largely accredited with reinvigorating awareness of stave churches and their precarious state at the time.

(AM), 624 quarto. It is also preserved incomplete in a fragment, Reykjavík, AM 237 a folio, which dates to the middle of the twelfth century (*c.* 1150) and is considered the earliest extant piece of Old Norse writing in the Latin alphabet. The homily books were written around 1200 — NHB (*c.* 1200–25) perhaps a decade or two later than IHB (*c.* 1200) — and represent the earliest complete codices in a Scandinavian vernacular now extant. AM 624 quarto was written close to the turn of the sixteenth century (*c.* 1500).[7] Consequently, copies of the work span almost entirely the written vernacular (in the Latin alphabet) of the medieval period.[8]

Academic attention to this specific work has largely approached the homily in relation to two issues that are of recurrent concern in the broader arena

---

[7] For dates, see Hall, 'Old Norse-Icelandic Sermons', nos 1, 2, 4, and 28. These dates are taken from Degnbol and others, *Ordbog over det norrøne prosasprog*, I.

[8] Hall, 'Old Norse-Icelandic Sermons', pp. 664–65.

of Old Norse studies, namely the question of whether the homily is Icelandic or Norwegian and whether its prose style deserves to be considered 'native' or Latinate.[9] However, the dichotomy between prose forms is difficult to maintain, and a definitive answer to the work's origin has proved elusive. In providing an overview of scholarship to date in 1969, Hans Bekker-Nielsen effectively quieted the debate, proposing

> that the Dedication Homily be characterized as an Old Norse attempt to use symbolic interpretations that were in vogue throughout Western civilization during and before the twelfth century, written by an anonymous author who had learned of this tradition in the course of his formal education or through his personal study of ecclesiastical literature in Latin and who composed his homily somewhere in the Old Norse world.[10]

As the debate around these seemingly central issues has dwindled so has relative interest in the homily itself.[11] Nevertheless, this homily, and the corpus of Norse sermon material in general, offers considerable insight into the world of manuscript culture as this European phenomenon made its way north. As a work (presumably) destined for oral presentation in an ecclesiastical setting, the homily represents a type of performance inextricably linked to the relatively new import of Christianity. As a written text, it was consulted, transmitted, and reproduced in a medium that was likewise bound to this religion of the book. Once given shape by an individual homilist, the work soon escaped authorial control and could be adapted and appropriated by subsequent readers and preachers. Consequently, as a form that bridges oral and written, Latin and vernacular, authorial and anonymous, the sermon, although not frequently considered canonical literature by belletristic standards, represents par excellence medieval literary production.

The dedication homily itself, which has been frequently summarized and translated, frames the dedication of a church in terms of Solomon's dedication of the first temple in Jerusalem, and offers a twofold explanation for the signification of the church: the first as the entire body of Christians, both living and dead; the second as a symbol of the characteristics that the Christian

---

[9] Bibliographic overviews are found in Bekker-Nielsen, 'The Old Norse Dedication Homily'; Magerøy, 'In dedicatione ecclesiæ sermo'; and Hall, 'Old Norse-Icelandic Sermons', pp. 682–85.

[10] Bekker-Nielsen, 'The Old Norse Dedication Homily', pp. 133–34.

[11] See Hall, 'Old Norse-Icelandic Sermons'. One notable exception is Schumacher, '"Den hellige ånds port"'.

individual exhibits. The homily surveys the prominent features of the church's architecture and offers an explication of each element within the framework of the larger Christian community and then within the role of the individual. For example, as part of the Christian community the foundation timbers represent the apostles; for the individual Christian they represent faith. With few exceptions an element elaborated within the first framework is taken up again in the second.[12] In many cases, the two explanations are nearly identical, such as that for the floorboards, which represent the humble within the Christian community and humility within the individual. As a result, while the homily yields a fair degree of repetition, the work also offers a striking degree of rhetorical balance. The homily's conclusion relates the ritual and traditional gestures of the feast of the dedication to reflect the way in which individuals should perform Christian duties, stating:

> Oc sva sem vér føðum ós itarlegre føzlo umm hǫtiðir. sva scolum vér føða ond vara hotiðlegre føzlo. þat er orð guðs. þvi at osómt er at licamr føðesc ok clęðesc itarlega. en hinn iðre maðr se u-prvðr ok missi sinnar føzlo [...] Oc sva sem vér tǫ cum í kirkiu himnesca føzlo þat er corpus domini. sva scolum ver væita þorfǫndum licamlega føzlo
>
> [just as we feed ourselves with fine meats on feast days, so we must feed our spirits with festive food, that is the word of God; for it is unseemly that the body should be finely fed and clothed and the inner man be threadbare and go without food [...]. And just as we receive spiritual food in church, i.e. *corpus domini*, so must we give bodily food to those in need.][13]

Finally, the homilist relates the audience's action to salvation, asserting 'if we celebrate temporal festivals with such devotion, then we shall win the eternal festival in heaven with our Saviour' ('Ef vér holdum með slicum á-huga stundlegar hotiðir á iorðu. þa munum vér æignasc ei-lifa hǫtið á himni með lausnara varum drotne').[14]

---

[12] Notable exceptions are the nave, which represents Christians on earth with no direct counterpart representation in the individual Christian, and the churchyard, which signifies the custody of the good qualities of the individual but is not elaborated as part of the Christian community.

[13] *In dedicatione templi sermo*, ed. by Indrebø, p. 99, ll. 10–13 and 29–31; and Kolsrud, *Messuskýringar*, p. 104, col. B and p. 106, col. B. The translation is from *The Old Norse Homily on the Dedication*, trans. by Turville-Petre, pp. 98–99.

[14] *The Old Norse Homily on the Dedication*, trans. by Turville-Petre, p. 99 (*In dedicatione templi sermo*, ed. by Indrebø, p. 99, ll. 32–34; and Kolsrud, *Messuskýringar*, p. 107, col. B).

The Ritual of the Homily

The dedication of a medieval church involved an elaborate liturgical ritual in the form of the Mass required of the celebration. While local entities likely experienced some variation, we can reasonably expect that celebrants participated in a procession around the church, a ritual entrance into the church, and a procession for the transfer of relics, if available.[15] Thereafter, the annual celebration of the dedication represented a date of primary significance for the local community within the liturgical year. For Pál Jónsson, Bishop of Skálholt (1195–1211), it was one of four occasions on which this rather reluctant preacher was sure to deliver a sermon, according to the saga bearing his name:

> Páll byskup lét sjaldan, nema þá er hátíðir væri, kenna kenningar hjá því sem áðr var; ok virði hann þá enn ǫllum meira at vera er sjaldan næði. En hann lét náliga hvern helgan dag tvær messur syngja. Fjóra daga kenndi hann sjálfr kenningar á hverjum tólf mánuðum: jóladaginn fyrsta ok miðvikudaginn fyrstan í fǫstu, skírdag, ok kirkjudag, en því at eins fleiri daga at honum þótti nǫkkur nauðsyn til bera.
>
> [Compared to the past, Bishop Pál seldom allowed preaching unless it was an important service; for he thought that they would care for it more if they could seldom get it. But he had two masses sung almost every saint's day. On four days he preached sermons himself in the course of each year: the first day of Christmas, the first Wednesday of the fast (Ash Wednesday), Maundy Thursday and the day of the (dedication of the) church, and other days that something seemed necessary to deliver to him.][16]

The relative infrequency of Pál's preaching highlights what is often seen as a potential dichotomy in Christian life, namely that a surfeit of preaching can infringe on the ritual solemnity of Mass. So, for example, the early Puritans (and many present-day evangelical denominations) promoted services that focused on the moral teaching of the church, most clearly realized in the prominence of the sermon and the emphasis on its message. By contrast, the medieval Mass is frequently considered a rich liturgical performance that directs the audience's attention to rite and mystery, but leaves little room for preaching and its attendant explicative function. The portrayal is commensurate with the idea that in Protestantism the sermon replaced the Eucharist as the focal point

---

[15] For a detailed description of the ceremony, see Spatz, 'Church Porches and the Liturgy', pp. 347–50.

[16] *Páls saga byskups*, ed. by Ásdís Egilsdóttir, in *Biskupa sögur*, ed. by Gudrún Á. Grímsdóttir and Jónas Kristjánsson, II, 319 (chap. 14).

for Christian worship.[17] The success of the Franciscans and the Dominicans in their popular preaching outside the Mass is often seen as proof of the dearth of clerical teaching available to the medieval public before the middle decades of the thirteenth century. That Latin served as the vehicle for much preaching in the twelfth century evinces further support.[18]

In so much as the portrait relates to the period before the composition of the dedication homily, it is furthered by the relative paucity of vernacular sermons in preserved manuscripts (before *c.* 1200) and the absence of specific instructions for preaching within the Mass. However, extensive Carolingian legislation promulgated the ideal of the systematic exposition of biblical readings based on the annual liturgical cycle,[19] an ideal reiterated in Anglo-Saxon England where much homiletic material was reworked into the vernacular.[20] Indeed, notable Carolingian homiliaries contain dedications indicating that the works were intended for the instruction of the laity.[21] Rather famously the St Père de Chartres homiliary, designed to provide preachers with models for doctrinal teaching and moral education, yielded both Old English and Old Norse adaptations of its homilies.[22]

---

[17] Compare, for example, McCullough, *Sermons at Court*, p. 71: 'sermons in the context of the medieval mass — *inter missarum solemnia* — were probably rare'. McCullough notes that scholarship varies, but in adopting this line accepts earlier rather than more recent scholarship, which takes issue with denigrating portrayals of the medieval preacher; see, for example, Spencer, *English Preaching in the Late Middle Ages*, p. 328.

[18] On Latin preaching in the twelfth century, see Constable, 'The Language of Preaching in the Twelfth Century', and Hall, 'Latin Sermons and Lay Preaching'.

[19] See Amos, 'The Origin and Nature of the Carolingian Sermon' and Amos, 'Preaching and the Sermon in the Carolingian World'; Clayton, 'Homiliaries and Preaching in Anglo-Saxon England'.

[20] For example, Ælfric's *Pastoral Letter to Wulfsige* directs that on Sundays and Mass days the priest must relate the sense of the meaning of the Gospel in English to the people ('Se mæssepreost sceal secgan sunnandagum and mæssedagum þæs godspelles angyt on englisc þam folce'); Ælfric, *Pastoral Letter to Wulfsige*, ed. by Fehr, § 61 (p. 14).

[21] For example, the homiliaries of Hrabanus Maurus, Archbishop of Cologne, on which see Woods, 'Six New Sermons by Hrabanus Maurus', and Landpertus of Mondsee, on which see Clayton, 'Homiliaries and Preaching in Anglo-Saxon England', p. 215; Barré, 'L'Homéliaire carolingien de Mondsee', p. 80.

[22] On the adaptations, see Cross, *Cambridge, Pembroke College MS 25*, and Hall, 'Old Norse-Icelandic Sermons', pp. 672–73. On the St Père homiliary, see Cross, *Cambridge, Pembroke College MS 25*, pp. 57–61; Barré, 'L'Homéliaire carolingien de Mondsee', p. 24; Dolbeau, 'Du nouveau sur un sermonnaire de Cambridge'. An electronic edition of this homiliary, based on Cambridge, Pembroke College, MS 25 is in progress under the direction of Tom Hall.

In early medieval Iceland, Bishop Pál's depicted reservation notwithstanding, preaching appears to have been frequent, perhaps even 'practically speaking a daily occurrence'.[23] Pál's predecessor as bishop of Skálholt, Thorlákr Thórhallsson (1178–93), was renowned for his preaching, as is implied by the comparison to the past in *Páls saga byskups*.[24] Guðmundr Arason is said to have delivered a memorable sermon for the feast of All Saints at Þingeyrar in 1200.[25] Perhaps the most well-known example of early medieval Scandinavian preaching is the portrait of Gísli, a Swedish priest engaged as master of the school at Hólar under its first bishop, Jón Ögmundarson (1106–21):

> Ok ávallt er hann prédikaði fyrir fólkinu, þá lét hann liggja bók fyrir sér ok tók þar af slíkt er hann talaði fyrir fólkinu, ok gerði hann þetta mest af forsjá ok lítillæti, at þar hann var ungr at aldri þótti þeim meira um vert er til hlýddu at þeir sæi þat at hann tók sínar kenningar af helgum bókum en eigi af einu saman brjóstviti. En svá mikil gipt fylgði þó hans kenningum at menninir, þeir er til hlýddu, kómusk við mjǫk ok tóku mikla skipan ok góða um sitt ráð. En þat er hann kenndi í orðunum þá sýndi hann þat í verkunum.
>
> [And whenever he preached before the people, he had a book before him and took from it that which he told the people, and he did this mostly from prudence and humility, because, as he was young in years those who listened would value it more if they saw that he took his teaching from holy books and not from his own native wit. And so much benefit accompanied his teaching that the men who listened to it were much moved and made great and good changes in their behaviour. And that which he taught in words he showed in works.][26]

This portrayal of the young Swede emphasizes the idea that the authority of the sermon derives not from the insight or the rhetorical abilities of the individual preacher, but rather from books, from which the preacher can impart learning that has been preserved in a seemingly immutable form and in a code decipherable only by those trained by the Church. If the detail indicating Gísli's youth suggests that an older figure would not have needed the legitimizing presence of the book, the implication seems to be that an older preacher's authority

---

[23] Paasche, *Homiliu-Bók*, p. 11.

[24] *Páls saga byskups*, ed. by Ásdís Egilsdóttir, in *Biskupa sögur*, ed. by Gudrún Á. Grímsdóttir and Jónas Kristjánsson, II, 319 (chap. 14); see the quotation at note 16, above.

[25] *Guðmundar biskups saga*, ed. by Jón Sigurðsson and others, I, 465 (chap. 35): 'Þar telr hann merkilega tölo allra heilagra messo.'

[26] *Jóns saga ins helga*, ed. by Sigurgeir Steingrímsson, Ólafur Halldórsson, and Peter Foote, in *Biskupa sögur*, ed. by Gudrún Á. Grímsdóttir and Jónas Kristjánsson, I, 205–06 (chap. 8).

would be conferred by age and years of experience. In addition to the presentation of Gísli as a conduit for teaching from holy books, the portrayal emphasizes teaching as a catalyst for motivating the moral behaviour of his audience. Towards this end, Gísli not only uses the rhetorical force of verbal admonition and suasion, but also demonstrates the realization of a Christian ideal in his own actions, *í verkunum*. In this case, the preacher is not only a teacher, charged with revealing mysteries of ecclesiastical doctrine and imparting knowledge of the Bible, but also a model; his very life serves as an exemplum. Words and works represent an idealized norm; exhortation and illustration serve to mould the actions of the congregation which are the basis of grace.

In the dedication homily, not surprisingly, grace is linked to participation in the rituals of the Church: baptism, the Eucharist, prayer, penance, and burial.

> En með því at vér hɔldum kirkiu hælgi í dag goðer brøðer. þa er os fyrst nauðsyn at vita hversu myccla miscun vér tɔcúm í kirkiunni. Fyrst er maðr cømr í hæim. þa scal hann til kirkiu bera. ok þar skira. ok geresc hann þa guðs sonr er hann var áðr syndar þræl. I kirkiu scal vígia hold ok bloð drotens várs Iesu Crist þat er allr cristin lyðr scal bergia til lausnar [...]. I kirkiu er setr satar-fundr á milli guðs ok manna. ok verða þar allar bøner þægstar guði þǽr er vér biðium fyrir os. Ef ver fɔllum í stor-syndir ok verðum mis-sátir við guð. þa sculu vér en til kirkiu fara ok taka þar scriptir af kennimɔnnum ok sætasc við guð. En þa er maðr andasc þa scal licam hans til kirkiu føra ok þar grafa. ok sculu þar kenni-menn fela á hende guði ɔnd hans.

> [And since, dear brethren, we are holding the feast of dedication today, it is of great importance that we realize how great is the grace we receive in church. When a man first comes into the world, he shall be brought to church and shall there be baptized, and he then becomes the son of God, he who was until then the slave of sin. In the church, the flesh and blood of Our Lord shall be consecrated, and all Christians shall taste of it for their salvation [...]. In church meetings of reconciliation are held between God and men, and all the prayers which we offer in church are those most pleasing to God. If we fall into mortal sin and are in disagreement with God, we must go again to church and accept the penance imposed by the clerks and so be reconciled with God. And when a man dies, his body shall be brought to church and buried there and the clerks shall commit his soul to God's keeping.][27]

The homily enjoins the audience to consider its participation not only within the framework of the institutional Church but also in terms of the physical church of the congregation, reminding that 'we should take great care of our

---

[27] *In dedicatione templi sermo*, ed. by Indrebø, p. 95, ll. 19–33 (Kolsrud, *Messuskýringar*, pp. 86–88, col. B); *The Old Norse Homily on the Dedication*, trans. by Turville-Petre, p. 94.

churches for [there we beseech God's mercy] [...] when we come into the world, and while we are in the world, and when we depart from the world' ('Af því æigum vér [...] at leggia myccla røct á kirkior værar. at vér søkium þangat miscum guðs þegar er ver cumum í haeim. ok þengat meðan vér erom í hæimi. ok þingat þa er vér færum ór hæmi').[28] Care for the physical setting in which grace is sought reflects a commitment to earning grace itself. Focus on the individual architectural elements of the local church offers a physical and rhetorical framework for situating the individual within the Christian community and moreover directs the actions by which the congregant is to lead a Christian life.

The Performance of the Text

These brief portrayals of medieval preaching suggest that as a performance the act occurred more frequently than the number of contemporary manuscripts of homiletic material in the vernacular initially suggest. Yet the relationship between the oral performance, its ritual, and the written record that represents the material of the performance is difficult to ascertain. The depiction of Gísli suggests that he took material from books and that the authorizing presence of the object lent legitimacy to his expression, but does not indicate that he read verbatim from the book. Indeed, the very notion that the young Swede required a book on account of his youth suggests that it was anomalous and that others did not require such supplemental authority. As a result, the words expressed in an individual preaching performance need not match the words of a given sermon in its manuscript form. This written presentation serves not as a literal transcript, but as an indication of a type of performance.

Moreover, as a handwritten medium prone to human error and often not bound to authorial control, the manuscript itself constitutes a performance produced (for the present purposes) most notably by its scribes, but also by compilers and book makers. Scribal performance has been used to describe several vantages on the medieval copyist. From one angle, the phrase may be used as a rough synonym for 'competence'.[29] From another, it suggests the scribe as author based on the idea that in 'the act of copying a text, the scribe supplants the original poet, often changing words or narrative order, suppressing

---

[28] *The Old Norse Homily on the Dedication*, trans. by Turville-Petre, p. 94 (Turville-Petre's translation has been altered to mirror the Old Norwegian text); *In dedicatione templi sermo*, ed. by Indrebø, pp. 95, l. 33–96, l. 4; and Kolsrud, *Messuskýringar*, p. 88, col. B.

[29] See, for example, Moffat, 'Anglo-Saxon Scribes and Old English Verse'.

or shortening some sections, while interpolating new material in others'.[30] Undoubtedly, in some situations the scribe was responsible for the very changes to which the manuscript attests, and thereby supplants the original poet. In others, one imagines that the scribe was a diligent, or not so diligent, copyist and little engaged with the meaning of the text. However, the most likely predominate situation is one in which any given extant manuscript represents the consummation of a complex series of interactions among antecedent authors, scribes, compilers, and revisers. In other words, the scribe physically responsible for the writing of any given extant manuscript need not be responsible for the revisions and alterations to which the manuscript attests. Furthermore, as a general rule it is difficult to assign responsibility to a particular preceding scribe, reviser, or compiler.

Nevertheless, we can see the results of the process, if not the specific dynamics of the process itself; the performance of the manuscript represents but one point of completion, 'the fruit of a long gestation in the manuscript matrix'.[31] As such, the performance of an individual manuscript offers an individual 'text' that fits within a broader pattern of the 'work', to employ a useful distinction.[32] Appreciation of the dynamic between text and work considers medieval literature and its aesthetics in relation to medieval media and processes of textual transmission. Within this dynamic, the individual performances exemplify how the manuscript culture of the Middle Ages 'did not simply live with diversity, [...] [but] cultivated it'.[33] The broader picture of the transmission of the work offers points of contingency within the cultivation of variation.

Against the background of variation within unity, the dedication homily represents an interesting case among Old (West) Norse homilies. Preserved complete in IHB (under the title *Kirkioda(g)smal*), in NHB (as *In dedicatione templi sermo*), and in Reykjavík, AM 624 quarto (without a title, but beginning *Salamon konongr gerði*), as well as partially in AM 217 a folio (beginning with *[...] trú rétta. þa es oss leiþer inn til*), these copies, as noted above, span almost entirely the period of the medieval vernacular written in the Latin alphabet. In keeping with the work's status as a reflection of the region's unique contribution to the Middle Ages, the homily has been the subject of frequent editorial concern. The three earliest manuscript versions have been separately

---

[30] Nichols, 'Introduction: Philology in a Manuscript Culture', p. 8.

[31] Symes, 'Manuscript Matrix, Modern Canon', p. 19. The phrase 'manuscript matrix' is borrowed from Nichols, 'Introduction: Philology in a Manuscript Culture'.

[32] Zumthor, *Essai de poétique médiévale*.

[33] Nichols, 'Introduction: Philology in a Manuscript Culture', p. 9.

edited.[34] All four versions have been printed in a parallel edition.[35] And the parallel edition has been further recollated, corrected, and analysed in light of every variant.[36]

In exploring the dedication homily's place within the parameters of manuscript variation, it is important to recognize that although many contemporary and antecedent Latin parallels have been suggested for details within the homily, no single or predominating Latin source has been identified.[37] Consequently, no authoritative source controls the transmission of the homily or dictates analysis of its variation. Nevertheless, the homily does place itself within the framework of Latin learning. The basis for the explication relies on a double meaning inherent in a Latin word, *ecclesia*, which, as the homily remarks, can be used to designate the whole Christian community or congregation as well as the church as a building:

> En með því at æino nafne callasc á bocum kirkian ok allr saman cristin lyðr. þa monum vér sægia hvessu kirkian merkir lyðen. eða hvessu cristin lyðer ma callasc holl guðs.
>
> [Now, since the church and the whole Christian community is denoted by the same name in books, we may explain how the church symbolizes the people and how the Christian people may be called the place of God.][38]

In the latest version of the homily (AM 624 quarto) *Salamon konongr gerði*, the word in question is spelled out, *þat is ecclesia*, informing the audience of the learned background to the discourse. The homily invokes its own status as a learned exposition by recourse to 'books' and the semantics of their sacred language; the work uses the vernacular to convey that background, some of its concern and issues, to a broader audience, thereby granting to that audience (rather limited) access to the sacred learning of the faithful.

Interestingly, in addressing its audience the dedication homily reveals one of its most significant points of variation. Broadly speaking, the audience for

---

[34] Indrebø, *Gamal norsk homiliebok* for NHB; de Leeuw van Weenan, *The Icelandic Homily Book, Perg. 15 4to* for IHB; Þorvaldur Bjarnarson, *Leifar fornra kristinna fræða íslenskra* for AM 217 a folio; Kolsrud, *Messuskýringar*, for *Salamon konongr gerði* and *[ ] trú rétta. þa es oss leiþer inn til*.

[35] Kolsrud, *Messuskýringar*.

[36] Magerøy, 'In dedicatione ecclesiæ sermo'.

[37] See Hjelde, *Norsk preken i det 12. århundre*; Turville-Petre, 'The Old Norse Homily on the Dedication'.

[38] *In dedicatione templi sermo*, ed. by Indrebø, p. 96, ll. 4–6 (and Kolsrud, *Messuskýringar*, pp. 88–89, col. B); *The Old Norse Homily on the Dedication*, trans. by Turville-Petre, p. 93.

individual vernacular homilies is frequently conjectured on the basis of internal clues.[39] In this respect, an addition in *Kirkioda(g)smal*, which emphasizes the way in which the addressed should take care of churches, namely 'with frequent prayers and offerings and attendance at service' ('í oftlegum béonom oc fórnom oc tíþa til sǿcnom'),[40] suggests a lay audience. Moreover, the addition coincides with less explicit indications, such as the condition stating 'if we fall into mortal sin and are in disagreement with God, we must go again to church and accept the penance imposed by the clerks' ('Ef ver fǿllum í stor-syndir ok verðum mis-sátir við guð. þa sculu vér en til kirkiu fara ok taka þar scriptir af kennimǿnnum').[41] In principle, these internal clues to an audience often stand in seeming contradiction to the standard homiletic address *fratres karissimi* (or a vernacular version thereof), a form that at least upon initial consideration suggests a work within a religious order. However, most commonly the internal evidence is considered more persuasive, and scholars are inclined to interpret the address to 'brothers' in its broadest connotation.[42]

Significantly, the manuscript performances of the dedication homily endeavour to expand the forms of address. The homily invokes its audience at three points (noted by an ellipsis in the following quotations). The first follows the summary of Solomon's dedication and reminds listeners or readers of the feast of the dedication: 'And since [...] we are holding the feast of the dedication today, it is of importance that we realize how great is the grace we receive in church.'[43] The second follows shortly thereafter as the homilist reminds the audience of caring for the church, preceding the discussion of the double significance of *ecclesia*: 'Therefore [...] we should take great care of our churches, for we go to them when we come to the world, and while we are in the world, and when we depart from it.'[44] The final example occurs within the conclusion of the homily after the signification of the church has been elucidated: 'Therefore it is necessary for us [...] when we celebrate this feast of dedication, to purify

---

[39] See, for example, Clayton, 'Homiliaries and Preaching in Anglo-Saxon England'.

[40] *Kirkioda(g)smal*, ed. by Kolsrud, p. 88, col. C.

[41] *In dedicatione templi sermo*, ed. by Indrebø, p. 95, ll. 29–31 (and Kolsrud, *Messuskýringar*, p. 88, col. B); *The Old Norse Homily on the Dedication*, trans. by Turville-Petre, p. 94.

[42] See, for example, OED, s.v. brother, n., 3. 'A fellow-member of a Christian society, or of the Christian Church as a whole; a fellow-christian; a co-religionist generally.' The definition is supported by a citation from the Lambeth homilies, preserved in a manuscript from the end of the twelfth or the early thirteenth century.

[43] *The Old Norse Homily on the Dedication*, trans. by Turville-Petre, p. 94.

[44] *The Old Norse Homily on the Dedication*, trans. by Turville-Petre, p. 94.

the churches of our hearts so that God shall not find in his temple, which we are ourselves, anything which may anger him.'[45]

In the first instance, *In dedicatione templi* invokes 'good brothers', *góðer brøðr*; *Salamon konongr gerði* omits any address; and *Kirkioda(g)smal* calls out the more inclusive brothers or sisters, *góþ systkin*. In the second instance, *Kirkioda(g)smal* and *Salamon konongr gerði* present forms of 'good brothers', *góþer bréoþr*, but *In dedicatione templi* invokes 'good friends', *góðer vinir*. In the final example, the manuscript versions in IHB and NHB have forms of 'good brothers', *góþer bréoþer*; the fragmentary homily has 'good brothers and sisters' using the group noun, *góþ sýstken*; and *Salamon konongr gerði* addresses 'good brothers and sisters' using the individual words for either sex, *brǿdr ok systur*. Remarkably, none of the manuscript performances consistently construe the forms of address, nor does any maintain a consistent form of address throughout. It appears that, despite the prevalence of 'good brothers' as a universal form of address, practitioners of the dedication homily felt compelled to broaden the invocation to be more explicitly inclusive, and yet the predominance of the traditional form acted as a constraint so that a single form of address is not uniformly employed in an individual text; the possibility of a preacher using the more all-encompassing invocations for explicitly mixed congregations is suggested in the alternation.

In addition, the audience for any given homily was potentially twofold. Besides the ultimate addressees, presumably in this case laity, who would experience the text orally, the homily also informed those presbyters who encountered the work as a written text. For this latter group reception was an activity that involved the interpretation and revision of the material. The dedication homily offers specific examples demonstrating the nature of potential revision, most notably in appeals to scriptural authority. For example, *In dedicatione templi* states that 'the foundation timbers of the church signify the Apostles of God, who are the foundations of all Christendom' ('Syllo stoccar kirkiunnar merkia postola guðs. en undirstoccar ero allar christni').[46] *Kirkioda(g)smal* on the other hand, offers a longer explanation, stating that the timbers represent both the 'apostles and prophets who are foundations of all faith, as Paul the Apostle said: You are built upon the foundation of the apostles and prophets' ('postola oc spámen. er understockar ero allrar tru sem paulus mælte. Ér eroþ

---

[45] *The Old Norse Homily on the Dedication*, trans. by Turville-Petre, p. 98.

[46] *In dedicatione templi sermo*, ed. by Indrebø, p. 96, ll. 19–20 (and Kolsrud, *Messuskýringar*, p. 90, col. B); *The Old Norse Homily on the Dedication*, trans. by Turville-Petre, p. 95.

smíþaþer yuer grundvoll postola oc spámenna'),[47] showing (in this case correct) recourse to Paul's letter to the Ephesians (2. 20: 'superaedificati super fundamentum apostolorum et prophetarum').

Assigning priority to either reading is problematic. An initial assessment might consider the reference to Paul in *Kirkioda(g)smal* as an addition; the shorter version appears in two manuscripts and the longer only in IHB.[48] Yet, on the other hand, it is not impossible that the shortened version represents the subsequent stage and is merely reflected in more manuscripts by the chances of survival. Indeed, the longer version provides a rhetorical rejoinder that verbally mirrors the later explanation of the foundation timbers of this church within the second part of the homiletic exposition. There, in relation to the individual Christian 'the foundation timbers [...] signify faith, for over this foundation and basis we shall fashion all our good works' ('Syllu-stoccar þessar kirkio merkia trv. þvi at yfir þann grund-voll ok unndir-stocscolum vér smiða oll góð værc').[49] In other words, within the long version the two expositions of the foundation timbers provide an appealing verbal contrast, especially in the reuse of words for foundations and building (*grundvoll* and *eroþ smíþaþer [ ] vér smiða*). However, the longer formulation fails to contrast the essence of the foundations of the congregation and the individual; both are, ultimately, faith, *tru*. The shorter version of the explanation provides fewer verbal parallels, but more substantial contrast: the apostles are the foundations for the Christian body, faith the foundation for personal Christianity. Whichever version, if either, represents the authorial original matters less than the types of revision that either process might represent. In the one, a small element of the homily has been expanded in conjunction with scriptural authority. In the other, reference to scriptural authority has been excised in order to provide a more distinct contrast.

A similar example further demonstrates the manner in which variation attends to authority. All texts of the homily relate that the doorway before the portal signifies control of the tongue and allude to Psalm 140(141). 3 ('pone Domine custodiam ori meo et ostium circumstantiae labiis meis'), stating: 'The

---

[47] *Kirkioda(g)smal*, ed. by Kolsrud, p. 90, col. C; *The Old Norse Homily on the Dedication*, trans. by Turville-Petre, p. 95, n. 68.

[48] Turville-Petre, 'The Old Norse Homily on the Dedication', p. 92, on the other hand thought IHB followed the original text and that that in NHB had been shortened (in 1949 at the time the observation was made, however, the existence of the version in AM 624 quarto was not known).

[49] *In dedicatione templi sermo*, ed. by Indrebø, p. 98, ll. 12–14 (and Kolsrud, *Messuskýringar*, p. 99, col. B); *The Old Norse Homily on the Dedication*, trans. by Turville-Petre, p. 97.

doorway before the portal signifies control of the tongue as David said in a psalm [*or* as the psalmist said]: Set a watch, O Lord, before my mouth, and a door to guard my lips' ('Hurð fyrir durum merkir tungu stilling sva sem david mælte í salme. Sett þu varð halð munni mínum droten. oc hurð at giata varra minna').[50] Three manuscripts continue with a passage omitted by *Kirkioda(g) smal*: 'As he spoke in these words: Open my mouth when it befits better to speak than to be silent, but close it when it is better to be silent than to speak' ('Sva sem hann þetta mælte. Luc up þun mun min þa er bætr gægnir at mæla an þegia. en þu byrg hann þa er bettre er þagat an mælt').[51] In this case, the situation with respect to length is reversed; the text in IHB represents the shorter version. The attributed quotation in the longer texts, however, is not found in the Bible. The words may well be a studied conflation of the sentiments found in Psalm 50(51). 17 ('Domine labia mea aperies et os meum adnuntiabit laudem tuam') and Ecclesiastes 3. 7 ('tempus tacendi et tempus loquendi').[52] Nevertheless, barring the unlikely event that the intermediary worked from a version of the Bible that made the conflation itself, strictly speaking the attribution is erroneous. Priority for one reading over another is again difficult to assign.

In addition to these forms of variation relating to audience and authority, the dedication homily exhibits variation that impinges on the manuscript as a textual technology, and more specifically the role of human engagement (as opposed to mechanical or digital reproduction) in the role of textual transmission. In explicating the tie beams in relation to the Christian community, two distinct significations emerge:

In dedicatione templi:

Ðværtre er scorða staflægiur ok up halda þæim triom er asa styðia. merkia þa menn í cristnínní er sætta veraldar hofðingia í raðum sinum. en þæir efla munc-lif ok hælga staðe með æuðǽfum.

[The tie-beams, which support the wall-plates and uphold those timbers which support the ridge-beams, signify those Christians who reconcile worldy chiefs by their counsels, for these support monasteries and holy places with their wealth.][53]

---

[50] *In dedicatione templi sermo*, ed. by Indrebø, p. 98, ll. 5–8; and Kolsrud, *Messuskýringar*, p. 98, col. B; *Kirkioda(g)smal* and *Salamon konongr gerði* have variations of *sva salmaskadlit mælte*; *The Old Norse Homily on the Dedication*, trans. by Turville-Petre, p. 97.

[51] Quoted from *In dedicatione templi sermo*, ed. by Indrebø, p. 98, ll. 8–10 with variants printed in Kolsrud, *Messuskýringar*, p. 98, under cols A and D; *The Old Norse Homily on the Dedication*, trans. by Turville-Petre, p. 97.

[52] As suggested by Gunnes in Salvesen, *Gammelnorsk homiliebok*, p. 177 n. 8.

[53] *In dedicatione templi sermo*, ed. by Indrebø, p. 97, ll. 17–20 and Kolsrud, *Messuskýringar*,

Kirkioda(g)smal:

þuertré es scorþa staflǽgior oc upphalda dvergom es ása styþia. merkia þa meɴ i cristnenne es efla veraldar hǫfþingia i ráoþom en heilog munclíf i ᴂuþéofom.

[The tie-beams, which support the wall-plates and uphold the king-posts which support the ridge-beams, signify those Christians who strengthen worldly chiefs by their counsels and holy monasteries by their wealth.][54]

The variation hinges on those 'who reconcile' (*er sætta*) and those 'who strengthen' (*es efla*). Putting aside, once again, the question of priority, one can readily imagine how ocular misapprehension (in which *tt* and *fl* might be confused), aural miscues (in which the ear might confuse *er s* and *es*), or a combination thereof (confusion between *r* and *s*; conflation of *æ* and *e*) might prompt the writing of one phrase for another; the substitution might take place during the course of several acts of copying or be the reflection of a single scribe. Subsequent intermediaries might then have reconstrued the remainder of the clause to coincide with their understanding or to remedy errors in transmission. Such a process corresponds roughly to the mechanics described by Alphonse Dain whereby an initial misreading might prompt a change or error of greater significance, which in turn demands a correction, but one supplied based on the conjecture of an intermediary rather than the authority of an archetype.[55]

As much as the types of variation found in the dedication homily relate this work to homiletic performance and the manuscript matrix, equally telling against this backdrop is the way in which the dedication homily lacks variation in its manuscript presentations. The lengthiest variant, indeed the only variant that comprises a number of sentences, is found in *Kirkioda(g)smal* just before the last sentence of the homily as a whole:

Pryþom vér oc þa aɴder órar góþum siþom. en kirkior órar oftlegom fórnom oc líose oc tíþa halde. þa es vér komom til kirkio oc seókiom tiþer. þa hǫfom vér óst oc friþ hverʀ vaʀ viþ aɴan. þuiat óseómt es at vér hafem hatr i hiotrom órom þa ér vér stǫndom at sáttar funde guþs oc maɴa.

---

p. 95, col. B with spelling variants in cols A and D; English translation with slight modifications from *The Old Norse Homily on the Dedication*, trans. by Turville-Petre, p. 96.

[54] *Kirkioda(g)smal*, ed. by Kolsrud, p. 95, col. C; *The Old Norse Homily on the Dedication*, trans. by Turville-Petre, p. 96, n. 72.

[55] Dain, *Les Manuscrits*, p. 54.

[And then let us adorn our souls with good customs and our churches with frequent offerings and light and performing services. When we come to church and frequent services, then we have love and peace, each of us towards the other, because it is improper that we have hate in our hearts when we stand at a meeting of reconciliation of God and man.][56]

Although significant in itself, this passage does little to change the thematic emphasis of the homily. Rather the sentences recapitulate in hortatory form themes iterated throughout the work: the importance of proper behaviour and church attendance as enabling reconciliation between man and God. Echoing the emphasis on the rites of the church as part of the life of the individual, this exhortation stresses the physical church building and attendance as a mediator between people and between the divine and the human; its rituals perpetuate social and spiritual harmony.

The variation (or lack thereof) in the manuscripts of the dedication homily contrasts with the full range of compositional techniques employed by many homilists of the period. The difference in character is highlighted by comparison with the vernacular use of the Gregorian categorization of the orders of angels set out in *Homilia 34* of his homilies on the Gospel.[57] This motif is translated in whole or in part in Old Norse homilies found in four manuscripts (three of which also contain the dedication homily): IHB (fols 40ᵛ–42ᵛ), NHB (fols 66ᵛ–68ᵛ), AM 237 a fol (fol. 2), and København, Det Arnamagnæanske Institut, 677 quarto (*c.* 1200–25) (fols 18ʳ–19ᵛ).[58] In AM 677 quarto, the exposition of the orders is found within a context that most closely mirrors the Latin source, namely a translation of *Homilia 34* among ten translated *Homiliae in evangelia*.[59] In IHB, Gregory's exposition has been reappropriated under the title *De sancto Michaele et omnium angelorum*. The relevant text of these two manuscripts follows that of Gregory to such an extent that the material may be characterized as a translation. Similar to IHB, NHB (and presumably AM 237 a folio, which corresponds closely to the text of NHB) employs the orders of

---

[56] *Kirkioda(g)smal*, ed. by Kolsrud, p. 106, col. C.

[57] Gregory I, *Homiliae in evangelia*, ed. by Étaix, pp. 299–319.

[58] For a full discussion of the use of Gregory's exposition, see Frederiksen, 'Til engleafsnittet i Gregors 34. evangeliehomilie i norrøn oversættelse', and also Hjelde, *Norsk preken i det 12. århundre*, pp. 347–66. The homily found in the last of these manuscripts is edited in Þorvaldur Bjarnarson, *Leifar fornra kristinna fræða íslenskra*, pp. 57–68.

[59] Under the system of pericopes known as Roman 3, the homily corresponds to the fourth Sunday after Pentecost; Gregory himself may have preached it on 29 September 591 (compare Gregory I, *Homiliae in evangelia*, ed. by Étaix, pp. lxvii–lxviii), St Michael's day.

angels within a work intended for St Michael's day (*Admonitio valde necessaria. Sanctorum angelorum. in die sancti Michaelis*). However, in NHB and AM 237 a folio the vernacular follows Gregory's exposition more loosely; rather than translation these versions appear to be a paraphrase.[60] This kind of textual mobility — whereby a Latin homily serves as the basis for a translation, an extended motif therefrom can be excised to serve as a stand alone homily for another occasion, but also can be recast as part of a larger exposition in a different manuscript context — is common in homiletic composition to such an extent that modern critics speak of 'cut-and-paste works'.[61] Despite the clumsiness of this metaphor, the gathering, adaptation, and adoption of ideas, motifs, and phrases from a wide range of antecedents is readily transparent in the techniques often used within variant texts of a single work. Indeed, even homilies that are considered translations can reveal adaptations that invert the emphasis of the original.[62]

With this example in mind, the dedication homily as it appears in its extant manuscripts offers a relatively unaltered textual core. The texts show adaptations relating to the terms used to address the audience, the configuration of authoritative sources, and as reactions to potential miscopying, but maintain a striking consistency in outlining the significance of individual elements of the church. Indeed, from the point of view of transmission the rhetorical repetition displayed in the homily represents a potentially fecund source of scribal error. For example, in the final lines before the concluding formula, the homilist structures four sentences around the co-ordinating elements 'just as […] so must we' ('[oc] sva sem […] sva scolum vér'); this is the type of repetition to which haplography as the result of scribal eye-skip is endemic. Yet the dedication homily avoids this pitfall. In other cases, we might attribute such consistency to the controlling restraint of an author or perhaps fidelity to an authoritative source. In this case, the (relative) uniformity might well be a function of the work's strong attachment to the individual parts of the church building. The dedication homily does not centre around narrative elements related to, for example, Jesus's life or the *vita* and *passio* of a distant saint, stories that

---

[60] Frederiksen, 'Til engleafsnittet i Gregors 34. evangeliehomilie i norrøn oversættelse', p. 72.

[61] See Abram, 'Anglo-Saxon Influence on the Old Norwegian Homily Book' for the technique in relation to the first NHB *Sermo ad populum*. For a critique of the 'cut-and-paste' metaphor, see Scragg, *Dating and Style in Old English Composite Homilies*.

[62] Compare, for example, studies of the Old Norse and Old English renderings of Ralph d'Escures's Assumption homily; Conti, 'The Old Norse Afterlife of Ralph d'Escures' *Homilia de assumptione*', pp. 228–29; Treharne, 'The Life of English in the Mid-Twelfth Century'.

an audience might grasp from a distance consisting of elements that might be expanded, reduced, or amended. Rather, the work meditates on a fixed set of architectural details peculiar to a locally distinct type of church, arguably intimately known to the congregation. Perhaps, if new elements were added, the church of the homilist's exposition would fail to relate to the church experienced by and known to the audience. Alternatively, the removal of any given architectural detail might frustrate the expectations of the audience. Although the architectural details of the dedication are not specific enough to identify the work with any particular church — indeed, the church likely 'never existed anywhere except the homilist's imagination'[63] — the architectural description matches a type of edifice that continued to proliferate in the West Norse world when wooden churches were long supplanted elsewhere.

Like a number of medieval vernacular works, the dedication homily owes much of the attention paid to it to a modern interest in texts that appear to illustrate the quintessential characteristics and unique nature of the vernacular culture from which a given work was born. Yet, if past studies focusing on the dedication homily for its Norwegian (or Icelandic) qualities can be seen as tied to national desires for *le patrimoine*, present fascination with textual technology and media must recognize the influence of the digital revolution and its electronic formats on our conceptualization of the handwritten world, even as the postmodern medievalist claims an appreciation of medieval cultural and aesthetic values as the primary objective for the promotion of manuscript culture. Within a model of understanding the past that claims to appraise that past on its own terms, the dedication homily is in many ways characteristic of composition in the age of the manuscript, of a 'literature' that embraces the oral and aural as well as the written. And yet its relative consistency, while not entirely atypical, is noteworthy in this context. Indeed, much as the variation of the text of the homily reveals distinctive features of the manuscript medium, the repetition of architectural elements and the fixity of the text pertaining to these details remind the reader of the routine nature of much medieval life. As a performance, both textual and possible, among the rituals that punctuated the annual cycle promulgated by the medieval Church, a reading of the dedication homily facilitates a picture of canonicity in an age before the typesetter supplanted the scribe and the national hero displaced the preacher.

---

[63] Bekker-Nielsen, 'The Old Norse Dedication Homily', p. 130.

Works Cited

Primary Sources

Ælfric of Eynsham, *Pastoral Letter to Wulfsige*, in *Die Hirtenbriefe Ælfrics*, ed. by Bernhard Fehr, with a supplementary introduction by Peter Clemoes, Bibliothek der angelsächsischen Prosa, 9 (Darmstadt: Wissenschaft, 1966; orig. publ. Hamburg: Grand, 1914), pp. 1–34

Biskupa sögur, ed. by Gudrún Á. Grímsdóttir and Jónas Kristjánsson, 3 vols, Íslensk fornrit, 15–17 (Reykjavík: Hið íslenzka fornritafélag, 1998–2003)

Gregory I, *Gregorius Magnus: Homiliae in evangelia*, ed. by Raymond Étaix, Corpus Christianorum Series Latina, 141 (Turnhout: Brepols, 1999)

Guðmundar biskups saga, ed. by Jón Sigurðsson and others, 2 vols (København: Møller, 1858–78)

In dedicatione templi sermo, in *Gamal norsk homiliebok: Cod. AM 619 4to*, ed. by Gustav Indrebø (Oslo: Universitetsforlaget, 1966; orig. publ. Dybwad, 1931), pp. 95–99

Kirkioda(g)smal, ed. by Oluf Kolsrud, in *Messuskýringar, liturgisk symbolik frå den norskislandskekyrkjaimillomaderen* (Oslo: Dybwad for Kjeldeskriftfondet, 1952), pp. 85–101

The Old Norse Homily on the Dedication, trans. by Gabriel Turville-Petre, in *Nine Norse Studies*, Viking Society for Northern Research Text Series, 5 (London: University College London, 1972), pp. 93–99

Secondary Works

Abram, Christopher, 'Anglo-Saxon Influence on the Old Norwegian Homily Book', *Mediaeval Scandinavia*, 14 (2004), 1–34

Amos, Thomas Leslie, 'The Origin and Nature of the Carolingian Sermon' (unpublished doctoral dissertation, Michigan State University, 1983)

——, 'Preaching and the Sermon in the Carolingian World', in *De ore Domini: Preacher and the Word in the Middle Ages*, ed. by Thomas L. Amos and others (Kalamazoo: Medieval Institute Publications, 1989), pp. 41–60

Barré, Henri, 'L'Homéliaire carolingien de Mondsee', *Revue Bénédictine*, 71 (1961), 71–107

Bekker-Nielsen, Hans, 'The Old Norse Dedication Homily', in *Festschrift für Konstantin Reichardt*, ed. by Christian Gellinek (Bern: Franck, 1969), pp. 127–34

Berend, Nora, ed., *Christianization and the Rise of Christian Monarchy: Scandinavia, Central Europe and Rus' c. 900–1200* (Cambridge: Cambridge University Press, 2007)

Christie, Håkon, 'Da Fortidsminnesmerkeforeningen reddet stavkirkene', *Foreningen til norske fortidsminnesmerkers bevaring (årbok)*, 132 (1978), 43–62

Clayton, Mary, 'Homiliaries and Preaching in Anglo-Saxon England', *Peritia*, 4 (1985), 207–42

Constable, Giles, 'The Language of Preaching in the Twelfth Century', *Viator*, 25 (1994), 131–52

Conti, Aidan, 'The Old Norse Afterlife of Ralph d'Escures' *Homilia de assumptione Mariae*', *Journal of English and Germanic Philology*, 107 (2008), 215–38

Cross, James, *Cambridge, Pembroke College MS 25: A Carolingian Sermonary Used by Anglo-Saxon Preachers*, King's College London Medieval Studies, 1 (Exeter: King's College London, 1987)

Dahl, J. C. C., *Denkmale einer sehr ausgebildeten Holzbaukunst aus den frühesten Jahrhunderten in den innern Landschaften Norwegens* (Dresden: Dahl, 1837)

Dain, Alphonse, *Les Manuscrits*, 3rd edn (Paris: Société d'édition 'les belles lettres', 1975)

Degnbol, Helle, and others, eds, *Ordbog over det norrøne prosasprog*, 3 vols (København: Arnamagnæanske kommision, 1989–2004), I: *Registre* (1989)

Dolbeau, F., 'Du nouveau sur un sermonnaire de Cambridge', *Scriptorium*, 42 (1988), 255–57

Frederiksen, Britta Olrik, 'Til engleafsnittet i Gregors 34. evangeliehomilie i norrøn oversættelse', in *Opuscula*, VII, Bibliotheca Arnamagnæana, 34 (København: Reitzel, 1979), pp. 62–93

Hall, Thomas N., 'Latin Sermons and Lay Preaching from Post-Reform Canterbury', in *The Power of Words: Anglo-Saxon Studies Presented to Donald G. Scragg*, ed. by Hugh Magennis and Jonathan Wilcox (Morgantown: West Virginia University Press, 2006), pp. 132–70

——, 'Old Norse-Icelandic Sermons', in *The Sermon*, ed. by B. M. Kienzle, Typologie des sources du Moyen Âge occidental, 81–83 (Turnhout: Brepols, 2000), pp. 661–709

Hjelde, Oddmund, *Norsk preken i det 12. århundre: studier i gammel norsk homiliebok* (Oslo: [n. pub.], 1990)

Indrebø, Gustav, *Gamal norsk homiliebok: Cod. AM 619 4to* (Oslo: Universitetsforslaget, 1966; orig. publ. Dybwad, 1931)

Kolsrud, Oluf, *Messuskýringar: liturgisk symbolik frå den norsk-islandske kyrkja i millomalderen* (Oslo: Dybwad for Kjeldeskriftfondet, 1952)

Lidén, Hans-Emil, 'Stave Church', in *Medieval Scandinavia: An Encyclopedia*, ed. by Phillip Pulsiano (London: Garland, 1993), pp. 609–10

Magerøy, H., 'In dedicatione ecclesiæ sermo: om overleveringa av "Stavkyrkjepreika"', in *Opuscula*, VIII, Bibliotheca Arnamagnæana, 38 (København: Reitzel, 1985), pp. 96–122

McCullough, Peter, *Sermons at Court: Politics and Religion in Elizabethan and Jacobean Preaching*, Cambridge Studies in Early Modern British History (Cambridge: Cambridge University Press, 1998)

Moffat, Douglas, 'Anglo-Saxon Scribes and Old English Verse', *Speculum*, 67 (1992), 805–27

Nichols, Stephen, 'Introduction: Philology in a Manuscript Culture', *Speculum*, 65 (1990), 1–10

Paasche, Fredrik, *Homiliu-Bók [Icelandic Sermons]*, Corpus codicum Islandicorum medii aevi, 8 (København: Levin, 1935)

Salvesen, Astrid, *Gammelnorsk homiliebok*, with introduction and commentary by Erik Gunnes (Oslo: Universitetsforlaget, 1971)

Schumacher, Jan, '"Den hellige ånds port": til belysning av et særpreget motiv i Stavkirkiprekenen', in *Transformasjoner i vikingtid og norrøn middelalder*, ed. by Gro Steinsland, Møteplass Middelalder, 1 (Oslo: Unipub, 2006), pp. 153–68

Scragg, D. G., *Dating and Style in Old English Composite Homilies*, H. M. Chadwick Memorial Lectures, 9 (Cambridge: Department of Anglo-Saxon, Norse and Celtic, 1998)

Spatz, Nancy, 'Church Porches and the Liturgy', in *The Liturgy of the Medieval Church*, ed. by Thomas Heffernan and E. Ann Matter (Kalamazoo: Medieval Institute Publications, 2001), pp. 327–67

Spencer, Helen, *English Preaching in the Late Middle Ages* (Oxford: Oxford University Press, 1993)

Symes, Carol, 'Manuscript Matrix, Modern Canon', in *Oxford Twenty-First Century Approaches to Literature: Middle English*, ed. by Paul Strohm (Oxford: Oxford University Press, 2007), pp. 7–22

Þorvaldur Bjarnarson, *Leifar fornra kristinna fræða íslenskra: Codex Arna-Magnæanus 677 4to auk annara enna elztu brota af ízlenzkum guðfræðisritum* (København: Hagerup, 1878)

Treharne, Elaine, 'The Life of English in the Mid-Twelfth Century: Ralph d'Escures' Homily on the Virgin Mary', in *Writers in the Reign of Henry II*, ed. by Ruth Kennedy and Simon Meecham-Jones (New York: Palgrave, 2006), pp. 169–86

Turville-Petre, Gabriel, 'The Old Norse Homily on the Dedication', in *Nine Norse Studies*, Viking Society for Northern Research Text Series, 5 (London: University College London, 1972), pp. 79–101 (first publ. in *Mediaeval Studies*, 11 (1949), 206–18)

Weenan, Andrea de Leeuw van, *The Icelandic Homily Book, Perg. 15 4to in the Royal Library, Stockholm* (Reykjavík: Stofnun Árna Magnússonar, 1993)

Woods, Jennifer, 'Six New Sermons by Hrabanus Maurus on the Virtues and Vices', *Revue Bénédictine*, 107 (1997), 280–306

Zumthor, Paul, *Essai de poétique médiévale*, Collection poétique (Paris: Seuil, 1972)

The Performative Non-Canonicity of the Canonical: *Íslendingasǫgur* and their Traditional Referentiality

Slavica Ranković

The texts considered in this article can hardly be more canonical. Indeed, what kind of origin stories would the sagas of Icelanders be if they were not canonized, that is, recommended as true and genuine? The reason these narratives figure in a volume on non-canonical texts, however, is that they teach us to distinguish between the sense of canon (from Greek *kanōn*, 'rule,' 'standard')[1] derived from the academic practice of appraising, of setting ideals of literary achievement, and a sense of canon as a rule of thumb that gathers multiple performed identities of a living tradition into a working template for a social contract, that is, the 'spirit of a nation'. In particular, I will suggest that the dark overtones of discipline (as in 'discipline and punishment') that inform our intuitions about modern educational, normative, and canonical texts might serve us poorly when studying what we commonly call 'traditional texts'.

For a body of texts to fully perform such rigorous canonical duties, to communicate (as textbooks often do) particular sets of social, ethical, and aesthetic norms, to educate and discipline a community of its subscribers, one would expect it to be disciplined itself, in the sense that it should at least be definable as that — a body — to begin with. But where (and when) exactly are the sagas

---

[1] See <http://www.merriam-webster.com/dictionary/canon> [accessed 5 September 2012].

Slavica Ranković, University of Bergen, Postdoctoral Researcher, slavica@milos-and-slavica.net

of Icelanders? What constitutes their normative corpus? The searching gaze instantly falls on the beautifully engraved leather spines of the *Íslenzk fornrit* editions. While in their binding uniformity they lend the sagas unity and an undisputable corporeity — concrete and heavy, to be sure, so that even a slight tremor of the library shelf would set a doubting scholar running for cover — they nevertheless do so only strenuously. Their introductions and footnotes feature multiple sites of exclusions ('such and such a manuscript is taken as a basis of this saga text, but all these late/derivative/incomplete/fragmentary are not'; 'for an alternative wording/divergent version of this part of the story, see manuscript x'), and abound with referrals ('this event/episode/character is treated differently in the sagas x and y') and with caveats ('even though this saga does not take place on the Icelandic soil, it is still included here because [...]', 'the strong fantastic and supernatural elements actually place this saga within the generic vicinity of the *fornaldarsǫgur*, yet [...]'). The bulky corpus is thus replete with proportionately bulky provisos that pull apart from within its stylishly encrusted unity and are continually forcing the genre's canonical self to face up to its non-canonical self.

If as textually performed 'multiforms'[2] the sagas already problematize their own canonicity, they do so even more forcefully if their (now widely accepted) oral background is also taken into account. With each performance (return, repetition), a saga would have at once been the site of iteration and change, a place where communal identity, ideals, and values were not simply passed down, 'taught' to the young, but were simultaneously being learnt from these 'pupils' in the live interactions in which the very confirmation of one's identity vitally depends on continual renegotiation and readjustment in order for it to fit a changing world. In other words, in oral performance there is no such thing as a safe or innocent handling of living traditional narratives and identity stories. By focusing on the formulaic features of the sagas, showing how through usage and mutual referentiality even these most regulatory and regulated elements of the saga master narratives, in their very regularity and iterability, already enable diversity and are susceptible to change, I also hope to show that, as both textually and orally performed narratives, as lived storyworlds, the canonical sagas in an important sense resist canonization through the dialogism that they engender.

---

[2] This is how Lord describes oral forms, but the concept (as discussed below) is also applicable to various manuscript realizations of the 'same' story, i.e. textual performances; Lord, *The Singer of Tales*, p. 100.

Traditional Formulae are not Literary Clichés

The common prejudice regarding the formula — that it is an oral counterpart of a literary cliché — needs to be addressed first. In *The Singer of Tales*, Albert B. Lord, aware that his theory of oral-formulaic composition might carry this unwanted connotation, already draws attention to their remarkable adaptability/flexibility and cautions that 'usefulness of composition carries no implication of opprobrium'.[3] His defence of formulae has, however, mainly emphasized their utility: formulaic technique is there to enable the singer, 'to serve him as a craftsman, not to enslave him'; 'without this usefulness the style [...] the whole practice would collapse or would have never been born'.[4] Seductive on the one hand, this insistence on the formulae's ultimate role as mnemonic/improvisational devices has, on the other, given rise to a need to defend the artiness of traditional art against the utilitarian tedium: if something is primarily useful, then it cannot be all that beautiful; and if the singer is indeed a craftsman, then he is not much of an artist, a genius.

Such reaction has in turn led to overemphasizing the role of the last contributor in the development of the traditional text, splitting the studies of oral and orally derived literature into two camps. That for Lord himself this 'mechanism versus aesthetic'[5] dichotomy does not exist (i.e. the utility of formulae does not in itself contradict or jeopardize the artistry of the traditional idiom) might be discerned from the following passage:

> [The singer's] oft-used phrases and lines lose something in sharpness, yet many of them must resound with overtones from the dim past whence they come. Were we to train our ears to catch these echoes, we might cease to apply the clichés of another criticism to oral poetry and thereby become aware of its own riches.[6]

Still, Lord's main preoccupation is the working of oral tradition; he does not have the time to engage further with its aesthetics, trace the echoes and the riches that he intuits are there. As with any pioneering work (and *The Singer of Tales* was such a work, at least in the West), the main task is not to meet all the challenges but to outline them, to prompt a development of new sensitivities, as well as to designate the possibilities for further research.

---

[3] Lord, *The Singer of Tales*, p. 65.
[4] Lord, *The Singer of Tales*, pp. 54, 65.
[5] See Foley, *Immanent Art*, p. 3.
[6] Lord, *The Singer of Tales*, p. 65.

On Traditional Referentiality:
The Aesthetic and Semantic Acumen of Formulae

Thirty years after the publication of *The Singer of Tales*, John Miles Foley started from where Lord had left off — with the question of how traditional idioms signify, how they produce aesthetic effects. For Foley, as for Lord, there is no rupture between the utility and aesthetics of formulae: traditional narratives produce meaning and achieve their literary effects because rather than in spite of their formulaity. It is the power of formulaic features to evoke the complex webs of traditional associations that enables them to signify beyond any of their particular (oral or textual) realizations. The shared context, the common identity of the particular interpretative community enables formulae to do so with the utmost economy. Note how the following quotation closely mirrors the points Lord makes above about the traditional art being an echoic and resounding, rather than enslaving, medium:

> Traditional elements reach out of the immediate instance in which they appear to the fecund totality of the entire tradition, defined synchronically and diachronically, and they bear meanings as wide and deep as the tradition they encode. The 'how' of the traditional idiom, while overlapping at some points with the 'how' of the literary text, also and crucially includes an extratextual dimension uniquely the domain of oral traditional art. This idiom is liberating rather than imprisoning, centrifugal, rather than centripetal, explosively connotative, rather than claustrophobically clichéd.[7]

Even though the dynamic discussed in this particular passage is related to oral traditional art, it also applies to orally derived texts written at the interface of orality and literacy, texts that both rely on oral lore and are in turn accepted back and recycled by oral tradition. These are the texts whose authors and scribes still very much work under oral precepts and attitudes to art, and texts that are still received orally by the majority of the audience. Rather than being discrete entities, fixed objects, medieval traditional narratives such as the sagas are, much like their oral counterparts, entities distributed across their various oral and manuscript instances of realization (textual performances) — they are multiforms that forever exist as potentialities. In fact, a special virtue of Foley's study of oral poetics and aesthetics is the wealth of examples that show how different oral traditions (Muslim and Christian Serbo-Croatian oral epic), but also different orally derived literary works (the Ancient Greek *Iliad* and

---

[7] Foley, *Immanent Art*, p. 7.

the Anglo-Saxon *Beowulf*), rely in various degrees on traditional referentiality and in their own unique ways trigger this metonymic process by which the whole 'immanent'[8] tradition is summoned by its parts (i.e. orally or textually performed instances) and brought to bear on their interpretation.

How does traditional referentiality work within the sagas? For example, as an audience gathers to hear about the quarrel between Jǫkull Ingimundarsson of Vatnsdalr and the relative of Finnbogi the Mighty, the Norwegian Bergr,[9] the reception is not merely conditioned by the immediate sentences that the saga-teller or reader utters. Rather, each audience member receives this particular incarnation of the story against as many of its previous realizations (whether read or told) as s/he has experienced before, from, let us say, a different saga-teller or reader, in a different mood, under different circumstances, from a different perspective. Consider, for instance, *Finnboga saga ramma*, which favours Finnbogi the Mighty over the Ingimundarssons: the two local traditions are here caught battling over the canonicity of their versions of the same event.[10] Thus, this particular related episode from *Vatnsdœla saga* is an instance of the text which is not all contained in this single performance; it is rather distributed across its previous performances and even those yet to be realized, for at the heart of the complex unity of their immanent existence they maintain the diversity of the future.[11]

---

[8] On the immanent nature of the sagas, see Clover, 'The Long Prose Form'. In fact, John Foley acknowledges his debt to Clover for the inspiration for the title of his book *Immanent Art: From Structure to Meaning in Traditional Oral Epic* (p. ix). Underlying Foley's views on the relation between the epic tradition and a performed piece (an epic poem) is the Saussurean model of language (more explicitly discussed in Foley, *Homer's Traditional Art*, pp. 19–20). Kellogg, 'The Prehistory of Eddic Poetry', also considers tradition as a cultural competence, a sort of *langue*, and its performed instances as *parole*, but the connection was already made about sixty years earlier in 1929 by the Russian Formalists Roman Jakobson and Petr Bogatyrev; see Jakobson and Bogatyrev, 'On the Boundary between the Studies of Folklore and Literature'. In Ranković, 'The Temporality of the (Immanent) Saga', I argue for a revision of the concept of immanence in accordance with the post-structuralist (Derridean) revision of structuralism, i.e. no *langue* (read: tradition/saga/formula) is immune from *parole* (read: performed instance of a tradition/saga/formula), and so no *parole* exists that is not already a *langue*, and vice versa.

[9] *Vatnsdœla saga*, ed. by Einar Ól. Sveinsson, chaps 32–35.

[10] *Finnboga saga ramma*, in *Íslendinga sögur og þættir*, ed. by Bragi Háldorsson and others, i, 625–73. For more about the differences between the two sagas in their reporting of the same events, see Gísli Sigurðsson, 'Another Audience — Another Saga'; Gísli Sigurðsson, *The Medieval Icelandic Saga and Oral Tradition*.

[11] On traditional texts' evolutionary dynamic of production, and their distributed authorship, see Ranković, 'The Distributed Author'; Ranković, 'Who Is Speaking in Traditional

Furthermore, this account of Jǫkull's dealing with Bergr will be considered against his other feats, as well as other kinds of virtual entries to be found under the reference 'Jǫkull' within the tradition. One of the more obvious ones would have to be his giant great-uncle and a namesake whose appearance, temper, and prodigious strength the younger Jǫkull closely mirrors.[12] There are, however, others against whom he could be measured too: his grandson, Jǫkull Bárðarsson is similarly 'mikill maðr ok sterkr ok inn mesti ofsamaðr [...] mjǫk ódæll, en þó mikilhœfr maðr' ('a big, strong man and exceptionally arrogant [...] very overbearing, but a man of many gifts'),[13] and other Jǫkulls in the sagas, even if unrelated by blood, still show the same supreme strength and irascibility of the hero at hand. Jǫkull Búason (*Kjalnesinga saga*, *Jǫkuls þáttr Búasonar*), for example, is also prodigiously endowed with muscle and prowess, and is even a descendant of giants himself (although he is not as quick-tempered), while Jǫkull Hólmkelsson from *Víglundar saga*, and Jǫkull Þorgrímsson and Jǫkull the Viking from *Gunnars saga Keldugnúpsfífls*, seem to be pure hotheads and troublemakers, mirroring (even augmenting) Jǫkull Ingimundarsson's own shortcomings.[14] All these Jǫkulls represent strong reverberative points within the echoic saga medium and have potential bearing on the interpretation of our particular Jǫkull under scrutiny.

Texts?'. I see this production dynamic as the facilitator of the interpretative strategy of traditional referentiality.

[12] Name giving in traditional cultures is, of course, hardly ever arbitrary. The baby either showed resemblance to a person (usually a relative) from birth whose name s/he would then be given, or it was given the name in the hope that s/he would take on the characteristics of the namesake. It is not by accident that Jǫkull's wise but physically weaker and smaller elder brother came to be named Þorsteinn, just like their great-grandfather whose stature and wisdom he inherited. The two Þórólfrs from *Egils saga* are also classic cases in point. Names in the sagas can sometimes also act as descriptions of their bearers. I am grateful to Jonas Wellendorf for drawing my attention to the fact that, since the word *jǫkull* means glacier, the connotation of strength and the association with giants (who tend to dwell on glaciers) are present in the very names of the above discussed heroes.

[13] *Grettis saga Ásmundarsonar*, ed. by Guðni Jónsson, p. 117; *The Saga of Grettir the Strong*, trans. by Scudder, II, 104. Interestingly enough, this similarity is not commented on in *Vatnsdæla saga*, but there is no need for it either: the saga writer can rely on his 'silent but ever-present partner' (Foley, *Immanent Art*, p. 60) — tradition — to supplement his account. In other words, he could have counted on his audience's ability (or at least the ability of some of its members) to make the appropriate connection.

[14] *Kjalnesinga saga*, in *Íslendinga sögur og þættir*, ed. by Bragi Háldorsson and others, II, 1437–59; *Jökuls þáttr Búasonar*, in *Íslendinga sögur og þættir*, ed. by Bragi Háldorsson and others, II, 1459–66; *Víglundar saga*, ed. by Jóhannes Halldórsson; *Gunnars saga Keldugnúpsfífls*, in *Íslendinga sögur og þættir*, ed. by Bragi Háldorsson and others, II, 1144–65.

At the same time, the 'bearings' of these characters are always yet to be synchronized into a unidirectional commitment. 'All these Jǫkulls' are pulling *the* Jǫkull apart from inside out by competing attitudes. This emerging, immanent Jǫkull is thus a gathering together and a tearing apart all at once, heartfelt and lived through 'for real' by the community's every stakeholder. 'All these Jǫkulls' are brought together and maintained in their gathering by the common question: 'who am I'/'who are we', 'what would I/we do in Jǫkull's shoes', 'what should I/we do'? Yet this very gathering disperses the unity of the identity question/explanation across time and space and so many performances. This immanent Jǫkull is thus a unity whose claim to oneness rests upon its ongoing cultivation of diversity, of a certain productive spacing or distancing right at the heart of its own gathering.

To complicate even further the referential webs, the very structure of which resists the vectorial disciplinarity of a canon, just as the audience hears how our hero swings his sword at Bergr (*Vatnsdæla saga*, chap. 32), without the saga writer/teller/reader adding any extra words, a completely different epic career could be summoned — that of yet another famous saga firebrand and the great-grandson of Jǫkull Ingimundarsson, the outlaw Grettir the Strong. The informed audience members could derive enhanced pleasure from knowing that the object which is now threatening Bergr is destined to have an extended and glorious epic life long after its present bearer is dead and gone. Being one of those exceptional weapons that get to be named, *Ættartangi* ('Sword of Generations'; *Vatnsdæla saga*, chap. 32) proves worthy of its appellation: it famously inaugurates Grettir's epic career and enables the first (if also the last) heroic deed of the outlaw's temperate brother Atli (chap. 43) on whom Grettir bestows the sword after winning his own in Norway. A family heirloom, the 'sword of generations' is renamed *Jǫkulsnautr* by Grettir ('Jǫkull's Gift'; *Grettis saga*, chap. 18) and thus becomes strongly linked to two particular family members: a heroic ancestor whose feats have impressed a stamp onto the weapon too strongly to associate it with anyone else, and the first descendant who does proper justice to the sword he is carrying, the worthy heir of Jǫkull and his prodigious gifts — Grettir the Strong. The two heroes are thus, in the most economic yet the most effective way, brought to bear upon each other; *Vatnsdæla saga* and *Grettis saga* spill over their immediate borders, with the former acting as a prologue of sorts to Grettir's epic biography, while in turn his stories act as epilogues to the one presently told.

It is perhaps interesting to note in addition that not only fictional swords are capable of acting as catalysts of traditional referentiality. Real-life objects and landscape features that were often appropriated into the sagas for authenticating purposes[15] are all potential story engines as well. If one happened to be passing Spjótsmýrr ('Spear-Mire') or Kambsnes ('Comb Point'), it would have been difficult not to think of the spearhead that Grettir the Strong lost when he had slain Þorbjǫrn Ox-might and his son (*Grettis saga*, chaps 48 and 49), or the land-taking journey of Unnr/Auðr the Deep-minded during which she famously lost her comb.[16] A big boulder with a grooved surface somewhere at Borg might well have prompted a person to ponder on whether this could be that same rock for which Skalla-Grímr had to sail all the way to Miðfjarðareyjar and which he used to forge his iron upon.[17] Even sitting with one's kinsmen in the booth at Þingvellir awaiting the next day's presentation of one's case at the Assembly might have occasioned the (silent or loud) recollection of various legal duels of Njáll, Snorri, Sturla, and other gifted and sly lawmen, which could have affected the course of the next day's legal proceedings themselves. And conversely, someone's stunning legal feat would have in turn affected the retelling of the *þing* triumphs of these famous saga lawmen. Thus as the saga heroes and luminaries are summoned to teach, be role models, invite identification, so are they in turn being 'taught' contemporary history, heroism, ethics, values, law, etc., in order to remain serviceable role models. This kind of interactive and ongoing canonization defies the more vertical disciplining that we associate with modern educational systems and the canonical works they promulgate.[18]

One could perhaps concede that the arguments presented above relating to traditional referentiality might work fine for the original audiences and the sagas as they were, but could wonder nevertheless about the relevance of this meaning-generating engine and an interpretative strategy to us today. To be sure, the sagas that we encounter now are no longer a part of a living tradition

[15] For more on the use of objects and landscape features as authenticating devices, see Ranković, 'Golden Ages and Fishing Grounds'; Ranković, 'Authentication and Authenticity in the Sagas of Icelanders'.

[16] *Laxdæla saga*, ed. by Einar Ól. Sveinsson, chap. 5.

[17] *Egils saga Skalla-Grímssonar*, ed. by Sigurður Nordal, chap. 30.

[18] Of course, a feedback loop also exists in modern educational systems. However, it is subject to a number of levels of remove and of generalization. The master narrative passed down (or rather, downloaded) to young minds is thus still very responsive to them, but in the sense that, for example, 64 per cent of girls as opposed to only 31 per cent of boys are enrolling at a particular higher education programme, or in the sense that 24 per cent of pupils with special needs end up moving to private schools which roughly corresponds to the percentage of parents who can afford it, and so on.

and, unlike the original audiences, we do not approach these orally derived texts with the entire immanent tradition in our bones. This, however, does not mean that all aspects of the interpretative dynamics inherent in it (i.e. traditional referentiality) are lost to us. Each of the separate works we encounter is in a lively dialogue with the rest of the works in the extant corpus (even if only as represented by Íslenzk fornrit), continuing to create an abundance of interpretational possibilities. The more of the corpus we know, the better our chance to enjoy the separate works.

For example, just as the modern reader engages with Þorgerðr Egilsdóttir in *Laxdæla saga* — the powerful, slightly avaricious matriarch and the avenger of her son's death — without any effort whatsoever on the saga writers'/scribes' part, another, rather different Þorgerðr is conjured instantaneously: the benevolent, if mischievous, sharply witted young woman who manages to trick her headstrong father into taking some food after, deeply bereaved by the loss of his favourite son, he had decided to starve himself to death (*Egils saga*, chap. 79). This 'second' Þorgerðr from *Egils saga* adds new dimensions to the 'first', making her a complex character and thus nuancing our response. Moreover, her father Egill's own temper, cunning, and avarice (summoned in the minds of the reader by her very patronymic, *Egilsdóttir*) offers more clues as to how the young, lively Þorgerðr from *Egils saga*, becomes the embittered Þorgerðr of *Laxdæla saga*. It is through this fierce economy of traditional referentiality, relying on the readers'/listeners' knowledge of tradition to expand the immediate borders of the text at hand, that the ever-incomplete text achieves an amazing opulence and vibrancy of meaning: the experience of the immanent story is itself complete. It is precisely this immanence of her character, the incompleteness of any particular realization of it (an incompleteness that would be intolerable in modern-day identity stories) that allows us to treat Þorgerðr as one and the same character across the saga corpus.

Traditional Referentiality = Intertextuality?

Herein also lies an important nuance between otherwise very similar dynamics of signification and interpretation: the one just discussed, pertaining to oral and orally derived texts; the other — intertextuality — pertaining to the now more familiar, post-Gutenbergian literary texts. While both models acknowledge the relational nature of interpretation and meaning in general, they are nevertheless distinct in the context in which this relational intuition is applied, with 'the anxiety of influence'[19] (and the anxiety of interpretation) being at the heart of this contextual distinction. Namely, the two kinds of reproduction technologies — content-sensitive, involving more fluid texts (e.g. oral, manuscript, early print, electronic-interactive), and content-insensitive, involving more fixed texts (e.g. modern print, electronic-static) — put different pressures on the singers/storytellers/scribes and on modern literary authors, as well as build up different attitudes and expectations in their respective audiences.[20]

To be sure, as with the mentioned immanent traditional reference 'Þorgerðr Egilsdóttir' we can easily think of an analogous virtual reference within the literary tradition, for example 'Ulysses'. Along with its more straightforward entries such as 'Homer's' Odysseus,[21] Dante's Ulysses, and Tennyson's Ulysses, this virtual reference would equally include Joyce's Leopold Bloom, and even Everett McGill, or rather, Ulysses Everett McGill, from the Coen Brothers' 2000 film *O Brother, Where Art Thou?* Just as the traditional audience is invited to draw and revel in various relations between these characters, so is the modern one, but quite unlike its traditional counterpart, the modern audience does so by emphasizing what distinguishes these characters from one another. For all the interactions that occur between the entries that comprise the literary 'Ulysses' reference, they remain discrete, autonomous (if not independent) entities; in fact, it is only because Joyce and the Coen Brothers rely on their relatively safe, separate existence that they can name their characters Leopold or Everett (and yet expect them to be recognized as some kind of Ulysses figures) to begin with.

While it is not up to either of these works to keep *The Odyssey* or Dante's 'Canto of Ulysses' alive, the oral entries that contribute to the traditional virtual reference 'Þorgerðr Egilsdóttir' are, on the other hand, in constant need of resuscitation because they are virtual/ephemeral themselves. Their basic physics is vitally dependent on the continual retelling of stories about Þorgerðr, good or bad renderings, inspired or not.[22] Until writing becomes fully interiorized as

[19] See Bloom, *The Anxiety of Influence*. On my usage of this term as distinct from Bloom's, see Ranković and Ranković, 'The Talent of the Distributed Author'.

[20] For more on the distinction between the content-sensitive and the content-insensitive technologies of reproduction (as preferred to the outdated orality-literacy divide), see Ranković, 'The Oral-Written Continuum as a Space'; Ranković and Ranković, 'The Talent of the Distributed Author'.

[21] The oral background of *The Odyssey* is here momentarily neglected and the epic is treated as in popular perception — as a canonical work of classical literature attributable to a lone author-genius.

[22] This is not to say that an oral audience is aesthetically indifferent, but that, for a story to survive, it does not matter whether it is well or badly performed. Just as long as it is around,

a technology,[23] the same rules apply to the saga characters as developed within the manuscript culture, since, as previously mentioned, this is still being done under the auspices of oral poetics, affecting the process not only of composition, but of transmission and reception too.

Whether as an oral or a manuscript multiform, when a text is perpetually fluid, impossible to grasp as a fixed object, the variability is a given. As Lord notes: 'the differences are inherent in the very process of transmission and composition',[24] and so the pressure is on preservation. This pressure will produce a situation in which an emulation of tradition (and a reliance on formulae) never comes close to resembling a literary cliché because it always implies a recreation. A true repetition, or, to be more precise, reduplication, only becomes possible when the text one repeats is safely stored somewhere, available for inspection. It is only when the fixity of the text is granted (ultimately by print[25]) that cliché is born, and that the anxiety of influence sets in. Thus, even though the literary tradition is as much formative for the individual talent as is the oral tradition, as Judith Still and Michael Worton point out, 'the writer's (and the reader's) relationship with this tradition is usually, perhaps necessarily, one of contestation'.[26] Freed from the pressure to preserve, writers face the pressure for variation, and so originality — if not origination[27] — becomes

---

surprisingly little seems to be lost by a bad performance. As the nineteenth-century Serbian collector of oral lore, Vuk Stefanović Karadžić, remarks: 'a good singer mends even a bad song, in accordance with other songs he knows. Thus, I think, were some Podrugović [Vuk considered this singer the best among those from whom he collected epic songs] to hear the worst song today, he would, after a few days, say it nicely and in the right order, the way his other songs are'. Karadžić, 'Preface', p. 378, my translation.

[23] Ong, *Orality and Literacy*, pp. 82, 56, defines interiorization as the point at which new technologies such as writing stop being 'mere exterior aids but also interior transformations of consciousness'. 'Writing has to be personally interiorized to affect thinking processes.'

[24] Lord, *The Singer of Tales*, p. 112.

[25] This remark, of course, does not encompass the early days of print, when publishers and printers, yet unburdened by copyright laws and authorship issues, intervened with more freedom in the manuscripts they were printing, and editions of one and the same work varied; see, for example, Ezell, *Social Authorship and the Advent of Print*. Ong's ideas regarding interiorization of new technologies are highly applicable in this context too (compare note 23 above).

[26] Worton and Still, 'Introduction', p. 10.

[27] Structuralist and post-structuralist scholars such as Roland Barthes, Michel Foucault, Jacques Derrida, Stanley Fish, and others have successfully challenged the author as the absolute origin of meaning, but have not necessarily denied him/her 'the power to mix writings' in an original way; Barthes, 'The Death of the Author', p. 128.

an expectation. It is with this expectation that the modern reader approaches Joyce's or the Coens' Ulysses figures.

For Þorgerðr, however, an interpretative alternative exists, as she was treated and developed according to the traditional poetics, projecting the model of authorship as apprenticeship rather than Oedipal rebellion. Instead of endeavouring to distinguish itself from the previous ones, each new rendering (whether in oral or manuscript form) of her character strives to come as close as possible to the traditional, immanent Þorgerðr as conceived of by each contributor at a particular time and place. Her perpetual immanence, however, and adaptivity to the ever-changing needs, views, and attitudes of her interpretative community will, without the necessity for any deliberate effort, lead to such different portrayals as those encountered in *Laxdæla saga* and *Egils saga*,[28] adding to Þorgerðr's complexity as one and the same character at the level of the saga corpus. It is these inverted attitudes and expectations of modern and traditional authors as well as their respective audiences that mark the points of divergence between principally related strategies of interpretation — intertextuality and traditional referentiality.[29] These same attitudes and expectations also mark a difference between traditional and modern master narratives, with the implication that the former are never mastered and are forever in the process of remastering themselves through performance. As the sections to follow attempt to demonstrate, the intricate workings of traditional referentiality at various narrative scales and in various components of the sagas (formulaic plot, character, motif), they should also serve to further illuminate this adaptational dimension that characterizes traditional canons.

Traditional Referentiality and Paths of Emplotment

As argued earlier, formulae that today to an untrained eye may indeed appear as 'claustrophobically clichéd' had the opposite effect. What is more, the more of the corpus one knows, the less likely the formulaic expressions are to sound — even to the modern reader — as the inarticulate muttering of a lover who cannot muster a better compliment than that his beloved has beautiful eyes. While the beloved might pout at the emptiness of the tired expression, the unstinting reader will become embroiled in an intricate web, which may not

---

[28] This is not to say that such deliberate effort cannot or does not occur within tradition, only that it does not have to in order for such different portrayals to emerge.

[29] For more on the relationship between intertextuality and traditional referentiality, see Ranković, 'The Distributed Author', pp. 108–31.

be as immense as the living tradition had once been, but which will still have preserved the ability to reward the richness of content. Whether we consider the small-scale formulaic features in the sagas, such as the blue-black[30] cloak/clothes that heroes tend to wear as they set off to kill,[31] or their blisters bursting before a disaster, or the formulaic themes (such as that of a young Icelander venturing on a journey, or the troublesome weddings), the special way in which these instances resonate with the similar in the corpus does not allow for tedium to set in.

For instance, when Kjartan from *Laxdæla saga* heads for Norway and forms a close friendship with the Norwegian princess Ingibjǫrg, the audience would indeed not have been in suspense as to whether or not this would (negatively) affect his relationship with his intended, Guðrún Ósvífrsdóttir, whom he leaves behind in Iceland. From the experience of other Icelandic saga heroes (e.g. Egill, Þórólfr, Hrútr) the reader/listener would know that Norwegian female royalty were often more trouble than they were worth, rather clingy and likely to curse you or do their best to have you killed. Suspense was, nevertheless, created in how it would all happen and what consequences would occur. Tradition again holds some clues to this puzzle. Although Chapter 19 of *Laxdæla saga* mentions both how Kjartan's great-uncle Hrútr was a lover of the Norwegian queen Gunnhildr and how his first marriage ended in a divorce, no causal connection is made between the two instances, nor is an indication given as to the reason

---

[30] The colour black/dark in Old Icelandic is designated by two adjectives: *blár* ('blue' in Modern Icelandic) and *svartr* ('black' in Modern Icelandic). It seems that the first adjective is used in the sagas mostly for the blue-black shade of the dye used to colour clothing; before the late fourteenth century it was not possible to produce a deep black colour (compare Wolf, 'The Color Blue in Old Norse-Icelandic Literature'), while *svartr* 'seems at this period to have referred to a brown-black colour' (*The Complete Sagas of Icelanders*, ed. by Viðar Hreinsson and others, v, 406). The situation described above usually calls for the use of *blár*, rather than *svartr* (see, however, note 56). In fact, some saga writers (and their audience) seem not only well aware of both the closeness and difference between the two shades of black, but also aesthetically exploit the edginess of these notions. Thus in the closing chapters of *Laxdæla saga*, it is said of Valla-Ljótr that for everyday pursuits he wore 'svartan kyrtil' ('a brown-black tunic'), while he wore 'blánn kyrtil' ('a blue-black tunic') when getting ready to fight (*Laxdæla saga*, ed. by Einar Ól. Sveinsson, p. 245; *The Saga of the People of Laxardal*, trans. by Kunz, v, 129). There is a nearly identical contrast about the hero's moods in *Valla-Ljóts saga* itself, only there he wears a *brúnan* ('brown'), rather than a *svartan kyrtil* when in a good mood, and a 'blán kyrtil [...] er víghugr var á honum' ('black tunic [...] when the killing mood was upon him') (*Valla-Ljóts saga*, ed. by Jónas Kristjánsson, p. 240; *Valla-Ljot's Saga*, trans. by Acker, IV, 135).

[31] See Wolf, 'The Color Blue in Old Norse-Icelandic Literature', p. 71.

for the divorce. But the reader familiar with *Njáls saga*[32] will remember that it is the promiscuous and vengeful Norwegian queen (quite a different Gunnhildr from the one sketched in *Laxdæla saga*) that has put a curse on Hrútr. With our hero not being able to consummate the marriage, his wife Unnr requests and is granted a divorce (chap. 7). Interestingly enough, Gunnhildr is surprisingly mindful of Hrútr's manhood in her curse, as the reason for the couple's inability to have sex is not that Hrútr is impotent, but rather that at the crucial moment he becomes overly endowed. In any case, Hrútr's affair with the queen not only affects his personal life, but breeds fatal consequences for the whole district: after Unnr marries another man, she gives birth to the greatest villain of the saga, Mǫrðr Valgarðsson, whose schemes eventually bring about the deaths of many noble people, the two heroes of *Njáls saga*, Gunnarr and Njáll, among them.

But what does this have to do with Kjartan? As opposed to Hrútr's liaison with Gunnhildr, Kjartan's with Ingibjǫrg seems rather platonic, yet it is hinted on several occasions that it might be more than that. When Kjartan's companion Bolli (a cousin, foster-brother, and also a rival) sets back for Iceland, he reproaches Kjartan for not joining him, accusing that it is not only the king's orders but also his beautiful sister that are keeping him in Norway: 'en hǫfum þat fyrir satt, at þú munir fátt þat, er á Íslandi er til skemmtanar, þá er þú sitr á tali við Ingibjǫrgu konungssystur' ('I also take it for granted that you remember little that might entertain you in Iceland when you're conversing with the king's sister Ingibjǫrg').[33] Kjartan does not deny the accusation, but simply asks Bolli not to go on saying such things (because it is nonsense, one wonders, or because he does not want to be found out?) and to give his regards to their family and friends instead. (Guðrún is presumably among the latter, although, in line with Bolli's own obliqueness, no explicit mention is made.) Later, when Kjartan himself decides to go back to Iceland, Ingibjǫrg clearly feels jilted and states that she knows it is of his own accord that he is leaving, not because others are urging him. We are further told that when the time came for Kjartan to leave he embraced Ingibjǫrg, and that 'þeim þœtti fyrir at skiljask' ('both of them regretted having to part').[34] The princess is so distressed that she cannot

---

[32] *Brennu-Njáls Saga*, ed. by Einar Ól. Sveinsson chap. 6.

[33] *Laxdæla saga*, ed. by Einar Ól. Sveinsson, p. 126; *The Saga of the People of Laxardal*, trans. by Kunz, v, 64.

[34] *Laxdæla saga*, ed. by Einar Ól. Sveinsson, p. 131; *The Saga of the People of Laxardal*, trans. by Kunz, v, 67.

even go to see Kjartan off. Moreover, the gift she sends for his bride-to-be (a richly embroidered headdress) is not only a generous and gallant gesture showing that she can rise above her present humiliation but is slightly spiteful and condescending, too: 'vil ek, at þær Íslendinga konur sjái þat, at sú kona er eigi þrælaættar, er þú hefir tal átt við í Nóregi' ('I want Icelandic women to know that the woman you have consorted with here in Norway is hardly the descendent of slaves').[35] The headdress could also be seen as the intended constant reminder for Kjartan's bride of the relationship he had in Norway with a woman of a higher birth: acting as Ingibjǫrg's metonymic extension, the headdress potentially becomes a way for her to come between the couple.[36]

Kjartan's relationship with the Norwegian princess, like Hrútr's with the Norwegian queen, proves fatal: not only does Bolli use it to persuade Guðrún to marry him instead, but the luxurious headdress that the princess sends becomes a catalyst for a series of vengeful acts that eventually lead to the deaths of both Kjartan and Bolli, as well as some of their close kin and friends. Of course, what augments the tragedy here is precisely the fact that Bolli and Kjartan are close relatives themselves; in their feud the rest of the kin are forced to choose sides, and thus everyone loses. The two separate involvements of Icelandic heroes with Norwegian female royalty (Kjartan's with Ingibjǫrg and Hrútr's with Gunnhildr) powerfully illuminate one another and bring gravity and further nuance to the interpretation of both *Laxdæla saga* and *Njáls saga* that would not have been available in any other way. At the same time, as the identity conundrums involving Icelandic ties with Norway bring these two instances together, any particular attitude towards the problem is also pulled apart from within by the diversity that is maintained by the gathering itself.

---

[35] *Laxdæla saga*, ed. by Einar Ól. Sveinsson, p. 131; *The Saga of the People of Laxardal*, trans. by Kunz, v, 67.

[36] An additional interpretation is, as Else Mundal persuasively argues, that the gift of a headdress was also a gesture intended to humiliate Kjartan personally; Mundal, 'Symbol og symbolhandlingar i sagalitteraturen', pp. 58–60. Even though the gift was outwardly dedicated to his betrothed, it is still given to Kjartan, a man, and as such intended as an insult, if a veiled one. In saga literature, presenting a man with a piece of women's clothing (even if it can only barely be read as specifically women's) carries a strong accusation of effeminacy. The author(s) of *Laxdæla saga* is (are) well aware of this, since it is with a similarly ambiguous gesture that, earlier in the saga (chap. 34), Kjartan's fiancée Guðrún gets rid of her first husband (i.e. she presents him with a shirt that is cut a tad lower than what is considered standard for men's garments).

Traditional Referentiality and Characterization

Observed from the perspective of traditional referentiality, some apparently contradictory features in characters, for example the violent temper of Grettir the Strong, become less arbitrary and inexplicable. Not constructed, created from scratch, but evolving over a long period of time, traditional characters such as Grettir often resound with the characteristics of their predecessors, both human, heroic (as we have shown earlier, in Grettir's case Jǫkull Ingimundarsson is among the important ones), as well as mythic — the rash and capricious ancient gods. In his appearance (red hair, enormous physique), in his explosive disposition, and in his role as a dispatcher of monsters and trolls, Grettir strongly evokes the Old Norse deity of thunder, Þórr.[37] In addition, through his role as a poet Grettir also shares some of the characteristics linked to the Norse chief god and the poet of poets — Óðinn. Óðinn (the name is derived from an adjective for 'furious', 'wild', 'mad')[38] famously steals the mead of poetry, pledges one eye in return for wisdom, and also hangs himself as a sacrifice to be able to learn the runes of wisdom.[39] Thus he ultimately becomes the patron of poets in the Scandinavian world who inherit some of his characteristics.

Considering another famous poet of saga literature, Egill Skalla-Grímsson, Margaret Clunies Ross points out that the 'extreme instability of temper [...] accompanies the gift of poetry'.[40] In her opinion, the connection to Óðinn and the old Scandinavian belief that relates the poet's talent with extraordinary mental states (shape-shifting, berserk frenzy, etc.) is further strengthened by the medieval theories of humours, which we may presume were in some form also floating among the common folk, not only the learned elite. Melancholy is the humour characteristic of poets, marked by 'a lack of moderation in [...] behaviour, [...] abrupt transitions from hostility, pettiness and avarice to sociability and generosity'.[41] Observed from this perspective, the responsibility for tempestuous outbursts is somewhat shifted away from the hero, as they are, among the audience with ears trained 'to catch these echoes', understood to be beyond the power of his will. The craft of poetry and the glimpses it affords into the most

---

[37] On Þórr's characteristics and godly attributes, see Branston, *Gods of the North*, pp. 120–23.
[38] See Branston, *Gods of the North*, p. 108.
[39] See Branston, *Gods of the North*, pp. 113–16.
[40] Clunies Ross, 'The Art of Poetry and the Figure of the Poet', p. 131.
[41] Clunies Ross, 'The Art of Poetry and the Figure of the Poet', p. 136.

intimate thoughts of its complex creators are the redeeming qualities of the hero-poets, including Grettir: consider the discrepancy in Chapter 47 of the saga between his simultaneous outward indifference, even cheerfulness, after hearing the news of his outlawry and the deaths of his father and elder brother, and the utter inner devastation expressed in the verses Grettir composes on the occasion. The melancholy humour that gives rise to profound emotions expressed in poetry (not only violent outbursts) is thus rendered a necessary evil, and so Grettir's contradictions resonate with those of other saga skalds.

Still, when Grettir in particular is in question, Margaret Clunies Ross has some reservations and contends that the most significant way in which Grettir diverges from the typical skald characters is that he is more pronouncedly anti-social and 'given to much more generalized aggression (including a sadistic interest in animals)'.[42] In his otherwise astute analysis of psychology in *Grettis saga*, Russell Poole also seems to agree that 'sadism or pathological cruelty' would be a fitting, albeit 'modern assessment'.[43] Modern or not, if this diagnosis were correct, Grettir would hardly have deserved such a strong iconic presence in Icelandic culture,[44] let alone have inspired Matthías Jochumsson to write those famous words: 'You, Grettir, are my nation.'[45] While the animals on his father's farm indeed suffer cruelly at his hands (he wrings the necks of innocent goslings, and flays the back off of his father's favourite mare, Kengála), we are never led to believe that Grettir takes pleasure in doing so. Thus, the crucial component in the definition of sadism is missing, not to mention that such a heavy modern condemnation seems misplaced to begin with, as the actual word used to categorize Grettir's deeds is *bernskubragð*[46] ('boyish/childish trick',[47] 'prank'[48]). Modern versus medieval sensibilities aside, if Grettir's disposition towards animals were generally cruel, it would be hard to explain that this cold-blooded torturer of animals could be disturbed by the desolate bleating of the ewe whose lamb he slaughtered to satisfy his hunger (chap. 61), or that the ram he encounters on Drangey Island becomes a sort of a playmate and

---

[42] Clunies Ross, 'The Skald Sagas as a Genre', p. 36.

[43] Poole, 'Myth, Psychology, and Society', p. 11.

[44] See Hastrup, 'Tracing Tradition — an Anthropological Perspective'; also Tulinius, *The Matter of the North*, p. 31.

[45] *The Saga of Grettir the Strong*, trans. by Scudder, ii, 49.

[46] *Grettis saga Ásmundarsonar*, ed. by Guðni Jónsson, p. 42.

[47] Zoëga, *Íslenzk-Ensk orðabók*, p. 39.

[48] *The Saga of Grettir the Strong*, trans. by Scudder, ii, 67.

is spared even when the food supplies on the island begin to run low (chap. 74). For all his 'antisocial behaviour', he puts up with a lot of impudence and slovenly behaviour to keep the company of Þorbjǫrn Noise and is congenial enough with good people such as the merry farmer Sveinn.[49]

Rather, the animals could be seen as victims of the vicious war going on between two figures in the household who actually closely resemble one another: young Grettir and his father, Ásmundr. We are told at the outset that Grettir was disliked by his father, his promising, even-tempered, and farming-oriented brother Atli being the favourite (chap. 14). By giving his proud son the tasks he knows must be humiliating for him, Ásmundr deliberately sets out to break Grettir's spirit. In addition, the father-and-son war is unequal, as one side (Ásmundr) has all the power, and the other (Grettir) can only ever strike indirectly, by hurting or ruining something precious to the enemy. As Russell Poole notes, it cannot be a coincidence that Kengála's skin comes off right after Ásmundr orders Grettir to scratch his back by the fire (the space designated for women's work), while heaping abuse on him. The mare's skin becomes the substitute for the one which the insulted Grettir may have really desired to take off at that moment, the one into which he pressed the wool-comb too strongly while scratching it (and barely escaped a beating as a result), the one belonging to his father. Unlike Poole, however, I do not see this in terms of venting, or deflecting anger,[50] but as exacting revenge, something closer to the conceptual world of the sagas.

This, of course, does not excuse Grettir's deeds, but it does put them into the framework of the age-old struggle between generations, and it is precisely at this point that the prism of traditional referentiality may offer new, alternative vistas. In saga literature, it is not only the disobedient children who are criticized, but also parents who disregard the nature of their offspring and impose their will on them too despotically.[51] Furthermore, Grettir is not the only one

---

[49] The episode that starts as a hot pursuit when Grettir 'borrows' Sveinn's horse, Saddle-head, turns into a humorous poetry contest between the pursuer and the pursued, and finally ends in friendship and a lot of merry-making between the two (*Grettis saga Ásmundarsonar*, ed. by Guðni Jónsson, chap. 47).

[50] Poole, 'Myth, Psychology, and Society', p. 11.

[51] Consider, for instance, Hǫskuldr's forceful arrangement of Hallgerðr's first marriage in *Njáls saga* that turns disastrous and forces the father to change his tactics the next time round (*Brennu-Njáls Saga*, ed. by Einar Ól. Sveinsson, chaps 10–13). In this respect, rather than being a mere litotes (Poole, 'Myth, Psychology, and Society', p. 11) or indication of a damaging motherly protectiveness, the even-handed assessment given by Grettir's mother, Ásdís,

to be not simply the second born, but also the second best to his father, or to incur his wrath. Egill Skalla-Grímsson is similarly slighted by his father in respect to his handsome, cheerful-tempered elder brother Þórólfr, and on one occasion only avoids being killed by his parent because his foster-mother draws the attention and the rage of the maddened Skalla-Grímr onto herself. Like Grettir, the twelve-year-old Egill has only limited and indirect options when it comes to avenging himself on his father; thus, after Skalla-Grímr kills Egill's foster-mother, the boy in turn kills his father's favourite servant at dinner later that evening (chap. 40). What makes these parallels particularly interesting (and difficult to discount as mere coincidences) is the fact that Skalla-Grímr was in turn slighted by his own father Kveld-Úlfr who preferred the other golden boy Þórólfr (Egill's uncle and the hero of the first thirty chapters of *Egils saga*), and that Ásmundr himself, like Grettir (and quite unlike the favoured Atli), was very adventurous in his youth, disliked farming, and was disliked by his own father in turn: 'var fátt um með þeim feðgum' ('father and son did not get on well together'),[52] we are told.

All these saga fathers and sons locked in strife seem to be destined to repeat the mistakes of their elders, and the loathing and anger that they feel towards the offspring that takes after them in appearance (and/or temperament) seems also to be self-loathing and self-directed anger. Thus, without the need for overt psychologizing, the character of Grettir the Strong becomes invested with a remarkable psychological depth and intricacy. It is through the complex journey in which the features absorbed from earlier mythic and heroic figures intertwine (more or less harmoniously) with newer layers of representation that traditional heroes such as Grettir gain multiple shades, dimensions. Grettir's character can thus be perceived as a site of social negotiation of contrasting values and attitudes, and as such, as still unfinished, still in the making, and hence not lending itself to the monologizing ethical/aesthetic ecology of the canonical.

---

is precise: 'Eigi veit ek, hvárt mér þykkir meir frá móti, at þú skipar honum jafnan starfa, eða hitt at hann leysir alla einn veg af hendi' ('I don't know which I object to more: that you [she addresses her husband] keep giving him jobs, or that he does them all the same way') (*Grettis saga Ásmundarsonar*, ed. by Guðni Jónsson, pp. 41–42; *The Saga of Grettir the Strong*, trans. by Scudder, II, 67).

[52] *Grettis saga Ásmundarsonar*, ed. by Guðni Jónsson, p. 34; *The Saga of Grettir the Strong*, trans. by Scudder, II, 63.

Traditional Referentiality between Stability and Change

Traditional referentiality works in the ways described because of the high degree of stability inherent in the traditional code. At the same time, one must not forget how relative this stability is. To be sure, when we read of Hrafnkell donning blue-black clothes before his encounter with Einarr Þorbjarnarson (*Hrafnkels saga*, chap. 5),[53] we can safely assume that the encounter will end in Einarr's death. This is not simply because the poor boy rode the horse he was not supposed to, but because, as remarked earlier, people wearing blue-black clothes or capes in the sagas do this regularly. Skarpheðinn wore them before killing Þráinn Sigfússon (*Njáls saga*, chap. 92), and so did Gísli when setting off to kill his brother-in-law Þorgímr.[54] All this goes on until, of course, something slightly different happens. Thus, when Síðu-Hallr wears a blue-black cloak upon meeting with Þorgeirr Skorargeirr and Kári Sǫlmundarson, it is to procure a settlement for his son-in-law Flosi (*Njáls saga*, chap. 147); in *Eyrbyggja saga* it is the good housewife Geirríðr rather than Arnkell goði who wears blue-black clothes as she rides with his party and helps him fight off the dark arts of the evil sorceress Katla;[55] and Þráinn Sigfússon wears a blue-black cloak every time he rides out (*Njáls saga*, chap. 91), regardless of whether or not he will end up killing someone. However, even in these cases where the ruptures and changes in the traditional code are perceptible, the undertones of the traditional meaning are also present: Síðu-Hallr's cloak adds extra gravity to the situation and stresses the importance of reaching a settlement; Geirríðr is joining an avenging party and, although a woman, she is still the crucial figure in defeating the most powerful enemy (appropriately, another woman) and in bringing about the death of the man (Katla's scoundrel son Oddr) who cut off the hand of Arnkell goði's noble, peace-loving wife Auðr (yet another woman, woman-victim, and the cause for the revenge). The fact that Þráinn Sigfússon always wears blue-black further points to his general arrogance, bullishness, and menacing behaviour (his clothing signals that he wants people to fear him) which, in addition to the trick he played in Norway, lands him in trouble with the Njálssons and eventually leads to his killing.[56]

---

[53] *Hrafnkels saga Freysgoða*, in *Íslendinga sögur og þættir*, ed. by Bragi Háldorsson and others, II, 1397–1416.

[54] *Gísla saga Súrssonar*, ed. by Guðni Jónsson and Björn K. Þórólfsson, chap. 16.

[55] *Eyrbyggja saga*, ed. by Einar Ól. Sveinsson and Matthías Þórðarson, chap. 20.

[56] Even though the adjective *svartr* rather than *blár* is used to describe the clothes of the young Snorri goði upon his return from Norway (he even rides a black mare; *Eyrbyggja saga*,

One of the most complex employments of the blue-black cloak device is to be found in *Vatnsdæla saga*. After their father's hospitality was repeatedly abused by the troublemaker Hrolleifr and his sorceress mother, the sons of Ingimundr find the latest impudent act of Hrolleifr (he infringes on their fishing rights and beats up their servants) too much to bear, and they go to confront him. In accordance with his earlier mentioned fiery nature, Jǫkull does not hide that his intention is to put a stop to Hrolleifr's acts once and for all, but Ingimundr entreats his sons to try and reach a settlement rather than fight. Knowing that Jǫkull will be hard to restrain, he sends along Þorsteinn, his wise and cunning eldest son, to keep his younger brother's temper in check. This, however, becomes impossible as Hrolleifr turns a deaf ear to all the Ingimundarssons' warnings and starts throwing stones over the river at them instead. They respond, of course; the stone and spear fight escalates, and when the old and blind Ingimundr is informed of this, he appears on the scene wearing a blue-black cloak (*Vatnsdæla saga*, chap. 22). Sobered by their father's appearance and remembering his earlier request, the sons withdraw, if reluctantly, and leave him to deal with the situation. (He is, after all, the head of the family and the district chieftain, and thus the proper person to resolve disputes.) For all the outward rhetoric of threat — the clothes that should signify his unequivocal intention to avenge the offence most severely, the fact that he rides into the river — all that Ingimundr does is give the rogue yet another warning and request from him to act as is right and proper. Instead of a response, Hrolleifr hurls a spear at the old man and runs him through. The mortally wounded Ingimundr is then led home by a servant boy to his high seat where his sons will find him dead later in the evening. Just before he dies, Ingimundr sends the boy to warn his

---

ed. by Einar Ól. Sveinsson and Matthías Þórðarson, chap. 13), and the cloak that Grettir the Strong begins wearing after being pronounced an outlaw is black (*Grettis saga Ásmundarsonar*, ed. by Guðni Jónsson, chap. 47), it is perhaps not too far-fetched to conceive that these instances may also have taken on some of the traditional semantic undertones usually connected with blue-black clothing. In the earlier example of Valla-Ljótr's clothes (compare note 30), the distinction is indeed overtly made, but the two shades are nevertheless related in the same breath, and it is conceivable that some slippages and overlaps of meaning could occur. To be sure, Grettir wears his black cloak as a means of disguise, and the black-clad Snorri does not kill his uncle-stepfather Bǫrkr, but tricks him out of property (*Eyrbyggja saga*, ed. by Einar Ól. Sveinsson and Matthías Þórðarson, chap. 14). Nevertheless, Snorri's battle arena involves more strategic manoeuvring and diplomacy than the usual heroics — therefore, tricking or socially ruining his opponent is quite on par with a killing — while Grettir's black clothes and outlawry go hand in hand; both past and future killings could thus be implied. For a more detailed discussion, see Ranković, 'The Temporality of the (Immanent) Saga'.

killer and bid him to flee before his sons catch up with him and exact revenge. He explains this extraordinary act as follows:

> mín er eigi at betr hefnt, þótt hann deyi, en mér samir at skjóta skjóli yfir þann, er ek hefi áðr á hendr tekizk, meðan ek má [um] mæla, hversu sem síðar ferr.[57]
>
> [I am no better avenged by his death and, no matter what happens later, as long as I have any say in things, it is right for me to protect the person whom I have previously agreed to help.][58]

It is only at this moment that the function of the blue-black cape can be fully appreciated, driving home the point that Ingimundr had no intention of killing the offender to begin with. He had, nevertheless, counted on both his sons and his killer to read (and so effectively misread) his blue-black attire the way tradition bid, the way we, the readers of the saga, would read it as well. It is only such a drastic gesture that would have persuaded his sons that he meant business and reassured them enough to leave; it is only this gesture that would have induced Hrolleifr to actually kill him, which, we might venture to argue now, could have been Ingimundr's aim after all. Tied by hospitality bonds yet wanting to get the troublemaker to leave his farm without endangering the lives of his sons in the process, Ingimundr puts himself forward as a willing victim. By offering his life as sacrifice he has the chance to reap the reward in the afterlife from that god who places so much value on forgiveness, the one whose faith had not yet arrived in Iceland, but who, the righteous, noble men like Ingimundr and Þorsteinn already intuit, is 'þeim, er sólina hefir skapt ok allan heiminn, hverr sem sá er' ('Him who created the sun and all the world, whoever He is').[59] In addition, Ingimundr is able to meet a warrior's end rather than die the humiliating death of old age. The use of the blue-black cloak in this passage (as a smokescreen of sorts) is particularly interesting because it becomes a metatextual as much as a formulaic device, and shows off the aesthetic potential of the interaction between the oral and written media.

---

[57] *Vatnsdæla saga*, ed. by Einar Ól. Sveinsson, p. 61.

[58] *The Saga of the People of Vantsdal*, trans. by Wawn, IV, 30.

[59] *Vatnsdæla saga*, ed. by Einar Ól. Sveinsson, p. 62; *The Saga of the People of Vantsdal*, trans. by Wawn, IV, 30. It is Ingimundr's son Þorsteinn who utters these words, as well as expresses hope that his father will be welcomed by this god.

Thinking Canons

Because the tradition is a living, shifting, ever-changing polygon of meanings and not a map that will take you from A to B, or a Morse code in which a particular letter of the alphabet always corresponds to a particular combination of dashes and dots, the 'anchorage of meaning'[60] it provides is of a complex sort. For one, the meaning is negotiated by each listener/reader, depending on the extent of his or her immersion in tradition. More importantly, as the examples above show, even the greatest knower of tradition cannot afford to grow complaisant. This is not only because tradition is always too vast, multilayered, and diverse for any single individual to possess, but because the meaning of traditional idioms, like the meaning of words in any living language, shifts, drifts, changes through usage, and was never set in the first place. While certainly delineated, the horizon of the audience's expectation is also transgressed, as the 'expressive ecology'[61] of the formulaic phrases, motifs, and themes expands, alters, adapts to the new needs of the community. As the examples with Síðu-Hallr and Ingimundr show, the traditional impulse for revenge is being overridden by another, increasingly important ethic impulse: the need to settle differences peacefully rather than seek redress by triggering new cycles of violence. Such transgressions, and the malleability of the traditional code in general, are crucial factors that make traditional narratives such as the sagas a means of renewal and negotiation of a social contract,[62] an active force in creating and recreating communal identity, not the mere reflection of it. Reading these passages, we find the tradition still evaluating the alternatives, still pondering the stakes — thinking. This then would be a different kind of canon: one that stutters, hesitates, a thinking canon, still enlisting the direct help of common folk to gather all of itself into a future.

Of course, strictly speaking, we now know the sagas as they are recanonized by the very different gathering efforts of the generations of scholars who have tirelessly attempted to resuscitate the fragile remains of a once living practice.

---

[60] The expression is appropriated from Barthes, 'Rhetoric of the Image', who introduced 'anchorage' to describe the tactics employed in advertising whereupon an image is accompanied with a caption for the sake of redundancy, i.e. in order to reduce its semantic possibilities and so lead the recipient to a particular interpretation/particular meaning of the image.

[61] Foley, 'Fieldwork on Homer', p. 27.

[62] For a similar perspective on the 'community-building' rationale of traditional literature (Kamsá ritual language), see McDowell, 'The Community-Building Mission of Kamsá Ritual Language'.

Nevertheless, fragmentary as it may be, the tantalizing glimpses of this living tradition call upon us to distinguish the two notions of canon, and likewise the educational/normative function that is peculiar to it. Where the mouth and the ear, the hand and the eye of the tradition are not metaphorical references to institutions and vast social processes but still actual body parts, where master narratives are still authored in performance, we may need to adjust our intuitions accordingly and try to shake off some of the acquired distaste with respect to the normative power of master narratives. Of course, in general, a canonical text is a text that is treated as such. No text can be canonical 'intrinsically'. What the sagas of Icelanders and their traditional referentiality remind us is that any such treatment is our own doing.

Works Cited

Primary Sources

Brennu-Njáls Saga, ed. by Einar Ól. Sveinsson, Íslenzk fornrit, 12 (Reykjavík: Hið Íslenzka fornritafélag, 1954)

The Complete Sagas of Icelanders, ed. by Viðar Hreinsson and others, 5 vols (Reykjavík: Leifur Eiríksson, 1997)

Egils saga Skalla-Grímssonar, ed. by Sigurður Nordal (Reykjavík: Hið íslenzka fornritafélag, 1933)

Eyrbyggja saga, ed. by Einar Ól. Sveinsson and Matthías Þórðarson (Reykjavík: Hið íslenzka fornritafélag, 1935)

Gísla saga Súrssonar, in *Vestfirðinga sǫgur*, ed. by Guðni Jónsson and Björn K. Þórólfsson (Reykjavík: Hið íslenzka fornritafélag, 1943), pp. 3–118

Grettis saga Ásmundarsonar, ed. by Guðni Jónsson (Reykjavík: Hið íslenzka fornritafélag, 1936)

Íslendinga sögur og þættir, ed. by Bragi Háldorsson and others (Reykjavík: Svart á hvítu, 1987)

Laxdæla saga, ed. by Einar Ól. Sveinsson (Reykjavík: Hið íslenzka fornritafélag, 1934)

The Saga of Grettir the Strong, trans. by Bernard Scudder, in *The Complete Sagas of Icelanders*, ed. by Viðar Hreinsson and others, 5 vols (Reykjavík: Leifur Eiríksson, 1997), II, 49–191

The Saga of the People of Laxardal, trans. by Keneva Kunz, in *The Complete Sagas of Icelanders*, ed. by Viðar Hreinsson and others, 5 vols (Reykjavík: Leifur Eiríksson, 1997), V, 1–130

The Saga of the People of Vantsdal, trans. by Andrew Wawn, in *The Complete Sagas of Icelanders*, ed. by Viðar Hreinsson and others, 5 vols (Reykjavík: Leifur Eiríksson, 1997), IV, 1–66

Valla-Ljóts saga, in *Eyfirðinga sǫgur*, ed. by Jónas Kristjánsson (Reykjavík: Hið íslenzka fornritafélag, 1956), pp. 233–60

Valla-Ljot's Saga, trans. by Paul Acker, in *The Complete Sagas of Icelanders*, ed. by Viðar Hreinsson and others, 5 vols (Reykjavík: Leifur Eiríksson, 1997), IV, 131–47

Vatnsdæla saga, ed. by Einar Ól. Sveinsson (Reykjavík: Hið íslenzka fornritafélag, 1939)

Víglundar saga, in *Kjalnesinga saga*, ed. by Jóhannes Halldórsson (Reykjavík: Hið íslenzka fornritafélag, 1959), pp. 63–116

Secondary Works

Barthes, Roland, 'The Death of the Author', in *Authorship: Plato to Postmodern*, ed. by Seán Burke (Edinburgh: Edinburgh University Press, 2001), pp. 125–30

——, 'Rhetoric of the Image', in Roland Barthes, *Image, Music, Text* (London: Fontana Press, 1977), pp. 32–51

Bloom, Harold, *The Anxiety of Influence: A Theory of Poetry* (Oxford: Oxford University Press, 1975)

Branston, Brian, *Gods of the North* (London: Thames & Hudson, 1980)

Clover, Carol J., 'The Long Prose Form', *Arkiv för nordisk filologi*, 101 (1986), 10–39

Clunies Ross, Margaret, 'The Art of Poetry and the Figure of the Poet in *Egils saga*', in *Sagas of the Icelanders: A Book of Essays*, ed. by John Tucker (New York: Garland, 1989), pp. 126–45

——, 'The Skald Sagas as a Genre: Definitions and Typical Features', in *Skaldsagas: Text, Vocation and Desire in the Icelandic Sagas of Poets*, ed. by Russell Poole (Berlin: de Gruyter, 2001), pp. 25–49

Ezell, Margaret J. M., *Social Authorship and the Advent of Print* (Baltimore: Johns Hopkins University Press, 1999)

Foley, John Miles, 'Fieldwork on Homer', in *New Directions in Oral Theory: Essays on Ancient and Medieval Literatures*, ed. by Mark C. Amodio (Tempe: Arizona Center for Medieval and Renaissance Studies, 2005), pp. 15–41

——, *Homer's Traditional Art* (University Park: Pennsylvania State University Press, 1999)

——, *Immanent Art: From Structure to Meaning in Traditional Epic* (Bloomington: Indiana University Press, 1991)

Gísli Sigurðsson, 'Another Audience — Another Saga: How Can We Best Explain Different Accounts in *Vatnsdæla Saga* and *Finnboga Saga Ramma* of the Same Events?', in *Text und Zeittiefe*, ed. by Hildegard L. C. Tristram (Tübingen: Narr, 1994), pp. 359–75

——, *The Medieval Icelandic Saga and Oral Tradition: A Discourse on Method*, Publications of the Milman Parry Collection of Oral Literature, 2 (Cambridge, MA: Harvard University Press, 2004)

Hastrup, Kirsten, 'Tracing Tradition — an Anthropological Perspective on *Grettis saga Ásmundarsonar*', in *Structure and Meaning in Old Norse Literature: New Approaches to Textual Analysis and Literary Criticism*, ed. by John Lindow, Lars Lönnroth, and Gerhard W. Weber (Odense: Odense Universitetsforlag, 1986), pp. 281–313

Jakobson, Roman, and Petr Bogatyrev, 'On the Boundary between the Studies of Folklore and Literature', in *Readings in Russian Poetics: Formalist and Structuralist Views*, ed. by Ladislav Matejka and Krystyna Pomorska (Cambridge, MA: MIT Press, 1971), pp. 91–93

Karadžić, Vuk Stefanović, 'Preface', in *Srpske narodne pjesme*, ed. by Vuk Stefanović Karadžić, 4 vols (Beograd: Prosveta, 1976), IV, 363–82

Kellogg, Robert, 'The Prehistory of Eddic Poetry', in *Poetry in the Scandinavian Middle Ages*, ed. by Teresa Pároli (Spoleto: Centro italiano di studi sull'alto medioevo, 1990), pp. 187–99

Lord, Albert B., *The Singer of Tales* (Cambridge, MA: Harvard University Press, 1960)

McDowell, John H., 'The Community-Building Mission of Kamsá Ritual Language', in *Native Latin American Cultures through their Discourse*, ed. by Ellen B. Basso (Bloomington: Folklore Institute, Indiana University, 1990), pp. 67–84

Mundal, Else, 'Symbol og symbolhandlingar i sagalitteraturen', in *Middelalderens symboler*, ed. by Ann Christensson, Else Mundal, and Ingvild Øye (Bergen: Senter for europeiske kulturstudier, 1997), pp. 53–69

Ong, Walter J., *Orality and Literacy: The Technologizing of the Word* (London: Methuen, 1982)

Poole, Russell, 'Myth, Psychology, and Society in *Grettis saga*', *Alvíssmál*, 11 (2004), 3–16

Ranković, Slavica, 'Authentication and Authenticity in the Sagas of Icelanders and Serbian Epic Poetry', in *Medieval Narratives between History and Fiction: From the Centre to the Periphery of Europe, c. 1100–1400*, ed. by Panagiotis A. Agapitos and Lars Boje Mortensen (København: Museum Tusculanum, 2012), pp. 199–233

——, 'The Distributed Author and the Poetics of Complexity: A Comparative Study of the Sagas of Icelanders and Serbian Epic Poetry' (doctoral thesis, University of Nottingham, 2006) <http://etheses.nottingham.ac.uk/2098/> [accessed 5 August 2012]

——, 'Golden Ages and Fishing Grounds: the Emergent Past in the Sagas of Icelanders', *Saga-Book*, 30 (2006), 39–64

——, 'The Oral–Written Continuum as a Space', in *Along the Oral-Written Continuum: Types of Texts, Relations and their Implications*, ed. by Slavica Ranković, Leidulf Melve, and Else Mundal, Utrecht Studies in Medieval Literacy, 20 (Turnhout: Brepols, 2010), pp. 39–71

——, 'The Temporality of the (Immanent) Saga: Tinkering with Formulas', in *Dating the Sagas: Reviews and Revisions*, ed. by Else Mundal (København: Museum Tusculanum, 2013), pp. 149–94

——, 'Who Is Speaking in Traditional Texts? On the Distributed Author of the Sagas of Icelanders and Serbian Epic Poetry', *New Literary History*, 38 (2007), 293–307

Ranković, Slavica, and Miloš Ranković, 'The Talent of the Distributed Author', in *Modes of Authorship in the Middle Ages*, ed. by Slavica Ranković and others (Toronto: Pontifical Institute for Mediaeval Studies Press, 2012), pp. 52–75

Tulinius, Torfi H., *The Matter of the North: The Rise of Literary Fiction in Thirteenth-Century Iceland* (Odense: Odense Universitetsforlag, 2002)

Wolf, Kirsten, 'The Color Blue in Old Norse-Icelandic Literature', *Scripta Islandica*, 57 (2006), 55–78

Worton, Michael, and Judith Still, 'Introduction', in *Intertextuality: Theories and Practices*, ed. by Michael Worton and Judith Still (Manchester: Manchester University Press, 1990), pp. 1–44

Zoëga, Geir T., *Íslenzk-Ensk orðabók* (Reykjavík: Sigurður Kristjánsson, 1904)

Provider of Prosperity: The Image of St Anne in Finnish and Karelian Folklore

Irma-Riitta Järvinen

Di contr' a Pietro vedi sedere Anna,	Opposite Peter I saw Anna sitting,
tanto contenta di mirar sua figlia,	so content to be gazing at her daughter
che non move occhio per cantare osanna.	that she did not move her eyes to sing hosanna.
Dante Alighieri, *La Divina Commedia*, *Paradiso*, xxxii, lines 133–35	Dante Alighieri, *The Divine Comedy*, trans. by Sisson, p. 494

Annikki, Tapion tytti,	Annikki, the daughter of Tapio,
piikaseni, pikkuseni, orjani alinomane,	my maid, my little one,
paras palkkalaisiani,	my permanent slave, my best servant,
jok' on kenkältä kepie, aina käyvä ahkerasta!	who has a light step, always diligent at work!
Kankas kultane kutohos, vaippa vaskine vanuta,	Weave a golden cloth, felt a copper quilt,
jolla karjana katamma,	With which we'll cover the cattle,
sontaseäret suojelemma [...].	protect the filthy legs [...]. (my translation)

Lukkańi Huotari, Ponkalahti, Archangel Karelia, 1877
(*Suomen kansan vanhat runot*, ed. by Niemi and others, I. 4, no. 1412)

In Finland the eastern and the western folklore traditions of St Anne meet, as is the case with many other folklore and cultural phenomena. St Anne, the grandmother saint of the late Middle Ages, is a constructed figure whose life history and features have been created, added to, and modified throughout the Middle Ages.[1] Ideas and motifs expressed by her legend have been recycled and passed

---

[1] In the 1990s, St Anne, as a cultural symbol, drew the attention of scholars interested in

Irma-Riitta Järvinen, Finnish Literature Society, Senior Researcher, University of Eastern Finland, Adjunct Professor, irma-riitta.jarvinen@finlit.fi

on throughout the centuries in the folklore process, supported by the numerous visual presentations of the saint, and by folk drama. In this sense, her image represents a perfect example of what folklore is about: expressing and varying old ideas in new forms.

My aim is to analyse the image of St Anne as it is presented in Finnish-Karelian agrarian folklore. What kind of impact did her image, which was greatly promoted especially by the Western but also by the Eastern Church have on people's conceptions and actions? Why did people appeal to her, and how did people conceive of the benefit of this saintly figure in their own lives? In the late Middle Ages St Anne had, after all, become an integral part of 'religion as it is lived',[2] everyday vernacular religion and practice.

Methodologically, the task is challenging. It is not plausible to speak of a clear continuity between a late medieval saint and late nineteenth- and early twentieth-century folklore documentation. We know that St Anne was an extremely potent figure in the late Middle Ages in Europe. As a cultural symbol, she had the power of triggering, setting forth, and nurturing peoples' imagination and ways of thinking, which led to activating various ideological formations.[3] Folklore data, no matter how odd or trivial it may seem, can be viewed as a source of 'clues' asking for an interpretation, as is seen in the way the Italian historian Carlo Ginzburg looks at his materials.[4] Folklore documentation is full of 'residues' of the past, archaic features, obscurities, and emotions, which Ginzburg defines as the special field of interest among the historians of mentalities.[5]

St Anne belongs to the group of miraculous mothers of the New Testament and the Apocrypha; the other two are Elizabeth and Mary.[6] Like the Virgin Mary, she gained widespread popularity in Finland, and elsewhere in Europe, in the late Middle Ages. By the late fourteenth century, Anne's popularity had

---

women's role in society, because the rise of her cult connects with ideologies concerning the family and the woman's role in the family; for example Ashley and Sheingorn, *Interpreting Cultural Symbols*; Atkinson, *The Oldest Vocation*; Riches and Salish, *Gender and Holiness*; Nixon, *Mary's Mother*.

[2] Primiano, 'Vernacular Religion and the Search for Method', p. 44.

[3] Ashley, 'Image and Ideology', p. 112.

[4] For example Ginzburg, *Clues, Myths, and the Historical Method*, trans. by Tedeschi and Tedeschi.

[5] Ginzburg, *Juusto ja madot*, p. 38.

[6] Larson, 'The Role of Patronage and Audience', p. 30.

spread throughout Germany, Switzerland, Flanders, and Holland, making substantial inroads into Poland, Bohemia, and Scandinavia.[7] In Finland, which as a Swedish province represented the remote edges of the Western Christian sphere, the strength of Anne's cult is shown by the number of her representations in Finnish medieval church art; only statues of Jesus and Mary exceeded the number of statues of St Anne.[8] In Sweden, and in Finland as well, the Birgittan Order promoted the cult of St Anne.[9] St Anne was the *patrona* of the Birgittan monastery in Naantali near Turku.[10] In Birgitta's writings, the value of the work of wives and mothers is strongly emphasized, with references to Mary and her mother Anne.[11] Anne had an altar in the Cathedral of Turku, and in fifteenth-century Finland her memorial day was celebrated in the category of *totum duplex*, the highest rank.[12] Anne's wooden statues — a number of them representing the 'Anna selbdritt'[13] type (Anne Herself the Third) — have existed or still exist in twenty-two medieval stone churches.[14] Paintings depicting St Anne or parts of her legend exist in five churches; she is the patroness of five churches or chapels, and one decorated chancel was dedicated to her.[15] Elina Räsänen's research material includes forty-five wooden statues of the

---

[7] Nixon, *Mary's Mother*, p. 41.

[8] Nygren, *Helgonen i Finlands medeltidskonst*, pp. 23–29.

[9] Helander, 'Anna', p. 148; Räsänen, 'Agency of Two Ladies', p. 253.

[10] Lamberg, *Jöns Budde*, p. 324.

[11] Atkinson, *The Oldest Vocation*, p. 173.

[12] Malin, *Der Heiligenkalender Finnlands*, p. 251; Edgren and Mäkelä-Alitalo, 'Anna, pyhimys, neitsyt Marian äiti'.

[13] The 'Selbdritt' type of statue presents Anne almost as a giant holding Mary and Jesus on her lap, as though they were her children. In Western Europe small devotional nesting dolls of St Anne also existed: inside St Anne was Mary and inside Mary was a figure of Mary with the infant Jesus (Atkinson, *The Oldest Vocation*, pp. 160–61).

[14] Hiekkanen, *Suomen keskiajan kivikirkot*; see also Nygren, *Helgonen i Finlands medeltidskonst*, pp. 23–29; Räsänen, 'Reviewing Research on Medieval Wood Sculptures'.

[15] The following is based on information provided by Hiekkanen, *Suomen keskiajan kivikirkot*. Paintings of St Anne exist in the following churches: Finström, Kalanti, Lohja, Rymättylä, and Turku Cathedral. Wooden statues or altarpieces exist, or have existed, in Kisko, Pöytyä, Rymättylä, Turku Cathedral, Franciscan Church of Rauma, Sastamala, Ulvila, Vesilahti, Hattula, Hauho, Hollola, Janakkala, Sysmä, Urjala, Finström, Jomala, Lemland, Espoo, Pyhtää, Helsinki Parish, Keminmaa, and Vöyri. St Anne is the patroness of the Birgittan Church in Naantali, Hattula Church. Churches or chapels dedicated to her are Salo, the Dominican Church of Turku, and Kumlinge. The Decorated Chancel of St Anne is at the Viipuri Town Church.

Figure 12. Wooden sculpture of St Anne with Mary in the Church of Urjala, Finland; an example of a fifteenth-century transformation of an older sculpture of Mary and Jesus into an 'Anna selbdritt' by changing the head of Mary into that of Anne. Helsinki, Suomen kansallismuseo. Fifteenth century. Reproduced with permission. Photo courtesy of Elina Räsänen.

'Anna selbdritt' type in Finnish medieval churches.[16] Thus, we have plenty of material proof of her importance in the religious life of fifteenth- and early sixteenth-century Finland, but as is the case in general with the veneration of saints, no accounts have survived of people's thoughts or feelings when viewing these sacred images.[17]

[16] Räsänen, *Ruumiillinen esine, materiaalinen suku*, p. 35.
[17] Räsänen, 'Agency of Two Ladies', p. 246.

Figure 13. Birchwood sculpture, carved in Finland, representing St Anne, Mary, and Jesus. Lokalahti Church, Finland. *c*. 1500. Reproduced with permission. Photo courtesy of Elina Räsänen.

The Finnish and Karelian[18] folklore data about St Anne is relatively scarce and very late; its main genres are charms or prayers, inscriptions of calendar customs, and calendar proverbs. This folklore data essentially comes from the late nineteenth and early twentieth centuries, when it was documented through interviews in an intensive collecting activity and archived at the Folklore Archives of the Finnish Literature Society. Still, as a reservoir of long-lasting conceptions, views, tendencies, and feelings, folk poetry and folk traditions

---

[18] When speaking of Karelia, I here refer to the Orthodox areas of Karelia, i.e. Ladoga Karelia, Border Karelia, and Archangel Karelia. Karelian Isthmus was Catholic, and Lutheran after the Reformation.

have their own value in suggesting how people have conceived things and what they have held in esteem.

The question remains: What conclusions can we draw, and how, from the folklore materials? We lack information about the praxis of vernacular piety in medieval Finland and, as well, on what was actually the concrete effect of the Reformation on the thinking and cultural behaviour of the laity. The important observation, however, is that some kind of a conception of St Anne has existed in Finland and Karelia from the Middle Ages until the twentieth century.

The Legend of St Anne and the Rise of her Cult

There is no mention of the Virgin Mary's parents, Anne and Joachim, in the Bible. Their story was first presented in the apocryphal text the Protevangelium of James in about 150 AD. In this text, Anne and Joachim were described as a pious, rich, and childless elderly couple. Due to their childlessness, both faced insults. They both prayed intensively for a child and were separately informed by an angel that a child would be born to them. Anne gave birth to a girl and called her Mary. At the age of three she was brought to the temple and stayed there. She was blessed by the priest and God bestowed grace upon her and 'she danced for joy with her feet, and the whole house of Israel loved her'. The Protevangelium ends with the words: 'And Mary was in the temple nurtured like a dove and received food from the hand of an angel.'[19]

In Finland, the apocryphal texts of Jesus, the Virgin Mary, Anne, and Joachim, *Meidän Herramme Jeesuksen Christuksen Lapsuuden Kirja, niin myös lyhykäinen tieto Wanhimmistansa Joakimista ja Annasta* (A Book about the Childhood of Our Lord Jesus Christ, and a Short Presentation of his Elderly Joachim and Anna), were not published in Finnish until 1835,[20] and the folklore collections of the Finnish Literature Society bear no sign that this text had any influence on the oral tradition of St Anne.

The nature of Anne's conception in her old age was a matter of great dispute. As a miracle, it was linked to the conception of the Virgin Mary. The question of whether Anne's conception was immaculate ('without sin') was contested at various points in the Middle Ages.[21] As a result, although the Conception

---

[19] For the English text of the Protevangelium of James, see Ashley and Sheingorn, 'Introduction', pp. 53–57.

[20] *Meidän Herramme Jesuksen Christuksen Lapsuuden Kirja*.

[21] See Knowles, *The Monastic Order in England*, pp. 510–14; Ashley and Sheingorn,

of Mary was celebrated in various parts of Western Europe, a feast for the Immaculate Conception of the Virgin Mary was not papally sanctioned until 1476; even then, those opposing the doctrine could not be accused of heresy. At any rate, as the grandmother of Jesus, Anne's relationship to Jesus was the basis for viewing devotion to her as a means for personal salvation, which was a great concern in various layers of society in the late Middle Ages.[22]

In the West, the legend of Anne and Joachim was included in *Legenda aurea* (*The Golden Legend*) by Jacobus de Voragine at the end of the thirteenth century.[23] This widespread and influential collection of saints' lives helped to promote the cult of St Anne, which became popular in the northern countries in the late fourteenth century and increasingly popular in the fifteenth and early sixteenth centuries.[24]

Legenda aurea also included an important addition to the story of Anne, which was called the Trinubium.[25] After Joachim died, Anne remarried twice, first to Cleophas, who was the brother of Mary's husband Joseph, and then to Salome. In both marriages she gave birth to daughters who were also named Mary. These daughters (Mary Cleophas and Mary Salome) were mothers to several disciples of Jesus (James the Greater and the Less, Joseph the Just, John the Evangelist, Simon, and Jude). In the late Middle Ages this story led to presenting the Holy Kinship, the extended family of St Anne, in church art.[26] The family members were related to each other in a very complicated way, which possibly satisfied the popular taste by binding the biblical stories together. In church art the Holy Kinship was pictured as a noble family, thus equating nobility with holiness.[27] On the other hand, the Trinubium cast an odd light on the immaculate conception of Mary, and towards the end of the fifteenth century its popularity declined.[28]

The cult of St Anne actually began in the sphere of the Eastern Church as early as in the fourth century. Justinian built a church in her honour at Constantinople in the sixth century, and the day of its consecration on 25 or

---

'Introduction', pp. 7–9; Nixon, *Mary's Mother*, pp. 76–79.

[22] Nixon, *Mary's Mother*, p. 42.

[23] See Jacobus de Voragine, *The Golden Legend*, ed. by Granger and Ripperger.

[24] Edgren and Mäkelä-Alitalo, 'Anna, pyhimys, neitsyt Marian äiti'.

[25] Nixon, *Mary's Mother*, pp. 121–28.

[26] Sheingorn, 'Appropriating the Holy Kinship'.

[27] Nixon, *Mary's Mother*, pp. 16, 52–53.

[28] Atkinson, *The Oldest Vocation*, p. 160.

26 July became the memorial day of St Anne in many parts of the Christian world. In the northern countries, her memorial day was celebrated as the day of Mary's conception, and thus the memorial day of St Anne was on 9 December. For an unknown reason, in the diocese of Turku the day was exceptionally one week later, on 15 December.[29] Since the end of the seventeenth century 'Anna' has been celebrated in Finland on 9 December, as in other northern countries.[30] In the Greek Orthodox Church the memorial day of St Anne (and of her husband Joachim) was, and still is, venerated on 9 September, one day after the birth of the Virgin Mary.[31] These dates are clearly reflected in the folklore and calendar customs of St Anne's Day in Finland and Karelia.

The promoters of St Anne's cult were manifold, not only the church and Anne's confraternities,[32] but also economic organizations like guilds. For example, in Denmark the rapid spreading of Anne's cult at the end of the fifteenth century could not have taken place without the channels of the guilds. Moreover, the guilds, having their own altars in the churches, were important promoters of church art, ordering statues of saints and altarpieces. St Anne was chosen to be the patron saint of salesmen, for example in Svendborg, so she could be a favoured theme of presentation in church art.[33] In medieval Turku, Finland, the Guild of St Anne was active and took care of her altar in the cathedral.[34]

Many of Anne's cultural roles were clearly linked to the narrative of her life: she was a protector of marital life, of marital prosperity, and a helper of childless couples. She was respected as the founder of a sacred family tree, as a symbol of fertility and the continuity of generations who was portrayed together with her extended family in numerous pictures of the Holy Kinship.[35] A popular theme linked to Anne in English medieval wall paintings in particular showed her teaching her daughter Mary how to read.[36] Teaching children in order to make them into good Christians was one of the ideals of parenthood promoted in the late Middle Ages.[37]

[29] Malin, *Der Heiligenkalender Finnlands*, p. 241.
[30] Vilkuna, *Vuotuinen ajantieto*, p. 326.
[31] *Kirkkovuoden pyhät*, I, 27–29.
[32] Nixon, *Mary's Mother*, pp. 93–94.
[33] Bisgaard, *De glemte altre*, pp. 318–19.
[34] Piippo, 'Kiltalaitos keskiajan Suomessa', p. 203.
[35] Ashley and Sheingorn, 'Introduction', pp. 48–49.
[36] Gill, 'Female Piety and Impiety', pp. 103–08.
[37] Atkinson, '"Your Servant, My Mother"', pp. 152, 164.

St Anne was prayed to as a protector against the plague, as a healer of melancholy, a helper in childbirth, a helper of mothers with sick children, and as a patron of a good death. Anne's healing powers are embodied in the healing water 'St. Annenwasser' in Germany, and also in France, Italy, and England.[38] Thus, in the late Middle Ages she embodied ideas of kinship, of connection, and of relationships.[39] Her prosperity in the legend links her to certain professions; she was venerated as the patroness of miners and of shippers. St Anne was associated with woodworkers, and with the grapevine in France.[40] Her cultural roles were so varied that she cannot be declared a patron saint of women only, even though there was a clear emphasis on her attention to women's issues in some areas in Europe, for example in the Rhineland area.[41]

St Anne in the Finnish Folk Calendar: Darkness and Women's Work

What kind of marks, then, has this great matriarch left in Finnish and Karelian folklore? What are the traces and conceptions that connect the Finnish 'Anna' to the great European tradition that has evolved around the figure of St Anne?

Proverbs and calendar customs regarding St Anne's Day mostly represent western Finland with its Roman Catholic background, whereas the charms and prayers connected with her come from eastern Finland and Karelia, originating in the Eastern Greek Orthodox tradition centring around St Anne.[42] Since the memorial day of St Anne was celebrated in Finland in the darkest time of the year, the celebrations could never have been as spectacular as those in countries who held her memorial day in July; in Central Europe, for example, roads were covered with roses and carnations. In the agrarian calendar of the northern countries the darkest time of the year was mainly a time for rest. The Finnish proverbs[43] continuously comment on the long night and the darkness of Anna's Day:[44]

---

[38] Sautman, 'Anna, Saint', p. 30; Wimmer, *Handbuch der Namen und Heiligen*, p. 115.

[39] Ashley and Sheingorn, 'Introduction', p. 53.

[40] Sautman, 'Saint Anne in Folk Tradition', pp. 76–77, 82–84.

[41] Nixon, *Mary's Mother*, p. 79.

[42] Vilkuna, *Vuotuinen ajantieto*, p. 331.

[43] The archived proverb materials on St Anne's Day are numerous, but they are clearly centred around the basic theme of darkness, and of the length of the night.

[44] *Vanhat merkkipäivät*, ed. by Hautala, pp. 366–67; Vilkuna, *Vuotuinen ajantieto*, pp. 324–27. In Finnish, the form 'Anna' is used.

> There is enough of night to sleep on Anna's Day. (Variants throughout the whole country)
>
> There's night to sleep in the times of Anna's Day, and there's night for eating and bathing. (Heinävesi)
>
> There's night, but there's also a wood shaving to light on Anna's Day. (Lammi)
>
> Anna's eye has a long sleep. (Ilomantsi)

In some proverbs the idea that Anna's Day is 15 December has been preserved:

> Lucy's night, Anna's eve, the rooster falls down from its stick three times. (Several variants)

St Lucy's Day was on 13 December. This proverb thus dates back to the time before the memorial day of St Anne was moved one week earlier.[45]

The calendar proverbs helped to keep track of time by expressing the order of saints' days. They commented on the phenomena of the weather and defined the agrarian working calendar: what should be done by a certain day or around it. Thus, apart from it being dark and the winter solace drawing close, Anna's Day stands out as it was fairly close to Christmas. It was the first day that actually reminded people of Christmas time drawing near. Although St Anne's memorial day was in the highest rank as a church holiday in the Middle Ages, and was not removed from the Swedish church calendar until 1571 in the reduction of holidays,[46] no work restrictions have been preserved in folklore.[47] On the contrary, Anna's Day connects with women's work in preparing Christmas food and drink.

St Anne's image as a prosperous lady of the house, as her legend recounts, includes the idea of abundance of food and drink, and the image of St Anne is that of a female model who takes care of her household by feeding them and preparing for the festival season. In this sense the Finnish calendar customs connect to Anne's role as a women's saint in many areas in Europe,[48] although St Anne was not only a women's saint, but also the patroness of male professions like mining, seafaring, and rope making.

---

[45] Vilkuna, *Vuotuinen ajantieto*, pp. 324–25.

[46] Malmstedt, *Helgdagsreduktionen*, pp. 67–68.

[47] The case of St Catherine is different: it was strictly forbidden to spin on St Catherine's Day (25 November). In Finland, St Catherine was known as the patroness of sheep, spinning, and weaving, which connects to her martyr legend in which she was threatened to be tortured on a wheel.

[48] Sautman, 'Saint Anne in Folk Tradition', p. 84.

Women's work in preparation for Christmas began on St Anne's Day. The folklore manuscripts on Finnish calendar traditions mention that on that day women were supposed to start baking for Christmas. For instance, on the island of Tytärsaari in the Gulf of Finland, Anne's Day was called 'Bread-Anna', which was 'nine nights before Christmas. That was when Anna's name day was celebrated'.[49] The baking began right after midnight, and the loaves baked were out of the ordinary; they were round and had 'faces' with 'eyes' on them. The eyes were pressed into the face with a thimble. The loaves of bread were saved and could only be eaten on Christmas Eve. At night, people went from house to house to ask for fresh bread, which had to be given in order to secure the abundance of bread and fish for the coming year.[50]

Brewing the Christmas beer also began on St Anne's Day. The calendar proverbs state: 'Anna is brewing the beer', or 'On Anna's Day the beer is made, and it is drunk together in the festival'. The custom of brewing the beer on Anne's Day also applies to the Swedish-speaking areas of Finland. In addition, the Swedish and the Finnish-Swedish calendar customs also mention making strong alcohol (*brännvin*).[51] The idea of making the Christmas drinks was expressed in small rhyming poems, such as 'Anna with her jug ('kanna') arrives fourteen days before Christmas'. In Sweden, and in the Finnish-Swedish tradition as well, the *lutefisk* (dried cod, a popular Christmas food) had to be put to soak on St Anne's Day.[52]

These traditions may seem trivial from today's perspective, but they pertain to the greatest festival of the year, with its idea of abundance of food and drink. Through the memorial day they relate to Anne, the powerful and rich lady of the house, who was the grandmother of the child to come. In a sense the myth is at work here, and it was made concrete through the action of preparing food. Food traditions inside the home are conservative in nature and are passed on through very long periods of time. The customs and traditions at home were not easily changed after the Reformation, unlike the changes in public life.[53]

---

[49] Helsinki, Folklore Archives of the Finnish Literature Society, Tytärsaari 1936: Aili Laanti 1699; Helsinki, Folklore Archives of the Finnish Literature Society, Tytärsaari 1936: Aili Laanti 1807; Helsinki, Folklore Archives of the Finnish Literature Society, Tytärsaari 1936: Lauri Laiho 3815.

[50] Vilkuna, *Vuotuinen ajantieto*, pp. 326–27.

[51] Helsinki, Folklore Archives of the Swedish Literature Society, Card Index of Calendar Customs.

[52] Data on St Anne's Day in the manuscript collections of DAG (The Dialect, Placename and Folk Tradition Archives), Gothenburg, Sweden.

[53] Bringéus, *Årets festseder*, p. 238.

St Anne in Karelian Charms: 'A hundred saints in the woods [...]'

There are no traces of the legend of St Anne in Finnish-Karelian epic oral tradition, as there are, for example, of St Catherine of Alexandria and the Virgin Mary. However, she is referred to as Santta Anni/Anna in a Kalevala-metric legend poem alongside St Peter and St Andrew.[54] She is not given any special characteristics in the poem, but mentioned only as a member of the group of saints. Annikki is also mentioned as the 'sister of Moses' in a text of the epic poem 'The Song of Mary',[55] which is the story of the birth of Jesus.[56] The names Anni or Annikki are frequently used elsewhere in epic poetry, but not in the context of a saint or of a supranormal helper.

St Anne has occupied the role of the Virgin Mary in two texts of Eastern Finnish (county of Savo) healing charms, which were used for healing twisted ankles and injuries to the legs. St Anne is referred to as 'Santta Anni, armas neito' ('Santta Anni, precious maiden') or 'Santa Anni, armas muori' ('Santa Anni, precious old wife').[57] The charm describes how Jesus is riding on horseback to the church and how the horse becomes frightened by a partridge and then breaks its leg. The Virgin Mary is called for help to weave a healing string and bind the broken leg with it.

In Eastern Finnish and Karelian hunting charms and prayers St Anne is encountered in an unexpected place: she is living in the forest. According to Lotte Tarkka, in the world view of Archangel Karelian folklore the forest belongs to the sphere of the supranormal 'other', it is an 'anti-world', in contrast to the village and its reality, but it was modelled and understood in terms of the human community.[58] St Anne is referred to as Annikki, Annikka, Annatar, or Anni, rarely Anna.[59] She is a female spirit of the forest and presented as the daughter of Tapio, or as the wife of Tapio, who was the male spirit of the forest in Finnish-Karelian ethnic religion. Tapio was presented in literary sources

---

[54] *Suomen kansan vanhat runot*, ed. by Niemi and others, I. 1, nos 339–339*; *A Trail for Singers*, ed. by Kuusi, pp. 74–79. The theme of the poem is the encounter of Jesus (the Creator) and Iku-Turso, a sea monster. The Creator, St Anne, St Peter, and St Andrew are in the boat when they meet the sea monster. Jesus commands the monster never to rise up to the surface again.

[55] *Suomen kansan vanhat runot*, ed. by Niemi and others, I. 2, no. 1098.

[56] Timonen, 'Karjalan naisten Maria-eepos'.

[57] *Suomen kansan vanhat runot*, ed. by Niemi and others, VI. 2, nos 4591, 4592.

[58] Tarkka, *Rajarahvaan laulu*, pp. 286–92, 527.

[59] Krohn, *Suomalaisten runojen uskonto*, pp. 178–80.

for the first time by Mikael Agricola in 1551 in his list of Finnish and Karelian old gods. In his *Mythologia Fennica* (1789) Christfrid Ganander also gives a description of Tapio as a 'god of the forest', but it is interesting that in his references there is no trace of the daughter or the wife of Tapio bearing the name Annikki. Ganander only speaks of 'Tapion waimo' or 'Tapiotar' (the wife of Tapio), or of 'Tapiolan tarkka neito' (the keen maiden of Tapiola).[60] Ganander's manuscript material was probably inadequate, and Annikki's presence in the charms was not an overall feature.

Finnish scholars have agreed that the Annikki who is mentioned in the hunting charms and cattle charms is the representation of St Anne.[61] Haavio formulates: 'In a special position among the daughters of Tapio is Annikki, Annikka, Annatar, Ainikki, which means St Anne.'[62]

As Annikki is frequently mentioned as a member of the group of the spirits of the forest, she is one of the powerful supranormal helpers, as in the text of a charmer from Suistamo, Ladoga Karelia (1845):

> Sata on santtia metsässä, tuhat on miestä Metsolassa puhumahan puoleltani, vierelläni virkkamahan, katehia kaatamahan tuonne helvetin tulehen. […] Annikki, tytär Tapion, ylennä yheksän tuolta, viisi viitarantehilta, kuusi kummulta ylennä […].[63]

> [There are a hundred saints in the woods, there are a thousand men in Metsola to speak for me, to utter from my side, to make those who envy me to fall into that fire of Hell. […] Annikki, daughter of Tapio, make nine (animals) rise up from there, five from the edges of the thicket, six from the hill […].]

The power of the helping spirits was intensified by naming several of them, for example, in a charm for protecting the cattle when they were let out into the forest pastureland: Jesus, God, Mary, Lord, Creator, Hongas the mistress of Pohjola, Kuituva the king of the forest.[64]

These charms and prayers were used in rituals preceding the hunt in order to make it successful, or during the hunt, for example when men surrounded a bear's nest while trying to force the animal to come out. St Anne's connection with hunting makes sense, as her memorial day, after the birthday of the Virgin

---

[60] Ganander, *Mythologia Fennica*, pp. 88–89.
[61] Krohn, *Suomalaisten runojen uskonto*, pp. 177–80; Harva, *Suomalaisten muinaisusko*, p. 363; Vilkuna, *Vuotuinen ajantieto*, pp. 328–31; Haavio, *Suomalainen mytologia*, pp. 68, 446.
[62] Haavio, *Suomalainen mytologia*, p. 68.
[63] *Suomen kansan vanhat runot*, ed. by Niemi and others, VII. 5, no. 3213.
[64] *Suomen kansan vanhat runot*, ed. by Niemi and others, VII. 5, no. 3850.

Mary, was celebrated in the Greek Orthodox tradition on 9 September, at the start of the hunting season.[65]

Annikki was appealed to in the hunting charms for bears,[66] hares,[67] otters,[68] and birds;[69] when taking healing water;[70] when healing the injuries caused by 'weasel bites';[71] when letting the cows out to the pasture, and protecting the cows from bears;[72] when looking for cows 'hidden' by the forest;[73] and commonly at the start of a hunt.[74]

How is Annikki, or St Anne, presented in the charms? What does she look like, what does she do, and what is the evidence that might connect Annikki to St Anne? First, she is a member of the family of forest spirits. Her position in that crowd resembles her position as the great mother figure of the Holy Kinship, although the Holy Kinship never was as important in the Greek Orthodox Church as it was in the Roman Catholic Church. Still, there were contacts between the two, and an exchange of ideas regarding the holy personage is possible. Second, she is a rich lady, as her apocryphal legend also states. Her wealth is emphasized in the charms through descriptions of her appearance and her jewellery, with references to gold and silver. She is holding the keys of her storehouses that are full of prey for the hunter, as in the following hunting charm from Ilomantsi (1845):

> Tapion talon isäntä, Tapion talon emäntä, kaikki kullassa kuhahu, hopeissa horjeksihen. Annikki tytär Tapion, käess on kultaset avaimet, renkahat on reiellähän. Nuo

---

[65] Vilkuna, *Vuotuinen ajantieto*, p. 331.

[66] *Suomen kansan vanhat runot*, ed. by Niemi and others, I. 4, nos 1197, 1412; VII. 5, no. 3403; XII. 2, nos 6479, 6480, 6481.

[67] *Suomen kansan vanhat runot*, ed. by Niemi and others, VII. 5, nos 3514, 3520, 3533, 3539; XII. 2, no. 6606.

[68] *Suomen kansan vanhat runot*, ed. by Niemi and others, II, no. 967; VII. 5, no. 3420.

[69] *Suomen kansan vanhat runot*, ed. by Niemi and others, VII. 5, no. 3580.

[70] *Suomen kansan vanhat runot*, ed. by Niemi and others, VII. 5, no. 1862.

[71] *Suomen kansan vanhat runot*, ed. by Niemi and others, XII. 2, no. 8470. The case of 'weasel bites' is curious. The weasel was respected as a guardian spirit of the cowshed, but it also had other mythological, and harmful, functions; see Hako, *Das Wiesel in der europäischen Volksüberlieferung*.

[72] *Suomen kansan vanhat runot*, ed. by Niemi and others, VII. 5, no. 4176.

[73] *Suomen kansan vanhat runot*, ed. by Niemi and others, VII. 5, nos 3847, 3849, 3850, 3964; XII. 2, nos 6756, 6831, 6846, 6855.

[74] *Suomen kansan vanhat runot*, ed. by Niemi and others, XII. 2, no. 6969.

hänen käsi helisi. Astu aittahan mäellä, keikuttele kellarihin, aukase Tapion aitta, metsän linna liikahuta, päästä vilja valloillahan minun pyytöpäivinäni ja ajanto aikonani![75]

[The master of Tapio's house, the lady of Tapio's house, they all go in gold, they stroll around in silver. Annikki, daughter of Tapio, is holding golden keys in her hand, rings are hanging on her thigh. They jingle in her hand. Step into the storehouse on the hill, swing into the cellar, open the storehouse of Tapio, make the castle of the forest move, let the grain flow out, in the days when I am hunting, when I am having the time to chase!]

Annikki's power as the lady of the house is emphasized through the report of the many servants in her household, who are all very busy:

Annikki, tytär Tapion, piti piikoo yheksän, viis, kuus käskyläistä. Sukat siäriltä kuluu, kengät kauvolta mänöö.[76]

[Annikki, daughter of Tapio, had nine housemaids, five, six servants. Stockings wear out in their legs, the heels of their shoes disappear.]

Annikki's extravagant riches — the same poetic images are used in wedding poems from the area[77] — are described in a most poetic way in the hunting charms of Archangel Karelia:

Annikki, salon aljo, juoksi kullaista kujaa, hopiaista tietä myöten, kaglassa heliät helmet, korvat kulta koltsukoissa, silmäripset simpsukoissa, parta kullan palmikoissa, pää kullan vipaleissa.[78]

[Annikki, the being of the deep forest, ran on the golden lane, along the silver way, wearing shiny pearls in her neck, having golden rings in her ears, her eyelashes covered with sea shells, her beard beaded with gold, her head covered with bits of gold.]

The language of the charms is full of references to Annikki's riches, her gold and her silver, which in practice means the animals with valuable furs. She is requested to give them to the hunter by opening the doors of her storehouse. Anne's role as a generous giver is, incidentally, included in her name Anna, which in the Finnish language is the imperative singular form of the verb 'to

---

[75] *Suomen kansan vanhat runot*, ed. by Niemi and others, VII. 5, no. 3308.

[76] *Suomen kansan vanhat runot*, ed. by Niemi and others, VII. 5, no. 3311.

[77] In the praise of the spokesman of the bridegroom, *Suomen kansan vanhat runot*, ed. by Niemi and others, I. 3, no. 1675.

[78] *Suomen kansan vanhat runot*, ed. by Niemi and others, I. 2, no. 1110.

give'. Anna is also appealed to as a protector of cattle herding in the forest; this is because she is the lady of the forest, whose 'dogs' are the bears and the wolves, and she has the power to control them.

Thus, Annikki is a helper, and a protector. She helps the men to get their prey, and the women to protect the cattle. She is asked to weave a protecting cloth[79] to hide the cattle from the beasts:

> Annikki, Tapion tytti, piikaseni, pikkuseni, orjani alinomane, paras palkkalaisiani, joka on kenkältä kepie, aina käyvä ahkerasta! Kankas kultane kutohos, vaippa vaskine vanuta, jolla karjana katamma, sontaseäret suojelemma [...].[80]

> [Annikki, the daughter of Tapio, my maid, my little one, my permanent slave, my best servant, who has a light step, always diligent at work! Weave a golden cloth, felt a copper quilt, with which we'll cover the cattle, protect the shit legs [...].]

The Viewpoint of Popular Piety

Folk religion should be regarded, as Lauri Honko, Finnish scholar of folklore and comparative religion, has suggested, as a total approach to life, which includes this world and the 'other world': the spirits, the dead, the devil, Christ, and the saints. There is no controversy between a 'superstition' and a 'doctrine', because belief is not a question of following rational rules but of experiencing religious expectations and answers to those expectations in everyday life.[81] These lines of thought help us to understand the way of thinking behind Finnish-Karelian charms, which receive their personages from various sources, without making any distinction between Christian and ethnic religions. St Anne is well suited to the family of forest spirits, belonging in the category of supranormal helpers. The saints were added to the category of helpers because they were potentially powerful, or even more powerful than the old spirits. In any case, their presence in the charms was adding to the number of potential helpers, thus increasing the effect of the charms.

---

[79] Spreading out a cloth for protection is usually associated with the Virgin Mary in the charms; see Timonen, 'Karjalan naisten Maria-eepos', p. 113. The Protection of the Virgin Mary, known as 'Pokrova' in Orthodox Karelia, was celebrated on 1 October. According to the legend, Mary miraculously appeared and saved the city of Constantinople in 903 from the attack of the Saracens by spreading her gown over the city (see *Kirkkovuoden pyhät*, I, 97–98).

[80] *Suomen kansan vanhat runot*, ed. by Niemi and others, I. 4, no. 1412.

[81] Honko, 'Miten luoda terminologia haltiaperinteen tutkimukselle?', p. 107.

In his article dealing with a Modenese witchcraft trial in 1519, Carlo Ginzburg observes striking similarities in the descriptions of the apparitions of the Devil and the Madonna. He comments: 'The convergence of orthodox and diabolical religion in common piety clearly shows how thin the line separating the two could be in the mind of the believer, especially in the rural areas [...]. In situations of isolation, extreme hardships, and absolute poverty, the invocation of the devil may have offered the only hope.'[82]

St Anne, and all the ideas that this holy woman represents, can be analysed as mental images that are very long-lasting in quality. These images penetrate through centuries; they show variation, but they still provide models for knowledge, experience, and action.[83] The image of St Anne includes certain features and qualities that have been carried on through time, although her figure as a 'person' or 'character' has certainly faded, as has her religious value. We do not have any concrete information on what this overwhelmingly popular saint might have meant for Finnish late medieval men and women of the laity. However, we can judge something from the fact that St Anne was still known in the Finnish folk calendar of the nineteenth and twentieth centuries, and that she was prayed to for help four hundred years after the Reformation, even though the saints had been discredited as false and powerless helpers and Martin Luther had bitterly attacked the cult of St Anne.[84]

What has remained of St Anne, which of her qualities have survived throughout the centuries? Her image originally represented the good qualities of old age: skill and wisdom. She was the strong matriarch, who looked after the prosperity of the family: having children, healing the sick, helping people on their deathbeds. She most likely had these roles in Finland as well at the time when her cult was flourishing in the fifteenth and sixteenth centuries, but there is no evidence for this. Proof of her significance can still be seen in her tasks in the woods: she was a protector of the cattle and a helper in hunting.

In Protestant Finland, her role obviously grew smaller. Regardless of the loss of the great religious influence of St Anne, she was important as a holy model from the viewpoint of women's work and livelihood, and this kept her image alive: Anne acted as a human, baking, brewing the beer, protecting the cows and sheep. She was associated with creating abundance of food and drink based on the success of domestic animals, and thus she provided the means for

---

[82] Ginzburg, *Clues, Myths, and the Historical Method*, trans. by Tedeschi and Tedeschi, p. 13.
[83] Siikala, *Suomalainen šamanismi*, pp. 25–27.
[84] Farmer, *The Oxford Dictionary of Saints*, p. 18.

living. Compared to the Virgin Mary, her image in Finnish and Karelian folklore more strongly reflects the promotion of the economic well-being of human life. Her role in Eastern Finnish and Karelian charms as a wealthy member of the family of forest spirits, and as a controller of the hunter's prey, was equally in accordance with her legendary origins as the prosperous lady of the house.

Works Cited

Manuscripts and Archival Documents

Helsinki, Folklore Archives of the Finnish Literature Society, Tytärsaari 1936: Aili Laanti 1699
——, Tytärsaari 1936: Aili Laanti 1807
——, Tytärsaari 1936: Lauri Laiho 3815
Helsinki, Folklore Archives of the Swedish Literature Society, Card Index of Calendar Customs

Primary Sources

Dante Alighieri, *The Divine Comedy*, trans. by C. H. Sisson, with introduction and notes by David H. Higgins, rev. edn (Oxford: Oxford University Press, 1993)
Ganander, Christfrid, *Mythologia Fennica eller förklaring öfver De nomina propria deastrorum, idolorum, locorum, virorum &c* (Turku, Frenckell, 1789; facsimile repr. Helsinki: Suomalaisen Kirjallisuuden Seura, 1984)
Jacobus de Voragine, *The Golden Legend of Jacobus de Voragine*, ed., trans., and adapted by Ryan Granger and Helmut Ripperger (New York: Ayer, 1969)
Kirkkovuoden pyhät, 2nd edn, 2 vols (Joensuu: Ortodoksisen kirjallisuuden julkaisuneuvosto, 1979–80)
Meidän Herramme Jesuksen Christuksen Lapsuuden Kirja, niin myös lyhykäinen tieto Neitsestä Mariasta ja hänen Wanhimmistansa Joakimista ja Annasta (Viipuri: Cederwaller, 1836)
Suomen kansan vanhat runot, ed. by Aukusti Robert Niemi and others, 34 vols (Helsinki: Suomalaisen Kirjallisuuden Seura, 1908–48, 1997)
A Trail for Singers: Finnish Folk Poetry. Epic, ed. by Matti Kuusi, trans. by Keith Bosley (Helsinki: Suomalaisen Kirjallisuuden Seura, 1995)
Vanhat merkkipäivät, ed. by Jouko Hautala, 2nd edn (Helsinki: Suomalaisen Kirjallisuuden Seura, 1974)

Secondary Works

Ashley, Kathleen, 'Image and Ideology: Saint Anne in Late Medieval Drama and Narrative', in *Interpreting Cultural Symbols: Saint Anne in Late Medieval Society*, ed. by Kathleen Ashley and Pamela Sheingorn (Athens: University of Georgia Press, 1990), pp. 111–30

Ashley, Kathleen, and Pamela Sheingorn, 'Introduction', in *Interpreting Cultural Symbols: Saint Anne in Late Medieval Society*, ed. by Kathleen Ashley and Pamela Sheingorn (Athens: University of Georgia Press), pp. 1–68
——, eds, *Interpreting Cultural Symbols: Saint Anne in Late Medieval Society* (Athens: University of Georgia Press, 1990)
Atkinson, Clarissa W., *The Oldest Vocation: Christian Motherhood in the Middle Ages* (Ithaca: Cornell University Press, 1991)
——, '"Your Servant, My Mother": The Figure of Saint Monica in the Ideology of Christian Motherhood', in *Immaculate and Powerful: The Female in Sacred Image and Social Reality*, ed. by Clarissa W. Atkinson, Constance H. Buchanan, and Margaret R. Miles ([Wellingborough]: Crucible, 1987), pp. 139–72
Bisgaard, Lars, *De glemte altre: Gildernes religiøse rolle i senmiddelalderens Danmark*, Odense University Studies in History and Social Sciences, 241 (Odense: Odense Universitetsforlag, 2007)
Bringéus, Nils-Arvid, *Årets festseder*, 4th rev. edn (Stockholm: LT, 1988)
Edgren, Helena, and Anneli Mäkelä-Alitalo, 'Anna, pyhimys, neitsyt Marian äiti', in *Kansallisbiografia* (Biografiakeskus, Suomalaisen Kirjallisuuden Seura) <http://www.finlit.fi/aineistot/verkkoaineistot.php> [accessed 16 July 2012]
Farmer, David Hugh, *The Oxford Dictionary of Saints* (Oxford: Clarendon Press, 1979)
Gill, Miriam, 'Female Piety and Impiety: Selected Images of Women in Wall Paintings in England after 1300', in *Men, Women and Saints in Late Medieval Europe*, ed. by Samantha J. E. Riches and Sarah Salih (London: Routledge, 2002), pp. 101–20
Ginzburg, Carlo, *Clues, Myths, and the Historical Method*, trans. by Johan Tedeschi and Anne C. Tedeschi (Baltimore: Johns Hopkins University Press, 1992)
——, *Juusto ja madot: 1500-luvun myllärin maailmankuva [Il formaggio e i vermi: il cosmo di un mugnaio del '500]*, trans. by Aulikki Vuola, foreword by Matti Peltonen (Helsinki: Gaudeamus, 2007)
Haavio, Martti, *Suomalainen mytologia* (Helsinki: Werner Söderström, 1967)
Hako, Matti, *Das Wiesel in der europäischen Volksüberlieferung mit besonderer Berücksichtigung der finnischen Tradition*, Folklore Fellows Communications, 167 (Helsinki: Suomalainen Tiedeakatemia, 1956)
Harva, Uno, *Suomalaisten muinaisusko* (Porvoo: Werner Söderström, 1948)
Helander, Sven, 'Anna', in *Kulturhistoriskt lexikon för nordisk medeltid: från vikingatid till reformationstid*, ed. by Ingvar Andersson and others, 22 vols (Helsinki: Akademiska bokhandeln, 1956–78), I: *Abbed–Blide*, ed. by Gunvor Kerkkonen (1956), pp. 147–53
Hiekkanen, Markus, *Suomen keskiajan kivikirkot*, Suomalaisen Kirjallisuuden Seuran toimituksia, 1117 (Helsinki: Suomalaisen Kirjallisuuden Seura, 2007)
Honko, Lauri, 'Miten luoda terminologia haltiaperinteen tutkimukselle?', in *Perinteentutkimuksen perusteita*, ed. by Outi Lehtipuro (Helsinki: Werner Söderström, 1980), pp. 77–129
Knowles, David, *The Monastic Order in England: A History of its Development from the Times of St Dunstan to the Fourth Lateran Council 940–1216*, 2nd edn (Cambridge: Cambridge University Press, 1963)

Krohn, Kaarle, *Suomalaisten runojen uskonto*, Suomalaisen Kirjallisuuden Seuran toimituksia, 137 (Porvoo: Werner Söderström, 1915)

Lamberg, Marko, *Jöns Budde: birgittalaisveli ja hänen teoksensa*, Suomalaisen Kirjallisuuden Seuran toimituksia, 1115 (Helsinki: Suomalaisen Kirjallisuuden Seura, 2007)

Larson, Wendy R., 'The Role of Patronage and Audience in the Cults of Sts Margaret and Marina of Antioch', in *Men, Women and Saints in Late Medieval Europe*, ed. by Samantha J. E. Riches and Sarah Salih (London: Routledge, 2002), pp. 23–35

Malin, Aarno, *Der Heiligenkalender Finnlands: Seine Zusammensetzung und Entwicklung*, Suomen Kirkkohistoriallisen Seuran toimituksia, 20 (Helsinki: Suomen kirkkohistoriallinen seura, 1925)

Malmstedt, Göran, *Helgdagsreduktionen: övergång från ett medeltida till ett modernt år i Sverige 1500–1800*, Avhandlingar från Historiska institutionen i Göteborg, 8 (Göteborg: Historiska Institutionen i Göteborg, 1994)

Nixon, Virginia, *Mary's Mother: Saint Anne in Late Medieval Europe* (University Park: Pennsylvania State University Press, 2004)

Nygren, Olga Alice, *Helgonen i Finlands medeltidskonst: En ikonografisk studie*, Suomen Muinaismuistoyhdistyksen aikakauskirja; Finska Fornminnesföreningens tidskrift, 46 (Helsinki: Suomen Muinaismuistoyhdistys/Finska Fornminnesföreningen, 1945)

Piippo, Mikko, 'Kiltalaitos keskiajan Suomessa', in *Suomen kulttuurihistoria*, ed. by Laura Kolbe (Helsinki: Tammi, 2002–04), I: *Taivas ja maa*, ed. by Tuomas M. S. Lehtonen and Timo Joutsivuo (2002), pp. 202–03

Primiano, Leonard Norman, 'Vernacular Religion and the Search for Method in Religious Folklife', *Western Folklore*, 54 (1995), 37–56

Räsänen, Elina, 'Agency of Two Ladies: Wellborne qvinna Lucia Olofsdotter and Veneration of Saint Anne in the Turku Diocese', in *Les Élites nordiques et l'Europe occidentale (XIIe–XVe siècle)*, ed. by Tuomas M. S. Lehtonen and Élisabeth Mornet (Paris: Publications de la Sorbonne, 2007), pp. 245–61

——, 'Reviewing Research on Medieval Wood Sculptures: The Encounter of Olga Alice Nygren and Carl Axel Nordman with the Crowned Saint Anne', in *The Shaping of Art History in Finland*, ed. by Renja Suominen-Kokkonen, Studies in Art History, 36 (Jyväskylä: Taidehistorian Seura, 2007), pp. 214–27

——, *Ruumiillinen esine, materiaalinen suku: tutkimus Pyhä Anna itse kolmantena – aiheisista keskiajan puuveistoksista Suomessa*, Suomen Muinaismuistoyhdistyksen aikakauskirja; Finska Fornminnesföreningens tidskrift, 116 (Helsinki: Suomen Muinaismuistoyhdistys/Finska Fornminnesföreningen, 2009)

Riches, Samantha J. E., and Sarah Salish, eds, *Gender and Holiness: Men, Women and Saints in Late Medieval Europe* (London: Routledge, 2002)

Sautman, Francesca, 'Anna, Saint', in *Medieval Folklore: An Encyclopedia of Myths, Legends, Tales, Beliefs, and Customs*, ed. by Carl Lindahl, John McNamara, and John Lindow (Santa Barbara: ABC-CLIO, 2000), pp. 29–30

——, 'Saint Anne in Folk Tradition: Late Medieval France', in *Interpreting Cultural Symbols: Saint Anne in Late Medieval Society*, ed. by Kathleen Ashley and Pamela Sheingorn (Athens: University of Georgia Press, 1990), pp. 69–94

Sheingorn, Pamela, 'Appropriating the Holy Kinship: Gender and Family History', in *Interpreting Cultural Symbols: Saint Anne in Late Medieval Society*, ed. by Kathleen Ashley and Pamela Sheingorn (Athens: University of Georgia Press, 1990), pp. 169–98

Siikala, Anna-Leena, *Suomalainen šamanismi: mielikuvien historiaa*, Suomalaisen Kirjallisuuden Seuran toimituksia, 565 (Helsinki: Suomalaisen Kirjallisuuden Seura, 1992)

Tarkka, Lotte, *Rajarahvaan laulu: tutkimus Vuokkiniemen kalevalamittaisesta runokulttuurista 1821–1921*, Suomalaisen Kirjallisuuden Seuran toimituksia, 1033 (Helsinki: Suomalaisen Kirjallisuuden Seura, 2005)

Timonen, Senni, 'Karjalan naisten Maria-eepos', in *Runo, alue, merkitys: kirjoituksia vanhan kansanrunon alueellisesta muotoutumisesta*, ed. by Pekka Hakamies, Karjalan tutkimuslaitoksen julkaisuja, 92 (Joensuu: Joensuun yliopisto, 1990), pp. 111–48

Vilkuna, Kustaa, *Vuotuinen ajantieto: vanhoista merkkipäivistä sekä kansanomaisesta talous- ja sääkalenterista enteineen*, 9th edn (Helsinki: Otava, 1983)

Wimmer, Otto, *Handbuch der Namen und Heiligen*, 2nd edn (Innsbruck: Haller, 1959)

(Re)Performing the Past: Crusading, History Writing, and Rituals in the Chronicle of Henry of Livonia

Linda Kaljundi

A few years ago a Nokia advertisement ran in every cinema in Helsinki in which the British actor Gary Oldman encouraged people to make films out of their everyday moments to tell a story and advised them to include in it a catchy score, spectacular location, compelling dialogue, love, conflict, mystery, a chasing scene, etc. The clip ended with him quoting from Shakespeare's *As You Like It* (II. 7), 'All the world is a stage, and all the men and women are merely players'. This, needless to say, above all echoes the modern understanding of (re) living 'a life worth remembering, a drama worth having lived for'.[1] However, in this article, I would like to claim that what works for selling mobile phones with integrated film cameras can also be useful for studying medieval historical writing.

During the past decade, research into performances, rituals, and gestures has become increasingly topical among historians. Recently the British cultural historian Peter Burke has even called for a 'performative turn' in historical and cultural studies.[2] This semiotic approach to culture as a symbolic system has been greatly inspired and influenced by the works of anthropologists. In 1973, Clifford Geertz claimed in his seminal work *The Interpretation of Cultures* that 'culture is a system of inherited conceptions expressed in symbolic forms by means of which people communicate, perpetuate, and develop their knowledge

---

[1] As aptly phrased in Lowenthal, *The Heritage Crusade*, p. 144.

[2] Burke, 'Performing History'.

Linda Kaljundi, University of Tallinn, Coordinator of the Centre for Medieval Studies, Finnish Literature Society, Researcher, linda.kaljundi@tlu.ee

about and attitudes toward life'.[3] Since the function of culture is to impose meaning on the world and make it understandable (creating the conceptual world in which the subjects live), it consists of socially established structures of meaning, which also includes learned and symbolic behaviour. In medieval studies, this approach has been integrated and furthered by historical anthropologists, including Jean Claude Schmitt, Keith Thomas, Carlo Ginzburg, and others. Recently the works of the German medievalist Gerd Althoff have also pointed to the dominantly communicative role of medieval rituals and gestures, especially in the political life of the period: focusing mainly on royal and imperial rituals, he has argued that medieval public communication was ritual and demonstrative, demanding participation and audience.[4]

The performative acts can be extremely valuable for studying the mental world of any society: the patterns of life and thought, and the implicit mental rules governing social interaction. However, with regard to the medieval period, many difficulties still remain in applying the performative approach to the source material. Whereas the records of modern anthropologists cannot be taken for an objective report, the recollections of ritual action in medieval narrative and other texts, visual arts and music stretch the problematic relationship between perception and representation even more. On the one hand, it needs to be asked whether one can actually have access to medieval rituals since they are ultimately mediated by culturally and socially constructed narratives. On the other hand, one can also raise the question about the possibly strong structuring role of performances in the representation of historical events in narrative form.

Regarding the representational potential of the historiographical descriptions of performances, I would like to take as a starting point the ideas put forward by the American medievalist David A. Warner. In analysing the dichotomy between rituals as 'normally real' chronological events and remembered events, he at first admits that 'because the memories of medieval churchmen, our chief informants, were both malleable and subject to partisanship, the degree to which an account of a ritual corresponds with the actual event must always remain in doubt'.[5] However, he then continues: 'in any case, whether the ritual in question actually occurred or not, the ability to impose a particular reading on it implied a kind of power or authority'.[6] Thus, even when fac-

---

[3] Geertz, *The Interpretation of Cultures*, p. 89.
[4] For an introduction to his arguments, see Althoff, *Die Macht der Rituale*.
[5] Warner, 'Ritual and Memory in the Ottonian Reich', p. 256.
[6] Warner, 'Ritual and Memory in the Ottonian Reich', p. 256.

ing the uncertainty resulting from the above-mentioned dichotomy, 'the very fact that ritual exerted such a powerful influence on the historical imagination offers still other, potentially fruitful avenues of inquiry'.[7] In this article, I shall examine these avenues by focusing on the Chronicle of Henry of Livonia and discussing the role of the performative in the Christianizing as well as in the memory-making process.

The Chronicle of Henry of Livonia: A Founding Narration for the Frontier

The Chronicle of Henry of Livonia (*Chronicon Livoniae*) is a Baltic crusading chronicle that records what we might call the canonical period of the Livonian and Estonian crusade in around 1186–1227, that is, during the heyday of the crusading movement. The text was written between 1224 and 1228, likely by a local parish and missionary priest, Henry, who, after his arrival from Saxony to Livonia around 1205, had been an active partaker in the conquest and conversion.[8] The Chronicle, written in 'the praise of our Lord Jesus Christ who wishes His faith and His name to be carried to all nations', as 'through Him and with His cooperation and approval, these things were done',[9] is to record 'the many and glorious things [that] happened in Livonia at the time the heathen were converted to the faith of Jesus Christ'.[10] Its representation of the events is dominated by the theme of 'the enlargement of faith among the

---

[7] Warner, 'Ritual and Memory in the Ottonian Reich', p. 260.

[8] Henry is likely to have been born in around 1187–88 in Saxony, near Magdeburg; see Arbusow, 'Das entlehnte Sprachgut', p. 100; Johansen, 'Die Chronik als Biographie', p. 9; Bauer, 'Einleitung', pp. vi–ix. He was educated in Germany, probably at the monastery school at Segeberg under the tutorage of Abbot Rothmar, the brother of Bishop Albert of Riga (Johansen, 'Die Chronik als Biographie', p. 11). Henry came to Riga with Bishop Albert in around 1205 and was ordained a parish priest in 1208. He wrote his Chronicle between 1224 and 1226, and thereafter added one final chapter likely in 1227–28. Henceforth Henry remained a parish priest and died some time after the year 1259. For the latest research on the Chronicle, see Tamm, Kaljundi, and Jensen, *Crusading and Chronicle Writing*.

[9] *Heinrici Chronicon Livoniae*, ed. by Arbusow and Bauer, XXIX. 9: 'ad laudem eiusdem domini nostri Iesu Christi, qui fidem et nomen suum portari vult ad omnes gentes, ipso cooperante et confirmante, per quem talia sunt operata', citing John 20. 30–31; Acts 9. 15; *The Chronicle of Henry of Livonia*, trans. by Brundage, p. 237).

[10] 'multa quidem et gloriosa contigerunt in Lyvonia tempore conversionis gencium ad fidem Iesu Christi' (*Heinrici Chronicon Livoniae*, ed. by Arbusow and Bauer, XXIX. 9; *The Chronicle of Henry of Livonia*, trans. by Brundage, p. 237).

pagans' ('fidem dilatare in gentibus'),[11] which reflects the territorialization of the notion of *Christianitas* in medieval historical writing during the period of Christian expansion, if one is to follow the idea coined by the British medievalist Robert Bartlett in his influential and innovative work *The Making of Europe*.[12] Thus, next to being an exemplary crusading and missionary chronicle, Henry's Chronicle was designed as a founding narrative of the new bishopric, Riga, and aimed at establishing its legitimacy and identity.[13] Therefore it illustrates well what the American historian Patrick J. Geary has recently called the functionality of historiography in the construction of regional identities and in establishing the connections between things, persons, texts, and institutions.[14] This task included the construction of both new Christian identities at the frontier and of the otherness of local 'pagan' peoples. In studying how the medieval writers constructed their past at the edges of the known world, scholars have explained it as a process of establishing new self-identifications that would enable the inclusion of the local realms into the Christian scheme of things by integrating local historiography into universal history and local geography into the universal Christian space.[15] Furthermore, as Geary has remarked in the same connection, the authors' strong dependency on textual authorities reflects the pursuit of legitimacy and consolidation in a world lacking an alternative political hegemony.[16] Yet I believe to this one should add an aspect emphasized by Lars Boje Mortensen in the context of medieval Nordic history writing: in studying these founding narratives one should avoid the two-layer model where the primary field of politics simply uses or manipulates the secondary socio-cultural field (for example, religion or historical culture). Instead, we could study history as cultural memory that serves a similar function with the other modes of activating the dialogue with the past (such as, for example, ceremonies or liturgy).[17]

---

[11] Arbusow, 'Das entlehnte Sprachgut', pp. 12, 127–29.

[12] Bartlett, *The Making of Europe*, pp. 243–68.

[13] As has also been noted by Arbusow, *Liturgie und Geschichtsschreibung*, p. 5; see also Kattinger, 'Identität und Integration im Ostseeraum', pp. 118–19.

[14] Geary, 'Reflections on Historiography and the Holy'.

[15] For an expansion of this idea on the example of twelfth-century Scandinavian writing, see Mortensen, 'The Language of Geographical Description'. I have discussed the intertextual constructions of the new worlds in the Latin writings about the Saxon-Wendish frontier in Kaljundi, 'Waiting for the Barbarians'.

[16] Geary, 'Reflections on Historiography and the Holy'.

[17] Mortensen, 'Sanctified Beginnings and Mythopoietic Moments'.

Returning to Henry's narrative, it begins in the 1180s with the arrival and debated 'peaceful mission' of Meinhard, an Augustinian monk from Segeberg (Saxony) who also became the first bishop of Üxküll (Latv. Ikšķile) (1186–96).[18] The Chronicle then records the first crusade to Livonia in 1198 that was led by the next Bishop of Üxküll, Berthold (1196–98), and his martyrdom during the same campaign. Next Henry reports the conquest and conversion of the Livs and Lettgallians during the early years of the reign of Bishop Albert (1199–1229), his move of the see from Üxküll to Riga (which became the centre and the base for the Christians in this region), and the start of the regular crusading movement at the initiative of this energetic propagator of faith. Thereafter the Chronicle continues with the crusades to Estonia that started in 1208 and the descriptions of which take up more than two thirds of the text.[19] This first history of Livonia ends with the victorious crusading campaign to the islands of Moon (Est. Muhu) and Ösel (Est. Saaremaa) in 1227.[20]

If we assume that the priest Henry (*Henricus* or *Heinricus*), who is mentioned several times in the text, is the author of the Chronicle, then we must also take into account that the author had taken part in many of the events described: he had lived close to the mission and warfare in the lands of the Livs and Lettgallians, had been on the missions to Estonia, and taken part in crusading as a chaplain.[21] This has led some scholars to treat the text as a record of personal experiences, or even as an autobiography.[22] In addition to relying on his memory, he could also have used the testimonies of his fellow missionaries and crusaders; and even though his eye-witness arguments must be treated with care, it is not mere rhetoric when he claims 'Nothing has been put in this account except what we have seen almost entirely with our own eyes. What we have not seen with our eyes, we have learned from those who saw it and who were there'.[23]

---

[18] For recent discussions on the nature of the early mission to Livonia, see Helmann, 'Die Anfänge der christlicher Mission'; Helmann, 'Bischof Meinhard und die Eigenart der kirchlicher Organisation'; Jensen, 'The Nature of Early Missionary Activities'.

[19] *Heinrici Chronicon Livoniae*, ed. by Arbusow and Bauer, XII. 6 – XXIX.

[20] *Heinrici Chronicon Livoniae*, ed. by Arbusow and Bauer, XXX.

[21] Priest Henry is mentioned as a participant in the events in *Heinrici Chronicon Livoniae*, ed. by Arbusow and Bauer, XI. 7, XII. 6, XVI. 3, XVII. 6, XXIV. 1–2. In addition, different scholars have suggested that he also took part at the Lateran Council in Rome in 1215, travelled to Germany with Bishop Albert in 1222–24, and acted as an interpreter for the papal legate to the region, William of Modena in 1225–26.

[22] For an influential study of this text as an autobiography of the chronicler, see Johansen, 'Die Chronik als Biographie'.

[23] *Heinrici Chronicon Livoniae*, ed. by Arbusow and Bauer, XXIX. 9, citing I John 1. 1; The

Thus, to borrow a phrase coined by the British crusading historian Christopher Tyerman, Henry's Chronicle presents a viewpoint of 'a committed participant'.[24] Yet the text does offer a rare opportunity to gain insight into the crusading and missionary activities, as well as their symbolic universe — aspects of the Chronicle that have been emphasized, especially recently, and that have elevated Henry's text to a rather keen level of interest amongst crusading scholars.[25] However, an aspect that has gained but meagre attention is the Chronicle's description of the performative acts related to the mission and crusading. The Baltic German historian Leonid Arbusow has studied them in more depth in his analysis of Henry's use of liturgical language.[26] Alongside this, Henry's depictions of pagan rites have, of course, gained attention due to the Enlightenment and Romanticist and national interest in the distant past of local folk customs. Nevertheless, even when viewing the representations of the performative from an anthropological angle, finding a suitable approach is not easy. Indeed, Peter Burke has phrased the problem well in an introduction to his *Historical Anthropology of Early Modern Italy*: 'How can historians do "fieldwork" among the dead?'[27] To suggest one possible approach to tackling this question, I shall firstly discuss Henry's use of reperformance, and re-enactment of the past on a broader level, as an ontological principle for conceptualizing the present in a historical narrative. Secondly, I will look more closely into some of his representations of performative acts and ask how they vocalize the distant past during the crusading and Christianization process, and activate a dialogue with them.

Before doing so, however, one has to face the abundance of definitions for a 'performance'. Relying here on Burke's synthesis of various definitions,[28] one could claim that all human behaviour is learned, and thus use the term in a weaker sense to study the informal scenarios of everyday life. On the other hand, 'performance' in a stronger sense refers to formal rituals, ceremonies, and festivals; a scholar preferring this definition would explore more clearly identifiable symbolic actions and events, which are set apart from everyday life,

Chronicle of Henry of Livonia, trans. by Brundage, pp. 237–38.

[24] Tyerman, *The Invention of the Crusades*.

[25] See, first and foremost, Murray, *The Clash of Cultures on the Medieval Baltic Frontier*; Tamm, Kaljundi, and Jensen, *Crusading and Chronicle Writing*.

[26] Arbusow, *Liturgie und Geschichtsschreibung*; also Arbusow, 'Das entlehnte Sprachgut'.

[27] Burke, *The Historical Anthropology of Early Modern Italy*, p. 15.

[28] See Burke, 'Performing History', especially p. 43.

and place participants into a special situation — into a state where the world as experienced and the world as imagined meet more explicitly. I would like to remain in the middle and argue for the fluidity and flexibility of the performative quality in human experience. However, in the context of this article it seems important to point to one of the most significant elements of performances of any kind: they most often reperform and vocalize the past history of events which gives rise — as well as meaning and significance — to them. And, as I shall argue below, evoking the remembrance of the things past is exactly the feature that is common to the general structure and function of both the medieval historical discourse and the performative instances recorded in the text.

Taking the Typological Principle Seriously: Re-enacting the Past and Conceptualizing the Present

Henry's Chronicle begins with the lines 'Divine Providence, "by the fire of His love", and "mindful of Raab and Babylonia", that is, of the confusion of paganism, aroused in our modern times the idolatrous Livs from the sleep of idolatry and of sin in the following way'.[29] This sentence refers to the sacred history via both the Roman breviary[30] and the biblical Psalms (Psalm 86. 4). Thus, already in its beginning, the Chronicle presents a vivid example of an understanding that the present gains significance and meaning as an imitation of the things past. While we can interpret even the very act of historical writing as a kind of a performative act — an imitation of the works of previous authors, and of the very act of writing history — in medieval historical writing this is most eminently accompanied by a strong degree of textual imitation, intertextuality. In Henry's Chronicle, the quotations from textual authorities (as verses, words and phrases, or images and topoi) are almost omnipresent. This relates closely to the chronicler's considerable concern for 'inventing a tradition' for the frontier and to his aim of including the region, its pagan peoples, and Christian newcomers to the ancient and sacred past. Indeed, there being no previous narrative for Livonia (according to our present knowledge), he was the first to take up this task in this area.

---

[29] *Heinrici Chronicon Livoniae*, ed. by Arbusow and Bauer, I. 1: 'Divina providencia, memor Raab et Babilonis, videlicet confuse gentilitatis, nostris et modernis temporibus Livones ydolatras ab ydolatrie et peccati sompno taliter igne sui amoris excitavit'; *The Chronicle of Henry of Livonia*, trans. by Brundage, p. 25.

[30] *Officium Matutini in Tempore Adventus, Benedictio ad Lect. vi.* and often elsewhere in the Roman Breviary. See *Heinrici Chronicon Livoniae*, ed. by Arbusow and Bauer, p. 2.

In the text, biblical and classical words and phrasing are constantly used for describing the present course of events, and another significant type of textual authority is provided by the liturgy — the quotations from this realm, as convincingly demonstrated by Leonid Arbusow, had a major impact on the structure and rhythm of the Chronicle.[31] On a broader level, the omnipresent quotations are linked to the tradition of medieval historical writing that favours analogical and typological rather than causal explanations. The present history gains (spiritual) meaning as a reperformance of the past, which links the current course of events to the universal course of Salvation history, both as a continuation and as an imitation of it, and treats them as manifestations of the same eternal truth.[32] Thus historical facts can achieve spiritual meaning when typologically related to the sacred past. And, of course, one could add that conceptualizing continuity with and an imitation of the (authoritative) past does not characterize medieval historical writing alone, but is a crucial feature of the historical identity of any group.

Not surprisingly, in Henry's Chronicle the re-presentation of the current events of 'our modern times' ('nostris et modernis temporibus') as a recollection and repetition of the biblical wars of the people of Israel, and the Apostolic and saintly mission, serves the goal of bringing the present Livonia and Estonia into the mainstream of universal history and of establishing 'us' as credible historical agents. Along the same line, the mission of the Church in Riga is presented as part of the task of fulfilling the baptismal command Christ gave to the Apostles, most explicitly when Bishop Albert of Riga is said to follow the Lord 'as He commands in His gospels, saying "Go ye therefore, and teach all nations, baptizing them in the name of the Father, and of the Son, and of the Holy Ghost"'.[33] In addition, the small number of Livonian Christians[34] draws an analogy between them and members of the first congregations who lived at times when 'the harvest truly is plenteous, but the labourers are few' (Matthew

---

[31] See Arbusow, *Liturgie und Geschichtsschreibung*.

[32] As argued, for example, in Mégier, '"Ecclesiae sacramenta"', pp. 625–29, and Bagge, 'Ideas and Narrative in Otto of Freising's Gesta Frederici'.

[33] *Heinrici Chronicon Livoniae*, ed. by Arbusow and Bauer, XVI. 2, ref. Matthew 28. 29; *The Chronicle of Henry of Livonia*, trans. by Brundage, p. 122. Also the epilogue of the Chronicle (*Heinrici Chronicon Livoniae*, ed. by Arbusow and Bauer, XXIX. 9) refers to the same command, as given in Mark 16. 20.

[34] The small number of the Germans is emphasized in *Heinrici Chronicon Livoniae*, ed. by Arbusow and Bauer, IX. 3, X. 12, XXI. 7, XXII. 3, XXV. 4, XXVIII. 1, and that of the crusaders in general in ibid., VI. 1, XXV. 1.

9. 37). Similarly, the image of Riga as a new church (*novella ecclesia*) relies on 'such tribulation' and on the small number of Christians who, surrounded by pagans, are relieved by the help of God who 'with so few men and in the midst of pagans, always maintained His church'.[35]

The very same emphasis on Christians threatened by the unbelievers also formed the core of the crusading rhetoric, as these campaigns were understood as quintessentially protective. Thus, not surprisingly, this also forms the basis of the Livonian crusading rhetoric, as illuminated well in Henry's description of the Lateran Council (1215). There, according to him, Pope Innocent III (1198–1216) renewed for the Livonian clergy 'their authority to preach and to enlist, for the remission of their sins, pilgrims who would go to Livonia with them to secure the new church against the assaults of the pagans'.[36] The endeavour lies on the shoulders of the crusaders and the military order of the Sword Brethren (est. in Livonia in 1201). Their campaigns, and the victories achieved over many through the hands of the few, are compared to the wars of Israel, and especially those of the Maccabees in which the few elected people fought the wars of the Lord over many.[37]

---

[35] *Heinrici Chronicon Livoniae*, ed. by Arbusow and Bauer, X. 13: 'in medio gencium in tanta paucitate virorum suam semper conservat ecclesiam'; *The Chronicle of Henry of Livonia*, trans. by Brundage, p. 64. For the church of Livonia depicted as *adhuc parva*, see *Heinrici Chronicon Livoniae*, ed. by Arbusow and Bauer, XII. 5, for the Estonian church as *parvula adhuc infirma*, see ibid., XXVIII. 4. For the notion of *novella ecclesia*, see ibid., X. 8, XVI. 2, XIX. 7, XXII. 1, XXIV. 4.

[36] *Heinrici Chronicon Livoniae*, ed. by Arbusow and Bauer, XXII. 1: 'renovata auctoritate predicandi et peregrinos in remissionem peccatorum signandi, qui Lyvoniam secum proficiscentes novellam ecclesiam a paganorum tuerentur insultibus' (*The Chronicle of Henry of Livonia*, trans. by Brundage, p. 152). See also 'defenderunt ecclesiam novellam ab impetu paganorum'. It is also described as the church as 'beset with many tribulations' and situated 'in the midst of many nations and the adjacent Russians, who all took counsel together over ways to destroy it' in *Heinrici Chronicon Livoniae*, ed. by Arbusow and Bauer, XIV. 7, ref. Psalm 71. 10, Acts 9. 23; *The Chronicle of Henry of Livonia*, trans. by Brundage, p. 100. Similar images are used in *Heinrici Chronicon Livoniae*, ed. by Arbusow and Bauer, VI. 4, VII. 2, VIII. 1, X. 13, XII. 6, XIV. 4, XIV. 7, XVII. 1, XIX. 7, XXII. 1. Likewise, the legitimation for the founding of the Sword Brethen (in 1202) relies on the fear that otherwise the local Christians and the clergy, 'foreseeing the treachery of the Livonians' would be 'unable to resist the multitude of pagans', and on the need 'to preserve the church among the pagans' ('ad conservandam in gentibus ecclesiam') (*Heinrici Chronicon Livoniae*, ed. by Arbusow and Bauer, VI. 6; *The Chronicle of Henry of Livonia*, trans. by Brundage, p. 40).

[37] This idea is emphasized also in the thanksgiving to God after the battles: 'qui per paucos "operatus est salutem" ecclesie sue' citing from Psalm 73. 12 (*Heinrici Chronicon Livoniae*, ed. by Arbusow and Bauer, X. 8, 9, X. 14, XXI. 7, XXIII. 9); see also ibid., X. 12, 13, XXII. 3, XXV. 2,

Nevertheless, this structure also includes the local peoples, presented according to the model of the antagonists in those sacred stories: the pagans and apostates of the Old and New Testament. On the narrative level, this is also represented through the inclusion of several scenes and utterances from sacred writing. The newly converted Livs, depicted as 'stubborn' and 'treacherous', at first 'deceitfully with guile and tears' ('dolis et lacrimis [...] ficte'), ask Bishop Meinhard not to abandon them (as the Bishop was about to sail off), yet thereafter 'greeted the bishop on his return like Judas, and said: "Hail, rabi!"'.[38] As the chronicler compares the Livonian Christians and the crusaders to the people of Israel, he also establishes an analogy between the Livs and the Philistines, the enemies of the Israelites. To give just one example, the chieftain of the revolting Livs 'comforted and encouraged' his men, 'saying, as the Philistines once did: "Take courage and fight, ye brothers Philistines, lest you come to be servants to the Hebrews"'.[39] The utterances of the antagonists of the Old Testament are also used to represent other rivals: for example, one of the Lithuanian chieftains uses the voice of the Syrian king Ben-Hadad who fought against Israel.[40] Thus, in a text that is aimed at creating history and identity for the new Christian col-

XXVII. 6. A direct comparison to the wars of Israel is made as Henry states: 'ut unus persequeretur mille et duo fugarent decem milia' (ibid., XXV. 4: citing Deuteronomy 32. 30); and 'qui quondam exterruit Philisteos, ut fugerent coram David, or qui David a Philisteis semper defendit' (ibid., XXVII. 1, XXX. 4: citing I Samuel 17. 35–53). Heinrich Hildebrand was one of the first to draw attention to the comparison between the Rigans and the Israelites; Hildebrand, *Die Chronik Heinrichs von Lettland*, p. 38; later Leonid Arbusow has argued that the motif of the great victory achieved through the hands of the few is one of the dominant ones in the text (Arbusow, *Liturgie und Geschichtsschreibung*, p. 51).

[38] *Heinrici Chronicon Livoniae*, ed. by Arbusow and Bauer, I. 11: 'redeuntem episcopum Holmenses salutatione et animo Iude salutant, dicentes "Ave, rabbi"', citing Matthew 26. 49; *The Chronicle of Henry of Livonia*, trans. by Brundage, pp. 28–29. Later the Estonians are also presented as giving a Judas's greeting to their priest, as 'he was hailed with greetings from the mouth and not from the heart' ('salutatusque est salutatione oris et non cordis, qualiter Iudas Dominum salutavit') (*Heinrici Chronicon Livoniae*, ed. by Arbusow and Bauer, XV. 9; *The Chronicle of Henry of Livonia*, trans. by Brundage, p. 119).

[39] *Heinrici Chronicon Livoniae*, ed. by Arbusow and Bauer, X. 10: 'Confortabant enim eos Dabrelus, senior ipsorum, et animabat, quemadmodum Philistei quondam dicentes: "Confrontamini, Philistiim, et pugnate, ne serviatis Hebreis"', citing I Kings 4. 9; *The Chronicle of Henry of Livonia*, trans. by Brundage, p. 61).

[40] Mocking the Rigans, he says 'For the dust of this city [Riga] will scarcely satisfy the fist of our people'. *Heinrici Chronicon Livoniae*, ed. by Arbusow and Bauer, IX. 1: 'Vix enim pulvis civitatis illius pugillo populi nostri sufficiet', citing III Kings 20. 10; *The Chronicle of Henry of Livonia*, trans. by Brundage, p. 47.

ony, this dominantly mimetic representation of events, agents, and even places had a clearly legitimizing and authority-forming function.

Vocalizing and Re-enacting the Past

Is it possible to move on from these broader analogies and comparisons to look for more distinct representations? I would like to argue that the Chronicle does indeed represent several (types of) performative acts, which show an understanding that the sacred past also needs to be vocalized and acted out. This is most clearly made manifest by what is likely the best-known example of the uses of the performative in the Chronicle, namely Henry's account of the liturgical 'Play of the Prophets', which took place in Riga in the winter of 1204.[41] As pointed out by Brenda Bolton, during the twelfth and thirteenth centuries the liturgical drama was practised in many of the eastern frontier areas, where the dramatization of the liturgy and biblical events was to lay the foundations for the continuity of worship amongst the neophytes.[42] The play was addressed to the neophytes; it was performed 'in order that the pagans (*gentilitas*) might learn the rudiments of the Christian faith by an ocular demonstration'.[43] Here the analogy with the sacred history is made manifest: 'This play was like a prelude and prophecy of the future; for in the same play there were wars, namely those of David, Gideon, and Herod, and there was the doctrine of the Old and New Testaments.'[44] Moreover, it is also claimed to have been acted out with the participation of the pagan audience, as when 'the army of Gideon fought the Philistines, the pagans began to take flight, fearing lest they be killed'.[45]

---

[41] *Heinrici Chronicon Livoniae*, ed. by Arbusow and Bauer, IX. 14. See Schneider, 'Strassentheater im Missionseinsatz'; Petersen, 'The Notion of a Missionary Theatre'.

[42] Bolton, 'Message, Celebration, Offering', pp. 93–97. Bolton's article emphasizes Pope Innocent III's role in the use of and regulations for 'liturgical dramas' in the frontier areas.

[43] *Heinrici Chronicon Livoniae*, ed. by Arbusow and Bauer, IX. 14: 'ut fidei christiane rudimenta gentilitas fide disceret oculata'; *The Chronicle of Henry of Livonia*, trans. by Brundage, p. 53.

[44] *Heinrici Chronicon Livoniae*, ed. by Arbusow and Bauer, IX. 14: 'Iste autem ludus quasi preludium et presagium erat futurorum. Nam in eodem ludo errant bella, utpote David, Gedeonis, Herodis; erat et doctrina Veteris et Novi Testamenti'; *The Chronicle of Henry of Livonia*, trans. by Brundage, p. 53.

[45] *Heinrici Chronicon Livoniae*, ed. by Arbusow and Bauer, IX. 14: 'Ubi autem armati Gedeonis cum Phylisteis pugnabant, pagani timentes occidi fugere ceperunt'; *The Chronicle of Henry of Livonia*, trans. by Brundage, p. 53.

Several other passages of the Chronicle also refer to a need for 'ocular demonstrations' and participation in rituals, which, I believe, can be especially revealing in the context of conquest and conversion regarding an understanding of the efficiency and authority of symbolic behaviour and interaction. Furthermore, the emphasis on and the accompanying anxiety regarding the performative aspects suggests the importance of symbolic behaviour in the process of crusade and Christianization. The *legatio in gentibus* is something that needs to be performed. First and foremost, the dominant feature of those acts is their ability to link the present to the past (as did the analogical and typological models discussed above). Even though Henry abundantly uses quotes to represent those acts, he also constantly modifies the biblical, liturgical, hagiographical, and other patterns to fit different occasions. Indeed, the ability to fluidly adapt is an essential and vital feature of any performance, including medieval ritual performances.[46] In the following my interest lies in these questions: On what occasions and where do those performances take place? Who are the performers? What is their function (i.e. what is communicated by the rituals and through the agency of their participants)?

Firstly, one should begin by emphasizing that partaking in a mission, or a crusade, in itself has the quality of taking part in a ritual. Similarly crusading warfare is re-presented as imitation: it is presented as a re-enactment of the wars of Israel and especially the Maccabees. Like the Israelites the crusaders are also 'to fight the battles of the Lord against the pagans'[47] and act as agents through whom the divine plan and the grace of God are made manifest: He is said to have been fighting for them, as He fought for the chosen people.[48]

---

[46] As has been stressed by, for instance, Althoff, 'The Variability of Rituals'.

[47] For 'prelia Domini preliari contra paganos' citing from I Samuel 25. 28, see, for instance, *Heinrici Chronicon Livoniae*, ed. by Arbusow and Bauer, XXV. 1; and for 'the battles of the Lord' ('prelia Domini') citing from I Kings 25. 28, see ibid., XI. 5, XIII. 2, XXI. 2, XXV. 1, XXVII. 1. See also 'preliabatur prelia Domini cum leticia' (ref. I Maccabees 3. 2) in ibid., XIII. 2, XXVII. 1.

[48] For the battles where the Lord 'fought for them' ('pro eis pugnavit'), citing from Exodus 14. 25 and Judith 5. 16, see *Heinrici Chronicon Livoniae*, ed. by Arbusow and Bauer, XV. 3, XXV. 4, XXVII. 1, XXVIII. 7. The idea extends also to the Church as a whole: after one victorious battle 'the Livonian church knew truly that God was fighting for it'. See *Heinrici Chronicon Livoniae*, ed. by Arbusow and Bauer, XV. 3: 'ecclesia Lyvonensis Deum vere pugnare pro se intellexit', citing Exodus 14. 25; *The Chronicle of Henry of Livonia*, trans. by Brundage, p. 113. Similarly, the crusaders go into battle 'in quo confidentes' (*Heinrici Chronicon Livoniae*, ed. by Arbusow and Bauer, XI. 5, XXIII. 9, XXV. 4, XXX. 4: ref. Psalm 10. 1); and ibid., XII. 3 and XXV. 4: 'in Domino sperandum or spem totam ponebant in Domino', ref. Psalm 73. 28, 78. 7. Also, the Sword Brethren are called the 'army of the Lord' ('exercitus Domini') that is fighting

The Maccabees were a significant model for the crusading ideology as a whole, which relied heavily on the idea of reperforming the biblical past and also the past of the previous crusades. Furthermore, the crusading movement turned the experience of conquest and conversion into what we might call a collective performative act, one that places participants in a special situation. When looking at the Nordic missionary tradition one notices that in the pre-crusading period the past is mainly reperformed by the individual members of the elite: missionaries (and, to a great extent, even missionary bishops who are compared to Elisha, Elijah, Moses, and the great missionaries of the past), and princes and kings (compared for instance to David). During the crusades, however, the group presented to take part in the imitation of the authoritative figures of the past (Christ, the Apostles, the Maccabees, etc.) grows significantly larger.[49] In addition, as a penitential ritual and a way of gaining spiritual reward, crusading was closely interlinked with the pilgrimage tradition, and thus its authority also relied on following in the earthly footsteps of Christ. As a result, this 'monasticization of war' included not only campaigning, but also several sequential phases of the ritual of repentance and redemption (moving from a grief and fear of God to joy): taking the vow and taking part in the crusading ceremonies (for instance, Masses), showing individual devotion and penance, experiencing suffering and perils, acknowledging the longing for God, and achieving His grace. It was in the late twelfth and early thirteenth centuries that the crusading rhetoric and practices gained significant coherence, including its legislative, legitimizing, and also ritual strategies (crusading indulgence, privileges, sermons, vows, etc.), and Henry's Chronicle illuminates this process well: authors like him played a crucial role in creating the phenomenon they were describing, as they provided both the description and the definition for it.[50] In his representation crusading makes the expansion performative: with the help of biblical as well as liturgical quotations, the presentation of campaigning is ritualized and adjusted to the structure of a penitential ritual.

Firstly, the Chronicle reflects the initiating rituals of crusading campaigns: bestowing and taking the sign of the cross. A good example of this is offered,

---

'with joy the battles of the Lord'. See ibid., XIII. 2: 'preliabatur prelia Domini cum leticia', citing 1 Maccabees 3. 2; *The Chronicle of Henry of Livonia*, trans. by Brundage, p. 89; in the same passage Henry also states that 'the aid and victory of the Lord was always with them [the Sword Brethren]'. See *Heinrici Chronicon Livoniae*, ed. by Arbusow and Bauer, XIII. 2: 'auxilium et victoria Domini semper erat cum eis'; *The Chronicle of Henry of Livonia*, trans. by Brundage, p. 89.

[49] For an initial sketch of this idea, see Kaljundi, 'Waiting for the Barbarians'.

[50] Tyerman, *The Invention of the Crusades*, p. 35.

for instance, in the description of the crusade to Ösel in 1206, in the beginning of which Andreas Sunesen, the Archbishop of Lund (1201–28) 'bestowed the sign of the cross (*signo crucis signaverat*) upon a great multitude, which were to take vengeance on the pagans and subject the nations to the Christian faith'.[51] Other traces of crusading sermons also exist in the text,[52] the rhetoric of which is likewise revealed in an emphasis on the need to protect the young Church and the small number of Christians from the manifold dangers to which they are exposed in the barbarian lands. Henry also pays attention to the indulgence and privileges granted to the crusaders, stressing that they are equal to those given to the crusaders to the Holy Land.[53] These initiating markers of crusading are followed by yet another symbolically loaded element: the beginning of the crusading performance is also marked by a crossing of the sea (the maritime voyage to Riga via Lübeck and Visby). Every year around Easter the ships arrived with crusaders and provisions, and other ships transported the crusaders back after they had spent one year in Livonia. As the Chronicle is also structured according to the Easter season, most of the books begin either with the crusaders coming or leaving by sea, often accompanied by Bishop Albert of Riga.[54] Henry describes Bishop Albert's crusading sermons as a call 'to take on the sign of the cross in order to go by sea to Livonia', and, likewise, explicitly defines Livonia and Estonia as 'the lands beyond the sea' ('terrae transmarinae').[55]

[51] *Heinrici Chronicon Livoniae*, ed. by Arbusow and Bauer, x. 13: 'qui in remissionem peccatorum infinitam multitudinem signo crucis signaverat ad faciendam vindictam in nationibus et ad subiugandas gentes fidei christiane', ref. Psalm 149. 7; *The Chronicle of Henry of Livonia*, trans. by Brundage, p. 14.

[52] For example, the last book of the Chronicle describes how the papal legate William of Modena preached the crusade to Ösel: he 'displayed the sign of the holy cross for the remission of sins to all who bore the Christian name, that they might take revenge upon the perverse Oeselians'; and whilst the Gothlanders and Danes arguably refuse, 'the Germans obeyed and took the cross (*crucem recipiunt*)' (*Heinrici Chronicon Livoniae*, ed. by Arbusow and Bauer, xxx. 1; *The Chronicle of Henry of Livonia*, trans. by Brundage, p. 239). For indications to crusading sermons, see also *Heinrici Chronicon Livoniae*, ed. by Arbusow and Bauer, x. 8, 13, xii. 1, xiv. 4.

[53] For the mentioning of the crusaders' privileges and indulgence, see *Heinrici Chronicon Livoniae*, ed. by Arbusow and Bauer, i. 12, iii. 2, vii. 2, x. 13, xi. 9, xix. 7, xxii. 1, xxx. 1.

[54] Several scholars have pointed out that the Chronicle's structure follows the rhythm of pilgrims' seafaring, or 'pilgrimage-years'. See, for instance, Jensen, 'The Nature of Early Missionary Activities'.

[55] *Heinrici Chronicon Livoniae*, ed. by Arbusow and Bauer, xiv. 4: 'crucis signum sibi affigeat, ut mare transeat'; *The Chronicle of Henry of Livonia*, trans. by Brundage, p. 96. Livonia and Estonia are called *terra transmarinae* in *Heinrici Chronicon Livoniae*, ed. by Arbusow and Bauer, xv. 4, xxv. 2.

In the crusading literature, going to sea signifies giving oneself to perils and also recalls the symbolic importance the Bible ascribes to sea travel. The clerics and crusaders are 'committing themselves to the dangers of the sea (*periculis maris*)'[56] by travelling to Livonia. In particular, the endeavour of Bishop Albert, who travelled to Germany almost annually to recruit another levy of crusaders, is emphasized; as Henry claims, 'Not fearing to undergo prosperity and adversity for God, he [Bishop Albert] committed himself to the raging sea.'[57] In addition, Henry presents the sea voyage as dangerous not only because of the storms, but also due to the pagan pirates[58] — a motif which is not rare in the Baltic crusading tradition which previously made use especially of the threat that the Wendish pirates posed to their Danish and Saxon neighbours.[59] Yet the symbolic value of the seascape is not only defined by negative characteristics. The sea is also a place where the will of the Lord is made manifest, and therefore seafaring is an activity governed from on high: there the Lord keeps his people from dangers.[60] Moreover, the sea is closely connected to the Virgin Mary, the patroness of the Livonian mission, whom Henry also calls 'The Star of the Sea' ('maris stella') after the church anthem *Ave Maris Stella*. The one or two years' crusading experience is conclusively turned into a penitential ritual by the further perils that await the crusaders in Livonia and Estonia, concep-

---

[56] *Heinrici Chronicon Livoniae*, ed. by Arbusow and Bauer, XIII. 1; *The Chronicle of Henry of Livonia*, trans. by Brundage, p. 88.

[57] *Heinrici Chronicon Livoniae*, ed. by Arbusow and Bauer, VII. 1: 'pro prospera et adversa pro Deo pati non formidans fluctuanti pelago se committit'; *The Chronicle of Henry of Livonia*, trans. by Brundage, p. 41. In another passage, Henry adds that 'He [Bishop Albert] was not burned by the sun of prosperity by day nor saddened by the moon of adversity by night, and thus kept from the work of God on land and sea'. See *Heinrici Chronicon Livoniae*, ed. by Arbusow and Bauer, X. 11, citing Psalm 120. 6: 'quem nec sol adurit prosperitatis per diem, neque luna contristat adversitatis per noctem, ut a Dei negocio non desistat terra marique'; *The Chronicle of Henry of Livonia*, trans. by Brundage, p. 62. For the Bishop's valiant seagoing, see also *Heinrici Chronicon Livoniae*, ed. by Arbusow and Bauer, VIII. 1.

[58] The pagan pirates are mentioned, for instance, in *Heinrici Chronicon Livoniae*, ed. by Arbusow and Bauer, XIX. 5.

[59] See Jensen, 'The Blue Baltic Border of Denmark' for the Danish perspective, and Scior, *Das Eigene und das Fremde* for the viewpoint of Saxon history writing.

[60] He 'who commands the winds and the sea' ('qui imperat ventis et mari') (*Heinrici Chronicon Livoniae*, ed. by Arbusow and Bauer, IX. 6: citing Luke 8. 25; *The Chronicle of Henry of Livonia*, trans. by Brundage, p. 50) rescues the crusaders from the stormy sea as well as from the Estonian pirates, for example, in *Heinrici Chronicon Livoniae*, ed. by Arbusow and Bauer, VII. 2, VIII. 3, XI. 6.

tualized for the frontier Christian community as follows: 'Although Almighty God does not cease to test his elect ones, now placed in various tribulations (*tribulationes*), like gold in fire, nevertheless He does not desert them entirely, but rather, rescuing them from all evils, puts their enemies in greater fear.'[61]

Similarly the mission can be interpreted as an imitating act, during which the missionaries travelling to Livonia or Estonia place themselves in a situation for which the framework is given by the scriptural, apostolic, and hagiographic tradition. The process includes a series of acts to be performed: crossing the symbolic physical barriers (for instance the sea or rivers), entering the unknown desert-like environment haunted by demons, showing willingness to face perils, threats, and death for Christ, and going about and preaching 'in the midst of a crooked and perverse nation' (Philippians 2. 15). For better or for worse the undertaking often ends in martyrdom, an act which, needless to say, is also understood in the light of the earlier sacred models. Indeed, the first chapters of Henry's Chronicle emphasize the individual suffering of the first missionaries, especially of the first bishops of Üxküll, Meinhard and Berthold: according to Henry, the first was repeatedly betrayed and threatened by the locals, and the second became a martyr.[62] With regard to the clerics, one should mention that the Chronicle does not fail to mention the perils of priest Henry, the supposed author of the text: later on it stresses that after his consecration he, 'although exposed to many dangers (*plurimis periculis expositus*), did not cease to point out to them the blessed future life'.[63] However, after the beginning of regular crusading in early thirteenth-century Livonia, the threshold of penitential ritual opens up to the whole Christian community, including the crusaders and the Sword Brethren, the citizens and merchants of Riga, as well as the missionaries. This is well illustrated by the chronicler's remark on how

---

[61] *Heinrici Chronicon Livoniae*, ed. by Arbusow and Bauer, VIII. 3: 'Licet enim omnipotens Deus electos suos in variis tribulationibus positos quasi aurum in igne probare non desinat, nunquam tamen omnino deserit, immo ex omnibus malis eos eripiens maiorem hostibus eorum timorem ingerit', citing Job 23. 10, Genesis 48. 16; *The Chronicle of Henry of Livonia*, trans. by Brundage, p. 46.

[62] For the labours and troubles of Meinhard, see esp. *Heinrici Chronicon Livoniae*, ed. by Arbusow and Bauer, I. 9, I. 11, and for those of Berthold, ibid., II. 2; the martyrdom of the latter is described in ibid., II. 6. For the perils of other early missionaries, see ibid., I. 10, II. 9–10, IV. 2, VII. 6.

[63] *Heinrici Chronicon Livoniae*, ed. by Arbusow and Bauer, XI. 7: 'plurimis periculis expositus, future eis beatitudinem vite non desiit demonstrare'; *The Chronicle of Henry of Livonia*, trans. by Brundage, p. 75. The misfortunes of priest Henry are also vividly described in *Heinrici Chronicon Livoniae*, ed. by Arbusow and Bauer, XXIV. 5.

Sword Brethren 'bore the burden of the day, and the heats, in wars and other continual labors'.[64] Furthermore, the Chronicle points to the flexibility of performing the crusading ritual: one group of the Livonian crusaders fulfil their crusading vow by building the city walls of Riga.[65]

Finally, one ought not to forget that suffering also had a prominent legitimizing potential. This was, for instance, used to strengthen the claims of the new church at the Lateran Council (1215) where Bishop Albert 'reported the troubles (*tribulationes*), the wars, and the affairs of the Livonian church'.[66] The same argument was also used on the local level, as during the rivalry of the Danish and Riga churches over northern Estonia. The clerics from Riga (according to Henry) pointed out that 'this vineyard had been planted by the zeal of the pilgrims and the labor of the Rigans through the Blessed Virgin's Banner' and 'it had been cultivated by the blood of many men and by the many sufferings of war'.[67] Furthermore, not only does suffering serve to give legitimacy to the conquest, as well as meaning and significance to the crusading experience, but Henry also presents it as the experience and emotion that unites the crusaders and Christians with the local Livish neophytes. After the assaults by the Estonians in 1223, Henry argues: 'In Riga the word became known about all the evils which had been brought upon the Livonians and Letts and everyone wept and mourned over their colleagues who had been killed.'[68] At the end of

---

[64] *Heinrici Chronicon Livoniae*, ed. by Arbusow and Bauer, XI. 3: 'qui in bellis et in alia laboribus continuis portabant pondus diei et estus', citing Matthew 20. 2, 12; *The Chronicle of Henry of Livonia*, trans. by Brundage, p. 69. In the same passage, the Sword Brethren are also characterized as 'men who day and night set themselves up as a wall for the house of the Lord' ('viros, qui se murum pro domo Domini die ac nocte ponerent', citing Ezechiel 13. 5).

[65] *Heinrici Chronicon Livoniae*, ed. by Arbusow and Bauer, XIII. 3. Henry also describes the building of the city walls in ibid., XI. 1 and XII. 1. The metaphor of 'standing as the wall in front of the house of God' ('murum se pro domo Domini ponere') derives from Ezechiel 13. 5, and is used in relation to both the crusaders and the Sword Brethren in ibid., XI. 5, 9, and also in ibid., XI. 3, XIV. 4.

[66] *Heinrici Chronicon Livoniae*, ed. by Arbusow and Bauer, XIX. 7; *The Chronicle of Henry of Livonia*, trans. by Brundage, p. 152.

[67] Accordingly 'studio peregrionrum et Rigensium labore and sanguine multorum et bellorum incommodis multis' (*Heinrici Chronicon Livoniae*, ed. by Arbusow and Bauer, XXIV. 2; *The Chronicle of Henry of Livonia*, trans. by Brundage, p. 189).

[68] *Heinrici Chronicon Livoniae*, ed. by Arbusow and Bauer, XXVII. 1: 'Et innotuit sermo in Riga de omnibus malis, Lyvonibus et Lettis illatis, et fleverunt et doluerunt omnes de confratribus suis occisis', citing 1 Maccabees 7. 30, 8. 9; *The Chronicle of Henry of Livonia*, trans. by Brundage, p. 213. Also after the defeat at the Ümera battle (1210) the Livs and Lettgallians

the Chronicle, when the papal legate William of Modena met the Lettgallians during his trip to Livonia (1225), he 'praised highly their humility and patience, for they had gladly borne the name of our Lord Jesus Christ to the Esthonians and other peoples' and, furthermore, elevated the local neophytes to martyrdom, claiming according to Henry that they 'had sent many of their people, slain for the Christian faith, into the company of martyrs'.[69]

The Performances of Alterity and Rituals of Inversion

Ritual actions and ceremonial occasions can also function as promises about the future, as proof of making a commitment and fulfilling an obligation; moreover, they can be an expression of consensus or discord, play a role in disputes, or fail to do so. The above-described experience, however, has an inevitable precondition: the pagan barbarians. Likewise in this Chronicle performing paganism defines a pagan. For example, the Livs are defined as 'untamed people, overly given to pagan rites (*paganorum ritibus*)'.[70] Yet when taking a closer look at these rites one easily notices that they are presented in close interplay with Christianity, Christians, and Christian performances. Firstly, a significant amount of the pagan rituals in Henry's Chronicle underline the threat that the idolatrous cult poses to the missionaries or to the Christians in general. On the physical level, the most outstanding threat is the practice of human sacrifice. For example, Henry claims that the pagan Livs attempted to sacrifice their missionary Theoderic to pagan gods, and that they even sacrificed a group of cap-

'returned from the fight, bewailed their dead, and were joined by the whole church in grieving over the newly baptized who had been butchered by the pagans'. See *Heinrici Chronicon Livoniae*, ed. by Arbusow and Bauer, XIV. 7: 'reversi de prelio planxerunt interfectos suos, tristes eo quod nuper baptizati a paganis sint trucidati'; *The Chronicle of Henry of Livonia*, trans. by Brundage, p. 102. The inclusion of the local neophytes into the suffering threshold is also described in *Heinrici Chronicon Livoniae*, ed. by Arbusow and Bauer, XII. 6, XIV. 8, XV. 3.

[69] *Heinrici Chronicon Livoniae*, ed. by Arbusow and Bauer, XXIX. 3: 'humilitatem et patientiam eorum collaudavit, qui nomen domini nostri Iesu Christi ad Estones et ad alias gentes lete portantes, multos de gente sua propter eandem fidem christianam occisos in martyrum [...] consorcium transmiserant'; *The Chronicle of Henry of Livonia*, trans. by Brundage, p. 232. For the depiction of martyrdoms and the 'poetics of death' in general in Henry's Chronicle, see Tamm, 'Martyrs and Miracles'.

[70] *Heinrici Chronicon Livoniae*, ed. by Arbusow and Bauer, IX. 13: 'gens indomita et paganorum ritibus nimis dedita', citing from the Breviary; *The Chronicle of Henry of Livonia*, trans. by Brundage, p. 53.

tured crusaders.[71] Apart from the obvious rhetoric regarding them as a threat, one could also explain these representations with the American literary scholar Stephen Greenblatt's poignant remark about the discourse on 'the marvellous possessions' of the New World: the emphasis on the violent and primitive nature of the others' rites (human sacrifice is an example par excellence) implies a radical distinction between the pagan and Christian religious practices which can otherwise be depicted as disturbingly homologous.[72]

In addition to this, the impact of another significant 'strategy of alteration' is visible:[73] the presentation of a society devoted to irrational rituals, where the belief in the efficiency of rites and divination forms a significant part of their social order. Henry does not present what we might call a comfortable and stable relationship with a community deity, but instead pagan religion and rites are inspired by and confused with fear: pagans are led by magical superstitions, and they practice rites that are intended to placate demonic gods. Not surprisingly, in Henry's presentation a prominent rite is the casting of lots. This pagan ritual is, again, closely related to the Christians: the pagans are depicted as casting lots before going to the campaigns against the Christians of Riga,[74] or even when deciding whether or not Christians should be sacrificed to pagan gods.[75]

---

[71] Accordingly, 'diis suis immolare proponunt' (*Heinrici Chronicon Livoniae*, ed. by Arbusow and Bauer, I. 10), and 'diis suis immolantes' (*Heinrici Chronicon Livoniae*, ed. by Arbusow and Bauer, IX. 12).

[72] Greenblatt, *Marvellous Possessions*, pp. 30–32.

[73] In describing this I have taken inspiration from the ideas put forth by Mary Douglas in her analysis of the Old Testament; see Douglas, *Purity and Danger*, pp. 8–35.

[74] For example, Henry argues that the Estonians decide not to siege Riga because the lots of their gods had fallen to the opposite (*Heinrici Chronicon Livoniae*, ed. by Arbusow and Bauer, XX. 2); and he ascribes the same custom also to the Semigallians (ibid., XII. 2). Similarly to the rituals, which precede the wars, Henry also mentions the rituals for making peace and describes the changing of pikes or blood for signifying peace 'according to the customs of the pagans (*more gentilium*)' for instance, when the Semigallians confirm peace with the Christians (ibid., VI. 5). Also the Curonians are said to have had 'confirmed the peace with the effusion of blood, as is the pagan custom' ('mos paganorum') (ibid., V. 2; *The Chronicle of Henry of Livonia*, trans. by Brundage, p. 39). When the peace treaty was made with the Livonians, it is done by 'exchanging lances, according to the custom (*morem*)' (*Heinrici Chronicon Livoniae*, ed. by Arbusow and Bauer, II. 5; *The Chronicle of Henry of Livonia*, trans. by Brundage, p. 33). Likewise Bishop Berthold sends the pike back to the Livonians to tell them of his wish to end the peace (*Heinrici Chronicon Livoniae*, ed. by Arbusow and Bauer, II. 5); and the Lithuanians tell the Christians about the ending of the peace in a similar manner (ibid., XVII. 2).

[75] This Henry presents as taking place among the Livs; yet in his story the lots favour the missionary and the latter is saved (*Heinrici Chronicon Livoniae*, ed. by Arbusow and Bauer, I. 10).

An even closer interweaving is also mentioned: when the Lettgallians decide on whether they should accept the baptism from the Rigan priests 'they cast lots and asked the opinion of their gods as to whether, [...] they should submit to the baptism of the Russians of Pskov or, on the other hand, to that of the Latins'.[76] This scene is even more interesting as the lots fell, indeed, in favour of the Latins, and later in the narrative the Lettgallians are given the role of 'good neophytes'.

Nevertheless, the text contains but few detailed descriptions of the 'original' pagan religion or idolatry before the period of the initial conversion of the local peoples.[77] While interpreting these representations, one should take into account that the main legitimizing strategy of the Rigan mission and crusade is, according to Henry, the (repeated) apostasy of the Livs and Estonians. The core basis of the legitimacy of the crusades and forced mission is the model which first depicts a peaceful mission taking place among the heathens, followed by the treachery and apostasy of at least some of the neophytes. This allows the use of force to make the relapsed rejoin the faith and Church, as a forced conversion of the pagans would have run counter to canonical law. In this structure, the pagan rites Henry describes function above all as signifiers of the declining of the true faith. Thus, in this Chronicle where 'primitive pagans' use rituals magically and the neophytes are also prone to magic, the majority of magic rites are presented as inversions of Christian rituals and ceremonies. This, furthermore, suggests that the keen demarcation of pagan and blasphemous rites is related to establishing a difference between sainthood and magic (or witchcraft), as well as to anxiety regarding the orthodoxy of the Christian cult (and rites). As the anthropologist Mary Douglas has well pointed out, inverted rituals can reveal a concern for ritual purity in performing an act of worship that is already present in the scripture's history of the Israelites as a struggle between the prophets who demanded interior union with God and the people who were continually susceptible to sliding back into primitive magicality.[78]

Already from the beginning of Henry's narrative, which starts with the mission of Bishop Meinhard among the Livs, the locals are presented as having allowed themselves to be baptized only falsely in the hope of having the missionary build a stone castle to them as a reward.[79] Later, they are said to surren-

---

[76] *Heinrici Chronicon Livoniae*, ed. by Arbusow and Bauer, XI. 7: 'missis tamen prius sortibus et requisito consensu deorum suorum, an Ruthenorum de Plicecowe [...], an Latinorum debeant subire baptismum'; *The Chronicle of Henry of Livonia*, trans. by Brundage, p. 75.

[77] The only exception is the Lithuanians, to whom the mission was not addressed.

[78] Douglas, *Purity and Danger*, p. 32.

[79] So did the Livonians in Üxküll who 'all promised, though deceitfully, to be baptized'.

der and accept baptism only from a fear of the crusaders.[80] Furthermore, after the beginning of regular crusading, the Livs are marked as liable to apostasy (a greater sin than the original paganism); when depicting their conflicts with the new lords, Henry claims that the Livs are 'inconstant and of two minds';[81] 'although they had been baptized, [they] were nevertheless still rebels and unbelievers'.[82] They have either forgotten the faith or care little for baptism. For example in this model description of a pagan revolt the Livs are argued 'having accepted the grace of baptism from Meinhard, the first bishop of Livonia', yet then they 'scorned the faith of Christ and often said they had removed it by bathing in the Dvina'.[83]

Another important element for legitimizing the crusades are the few local neophytes whom Henry presents as remaining true to their new faith, hence creating a cause for the protection of Christianity from the 'hatred' (*odium*) of the revolting Livs.[84] A greater part of the Livs are, nevertheless, depicted as

See *Heinrici Chronicon Livoniae*, ed. by Arbusow and Bauer, I. 6: 'universitas se baptizandam, licet mendaciter, pollicetur'; *The Chronicle of Henry of Livonia*, trans. by Brundage, p. 26; and the ones in Holm 'cheated Meinhard by making a similar promise (*simili promissione*)' (*Heinrici Chronicon Livoniae*, ed. by Arbusow and Bauer, I. 7; *The Chronicle of Henry of Livonia*, trans. by Brundage, p. 27). After the forts are completed, the treachery is described in *Heinrici Chronicon Livoniae*, ed. by Arbusow and Bauer, I. 9 (*The Chronicle of Henry of Livonia*, trans. by Brundage, p. 27) as follows: 'in their inquity they [the Livs] forgot their oath and perjured themselves, for there was not even one of them who accepted the faith' ('oblita iuramenti mentita est iniquitas sibi, nec est usque ad unum, qui fidem suscipat'); citing Psalm 27. 12, 13. 3.

[80] Quite tellingly, indeed, Henry claims about Bishop Albert of Riga, the energetic propagator of the crusades: 'But the bishop, knowing the wickedness (*maliciam*) of the Livonians and seeing that he could not make progress among that people without pilgrims (*videns se sine auxilio peregrinorum in gente illa non posse proficere*), sent Brother Theoderic of Treiden to Rome for letters authorizing an expedition (*pro litteris expedicionis*)' (*Heinrici Chronicon Livoniae*, ed. by Arbusow and Bauer, IV. 6; *The Chronicle of Henry of Livonia*, trans. by Brundage, p. 38). The idea, however, is noted already during the mission of Meinhard (*Heinrici Chronicon Livoniae*, ed. by Arbusow and Bauer, II. 7) and developed later in ibid., IV. 4, IX. 9.

[81] 'duplici corde et inconstantes' (*Heinrici Chronicon Livoniae*, ed. by Arbusow and Bauer, XVI. 4; *The Chronicle of Henry of Livonia*, trans. by Brundage, p. 130).

[82] *Heinrici Chronicon Livoniae*, ed. by Arbusow and Bauer, IX. 11: 'rebelles et increduli', citing Numbers 20. 10; *The Chronicle of Henry of Livonia*, trans. by Brundage, p. 52.

[83] *Heinrici Chronicon Livoniae*, ed. by Arbusow and Bauer, IX. 8: 'acceptam baptismi graciam a primo Lyvonum antistite Meynardo fidem Christi [...] in Duna se lavantes delere sepe dicebant'; *The Chronicle of Henry of Livonia*, trans. by Brundage, p. 51.

[84] For an illuminating example of such arguments see, for example, *Heinrici Chronicon Livoniae*, ed. by Arbusow and Bauer, X. 5: 'Qui constantes in dilectione Dei fidem susceptam

weak in faith and liable to apostasy, and their many revolts against the Rigans are argued to have been primarily targeted not against the new supremacy, but against the new faith. These claims necessitate a depiction of the relapses into paganism as well, in which the performances of apostasy have a crucial role to play. Firstly, neglecting Christian rites already signifies neglecting the faith. Neglecting the sacraments, in particular, becomes a signifier that marks the beginning of the revolts, as when, for instance, the Livs are depicted, 'neglecting the sacraments (*immemores sacramentorum*), forgetful of their baptism, casting off the faith, not keeping the peace, beginning war again'.[85] Similarly, as in the case of the few loyal neophytes, accepting and practising Christian rites signify baptism and remaining loyal to the Christian church. Likewise apostasy is, of course, also marked by performing blasphemous rites. For instance, Bishop Albert of Riga blames the rebelling Livs 'because you rejected the sacraments of faith' and 'especially because, out of contempt of the most high God and in order to mock us and all Christians, you threw the goats and other animals

---

se omni caritatis affectu amplectere profitentur, ab amore et societate christianorum testantur nulla eos posse genera tormentorum separare. Unde nimirum eciam cognatorum tantum in eos excrevit odium, ut exinde maius esset odium amore, quo ante dilexerant. [...] Quos acerrimis penis afficientes [...]. De quibus non est dubium, quin cum sanctis martiribus pro tanto martyrio vitam receperint eternam' (*The Chronicle of Henry of Livonia*, trans. by Brundage, p. 57: 'Constant in the love of God, they confessed that they had embraced the faith they had received with all devotion and affirmed that no kind of torture could separate them from the love and society of the Christians. Because of this, naturally, the hatred even of their kinsmen grew so great against them that henceforth this hatred was greater than the love which they had previously felt. [...] They afflicted them with most cruel punisments [...]. There is no doubt that they received eternal life with the holy martyrs for such a martyrdom'). The importance of the early neophytes is similarly reflected in the mentioning of the names of the first Livs baptized by Meinhard. Henry lists the names of the first Livs baptized in both Üksküll (*Heinrici Chronicon Livoniae*, ed. by Arbusow and Bauer, I. 4) and Holm (ibid., I. 7), as well as of the two martyred Livish neophytes (ibid., X. 5), and of the chieftans who remained faithful during the revolts (ibid., X. 8, XIV. 10). Among them especially the Livish chieftain Caupo stands out; he was even taken to Rome to meet Pope Innocent III (ibid., VII. 3); Caupo is also praised in ibid., X. 10, XIV. 5, 8.

[85] *Heinrici Chronicon Livoniae*, ed. by Arbusow and Bauer, X. 6; *The Chronicle of Henry of Livonia*, trans. by Brundage, p. 57 (here partly my translation). Later similar claims are made also about the Estonians, as when they, for example, 'baptismi sui sacramenta violaverant, qui fidem Iesu Christi reiciendo ad paganismum redierant' (*Heinrici Chronicon Livoniae*, ed. by Arbusow and Bauer, XXVIII. 3) (*The Chronicle of Henry of Livonia*, trans. by Brundage, p. 221: 'who had violated the sacraments of their baptism, who had cast off the faith of Jesus Christ and returned to their paganism'). See also ibid., XXI. 5.

which you had immolated to the pagan gods in our face and in the face of the whole army'.[86]

Parallel to this, as the conquest and conversion proceed, the success of the Christians is presented in the rituals of submission, as well as in the accompanying performances of power. Indeed, they seem to reveal an understanding of a political culture where an eminent role is played by the symbolic elements: acts of recognition and submission, demonstrations of secular and especially ecclesiastical power, as well as other expressions of authority. As a founding narrative the text has to deal with continuous struggles concerning ecclesiastical and secular rulership over newly conquered lands, which also determines its key concern: confirming territorial authority and legitimizing the act of taking possession of lands and peoples. The interlinking of the Christian and feudal traditions and the subjugating of converts to the Christian Church and secular rulers (as well as tributes) rely heavily on the successful performance of various rituals: the rites of baptism and submission, along with the accompanying gestures that are to show humility (for example, tears and grieving) and fidelity to the new rule. Thus, the baptism ceremonies in particular may also be interpreted as reflecting an understanding that power can, or even must, be manifested and legitimized via the performative. As moments of submission they reflect the role of ritual and ceremonial occasions in conveying the message — in this case, in representing and establishing rule and authority. Similarly, the subjugation is marked by the replacement of old pagan rituals with new Christian ones.

---

[86] *Heinrici Chronicon Livoniae*, ed. by Arbusow and Bauer, XVI. 4: 'Pro eo, quod fidei sacramenta reiecistis [...] maxime in contemptum Dei altissimi et ad nostram et omnium christianorum illusionem hircos et cetera animalia diis paganorum immolantes in faciem nostram et tocius exercitus proiecistis'; *The Chronicle of Henry of Livonia*, trans. by Brundage, p. 129. For this, the Bishop claims, according to Henry, 'modicam summam argenti, centum videlicet oseringos vel quinquaginta marcas argenti, ab omni provincia vestra requirimus' ('we demand a moderate sum of silver from your entire province, namely one hundred oseringi, or fifty silver marks') (*Heinrici Chronicon Livoniae*, ed. by Arbusow and Bauer, XVI. 4; *The Chronicle of Henry of Livonia*, trans. by Brundage, p. 129). The mockery itself is also described in the same passage: 'clamor magnus fit et exultatio in castro, diisque suis secundum antiques consuetudines honorem impendentes animalia mactant, canes et hircos immolantes ad illusionem christianorum in faciem episcopi et tocius exercitus de castro proiciunt. Sed frustratur omnis labor eorum' ('At this there was great noise and rejoicing in the fort and the Livonians sacrificed animals, paying honor to their gods according to their old customs. They immolated dogs and goats and, to mock the Christians, they tossed them from the fort, in the face of the bishop and the whole army. But all of the Livonians' work was wasted') (*Heinrici Chronicon Livoniae*, ed. by Arbusow and Bauer, XVI. 4; *The Chronicle of Henry of Livonia*, trans. by Brundage, p. 127).

Taking the Spatial Turn

Pagan and blasphemous rites are thus often represented as inverted versions of Christian rituals (one could also interpret them as counter-rituals, or even rituals of erasure). Moreover, the rites that become prominent in Henry's representation of this ritual rivalry are connected not so much to individual conversion or apostasy, but rather to the Christianization and heathenization of the landscape. Recently (and probably at least partly influenced by the 'spatial turn' in cultural studies), several scholars have pointed to the chronicler's interest in the sacralizing and desacralizing aspects of space. Carsten Selch Jensen has well phrased this perpective in relation to Henry: during the process of Christianization 'not only peoples but entire physical landscapes were Christianized' and centres of power had to do with military and political, as well as spiritual, dominance.[87] Or, to put it the other way around: the conversion of a large number of people requires a redefinition of the physical landscape in accordance with the new religious beliefs.[88] In Henry's Chronicle, not surprisingly, the spatial technologies first and foremost include the demolishing of old pagan space, and establishing new sacred centres on a physical as well as on a symbolic and semantic level[89] (the inclusion of the land into Christian geographies, the naming of the Virgin Mary as the patroness of the land, etc.).

Firstly the demonic or diabolic nature of the local space gains an inevitable role in the Chronicle. Henry describes how the priest Daniel met a Liv coming out from one of the 'dark hiding places of the woods' and told him of a vision he had seen during the night. 'I saw the god of the Livonians (*deum Lyvonum*), who foretold the future to us. He was, indeed, an image (*ymago*) growing out of a tree from the breast upwards.'[90] The god had told him that a Lithuanian army would be coming the next day, and out of fear for that army the Livs did not dare to assemble for preaching. However, as the prophecy did not come

---

[87] Jensen, 'How to Convert a Landscape', pp. 155–56. For a recent discussion on Henry's view on such symbolic elements of the landscape as wilderness, see Nielsen, 'Henry of Livonia on Woods and Wilderness'. The spatial aspects have been discussed also in relation to the other Baltic crusades, such as the Danish crusades against the Wends; see Jensen, 'Sacralization of the Landscape'.

[88] Jensen, 'How to Convert a Landscape', pp. 156–57.

[89] The inclusion of Livonia into 'the cultural geography of medieval Europe' has recently been analysed in Tamm, 'A New World into Old Words'.

[90] *Heinrici Chronicon Livoniae*, ed. by Arbusow and Bauer, x. 14: '"Vidi", inquit, "deum Lyvonum, qui nobis future predixit. Erat enim ymago excrescens ex arbore a pectore et sursum"'; *The Chronicle of Henry of Livonia*, trans. by Brundage, p. 66.

true, the Livs came to the priest who 'execrated their idolatry and affirmed that a phantom (*fantasmata*) of this kind was an illusion of the demons (*demonum illusionem*)'.[91] '[He [priest Daniel] preached that there was one God, creator of all, one faith, and one baptism, and in these and similar ways invited them to the worship of one God.'[92] Including in his text quotations from the baptismal vow, Henry now depicts how the Livs, 'After hearing these things, [...] renounced the devil and his works, promised to believe in God, and those who were predestined by God were baptized.'[93] The demonic space, however, can also be acted against on the physical level, to break with the pagan past and root out old habits. Describing the campaigns to Estonia, Henry represents the sacred woods of the Estonians in Vironia (Est. Virumaa) where 'there was a mountain and a most lovely forest in which, the natives say, the great god (*magnum deum*) of the Oeselians, called Tharapita, was born, and from which he flew to Ösel. The other priest went and cut down the images and likenesses which had been made there of their gods (*imagines et similitudines deorum suorum*). The natives [the Estonians] wondered greatly that blood did not flow and they believed the more in the priest's sermons'.[94]

---

[91] *Heinrici Chronicon Livoniae*, ed. by Arbusow and Bauer, x. 14: 'quibus sacerdis ydolatriam detestans, huiusmodi fantasmata denonum illusionem affirmata'; *The Chronicle of Henry of Livonia*, trans. by Brundage, p. 66 (here partly my translation).

[92] *Heinrici Chronicon Livoniae*, ed. by Arbusow and Bauer, x. 14: 'unum Deum, creatorem omnium, unam fidem, unum baptisma esse predicat et his et aliis similibus ad culturam unius Dei eos invitat'; *The Chronicle of Henry of Livonia*, trans. by Brundage, p. 66.

[93] *Heinrici Chronicon Livoniae*, ed. by Arbusow and Bauer, x. 14: 'diabolo et operibus eius abrenunciant et in unum Deum credere se promittunt. Compare with the vow: Abrenuntias Satanae? Abrenuntio. Et omnibus operibus eius? Abrenuntio /--/ Credis in unum Deum /--/ Credo'; *The Chronicle of Henry of Livonia*, trans. by Brundage, p. 66.

[94] *Heinrici Chronicon Livoniae*, ed. by Arbusow and Bauer, xxiv. 5: 'ubi erant mons et silva pulcherrima, in qua dicebant indigene magnum deum Osiliensium natum, qui Tharapita vocatur, et de illo loco in Osiliam volasse. Et ibat alter sacerdos succidens imagines et similitudines deorum suorum ibi factas, et mirabantur illi, quod sanguis non efflueret, et magis sacerdotum sermonibus credebant'; *The Chronicle of Henry of Livonia*, trans. by Brundage, pp. 193–94. The phrase *imagines et similitudines* is a quotation from Genesis 1. 26. The spatial metaphors are also used when depicting the conversion of the Öselians: after the conqest of Waldia (Est. Valjala) 'The priests were led with joy into the town in order to preach Christ and to throw out Tharapita, the God of the Oeselians' ('qui in urbem cum gaudio ducuntur, ut Christum predicent, ut Tharapitam, qui deus fuit Osilianorum, eiciant'). A description of mass baptims follows, for which 'They consecrated a fountain in the middle of the fort' ('qui per medium castrum fontem consecrantes'). The same is claimed to recur all over Ösel: 'They brought priests with them to their forts to preach Christ, throw out Tharapita and the other pagan gods, and wash the people with holy baptism' ('presbyteros secum ad castra sua ducunt, qui Christum predicent, qui

Yet in addition to negative overtaking one also finds the positive signs of the Christianization, or conversion of landscape.[95] Next to the baptism of the peoples, an even more important part of Henry's representation of conversion is the 'moistening' (*tingere*) or 'besprinkling' (*aspergere*) of the local villages and fortifications with baptismal water.[96] A similar emphasis is often given to the raising of the flag of the Virgin Mary (*vexillum beate Marie*) in the conquered strongholds. For instance, after conquering a fort of the Selonians in 1208, the priests went into the fort, 'instructed them [the Selonians] in the beginnings of the faith, sprinkled the fort with holy water, and raised the banner of Blessed Mary over it'.[97] The banner becomes prominent especially during the conquest of Estonia, and then, quite tellingly, not only regarding the pagan Estonians, but also the Danish rivals of the Rigan mission are repeatedly told that these lands are already subjected to the Rigans under the banner of the Blessed Virgin.[98] Likewise, the erection of new fortifications, churches, and monasteries signifies the next step in the Christianization of the landscape; the first instances of this physical as well as symbolic appropriation were already present in Henry's account of the first bishop, Meinhard, who built a church and two castles in Livonia.[99] Furthermore, as Alan V. Murray has recently argued, the ways in which landscape was marked out as Christian could also

Tharapita cum ceteris paganorum diis eiciant, qui populum sacro baptismate tingant') (*Heinrici Chronicon Livoniae*, ed. by Arbusow and Bauer, XXX. 5; *The Chronicle of Henry of Livonia*, trans. by Brundage, pp. 244–45).

[95] In parallel to the general rise of interest towards space, also the idea of 'the conversion of landscape' has been quite widely launched in medieval studies; for an introduction, see Howe, 'The Conversion of the Physical World'.

[96] The besprinkling of strongholds is mentioned, for instance, in *Heinrici Chronicon Livoniae*, ed. by Arbusow and Bauer, XI. 6, XIV. 11, XXX. 5.

[97] *Heinrici Chronicon Livoniae*, ed. by Arbusow and Bauer, XI. 6: 'ad fidem iniciando eos instruunt et aspergentes castrum aqua benedicta et vexillum beate Marie in acre figunt'; *The Chronicle of Henry of Livonia*, trans. by Brundage, p. 74. Descriptions of similar action occur elsewhere in the Chronicle, for example in *Heinrici Chronicon Livoniae*, ed. by Arbusow and Bauer, XIII. 3, XVI. 4, XXIII. 8.

[98] Henry mentions the banner in relation to the Rigan-Danish disputes in *Heinrici Chronicon Livoniae*, ed. by Arbusow and Bauer, XXIII. 10, XXIV. 2, XXIX. 6. He uses the motif already for depicting the start of the crusades to Estonia, writing that 'the banner of the Blessed Virgin was carried [...] to all the Esths and the tribes round about' (ibid., XII. 3).

[99] Bishop Meinhard is said to have built a church (*Heinrici Chronicon Livoniae*, ed. by Arbusow and Bauer, I. 3) and a stone castle (ibid., I. 5–6) in Üxküll, and a stone castle in Holm (ibid., I. 7–9). For the churches built during the later period, see ibid., X. 14, X. 15, XI. 2, XI. 7, XIII. 3; and for the Cistercian monastery in Dünamunde (Latv. Daugavgriva), ibid., VI. 3, IX. 7.

rise above the ground and include the soundscape: during the colonization and conversion period in Livonia and Estonia the sounds of church bells and music (especially in battle) were deployed in the manifestation and propagation of the new faith.[100] For instance, during the siege of Riga in 1210 the Kurs, 'When they [the Kurs] heard the sound of the great bell [of Riga], they said that they were being eaten and consumed by this God of the Christians'.[101] Yet the construction of new strongholds could be accompanied by the demolishment of the former ones, as is well illustrated in the case of the Russian stronghold in Kokenhusen (Latv. Koknese), which the crusaders found in 1209 'deserted, and because of the filthiness of the former inhabitants full of snakes and worms' so that Bishop Albert 'ordered and asked that it be cleansed and renovated, and had it strongly fortified'.[102]

There is, furthermore, also a corporeal level in this overtaking of space: the Christian blood shed on the Livonian soil, as well as the remains and burial places of the local martyrs. The most eminent martyr of the new church was Bishop Bertold, yet Henry also recounts many other martyrdoms suffered by the missionaries and crusaders that all contribute to the Christianization of the landscape and the making of Christian geographies.[103] In addition, it is worth noting the fact that Henry also mentions the burial place of some Livish neophytes: he tells that the bodies of the two martyred converts, Kyrian and Layan, 'rest in the church of Üxküll and are beside the tombs of the bishops Meinhard and Berthold'.[104] An illuminating example of the functionality of martyrdom and the bodily remains of martyrs is a story about John, an arguably Estonian-

---

[100] Murray, 'Music and Cultural Conflict'.

[101] *Heinrici Chronicon Livoniae*, ed. by Arbusow and Bauer, XIV. 5: 'Et cum audirent sonitum campane magne, dicebant se ab illo Deo christianorum commedi atque consumi'; *The Chronicle of Henry of Livonia*, trans. by Brundage, p. 98.

[102] *Heinrici Chronicon Livoniae*, ed. by Arbusow and Bauer, XIII. 1: 'Et inveniens montem ipsum desertum et pre immundicia quondam inhabitantium vermibus ac serpentibus repletum iussitque et rogavit eundem montem mundari ac renovari et firmis fecit munitionibus muniri'; *The Chronicle of Henry of Livonia*, trans. by Brundage, p. 88.

[103] For the martyrdom of Bishop Bertold, see *Heinrici Chronicon Livoniae*, ed. by Arbusow and Bauer, II. 6. However, Henry also recounts martyrdoms of crusaders (for example, ibid., IX. 1, XIV. 1), of Sword Brethren (ibid., XIV. 11), and of other clerics (ibid., XXIII. 4). On the 'instrumentality' of the local martyrs in creating sacred zones in an otherwise pagan landscape, see also Jensen, 'How to Convert a Landscape', pp. 162–64.

[104] *Heinrici Chronicon Livoniae*, ed. by Arbusow and Bauer, X. 6: 'Horum corpora in Ykescolensi quiescunt ecclesia atque apposita sunt tumbe episcoporum Meynardi et Bertoldi'; *The Chronicle of Henry of Livonia*, trans. by Brundage, p. 57.

born priest of Holm. Henry claims that 'the people of Holm, who are quick to shed blood, took their priest, John, cut off his head, and cut the rest of his body into pieces'. Stating that he 'attained eternal life through the martyr's palm', Henry continues: 'The lord bishop [Albert] with his chapter devotedly buried his body and bones, which were collected afterwards by other priests, in the church of Blessed Mary at Riga.'[105]

Likewise the Chronicle's most eminent cases of religious as well as performative rivalry are closely connected to space. Firstly, the sanctuaries, sacred objects, and rites of the polytheistic pagan religion are presented as being most closely linked to nature and sacred forests, differentiating the primitive cult from monotheistic Christianity. Thus, the Chronicle argues for what we would nowadays call an evolutionary view on religion, where the primitive savage cult is seen as radically different from the higher forms of religion. Whenever Henry argues that the locals relapse into paganism, he depicts this as occurring through the expulsion of the Christian signs from the landscape. Interestingly, this poses an exact counterpart to the Christianization rituals. In the beginning of the Chronicle, after the withdrawal of the participants of the first Livonian crusade lead by Bishop Berthold (in 1198), Henry depicts the Livs performing a kind of ritual cleansing: 'lo! the treacherous Livonians, emerging from their customary baths, poured the water of the Dvina River over themselves, saying: "We now remove the water of baptism and Christianity itself with the water of the river. Scrubbing off the faith we have received, we send it after the withdrawing Saxons."'[106] The same passage gives another good example of the understanding that symbolic action can have a profound effect on the landscape:

> Those who had gone away [that is, the crusaders] had cut the likeness of the head of a man on a branch of a certain tree. The Livonians supposed this to be the god of the Saxons (*Saxonum deum*) and they believed that it was bringing flood and

---

[105] *Heinrici Chronicon Livoniae*, ed. by Arbusow and Bauer, x. 7: 'Porro Holmenses, quorum pedes veloces ad effundenudm sanguinem, capto Iohanne sacerdote suo, caput eius abscidunt, corpus reliquum mebratim dividunt. [...] per martyrii palmam ad vitam eternam. Cuius corpus et ossa, postea ab aliis sacerdotibus collecta, in Riga in ecclesia beate Marie domnus episcopus cum suo capitulo devote sepelivit'; *The Chronicle of Henry of Livonia*, trans. by Brundage, p. 58.

[106] *Heinrici Chronicon Livoniae*, ed. by Arbusow and Bauer, II. 8: 'ecce perfidi Lyvones de balneis consuetis egressi Dune fluminis aqua se perfundunt, dicentes: "Hic iam baptismatis aquam cum ipsa christianitate removemus aqua fluminis et fidem susceptam exfestucantes post Saxones recedetnes transmittimus"'; *The Chronicle of Henry of Livonia*, trans. by Brundage, p. 34. This event is mentioned once more in *Heinrici Chronicon Livoniae*, ed. by Arbusow and Bauer, IX. 8.

pestilence upon them. Accordingly, they cooked mead according to the rite, drank it together, and, having taken counsel, took the head from the tree, placed it on logs which they had tied together, and sent it as the god of the Saxons, together with their Christian faith, after those who were going back to Gothland by sea.[107]

Earlier in his text, Henry had already attributed the custom of washing off baptismal water to the Livs, quite clearly presenting it as an inverted baptismal rite (also a form of ritual purification): 'They thought that since they had been baptized with water, they could remove their baptism by washing themselves in the Dvina and thus send it back to Germany.'[108] Later Henry also claims about the apostatized Estonians that 'they washed themselves, their houses, and their forts with brooms and water, trying thus to erase the sacrament of baptism in their territory'.[109] The Estonian folklorist Ülo Valk has analysed the depiction of ritual washing in later folklore material,[110] maintaining that as purifying and sanctifying actions they were once of crucial importance as part of the rites of passage (such as childbirth, baptism, marriage, death), that is, in the passage of a human being from one status into another. As in such performances archaic tradition became connected with baptism, one can speak of the syncretism of heathen tradition and Christianity. Valk also asks whether the heretical practice of washing away baptismal water (in addition to Henry's Chronicle they are also found in late medieval resolutions[111]) can be linked to the popular cus-

---

[107] *Heinrici Chronicon Livoniae*, ed. by Arbusow and Bauer, II. 8: 'Illi autem, qui recesserant, in cuiusdam arboris ramo quasi caput hominis inciderant, quod Lyvones Saxonum deum putantes et ex hoc inundanciam et pestilenciam sibi immittere credentes, cocto iuxta ritum medone combibentes, captato consilio caput ab arbore ponentes ligna connectunt, quibus capus superpositum, quasi deum Saxonum, cum fice christianorum pos recedentes Gothlandiam per mare transmittunt'; *The Chronicle of Henry of Livonia*, trans. by Brundage, p. 34.

[108] *Heinrici Chronicon Livoniae*, ed. by Arbusow and Bauer, I. 9: 'baptismum, quem in aqua susceperant, in Duna se lavando removere putant, remittendo in Theuthoniam'; *The Chronicle of Henry of Livonia*, trans. by Brundage, p. 27.

[109] *Heinrici Chronicon Livoniae*, ed. by Arbusow and Bauer, XXVI. 8: 'se et domos suas et castra lavantes aquis et scopis pugnantes, taliter baptismi sacramenta de finibus suis omnino delere conabatur'; *The Chronicle of Henry of Livonia*, trans. by Brundage, p. 210. Next to this, abandoning the marital sacrament and going back to old social customs also demarcate the apostasy of the Estonians: 'They [the Estonians] took back their wives, who had been sent away during the Christian period' (ibid., p. 210).

[110] Valk, 'The Significance of Baptism'.

[111] The resolutions of Valga diet (*landtag*) in 1422 demanded that Estonians 'have their children baptized after the ways of the church within a month from their birth' and that 'no one should elude baptism or wash it away on pain of death'. At Valmiera diet in 1504, the resolutions

toms. Of course, they could indicate a mere groundless distrust of some too vigilant clerics towards the people. If baptism replaced the functions of heathen rites, it probably had to be combined with an additional purification rite, one that did not suggest washing away the baptismal water. In baptism as a ritual act of washing away the original sin and in the ritual act of washing in the sauna we can see a blending of two levels: a Christian and a heathen one. Moreover, the question remains whether, according to magical thought, it was at all possible to entirely wash away the baptismal water. Nevertheless, Valk concludes that Henry's reports about the Estonians washing away the baptismal water can hardly be explained in the same way: in the thirteenth century forceful christening could indeed be interpreted as surrendering to a foreign power, and people tried to get rid of it.

What is more, these kinds of rites of apostasy are placed into the context of the Chronicle's broader structure of watering topoi. The alliterative association of the place name Riga with the verbs *rigare* ('to water') and *irrigare* ('to irrigate') enables Henry to stress throughout his Chronicle that Riga's main aim is to baptize the heathens, in other words, to water them with baptismal water.[112] This association frames the text as a whole: it occurs in the opening verse of the Chronicle and claims the purpose of Riga is 'to irrigate (*irrigui*) and to give the holiest heavenly gifts to the land';[113] thereafter the verbs *rigare* and *irrigare* are frequently used in the descriptions of missions and the appeals to accept

of the Valga diet were pronounced again. Valk, 'The Significance of Baptism'; see also Vahemetsa, *Eestlaste võitlusest ristiusu*, pp. 161–62 (cited in Valk, 'The Significance of Baptism').

[112] *Heinrici Chronicon Livoniae*, ed. by Arbusow and Bauer, IV. 5 (ref. 1 Corinthians 3. 6; Josue 15. 19: 'quam et Rigam appellant, vel a Riga lacu vel quasi irriguam, cum habeat inferius irriguum ac irriguum superius. Irriguum inferius, eo quod sit aquis et pascuis irrigua vel eo quod ministratur in ea peccatoribus plenaria peccaminum remissio et per eam irriguum superius, quod est regun celorum, per consequens ministratur; vel Riga nova fide rigata et quia per eam gentes in circuitu sacro baptismatis fonte rigantur' (*The Chronicle of Henry of Livonia*, trans. by Brundage, p. 37: When Riga was established in 1201, the Livs are said to have called the place Riga, 'either from Lake Riga, or from irrigation (*irriguam*), since it is irrigated both from below and from above (*inferius irriguum ac irriguum superius*). It is irrigated from below, or, as they say, well moistened in its waters and pastures; or, since the plenary remission of sins is administered in it to sinners, the irrigation from above, that is, the kingdom of heaven is thus administered through it. Or, in other words, Riga, refreshed (*rigata*) by the water of the new faith, waters (*rigantur*) the tribes round about through the holy font of baltism'). I have analysed the functionality of watering motifs and their relation to the overall fertility imagery in Henry's Chronicle also in Kaljundi, 'The Motifs of Growth and Fertility'.

[113] *Heinrici Chronicon Livoniae*, ed. by Arbusow and Bauer, p. 1: 'irrigui sacra donaque celicavult dare terra'; my translation, as the opening verse is not included in the English translation.

baptism. In total the Riga-*rigare* motif occurs about thirty times and reaches its triumph in the last chapter, where the author rejoices over the fulfilment of the goal of the Riga church, as after the conversion of Mohn (Est. Muhu) and Ösel (in 1227) it watered all the neighbouring heathens.[114] In this case, the author interestingly linked the watering topoi with spatial metaphors: after the conquest the priests are twice remarked to have 'thrown out Tharapita'.[115] Throwing out Tharapita, however, also signifies the drowning of Pharaoh.[116] Hence the conversion of the Ösel is linked to the Old Testament histories: the submersion of the Pharaoh refers to the Israelites crossing the Red Sea (Exodus 14. 23–29), but it also symbolizes the submersion of the devil in the waters of baptism, as Henry is here drawing on the Easter Liturgy.

There is yet another prominent group of landscape-related religious performances: burial rites. At its start the Chronicle already indicates that, at least according to Henry's understanding, burials and cemeteries can easily rise to the centre of military and cultural conflict. Considering the episcopal nature of his text, this is not surprising: as argued by the French medievalist Michel Lauwers, the evolution of Christian European cemeteries in the Middle Ages reflects the development of an idea according to which the Church is not only a spiritual but also a spatial concept, closely bound to material constructions.[117]

---

[114] 'Thus does Riga always water the heathens! Thus did she now water Oesel in the middle of the sea. By washing she purges sin and grants the kingdom of the skies. She furnishes both the higher and the lower irrigation' ('Sic, sic Riga semper rigat gentes! | Sic maris in medio nunc rigat Osiliam | Per lavacrum purgans vitium, dans regna polorum | Altius irriguum donat et inferius') (*Heinrici Chronicon Livoniae*, ed. by Arbusow and Bauer, xxx. 6: ref. Josue 15. 19; *The Chronicle of Henry of Livonia*, trans. by Brundage, p. 245).

[115] Firstly, after the conquest of the fort of Waldia (Est. Valjala) 'The priests were led with joy into the town in order to preach Christ and to throw out Tharapita, the god of the Oeselians'. Secondly, Henry argues that the other Öselians also 'brought priests with them to their forts to preach Christ, throw out Tharapita and the other pagan gods, and wash the people with holy baptism'. *Heinrici Chronicon Livoniae*, ed. by Arbusow and Bauer, xxx. 5; *The Chronicle of Henry of Livonia*, trans. by Brundage, pp. 244–45. See also note 94.

[116] *Heinrici Chronicon Livoniae*, ed. by Arbusow and Bauer, xxx. 6, citing Exodus 15. 4: 'Quo complete, quo facto, populo videlicet cuncto baptizato, Tharapita eiecto, Pharaone submerse, captives liberatis, redite cum gaudio Rigenses' (*The Chronicle of Henry of Livonia*, trans. by Brundage, p. 246: 'When this is finished, when it is done, when all the people are baptized, when Tharapita is thrown out, when Pharaoh is drowned, when the captives are freed, return with joy, O Rigans!'). For the liturgical background of this passage, see Arbusow, 'Das entlehnte Sprachgut', p. 125.

[117] See Lauwers, *Naissance du cimetière*.

It is noteworthy that the second Bishop of Üxküll, Berthold, was at first received cordially, but that his discord with the Livs began at the consecration of the cemetery at Holm, where 'some [Livs] conspired to burn him in the church, others to kill him, and others to drown him'.[118] During the crusades to Estonia Henry makes claims about the Estonians' aggression towards Christian cemeteries, which, of course, also serves to strengthen the crusading call: during a raid to Livonia in 1211 'they burned the empty villages and churches and, with their pagan sacrifices, committed many abominations around the churches and tombs of Christians'.[119] Thus in the Chronicle, remaining true to the Christian funeral habits functions on the one hand as a sign of remaining true to the true faith. The most outstanding examples of this are the careful descriptions of the faithful neophytes attending the Christian funerals of the first Livonian missionaries and clerics. When a certain monk named Siegfried died, 'A group of weeping converts bore and followed his little body to the church, as is customary among the faithful (*fidelium more*)'. To this Henry adds a widespread hagiographical topos, continuing: 'As sons for a beloved father, they made a coffin for him out of good timber.' They then discovered that one plank was too short and report how the plank was miraculously lengthened.[120]

On the other hand, restoring pagan burial customs becomes an important symbolic signifier of apostasy. Indeed, the Chronicle in general also emphasizes the attention that the local peoples pay to the remains of their deceased, for instance during the siege of Riga when the Kurs are presented as being more worried about the dead than about continuing the fight: after collecting their fallen comrades 'they rested for three days while cremating their dead and

---

[118] *Heinrici Chronicon Livoniae*, ed. by Arbusow and Bauer, II. 2: 'alii in ecclesia concremare, alii occidere, alii submergere concertabant'; *The Chronicle of Henry of Livonia*, trans. by Brundage, p. 32.

[119] *Heinrici Chronicon Livoniae*, ed. by Arbusow and Bauer, XIV. 10: 'villas vacuas et ecclesias incenderunt et nequicias multas circa ecclesias et sepulchra mortuorum christianorum immolaticiis suis exercuerunt'; *The Chronicle of Henry of Livonia*, trans. by Brundage, p. 104.

[120] *Heinrici Chronicon Livoniae*, ed. by Arbusow and Bauer, VII. 6: 'Cuius corpusculum more fidelium ad ecclesiam deferens cum lacrimis neophitorum turba prosequitur. Cui tamquam filii dilecto patri sarcofagum de bonis lignis facientes'; *The Chronicle of Henry of Livonia*, trans. by Brundage, p. 44. For a thorough analysis of the mortuary rituals and posthumous miracles in Henry's Chronicle, see Tamm, 'Martyrs and Miracles'. The Chronicle also remarks that after the passing of Bishop Meinhard 'The funeral was held according to custom (*morem*)' even though 'the bishop was buried to the false wailing and tears of the Livonians' (*Heinrici Chronicon Livoniae*, ed. by Arbusow and Bauer, II. 1: 'Celebratis secundum morem exequiis et episcopo qualicunque Lyvonum planctu et lacrimis sepulto'; *The Chronicle of Henry of Livonia*, trans. by Brundage, p. 31).

mourning over them'.[121] Pagan funerary rites are presented as the opposite of the Christian burials. For instance, Henry presents the Estonians celebrating funerals 'according to their custom, with much wailing and much drinking'.[122] The distinction of pagan and Christian customs is underlined by the emphasis on the radical difference between cremation and inhumation: the above-mentioned Estonians who arguably held funerals with drinking feasts are also said to have had 'cremated the pitiful bodies'.[123] This conflict of different burials is furthermore developed in a passage that presents how the revolting Estonians 'disinterred the bodies of their dead, who had been buried in cemeteries, and cremated them according to their original pagan custom (*more paganorum*)'.[124]

These and other similar passages can be interpreted as instances where physical elements of landscape, symbolic meaning, and textual tradition intermingle. It is worth briefly mentioning, however, that Henry's interest in the landscape and the concomitant images is also reflected on a more metaphorical and analogical level: while the clerics and crusaders of Riga are presented as planters, sowers, and waterers, the baptized lands and peoples are depicted as a virginal farmland (or vineyard) in need of cultivation.[125] With the help of these widespread biblical metaphors, conversion is presented as a cultivation process. On the one hand, this imagery has obvious colonial features, as it represents the missionaries and crusaders as active and authoritative agents (cultivators), and the baptized land and peoples as the passive and receptive agents (the ones that need to be cultivated). On the other hand, it seems to be yet another example of the biblical cerealization imagery that was so often used during the expansion of Latin Christianity and the territorialization of the notion of *Christianitas*, as argued by Robert Bartlett.[126] Nevertheless, the emphasis on the many land-

---

[121] *Heinrici Chronicon Livoniae*, ed. by Arbusow and Bauer, XIV. 5: 'triduo quiescentes et moruos suos cremantes fecerunt planctum super eos'; *The Chronicle of Henry of Livonia*, trans. by Brundage, p. 98.

[122] *Heinrici Chronicon Livoniae*, ed. by Arbusow and Bauer, XII. 6; *The Chronicle of Henry of Livonia*, trans. by Brundage, pp. 86–87. See the next note for the Latin text.

[123] *Heinrici Chronicon Livoniae*, ed. by Arbusow and Bauer, XII. 6: 'tristia funera […] multis diebus colligentes et igne cremantes, exequias cum lamentationibus et potationibus multis more suo celebrabant'; *The Chronicle of Henry of Livonia*, trans. by Brundage, pp. 86–87.

[124] *Heinrici Chronicon Livoniae*, ed. by Arbusow and Bauer, XXVI. 8: 'corpora moruorum suorum, in cemeteriis sepulta, de sepulchris effoderunt et more paganorum pristino cremaverunt'; *The Chronicle of Henry of Livonia*, trans. by Brundage, p. 210.

[125] For an analysis of this imagery, see Kaljundi, 'The Motifs of Growth and Fertility'.

[126] See Bartlett, *The Making of Europe*, pp. 133–66.

scape-related rituals, both Christian and pagan, seems to reflect an idea that sanctity (as well as paganism) needs to be physically present and performed in order to effect a change, and that specific rites are to be performed with the people as well as to lands under conquest and conversion.

What is more, apart from the relationship between the Christian and pagan religion, ritual rivalry also charactizes the different missions to Livonia and Estonia, as during the course of her mission the Rigan church collided with the Russians, Danes, and, to a lesser extent, also Swedes. Henry's emphasis on the unorthodox baptismal practices of the Danish priests during the rivalry of the Danish and German-Rigan mission in northern Estonia in the early 1220s offers a particularly good example of the representational and rhetorical value of (arguably) unorthodox performances. According to Henry, the Danes made two attempts to establish their rule in Estonia with the campaigns to Ösel (1206) and Lindanise (1219); yet one must take into account that the Danes already had interests in the area prior to this, and that the Chronicle greatly downplays their role in the crusades.[127] The campaign to Ösel failed, but after the Danes had established themselves in northern Estonia (1219) and many of the Estonians were to accept Christianity from the Danes, the rivalry over the ecclesiastical rule in the region grew serious; among other strategic moves, Bishop Andreas Sunesen of Lund and Bishop Albert of Riga both appointed their own bishop for Dorpat (Est. Tartu). On a verbal and representational level also Henry takes part in this quarrel, presenting the Danes as performing their mission in an unorthodox manner: according to him,

> the Danes desired to take this neighbouring land for themselves and sent their priests, as it were, into a foreign harvest. They baptized some villages and sent their men to the others to which they could not come so quickly, ordering great wooden crosses to be made in all the villages. They sent the rustics with holy water and ordered them to baptize the women and children. They tried thereby to anticipate the Rigan priests and sought in this manner to put the land into the hands of the king of the Danes.[128]

---

[127] For the Danish crusades in the region, see first and foremost Lind and others, *Danske korstog*.

[128] *Heinrici Chronicon Livoniae*, ed. by Arbusow and Bauer, XXIV. 2: 'Sed Dani impsam terram sibi vicinam preoccupare cupientes sacerdotes suos quasi in alienam messem miserunt. Qui baptizantes villas quasdam et ad alias suos mittentes, ad quas ipsi venire tam subito non potuerunt, et cruces magnas ligneas in omnibus villis fieri precipientes et aquam benedictam per manus rusticorum mtitentes et mulieres ac parvulos aspergere iubentes, sacerdotes Rigenses taliter prevenire conabantur et hodo modo totam terram ad manus regis Danorum preoccuupare studebant'; *The Chronicle of Henry of Livonia*, trans. by Brundage, p. 189.

In addition, in describing the next Rigan mission to northern Estonia, Henry argues that the Danes encouraged the Estonians themselves to baptize their countrymen: when the Rigan priests sent to summon people from villages,

> A rustic, who was their elder, said: 'We are already all baptized.' When they [the Rigan missionaries] asked him by whose baptism they had been baptized, he replied: 'Since we were in the village of Ialgsama when a priest of the Danes performed the sacrament of baptism there, he baptized some of our men and gave us holy water. We returned to our own villages and each of us sprinkled our families, wives and children, with that same water. What more should we do? Since we have been baptized once, we will not receive it again.'[129]

The Russian interest was likewise present in Livonia before the German crusaders, and this is also reflected in the Chronicle. In this relation Henry does not fail to mention the differences in religious customs: when speaking of the Tholowa (Latv. Tālava) Livs who submitted to the power of the bishop of Riga in 1214, he writes 'They promised to change over from the Christian faith as they had received it from the Russians to the Latin use (*Latinorum consuetudinem*)', and that Bishop Albert of Riga sent his priest 'back with them to administer the sacraments of faith to them and to initiate them into Christian discipline'.[130] Of course, cooperation with the Russians was not rare especially

---

[129] *Heinrici Chronicon Livoniae*, ed. by Arbusow and Bauer, XXIV. 5: 'Et ait rusticus, qui fuit senior eorum: "Iam omnes", inquit, "baptizati sumus." Et requirentibus illis, cuius baptismate baptizati essent, respondit ille: "Cum essemus in villa Iolgesim, quando sacerdos Danorum ibi baptismi sui tractavit sacramenta, baptisavit viros quosdam ex nostris et dedit nobis aquam sanctam, et reversi sumus ad proprias villas et cum eadem aqua aspersimus et baptizavimus unusquisuque nostram familiam, uxores et parvulos, et vobis ultra quid faciemus? Cum enim semel baptizati sumus, vos ultra non recipiemus"'; *The Chronicle of Henry of Livonia*, trans. by Brundage, p. 193. In the same passage Henry states that the Danes have arguably also taken part in the rivalry over the Christianization of the landscape: telling how the Rigan missionaries baptized one village, the chronicler adds that 'The Danes afterwards built a church there, as they did in many other villages baptized by us' (ibid., p. 193).

[130] *Heinrici Chronicon Livoniae*, ed. by Arbusow and Bauer, XVIII. 3: 'promittentes se fidem christianam a Ruthenis susceptam in Latinorum consuetudinem commutare […] remittentes cum eis sacerdotem suum […] qui eis fidei sacramenta ministrando discipline christiane dare inicia'; *The Chronicle of Henry of Livonia*, trans. by Brundage, p. 136. The same passage also indicates well the practical and material terms of the confessional change, as 'they also promised to pay one measure of grain annually for each two horses, because they were protected by the bishop in peacetime as well as in war, were one heart and one spirit with the Germans, and rejoiced in the German's defence against the Esthonians and the Lithuanians' ('de duobus equis mensuram annone per singulos annos persolvere, eo quod tam pacis quam belli tempore semper

in the early phase of the mission, and the later confrontation of the Catholic and Russian Orthodox Church in the area was also about ecclesiastical and political power, not theology.[131] Yet the different views on orthodoxy of the rites (especially the baptismal rite, considering the context of conquest and conversion) were useful when there was a need to downplay the rivals on the representational level. Thus, on the one hand the Chronicle does not hesitate to name the Russians 'fellow Christians' (*conchristianos*) when describing making alliances with them.[132] On the other hand, when discussing the rivalry of the Russian princes and Riga over the tributary Livs and the Lettgallians, Henry stresses that the Russians neglect baptizing the natives, arguing in the case of Prince Vladimir of Polotsk: 'It is, indeed, the custom of the Russian kings not to subject whatever people they defeat to the Christian faith, but rather to force them to pay tribute and money to themselves.'[133] Moreover, Henry expands this

tuerentur ab episcopo et essent cum Theothonicis cor unum et anima una et contra Estones et Letones eorum semper gauderent defesione') (*Heinrici Chronicon Livoniae*, ed. by Arbusow and Bauer, XVIII. 3; *The Chronicle of Henry of Livonia*, trans. by Brundage, p. 136).

[131] As also argued in a recent thorough study on the relationship between the Rus and the Christian Livonians; see Selart, *Livland und die Rus'*. The impact of this political opposition on Henry's image of the Rus has been analysed in Schmidt, 'Das Bild der "Rutheni" bei Heinrich von Lettland', and Nielsen, 'Sterile Monsters? Russians and the Orthodox Church'.

[132] For example, when describing how a peace treaty was made with prince Vsevolod (*Heinrici Chronicon Livoniae*, ed. by Arbusow and Bauer, XIII. 4).

[133] *Heinrici Chronicon Livoniae*, ed. by Arbusow and Bauer, XVI. 2: 'Est enim consuetudo regum Ruthenorum, ut quamcunque gentem expugnaverint, non fidei christiane subicere, sed ad solvendum sibi tributum et pecuniam subiugare'; *The Chronicle of Henry of Livonia*, trans. by Brundage, p. 122. The whole scene is developed to illustrate this idea: 'The king [Vladimir] asked, now blandly, now with pointed threats, that the bishop [Albert of Riga] cease baptizing the Livonians. The king maintained that the Livonians were his servants and that it was in his power to baptize them or to leave them unbaptized' ('Rex vero modo blandiciis, modo minarum asperitatibus episcopum conveniens, ut a Lyvonum baptismate cessaret, rogavit affirmans in sua esse potestate, servos suos Lyvones vel baptizare vel non baptizatos relinquere') (*Heinrici Chronicon Livoniae*, ed. by Arbusow and Bauer, XVI. 2; *The Chronicle of Henry of Livonia*, trans. by Brundage, p. 122). Also the Novgorodians, after subjugating the Estonian fort of Odenpäh (Est. Otepää) in 1210, 'baptized a few of them [the Estonians] with their baptism (*baptismate suo quosdam ex eis baptizaverunt*), received four hundred *nogata* marks, left them, and went back to their country, saying that they would send back their priests to them to finish the holy regeneration of baptism'. Nevertheless, Henry continues, 'This they afterwards neglected, for the Ungannians later received priests of Riga, were baptized by them, and were numbered (*connumerati*) among the Rigan Christians' ('quod tamen postmodum neglexerunt. Nam Ugaunenses postea sacerdotes Rigensium susceperung et baptizati sunt ab eis et connumerati sunt cum Rigensibus') (*Heinrici Chronicon Livoniae*, ed. by Arbusow and Bauer, XIV. 2; *The Chronicle of Henry of Livonia*, trans. by Brundage, p. 95).

idea to the Russian Church as such, speaking of the 'Russian mother always sterile and barren, for she always attempted to subject lands to herself, not with the hope of the regeneration in the faith of Jesus Christ, but with the hope of loot and tribute'. Not surprisingly, this is contrasted with the Livonian church, the fertile, true, and original mother.[134]

In addition to the use of inverted and unorthodox performances as a legitimization strategy, I would like to refer to yet another idea from Mary Douglas — and one that is, to my mind, thought-provoking in the medieval context as well. Especially when exposed to boundaries and margins, one is subject to pressure and concerned with establishing hierarchies and order, and dreaming of internal coherence; one is concerned with what is not with it, part of it, and subject to its laws and hence potentially against it. Ideas about separating, purifying, demarcating, and punishing transgressions have as their main function the imposition of order on an inherently untidy experience; it is only by exaggerating the difference between within and without, above and below, with and against, that a semblance of order is created (and a meaning is imposed on the world).[135]

Conclusion

In conclusion, it is appropriate firstly to come back to these questions: Who carries out the performative acts, and equally importantly, Who records them? I would argue that it is significant to point out that the community behind texts like Henry's Chronicle, the frontier clergy (people devoted to history), was also the group who initiated, led, and influenced those processes. Like Henry, they staged the scenes both for missions and battlefields, as well as for the pages of history books. But could it be, then, that texts such as Henry's Chronicle represent the world view, concerns, and anxieties of a small clerical elite? I would like to argue that in Livonia (but also on a more general level) the crusading phenomenon brought along a significant change, and not only to the course of expansion in the uses of (inter)textuality, performativity, and past: as a shared experience of ritualization of present events, it changed the way in

---

[134] *Heinrici Chronicon Livoniae*, ed. by Arbusow and Bauer, XXVIII. 4, citing Exodus 23. 26, the Breviary: 'sterilis semper et infecunda, que non spe regenerationis in fide Iesu Christi, sed spe tribulotorum et spoliorum terras sibi subiugare conatur'; *The Chronicle of Henry of Livonia*, trans. by Brundage, p. 222.

[135] Douglas, *Purity and Danger*, p. 5.

which the history that was still being made was communicated to its participants, how its authoritative models were put into use in appropriation and how it was recorded in historical writing afterwards.

While a majority of the studies into the communicative role of rituals, performances, and gestures in medieval Europe have come to focus on the communicative role of ritual performances, could one claim that the same is also the case in this representation? How does the fact that common cultural and social knowledge (or sharing of meaningful structures and established codes) is needed in order to understand and take part in the performative public interactions relate to their use when the other party was presumably not provided with the code? For a long time, the Europeanization of the North was characterized as 'a clash of cultures', a notion that has lately been problematized (and to a certain extent replaced with the 'cultural encounter').[136] Many scholars, like Volker Scior in his recent article, have convincingly argued that 'the clash' is above all written into and by the textual tradition — relying on the authoritative model histories of clashing with the world of the Other.[137] What is more, when closely reading those 'clashes' one cannot but notice that the hostile party seems to share a profound knowledge of this tradition, because in their plundering and performances of idolatry they act according to the biblical scenery — and even speak with the voices of the antagonists of the Scripture: the Amorites, Philistines, Judas, etc. This, however, makes not only the whole concept of 'clashing cultures' highly problematical, but also the image of how these clashes were performed. On the other hand (and only when we stop looking for pagan rituals), this does not diminish its value with regard to the medieval European understanding of symbolic behaviour. Therefore, I would like to argue that the pagan rituals also gain meaning in the Christian system (or discourse), and as such can be revealing with regard to those modes of symbolic behaviour which are considered meaningful and relevant, or performances which have a power to impose changes and meaning upon the world, to effect a change.

In this sense the re-presentation and re-enactment of performances do reveal political realities. But can those performances also be revealing in regards to culture (or symbolic dimensions of social action)? In other words, are they above all means of not only textual, but also social representation? Perhaps we

[136] For the latest reflection on these issues in the Baltic context, see Murray, *The Clash of Cultures on the Medieval Baltic Frontier*.

[137] Scior, 'Kulturkonflikte? Christen, Heiden und Barbaren'. See also Scior, *Das Eigene und das Fremde* for a thorough analysis of the development of the pagan Other in the Saxon missionary chronicles.

can overcome the dichotomy by linking those two aspects. In our quest for the social and cultural dimension, we should treat Henry's accounts as valuable for the study of the principles involved in the universe of a particular culture, in this case the role of rituals for medieval Europeans and especially their frontier communities. They reflect what was considered important for the Christianization process and for making a Christian European identity at the frontier (for the others, it was a passage from the rites of alterity to the Christian rites; for 'us', it was a missionary and crusading process). Yet, even though social forms are the coordinates of the experienced world, in analysing them one should avoid constructing systematic rules. They are rather marked by fluidity, flexibility, and variability — a feature characteristic of performative practices that Peter Burke has recently called 'occasionalism'.[138] As Gerd Althoff has argued, especially in exceptional situations the medieval people 'varied, mixed, or updated them [the rituals] in keeping with the given situation or even invented new rituals if there was no suitable pre-existing ritual language at their disposal' which, of course, also produced new meanings.[139] Ritual elements (familiar gestures and actions) could be combined in a wide variety of ways, and their inherent innovation and modification becomes apparent when fitting them with circumstances or persons, or using known rituals in new places (or in an inverted manner), which sometimes can result in ambiguity, spontaneity, disputed outcomes and meanings.

In addition, I would also like to suggest that the abundance of rites refers to a special kind of memory culture (one closely connected with the understanding of an *imitatio*), which we might call a historicization of the frontier. Therefore the primary subject of this article is not in fact only the anthropology of crusade and mission, but also what could be called anthropology of historicization.[140] David A. Warner has argued that 'as historical events, medieval rituals are chiefly approached through accounts compiled by ecclesiastical literati, men and women who cultivated the art of memory and understood its capacity to inform both the present and future'.[141] These accounts are characterized by the active manner in which such communities addressed their history and the present affairs — as exemplified, for instance, by the facility by which monas-

---

[138] Burke, 'Performing History'.

[139] Althoff, 'The Variability of Rituals', pp. 73, 83–84.

[140] Faubion, 'History in Anthropology', p. 45. Or, of studying 'approches historciantes du monde', as Alain Délivré has put it (Faubion, 'History in Anthropology', p. 49).

[141] Warner, 'Ritual and Memory in the Ottonian Reich', p. 259.

teries altered their foundation legends or inscribed new meanings on relics and monuments. Furthermore, drawing on Patrick J. Geary, Warner reminds us that the act of remembering 'changed the very nature of what would be preserved'.[142] I would like to add that it also changed the way they were preserved. Thus in studying the performative, we could also treat it as a process of active memory-making, that is, of making current history memorable by linking it with the past via re-enacting and requoting past history. This reflects an understanding in which the reperformance of the past also means giving significance to our action and (re)affirming the continuity and coherence of the shared experience, thereby contributing to the establishment of memory and identity at the frontier. And, indeed, memory is something that can be made and shaped, both via writing it down and via reperforming it in new rituals — especially at the frontier, in areas and moments of crisis, where rituals and acts of continuity (as well as of possession) become crucial.

---

[142] Geary, *Phantoms of Remembrance*; cited in Warner, 'Ritual and Memory in the Ottonian Reich', p. 259.

Works Cited

Primary Sources

The Chronicle of Henry of Livonia, trans. by James A. Brundage (Madison: University of Wisconsin Press, 2003; orig. publ. 1961)

Heinrici Chronicon Livoniae, ed. by Leonid Arbusow and Albert Bauer, *Monumenta Germaniae Historica: Scriptores rerum Germanicarum in usum scholarum separatim editi*, 78 vols (Hannover: Hahn, 1871–), XXXI (1955)

Secondary Works

Althoff, Gerd, *Die Macht der Rituale: Symbolik und Herrschaft im Mittelalter* (Darmstadt: Primus, 2003)

——, 'The Variability of Rituals in the Middle Ages', in *Medieval Concepts of the Past: Ritual, Memory, Historiography*, ed. by Gerd Althoff, Johannes Fried, and Patrick J. Geary (Cambridge: German Historical Institute and Cambridge University Press, 2003), pp. 71–88

Arbusow, Leonid, 'Das entlehnte Sprachgut in Heinrich's "Chronicon Livoniae": ein Beitrag zur Sprache mittelalterlicher Chronistik', *Deutsches Archiv für Erforschung des Mittelalters*, 8 (1950), 100–53

——, *Liturgie und Geschichtsschreibung im Mittelalter: in ihren Beziehungen erläutert an den Schriften Ottos von Freising (1158), Heinrichs Livlandchronik und den anderen Missionsgeschichten des Bremischen Erzsprengels: Rimberts, Adams von Bremen, Helmolds* (Bonn: Röhrscheid, 1951)

Bagge, Sverre, 'Ideas and Narrative in Otto of Freising's Gesta Frederici', *Journal of Medieval History*, 22 (1996), 345–77

Bartlett, Robert, *The Making of Europe: Conquest, Colonisation, and Cultural Change, 950–1350* (London: Allen Lane, Penguin, 1993)

Bauer, Albert, 'Einleitung', in *Heinrici Chronicon Livoniae*, ed. by Leonid Arbusow and Albert Bauer, *Monumenta Germaniae Historica: Scriptores rerum Germanicarum in usum scholarum separatim editi*, 78 vols (Hannover: Hahn, 1871–), XXXI (1955), pp. vi–lxii

Bolton, Brenda, 'Message, Celebration, Offering: The Place of Twelfth- and Early Thirteenth-Century Liturgical Drama as "Missionary Theatre"', in *Continuity and Change in Christian Worship*, ed. by R. N. Swanson, Studies in Church History, 35 (Woodbridge: Boydell, 1999), pp. 89–103

Burke, Peter, *The Historical Anthropology of Early Modern Italy: Essays on Perception and Communication* (Cambridge: Cambridge University Press, 1987)

——, 'Performing History: The Importance of Occasions', *Rethinking History*, 9 (2005), 35–52

Douglas, Mary, *Purity and Danger: An Analysis of Concepts of Pollution and Taboo* (London: Routledge, 2006)

Faubion, James D., 'History in Anthropology', *Annual Review of Anthropology*, 22 (1993), 5–54

Geary, Patrick J., *Phantoms of Remembrance: Memory and Oblivion at the End of the First Millennium* (Princeton: Princeton University Press, 1994)

——, 'Reflections on Historiography and the Holy: Center and Periphery', in *The Making of Christian Myths in the Periphery of Latin Christendom (c. 1000–1300)*, ed. by Lars Boje Mortensen (København: Museum Tusculanum, 2006), pp. 323–29

Geertz, Clifford, *The Interpretation of Cultures* (New York: Basic Books, 1973)

Greenblatt, Stephen, *Marvellous Possessions: The Wonder of the New World* (Oxford: Oxford University Press, 2003)

Helmann, Manfred, 'Die Anfänge der christlicher Mission in den baltischen Länder', in *Studien über die Anfänge christlicher Mission in Livland*, ed. by Manfred Hellmann, Sonderband, 37 (Sigmaringen: Thorbecke, 1989), pp. 7–36

——, 'Bischof Meinhard und die Eigenart der kirchlicher Organisation in den baltischen Ländern', in *Gli Inizi del cristianesimo in Livonia-Lettonia: atti del colloquio internazionale di storia ecclesiastica in occasione dell'VIII centenario della Chiesa in Livonia (1186–1986), Roma, 24–25 giugno 1986*, Pontifico comitato di scienze storiche: atti i documenti, 1 (Città del Vaticano: Libreria editrice Vaticana, 1989), pp. 9–30

Hildebrand, Hermann, *Die Chronik Heinrichs von Lettland: ein Beitrag zu Livlands Historiographie und Geschichte* (Berlin: E. S. Mittler, 1865)

Howe, John M., 'The Conversion of the Physical World: The Creation of a Christian Landscape', in *Varieties of Religious Conversion in the Middle Ages*, ed. by James K. Muldoon (Gainesville: University Press of Florida, 1997), pp. 63–78

Jensen, Carsten Selch, 'How to Convert a Landscape: Henry of Livonia and the Chronicon Livoniae', in *The Clash of Cultures on the Medieval Baltic Frontier*, ed. by Alan V. Murray (Aldershot: Ashgate, 2009), pp. 151–68

——, 'The Nature of Early Missionary Activities and Crusades in Livonia, 1185–1201', in *Medieval Spirituality in Scandinavia and Europe: A Collection of Essays in Honour of Tore Nyberg*, ed. by Lars Bisgaard and others, Odense University Studies in History and Social Sciences, 234 (Odense: Odense Universitetsforlag, 2001), pp. 121–37

Jensen, Kurt Villads, 'The Blue Baltic Border of Denmark in the High Middle Ages: Danes, Wends and Saxo Grammaticus', in *Medieval Frontiers: Concepts and Practices*, ed. by David Abulafia and Nora Berend (Aldershot: Ashgate, 2002), pp. 173–93

——, 'Sacralization of the Landscape: Converting Trees and Measuring Land in the Danish Crusades against the Wends', in *The Clash of Cultures on the Medieval Baltic Frontier*, ed. by Alan V. Murray (Aldershot: Ashgate, 2009), pp. 141–50

Johansen, Paul, 'Die Chronik als Biographie: Heinrich von Lettlands Lebensgang und Weltanschauung', *Jahrbücher für Geschichte Osteuropas*, n.s., 1 (1953), 3–24

Kaljundi, Linda, 'The Motifs of Growth and Fertility in Henry's Chronicle of Livonia', *Ennen ja Nyt*, 4 (2004) <http://www.ennenjanyt.net/4-04/referee/kaljundi.pdf> [accessed 11 August 2012]

——, 'Waiting for the Barbarians: Reconstruction of Otherness in the Saxon Missionary and Crusading Chronicles, 11th–13th Centuries', in *The Medieval Chronicle*, ed. by Erik Kooper (Amsterdam: Rodopi, 2008), pp. 113–27

Kattinger, Detlef, 'Identität und Integration im Ostseeraum im Hoch- und Spätmittelalter', in *The European Frontier: Clashes and Compromises in the Middle Ages*, ed. by Jörn Staecker (Lund: Almqvist & Wiksell), pp. 115–26

Lauwers, Michel, *Naissance du cimetière: lieux sacrés et terre des morts dans l'Occident medieval* (Paris: Aubier, 2005)

Lind, John H., and others, eds, *Danske korstog: krig og mission i Østersøen* (København: Høst, 2004)

Lowenthal, David, *The Heritage Crusade and the Spoils of History* (Cambridge: Cambridge University Press, 1998)

Mégier, Elisabeth, '"Ecclesiae sacramenta": The Spiritual Meaning of Old Testament History and the Foundation of the Church in Hugh of Fleury's "Historia ecclesiastica"', *Studi medievali*, 43 (2002), 625–49

Mortensen, Lars Boje, 'The Language of Geographical Description in Twelfth-Century Scandinavian Latin', *Filologia Mediolatina*, 12 (2005), 103–21

——, 'Sanctified Beginnings and Mythopoietic Moments: The First Wave of Writing on the Past in Norway, Denmark and Hungary, c. 1000–1230', in *The Making of Christian Myths in the Periphery of Latin Christendom (c. 1000–1300)*, ed. by Lars Boje Mortensen (København: Museum Tusculanum, 2006), pp. 247–73

Murray, Alan V., 'Music and Cultural Conflict in the Christianization of Livonia, 1190–1290', in *The Clash of Cultures on the Medieval Baltic Frontier*, ed. by Alan V. Murray (Aldershot: Ashgate, 2009), pp. 141–50

——, ed., *The Clash of Cultures on the Medieval Baltic Frontier* (Aldershot: Ashgate, 2009)

Nielsen, Torben K., 'Henry of Livonia on Woods and Wilderness', in *Crusading and Chronicle Writing on the Medieval Baltic Frontier: A Companion to the Chronicle of Henry of Livonia*, ed. by Marek Tamm, Linda Kaljundi, and Carsten Selch Jensen (Farnham: Ashgate, 2011), pp. 157–77

——, 'Sterile Monsters? Russians and the Orthodox Church in the Chronicle of Henry of Livonia', in *The Clash of Cultures on the Medieval Baltic Frontier*, ed. by Alan V. Murray (Aldershot: Ashgate, 2009), pp. 227–52

Petersen, Nils Holger, 'The Notion of a Missionary Theatre: The *ludus magnus* of Henry of Livonia's Chronicle', in *Crusading and Chronicle Writing on the Medieval Baltic Frontier: A Companion to the Chronicle of Henry of Livonia*, ed. by Marek Tamm, Linda Kaljundi, and Carsten Selch Jensen (Farnham: Ashgate, 2011), pp. 229–44

Schmidt, Christoph, 'Das Bild der "Rutheni" bei Heinrich von Lettland', *Zeitschrift für Ostmitteleuropaforschung*, 44 (1995), 509–20

Schneider, Richard, 'Strassentheater im Missionseinsatz: zu Heinrichs von Lettland Bericht über ein grosses Spiel in Riga 1205', in *Studien über die Anfänge christlicher Mission in Livland*, ed. by Manfred Hellmann, Vorträge und Forschungen, 37 (Sigmaringen: Thorbecke), pp. 107–21

Scior, Volker, *Das Eigene und das Fremde: Identität und Fremdheit in den Chroniken Adams von Bremen, Helmolds von Bosau und Arnold von Lübeck*, Orbis mediaevalis: Vorstellungwelten des Mittelalters, 4 (Berlin: Akademie, 2002)

——, 'Kulturkonflikte? Christen, Heiden und Barbaren im früh- und hochmittelalterlichen Nordeuropa', *Das Mittelalter: Perspektiven mediävistischer Forschung*, 10 (2005), 8–27

Selart, Anti, *Livland und die Rus' im 13. Jahrhundert* (Køln: Böhlau, 2007)

Tamm, Marek, 'Martyrs and Miracles: Depicting Death in Henry's Chronicle of Livonia', in *Crusading and Chronicle Writing on the Medieval Baltic Frontier: A Companion to the Chronicle of Henry of Livonia*, ed. by Marek Tamm, Linda Kaljundi, and Carsten Selch Jensen (Farnham: Ashgate, 2011), pp. 135–56

——, 'A New World into Old Words: The Eastern Baltic Region and the Cultural Geography of Medieval Europe', in *The Clash of Cultures on the Medieval Baltic Frontier*, ed. by Alan V. Murray (Aldershot: Ashgate, 2009), pp. 11–35

Tamm, Marek, Linda Kaljundi, and Carsten Selch Jensen, eds, *Crusading and Chronicle Writing on the Medieval Baltic Frontier: A Companion to the Chronicle of Henry of Livonia* (Farnham: Ashgate, 2011)

Tyerman, Christopher, *The Invention of the Crusades* (Basingstoke: Houndmills, 1998)

Vahemetsa, A., *Eestlaste võitlusest ristiusu vastu XII–XVI sajandil*, Religiooni ja ateismi ajaloost Eestis, 2 (Tallinn: Eesti Riiklik Kirjastus, 1961), pp. 150–72

Valk, Ülo, 'The Significance of Baptism in Estonian Folk Belief', *Folklore*, 5 (1997), 9–38

Warner, David A., 'Ritual and Memory in the Ottonian Reich: The Ceremony of Adventus', *Speculum*, 76 (2001), 255–83

Part IV

Oral Poetics through the Social Spectrum

Two Medieval Ballads on Betrayal and Deception: Interpreting the Story of the First Christian Bishop in Finland through the Story of Judas Iscariot

Pertti Anttonen

Introduction

This article deals with two historically unrelated narratives, one concerning the killing of the first Christian bishop in Finland, known as St Henry, in the twelfth century, the other the betrayal of Jesus of Nazareth by Judas Iscariot as it is depicted in a thirteenth-century English manuscript. The purpose of the article is to read the two medieval texts in a comparative context and theorize on the diffusion and reception of Christianity on the basis of their motifs, genre, and performative power.

The narrative of St Henry, a martyr saint in the medieval church in Finland and in the present-day Catholic Church in Finland, is based on two kinds of sources, clerical and oral.[1] According to the liturgical legend in Latin called *Legenda sancti Henrici*, which dates from the late thirteenth century, Henry was an Englishman who came to baptize heathen Finns on a crusade with the

---

[1] See Heikkilä, *Pyhän Henrikin legenda*; Heikkilä, 'Vörnaden av Sankt Henrik i det svenska riket'; Lehtonen, 'Finlands erövring och frälsningshistoria', and this volume.

Pertti Anttonen, University of Helsinki, Adjunct Professor, pertti.anttonen@helsinki.fi

Swedish king Eric and met his death by the hand of a local murderer to whom he had tried to give a canonical punishment.[2] A vernacular song or song text dealing with the same theme, commonly known in Finnish as *Piispa Henrikin surmavirsi*,[3] tells that the Bishop was killed by a local peasant who had been angered by the clergyman's visit to his home in his absence, without showing adequate respect for hospitality rules. In accordance with the folk ballad's testimony, the killing of Bishop Henry, regarded commonly as a major event in early Finnish history, is generally assumed to have taken place on the ice of Lake Köyliö in the lower Satakunta area, less than a hundred kilometres north of the city of Turku. The Catholic reading of the narrative prioritizes the medieval church legend over the folk ballad, but within the Protestant nationalistic reading of the killing, also encountered in the works of some historians, more emphasis and truth-value has been placed on the folk ballad than the church legend.[4]

In the medieval English manuscript, the narrated events deal with the betrayal of Jesus by Judas, but the story derives from non-biblical sources, possibly from apocryphal Coptic gospels written in Egypt during the first and second centuries. One of these gospels made headlines recently, as it was rediscovered after having been lost for 1700 years and published in English translation in the May 2006 issue of the *National Geographic* magazine. This is the Gospel of Judas Iscariot. In addition to its original source, the medieval text of Judas raises a number of other questions. One of them concerns the text as a piece of evidence of the circulation of non-ecclesiastical perspectives on Christian mythology. What does the text have to say about one of the central myths of Christianity, the betrayal that led to the killing of Jesus? How and why does it differ from the authorized biblical narrative? And how is it relevant when trying to understand the Finnish narrative of the killing of the first Christian bishop?

---

[2] In English translation, the Bishop had wished 'to impose on a certain murderer the corrective discipline of the Church in such a way that he would not regard a pardon easily acquired as encouragement to further criminal acts. Then that unhappy, blood-thirsty man attacked the servant of righteousness and cruelly killed him'. *Finnish Folk Poetry*, ed. by Kuusi, Bosley, and Branch, p. 555.

[3] A facsimile of the oldest recorded text, published in English in 1999, translates this as 'The Ballad of the Death of Bishop Henry'; *Piispa Henrikin surmavirsi*.

[4] The emphasis placed on the vernacular song over the liturgical legend in Finnish historical research has also been noted by Heikkilä, *Pyhän Henrikin legenda*, p. 246.

A Ballad of Betrayal in Medieval England: The Manuscript of Judas

In 1882, Francis James Child, professor of English at Harvard University, published the first volume of his five-volume collection of *English and Scottish Popular Ballads*.[5] The oldest of the ballad texts printed in this collection derives from a manuscript kept under the auspices of Trinity College Library in Cambridge, England (MS B.14.39 / MS 323). This is a text that is generally known as Judas, as it tells the story of Judas Iscariot in rhyming couplets and in heptameter (that is, with seven poetic feet in each line) and how he came to betray Jesus. It is no. 23 in Child's collection, and thus generally referred to as Child 23. The text has been linguistically dated to the end of the thirteenth century and it is written in Early Middle English. It was first published in 1841 in the collection entitled *Reliquiae antiquae* by Thomas Wright and James Orchard Halliwell.[6]

Many generations of ballad scholars have studied the Judas manuscript. It has gained attention among literary scholars as well, but the text has not received any general acclaim for having a high literary value. Most of the scholarly attention given to the text has dealt with the enigma of whether it can be regarded as a ballad or not, on the one hand, and its language and the principles to be followed in its textual presentation for modern readers, on the other. In addition to phonetics and spelling, these principles include questions concerning the text's structure and its stanza division. There are thirty-three lines in the original manuscript, with no stanza structure, but many modern publishers have chosen to present it in thirty-six lines, which make eighteen couplets. When the caesura in the middle of each line is used as a dividing device, the text falls neatly into quatrains, which is a common ballad metre. However, transforming the text into a four-line stanza structure does not do complete justice to the manuscript. There are actually three triplets, that is, units consisting of three rhyming lines.

Following is the text taken from the edition published by Karin Boklund-Lagopoulou:

        Hit wes upon a Screþorsday   þat ure lowerd aros,
        Ful milde were þe wordes   he spec to Iudas:

---

[5] Child, *The English and Scottish Popular Ballads*.
[6] Wright and Halliwell, *Reliquiae antiquae*, I, 144.

'Iudas, þou most to Iurselem,   oure mete for to bugge;
þritti platen of seluer   þou bere upo þi rugge.

þou comest fer i þe brode stret,   fer in þe brode strete;
Summe of þine cunesmen   þer þou meist imete.'

Imette wid is soster,   þe swikele wimon:
'Iudas, þou were wrþe   me stende þe wid ston.
For þe false prophete   þat tou bileuest upon.'

'Be stille, leue soster,   þin herte þe tobreke!
Wiste min louerd Crist,   ful wel he wolde be wreke.'

'Iudas, go þou on þe roc,   heie upon þe ston,
Lei þin heued I my barm,   slep þou þe anon.'

Sone so Iudas   of slepe was awake,
þritti platen of selver   from hym weren itake.

He drou hymselve be þe top,   þat al it lauede ablode;
þe iewes out of Iurselem   a wenden he were wode.

Foret hym com þe riche ieu   þat heiste Pilatus:
'Wolte sulle þi louerd,   þat hette Iesus?'

'I nul sulle my louerd   for nones cunnes eiste,
Bote hit be for the þritti platen   þat he me bitaiste.'

'Wolte sulle þi lord Crist   for enes cunnes gode?'
'Nay, bote hit be for þe platen   þat he habben wolde.'

In him com ur lord gon   as is postles seten at mete:
'Wol sitte ye, postles,   ant wi nule ye ete?
Ic am iboust ant isold   today for oure mete.'

Up stod him Iudas: 'Lord, am I þat /freke/?
I nas neuer o þe stude   þer me þe euel spec.'

Up him stod Peter,   ant spec wid al is miste:
'þau Pilatus him come   wid ten hundred cnistes,
Yet ic wolde, louerd,   for þi loue fiste.'

'Stille þou be, Peter,   wel I þe icnowe.
þou wolt fursake me þrien   ar þe coc him crowe.'[7]

---

[7] Boklund-Lagopoulou, *'I Have a Yong Suster'*, pp. 51–52.

TWO MEDIEVAL BALLADS ON BETRAYAL AND DECEPTION   345

A rough translation of the text in modern English follows:

> It was on Maundy Thursday / that our Lord arose
> Kind were the words / he spoke to Judas
>
> Judas you must to Jerusalem / to buy our meat
> Thirty plates of silver / you will bear upon your back
>
> You will come far in the broad street / far in the broad street
> Some of your kinsmen / there you might meet
>
> He came across his sister / the treacherous woman
> Judas you were worthy / that I should stone you with stones
> For the false prophet / that you believe in
>
> Be silent beloved sister / your heart you break
> If my lord Christ knew / he would be angry
>
> Judas go and climb on the rock / high upon the stone
> Lay your head on my lap / sleep for a while
>
> As soon as Judas / awakened from sleep
> Thirty pieces of silver / were taken from him
>
> He pulled himself by his hair / so that his head was all bathed in blood
> The Jews from Jerusalem / thought he was mad
>
> Before him came the rich Jew / by the name Pilate
> Would you sell your Lord / who is called Jesus
>
> I will not sell my Lord / for any kind of possession
> Except for the thirty plates / that he entrusted to me
>
> Would you sell you Lord / for any kind of gold
> No except for the pieces / that he would want
>
> In comes our Lord / as his apostles sat at their food
> How do you sit apostles / and why will you not eat
> I am bought and sold / today for our food
>
> Up stood Judas / Lord, am I that man?
> I was never in a place / where evil was spoken of you
>
> Up stood Peter / and spoke with all his might
> Though Pilate came / with ten thousand knights
> Yet I would Lord / for your sake fight
>
> Be silent Peter / I know you well
> You will deny me three times / before the cock crows

As already mentioned, there is no unanimity among scholars as to whether the textual item can be classified as a ballad or not.[8] One of the main reasons for scepticism is the known history of the ballad genre. Ballad scholars maintain that the genre was born in France in the fourteenth century and disseminated to Britain no earlier than the fifteenth century. Were the Judas text a ballad, it would precede its genre by two hundred years. Yet, there are factors that speak for its classification as a ballad. These include the following characteristics in the text: condensed, swift, poetic, and dramatic dialogue; stylistic repetition of narration; and a focus on depicting social relations, especially those between close relatives and lovers.

According to the Hungarian scholar Lajos Vargyas, the ballad is a 'concise, short epic story, which tells of a single short event, and often only a single scene of it, and that, too, with omissions, by hints, and in haste'.[9] Comparing three genres of oral poetry, the heroic song in verse, the prose tale, and the ballad, Vargyas has sketched a chronological sequence in which the ballad has replaced the heroic song. The essential method in defining ballad characteristics is, thus, to 'find out what is new in it compared with the heroic song'.[10]

Vargyas argues that what is new in content and style in the ballad is the emphasis on human behaviour and a concentration on human psychological motifs. This is where the heroic song and the ballad differ. Unlike the heroic epic, the ballad deals with the clashes originating in people's lives, positions, their relations with one another, and especially with the clashes that originate in their faults and passions.[11] An essential trait in the psychologically oriented ballad is, according to Vargyas, that the events take place in the nuclear family,

---

[8] For a concise summary of this debate, see Boklund-Lagopoulou, '"Judas": The First English Ballad?', and Boklund-Lagopoulou, *'I Have a Yong Suster'*, pp. 48–49. The most recent publication on the topic, by Thomas D. Hill, takes a firm standpoint in favor of the text being a ballad. Writes Hill: 'One has to choose between two possibilities. Either an English poet, writing about the history of the Passion in a popular mode, invented narrative techniques characteristic of later ballad tradition and a number of ballad conventions and these conventions and techniques were promptly forgotten and not reinvented until a century or more later, or "Judas" is indeed an early ballad. If one wishes, one can redefine "Judas" as a religious narrative poem that owes much to the ballad conventions and techniques, but from the literary historical perspective these two positions are the same, in that they presume an ongoing tradition of medieval balladry to which "Judas" is our earliest English witness' (Hill, 'The Middle English "Judas" Ballad and the Price of Jesus', p. 1).

[9] Vargyas, *Researches into the Mediaeval History of Folk Ballad*, p. 241.

[10] Vargyas, *Researches into the Mediaeval History of Folk Ballad*, p. 238.

[11] Vargyas, *Researches into the Mediaeval History of Folk Ballad*, p. 243.

or the persons involved are in conflict with the other members of their nuclear family. The latter aspect is also noted by two other major ballad scholars, Max Lüthi and Donald Ward. Lüthi regards the nuclear family setting as one of the generic features of the ballad.[12] Ward considers it one of the factors that have caused the genre to emerge:

> Whenever there is a conflict it almost invariably involves the protagonist's relationship with his or her brother, sister, father, or mother. There is virtually no mention of aunt, uncle, grandmother, or grandfather, as one would expect to be the case if the ballad originated in an area in which the extended family was still an important force.[13]

Judas Betrays Jesus because of his Sister

The story of Judas in the medieval English text can be divided into four parts or narrative episodes, beginning with events taking place on Maundy Thursday, continuing with a dialogue between Judas and his sister, and another one between Judas and Pilate, and ending in the biblical scene of the Last Supper. It may be a recording of a song or an oral performance, but we do not know among whom and for whom it was performed and for which purposes. Evidence from historical sound changes serves to suggest that the text was not composed by the person who wrote the surviving manuscript; it thus has a history as a text, but we do not know that history. Therefore we do not know the history of the text's reception either; we only have the text.

In narrative details, there are similarities to the story of Judas in the Bible, but the ballad text does not represent the popularization of the canonical Christian narrative tradition. Unlike the Bible and the oral tradition that follows its themes and motifs, the medieval text does not present Judas as an embodiment of evil and betrayal. Nor does he betray Jesus as a result of having been influenced by Satan.

Instead of demonizing Judas, the text offers explanations for his choices. As in the Bible, he receives thirty plates or coins of silver, but not as blood money from the priests or from Pilate. Jesus gives him the money, asking him to go to Jerusalem to buy food for their Passover festivities. As Jesus predicts, Judas encounters his relatives along the way and meets his deceitful sister, who scorns

---

[12] Lüthi, 'Familienballade', pp. 89, 96.

[13] Ward, 'The Origin of the Ballad', pp. 52–53.

him for believing in a false prophet. Judas's sister thinks that he deserves to be stoned for this reason. Judas defends Jesus, but the sister tempts him into falling asleep with his head on her lap. The sister in this story can be interpreted as signifying a mistress, as has been suggested by the literary scholar Peter Dronke, among others.[14] Another possible interpretation, suggested by Karin Boklund-Lagopoulou, is that the sister represents the relatives of Judas with whom he has a loyalty conflict because of his support for Jesus.[15]

One can conclude from the narrated incidents that the medieval English text humanizes Judas and presents him as a person both with and without agency, making choices and falling victim to deception and temptation. Instead of showing greediness, he sets the price of the betrayal no higher than the sum of money that he was entrusted and, as the text adds, that he lost while sleeping. In this respect, the ballad appears to differ from other texts in Early Middle English in which Judas is depicted as having been born bad. In some of the medieval texts his badness has been explained with references to his allegedly Oedipal background. This set of motifs has spread to the vernacular traditions of many European countries mainly because of the *Legenda aurea* collection by Jacobus de Voragine. In Finland it became known through the compilation entitled *Svenska Folkböcker*, which was published in Stockholm in the late 1840s. The legend of Judas was printed in its second volume.[16]

The Bible and the medieval ballad of Judas agree when depicting Judas as having betrayed Jesus for thirty pieces of silver. They differ in depicting the reasons that led to the betrayal. The ballad text presents the sister as a temptress and makes Judas, the arch-traitor in Christian narrative tradition, a victim of deception. The only person characterized in the text is the sister; she is said to be treacherous (*swikele*).

Even though the Bible does not place the blame for the betrayal of Jesus on a woman, the narrative device of depicting women as temptresses and agents of undesired consequences can be regarded as a biblical motif. This is because of the story of the original sin and the forbidden fruit of Paradise, which continues to serve for countless men in the Christian world as an aetiological myth about the political fundamentals of the heterosexual relationship. As phrased by

---

[14] Dronke, *The Medieval Lyric*; see also Axton, 'Interpretations of Judas in Middle English Literature', p. 194.

[15] Boklund-Lagopoulou, '"Judas": The First English Ballad?'; Boklund-Lagopoulou, *'I Have a Yong Suster'*.

[16] Bäckström, *Svenska folkböcker*, pp. 198–206.

Boklund-Lagopoulou, 'any medieval Christian would know that woman is the source of original sin, false and deceitful, the "swikele wimon" as the poem puts it'.[17] Boklund-Lagopoulou adds that 'a medieval audience would not miss the parallelism with Adam, who was also seduced by a woman away from his lord'.[18]

Yet, instead of the dissemination of gender-political attitudes or theological doctrines as its argumentative goal, we can view the Early Middle English ballad as a text that purports to address relevant social motives and tensions in conjunction with the betrayal of Jesus. In such a function the English text has a parallel which Francis James Child himself referred to.[19] This is a ballad called *Judašowa pšerada* (Der Verrath des Juden),[20] which was taken down from oral circulation in the nineteenth century among the Western Slavic Serbs or Wends in Lausitz.

In this narrative song, Jesus and his Apostles travel across the country and come to the house of a poor widower. They ask for lodging, which is granted to them, but the woman says that she has no bread to give them. Jesus tells her not to worry and asks his Apostles which one of them will volunteer to go and buy bread for thirty pieces of silver. Judas volunteers, and on his way he encounters Jews who invite him to gamble with them. Judas responds: whether I play or not, I will lose everything. He wins the first round and the second, but loses the third one. The Jews ask him why he is so sad and suggest that he sell his master for thirty pieces of silver.

Jesus then asks his Apostles who has sold him. 'Is it I?' asks John. 'No, John, it's not you,' says Jesus. 'Is it I?' asks Peter. 'No, Peter, it's not you,' says Jesus. 'Is it I?' asks Judas. Jesus responds: 'You false Judas, you know best.' Judas is then overcome by remorse and he hastens to hang himself. God tells him to turn back, since his sins are forgiven, but Judas continues to run until he comes to a fir tree and says: 'Soft tree, fir tree, don't you bear me?' He then runs to an aspen and says: 'Hard tree, aspen tree, you will bear me.' Judas hangs himself in the aspen tree, known consequently in many folk narrative traditions as the Judas tree, trembling in fear of Judgement Day.[21]

---

[17] Boklund-Lagopoulou, *'I Have a Yong Suster'*, p. 57.

[18] Boklund-Lagopoulou, *'I Have a Yong Suster'*, p. 57.

[19] Child, *The English and Scottish Popular Ballads*, p. 242. For comparisons, see also Baum, 'The English Ballad of Judas Iscariot'.

[20] See Haupt and Schmaler, *Volkslieder der Sorben in der Ober- und Niederlausitz*, pp. 276–78.

[21] For example Daniels and Stevans, *Encyclopaedia of Superstitions*, p. 767; Baum, 'The

A Ballad of Betrayal in Medieval Finland: The Killing of Bishop Henry

The motif of a set of trees that are being spoken to is well known internationally. In Finnish, it appears, for example, in the oral narrative tradition concerning the killing of Bishop Henry. The killer of the bishop, named Lalli in the seventeenth-century clerical songs[22] and oral sources, conducts a similar dialogue to Judas's in the Wendish ballad in many narratives, eventually hanging himself in an aspen tree. In some other narrative variants a flock of mice chase him up a tree, from where he falls into a lake and drowns.

The presence of migratory motifs in the narrative complex concerning the killing of the first Christian bishop in Finland may serve to partially prove the imaginary or semi-imaginary origins of the story. In any case, the medieval ecclesiastical authorities interpreted the story to be true, and they established a martyr cult to venerate the murdered clergyman, including a pilgrimage to the sites where he was martyred and first buried. The authorized narrative of the thirteenth-century liturgical *Legenda sancti Henrici* was recounted, for example, in the sermons held to commemorate the martyr and in the visual images on the St Henry sarcophagus in the Church of St Henry in Nousiainen in present-day south-western Finland.[23]

When promoting the authorized reading of the murder narrative, medieval church iconography depicted the bishop's killer as a small, bald, creature-like man holding an axe, the murder weapon, in his hand. He is being trampled beneath the feet of St Henry. This motif is reproduced, for example, in mural paintings in many medieval churches. It also appears on the index page of the first book published in Finland, entitled *Missale Aboense*, printed in Lübeck in 1488 for the diocese of Turku. The image is also printed on the brass-plated cover of the Bishop's sarcophagus in the church of Nousiainen, in addition to having been reproduced in a number of paintings and pieces of sculpture.[24] The apparent religious message in this motif is that the sacred power of the martyr has defeated the profane physical power of the murderer and his weapon.

Such visualizations of the martyred bishop have obvious similarities with the way in which other saints in Catholicism have been depicted. A sculpture of St Eric in the Knivsta church near Uppsala makes a reference to his legendary

English Ballad of Judas Iscariot', p. 183; Chuvyurov, 'Trees in Komi (Zyrian) Rituals', pp. 71–72.

[22] See Lehtonen, in this volume.

[23] For St Henry and his legend, see further Heikkilä and Lehtonen in this volume.

[24] For a thorough presentation of St Henry illustrations, see Heikkilä, *Pyhän Henrikin legenda*.

crusade to Finland by placing a defeated heathen under his feet.[25] Similar iconography is familiar from the many representations of St George and Holy Margaret, who are depicted as having defeated a dragon or the devil disguised as a dragon. In a wall painting in the Taivassalo church near Turku, St Henry and St Margaret are placed next to each other, and the former is trampling on the body of his killer, while the latter steps on the body of a dragon.[26] Similarities can also be found, as suggested by the church historian Kauko Pirinen, in the iconography representing St Olaf, originally King Olaf of Norway, who was the most popular saint in Finland in the early medieval period.[27] The Finnish folklorist Martti Haavio has pointed to the similarities between the popular narratives connected to their respective pilgrim routes.[28]

In addition to the church-centred ways of commemoration and ritualization, the legend of the death of Bishop Henry has lived for centuries in the songs and orally transmitted historical narratives of people living along the old pilgrim road and elsewhere in the vicinity. According to some sources, the killer owned the Köyliö manor house, which was (and still is, in rebuilt form) located on the island called *Saari* (Island) or *Kirkkosaari* (Church Island) in Lake Köyliö, close to the present-day centre of Köyliö municipality.[29] Next to the main building of the manor house is a ground cellar called *Lallin kellari* (Lalli's cellar), where the killer is said to have hid himself after the murder — except that the cellar apparently dates from the sixteenth century.[30] The manor house and the rest of the manorial property were confiscated by the bishopric — according to some information as a form of compensation for the murder.[31]

---

[25] Åberg, 'Helgonen och helgondagarna', p. 213; see also Aili, Ferm, and Gustavson, 'Den fromme S:t Erik. Erikslegenden', p. 91.

[26] See for example Klinge, *Muinaisuutemme merivallat*, p. 95.

[27] Pirinen, 'Piispa Henrikin muisto ja Köyliön seurakunta'; Suvanto, 'Keskiaika', p. 18.

[28] Haavio, *Piispa Henrik ja Lalli*, pp. 231–35. For the cult of St Olaf, see for example Krötzl, *Pilger, Mirakel und Alltag*, pp. 61–64, and passim; Svahnström, *St. Olav: seine Zeit und sein Kult*; Mortensen and Mundal, 'Erkebispesetet i Nidaros'; for his cult in Finland, see Harvilahti in this volume.

[29] There is also a Finnish folk poem dealing with a Viking Age warrior, who after killing another man escapes into a hiding place called 'the Island' (see *Finnish Folk Poetry*, ed. by Kuusi, Bosley, and Branch, pp. 538, 540–41). His name has been documented as early as in 1422 in Köyliö as Kaukamoinen or Kaukamely; see Jaakkola, *Suomen varhaishistoria*, p. 359. This could suggest that the murder of the Bishop is a narrative variant of the legend of Kaukamoinen, but due to lack of reliable evidence this suggestion must be taken as mere speculation.

[30] Suvanto, 'Ensimmäinen ristiretki — tarua vai totta?', p. 157 n. 11.

[31] For example Dahl and Gardberg, *Suomen kartanoita*, p. 37.

The bishops of Turku were the legal owners of the manor house until 1549, the time of the Lutheran Reformation, after which it became the property of the Swedish Crown. The king eventually handed it over to a noble family, and since then it has been in private ownership (since 1746 in the Cedercreutz family).

The major source documenting the popular oral tradition about the murder of Bishop Henry is the Kalevala-metric[32] epic song or ballad called *Piispa Henrikin surmavirsi* (Song of the Slaying of Bishop Henry). This is, according to the Finnish folklorist Matti Kuusi, 'the best known poem of the Roman Catholic period in Finland'.[33] Emphasizing its significance as national history, Kuusi called the text 'the national legend of Finland'.[34] According to Martti Haavio, the song was composed as early as the end of the thirteenth century in order to attract pilgrims to the church at Nousiainen and to propagate the pilgrim road as well as the significance of the Nousiainen church within the St Henry martyr cult.[35]

Many versions of the song start off by describing how King Eric and Bishop Henry are brothers who decide to 'go and christen lands'.[36] Since they decide to make a crusade to Häme, this could suggest that the legendary trip to Finland by King Eric and Bishop Henry refers to the factual raid made by the Swedes to Häme in 1239 or 1249. This can also have been confused, intentionally or unintentionally, with the unsuccessful raid that the Swedes made to Novgorod

---

[32] The term 'Kalevala-metric' denotes the traditional tetrametric verse format of Finnish-language folk poetry, named anachronistically after the *Kalevala* epic that Elias Lönnrot compiled in the 1830s on the basis of such folk poetry. A Kalevala-metric or 'Kalevalaic' folk poem is similar in metrics and style to those texts published in the *Kalevala* epic, but is not necessarily included in the epic.

[33] *Finnish Folk Poetry*, ed. by Kuusi, Bosley, and Branch, p. 555.

[34] Kuusi, 'Keskiajan kalevalainen runous', p. 307.

[35] Haavio, *Piispa Henrik ja Lalli*; see also *Finnish Folk Poetry*, ed. by Kuusi, Bosley, and Branch, p. 556; Järvinen, *Legendat*, pp. 11–12; Heikkilä, *Pyhän Henrikin legenda*, pp. 246–56: Lehtonen, 'Finlands erövring och frälsningshistoria'.

[36] The written documents of the song and their fragments are preserved at the Folklore Archives of the Finnish Literature Society. They are published as nos 985–1005 in vol. VIII (1932) of *Suomen kansan vanhat runot*, ed. by Niemi and others, nos 1–3 in vol. IX. 1 (1918), and as nos 20–27 in vol. X. 1 (1933). The texts are also available on the Internet in the *Suomen kansan vanhat runot* digital database, <http://dbgw.finlit.fi/skvr/> [accessed 7 September 2012]. For the English translation of two variants, see *Finnish Folk Poetry*, ed. by Kuusi, Bosley, and Branch, nos 66–67. The oldest known handwritten document of the song, discussed by Lehtonen in this volume, was printed in edited form as no. 990 in vol. VIII of *Suomen kansan vanhat runot*, ed. by Niemi and others, and has also been published by the Finnish Literature Society as a facsimile in 1999 (*Piispa Henrikin surmavirsi*).

in 1142. On their way they stop at Lalli's place near Lake Köyliö (Kiulo) and are served food and drink by his wife Kerttu. In another variant the Bishop is travelling by himself and makes a visit to Lalli's home in his absence. When Lalli returns home, his wife deceives him into believing that the visitors had only paid sand and gravel for hospitality (or ashes in another variant), and upon hearing this Lalli becomes outraged, takes his hatchet and spear, and goes after him — on skis or by horse, depending on the variant. When the Bishop hears the sound of the approaching pursuer he tells his servant — in a manner quite common in Christian hagiographical literature — that when he is killed, his bones should be picked up and put on an ox-sledge, and that a church should be built where the ox grows tired. The motif functions as an explanation as to why the church at Nousiainen was originally built. Lalli then returns home with the Bishop's cap on his head, but when he tries to take it off, his hair also comes off with it. As was also emphasized in the medieval sermons held to commemorate the martyred Bishop, and in the authoritative *Legenda sancti Henrici*, the song presents this occurrence as God's punishment to and revenge against the Bishop's murderer.[37]

As in the clerical tradition, the Bishop's murderer is presented in the folk ballad and in the recorded oral legends as an ill-natured man or an evil pagan. In contrast to some other popular narratives in the Nordic countries concerning killers of bishops,[38] the text does not depict the killing of Bishop Henry in any heroic light. On the contrary, as described by Johannes Messenius in the early seventeenth century, annual festivals were held in the parish of Köyliö in medieval times in which the local population, echoing the attitudes of the ecclesiastical authorities, cursed the local-born murderer of their holy bishop and apostle.[39]

The Sacralization of Land with the Martyr Cult

As regards the motive to the Bishop's murder, at least two interrelated alternatives are given in the orally circulated songs and narratives. One of them concerns the social norm of hospitality and reciprocal exchange, and the alleged failure of Bishop Henry to act according to the norm and the social expectation. This is said to have angered the hot-tempered person whose house the

---

[37] See Heikkilä, *Pyhän Henrikin legenda*, p. 411.
[38] See Palmenfelt, 'Prästdråpssägnen'.
[39] Messenius, *Suomen kronikka*, p. 35.

Bishop visited. According to Kauko Pirinen, this perspective gained clerical acceptance towards late medieval times, since motifs referring to it are lacking in the liturgical legends but are present in church paintings.[40]

The theme of violating a hospitality rule has also been interpreted as carrying political overtones, as some variants of the song speak of a *ruokaruotsi*, 'a Swede to feed', which refers to the right of the Swedish officials to claim free board and lodging when travelling on government business.[41] The Finnish historian Kimmo Katajala has studied how such right — or at least its abuse — was met with some economically and/or politically motivated resistance among Finnish-speaking populations.[42] Similarly, the historians Eino Jutikkala and Kauko Pirinen maintain that the Bishop was killed as a result of a violent reaction by Lalli to the Bishop's own provocative behaviour, on the one hand, and the economic burdens imposed on the people by the church, on the other.[43] A good number of present-day historians claim that the folk song serves as evidence for the Bishop having met his fate due to local resistance against taxation policies.[44]

Yet, as I have discussed elsewhere,[45] there is reason to doubt that the popular opposition to the abuse of such right could explain the legendary killing of Bishop Henry. A number of factors speak against such an explanation as well as its political motivation. The concept of *ruokaruotsi* refers to practices and privileges that, according to both historians and folklorists, originate in the beginning of the fourteenth century.[46] If this dating is accurate, the privileged social institution in question was established at least a hundred years later than the time of the said killing. For this reason, it is plausible that the song projects to the narrated time a social institution that belongs to the time of narration.

Moreover, as Martti Haavio has concluded, one of the motivations for composing the song about Bishop Henry's death was to argue against the local

---

[40] Pirinen, 'Keskiajan kulttuurin välittyminen Suomeen', p. 18.

[41] *Finnish Folk Poetry*, ed. by Kuusi, Bosley, and Branch, p. 556.

[42] See Katajala, *Suomalainen kapina*, pp. 92–94.

[43] Jutikkala and Pirinen, *A History of Finland*, p. 45.

[44] See, for example, Lehtonen, 'Suomi ennen Suomea', pp. 21–22; Lehtonen, 'Keskiajan kirjallinen kulttuuri', p. 23; Virrankoski, *Suomen historia*, pp. 65–66; Vahtola, *Suomen historia*, p. 35; Alifrosti, 'Veronmaksun ikeeseen — kohtuutta vai riistoa', p. 216.

[45] Anttonen, 'Myytin ja todennäköisyyden historiaa'.

[46] For example Katajala, *Suomalainen kapina*, pp. 92–93; *Finnish Folk Poetry*, ed. by Kuusi, Bosley, and Branch, p. 556.

claims according to which Henry had acted in the manner of a *ruokaruotsi*.[47] This would be in line with the historical-political sketch drawn by the historian Matti Klinge, according to whom the concept of *ruokaruotsi* was already familiar in the region in which the murder is said to have taken place and at the time of the said murder. In Klinge's sketch, the areas of Kalanti, Satakunta, Nousiainen, and Taivassalo comprised 'northern Finland' at that time and formed a state together with areas of present-day central Sweden.[48] Although 'less developed', the Finnish side was pro-Swedish and pro-Christian.[49] According to Klinge, the motive for the murder of Bishop Henry was his violation of the hospitality rule. The economic motivation, taking bread and beer from Lalli's house, gave Lalli a reason for revenge, but the murder did not carry any political overtones of anti-Swedishness or anti-Christianization, as the preaching trip on which the Bishop was killed occurred in territory that was part of the kingdom of Sweden.[50]

Another approach to the narrative and its performative aspects emerges from cultural meanings given to martyrdom. One of the greatest changes that

---

[47] Haavio, *Piispa Henrik ja Lalli*, pp. 220–21; see also Järvinen, *Legendat*, pp. 11–12.

[48] Klinge, *Muinaisuutemme merivallat*, pp. 96–97.

[49] Klinge, *Muinaisuutemme merivallat*, p. 53.

[50] Klinge, *Muinaisuutemme merivallat*, p. 74. In Klinge's historical sketch this was the state of Svea, or the kingdom of Sweden, which was comprised mainly of the Lake Mälaren area in present-day Sweden, including Uppsala and Stockholm, together with the island of Åland and the Kalanti and Satakunta areas of present-day Finland. Drawing on heroic oral poetry, Klinge names this state *Pohjola* (the North). Until the early thirteenth century, according to Klinge, Finland Proper and areas that comprise the present-day Baltic countries formed a loose state and an organized society, a pagan *civitas*, which was called Väinölä. Its centre was located in Estonia, while the town of Turku was close to the area's northern reaches (ibid., pp. 96–97). Klinge's sketch avoids a nationalistic projection to the medieval past and emphasizes a political and religious polarization between 'northern Finland' and 'southern Finland'. He also claims that this polarization matches with the opposition between Pohjola and Väinölä that forms the basic plot in the Finnish national epic, the *Kalevala*. Klinge takes as his starting point that the legendary trip made by King Eric and Bishop Henry actually took place. In his view this was a military-religious expedition from the territory of one state to that of another, from Pohjola to Väinölä, the main purpose of which was to annex the non-converted Turku area to the Swedish state (ibid., p. 72). The political context for the annexation was the competition over this area with the Novgorodians and the Danes. The transfer of the bishop's see from Nousiainen in 'northern Finland' in the Swedish territory to Koroinen in Maaria, present-day Turku, in 'southern Finland' or Finland Proper in 1229 was directly linked to these processes. This took place after Finland Proper had broken its ties with Estonia, which had been conquered by the Danes in the 1220s (ibid., pp. 63–64, 68–69). The see was transferred to the Turku Cathedral around 1280.

the conversion to Christianity has meant historically for non-Christian peoples concerns the conceptualization of sacrifice and its role in the relationship between human beings and supernatural powers. Instead of sacrificial killings, Christianity has promoted the institution of martyrdom. In addition to Christian martyrs having a direct model in the narrative of Christ (in *imitatio Christi*), they embody the narrative theme of the heroic or noble death, in accordance with the etymology of the word 'martyr' (Greek for 'witness'). In essence, 'martyr' is a category of recognition. As noted by the Dutch religious scholar Jan Willem van Henten, 'the martyr cannot exist without supporters and must function somehow as a model in regard to the values and identity of this group of supporters'.[51] Accordingly, as discussed by the French anthropologist Jean-Pierre Albert, a martyr is a sacrifice by a human community in exchange for the benefits that the community is believed to obtain from the supernatural power.[52] But in addition to the supernatural, the sacrifice also constitutes a debt vis-à-vis the martyr. The form of payment of this debt is the socially constructed martyr cult. In order to pay for its debt to the martyr, the Christian community has a social obligation to organize itself around the martyr cult.

It is worth noting here the link between 'victim' and 'sacrifice'. In the English language, according to the *American Heritage Dictionary*, a 'victim' is one 'who is harmed or killed by another', as well as a 'living creature slain and offered as a sacrifice to a deity or as part of a religious rite'.[53] Even though these two meanings tend to be kept separate by using 'victim' for the former and 'sacrifice' for the latter, they also refer to each other. In the Finnish language the two words are synonyms and both translate as *uhri*. In Christian mythology, Jesus Christ, as well as the legendary Bishop Henry in his imitation, are victims who, post factum, are made into sacrifices for the Christian community. Unlike sacrificial animals, neither one was killed to make a sacrifice to a deity or god.

It is the conceptualization of the victim as a sacrifice that constructs a community of beneficiaries with a sense of obligation to organize around the martyr victim/sacrifice. Accordingly, the life and death of Henry can be seen as a narrative that was composed —most probably out of both fact and fiction as well as by the appropriation of local pre-Christian mythical sites and times[54] — for the sake of creating a local martyr cult and a religious community that would be organized (or which would organize itself) around the martyr cult.

[51] Van Henten, 'Jewish and Christian Martyrs', p. 168.

[52] Albert, 'Héros et martyrs dans l'imaginaire de la nation'.

[53] *American Heritage Dictionary*, s.v. victim.

[54] See Anttonen, 'Pyhä Henrik, pyhä maa ja pyhä aika', pp. 32–39.

Its linking of myth with both geography and annual temporal structures would have been in line with the general practice of the Roman Church to organize and institutionalize religiosity through the system of saints and martyrs. It also corresponds to what the American folklorist Roger Abrahams has discussed as the control of land through its sacralization.[55] Indeed, the creation of the martyr cult for the symbolic construction and consolidation of a religious and civic community may have been more instrumental in the integration of the Finnish-speaking territories into the kingdom of Sweden since the thirteenth century than any use of force or forms of legislation.

It is also worth noting that all Nordic countries have a martyr king that is said to have died for the sake of Christianity. King Olaf Haraldsson (Olaf II) became St Olaf, the patron saint of Norway, after having fallen in the Battle of Stiklestad near Trondheim, possibly in 1030. Denmark's King Knut, canonized in 1101 as St Knut, was murdered in Odense in 1086. King Erik Jedvardsson became St Erik (St Eric), the patron saint of Sweden, after being murdered in Uppsala in 1160. One can view these deaths, as Simo Heininen and Markku Heikkilä suggest, as the high cost that Christians had to pay for their eventual victory over paganism.[56] Yet, they can also be viewed as manifestations of a martyr-centric narrative model on which Christianity was established and both the land and the control over it were sacralized.

Two Misogynistic Stories?

In addition to the theme of violating a social rule, the song of Bishop Henry blames the murder on a woman, the killer's wife, who is said to have informed her husband about Bishop Henry visiting their house on a preaching trip and consuming food and drink in his absence without paying for it. The storyline does not hide the fact that the wife's claim over the guests' failure to pay for their food has no foundation in the course of the events described in the song. Such a theme has a wide array of parallels, and the wife's behaviour can be regarded as a variation of the biblical theme about the original sin and the deceitfulness of women. As discussed above, it is also present in the medieval English text of Judas. In both narratives the bond (or the potential bond) between the two main protagonists (Judas and Jesus; Henry and Lalli) is destroyed by the

---

[55] Abrahams, 'Phantoms of Romantic Nationalism in Folkloristics', p. 17.

[56] See for example Heininen and Heikkilä, *Suomen kirkkohistoria*, p. 14. On Scandinavian martyr cults, see also Antonsson, *St. Magnús of Orkney*; DuBois, *Sanctity in the North*.

third person in the story, a female. While the medieval English ballad places the blame for the betrayal of Jesus by Judas on Judas's sister, the song about the death of Bishop Henry blames Lalli's wife.

It is possible to condemn these motifs as straightforward representatives of misogyny. But other thematic similarities are also present in the two texts. Both the Judas text and the Finnish oral tradition concerning Bishop Henry's death, when dealing with the act of betrayal, make use of the theme of exchanging food for money, and in both this leads to dire consequences. The motif of the bloody head is also present in both. Judas despairs over the loss of his money by pulling himself by the hair, while the killer of the Bishop loses his hair (and the top of his head) when pulling off the Bishop's cap that he had placed on his head after killing him. The narratives of Judas and the Bishop's killer are also linked by the fact that in the Catholic era in Finland the killer was given a similar role as Judas in being seen as the embodiment of evil. In addition to ritual cursing, his role as a Judas figure has also been expressed in poetic and symbolic parallelism: for example, the oldest handwritten document of the song contains the couplet 'Lalli sitten pahin pakanoista | julmin Juudasten seasta', which is translated as 'Then Lalli, worst of the pagans, | among the Judases the cruelest'.[57]

The narrative characters of Judas and Lalli share death as punishment for their respective sins. But what is, in my mind, even more interesting here is the shared manner of narration in the two texts or text cycles, a narration that seeks social logic in a deed that does not receive a full explanation in the clerical tradition. The authorized saints' legends concerning Bishop Henry describe the killer as an impenitent criminal who is first scorned by the Bishop. In contrast, the orally transmitted accounts of the murder events explain the violent deed as an outcome of a conflict in the application of hospitality rules. Regardless of which version, if any, is historically more accurate, this latter manner of narration can be regarded as being psychologically more appealing, as it calls for mental reflection regarding social and cultural rules and human behaviour.

Accordingly, I would like to stress the way in which the narrated incidents deal with the workings of the human mind and the problems in social life. The story of the killing of Bishop Henry makes a moralistic statement, but the story of the betrayal of Jesus by Judas does not. What is more interesting is that they both illuminate how easy it is for people to be misguided. I am inclined to argue that the common characteristics in these two texts represent a generic feature in the popular treatment of Christian narrative topics: the avoidance of theological questions and the emphasis on human drama. Consequently, I

---

[57] *Piispa Henrikin surmavirsi*. I thank Tuomas M. S. Lehtonen for reminding me of this detail.

would argue that it is the psychological edge in the narrative figures and their personal choices, supported by the narrative conventions of the new ballad genre, that made these and similar narratives interesting and worth recounting. Indeed, to fulfil the social preconditions for repetition and replication is the primary prerequisite for the emergence and continuation of a narrative tradition, of folklore.

This does not, however, apply only to the medieval narration of the Bishop's killing but also to the changes in the narrative complex after the Reformation. During the Protestant-minded nation-building process of the nineteenth century, nationalist intellectuals in Finland began moulding the killer's image to meet the interests of national heroism and national defence. At the same time, the image of the Bishop, as well as the whole Catholic form of Christianity, came to be seen as representing foreignness and cultural Otherness on Finnish soil.[58] Accordingly, the killer of the first Christian bishop in Finland is no longer an embodiment of evil, but considered a local freedom fighter and one of the great Finns of all times.[59]

We can easily formulate a political explanation for the historical change in interpretation, but attention should also be given to the continuing ambiguity concerning the question of who is the hero of the story and who is the victim. As regards the character of the Bishop's killer, the images that are created and reproduced today, for example in local festivals, differ greatly from those presented by the medieval church in its iconography. Instead of being an impenitent criminal and a creature-like human figure placed low under the feet of his saintly victim, the killer is now represented as a man of physical strength and ideological determination, signalling masculine values in the making and protecting of the local community. This view is presented most conspicuously in the larger-than-life statue that was erected in 1989 in the centre of the municipality of Köyliö, next to the now bankrupt Säästöpankki Savings Bank, which paid for the statue as a token of its hundredth anniversary. The killer of the Bishop has become a hero for Protestant Finnish nationalism, but at the same time he is its first martyr and sacrifice, and in more than one sense, its first victim.

---

[58] See Anttonen, 'Catholicism as an Other'.

[59] See Anttonen, 'Transformations of a Murder Narrative'. The story of St Henry and his killing is a narrative of many beginnings. In addition to pointing to the beginning of Christianity, it has become a national narrative about the situation of Finland in Europe and its location between East and West. With such performative power, it can be regarded as a political myth, and many politicized meanings have been given to the formulation of its origins. The latest addition to the institutional arenas of interpretation, ritualization, and performance is in the field of Christian ecumenism. See Anttonen, 'A Catholic Martyr and Protestant Heritage'.

A Question of World View: Do Social Agents Have Free Will or Do They Follow a Divine Plan?

The betrayal of Jesus by Judas is a narrative topic that is common cultural history in the Christian world. As such, the narrative topic calls for research on its variations and functions and their historical changes. For example, we can map out these changes and study the factors that make the topic attention-drawing and psychologically interesting. But in addition to these approaches, we can also look at the cognitive factors that either enhance or prevent the communicability and adaptability of narrative motifs within this narrative tradition. In other words, we can study why and how ideas transmit or do not transmit, and what makes them transmissible.

Judas is an attractive motif in the Christian narrative tradition. This means that his character shares features from many other narrative traditions and narrative figures. At the same time, the Church as an institution has tried to strengthen the canonical privilege of the Bible as a source for imagining Judas. While most of the orally circulated narratives on biblical figures follow the Bible, there are also those that do not derive their content from it. The term 'apocryphal gospel' denotes a text or a collection of texts that depict events relating to the early phases of Christianity, but does so in a manner that has not been authorized, for example, by inclusion in the New Testament. Some of the most famous of these unorthodox gospels are the Gospel of Thomas, the Gospel of Mary Magdalene, and now the Gospel of Judas. These are texts that were translated from Greek during the first and second centuries AD by the Coptic Church, an early Christian movement in Alexandria in Egypt.

In the recently rediscovered and translated Gospel of Judas Iscariot, Judas receives a more positive and significant role than he does in the Bible. The text argues that Judas and his betrayal had a meaningful purpose in the Messianic fate of Jesus. In other words, Judas did not spoil Jesus's plans but, on the contrary, made them materialize. This can be regarded as a novel perspective because there is no suggestion of a cooperative effort by Jesus and Judas in the Bible.

On the other hand, we may argue that there is not that much novelty in this perspective after all. I am here referring to the general processes in constructing martyrs and martyr narratives. If the goal is to argue for the fate of Jesus as a martyr and consequently to propagate the doctrine of redemption, the role that is given to the traitor of Jesus does not differ from the narrative role that the Bishop's killer in Finland has as an agent who made it possible for the Bishop to become a martyr. With reference to the narrative functions outlined by Vladimir Propp,[60] we can say that the traitor of Jesus and the killer of Bishop Henry are both the hero's opponents and his helpers.

But does the opponent of the hero know that he is also the hero's helper? Does this dual role mean that there is a grand plan that the opponent/helper is part of? The Gospels in the Bible make a reference to the Old Testament prediction of the betrayal of Jesus. Does this mean that the biblical figures, including Judas, are not seen as acting upon their own will and own agency? The recently discovered Gospel of Judas does not propagate the idea that Judas had a free will and that he made a free choice. The medieval English ballad text, however, appears to present his actions in this light. We may conclude that the question of free will and responsibility in the medieval ballad does not derive from the Coptic gospel.

Some other features in the medieval ballad do, however, appear to share features with the apocryphal gospel. One of these is the presentation of a deceitful woman as an important agent. The philologist Paull Franklin Baum has made reference to the insatiable wife of Judas in one of the Coptic texts dealing with the twelve Apostles.[61] This is the *Patrologia orientalis* collection that was edited by E. Revillout in 1907. Every day Judas would bring her a portion of the funds entrusted to him, but despite this she would continue to mock him. In her greediness she tells Judas to deliver Jesus to the Jews because they would, according to her, give him a great reward. Judas is tempted by his wife's words — as Adam was tempted by Eve — and he sells his master for thirty pieces of silver.

How is it possible that a medieval English manuscript could contain traces of a text written in Egypt a thousand years earlier? Instead of going into the question of cultural brokering and diffusion, I wish to focus here on the more general, and at the same time more theoretical, question of the narrative reflection of human acts and their consequences. The Gospel of Judas raises curiosity and debate because it brings forth a novel dimension to the image of Judas, to the motives behind his actions, and to the doctrinal differences in early Christianity. When the Bible and other liturgical texts fail to provide an explanation for the motives that led to the narrated actions, an interest in constructing alternative narratives emerges.

How good or bad these alternative narratives and the motives they offer are is an issue to be reflected upon by those who hear, interpret, and transmit

---

[60] See for example Propp, *Theory and History of Folklore*.

[61] Baum, 'The English Ballad of Judas Iscariot', p. 185.

these narratives. The agency that Judas possesses in these narratives can and, indeed, must be evaluated by any individual who hears or reads the story, and this evaluation takes place on the basis of his or her own social ability to make choices and to take responsibility for them. I would argue that it is such reflection that enables and ensures the narrative's continuity in social use in order for it to be decontextualized and recontextualized, that is, extracted from particular performance situations and reformulated for new communicative purposes. Boklund-Lagopoulou makes a somewhat similar suggestion: 'Everyman is the true hero of medieval drama: it is his choice between good and evil in his slightest everyday actions which constitutes the stage on which, in the medieval view, an epic struggle between cosmic forces is eternally acted out'.[62]

In fact, we can argue that these individual reflections and narrative repetitions signify one of the central innovations that made Christianity diffuse in the first place. By this innovation I mean the discursive, normative, and didactic relationship between cosmological and theological ideas and doctrines, on the one hand, and individual desires and actions, on the other. We may understand the actions by Judas in the biblical narratives as part of a divine plan to strengthen the doctrinal basis of Christianity, but the individual followers of Christianity cannot assign themselves the same position. The followers of Christian faith are not narrative agents, but agents in the social appropriation of narratives and in the constitution of their performative power. The followers of Christianity must evaluate their own human actions vis-à-vis the moral doctrines of Christianity as well as the narratives that purport to represent and propagate these doctrines. It is my contention that the social basis for the diffusion, intertextual linking, and transmission of both orthodox and unorthodox texts lies in the cognitive propensity to evaluate one's own social agency through narratives depicting other people's social agency. This may be regarded as a basic human propensity that materializes and gains power in historically specific contexts such as in the oral and textual performances of songs like the medieval ballad on Judas or the Finnish-language songs on the killing of Bishop Henry.

---

[62] Boklund-Lagopoulou, *'I Have a Yong Suster'*, p. 59.

Works Cited

Primary Sources

Finnish Folk Poetry: Epic. An Anthology in Finnish and English, ed. by Matti Kuusi, Keith Bosley, and Michael Branch (Helsinki: Suomalaisen Kirjallisuuden Seura, 1977)

Piispa Henrikin surmavirsi: Suomalaisen Kirjallisuuden Seuran kansanrunousarkiston vanhin käsikirjoitus – The Ballad of the Death of Bishop Henry: The Oldest Manuscript in the Folklore Archives of the Finnish Literature Society (Helsinki: Suomalaisen Kirjallisuuden Seura, 1999)

Suomen kansan vanhat runot, ed. by Aukusti Robert Niemi and others, 34 vols (Helsinki: Suomalaisen Kirjallisuuden Seura, 1908–48, 1997)

Secondary Works

Åberg, Alf, 'Helgonen och helgondagarna', in *Den svenska historien*, ed. by Gunvor Grenholm, 15 vols (Stockholm: Bonnier, 1993), I: *Från stenålder till vikingatid*, pp. 212–16

Abrahams, Roger D., 'Phantoms of Romantic Nationalism in Folkloristics', *Journal of American Folklore*, 106 (1993), 3–37

Aili, Hans, Olle Ferm, and Helmer Gustavson, 'Den fromme S:t Erik. Erikslegenden', in *Röster från svensk medeltid: latinska texter i original och översättning*, ed. by Hans Aili, Olle Ferm, and Helmer Gustavson (Stockholm: Natur och kultur, 1991), pp. 90–103

Albert, Jean-Pierre, 'Héros et martyrs dans l'imaginaire de la nation', unpublished paper given at the seminar on 'National Heroes', 5 December 1996, Wien

Alifrosti, Kari, 'Veronmaksun ikeeseen — kohtuutta vai riistoa', in *Muinainen Kalanti ja sen naapurit: talonpojan maailma rautakaudelta keskiajalle*, ed. by Veijo Kaitanen, Esa Laukkanen, and Kari Uotila, Suomalaisen Kirjallisuuden Seuran toimituksia, 825 (Helsinki: Suomalaisen Kirjallisuuden Seura, 2003), pp. 214–21

American Heritage Dictionary, 2nd college edn (Boston: Houghton Mifflin, 1982)

Antonsson, Haki, *St. Magnús of Orkney: A Scandinavian Martyr-Cult in Context* (Leiden: Brill, 2007)

Anttonen, Pertti J., 'Catholicism as an Other', in *The European Mind: Narrative and Identity*, ed. by Henry Frendo, 2 vols (Malta: Malta University Press, 2010), II.5, 741–47

——, 'A Catholic Martyr and Protestant Heritage: A Contested Site of Religiosity and its Representation in Modern Finland', in *Creating Diversities: Folklore, Religion and the Politics of Heritage*, ed. by A.-L. Siikala, R. Klein, and R. Mathisen, Studia Fennica folkloristica, 14 (Helsinki: Suomalaisen Kirjallisuuden Seura, 2004), pp. 190–221

——, 'Myytin ja todennäköisyyden historiaa — Piispa Henrikin surma viimeaikaisen suomalaisen historiankirjoituksen valossa', in *Historioita ja historiallisia keskusteluja*, ed. by Sami Louekari and Anna Sivula, Historia mirabilis, 2 (Turku: Turun historiallinen yhdistys, 2004), pp. 95–129

——, 'Pyhä Henrik, pyhä maa ja pyhä aika', in *Pyhä: raja, kielto ja arvo kansanomaisessa uskonnossa*, ed. by Ilkka Pyysiäinen, Teemu Taira, and Tiina Mahlamäki (Helsinki: Suomalaisen Kirjallisuuden Seura, 2008), pp. 13–41

——, 'Transformations of a Murder Narrative: A Case in the Politics of History and Heroization', *Norveg: Journal of Norwegian Folkore*, 40 (1997), 3–28

Axton, Richard, 'Interpretations of Judas in Middle English Literature', in *Religion in the Poetry and Drama of the Late Middle Ages in England*, ed. by Piero Boitani and Anna Torti (Cambridge: Brewer, 1990), pp. 179–97

Bäckström, Per Olof, *Svenska folkböcker*, 2 vols (Stockholm: Bohlin, 1845–48)

Baum, Paull Franklin, 'The English Ballad of Judas Iscariot', *Publications of the Modern Language Association*, 31 (1916), 181–89

Boklund-Lagopoulou, Karin, *'I Have a Yong Suster': Popular Song and the Middle English Lyric* (Dublin: Four Courts, 2002)

——, '"Judas": The First English Ballad?', *Medium Aevum*, 62 (1993), 20–34

Child, F. J., *The English and Scottish Popular Ballads*, 10 pts in 5 vols (Boston: Houghton Mifflin, 1825–96)

Chuvyurov, Alexander, 'Trees in Komi (Zyrian) Rituals and Beliefs', *Pro ethnologia*, 18 (2004), 69–85

Dahl, Kaj, and C. J. Gardberg, *Suomen kartanoita* (Helsinki: Otava, 1989)

Daniels, Cora Linn, and C. M. Stevans, eds, *Encyclopaedia of Superstitions, Folklore, and the Occult Sciences of the World* (Chicago: Yewdale, 1903)

Dronke, Peter, *The Medieval Lyric* (Cambridge: Cambridge University Press, 1968)

DuBois, Thomas A., ed., *Sanctity in the North: Saints, Lives and Cults in Medieval Scandinavia* (Toronto: University of Toronto Press, 2008)

Haavio, Martti, *Piispa Henrik ja Lalli: Piispa Henrikin surmavirren historiaa* (Porvoo: Werner Söderström, 1948)

Haupt, L., and J. E. Schmaler, eds, *Volkslieder der Sorben in der Ober- und Niederlausitz* (Berlin: Akademie, 1841)

Heikkilä, Tuomas, *Pyhän Henrikin legenda*, Suomalaisen Kirjallisuuden Seuran toimituksia, 1039 (Helsinki: Suomalaisen Kirjallisuuden Seura, 2005)

——, 'Vörnaden av Sankt Henrik i det svenska riket', in *Suomen Museo 2006: Pyhä Henrik ja Suomen kristillistyminen – Finskt Museum 2006: Sankt Henrik och Finlands kristnande*, ed. by Helena Edgren, Tuukka Talvio, and Eva Ahl (Helsinki: Suomen Muinaismuistoyhdistys; Glossa — Keskiajan tutkimuksen seura, 2007), pp. 101–26

Heininen, Simo, and Markku Heikkilä, *Suomen kirkkohistoria* (Helsinki: Edita, 1997)

Henten, Jan Willem van, 'Jewish and Christian Martyrs', in *Saints and Role Models in Judaism and Christianity*, ed. by Marcel Poorthuis and Joshua Schwartz (Leiden: Brill, 2004), pp. 163–81

Hill, Thomas D., 'The Middle English "Judas" Ballad and the Price of Jesus: Ballad Tradition and the Legendary History of the Cross', *English Studies*, 89 (2008), 1–11

Jaakkola, Jalmari, ed., *Suomen varhaishistoria: Heimokausi ja 'Kalevalakulttuuri'*, vol. II of *Suomen historia*, ed. by Jalmari Jaakkola and others, 2nd rev. edn (Porvoo: Werner Söderström, 1956)

Järvinen, Irma-Riitta, ed., *Legendat: kansankertomuksia Suomesta ja Karjalasta* (Helsinki: Suomalaisen Kirjallisuuden Seura, 1981)

Jutikkala, Eino, and Kauko Pirinen, *A History of Finland*, trans. by Paul Sjöblom (Helsinki: Werner Söderström, 1996)

Katajala, Kimmo, *Suomalainen kapina: talonpoikaislevottomuudet ja poliittisen kulttuurin muutos Ruotsin ajalla (n. 1150–1800)*, Historiallisia tutkimuksia, 212 (Helsinki: Suomalaisen Kirjallisuuden Seura, 2002)

Klinge, Matti, *Muinaisuutemme merivallat* (Helsinki: Otava, 1983)

Krötzl, Christian, *Pilger, Mirakel und Alltag: Formen des Verhaltens im skandinavischen Mittelalter* (Helsinki: Suomen Historiallinen Seura, 1994)

Kuusi, Matti, 'Keskiajan kalevalainen runous', in *Suomen kirjallisuus*, ed. by Matti Kuusi and others, 8 vols (Helsinki: Suomalaisen Kirjallisuuden Seura, 1963–70), I: *Kirjoittamaton kirjallisuus* (1963), ed. by Matti Kuusi, pp. 273–397

Lehtonen, Tuomas M. S., 'Finlands erövring och frälsningshistoria: Sankt Henrik, Finlands kristnande och uppbyggandet av det förflutna', in *Suomen Museo 2006: Pyhä Henrik ja Suomen kristillistyminen – Finskt Museum 2006: Sankt Henrik och Finlands kristnande*, ed. by Helena Edgren, Tuukka Talvio, and Eva Ahl (Helsinki: Suomen Muinaismuistoyhdistys; Glossa – Keskiajan tutkimuksen seura, 2007), pp. 7–26

——, 'Keskiajan kirjallinen kulttuuri', in *Suomen kirjallisuushistoria*, ed. by Yrjö Varpio, Lasse Koskela, and Liisi Huhtala, Suomalaisen Kirjallisuuden Seuran toimituksia, 724, 3 vols (Helsinki: Suomalaisen Kirjallisuuden Seura, 1999), I: *Hurskaista lauluista ilostelevaan romaaniin*, ed. by Yrjö Varpio and Liisi Huhtala, pp. 12–35

——, 'Suomi ennen Suomea: raja-alueen kiinnittyminen eurooppalaiseen kulttuuripiiriin', in *Suomi, outo pohjoinen maa? Näkökulmia Euroopan äären historiaan ja kulttuuriin*, ed. by Tuomas M. S. Lehtonen (Porvoo: PS-kustannus, 1999), pp. 18–49

Lüthi, Max, 'Familienballade', in *Handbuch des Volksliedes*, ed. by Rolf Wilhelm Brednich, Lutz Röhrich, and Wolfgang Suppan, 2 vols (München: Fink, 1973–75), I: *Die Gattungen des Volksliedes* (1973), pp. 89–100

Messenius, Johannes, *Suomen kronikka*, trans. by Eero Välikangas (Tampere: Sanasat, 1997)

Mortensen, Lars Boje, and Else Mundal, 'Erkebispesetet i Nidaros — arnestad og verkstad for Olavslitteraturen', in *Ecclesia Nidrosiensis 1153–1537: søkelys på Nidaroskirkens og Nidarosprovinsens historie*, ed. by Steinar Imsen (Trondheim: Tapir, 2003), pp. 353–84

Palmenfelt, Ulf, 'Prästdråpssägnen — ett tittrör ned i Kalmarunionens sociala strider', *Tradisjon*, 15 (1985), 35–48

Pirinen, Kauko, 'Keskiajan kulttuurin välittyminen Suomeen', in *Suomen kulttuurihistoria*, ed. by Päiviö Tommila, Aimo Reitala, and Veikko Kallio, 3 vols (Helsinki: Werner Söderström, 1979–82), I: *Ruotsin-vallan aika*, pp. 11–39

——, 'Piispa Henrikin muisto ja Köyliön seurakunta', mimeograph (1987)

Propp, Vladimir, *Theory and History of Folklore*, trans. by Ariadna Y. Martin and Richard P. Martin (Minneapolis: University of Minnesota Press, 1984)

Suvanto, Seppo, 'Ensimmäinen ristiretki — tarua vai totta?', in *Muinaisrunot ja todellisuus: Suomen kansan vanhojen runojen historiallinen tausta*, ed. by Martti Linna, Historian aitta, 20 (Helsinki: Historian ystäväin Liitto, 1987), pp. 149–60

——, 'Keskiaika', in *Suomen historia*, ed. by Yrjö Blomstedt and others, 8 vols (Helsinki: Weilin & Göös, 1984–88), II: *Keskiaika; Valtaistuinriitojen ja uskonpuhdistuksen aika; Kansankulttuurin juuretpp* (1985), pp. 11–225

Svahnström, Gunnar, *St. Olav: seine Zeit und sein Kult*, Acta Visbyensia, 6 (Visby: Museum Gotland, 1981)

Vahtola, Jouko, *Suomen historia: jääkaudesta Euroopan unioniin* (Helsinki: Suuri Suomalainen Kirjakerho, 2003)

Vargyas, Lajos, *Researches into the Mediaeval History of Folk Ballad* (Budapest: Akadémiai kiado, 1967)

Virrankoski, Pentti, *Suomen historia: ensimmäinen osa*, Suomalaisen Kirjallisuuden Seuran toimituksia, 846 (Helsinki: Suomalaisen Kirjallisuuden Seura, 2001)

Ward, Donald, 'The Origin of the Ballad, Urban Setting or Rural Setting?', in *Ballads and Ballad Research*, ed. by Patricia Conroy (Seattle: University of Washington Press, 1978), pp. 46–57

Wright, Thomas, and James Orchard Halliwell, *Reliquiae antiquae: Scraps from Ancient Manuscripts, Illustrating Chiefly Early English Literature and the English Language*, 2 vols (London: John Russell Smith, 1845)

Female Mourning Songs and Other Lost Oral Poetry in Pre-Christian Nordic Culture

Else Mundal

It is obvious that the written culture and Christianization introduced new genres in the Nordic societies.[1] The question which I will discuss here is whether the arrival of writing and the change of religion also resulted in the demise of some old oral genres. Genres whose existence could be undermined by the written culture and the new religion were first and foremost genres that were closely connected to rituals belonging to the heathen cult or to rites closely connected to the heathen culture. We have knowledge of genres that existed in the oral culture, for instance the Eddic mythological poems and heroic poems and the different subgenres of skaldic poems, because these poems — or some of them — were later written down on parchment. But even if they had not been written down, we would still have known about them, since a few stanzas are known from runic inscriptions, and skalds and the performance of skaldic poetry are often mentioned in different sources.

Among the different subgenres of skaldic poetry, the so-called *erfikvæði* which was performed in memory of a dead person, and probably sometimes in connection with a celebration of the dead, the *erfiol*, can be classified as — or come very close to — a religious ritual. This type of poetry is well documented in the sources, and it was produced and transmitted orally for a long time after Christianization.

---

[1] The word 'Nordic' is here used with reference to the areas where a Nordic (Scandinavian) language was spoken and thus it has a wider meaning than Old Norse, which is used with reference to the West Nordic area, Norway and Iceland.

Else Mundal, University of Bergen, Professor, else.mundal@cms.uib.no

As regards the poems of gods within the Eddic poetry there has been a discussion in the past of whether these poems — or some of them — could have been connected to religious rites and performed as a sort of religious drama.[2] Some of the mythological poems that have been preserved have a form that makes a performance as drama plausible, but it is, in my opinion, not easy to see how the preserved mythological poems can be connected to religious rites. In any case, they survived Christianization and were transmitted in the Christian culture — some of them may even have been composed in Christian times.

Genres in the pre-Christian Nordic societies that were more closely connected to cultural or religious rites than the poetry that has been preserved may, however, have existed. The genres I have in mind are female mourning songs and verses of the kind that Adam of Bremen mentions in his *Historia Hammaburgensis Ecclesiae*, Book IV, Chapter 27, scolion 141, which according to him were so obscene that he would not say more about them. The fact that these genres are lost — or nearly lost — may, especially in the latter case, be a result of the Christian culture. It is, however, also possible that their cultural function and the way they were performed indicate that these genres were not meant to be transmitted. The performance of these genres was bound to a certain occasion in an oral culture and an oral context.

In this article the main focus will be on the female mourning songs, but the 'obscene' songs mentioned by Adam of Bremen will also be included in the discussion. These two genres seem to be very different, but they have one important thing in common: they are both closely connected to rituals in pre-Christian culture. Therefore they may shed light on each other, and the reason why they are so poorly documented may, at least partly, be the same for both. Together these two nearly lost genres can contribute to a fuller picture of oral poetry in the Nordic areas.

The Mourning Songs

In 1944 Jón Helgason launched the theory, based on his reading of the runic inscription on the Swedish Bällsta stones, that a song of mourning called *grátr* had existed in Scandinavia. The inscription names three men who established a *þing* (an assembly place). These three men, who were sons of a certain Ulfr, raised the stones and worked the staff (*stafr*) — which was also part of the

---

[2] See Phillpotts, *The Elder Edda*; Gunnell, 'The Play of Skírnir'; Gunnell, *The Origins of Drama in Scandinavia*.

memorial monument — and the name of the man who cut the runes on the stone is mentioned. A woman is also mentioned in the inscription. The woman's name is Gýríðr, and she must be the widow of Ulfr. The lines about her read as follows:

> Ok Gyriði gats at veri.
> Þy man i grati getit lata.[3]
>
> [Likewise Gýríðr loved her husband.
> So [she] shall let [him] be spoken of in a *grátr*.]

Until 1944, when Jón Helgason published his reinterpretation of the inscription, there seems to have been consensus among the scholars that *í gráti* should be understood as 'in mourning'. Jón Helgason argued that *grátr* must have been the Nordic word for a type of poetry. The fact that the word *grátr* is used at the end of two Old Norse poems, the Eddic poem *Oddrúnargrátr*[4] and the poem about the Virgin Mary, *Maríugrátr*, was one of the arguments Jón Helgason used to support his theory, but he did not feel sure that the word *grátr* in the last stanza of *Oddrúnargrátr* should be understood as 'en beteckning för dikten' ('a genre term for the poem').[5] Jón Helgason's main argument was that the preposition *í* is not the preposition we should expect to find if the meaning of *í gráti* was 'in mourning', as in that case the preposition should have been *með*.

Jón Helgason's interpretation of *í gráti* has been accepted by the majority of scholars, but some scholars have argued against his interpretation of the word *grátr* in the Bällsta inscription as a word for a mourning song,[6] or against the existence of a genre of this kind in the Nordic culture in general.[7] The most recent scholar to comment on the Bällsta inscription is Joseph Harris.[8] In a very thorough discussion of the inscription he demonstrates that Jón Helgason's reading is the most logical in this context.[9]

---

[3] The two Bällsta stones are numbered U225 and 226, and the inscription is published in *Upplands runinskrifter*, ed. by Wessén and Jansson, Sveriges runinskrifter VII, 346–75. The translations of this and the following Old Norse/Old Nordic texts are my own.

[4] The title *Oddrúnargrátr* is preserved only in later paper manuscripts.

[5] Jón Helgason, 'Bällsta-inskriftens "i grati"', p. 162.

[6] Sävborg, *Sorg och elegi i Eddans hjältediktning*.

[7] Von See, 'Das Phantom einer altgermanischer Elegiendichtung'.

[8] Harris, 'The Bällsta-Inscriptions'.

[9] See especially Harris's discussion of *man getit lata* (Harris, 'The Bällsta-Inscriptions', pp. 228–30).

Before winding up the discussion of the meaning of *grátr* in the Old Nordic languages, I would like to add that the use of the word in the last stanza of *Oddrúnargrátr*, 'nú er um genginn | grátr Oddrúnar' ('now is Oddrún's *grátr* over'), shows that the word here cannot have the ordinary meaning 'crying'. Oddrún would of course be as sorrowful after she had performed her poem as before. Her grief for her miserable life would not be over, but only her poem would be. This way of ending a poem is very similar to the ending of *Hávamál*: 'Nú eru Háva mál kveðin.' The parallel in *Hávamál* supports the understanding of *grátr* as part of the name of the poem or as a poem of a special type. In both cases this is an argument in favour of Jón Helgason's theory, namely that in the Nordic societies mourning songs known as *grátr* existed.[10] If *Oddrúnargrátr* can be understood as an example of a mourning song, the ethnic genre term *grátr* seems, however, to cover a wider field than 'mourning songs for recently dead people'. Another word has also been preserved in the Old Norse language that must signify a poem that expresses sorrow for dead people. In *Helgakviða Hundingsbana* II, stanza 46, the dead Helgi, who has returned to his grave mound, says:

> skal engi maðr
> angrljóð kveða
> þótt mér á brjósti
> benjar líti; [...][11]

[No one should sing *angrljóð* though on my breast wounds can be seen.]

The meaning of *angrljóð* is 'song of sorrow'. The word characterizes a special type of poetry, and it is possible that this word was also used as an ethnic genre term with the same meaning as *grátr*. In the following, *grátr* in the narrow meaning 'female mouring song for dead people' will be discussed.

The strongest argument in favour of the theory for the existence of a female mourning song in pre-Christian Nordic culture is not the existence of the words — or terms — *grátr* and *angrljóð*, but the existence of a few stanzas and lines within the Eddic poetry which may be seen as reflections of the lost genre in my opinion. The stanzas and lines in question are discussed below.

---

[10] Von See seems to think that the word *grátr* in *Oddrúnargrátr* shows influence from Christian poetry (von See, 'Das Phantom einer altgermanischer Elegiendichtung', p. 98). It is, in my opinion, more likely that Old Norse Christian poetry (for instance in *Máríugrátr*) has taken over an older term.

[11] This and the following Eddic stanzas are quoted from *Norrøn Fornkvæði*, ed. by Bugge; the normalization of the text is mine.

Carol Clover, who has supported Jón Helgason's theory, argued that this genre must be seen in connection with revenge.[12] In her articles she focuses on three goading scenes in the sagas of the Icelanders (*Njáls saga*, chap. 116, *Harðar saga*, chap. 38, and *Heiðarvíga saga*, chap. 22) and on three poetic texts (*Guðrúnarhvǫt*, *Hamðismál*, and *Sonatorrek*). In the first five of these texts women's mourning and goading are connected. Clover's argument for the connection between the female mourning song, or lament,[13] and revenge is interesting indeed. I will not deny that mourning songs and goading could in some cases be connected, take place at the same time, and be performed by the same woman or women. Two of the stanzas I quote below as examples of the kind of poetry which in my opinion best reflects genuine mourning songs are in fact connected with goading. In principle, however, the act of performing mourning songs and the act of goading are different. It is not reasonable that mourning songs were performed only in cases when a person had been killed and when there was a demand for revenge; mourning songs must also have been performed when people died from sickness and old age. Mourning songs are closely connected with death and funerals, while in most cases goading would take place a long time after a person had been killed.

In my opinion it is more likely that the *grátr* was primarily a 'poem' in which a woman — or perhaps several women — expressed grief and praised the dead. In previous studies I have mentioned in passing that in searching for remnants of female mourning songs within Nordic culture we should look at stanzas in Eddic poems which describe scenes where women learn that a beloved man is dead.[14] Such stanzas are present in *Guðrúnarkviða* I and

---

[12] Clover, '"Cold are the Counsels of Women"'; Clover, 'Hildigunnr's Lament'. The former is a short version of the latter and was presented at the Saga Conference in 1985.

[13] In the discussion of the female mourning songs in the Nordic areas different English genre terms have been used. Carol Clover uses the term 'lament' the meaning of which covers expressions of grief from 'crying' to 'mourning poems', and she also discusses whether the Nordic lament took some fixed, poetic form (Clover, 'Hildigunnr's Lament', p. 180). The term 'elegy' is also used. This term is used both for mourning songs for dead people as well as for mourning songs for other unfortunate accidents than death. In the pre-Christian culture in the Nordic areas, as well as in other neighbouring cultures, there no doubt existed poetry which can be characterized as elegies; see Harris, 'Elegy in Old English and Old Norse'. A close parallel to the female mourning songs discussed here is found in the last lines of the Old English poem *Beowulf* (ll. 3150–52). There may even be a Nordic link here since the mourning woman is called *Geatisc meowle*, 'old woman from Götaland (or Jylland)'; *Klaeber's Beowulf*, ed. by Fulk, Bjork, and Niles, p. 107. Another Nordic area where female mourning songs have existed up to this day is Karelia.

[14] Mundal, 'Æ standa mér augo / of eld til gráfeldar', p. 128 n. 15; Mundal, 'The Position of Women in Old Norse Society', p. 8.

Helgakviða Hundingsbana II, and a few similar stanzas are placed in scenes where a woman remembers a dead beloved person. In the following I will present the type of stanza that, in my opinion, is the best source for knowledge about female mourning songs. These stanzas are not genuine mourning songs in the sense that they would have been recorded as they were performed by a real, historical woman. These stanzas were put in the mouth of women who, according to the tradition, lived long, long ago. Nevertheless, the model for the Eddic stanzas may very well have been real mourning songs that were known in Old Norse society at the same time as Eddic poems were composed and transmitted.

Eddic poems that give expression to women's grief have been regarded as late poetic creations by many scholars. Andreas Heusler argued that these poems belonged to a late layer of Eddic poetry that was composed under the influence of continental ballad traditions, and many scholars have since supported his theory.[15] The relationship between the male *erfikvæði* and the female stanzas of mourning in Eddic poetry, and the relationship of both these chategories to Old English elegies on the one hand and continental ballads on the other, is, however, as Clover put it 'one of the knottiest problems in Old Norse literary studies'.[16] The stanzas that I investigate here may belong to rather late Eddic poems, but that does not mean that these stanzas were composed under the influence of ballads. The word *grátr* in the Bällstad inscription is a very strong argument in favour of the view that female mourning songs were performed as part of the funeral ritual at the time this inscription was made in the eleventh century. We do not know when the genre died out in the Nordic regions. The change of religion probably had something to do with its disappearance, but customs connected to important rituals in life are normally hard to change or root out. It is therefore reasonable that the female mourning songs continued to live for some time after Christianization, and long enough to be reflected in late Eddic poems.

A typical stanza of the kind that I want to look at more closely in the search for female mourning songs in the Nordic areas is stanza 18 in *Guðrúnarkviða* I where Guðrún mourns Sigurðr's death:

---

[15] Heusler, 'Heimat und Alter der eddischen Gedichte'; Heusler, *Die altgermanische Dichtung*. On the discussion of this problem, see Vésteinn Ólason, 'Eddukvæði', pp. 152–57, and pp. 578–79 for references.

[16] Clover, 'Hildigunnr's Lament', p. 153.

> Svá var minn Sigurðr
> hjá sonum Gjúka,
> sem væri geirlaukr
> ór grasi vaxinn,
> eða væri bjartr steinn
> á band dreginn,
> jarknasteinn
> yfir ǫðlingum.

[So was my Sigurðr compared with the sons of Gjúki as if a leek were grown up out of the grass, or a bright stone were threaded onto a string, a precious gem above other noble men.]

In *Guðrúnarkviða* II, stanza 2, Guðrún expresses her grief for Sigurðr's death in a similar way:

> Svá var Sigurðr
> uf sonum Gjúka,
> sem væri grœnn laukr
> ór grasi vaxinn,
> eða hjǫrtr hábeinn
> um hvǫssum[17] dýrum,
> eða gull glóðrautt
> af grá silfri.

[So was Sigurðr beside the sons of Gjúki as if a green leek were grown up out of the grass, or a long-legged hart among the quick animals, or red-glowing gold next to grey silver.]

Another stanza of the same kind, except that the mourning woman also wants revenge, is stanza 38 in *Helgakviða Hundingsbana* II. Here Sigrún mourns the death of Helgi who was killed by her own brother:

> Svá bar Helgi
> af hildingum
> sem ítrskapaðr
> askr af þyrni,
> eða sá dýrkálfr
> dǫggu slunginn,
> er øfri ferr

---

[17] The meaning of this form is not clear. Some editors have changed the form *hvǫssum* to *hǫsum*, 'grey'. Others have understood *hvǫssum* (dat. of *hvass*) as 'sharp-eyed'. Neither of these interpretations fits the context. The best interpretation in my opinion is 'quick', 'fast-running'; in other words, Sigurðr is the best among the best.

> ǫllum dýrum
> ok horn glóa
> við himinn sjálfan.

[So much better was Helgi compared with other chieftains as the bright-growing ash compared with the thorn-bush, or the young deer, drenched in dew, that surpasses all other animals, and its horns glow against the sky itself.]

Stanza 15 in *Guðrúnarhvǫt* is an interesting example because here a mother is mourning her dead daughter. In this case there is also a connection between mourning and revenge since here Guðrún goads her sons to take revenge on their sister's killer. The scene where this poem is performed is a goading scene; however, after the mention of the dead daughter, a stanza suddenly appears in the same style as we find in other stanzas where a woman is mourning a recently dead person she loved dearly:

> Enn um Svanhildi
> sátu þýjar,
> er ek minna barna
> bazt fullhugðak;
> svá var Svanhildr
> í sal mínum,
> sem væri sœmleitr
> sólar geisli.

[Then still with Svanhildr sat her maids, the one of my children whom I loved the best with all my heart; so was Svanhildr in my hall as if there were an illustrious ray of the sun.]

The stanzas above are made up of a series of comparisons and clearly stand out from the surrounding parts of the poems. The style of these stanzas is in fact so different from the surrounding stanzas that they function as a poem within a poem. And that is exactly the point. The stanzas, which are composed of very stereotypical lines in which a woman praises a recently dead beloved person by comparing him — or her — to precious and beautiful things or beings, are meant to be associations to, or function in the context as, mourning songs.

Other stanzas than those in which the dead person is praised may also be associated with female mourning songs. The woman's praise of the dead was in all likelihood the main theme of these songs, but another theme was probably her complaint about her own miserable situation. We can find, in fact, a few stanzas with this content that are built up of a series of comparisons in the same way and in the same style as the stanzas which praise the dead. One example of such a stanza is stanza 19 in *Guðrúnarkviða* I, which follows the stanza quoted above that praises Sigurðr:

> Ek þóttak ok
> þjóðans rekkum
> hverri hærri
> Herjans dísi;
> nú em ek svá lítil,
> sem lauf sé
> opt í jǫlstrum,
> at jǫfur dauðan.

[I thought myself also, among the kings's warriors, to be higher than all of Óðinn's goddesses; now, when my man is dead, I am as little as a leaf in the bay-willows must often be.]

Another stanza with the same content and in the same style is *Hamðismál*, stanza 5. In this stanza it is also Guðrún who complains about her miserable life:

> Einstœð em ek orðin
> sem ǫsp í holti,
> fallin at frændum
> sem fura at kvisti,
> vaðin at vilja
> sem viðr at laufi,
> þá er in kvistskœða[18]
> kømr um dag varman.

[I have come to stand alone as an aspen in the grove, I have lost my kinsmen as a pine its branches, deprived of happiness as a tree of its leaves, when the woman cutting twigs comes on a warm day.]

It is also possible that echos of the female mourning songs can be found in inscriptions on memorial stones. The inscription on the Norwegian Dynna stone from the early Christian period is especially interesting in this connection. The stone was erected by a mother in memory of her dead daugher. In the inscription the mother names herself and her daughter, and says that she also had a bridge built in memory of her daughter. In connection with mourning songs it is interesting that the inscription ends in words that fit perfectly into two Eddic lines:

---

[18] Who *in kvistskæða* is, is difficult to say, but this woman cutting branches could be a picture of death, or even Hel.

> Sú vas mær hǫnnust
> á Haðalandi.[19]

[She was the most dexterous young girl in Hadeland.]

These lines in Eddic form could very well echo the mother's mourning song.

Women who performed mourning songs were in all likelihood ordinary women, not skalds who were trained in composing poetry. However, to be able to compose a mourning song did not, judging from the stanzas quoted above, require much skill in literary craftsmanship. Nevertheless, these stanzas are, in a way, great poetry. Emotions are expressed in beautiful images. The very stereotypical language where the same lines, or variants of the same lines, turn up again and again, however, indicates that mourning songs were not the work of an individual. They were improvised poems, comprised of lines that existed within the tradition and that were known by everyone. What images and lines a mourning woman would choose would depend on the situation: whether the dead person was young or old, a man or woman, on the dead person's place in society, and other factors.

The very special character of the mourning songs and the context of the performance of such songs may also offer a key to the understanding of some of the problems connected to this genre. One minor problem can be mentioned first. Most scholars will agree that mourning songs belong to the female sphere. The lines on the Bällsta stone ('Þy man i grati | getit lata') have, however, caused some problems. The implicit subject must be the widow, and the implicit object must be the dead husband, which gives the fuller form of the sentence ('Þy man [hon] i grati [hans] getit lata') the meaning: 'she shall let him be spoken of in a mourning song'.[20] This sentence does not state that Gýríðr herself had made or even performed the *grátr* mentioned in the inscription. It is perhaps a possible reading, but judging from the phrase *man getit lata* alone, a more likely possibility would be that she had commissioned someone to compose and/or perform the *grátr*. Gýríðr's role in the composition of the *grátr* has been compared to the role Gunnhildr, widow of King Eiríkr Bloodaxe, played when she had a poem composed about her husband after his death. According to *Fagrskinna*, Chapter 8, 'lét Gunnhildr yrkja kvæði um hann' ('Gunnhildr had a poem composed

---

[19] The inscription is published in *Norges innskrifter med de yngre runer*, ed. by Olsen, I, 192–202.

[20] The phrase *man getit lata* is thoroughly discussed by Joseph Harris with references to previous interpretations (Harris, 'The Bällsta-Inscriptions', pp. 228–30).

about him').[21] This poem is *Eiríksmál*, which can be characterized as an *erfikvæði*, and is certainly not a *grátr*. There is a general agreement among scholars that the sentence means that Gunnhildr commissioned a skald to compose the poem. Most scholars who have commented on *man getit lata* in the Bällsta inscription have understood this phrase in the same way, and they seem to have taken it for granted that the skald was a man.[22] This is also the reading favoured by Harris, but he sees it as a possibility that the widow was her own skald.[23] Clover seems to favour the reading that Gýríðr had made the poem herself.[24]

I agree with those who find it difficult to see Gýríðr in the Bällsta inscription as the sole composer of the *grátr*. At the same time I find it very hard to believe that a male skald would compose poetry of the same sort as we find in the stanzas quoted above, which in my opinion are the kind of poetry which best reflects the nearly lost genre. I also find it very unlikely that the genre term *grátr* could be used about poetry composed and performed by men in pre-Christian Nordic culture. The term may have covered a wider field than 'mourning songs for dead people', but the term *grátr* indicates that this must have been a female genre. There are elements of mourning in poems and stanzas that are known to have been composed by men. Egill Skallagrímsson's *Sonatorrek* has often been mentioned in this connection. Furthermore, this poem does in fact make use of a few of the same images as the Eddic stanzas mentioned above. *Sonatorrek* is, however, spoken of as an *erfikvæði* in Old Norse sources; it is not a *grátr*.

There are, however, other options than to draw the conclusion that Gýríðr had commissioned a male skald to make a poem in memory of her husband. One possibility is that Gýríðr commissioned a woman, a professional mourner, to perform the *grátr*. The problem is that we do not know whether professional mourners existed in Nordic culture in pre-Christian and early Christian times; and the stanzas quoted above were all performed by women who were emotionally attached to the deceased.

Another possibility, which would make the phrase *mun getit lata* sound very logical, offers itself if we think of what mourning scenes probably looked like and how mourning songs were performed. In the stanzas quoted above we only hear the voice of one woman. That is what we should expect to find within the frame of an epic/dramatic poem. However, mourning women and mourning

---

[21] *Fagrskinna*, ed. by Bjarni Einarsson, p. 77.

[22] Jón Helgason, 'Bällsta-inskriftens "i grati"'; Jansson, *Runinskrifter i Sverige*, pp. 136–37.

[23] Harris, 'The Bällsta-Inscriptions', pp. 225–26, 228–30.

[24] Clover, 'Hildigunnr's Lament', pp. 181–83.

songs are known from many cultures.²⁵ Normally a mourning widow, mother, daughter, or sister will not mourn alone, but will be joined by other women. If Gýríðr, as the widow, was the leader of the mourning ritual and opened the mourning song, other women, for instance other female relatives, could join in and perform some lines of praise or sorrow. If this was the normal mourning scene for the Nordic areas as well, the phrase *mun getit lata* falls into place.

A major problem concerning Nordic female mourning songs is explaining why this genre is so poorly documented. Carol Clover has suggested that Christianization undermined this sort of poetry, but she thinks that happened because the mourning songs were associated with blood feud.²⁶ Christianization may have weakened the position of female mourning songs even if they were only vaguely associated with revenge and blood feud — as I think — since the Church brought new funeral rites which replaced the old ones, and since there are reasons to believe that especially women's rituals would have been the most suppressed in the new culture. Clover also points out that women's mourning songs in general seem to have a poor rate of survival in all cultures, and that there is a lack of interest in the female sphere in the sources from Scandinavia.²⁷ Jón Helgason ends his article by stating that 'klagosången var endast muntlig och föll i glömskan' ('the mourning song had only oral form and was forgotten').²⁸

To explain what happened to the mourning songs within Nordic culture, I think we should take our point of departure in the scene where genuine mourning songs were performed. We do not know much about this scene, but the sources give us a few leads. The genre is called *grátr*, which probably indicates that these songs were performed with a tearful voice. The women who performed mourning songs would also express their sorrow through their body language — by crying in distress, by loosening their hair.²⁹ The mourning women probably also wore clothing that signalled that they were grieving. All these things connected with the mourning scene cannot be separated from the text, or the wording, of the mourning song. In other words, these songs could not be

---

[25] See Clover, 'Hildigunnr's Lament', pp. 162–73 with many references to literature about this phenomenon worldwide.

[26] Clover, 'Hildigunnr's Lament', p. 180.

[27] Clover, 'Hildigunnr's Lament', p. 180.

[28] Jón Helgason, 'Bällsta-inskriftens "i grati"', p. 162.

[29] *Guðrúnarkviða* I, stanza 1, mentions striking hands together and crying; stanza 15 mentions loosening of hair. The women's behaviour is also described in *Sigurðarkviða in skamma*, stanza 25 and 29. The last part of stanza 12 in *Baldrs draumar* probably describes a mythic mourning scene. In saga literature the most typical description of a mourning woman is the description of Hildigunnr in *Brennu-Njáls saga*, ed. by Einar Ól. Sveinsson, chap. 116.

performed as entertainment of any sort at a later occasion. The performance of the individual mourning song is, in my opinion, likely to have happened only once. What existed in the tradition were not individual mourning songs, but a large store of lines and poetic images from which these songs were made. Since they obviously did not live long enough to be written down by learned men in the Middle Ages who were interested in documenting the previous culture of their people, the closest we can hope to come to genuine mourning songs in the Nordic areas is stanzas in scenes describing mourning — as we find in Eddic poetry — and 'silent' mourning on a runic stone.[30]

The fact that female mourning songs are so scarcely documented is in my opinion a very logical consequence of the special nature and function of this poetry. The difference between the male *erfikvæði*, which was meant to be remembered and is well documented in Old Norse sources, and the female *grátr*, which was not meant to be remembered and transmitted orally, can perhaps be traced as far back in time as Tacitus's *Germania*. In Chapter 27 where he describes the Germanic funeral rites he says: 'Feminis lugere honestum est, viris meminisse' ('it is considered an honour for women to mourn, for men to remember').

Songs Connected to a Fertility Cult

The other type of oral songs I mentioned at the beginning are songs that were used in connection with a heathen cult, most likely a fertility cult. Adam of Bremen writes in Book IV, Chapter 27, scolion 141, that in connection with the offerings in Uppsala people sing songs so obscene that he cannot repeat them:

> Ceterum neniae, quae in eiusmodi ritu libationis fieri solent, multiplices et inhonestae, ideoque melius reticendae.[31]

> [Furthermore, the incantations customarily chanted in the ritual of a sacrifice of this kind are manifold and unseemly; therefore, it is better to keep silent about them.][32]

---

[30] Joseph Harris suggests that the *grátr* mentioned in the Bällsta inscription was carved on the *stafr*, which, like the stones, were erected by Ulfr's sons in memory of their dead father (Harris, 'The Bällsta-Inscriptions', pp. 233–35). This is an interesting point. A silent 'performance' on the *stafr* would have been a future possibility, an oral reperformance would not. However, a carving on a *stafr* would probably not have ensured that individual mourning songs would be remembered for long: a runic inscription on a wooden *stafr* standing in the open in the snow and rain would have been difficult to read after a short time.

[31] Adam of Bremen's text is quoted from Adam von Bremen, *Hamburgische Kirchengeschichte*, ed. by Schmeidler, p. 260.

[32] The English translation of Adam of Bremen is quoted from *History of the Archbishops of*

Since Adam has chosen to say no more about these songs it is difficult to have a good impression of them. It is also difficult to say how well-informed Adam was about the cult in Uppsala. As far as we know, he had never heard and seen what was going on himself; he was dependent on second-hand information, and his description of the heathen cult in Uppsala may have been coloured by a certain tendency of some Christian authors to describe the heathen culture in a negative light.[33] As a contemporary source for the Christianization of Sweden, Adam of Bremen cannot, however, be disregarded, especially as later sources may exist to support his mentioning of 'obscene' songs.

The songs mentioned by Adam of Bremen do not seem to fit a description of Eddic poems about gods of the kind which are extant. These poems contain a few lines here and there that may have offended the men of the Church, but as a whole this poetry cannot be characterized as obscene. This characterization could, however, match the stanzas found in the story called *Vǫlsa þáttr* in *Flateyjarbók*.[34] In this story we have a description of how King Óláfr the saint, in disguise, comes to a farm where a heathen sacrifice (*blót*) is taking place.[35] The penis of a horse, which is called *vǫlsi*, is handed over from one person to the other, and they all recite a stanza, some of which could undoubtedly fit Adam's description.

The farmer's son brings the penis of the horse from the place where a horse had been slaughtered to the house; he improvises a stanza saying to the women, and especially to the slave woman:

> Hér meguð sjá
> heldr rǫskligan
> vingul skorinn
> af viggs fǫður;
> þér er ambátt
> þessi vǫlsi
> allódaufligr
> innan læra.[36]

Hamburg-Bremen, trans. by Tuschan, p. 208.

[33] Some scholars have been very critical towards the source value of Adam of Bremen; see for instance Janson, *Templum nobilissimum*.

[34] *Flateyjarbók*, ed. by Unger and Guðbrandur Vigfússon, II, 331–36.

[35] For an analysis of the *þáttr*, see Steinsland and Vogt, '"Aukinn ertu Uolsi ok upp um tekinn"'.

[36] The stanzas from *Vǫlsa þáttr* are quoted from *Den norsk-islandske skjaldedigtning*, ed. by Finnur Jónsson, B II, 237–38.

FEMALE MOURNING SONGS AND OTHER LOST ORAL POETRY

[Here you may see a rather potent limb cut out of the horse father, for you, slave woman, this *vǫlsi* would be very lively between your thighs.]

Later, when the penis of the horse is handed over from one person to the other, the farmer's son gives the *vǫlsi* to his sister with the words:

> Beri þér beytil
> fyr brúðkonur;
> þær skulu vingul
> væta í aptan;
> þiggi mǫrnir
> þetta blæti,
> en dóttir bónda
> drag þú at þér vǫlsa.

[Take the limb to the bridesmaids, they shall wet it this evening; receive giantesses this sacrifice, but you, farmer's daughter, draw *vǫlsi* at you.]

The farmer's daughter is not very excited. She hands *vǫlsi* over to the male slave of the household. His comment is that he would much rather prefer a hunk of bread, and he hands the penis of the horse over to the slave woman asking her to receive the *vǫlsi*. She answers:

> Víst eigi mættak
> viðr of bindask
> í mik at keyra,
> ef ein lægim
> í andkætu;
> þiggi mǫrnir
> þetta blæti, [...]

]I could certainly not resist driving it into me if we were laying down in mutual lust; receive giantesses this sacrifice, [...]]

The stanza improvised by the slave woman is the most coarse. The whole situation is, however, rather unrestrained.

It is a matter of discussion whether the scene described in the late source *Flateyjarbók* has anything to do with heathen cult or not. If we look for genuine stanzas connected to heathen cult, the stanzas in *Vǫlsa þáttr* are probably not 'the real thing'. The whole scene and such stanzas as given here could, however, have been modelled on much older heathen rituals. Supporting this theory is the fact that we know of similar ceremonies connected to wedding parties or harvesting from the late Middle Ages and later. As early as in 1903, Andreas

Heusler pointed out in an article that stanzas like those which are found in the Icelandic *Vǫlsa þáttr* may have existed in a long-lived tradition connected to wedding parties and harvesting feasts.[37] A parlour game which included the sex organ of an animal (or something looking like it) being sent around among the guests, who had to recite a stanza or some rhymed words over it, is found in several places, and the custom is especially well documented in Iceland and in the Faeroe Islands.[38]

A very interesting Old Norse text which must be seen in connection with the parlour game mentioned above is called *Grettisfærsla*. Chapter 52 of *Grettis saga*, which is one of the later sagas of the Icelanders from around 1300, tells how Grettir, who was an outlaw, was once taken prisoner by the farmers in the district where he had committed many crimes. They planned to keep him imprisoned until they found the chieftain of the district, but the problem was that none of the farmers wanted to receive him, and therefore all of them tried to send him to someone else. The author of the saga comments:

> Ok eptir þessu viðtali þeira hafa kátir menn sett frœði þat, er Grettisfœrsla hét, ok aukit þar í kátligum orðum til gamans mǫnnum.[39]

> [And on the basis of their conversation lively chaps have composed the text of learning called *Grettisfærsla* and interpolated it with randy words for the amusement of men.]

This poem (*frœði*, 'text of learning', must be ironic) is only mentioned, not quoted, in all manuscripts except one. In the manuscript AM 556a 4to at the Stofnun Árna Magnússonar í íslenskum fræðum, Reykjavík, from the end of the fifteenth century a text with the title *Grettisfærsla* was added to the saga. The text is preserved in a very fragmentary state, and has in fact been erased, probably around the time of the Reformation. Today it is possible, however, to read some words in ultraviolet light. This text describes a certain Grettir, who is probably to be understood as a personified penis. He has sexual intercourse with everything that moves, both on two and four legs, old creatures and young and of both sexes, even with the pope in Rome.[40]

---

[37] Heusler, 'Die Geschichte vom Völsi'.

[38] See Ólafur Halldórsson, 'Grettisfœrsla', especially pp. 41–50 with references to sources and literature on the subject.

[39] *Grettis saga Ásmundarsonar*, ed. by Guðni Jónsson, p. 168.

[40] What is legible of the text has been edited by Ólafur Halldórsson, 'Grettisfœrsla', pp. 22–24.

Ólafur Halldórsson drew the conclusion that the text preserved in AM 556a 4to was not a poem about the hero of *Grettis saga*, but a text of the type mentioned above and documented in later Icelandic folk tradition. He suggests that the text was added to *Grettis saga* because of a misunderstanding. Since the personified penis is called Grettir, the writer of the manuscript AM 556a 4to wrongly identified this text with the text mentioned in *Grettis saga* Chapter 52. Ólafur Halldórsson hints at another possibility. He suggests that the scene where the farmers refuse to receive Grettir and send him on to the next one could be modelled on the parlour games mentioned above.[41] However, if the scene in the saga was modelled on such games, the poem made about this incident would also have been modelled on the kind of poetry connected to these games, making *Grettisfærsla* a sort of parody of that poetry and meaning that it is a poem about Grettir after all. The sexual excesses of the hero mentioned in the saga may have motivated the choice of model. However, what is important here is that if *Grettisfærsla* is a sort of parody, the poetry of which it is a parody must have been well known. A parody of unknown types of texts would make little sense.

Like female mourning songs, the type of songs which may have been rooted in the same tradition as the cult songs that are mentioned by Adam of Bremen are not well documented in the written sources from the Middle Ages. However, the sources we have indicate that this kind of poetry was both long-lived and vital in the oral culture.

Conclusion

Female mourning songs and cult songs connected to a fertility cult are of course very different kinds of poetry. However, if we take both of these two lost, or nearly lost, genres into consideration, a picture emerges of a pre-literate Old Norse society slightly different from the one we find in textbooks based on the written genres.

One striking difference is that female poetry was much more important in Nordic culture in pre-Christian and early Christian times than the written sources indicate. Female mourning songs must have been rather widespread. We do not know whether mourning songs were performed as part of the funeral ceremonies regardless of the status of the dead person, or whether only some dead persons were honoured with mourning songs. Most dead people,

---

[41] Ólafur Halldórsson, 'Grettisfærsla', pp. 48–49.

however, would have left grieving relatives behind, and to express grief over dead family members was most likely looked upon as the decent and right thing to do. It is therefore reasonable to think that female mourning songs were both an important and a frequently performed genre.

Whether, or to what degree, women took part in the performance of the 'obscene' songs mentioned by Adam of Bremen we do not know. The stanzas in *Vǫlsa þáttr*, which may be modelled on songs used in situations which shared some important features with fertility cult, or perhaps replaced fertility cult in Christian times, for instance at harvest celebrations and perhaps weddings, were, according to *Vǫlsa þáttr*, performed by men and women alike. That must also have been the case with the stanzas recited over an animal's sex organ, or something looking like a penis, which was sent from person to person around the table as a form of a parlour game known from later times. Such parlour games took place at gatherings where both men and women were present. The fact that these songs were 'obscene' does not indicate that women did not participate actively in them. There is a very good source that documents that women in the Old Norse society were not especially shy in contexts like this; the sagas about the twelfth-century Icelandic holy bishop Jón report that the Bishop tried to suppress a new kind of dance:

> Leikr sá var kærr mönnum, áðr en hinn heilagi Jón varð biskup, at kveða skyldi karlmaðr til konu í dans blautlig kvæði ok regilig, ok kona til karlmanns mansöngsvísur; [...] [42]
>
> [A game was popular among people before the holy Jón became bishop, namely that men sang mawkish and immoral songs to women in a dance, and women to men songs of love; [...]]

This kind of poetry, which must be different from the later ballads, seems to have been popular for awhile. Together with the genres mentioned above, women's participation in these dialogical songs highlights the fact that women played a more important role in literary life than Old Norse canonical genres indicate.

If we take them into consideration, the poorly documented genres also reveal other characteristics that contribute to a different picture of Old Norse literature: emotions are given more space than we previously thought in that type of literature, and the impression that Old Norse literature is somewhat

---

[42] This information is found with small variations in the different versions of the saga. Here the text is quoted from *Jóns saga*, ed. by Guðbrandr Vigfússon and Jón Sigurðsson, p. 237.

circumspect in regards to sexuality and sexual life is seriously undermined.[43] The mourning songs show that at the very least women were expected to give expression to their feelings. Men were supposed to control their feelings to a much higher degree, and since Old Norse written literature focuses on men much more than on women, we can easily get the impression that feelings were surpressed in Old Norse culture. If we take into consideration typical female genres and literature that focuses on women, we obtain a fuller picture of Old Norse literature and culture.

The songs that Adam of Bremen characterized as obscene and the texts mentioned above, although later and poorly documented, were, in my opinion, most likely related, and may have been much more popular and well known in the oral culture than we can deduce from the written record. One factor in explaining why such texts are scarcely transmitted in writing is obviously that the Church did not favour such expressions of popular culture.[44] Another reason for the scant documentation of both mourning songs and the more 'indecent' poetry has to do with the fact that these genres were improvised, and not memorized textual forms.

Correcting the impression that Old Norse culture was completely dominated by the type of poetry that has been characterized as memorized poetry is perhaps the most important insight gained by including mourning songs and the 'indecent' popular poetry into the material on which Old Norse poetry has to be judged. It is generally agreed that skaldic poetry must be regarded as memorized poetry. When skaldic stanzas were composed the skald could improvise by using stereotypical language, composing *kenningar* on the basis of older *kenningar*, and so on. However, when a skaldic stanza was later recited, there was in principle no place for improvisation. There has been discussion of whether Eddic poetry should be regarded as memorized or improvised poetry.[45] The Eddic metres would make minor changes to a stanza from one performance to another possible. The great majority of scholars will, however, agree that Eddic poetry must be characterized as memorized poetry. If we think of typical memorized and improvised poetry as the two extreme points at each end of a line, skaldic poetry would be very close to the end of the line marked 'memorized'. Eddic poetry would also — according to the view held by most scholars — be found on the line much closer to the 'memorized' end of the scale.

---

[43] Concerning the latter of these themes, see Mundal, 'Holdninga til erotikk i norrøn dikting'.

[44] See Mundal, 'Holdninga til erotikk i norrøn dikting', p. 39.

[45] For an overview of the discussion, see Thorvaldsen, '*Svá er sagt í fornum vísindum*', pp. 19–34.

The poetry discussed in this article must be placed closer to the other extreme. I have argued that female mourning songs were improvised poetry to the extreme degree that individual poems never existed in the oral tradition. The individual poems were a one-time performance that were made up of more or less fixed lines and stock phrases that existed within the tradition. This type of poetry was at least as close to the extreme 'improvised' point as the skaldic poetry was to the extreme 'memorized' point. The coarse oral poetry of the type found in *Vǫlsa þáttr* may also be a kind of poetry that did not exist as a poem in oral tradition. What existed were lines, stereotyped images, and stock phrases that were combined in continuously new variations when poetry of this kind was performed.[46] The same may be the case with the dances that the holy bishop Jón tried to stop, although this is difficult to say with certainty.

The nearly lost genres discussed in this article may not be literature of the same quality as skaldic and Eddic poetry; however, if we take these genres into consideration we will obtain a fuller picture of the oral poetry that existed in preliterate Nordic culture, which seems to have been much broader in both content and style than the poetry that was committed to writing.

---

[46] The rhymed text which is added to *Grettis saga* in one of the manuscripts was written down in the Middle Ages and seems to have existed as a poem or rhymed text in the oral tradition. However, this case may be special if the text is about Grettir, the hero of *Grettis saga*, and modelled on improvised poetry of the kind used at harvest feasts and wedding parties.

Works Cited

Primary Sources

Adam von Bremen, *Adam von Bremen: Hamburgische Kirchengeschichte*, ed. by Bernhard Schmeidler (Hannover: Hahn, 1917)

Brennu-Njáls saga, ed. by Einar Ól. Sveinsson, Íslenzk fornrit, 12 (Reykjavík: Hið íslenzka fornritafélag, 1954)

Den norsk-islandske skjaldedigtning, ed. by Finnur Jónsson, 4 vols in two sections (København: Gyldendal, 1912–15)

Fagrskinna, ed. by Bjarni Einarsson, Íslenzk fornrit, 29, (Reykjavík: Hið íslenzka fornritafélag, 1984)

Flateyjarbók, ed. by C. R. Unger and Guðbrandur Vigfússon, 3 vols (Christiania: Malling, 1860–68)

Grettis saga Ásmundarsonar, ed. by Guðni Jónsson, Íslenzk fornrit, 7 (Reykjavík: Hið íslenzka fornritafélag, 1936)

History of the Archbishops of Hamburg-Bremen, trans. by Francis J. Tuschan, Records of Western Civilization (New York: Columbia University Press, 2002)

Jóns saga hins helga eptir Gunnlaug múnk, in *Biskupa sögur*, ed. by Guðbrandr Vigfússon and Jón Sigurðsson, 2 vols (København: Hið íslenzka bókmentafélag, 1858–78), I, 213–60

Klaeber's Beowulf and the Fight at Finnsburg, ed. by R. D. Fulk, Robert E. Bjork, and John D. Niles, 4th edn (Toronto: University of Toronto Press, 2008)

Norges innskrifter med de yngre runer, ed. by Magnus Olsen, 6 vols (Oslo: Kjeldeskriftfondet, 1941–90)

Norrøn Fornkvæði: Islandsk Samling af folkelige Oldtidsdigte om Nordens Guder og Heroer almindelig kaldet Sæmundar Edda hins fróða, ed. by Sophus Bugge (Oslo: Universitetsforlaget, 1965)

Upplands runinskrifter, ed. with commentary by E. Wessén and S. B. F. Jansson, vols VI–IX of *Sveriges runinskrifter* (Stockholm: Almqvist & Wiksell, 1940–78)

Secondary Works

Clover, Carol J., '"Cold are the Counsels of Women": The Tradition Behind the Tradition', in *The Sixth International Saga Conference 28.7.–2.8. 1985, Workshop Papers* (København: Arnamagnæanske Institut, 1985), pp. 151–75

——, 'Hildigunnr's Lament', in *Structure and Meaning in Old Norse Literature: New Approaches to Textual Analysis and Literary Criticism*, ed. by John Lindow, Lars Lönnroth, and Gerd Wolfgang Weber, The Viking Collection, 3 (Odense: Odense Universitetsforlag, 1986), pp. 141–83

Gunnell, Terry, *The Origins of Drama in Scandinavia* (Cambridge: Brewer, 1995)

——, 'The Play of Skírnir: A New Look at the Old Idea of Ancient Scandinavian Drama', *Nordic Theatre Studies*, 7 (1995), 21–35

Harris, Joseph, 'The Bällsta-Inscriptions and Old Norse Literary History', in *International Scandinavian and Medieval Studies in Memory of Gerd Wolfgang Weber*, ed. by Michael Dallapiazza and others (Trieste: Pernaso, 2000), pp. 223–39

——, 'Elegy in Old English and Old Norse: A Problem in Literary History', in *The Vikings*, ed. by Robert T. Farrell (London: Phillimore, 1982), pp. 157–64

Heusler, Andreas, *Die altgermanische Dichtung*, 2nd edn (Potsdam: Athenaion, 1941)

——, 'Die Geschichte vom Völsi, eine altnordische Bekehrungsanekdote', *Zeitschrift des Vereins für Volkskunde*, 13 (1903), 24–39

——, 'Heimat und Alter der eddischen Gedichte: das isländische Sondergut', in *Kleine Schriften*, 4 vols (Berlin: de Gruyter, 1969–78), II, 165–94

Janson, Henrik, *Templum nobilissimum: Adam av Bremen, Uppsalatemplet och konfliktlinjerna i Europa kring år 1075*, Avhandlingar från Historiska institutionen i Göteborg, 21 (Göteborg: Historiska institutionen, 1998)

Jansson, Sven B. F., *Runinskrifter i Sverige* (Stockholm: AWE/Gebers, 1963)

Jón Helgason, 'Bällsta-inskriftens "i grati"', *Arkiv för nordisk filologi*, 59 (1944), 159–62

Mundal, Else, 'Æ standa mér augo / of eld til gráfeldar: ein mansong til Haraldr gráfeldr?', in *Festskrift til Alfred Jakobsen*, ed. by Jan Ragnar Hagland, Jan Terje Faarlund, and Jarle Rønhovd (Trondheim: Tapir, 1987), pp. 120–29

——, 'Holdninga til erotikk i norrøn dikting', in *Kjønn – erotikk – religion*, ed. by Einar Ådland and Kirsten Bang, Bergen Museums skrifter, 9 (Bergen: University of Bergen, 2001), pp. 28–40

——, 'The Position of Women in Old Norse Society and the Basis for their Power', *NORA: Nordic Journal of Women's Studies*, 1 (1994), 3–11

Ólafur Halldórsson, 'Grettisfœrsla', in *Grettisfœrsla: safn ritgerða eftir Ólaf Halldórsson gefið út á sjötugsafmæli hans 18. Apríl 1990*, ed. by Sigurgeir Steingrímsson, Stefán Karlsson, and Sverrir Tómasson (Reykjavík: Stofnun Árna Magnússonar, 1990), pp. 19–50

Phillpotts, Bertha, *The Elder Edda and Ancient Scandinavian Drama* (Cambridge: Cambridge University Press, 1920)

Sävborg, Daniel, *Sorg och elegi i Eddans hjältediktning*, Acta Universitatis Stockholmiensis, Stockholm Studies in History of Literature, 36 (Stockholm: Almqvist and Wiksell, 1997)

See, Klaus von, 'Das Phantom einer altgermanischer Elegiendichtung: Kritische Bemerkungen zu Daniel Sävborg, "Sorg och elegi i Eddans hjältediktning"', *Skandinavistik*, 28 (1998), 87–100

Steinsland, Gro, and Kari Vogt, '"Aukinn ertu Uolsi ok upp um tekinn": en religionshistorisk analyse av Vǫlsaþáttr i *Flateyjarbók*', *Arkiv för nordisk filologi*, 96 (1981), 87–106

Thorvaldsen, Bernt Øyvind, '*Svá er sagt í fornum vísindum*: tekstualiseringen av de mytologiske eddadikt' (unpublished doctoral dissertation, Universitetet i Bergen, 2007)

Vésteinn Ólason, 'Eddukvæði', in *Íslenzk bókmenntasaga*, ed. by Guðrún Nordal, Sverrir Tómasson, and Vésteinn Ólason, 2 vols (Reykjavík: Mál og Menning, 1992–93), I, 75–187 and 576–80

'She was fulfilled, she was filled by it...': A Karelian Popular Song of St Mary and the Conception of Christ

Senni Timonen

The Song of Mary

The Song of Mary or Christ is an epic folk song composed in indigenous Finnish-Karelian Kalevala metre, depicting the life of Christ from conception to resurrection. The name of the protagonist varies depending on who is understood as the main hero or heroine of the song.

Scholars have agreed that this song — or, more accurately, song cycle — was composed in the Middle Ages. Yet opinions concerning exact dates and sources vary. This song was originally thought to be of Roman Catholic origin.[1] In 1963, when more eastern parallels had been found,[2] Matti Kuusi, a folklorist, presented a new theory: the song may have been created by an early missionary of the Eastern Church, before the activity of the Western Church in Finland began.[3] Later Heikki Kirkinen, a historian, could date at least the Karelian

---

[1] Borenius, 'Suomen keskiaikaista runoutta I'; Krohn and Krohn, *Kantelettaren tutkimuksia*, II; Haavio, *Suomalaisen muinaisrunouden maailma*, p. 67.

[2] See especially Haavio, 'Jumala-kuningas ja hänen vastustajansa', and Haavio, 'Jeesus-lapsi ja hänen ahdistajansa'.

[3] Kuusi, 'Keskiajan kalevalainen runous', p. 297. The theory of early Eastern Christian influence in Finland is based mainly on linguistic evidence: the Finnish words *pappi* (priest), *risti* (cross), *raamattu* (Bible, book), and *pakana* (pagan) are thought to derive from Old Russian. In addition, some archaeological eastern material is found in western parts of Finland. Finnish

form of the cycle to the late Middle Ages (in Karelia *c.* 1400–1500), because by that time the Eastern form of Christianity had been established in Archangel Karelia, where the fullest cycles of the song have been recorded.[4]

In its preserved forms the song consists of six or seven main sections, which are supposed to originally have been separate songs. In the course of time singers formed more or less fixed chains of them, in some regions coherent epics; this is how other epic cycles also evolved.[5] A single variant is usually composed of two, three, four, or five of these sections, depending on the local tradition or on the singer.[6]

The main parts of the epic are as follows:

1. *The Song of the Berry* tells how the Virgin becomes pregnant by eating a berry, an apple, or a nut.

2. *The Song of the Search for a Bathhouse* tells how Mary is looking for a *sauna* where she can give birth to her son (or wash him), but is driven away to a stable.

3. *The Song of St Stephen* tells how Tapani, a stableman of Ruotus (Herodes), sees a star while giving water to his horse and leaves Ruotus because a new lord is born.

4. *The Song of the Sowing Miracle* tells how Mary, escaping the Jews with her son, meets a sower; a moment later the corn is miraculously ripened, and the sower saves the mother and child by telling the Jews that he saw them long ago, in sowing time.

5. *The Song of the Search for the Lost Child* tells how Mary loses her child and sets off to look for him, asking everything she encounters on her way — the road, the moon, the star, and the sun — whether they have seen him. The sun tells the truth: he is in the grave.

---

historians still believe today that even if these facts point to eastern contacts they are too random to give proof of any systematic missionary activity, not to mention Christianization (compare, for example, Purhonen, *Kristinuskon saapumisesta Suomeen*, pp. 142–45; Hiekkanen, *Suomen keskiajan kivikirkot*, p. 12).

[4] Kirkinen, *Pohjois-Karjalan kalevalaisen perinteen juuret*, p. 112.

[5] The most famous Kalevala-metre cycle is the Sampo cycle, which contains myths (for example the beginning of the world) and heroic adventures; see *Finnish Folk Poetry*, ed. by Kuusi, Bosley, and Branch, pp. 110–34, 525–29.

[6] See *Finnish Folk Poetry*, ed. by Kuusi, Bosley, and Branch, pp. 283–302 for texts, English translations, and commentaries of some representative variants.

6. *The Song of the Resurrection* is the Christ-oriented part of the cycle. The sun melts the rocks allowing Christ to rise up from the grave. However, in many variants it is Mary who becomes the subject and asks the sun for help.

7. *The Song of the Shackling of the Devil (Hiisi)* tells how, after rising from the tomb, Christ goes to the forge of the Devil's smith (i.e. Hell), and by means of a trick shackles him to a rock for eternity. But again, Mary has often become the protagonist of this song — it is she who goes to Hell and captures the Devil.

A thorough study of this song cycle has not yet been undertaken. Nevertheless, its contents have been defined, the relations of some of its parts to the Bible have been discussed, and its possible contacts with other Kalevala poetry themes, church paintings, and some European legends and songs have been outlined.[7] The background is biblical, but as can be seen, the Bible story is often quite distant. For songs 2, 4, and 5 of the central 'Marian' songs the nearest folk-song parallels have been found from Romania and Ukraine,[8] for song 6 from the Orthodox Setu tradition in Estonia,[9] and for song 7 from the Eurasian myth tradition and its popular Christian variations in Ukraine, Estonia, and Livonia.[10] The Song of St Stephen (3), known as a separate song in Lutheran Finland and only seldom connected to our song, is the only theme clearly of Scandinavian origin (cf. Staffansvisa).[11] But sources or near parallels have not been found for all features in this cycle; for example, the active role of the sun is perhaps of Finnish or Karelian origin, or derives from an unknown source.

A problem is that the closest folk-song parallels for some Marian parts of the song have been found from White Russia and the South Slavs, but not from northern Russia. Was the north Russian religious folklore not well collected or published, or had it vanished before the time of collecting? Heikki Kirkinen, the only historian who has written of this song, considers it possible that the sources of information and inspiration may have come to Karelia directly

---

[7] Borenius, 'Suomen keskiaikaista runoutta I'; Krohn and Krohn, *Kantelettaren tutkimuksia*, II; Haavio, *Kirjokansi*, pp. 349–67; Haavio, 'Jumala-kuningas ja hänen vastustajansa'; Haavio, 'Jeesus-lapsi ja hänen ahdistajansa'; Kuusi, 'Keskiajan kalevalainen runous', pp. 292–97; Kirkinen, *Pohjois-Karjalan kalevalaisen perinteen juuret*, pp. 110–12; Oinas, 'The Search for the Lost Child'; Asplund, 'Legendenlieder'.

[8] Kuusi, 'Keskiajan kalevalainen runous', p. 295; Haavio, 'Jeesus-lapsi ja hänen ahdistajansa'; Oinas, 'The Search for the Lost Child'.

[9] Krohn and Krohn, *Kantelettaren tutkimuksia*, II, 189–92.

[10] Haavio, 'Jumala-kuningas ja hänen vastustajansa'.

[11] Krohn and Krohn, *Kantelettaren tutkimuksia*, II, 8–43; Haavio, *Kirjokansi*, pp. 354–60.

from the South Slavs or Byzantium. In the Middle Ages the main route from Constantinople to the north and vice versa went through the economically and spiritually powerful Kiev, the medieval Russian centre where Christianity had entered from Byzantium. From these southern routes the traders, pilgrims, monks, and itinerant singers may have brought some of the core ideas from these songs — or even complete songs — to Karelia.[12]

It must be emphasized that no medieval texts of the song exist to support any of the datings which have been presented. The oldest references to the Song of Mary/Christ are from the end of the seventeenth century. In 1690 Matthias Salamnius, a priest, wrote his *Ilo-laulu Jesuxesta* (Joy Song of Christ), written in flawless Kalevala metre and with allusions to traditional songs, among them the Song of Christ.[13] And in 1697 Erik Cajanus, a future priest, presented in his academic study two lines from our folk song in which, he said, the whole history of the Passion is told in an utterly elegant way by an unknown author ('tota historia passionis Christi elegantissime tractatur, autore nescio quo').[14] These references to the song show that it was known as a cycle at least in the latter half of the seventeenth century.

Fragments of the song are known from the eighteenth century,[15] but the first complete text was not recorded until 1825 in Archangel Karelia by the young A. J. Sjögren, later a linguist and academician in St Petersburg.[16] After him, generations of collectors recorded its variants, and it is richly represented in the archive materials: 356 variants of the song have been found from Karelia and Ingria. Almost all of its singers have been Russian Orthodox, and most of them women.

Even if it is uncertain whether these songs were originally composed in Roman Catholic pre-Finland or in Orthodox Karelia, and whether this happened in the

---

[12] Personal discussion with Heikki Kirkinen, 2007. Compare Kirkinen, *Karjala idän kulttuuripiirissä*, pp. 41–51. Kirkinen is himself Karelian and has concentrated in his research on the early history of Karelia.

[13] Tarkiainen, 'Suomalainen messiadi', pp. 69–71; Sarajas, *Suomen kansanrunouden tuntemus*, pp. 86–88; Kuusi, 'Salamnius, Matthias'.

[14] Sarajas, *Suomen kansanrunouden tuntemus*, pp. 92–93; Krohn and Krohn, *Kantelettaren tutkimuksia*, II, 117–18. These writers were born in northern Finland in regions where Kalevala poetry still flourished, and Salamnius worked as a priest in central Ingria, near the villages from which the Izhor Song of Mary was later recorded.

[15] *Suomen kansan vanhat runot*, ed. by Niemi and others, XV, nos 79–80; compare Krohn and Krohn, *Kantelettaren tutkimuksia*, II, 115–17.

[16] *Suomen kansan vanhat runot*, ed. by Niemi and others, I. 2, no. 1117.

early or later Middle Ages or even later, it is nevertheless a fact that they were remembered in Orthodox Karelia and Ingria, and it was there they flourished and reached the forms in which we know them now.

I have previously analysed this entire epic from a feminist viewpoint, that is, by focusing on the meanings that the Karelian singers, women from whom the texts were written down, gave to Mary in the nineteenth century.[17] The Virgin in the song seemed to me to have been both a representative of holiness and of human, bodily femininity. Most astonishing was the centrality of St Mary and her heroic activity in this epic, which struck me as utterly non-canonical: the complete opposite of the St Mary in the Bible and in the ecclesiastical tradition.[18] In my eyes this song was a brilliant demonstration of the twofold nature of great folk art and myth as both an ideal (a model) for and a self-portrait (a picture) of its singers.[19]

In my current research of the St Mary songs, I will not ignore the feminist point of view, but will expand on the research problems. My intention is to analyse the song's construction through a textual analysis of each part of the epic in order to identify the Christian and indigenous elements on the basis of which the song is composed and to understand the cultural backgrounds of the motifs and especially their meanings in these particular songs. In this article I shall concentrate on the first part of the epic, that is, on narration in the song telling of the conception of Christ: the Song of the Berry.

Context: The Kalevala-Metre Tradition

The central background and context of this song, and the cycle as a whole, is the so-called Kalevala metre and the traditional culture expressed in it. This metre is a Finnic phenomenon used in the old folk songs of Finns, Karelians, Izhors, Votes, and Estonians. Its prosodic structure is unrhymed, non-strophic, trochaic tetrameter, based on both the length of the syllables and on their stress.[20]

---

[17] Timonen, 'The Mary of Women's Epic'.

[18] I later found that feminist theologians have also found St Mary's hidden female strength in the Bible; compare for example Vuola, '*La morenita* on Skis'.

[19] This view was influenced by Clifford Geertz's famous article 'Religion as a Cultural System' (1973): religious symbols provide a 'model of' and 'model for' the life of the believers.

[20] The metre is enlivened by a balanced alternation of normal (in which the word stress and the poetic stress coincide) and broken (in which they do not coincide) trochaic lines: '*läk*si / *mar*jam / *poi*min/*ta*ha' (normal, = she went to pick the berry); '*mar*ja/ṅi mä/*jel*tä / *huu*si' (broken, = a berry called from the hill).

Kalevala metre is thought to have evolved during the Proto-Finnic period.[21] Although its exact prehistory remains unclear, it is now assumed to have developed in the context of singing and to have emerged 'as a spontaneous reaction to the phonetic and prosodic development of Proto-Finnic'.[22] The classical form of the metre seems to have travelled with Finnish settlers in the ninth century to Ancient Karelia in the northern and north-western shores of Lake Ladoga, where its richest forms were developed and spread towards the north, south, and west. The metre became so popular and flexible that it served as the main prosodic form of most sung and recited genres. It had vanished almost completely in western and southern Finland by the time of the Reformation, but in eastern Finland, Karelia, and Ingria it was more or less in use until the beginning of the twentieth century.[23]

There are about 150,000 texts representing Finnish, Karelian, Izhor, and Vote forms of this poetry in the archives of the Finnish Literature Society; in Estonia (Tartu) they probably have even more Estonian material, and in Russia (Petrozavodsk) there is plenty of Karelian material.[24] Abundant material is thus available. But if our intention is to study medieval poetry, for example, we face a problem. The main bulk of the texts were collected in the nineteenth century. How do we know what songs, and what features, images, perhaps lines, in these songs, are of medieval origin? The situation is in a way similar when we speak, for example, of the medieval ballads of Scandinavia, or of the medieval Christian traditions preserved in modern European folklore.[25] On the

---

[21] The dating is based on many factors, for example the areal/demographical distribution of the metre and the historical evolution of the Finnic languages.

[22] Leino, *Language and Metre*, p. 140; Leino, 'The Kalevala Metre'; personal discussion with Pentti Leino, 2008. This means that the metre is of indigenous origin. Compare Matti Kuusi's opinion that the Kalevala metre emerged as a result of early contacts between western Proto-Finns and ancient Balts; Kuusi, 'Questions of Kalevala Metre', p. 54.

[23] For the metre, see e.g. *Finnish Folk Poetry*, ed. by Kuusi, Bosley, and Branch, pp. 62–65; Kuusi, 'Questions of Kalevala Metre'; Leino, *Language and Metre*, pp. 129–49; Leino, 'The Kalevala Metre'; for the melody and the metre together, see Laitinen, 'Anni Tenisovan Marian virsi'.

[24] Most of the material in Finland is published in *Suomen kansan vanhat runot*, ed. by Niemi and others. Of the editions of the Karelian material in Petrozavodsk, see for example *Karjalan kansan runot*, ed. by Jevsejev; of the Estonian materials Ülo Tedre's anthology *Eesti rahvalaulud: antoloogia*, ed. by Tedre gives a general picture; comprehensive areal editions are published in the series Vana Kannel (Old Kantele) and Setukeste laulud (The Songs of the Setu People).

[25] For example, for the Hungarian religious folklore, see Kriza, 'The Survival of Medieval Tradition'.

other hand, the Finnish-Karelian case is different because the Kalevala-metre materials also contain layers from older eras.

Generations of Finnish folklorists have made efforts to create a chronology of the Kalevala poetry. The datings differ from each other a lot, because they depend on current research trends and also on individual backgrounds and ideologies. Yet all agree that Christian themes began to be cast in the Kalevala metre in the Middle Ages, and that their expansive adaptation in this oral local culture proves that the Christianization process took root among Finns and Karelians. As Christianity came to Finland and Karelia partly from the West and partly from the East, the Christian themes and features are here partly of western, partly of eastern origin. Christian features appear in the Kalevala-metre poetry mainly in incantations (charms) and narrative songs. God, Jesus, Mary, and the saints began to be prayed to for help and occupy heroic positions, together with or fighting against the indigenous pre-Christian gods, spirits, and heroes.[26]

All this is logical: before the Christianization of the singers (or before they adopted Christian ideas) these themes could not have occurred in the Kalevala poetry. Another, more complicated problem is when, how, and to what extent Christianity was internalized, and when and how these songs and charms evolved and reached the forms in which they were written down so much later.

In Lutheran Finland the Reformation has given another dating point: the core of the Kalevala-metre prayers to St Mary, for example, is certainly of Catholic origin. The abundance of these prayers to Mary in the materials collected in Finland in the nineteenth and twentieth centuries bears witness to the depth and long duration of popular internalization of St Mary.[27] Thus she was not forgotten even under the pressure of the Reformation and the centuries of Lutheran teaching.

The dating of Karelian and Izhor religious folk poetry is different, because in Orthodox Karelia and Ingria Eastern Christianity, and with it the veneration of Mary, has continued uninterrupted from the Middle Ages up to the nineteenth century. It is there and only there that the epic song depicting the life of Mary and her son has been recorded.

[26] Compare for example Haavio, *Suomalaisen muinaisrunouden maailma*, pp. 62–64; Kuusi, 'Pakanuuden ja kristinuskon murros'; Kuusi, 'Keskiajan kalevalainen runous'; Sarmela, *Volksüberlieferung*, trans. by Mahringer and others, pp. 28–29; Siikala, *Mythic Images and Shamanism*, pp. 339–42.

[27] St Mary is the person who is most often prayed to in Kalevala-metre incantations and charms; see Vilkuna, 'Maria i folketraditionen', p. 373.

The Distribution of the Conception Song

The structure of the Song of Mary/Christ varies greatly; thus the number and distribution of the variants of single themes vary, too. The conception theme does not occur in all texts, and when it does, the forms of narration can differ from each other. This is interesting for many reasons, not least because different variations can tell of the history of the songs as well as of the varying circumstances and interpretations of the singers.

There are three important areal traditions or forms of the Song of the Berry (see Map 2). The first and richest form has flourished in Archangel Karelia in the North (eighty-three variants). The second form, sung in Olonets Karelia (twenty-two variants) and to a certain extent in Ladoga Karelia (thirteen variants), shows that this epic was in a dynamic process of change in these regions at the time of collection. The third, southern tradition, that of Izhors, was recorded only in two Ingrian coastal villages, where other archaic versions of Kalevala poetry have also survived (seven variants).[28] It is worth noting that all these areas are borderlands between Eastern and Western Christendom, between two states, and accordingly, between two cultures. Archangel and Olonets Karelia have belonged to Novgorod and later to Russia from the Middle Ages, as has Ingria, with the exception of a hundred-year episode of Swedish rule (1617–1721). Ladoga Karelia, originally under Novgorod and Russia, has at times been incorporated into Swedish realms and later Finland (e.g. from 1617–1721 it belonged with the rest of Finland to Sweden), at times to Russia.[29]

Of all these regions, the Karelians and Izhors have, nevertheless, a more or less common prehistory. They derive from the same Eastern Finnic group, living around Lake Ladoga and evolving during the first millennium into Karelians along the northern and western shores of Lake Ladoga (and later expanding to Archangel and Olonets), and into Izhors on the southern coast of the Gulf of Finland.[30] Both the Karelians and Izhors were Christianized slowly from the

---

[28] Most of this material is published in the *Suomen kansan vanhat runot*, ed. by Niemi and others; unpublished texts and tape recordings are in the Folklore Archives of the Finnish Literature Society, with some also in the publications and archives of the Karelian Research Center of the Russian Academy of Sciences, Petrozavodsk.

[29] See for example Kirkinen, *Karjala idän kulttuuripiirissä*; Kirkinen, *Karjala taistelukenttänä*, II; Korpela, *Viipurin linnaläänin synty*.

[30] Vepsians also belonged to this supposed pre-group. See Uino, 'Viikinkiaika n. 800–1100 jKr.', p. 380; Leskinen, 'Karjalaisten kielimuotojen alkuperän arvoitus', p. 448. Earlier it was

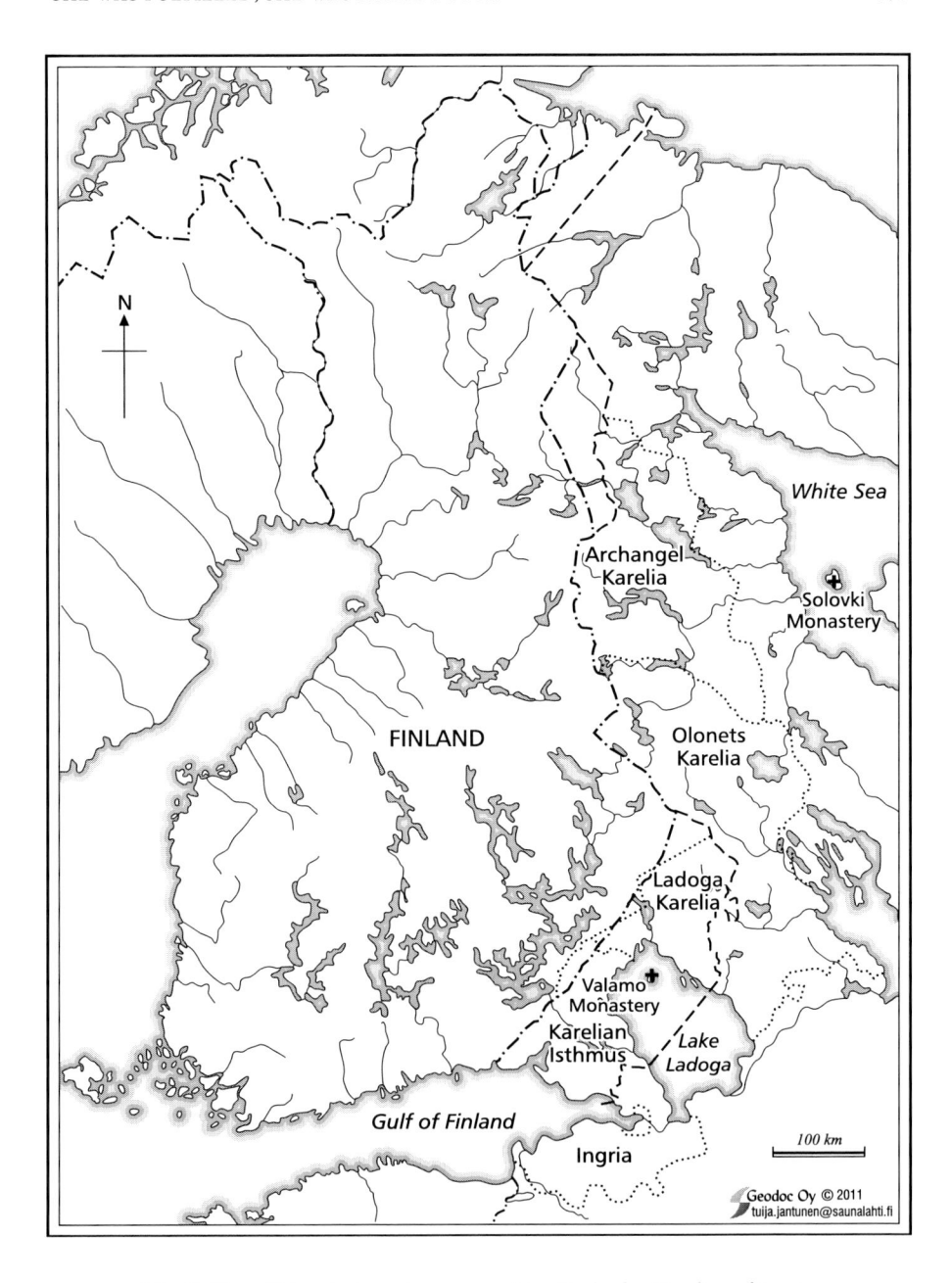

Map 2. Map of historical provinces comprising Orthodox Karelia and Ingria. The influential monasteries of Valamo and Solovki were founded in the Middle Ages. Here, both the present-day border and the course of the border in the period 1920–39 between Finland and Russia have been given. © Geodoc Oy, tuija.jantunen@saunalahti.fi

beginning of the second millennium on.[31] By 1500 the Karelian and Izhor areas seem to have had quite systematic networks of Orthodox churches, chapels, and monasteries,[32] although the internalization process took place over a much longer period. From the seventeenth century onwards many Karelians, and to some extent Izhors as well, joined to the Old Belief sect,[33] which may be reflected in their religious songs.

The material — 118 variants in all of the Song of the Berry — was collected between 1825 and 1970. Of the singers, eighty-six are identifiable.[34] As guides to the songs I will follow three singers, one from each tradition. The Archangel Karelian version is represented by a famous singer in Vuokkiniemi in the village of Latvajärvi, Arhippa Perttunen (1769–1839), whose songs have perhaps had the most influence on Elias Lönnrot's *Kalevala*. His variant from 1834 is 294 lines long in its entirety, and also contains the Song of the Search for a Bathhouse, and the Song of the Search for the Lost Child. The Olonets Karelian version is represented by Okuli (Okki) Gordeinen (born *c*. 1835) in Repola in the village of Suulaansaari. Her variant from the year 1897 is 145 lines long, and it also includes the Song of the Search for a Bathhouse, the Song of the Search for the Lost Child, and the Song of the Shackling of the Devil. The Izhor tradition is represented by Taroi, Päntty's daughter (b. 1819), in Hevaa, Lenttisi village. The length of her variant from the year 1891 is 251 lines, including also the Song of the Search for a Bathhouse, the Song of St Stephen, the Song of

thought that the Izhors had separated from the Karelians, but new archaeological evidence seems to show the continuity of the Izhor settlements in Ingria. Nevertheless, these questions remain debated — for example Jukka Korpela considers that it is not wise to set up ethnic boundaries between the Izhors, Karelians, Votes, etc. of these times (Korpela, *Viipurin linnaläänin synty*, p. 23).

[31] Christian ideas may have reached them very early because they were living near the trade routes to the south (compare note 12 above). After reading Janson, *Från Bysans till Norden* and having conversations with Henrik Janson, I began to understand how much international movement there was at that time; thus the Izhors and Karelians must have also adopted Western Christian motifs. Compare also Korpela, *Viipurin linnaläänin synty*, pp. 43–47.

[32] Kirkinen, 'Inkerin keskiaika ja uuden ajan alku vuoteen 1616', pp. 58–60.

[33] See for example Kuujo, 'Ruotsi vai Venäjä Antikristuksen valtakunta?'; Pentikäinen, *Oral Repertoire and World View*, pp. 100–20; Shikalov, 'Old Believers in the Kemi Jurisdictional District'.

[34] Earlier collectors seldom mentioned singers, but later collectors, on the other hand, recorded this song multiple times from some singers. All this means is that the number of the texts is not the same as that of the singers.

the Search for the Lost Child, the Song of the Resurrection, the Song of the Shackling of the Devil, and also additional legend songs.[35]

With these singers, and by seeking additional information from others, I shall present, scene by scene, a popular interpretation of one of the greatest mysteries of the Christian doctrine: the Incarnation.

The Berry Speaks

Marjanen mäeltä huuti	A berry called from the hill
punapuola kankahalta:	a red-berry from the heath:
'Tule neiti poimomahan	'Come, maid, and pick me
vyövaski valitsemahan	copper-belted one, choose me
ennen kun etona syöpi	before the slug devours me
mato musta muikkoali.'	and the black worm gobbles me.'
	(Arhippa, ll. 1–6)

Marjane mäjellä kirgu	A berry shrieked on the hil
buolungaine kangahalla:	A red-berry on the heath:
'Tule vain neiti poimomaha	'Come, maid, and pick me,
sormuskäsi suoltamaha	ring-handed, pull me,
tinarinta riipimähä!'	tin-breasted, pluck me!'
	(Okuli, ll. 24–28)

In Archangel Karelia the text most often begins with this monologue of the berry. A red-berry (*punapuola*)[36] is calling or shouting or shrieking on the hill, on the heath. The berry calls the one it is speaking to *neiti* (a maid) and also describes her appearance by addressing her as 'copper-belted' or 'tin-breasted' or 'ring-handed'; this means that she is unmarried and beautifully adorned with brooches, rings, and belts made of tin and copper.

The berry's suggestion — come and pick me! — is often followed by the lines Arhippa gives above: come before a slug or a black worm eats me. The idiom of the gobbling 'black worm' usually refers to a dangerous snake in

---

[35] The English translations of these texts are by Keith Bosley and taken from *Finnish Folk Poetry*, ed. by Kuusi, Bosley, and Branch, nos 59 (Arhippa, from *Suomen kansan vanhat runot*, ed. by Niemi and others, I. 2, no. 1103), 61 (Okuli, from ibid., II, no. 323a), and 62 (Taroi, from *Suomen kansan vanhat runot*, ed. by Niemi and others, IV. 3, nos 4022–25). I am grateful to Keith Bosley for checking the final texts. Other translations are mine, unless otherwise noted.

[36] Keith Bosley has translated the Karelian word *puola*, *buolungaine* (Vaccinium vitis idaea) as 'red-berry', but in my discussion I use the usual English translation 'lingonberry'.

Finnish-Karelian poetry.[37] Idioms of slugs and maggots refer to the grave, that is, death, in lyric songs in which the singer encourages his/her tongue (i.e. him/herself) to sing: in the grave it cannot sing any more, there 'the maggots of death' and 'the worms of death' will eat it.[38] In the same way the climax of the berry's monologue is dramatic: *Memento mori* — act before it is too late!

A similar monologue from a berry, but in this case a strawberry, was sung in Finland, in Ingria and Karelia as a separate song, without any reference to pregnancy or to St Mary. It could be sung when going to pick berries, or as a lullaby, or when speaking of the relationships of young women and men, especially in wooing or seduction situations.[39] Some scholars have assumed that this little song was adapted in Karelia to the Song of Mary.[40]

The Karelian song does not always begin with the speech of the berry. In Olonets Karelia singers often first describe the girl's long history at home, using exaggerated metaphors: 'sitting in her father's house' she wore trinkets and chains, floorboards, thresholds, and lintel timbers. At last she went out to the field beside the yard, and there she heard the voice of the berry, tells Okuli (ll. 5–23). Occasionally singers describe the girl's everyday work at home in an introduction: Mary was sweeping the floor, and when she carried the rubbish to the field behind the yard she heard the berry's voice from the forest.[41]

These motifs are found in other contexts as well. A girl who has lived long at her parents' home is an introduction to many songs in which the girl later becomes seduced.[42] The floor-sweeping formula works as an introduction in different women's songs; it can be interpreted as flexible poetic material of women. A perhaps random parallel is a Bulgarian Annunciation folk legend, in which Mary is sweeping the floor of the temple where she is living;[43] in a Karelian

---

[37] The 'black worm' as a snake occurs constantly in charms and incantations in Savo and Karelia, see e.g. *Suomen kansan vanhat runot*, ed. by Niemi and others, I. 4, no. 411 in which Arhippa Perttunen tells about the origin of the snake: 'Sai kärmes kähäjämähän, mato musta muikkamahan' (the snake began to wheeze, the black worm to gobble).

[38] See e.g. *Suomen kansan vanhat runot*, ed. by Niemi and others, I. 3, nos 1316, 1405.

[39] See e.g. *Suomen kansan vanhat runot*, ed. by Niemi and others, XIII, no. 748 (when picking berries), III, no. 635 (wooing), IV, no. 2147 (wooing or seduction), XIII, no. 754 ('Is sung meaning that a young woman is wanting suitors'), nos 5165 and 5168 (as a lullaby).

[40] Krohn and Krohn, *Kantelettaren tutkimuksia*, II, 52–53. This view, which indicates that the small song is older, is based on its more extensive distribution, also in Finland and among Lutherans.

[41] *Suomen kansan vanhat runot*, ed. by Niemi and others, I. 2, no. 1098, also in Ladoga Karelia (ibid., VII. 1, no. 738; VII. 4, no. 3013).

[42] Compare for example *Finnish Folk Poetry*, ed. by Kuusi, Bosley, and Branch, no. 71.

[43] Mansikka, 'Legendat ihmeellisestä synnyttämisestä', p. 9.

Figure 14. Icon representing the Annunciation; the icon has been enlarged, the edge has been broadened, and Lord Sabaoth has been added at a later date. Originally from Valamo Monastery, Ladoga Karelia, now held in Kuopio, Suomen Ortodoksinen Kirkkomuseo. Seventeenth century. Reproduced with permission.

version she goes to the shore to moisten her floor brooms.[44] In the apocryphal Book of James she is also performing the traditional tasks of women. When she hears Gabriel's voice for the first time she is going to fetch water from a well; in the second meeting she is weaving a temple cloth.[45] These homely apocryphal scenes were frequently presented in iconography and church art. The singers must have known some forms of these pictorial traditions.

Berry-picking was a domestic chore of Karelian women in late summer and early autumn, so it is no wonder that it occurs as an image in other women's songs too; it is interesting that the berry-picking motif is often connected with danger. One tragic song tells of a mother's death caused by eating the berries her daughter has picked,[46] and in another song the speaker foretells her own death from picking lingonberries.[47]

A touch of danger may even be sensed in the Song of Mary. But it is the motif of addressing and listening that makes this story exceptional. It breaks with everyday routines and common sense. The miracle begins to happen through the voice and through the ear. I posit that before their eyes the singers may have had, among other things, the image of the listening Mary and the angel who is addressing her in the pictorial and verbal Annunciation scenes. Berry's speech and Angel's speech are not necessarily identical, but in some way they echo and continue each other. As the Mary of Annunciation, so the Mary of our song must act instantly — or the crucial moment will be over, and her chance lost.

Mary's Response

Neitsy Maaria emonen	The virgin mother Mary
rakas äiti armollinen	the dear merciful mother
viitisekse vaatisekse	dressed herself and decked herself
pääsomille suorieli	prettily adorned her head
vaattehilla valkehilla.	with a fair white cloth:
Läksi marjan poimentaan	she went to pick the berry
punapuolan katsontaan.	to look for the red-berry.
Niin meni mäille — sano! —	So — she went to the hill — tell! —

(Arhippa, ll. 7–14)

---

[44] Järvinen, *Legendat*, p. 27. It is not yet the Annunciation here, but the first sign referring to it — this double structure may reflect that of the Book of James.

[45] Compare Tuominen, 'The Mother of God Image', pp. 149–50.

[46] Compare *Finnish Folk Poetry*, ed. by Kuusi, Bosley, and Branch, pp. 402–04.

[47] Compare *Suomen kansan vanhat runot*, ed. by Niemi and others, IV, no. 2992; VII.2, no. 2163.

Koppai koisan kobrahase	She snatched a basket
silkin peähäsä sivalti:	slapped a silk scarf on her head:
meät on mätky männessähä	the hills boomed with her going
voarat on notku nousessa.	mountains bent with her climbing.

(Okuli, ll. 29–32)

It now becomes clear of whom the singer speaks and to whom the berry speaks: 'The virgin mother Mary, the dear merciful mother'. This is one of the most popular Mary formulae in the Kalevala-metre poetry; it occurs not only in the Song of Mary but also in numerous incantations in which Mary is asked for help, and not only in Karelia but also in Finland. Interestingly it combines two words for 'mother': the older *emo(nen)* and the newer *äiti*, with *neitsyt* 'virgin', 'girl'; the latter is thought to be a Finnish and not a Karelian form. Some researchers have interpreted the first line as a translation from the Roman Catholic Sanctus Mass from the eleventh century ('Virgo mater Maria'), and 'merciful mother' as an adaptation from Latin *gratia plena, mater gratiae*,[48] but in fact the Eastern hymns combine the words 'virgin' and 'mother' in parallel ways.[49] This simple expression ought to be studied more thoroughly.[50] Other Mary formulae also occur in the variants of this song and in prayers as well: 'Pyhä piika pikkarainen, vaimo valkian verinen' (holy little maid, fair-skinned woman);[51] 'Maaria pyhhäinen vaimo, itse Maaria vahhainen' (Mary holy woman, herself Mary made of wax);[52] 'Muarie matala neiti' (Mary the low/small maid);[53] 'Se oli vanhin vaimoloista, eläjien ensimäinen' (She was the oldest of women, the first of those who live);[54] etc. These formulae emphasize her holiness, her beauty, her purity, her humbleness, and her mythical status as the first of women.

Mary's response to the call of the berry is always immediate, unhesitating, and determined. Here her attitude seems to deviate from that of the scared

---

[48] Krohn, *Suomalaisten runojen uskonto*, p. 216; Haavio, *Suomalaisen muinaisrunouden maailma*, p. 190.

[49] Kirkinen, *Pohjois-Karjalan kalevalaisen perinteen juuret*, p. 113.

[50] A similar problem is the expression 'guds moder' (God's mother) and its variations in early Swedish rune stones; even if Per Beškow has found quite convincing western parallels, the sources are not really resolved until *both* texts, those of the Eastern and Western churches, are compared side by side; see Beškow, 'Runor och liturgi'.

[51] *Suomen kansan vanhat runot*, ed. by Niemi and others, I. 2, no. 1120.

[52] *Suomen kansan vanhat runot*, ed. by Niemi and others, III, no. 1986. The singer explained that *vahhainen* (waxy, made of wax) means 'As pure as a candle made of wax'.

[53] *Suomen kansan vanhat runot*, ed. by Niemi and others, I. 2, no. 1119.

[54] *Suomen kansan vanhat runot*, ed. by Niemi and others, I. 2, no. 1103a.

Mary in many pictorial representations of the Annunciation.⁵⁵ She is not afraid. She wants to go to the hill, to the berry. Her departure is given further significance by the accounts of how she dresses and prepares herself. In Arhippa's variant she puts a *pääsoma* on her head, that is, a beautiful maiden's ribbon, and white clothes; in Okuli's variant she puts a silk scarf on her head; in many others she puts on blue shoes and red laces. Some singers bring formulae from heroic and mythic epics that recount Mary putting on an iron shirt.⁵⁶ The preparations lead up to the verb *went*, which emphasizes Mary's activity and the irresistibility of the call of the berry. The sudden, frenzied nature of departure is emphasized: 'She *snatched up* the basket'; 'She *slapped* a silk scarf on her head.' Sometimes the singers shift to the first person singular: 'I went to pick the berry.'⁵⁷

Arhippa does not describe the journey in more detail, but many others do, and this happens again with lines and phrases reminiscent of men's heroic epics. Okuli says that the hills and mountains were moving under her steps, thus giving the journey a mythic character. In other variants the journey may be of immeasurable length and proceed with giant steps: 'Moved her feet; she was on the third hill. Moved them a second time: she was on the sixth hill. Moved them a third time: she was on the ninth hill.'⁵⁸

The landscape turns into a magnificent creation scene. What she approaches can be interpreted as a mythic world mountain, the centre of the world. It has many parallels in epic Kalevala-metre poetry, in the context of the male hero Väinämöinen, and in the incantations as well: important, mythical things tend to take place on a hill.⁵⁹

The Izhor singers begin from this point, from Mary's journey — in their versions there is no speech by a berry (actually there is no berry at all), nor is there a hill:

Maaria pyhhäin vaimo	Mary the holy woman
vaimo valkiaveriin	the fair-skinned woman
kääyy käpäelöö	went strolling along:
hietroin helmoin heutaisoo	her fine skirt-hems were swaying
puhas paitain povees	on her bosom a clean shirt
silkkiliinain sisääs	under it a silken cloth
vitsa kultainen käees	a golden lash in her hand

---

⁵⁵ See, for example, Hirn, *The Sacred Shrine*, pp. 284–85, and Tuominen, 'The Mother of God Image', p. 150: in the icons Mary is often afraid.

⁵⁶ *Suomen kansan vanhat runot*, ed. by Niemi and others, I. 2, no. 1107.

⁵⁷ *Suomen kansan vanhat runot*, ed. by Niemi and others, II, no. 320.

⁵⁸ *Suomen kansan vanhat runot*, ed. by Niemi and others, I. 2, no. 1111.

⁵⁹ For example Siikala, *Mythic Images and Shamanism*, pp. 58, 418 (mountain).

hopeain ruoska vööl.	a silver whip at her belt.
Mäni odroipellolleen	She went to her barley field
kagroikaapunaiselleen.	to her small oat-rick.

(Taroi, ll. 1–10)

The Izhor Mary is described as an especially clean, pure, and shining female creature, in silk clothes, a silver or golden staff or lash or whip in her hand, walking peacefully in her corn fields. Compared with the Karelian Mary she is not heroic but delicate, and she does not act with ardour but — at least in the beginning — with dignity. Her surroundings are agricultural. This difference is due to the lifestyle and circumstances of the singers. The Ingrians lived in the middle of their open, agricultural fields; the Karelians hunted, fished, and burn-beat their land in the middle of their enormous forests. In Ingria Mary's special attribute is the staff or whip made of gold or silver in her hand, an item which is lacking in Karelia. It may have come from church paintings or icons; the same motif is found also in Bulgarian songs.[60] There its function is to protect her against evil powers (which may also be the case here, but it is not mentioned). In every case, the Izhor Mary walks with the staff in her hand, and even if her landscape does not have any hills, she approaches something that is as mythic as the holy mountain.

She Eats the Berry from which She Becomes Pregnant

keksi marjasen meältä	found the berry on the hill
punapuolan kankahalta:	the red-berry on the heath:
on marja näkemiehen	it was a wondrous berry
puola ilman luomeehen,	a heaven-sent red-berry:
alahahko ois maasta syöä	too low to eat off the ground
ylähähkö puuhun nosta.	too high to climb a tree for.
Tempo kartun kankahalta	She dragged a pole from the heath
senni päällä seisataksen:	and stood upon it
heitti marjan helmohinsa	threw the berry in her lap
helmoiltansa vyönsä päälle	from her lap up to her belt
vyönsä päältä rinnoillensa	from her belt up to her breasts
rinnoiltansa huulellensa	from her breasts up to her lip
huuleltansa kielellensä	from her lip on to her tongue:
siitä vatsahan valahti.	thence it slipped to her belly.

(Arhippa, ll. 15–28)

---

[60] Information received from Katja Mikhailovna.

> Otti marjan sormillaha
> sormilta huulillahe
> huuliltahe kielillähä:
> tuosta vatšaha vajuupi
> kulkkuhu kureksisehe.
>
> A berry in her fingers
> she took, from fingers to lips
> from her lips on to her tongue:
> thence to her belly it sank
> was swallowed up in her throat.
>
> (Okuli, ll. 33–37)

> näki tuolt oksalt omeenan
> näki puult päähkinäisen,
> otti oksalta omeenan
> otti puult päähkinäisen,
> loi omeenan huuloilleen
> huuloiltaan kieloilleen
> kieloilt kerukselleen.
>
> saw an apple on that bough
> saw a nut upon the tree
> took the apple from the bough
> took the nut from off the tree
> put the apple to her lips
> from her lips on to her tongue
> from her tongue into her throat.
>
> (Taroi, ll. 11–17)

Some singers tell that when Mary reached the hill or field and saw the berry (in Ingria, as is seen in Taroi's song, it is an apple or nut), she simply took it in her hand and put it on her lips, from where it went into her belly. But more often the meeting of Mary and the berry is more dramatic. In many Archangel Karelian variants Mary realizes that the berry has gone into a tree, or grows in a tree, and is sometimes so high that it is in the middle of the sky and the earth.[61] In Arhippa's version, Mary sees that it is too high for her to reach yet is determined to get it, and so she acts: she takes a pole from the heath to stand on. When she is high enough, she throws the berry into her lap, her belt, her breasts, her lips, her tongue, from where it finally slips into her belly.

Many singers emphasize Mary's ecstatic state by making her even more active. Some tell that she takes a pine tree and shakes the berry with it so that it falls down.[62] In many variants Mary begins to address the berry which has now fallen down or is on the ground. She commands: 'Rise up, rise up, my little berry, roll up on my bright hems! Rise up, rise up, my berry on tips of my brass belt, on to my fair breasts, my silver lips, my golden tongue!' Some singers describe the event as the immediate alternation of the words and their consequences: '"Rise up, berry, on the balls of my feet!" The berry rose up on the balls of her feet. "Rise up, berry, on my belt!" The berry rose up on her belt. "Rise up, berry, on my lips!" The berry rose up on her lips, and slid down into the belly.'[63]

---

[61] *Suomen kansan vanhat runot*, ed. by Niemi and others, I. 2, nos 1117–18.

[62] *Suomen kansan vanhat runot*, ed. by Niemi and others, I. 2, no. 1117.

[63] *Suomen kansan vanhat runot*, ed. by Niemi and others, I. 2, nos 1107–08, 1109, 1116, 1118.

In Ladoga Karelia the passus sometimes also mentions Mary's inner state of mind: 'She took a berry to her lips, another to her mind, a third she devoured into her belly.'[64] But on the whole a strong feeling of physicality dominates this description, adding more and more details of Mary's body, culminating at her mouth. Some singers conclude the berry-eating with Mary's remark on the delicious taste of the berry. She delays swallowing, feels the berry with her lips and tongue, not having the heart to let it slip into her stomach: 'Many have I picked, many plucked, many fingered, but never one so good!'[65]

The berry-eating episode is, also in the basis of its aesthetic structure, the centre of the Song of the Berry. Thomas DuBois has shown through his ethnopoetic analysis of Arhippa's four versions that here the singer uses a succession of five parallel lines, but normally uses shorter successions. This means that Arhippa accentuates 'key narrative moments' with longer sets of parallel lines.[66] This tendency is also discernible in many other singers' performances, as has been shown above. The moment of eating the berry is utterly crucial in Mary's life. But why is it so central?

Scholars have found a model for this description from images of mythical tears in Karelian epic poetry. For example, Aino's mother's tears in the *Kalevala* and in the corresponding folk song move in a parallel, though inverse, way: 'Roll, a tear, roll, another [...] on my fine skirt-hems, on my gorgeous breasts; roll, a tear, roll, another [...] on my silk belt-ends [...] lower still than that, upon my fair heels.'[67]

I think that even if this description is a parallel, it is so only stylistically, that is, it has nothing to do with the meaning of the Song of Mary. But another description has more in common with the intention as well as the form of the description of the berry. In this formula something is also asked, or commanded, to *rise up* on a maiden's body. It is used in love spells, especially in those which try to rouse men's sexual desire and potency. In these spells the healer can utter, for example, the following lines: 'Rise up pin, stand up smith, come up men's prow!'

---

[64] The expression *otti mielillä* (or *mielellä/hän*, Suomen kansan vanhat runot, ed. by Niemi and others, VII. 1, nos 737, 738, 742) is difficult to understand exactly. The singer may simply mean that it pleased her to take it, but textually the line follows the parallelism used in the other lines and says that she took the berry in or to her mind.

[65] *Suomen kansan vanhat runot*, ed. by Niemi and others, I. 2, no. 1098.

[66] DuBois, 'An Ethnopoetic Approach to Finnish Folk Poetry', pp. 147–50.

[67] Krohn and Krohn, *Kantelettaren tutkimuksia*, II, 62; Kuusi, 'Keskiajan kalevalainen runous', pp. 295–96. Keith Bosley's translation: *Finnish Folk Poetry*, ed. by Kuusi, Bosley, and Branch, pp. 412–13; compare also *The Kalevala*, trans. by Bosley, Poem 4, lines 451–72.

Noppa (pin), *seppo* (smith), and *urosten kokka* (men's prow) are penis metaphors in love magic.[68] The following lines of a love spell express exactly how the penis must act: 'Rise without lifting, stand up without touching, stay up like a hay pole, move up like an iron pole — rise on this maid's cunt, rise on this child's loins!'[69] Sometimes metaphors are also used for the girl's genitals: the penis must rise 'to the mouth of a hairy river, to the side of a furry pond'.[70]

This parallel theme in love magic gives the Karelian berry episode of the Virgin Mary an actively erotic and sexual flavour. But it is the woman, Mary herself, who is active, not others, as is the case in love magic. The sexual undercurrent is strengthened by the symbolism of the forest. As Lotte Tarkka has pointed out, in ballads sung by women that tell about young women 'the threat of the forest is interpreted as markedly erotic'. A girl's departure to the forest is dangerous, because the erotic encounter happens outside the control of the community.[71] In this light Mary is not only active but also courageous: she is not afraid; on the contrary, she wants to go to the forest.

In Ingria the apple episode does not seem to have been experienced and described as intensively as the berry episode in Karelia: Mary simply sees the apple or nut and eats it. But the case is not so simple. These Izhor lines obtain powerful signifiers from similar images in other songs. In Ingrian women's love and wedding songs a desirable young man is frequently described as an apple, a nut, or a berry. A mother warns of beautiful men, but the daughter nevertheless falls in love with a man who is 'like a strawberry on the ground, or an apple on the bough, or a nut on a tree', uttering: 'I have somebody in my mind, like an apple on the bough, or a nut on a tree.'[72] Sexual berry and apple symbolism is also developed in seduction contexts in Ingrian women's songs. Often a woman speaking in a song remembers her youth, when no man was good enough for her, but alas, 'A man came and changed my mind with blueberries, altered my mind with raspberries, persuaded with strawberries'.[73] Similarly, in an Ingrian incest ballad the protagonist addresses his sister (unaware of who she is):

---

[68] Virtaranta and others, *Karjalan kielen sanakirja*, III, 522; V, 338.

[69] *Suomen kansan vanhat runot*, ed. by Niemi and others, I. 4, no. 2502; VII. 5, no. 4645.

[70] *Suomen kansan vanhat runot*, ed. by Niemi and others, I. 4, no. 2502.

[71] Tarkka, *Rajarahvaan laulu*, pp. 282–86.

[72] *Suomen kansan vanhat runot*, ed. by Niemi and others, III, nos 917, 975. Berry, apple, and nut imagery can also refer to beautiful young women; for example ibid., III, nos 3075, 3078.

[73] *Suomen kansan vanhat runot*, ed. by Niemi and others, V. 2, no. 2404; V. 3, no. 615.

> 'Step, maiden, into my sledge
> into the back of my sleigh
> to eat my apples
> and to bite my nuts!'[74]

Tarja Kupiainen, a folklorist, has noticed that this young man describes his desirability through food metaphors — he is 'made of honey, created of sugar'. She continues: 'The images connected with eating and especially with the oral satisfaction received from delicacies refer to sex appeal and virility.'[75]

With these parallels in mind, the short lines describing how Mary 'saw an apple on the bough — took the apple from the bough — put the apple to her lips' receive significant meanings. In a nutshell, they symbolically express the female experience of erotic and sexual desire and pleasure. In this case the girl is not seduced, timid, or defiant — she makes her decision to take the apple from the tree freely and independently.

The erotic tones, so explicit in the berry and apple episodes in the Song of Mary, are not unknown in Church art either. Many Western pictorial representations of the Annunciation express human erotic tension in this scene.[76] Eastern icon tradition seems to be different in this respect, but physicality may be seen to be present in icons in which Mary's pregnancy is depicted as having occurred at that very moment.[77]

The berry/apple episode is the climax of this song, full of variation, expressing wonder, joy, desire, shifting with different viewpoints and additional details. But the conclusion, the description of becoming pregnant, is calm and realistic, showing minimal variation:

Siitä tyyty, siitä täyty	She was fulfilled, she was filled
siitä paksuksi panihen	by it, grew thickset from it
lihavaksi liittelihen.	put on flesh from it.

(Arhippa, ll. 29–31; cf. Okuli, ll. 38–40, and Taroi, ll. 18–20)

Every singer repeats this approximately in the same manner. This formula is used to some degree in other poems as well, in various contexts and describing

---

[74] *Finnish Folk Poetry*, ed. by Kuusi, Bosley, and Branch, p. 254. Translation by Keith Bosley. See also *Suomen kansan vanhat runot*, ed. by Niemi and others, III, no. 458; IV, nos 2002, 3061.

[75] Kupiainen, *Kertovan kansanrunon nuori nainen*, pp. 166–67.

[76] Hirn, *The Sacred Shrine*, pp. 290–93.

[77] *Annunciation*, p. 21.

pregnancy as well as illness.[78] In the context of the Song of the Berry it is, nevertheless, most systematically present.

Proofs of Virginity

<table>
<tr><td>

'Voi milma poloista porttoa:
en istunut hevolla reessä
ubehilla olluzilla
engä syönyt mahon maiduo
härillä halissehien,
en syönyt kanan munoa
poigakukon polgomia! [...]
Täm on kohtu Luojan luoma
seädämä pyhän Jumalan!'

</td><td>

'Wretched harlot that I am:
I've sat in no horse's sledge
that has been among stallions
nor drunk a barren cow's milk
that has been around with bulls
I have eaten no hen's eggs
mounted by a cockerel! [...]
This is the Creator's work
begotten by holy God!'

</td></tr>
</table>

(Okulina, ll. 69–81)

Here Arhippa Perttunen is silent, so we follow Okulina. The local song in Olonets Karelia extends the conception and pregnancy story with a dramatic episode, which commonly occurs in another song telling of a young woman who fetches water from a spring and then offers it to her relatives.[79] In Okulina's song, as in many other Olonets variants of the Song of Mary, it is Mary who comes home from the forest and offers not water but berries to her relatives. They refuse to eat them claiming that she is a whore and had gone to the hill to meet young men, not to pick berries.

The accusation of being a whore is exceptionally hard when it comes from Mary's own family and own mother. This theme is also emphasized in other women's songs. As Tarkka says, it reflects the fact that 'the threat of becoming labelled as a whore was an emotionally heavy factor which restricted women's action'. Nevertheless, Mary's fate in this song must have given young women 'moral support'.[80]

In our song Mary defends herself emphatically, uttering the words above: she has not done or eaten anything related to male sexuality. It is interesting

---

[78] Pregnancy: *Suomen kansan vanhat runot*, ed. by Niemi and others, VII. 1, no. 101; I. 4, no. 584; IV, no. 329; illness caused by eating berries: ibid., IV, no. 384. See also Tarkka, *Rajarahvaan laulu*, p. 170 and her n. 1191 (this formula can also be used in the description of how the miraculous *Sampo* became rooted in earth).

[79] Of the song The Girl Who Lingered at the Spring, compare *Finnish Folk Poetry*, ed. by Kuusi, Bosley, and Branch, pp. 455–64.

[80] Tarkka, *Rajarahvaan laulu*, p. 223.

that sexuality is here connected with animals: horses, cocks, fish. These words also occur in some Archangel Karelian variants in the introduction of the song, but there the last two exceptionally religious lines are lacking — of course, because Mary is not yet pregnant.[81] In Ingria this episode is unknown.

This declaration of virginity is again a formula used in other songs telling of young women who give birth illegitimately or miraculously.[82] In these non-religious connections the passage may contain a flavour of humorous exaggeration, perhaps a bit of it here as well — who could eat eggs or drink milk without the prior participation of a cock or bull? Or is she saying that she has totally refused drinking milk and eating eggs? But these lines also express something else: a feeling of deep solemnity, and of wonder.

The latter attitude can be compared both to the Bible and especially to the apocryphal Book of James. In these Christian traditions the pregnant Mary is likewise cruelly accused of impurity, and she defends herself saying: 'I am pure, and know not a man.' And in his sleep, Josef, suspecting Mary's virginity, hears an angel say: 'For that which is in her is of the Holy Spirit.'[83] The Book of James has been seen as one of the central texts in constructing the idea of Mary's virginity.[84] The angel's words in it are almost identical to Mary's words in the Karelian song, yet their theological interpretation of virginity does not seem to be the point of the folk song.

Proof of Mary's innocence can also be transmitted in another way in our song, again in Okulina's version. After her family has driven her out of their home, Mary walks alone in the forest. With her heart full of despair, she approaches a river, intending to drown herself:

'Vie virta, kohota koski!'	'Take me, stream, lift me, rapids!'
'Eipä silma virta vie	'No, the stream will not take you
eigä koski kohota	nor will the rapids lift you:

---

[81] *Suomen kansan vanhat runot*, ed. by Niemi and others, I. 2, nos 1113, 1115.

[82] In the songs of Marketta (Margaret) and Iro (Irina) the protagonists declare themselves, or the singer declares them to be, so chaste that they do not eat eggs, milk, or spawning fish, etc. But Marketta is seduced, and Iro eats berries as Mary does, and both become pregnant. The declaration on virginity in these songs seems to occur only in Orthodox Karelia. See for example *Suomen kansan vanhat runot*, ed. by Niemi and others, I. 1, nos 687, 689; II, nos 333–35; VII. 2, nos 700–31 (Marketta); ibid., I. 4, nos 2155–56; II, nos 95–102, VII. 1, nos 98–131 (Iro). Some of the texts seem to refer in this connection to the Lent: the girl is so religious that she is fasting all the time (Krohn and Krohn, *Kantelettaren tutkimuksia*, II, 58).

[83] Hennecke, *New Testament Apocrypha*, ed. by Schneewelcher, I, 381.

[84] Foskett, *A Virgin Conceived*.

kuin on poiga polvillase	you'll have a boy on your knees
herra Kristus helmoillase'.	the Lord Christ upon your lap.'
	(Okulina, ll. 87–91)

In many other variants it is even clearer that it is the stream speaking here. Nature itself gives proof of Mary's purity and the holiness of her state. This motif is known only in the parish of Repola in Olonets.[85] Its source is unknown; its spirit has something in common with the water evidence in the Book of James, where Mary and Joseph have to drink God's water, go up to a mountain, and return undamaged to prove her virginity.[86]

Despair and suicidal thoughts increase the human atmosphere around the Karelian Virgin. In this respect Mary resembles the girls of some other Karelian songs who try to commit or succeed in committing suicide in comparable situations.[87] But she is the only one whose attempt is hindered by a miracle. I have only found parallels to this item in Marian folklore from Romanian songs, in which Mary tries to commit suicide by throwing herself against a sharp rock, but, like the stream in Karelia, the rock in Romania refuses to kill her: it melts away![88] Even more reminiscent of the Karelian Mary's despair is that of Psyche in Apuleius's *Eros and Psyche*. Bearing a child and desperate because her god-lover Amor has abandoned her, Psyche

> threw herself from the bank of a nearby stream. But the gentle river, in respect it would seem for the god who is wont to scorch even water, and fearing for himself, immediately bore her unharmed on his current and landed her on his grassy bank.[89]

---

[85] *Suomen kansan vanhat runot*, ed. by Niemi and others, II, nos 320, 323–25a, 329–30a, 332. The episode is sometimes depicted in a later phase, i.e. in connection with the birth of the child.

[86] Hennecke, *New Testament Apocrypha*, ed. by Schneewelcher, I, 382–83. Because many Old Believers were living in Repola, it is possible that the suicide motif in our song is connected with their knowledge of apocryphal literature; compare Tshernjakova, 'Repolan seurakunta 1800-luvulla', pp. 78–82.

[87] The most famous of these songs is The Song of the Hanged Maid; see *Finnish Folk Poetry*, ed. by Kuusi, Bosley, and Branch, pp. 410–15; Kupiainen, *Kertovan kansanrunon nuori nainen*, pp. 123–31.

[88] Gaster, 'Rumanian Popular Legends of the Lady', p. 1125. The Song of the Search for a Bathhouse also has parallels in these Romanian songs; see Kuusi, 'Keskiajan kalevalainen runous', p. 295. In Greek tradition, St Mary's violent grief and threats to commit suicide are essential in the context of Christ's death, but instead of a miracle it is the words of Christ that stop her from killing herself; see Alexiou, *The Ritual Lament in Greek Tradition*, pp. 64–65, 68–69.

[89] Apuleius, *Cupid & Psyche*, ed. by Kenney, p. 79. I am grateful to Satu Apo, who provided

Basically, the emphasis on Mary's virginity, her momentary despair and doubts (but not the wish to die) are in line with the Orthodox interpretation of Mary. This is richly expressed in the Byzantine Akathistos hymn, a central Marian text in the Eastern Church. The hymn concentrates on the mystery of Incarnation and its crucial realization point, Annunciation, and does so entirely from Mary's point of view — just like our folk song. In the discussion with Gabriel Mary utters her doubts, crying: 'The paradox of your words | I find hard for my soul to accept, | for you speak of childbirth from a conception without seed [...].' Joseph is even more troubled, suspecting 'illicit love'. The focus of the song is the praise of Mary's virginity: 'Hail, you who bring opposites together, | Hail, you who unite virginity and childbirth [...].'[90]

Even if the basic interpretation of the Incarnation as a mystery of the Virgin's conception is the same in these two languages, the written version of the church and the orally created and reproduced version of common people, something still seems to be totally different. This difference is most dramatically visible in the symbol of the fruit.

Why a Berry, an Apple, a Nut?

Where did the central idea of this song, that of becoming pregnant by eating a berry, or an apple, come from? It seems to be exceptional in connection with Mary; or at least no indisputable sources have been found. In the neighbouring traditions, in Scandinavian, Estonian, and north Russian legend songs, the conception of Christ is rarely described, and when the theme occurs, it is presented as a quite canonical depiction of Gabriel's visit to Mary.[91]

---

me with information about this source. Psyche tries several times to kill herself, but the 'helper' (e.g. knife, stream) always refuses to do it. The description has been compared with Ovid's similar story of Ilia, a Vestal Virgin seduced by the god Mars, mother of Romulus and Remus. In Greek romances aborted suicide was also a common theme. See E. J. Kenney's commentary in Apuleius, *Cupid & Psyche*, ed. by Kenney, pp. 174–75.

[90] See for example Peltomaa, *The Image of the Virgin Mary*, p. 33; for her translation of the hymn, see pp. 3–19. In our song St Mary is not in fact doubtful, others are, and this is why she is desperate. But a Danish song about the Annunciation gives an example of a doubtful Mary who does not believe she is pregnant — unless stone becomes iron, she says, which does indeed occur; *Danmarks gamle folkeviser*, ed. by Grundtvig and others, IV, 531–32.

[91] See, for example, *Danmarks gamle folkeviser*, ed. by Grundtvig and others, IX, 188–89; ibid., X, 194–98; Bezsonov, *Kaleki perekhozhie*, pp. 6–15. In *Sveriges medeltida ballader* the theme is lacking; see *Sveriges medeltida ballader*, ed. by Jonsson, I. Compare Batho's remark on

Some scholars have assumed, and I agree, that in the Song of Mary the Izhor apple image is original. The Izhor version is short and simple; following the Kalevalaic parallelism aesthetics, the word 'nut' is added simply to repeat the word 'apple' and to emphasize its fruit-in-a-tree character. It is evident that even the Karelian berry version still carries traces of the apple tree, as was seen in Arhippa's version: the berry was growing in a tree or jumped up into a tree.[92] The metamorphosis of the apple into the berry has been also explained by the fact that the Finnish-Karelian forms of Mary, *Maria* (*Marja*) resemble the word *marja*, 'berry'.[93] As a whole, this is an example of 'milieu-morphological adaptation' typical of oral traditions — singers replace an unknown thing with one they know well.[94] In Karelia apple and nut trees do not grow, but the forests are full of lingonberries, and one of women's important tasks has always been to pick berries, prepare food with them, and preserve them for winter. On the contrary, in the more southern Ingria, apple and nut trees thrive.

Above I have compared the berry and the apple in the Mary songs to the erotic and sexual imagery familiar to the creators and singers of these songs in their local poetic traditions. This erotic frame receives further support from European folk songs, in which berry metaphors are emphatically erotic: picking berries is a well-known metaphor for a love affair, and eating berries is a metaphor for sexual pleasure, for coitus, and — especially in women-centred cultures — for conception.[95] In addition, the apple is an age-old symbol of love, life, and fertility.[96]

European religious balladry: 'The Annunciation is treated with too close fidelity to canonical history for quotation to be necessary' (Batho, 'The Life of Christ in the Ballads', p. 72). Prose legends seem to offer more fabulous stories. A Karelian legend tells that Mary yawned in the temple, and thus 'the power of the Holy Spirit' went to her mouth. Another informant tells that the child came into Mary 'as if out of nothing: She did not know from where it came' (Järvinen, *Legendat*, pp. 27–28).

[92] Krohn and Krohn, *Kantelettaren tutkimuksia*, II, 63. Did the Karelian singers associate the berry tree with rowan, with its red berries? The rowan has been a holy tree in Finnish and Karelian pre-Christian traditions, and it has been associated with female sexuality and fertility, later sometimes also with the Virgin; compare Anttonen, 'Pihlaja, naisen kiima ja kasvuvoiman pyhä locus'.

[93] Borenius, 'Suomen keskiaikaista runoutta I', p. 77.

[94] Honko, 'Rethinking Tradition Ecology', pp. 69–75; compare also Harvilahti in this volume.

[95] Danckert, *Symbol, Metapher, Allegorie im Lied der Völker*, III, 1085–90. Berries can of course have other meanings, too, but the erotic/sexual ones seem to dominate.

[96] Danckert, *Symbol, Metapher, Allegorie im Lied der Völker*, III, 1016–32.

Nevertheless, the use of these images in our song deserves a little more examination. Even if Mary does not seem to become pregnant from eating a berry or an apple in neighbouring poetic traditions, many parallels have been offered from other genres, and from more distant cultures, about which I will say some more.

First, a tree whose berries or fruits are too high up to be reached is also vividly depicted in an apocryphal text: Pseudo-Mattheus tells of a palm tree which bent its branches and fruits for hungry Mary to eat during the flight to Egypt. Many European folk legends, songs, church paintings, and icons depicting this miracle are known. In these it can be Jesus who commands the tree, or the tree bends itself without asking. The earlier folklorists Julius and Kaarle Krohn thought that this was the source of our song,[97] but later Martti Haavio rejected this idea, arguing that the stories are too different, and the fruit motif has a different function.[98]

Secondly, an almost identical parallel to the conception of Mary from a berry is represented in Ladoga Karelia and Southern Olonets in a Kalevala-metre song telling of the birth of three hero-sons: Väinämöinen, Ilmarinen, and Lemminkäinen. These well-known Kalevala poetry heroes are here conceived from three berries eaten by their virgin mother Iro.[99] This version is so local and deviates so much from other heroic epics that it is considered to have been composed under the influence of the Song of the Berry, that is, it seems to be an example of the 'paganizing' of Christian folk tradition.[100] In this area the Song of the Berry seems to have more or less disappeared and incorporated, in addition to the Song of Iro, also to the Song of Marketta,[101] and occasionally

---

[97] The Krohns (Krohn and Krohn, *Kantelettaren tutkimuksia*, II, 48–49) were glad to notice that in France the tree is an apple tree. They cite the English 'Cherry Tree Carol' in which Jesus speaks from the womb: 'From that it is not a long step to the idea of the Finnish poem.'

[98] Haavio, *Kirjokansi*, p. 350. About the legend, see for example Bringéus, 'The Rest on the Flight into Egypt'; Kriza, 'The Survival of Medieval Tradition', p. 95; Royston, '"The Cherry-tree Carol"'.

[99] For the Song of Iro, see also note 82 above.

[100] Krohn and Krohn, *Kantelettaren tutkimuksia*, II, 54–56; Kuusi, 'Pakanuuden ja kristinuskon murros', pp. 149–50. Other examples of this phenomenon are also known in Kalevala poetry; compare also Henrik Janson's article in this volume.

[101] For example *Suomen kansan vanhat runot*, ed. by Niemi and others, VII. 1, nos 731, 737, 738. In most variants in Ladoga Karelia it is uncertain whether the singer is really speaking of St Mary, Iro, or Marketta.

to birth-giving charms.[102] This phenomenon is interesting, because otherwise these areas were, at least in the nineteenth century, more markedly Orthodox Christian than the Karelian areas in the North, where the berry song and mythic poetry in general still flourished.[103]

Thirdly, inverted versions of the miraculous conception theme also exist. In Kalevala-metre poetry they are represented in the description of the birth of terrible diseases. This poem, used as a spell against diseases, begins as follows:

Loviatar, vaimo vanha,	Loviatar, old woman
portto Pohjolan emäntä	whore, mistress of Pohjola
selin tuuleen makasi,	laid her back against wind
p-in pahaan säähän,	her arse against bad weather
kalten kaarna-pohjoseen.	sideways against the north wind.
tuuli tuuli kaksi vuotta,	The wind blew for two years
seuro seihtemän kesee	churned for seven summers
yhen porton p-een;	to the arse of one whore;
teki tuuli tiineeksi,	the wind made her pregnant
ahava kohulliseksi.	the march-wind with the womb.[104]

These two birth poems interact with each other so closely that in some variants of the Mary song Mary also becomes pregnant by the wind. Anna-Leena Siikala and Lotte Tarkka have noticed that in Kalevala poetry pregnancy without a man is a myth theme in which, according to Tarkka, 'illegitimate sexuality is discussed in a mythical frame of reference'.[105]

The miraculous or mythical conception of a hero or a deity is in fact a common theme in heroic, fantastic, and religious traditions all over the world.[106] One of its recurring models is conception through smelling a flower or eating a fruit.

---

[102] *Suomen kansan vanhat runot*, ed. by Niemi and others, VII. 5, nos 3013, 3046.

[103] Compare Järvinen, *Karjalan pyhät kertomukset*; Siikala, *Mythic Images and Shamanism*, p. 339.

[104] *Suomen kansan vanhat runot*, ed. by Niemi and others, VII. 4, no. 2401; translation modified on the basis of Keith Bosley's (cf. *The Kalevala*, trans. by Bosley, Poem 1, lines 125–36; Poem 45, lines 35–44) and Anna-Leena Siikala's translations of other versions of this theme (Siikala, *Mythic Images and Shamanism*, p. 262).

[105] Tarkka, *Rajarahvaan laulu*, p. 452 n. 2280. According to this interpretation, illegitimate sexuality was a problem which had to be lifted up to a mythical sphere in its totality — i.e. containing both its evil (devilish) and good (holy) dimensions — in order to ponder it. I think that this might not only be a question of illegitimate sexuality, but of female sexuality in more general terms.

[106] See, for example, Dundes, 'The Hero Pattern and the Life of Jesus'; Leeming, 'Virgin Birth'; Weigle, *Creation and Procreation*, pp. 77–84.

The Karelian and Izhor Marys are popular Christian variations of this mythical theme. Their parallels seem to appear frequently in the Marys of South and Balkan Slavic religious folksongs and legends — this may or may not be a coincidence.[107] For example, some Slovenian, Romanian, and Bulgarian Marys smelled a flower;[108] a Romanian Ann, Mary's mother, smelled an apple leaf;[109] a Slovenian Mary inhaled a grape;[110] and, last but not least, a Grusian Mary ate an apple into which God had blown his spirit.[111] Many Bulgarian Marys just ate an apple.[112]

If we accept the theory of the originality of the apple in our tradition, the apple image becomes important in this connection. The fertilizing power of the apple is generally known also in the non-Christian miraculous birth traditions, in Russia as well as in Scandinavia, in fairy tales as well as in Old Norse literature. In *Völsunga saga* the Volsungs descend from an apple: King Rerir was married, but could not have a child. He and his wife prayed with their heart and soul to have one. Frigg asked Odin to help, and he sent them an apple, which they ate. That is how the hero Volsung was born.[113] These stories can exaggerate the erotic, sexual tone of the apple conception model. According to Old Norse humorous folk etymology these Volsungs are 'sons of (a horse's) penis'.[114]

---

[107] One reason for the many South Slavic parallels presented above is my good group of advisors from these cultures. I am especially grateful to Antoaneta Granberg for all her aid when I visited Gothenburg, and Florentina Badalanova who generously informed me of her work on the Bulgarian materials. Also Matej Gorsic, Monika Kropej, Slavica Rancović, Katja Mikhailovna, and Sonja Miladinovic have given valuable references.

[108] Mansikka, 'Legendat ihmeellisestä synnyttämisestä', p. 9; *Slovenske narodne pesmi iztiskanih in pisanih virov*, ed. by Štrekelj, III, 10, 12–13; Vranska, *Apokrifite za Bogoroditsa i Blgarskata narodna pesen*, pp. 94–96; the flower can be a lily, an iris, or a bunch of pinks (carnations?). According to Badalanova, 'The Spinning Mary', p. 226, the flower model is inspired by the Annunciation icons in which Gabriel gives a flower to the Virgin.

[109] Mansikka, 'Legendat ihmeellisestä synnyttämisestä', p. 8. Compare also the medieval Funuel legend in which St Ann herself descends from an apple leaf; this type has flourished in the Western traditions (ibid., pp. 8–9).

[110] *Slovenske narodne pesmi iztiskanih in pisanih virov*, ed. by Štrekelj, III, 11–13. The grape was given to her by Gabriel or Josef.

[111] Mansikka, 'Legendat ihmeellisestä synnyttämisestä', p. 9. I have not yet been able to identify Mansikka's source.

[112] Badalanova, '"Zavetnii fol'klor"', p. 78.

[113] Danckert, *Symbol, Metapher, Allegorie im Lied der Völker*, III, 1025; Davidson, *Roles of the Northern Goddess*, pp. 146–47.

[114] I am grateful to Jonas Wellendorf who informed me about this. See also Else Mundal's article in this volume.

Speaking of the Marian traditions, the Grusian and Bulgarian apple versions mentioned above are of special interest here. Many of these variants have been recorded quite recently from the Bulgarian villages in the Ukraine.[115] In these stories the Virgin Mary is said to have swallowed a *blaga* (good, sweet, pleasant) apple on Annunciation day, which is how she became pregnant. Florentina Badalanova, the collector of these stories, has noticed that the key word in them is precisely the word *blaga*, which demonstrates 'the merging of culinary and sexual codes', a characteristic feature of the apple legend. The profound connotations of the sexual images presented here arise from the fact that, according to Badalanova, these stories combine, by implicit parallelism and antithesis, two mythical events and two mythical women: Mary and Eve.[116] This merging explains, for instance, why the concept of sin can appear in the scene, as in the text recorded from Ana Vezirskaja in 1989:

> The holy God-Bearer gave birth from a tree [...] such a tree which had a fruit [...] she had been in the forest [...] and she sank into vice [...] she sinned with this tree, which had had the fruit [...] she was pregnant for nine months and then she gave birth to the God.[117]

The idea of Mary as the second Eve and the parallelism and merging of these female figures is present in many forms of Bulgarian folk culture.[118]

Earlier Finnish scholars have also connected the Karelian-Izhor berry/apple to Eve's apple;[119] thus Matti Kuusi asks: 'Or did he [the poet] proportion the painting of Eve and the apple or the life tree symbol he saw in the church walls to the Virgin Mary's conceptio immaculata?'[120] The meaning of this connection was, nevertheless, not pondered. Considering all the sexual connotations presented above in our song, remembering the central oral formula describing

---

[115] Badalanova, 'Notes on the Cult of the Virgin Mary', pp. 184–85, 190–91.

[116] Badalanova, '"Zavetnii fol'klor"', p. 78.

[117] *Folkloren erotikon*, ed. by Badalanova, III, 118.

[118] Compare Badalanova, 'Notes on the Cult of the Virgin Mary', and Badalanova, 'The Spinning Mary'.

[119] The Krohns (Krohn and Krohn, *Kantelettaren tutkimuksia*, II, 63) express the idea as complicated: 'One could think that the biblical story of the apple of Paradise has influenced the palm tree legend, after it was adapted as the beginning of the song.' According to the Krohns, the analogy was first presented by K. A. Gottlund, handwritten in page 225 of his copy of the Old Kalevala: 'Adam och Eva, junfru Maria' (Adam and Eve, the Virgin Mary).

[120] Kuusi, 'Keskiajan kalevalainen runous', p. 295.

Mary as 'the oldest of women, the first of those who live',[121] and comparing the Bulgarian apple version and its interpretation by Badalanova, the implicit presence of Eve is obviously here as well. In our song Mary's active response to the berry's call, the delicious taste of the berry, and the experience of happiness under the fruit tree can with good reason be connected to the tree of paradise. The Karelian and Izhor singers thought in terms of antithesis even less than the Bulgarian informants. For them Eve's paradise was never lost nor brought back by Mary. In this song those two were one. This Mary-Eve of the Karelian and Izhor singers dwelled in mythical time, free of linearity and its logic.

Badalanova interestingly connects the Bulgarian parallelism and combination of Eve and Mary with the first patristic writings on the theme (from the second century onwards), and assumes the antiquity of the folklore versions. She concludes that new research on the complicated and layered dialogue and the coexistence of the 'written' and the oral spheres of the Slavic Orthodox world is required.[122]

The combination of Eve and Mary has nevertheless flourished in Eastern and Western Christianity through centuries; thus the singers may have elaborated the theme in dialogue with the Church in later times. In Western Christian art Eve with her apple tree and Mary with Gabriel in an Annunciation scene are often presented side by side.[123] The apple, the symbol of Eve, became one of the symbols of Mary, too, and was depicted in her hand or somewhere near her, or in the palm of her child.[124] In addition, Eastern Marian theology, as richly expressed in the Akathistos hymn and in the liturgical texts of Annunciation Day, is full of references to Mary as the second Eve who wins back the fruits of Paradise, transforming the apple of sin into the apple of salvation.[125]

On the basis of the materials presented above, it seems possible that the Karelian-Izhor motif of the Mary who becomes pregnant by an apple is an early adaptation from South Slavic religious traditions. Did the traders or the pilgrims using the route via Novgorod and Kiev to Constantinople bring it, among other things, to the Baltic Sea? There is no certain answer. As Anna-Leena Siikala has stated, to determine the origin of individual images is an almost impossible

---

[121] *Suomen kansan vanhat runot*, ed. by Niemi and others, I. 2, no. 1103a.

[122] See Badalanova, 'Notes on the Cult of the Virgin Mary', pp. 173–86; Badalanova Geller, 'The Spinning Mary', pp. 245–46.

[123] See for example Guldan, *Eva und Maria*; Lindgren, 'Gideons fäll och Arons grönskande stav'.

[124] Guldan, *Eva und Maria*, pp. 108–16.

[125] Peltomaa, *The Image of the Virgin Mary*, pp. 130–33.

task.[126] At any rate, in this connection it is interesting to note that many other motifs in the Song of Mary have their nearest parallels in South Slavic traditions.[127] There must be a reason for this cluster of related features.

Nevertheless, caution is required. As was seen above, conception by an apple was known in northern non-Christian folklore. Figures of Eve and Mary could also be combined spontaneously in different eastern as well as western oral cultures. Elina Vuola, a Finnish theologian, has recently noticed an interesting parallel in the *Popol Vuh* epic of the Quiché Maya Indians: A virgin hears of a mythical, dangerous tree with sweet fruits. She stretches her hand and takes the fruit and is fertilized by the saliva spit out by the stone in the fruit. Like Mary, she defends herself against accusations: 'There is no man whose face I've known'. Vuola states that here 'the images of Eve and Mary are mixed, as are Christian and pre-Christian elements, just as in the Karelian myths'.[128]

A Synthesis of Sacred and Profane

The connection of virginity and holiness with the eating of a fruit may thus be interpreted symbolically as an exploration of aspects of sexuality and conception raised in a mythic sphere. In the Mary of these songs female sexuality and a life-giving capacity were both liberated and sacralized. The women who sang these songs and listened to them may have seen, at least momentarily, sexuality in their own life as pure and symbolically virginal as that of the divine mother. And like her, they may have experienced the outside world, even their own families, as cruel and unsympathetic as she did.

Is this an example of a special women's religion? I have considered this possibility and it does seem to fit with such a phenomenon. The singers were mostly women. The heroine is a holy woman. The Kalevala-metre parallels of the central motifs appear mostly in women's songs. From this angle the focus of the song arises from the female experience of sexuality and its social implications.

Vuola also connects the Indian as well as the Karelian stories to women's life. She sees in these texts female reinterpretations of the image 'woman-tree-sexuality', which 'might be reflective of women's cultural resistance against the demonization of their sexuality, and — theologically speaking — of a possibility of a life-affirming, bodily image of Virgin Mary based on women's concrete experiences'.[129]

---

[126] Siikala, *Mythic Images and Shamanism*, p. 336.

[127] See above.

[128] Vuola, '*La Morenita* on Skis'.

[129] Vuola, '*La Morenita* on Skis'.

Yet a problem remains: men also sang this song. This is relevant, even if only seven male singers are known. Arhippa Perttunen's variants belong to the finest texts of the song. He did not remember and compose his versions of it just to please women. It must have been important to him personally, even though he was a man — and to many other men, too, over the course of hundreds of years. Thus the song is a poetic expression of both women's and men's religion, that is, folk religion, in Karelia.

When the concept of folk religion is intended to be understood from the angle of those who believed, as we currently do, we are dealing with the world view and experience of the singers. Their religion, and this song as one of its manifestations, was a comprehensive whole from their perspective — not syncretism, not a mixture constructed of indigenous and ecclesiastical elements, as can be assumed from the outside. Karelian folk religion is regarded as a special creation, which differs sharply from Christianity, but nevertheless has been in close contact with it from the Middle Ages on. One of the special features of it and folk religion generally is thought to be the fact that people did not internalize the ultimate goal of Christianity: the individual's salvation in the afterlife. Folk religion operates in a pragmatic this-world, where help for needs and advice on how to live right with others is asked and received from the world beyond.[130]

This does not mean that folk religion is simple; it is just different. Its poetic manifestations can be highly symbolic and profound, as is the case in the Song of the Berry. To bind the berry/apple symbol to women's sphere and female sexuality is only one way to interpret it, because, as we know, a special characteristic of an important symbol is its inexhaustibility. Caroline Walker Bynum, an expert of the Western European Middle Ages, emphasizes the polysemic nature of a religious symbol by saying that in fact it has no meaning, it just 'gives rise to thought'.[131] From another angle, Anna-Leena Siikala states: 'The search for the "meaning of a word", characteristic of literate cultures is, however, alien to non-literate religions.'[132]

---

[130] Karelian folk religion (folk piety, popular religion) has been largely discussed in Finland in recent years; the lines above are based on Järvinen, *Karjalan pyhät kertomukset*, pp. 17–23; Keinänen, *Creating Bodies*, pp. 18–27, 47–50; Laitila, 'Vienan kansanomainen ja kirkollinen uskonnollisuus'; Stark, *Peasants, Pilgrims, and Sacred Promises*, pp. 20–72; Tarkka, *Rajarahvaan laulu*, pp. 22–27.

[131] Bynum, 'Introduction: The Complexity of Symbols', pp. 9–10, follows the views of Victor Turner and Paul Ricoeur. Compare also Badalanova, '"Zavetnii fol'klor"'.

[132] Siikala, *Mythic Images and Shamanism*, pp. 55–56.

All this fits well to the exceptionally layered Kalevala-metre material, where symbols have resonance in many poetic genres and spheres and eras of experience and culture. Thus, let us suppose, to begin with, that the image of Mary eating the apple/berry does not signify anything; instead, it sets the mind in motion towards different spheres of meaning.

Bynum has shown how the same symbols can be constructed differently in the writings of medieval men and women. To women the symbols of food and eating and female figures in general were a continuation of their own action in everyday life, whereas to men these symbols were reversals of their spheres and of themselves. In other words, men's use of female gender symbols was more complicated than women's use of them. In every case, both sexes were active in creating the religious language in the late Middle Ages, when symbols became more and more gendered and female.[133]

A woman picking and eating a berry/apple and becoming pregnant is from this perspective an utterly gendered symbol. How did male singers interpret it? And did all women in fact comprehend it in the same way, through their womanliness? What kinds of other possibilities does this image offer?

Even if abstract thought does not seem to belong to folk religion, an understanding of symbolism does, as do dialogues between 'high' and 'low' symbolism. Literati have always offered their symbol interpretations to non-literati, and they have further recreated them. An Old Norse text gives an example of such an explanation. It tells a story about two men who walk in a desert and carry a grape on a pole between them. The writer explains: the grape is Christ, and the pole is the cross on which he is thrown. The moral of the parable is, as the grape gives the highest drink to the spiritual life of people, so does the son of God, through his blood, give spiritual life to people.[134] In medieval theological texts the symbol of Christ on the cross could further be compared to an apple on a tree, and this image created, by an analogy, another: Mary was the mystic tree which carried the Christ-apple.[135]

The Karelians and Izhors could also have heard of such and other comparable fruit symbolism explanations. Why does Mary, later in our song,

---

[133] Bynum, 'Introduction: The Complexity of Symbols'.

[134] '[S]o wie die Weintraube den höchsten Trank gibt für das spirituelle Leben der Menschen, so gibt der Sohn Gottes allen rechtgläubigen Menschen das spirituelle Leben durch das Vergeissen seines Blutes, das ist im allgemeinen die Verwandlung von Wein und Wasser zu jedem Mass': Oláfr Thordarson Hvítaskáld, *Dritte grammatische Abhandlung*, ed. by Olsen, p. 241. I am grateful to Jonas Wellendorf for sending me this text.

[135] Guldan, *Eva und Maria*, pp. 110–12.

systematically call her son 'my golden apple'?[136] Later in this song why does one singer recount, between poetic lines, a strange story: When Christ had risen up from the grave he went to a pond to wash himself of blood, and ordered his blood to be 'food for sinners'. But soon he realized that the rich would take it. 'So he threw all his blood upon the heath to become red lingonberries. That is how these berries came into existence.'[137]

Lingonberries — sacred food for poor people? I do not claim that the singer and the listeners tasted Christ's blood when they ate lingonberries. The point is that this is how the imagery works: berry symbolism is here continued by connecting it to Christ's blood, to the Communion wine, to sin, and to the opposition of rich and poor, the singer being on the side of the poor. The fact that the berries were already on the heath in the beginning of the song, before the conception of Christ, does not create a contradiction: the song operates in the world of mythical logic. Even if the doctrine of salvation and the meaning of the Communion were perhaps not internalized in Karelian culture, symbols referring to them were appropriated and recreated in new ways, loaded with experiences and values important in the singers' lives.

Tom DuBois has analysed Arhippa Perttunen's Song of Mary as a work of oral art. Comparing Arhippa's text with that of Lönnrot's in the *Kalevala*, he concludes that Arhippa's text is 'a complex oral meditation', while Lönnrot's is 'a complex literary explanation'. He characterizes Arhippa's complexity as follows:

> The plot is already known: it exists in the Bible. The *Nativity* is an intertextual, metonymic meditation on that plot [...] the sacred events within the narrative — the Annunciation, the Nativity, the Crucifixion — are camouflaged within metaphorical structures that operate as a somewhat puzzling allegorical narrative, sensible, nonetheless, to an audience 'alive to the encoded signals for interpretation'.[138]

---

[136] For example in Arhippa's song Mary repeats this idiom when she is searching for her son. (It is odd that the apple appears here, but not as the medium of fertilization in Archangel Karelia!) The same idiom has equivalents at least in Serbian and Bulgarian folklore. For example in Serbian songs the loved one, most often a child, is often addressed as 'my golden apple' (information from Slavica Ranković). The Bulgarians have a church called 'The Golden Apple', outside of which grows an apple tree from which barren women eat apples and pray to Mary to help them become pregnant (Badalanova, 'Notes on the Cult of the Virgin Mary', pp. 184–85).

[137] *Suomen kansan vanhat runot*, ed. by Niemi and others, I. 2, no. 1098. The text from the year 1825 is a very rich combination of the Song of Mary/Christ and other legends of Christ.

[138] DuBois, 'From Maria to Marjatta', pp. 265–66 (DuBois cites John Miles Foley).

Those 'encoded signals' — underlying references to indigenous and ecclesiastical images — are hints to possible meanings, pathways which give rise to thought.

This is a special kind of thought. The characterization of the song as 'a meditation' is excellent and holds true for many other variants of the song as well. It helps to discuss the berry/apple symbolism further. Religious meditation is a way to reach mystic union with the sacred. In Christianity this sacred is God. The yearning for and realization of this union was, in medieval mystics' texts, for instance, presented in utterly physical images, those of sexual desire and intercourse, hunger and eating, thirst and drinking. Symbolism of the same kind works in the mystery of the Eucharist.[139]

The folk religious imagery of berry/apple-eating, and female sexuality used in the Song of Mary can, from one possible angle, be seen as a folk parallel to these Christian mystical traditions. By eating the berry Mary experiences the meeting of and the union with the sacred. Even if the description of this meeting uses female images, men could also internalize it, and in this basic sense this gender-related image could transcend gender: to become — for men as well as for women — genderless.

What kind of sacred does Mary respond to and unite with? At this point the research ends. It is not possible to see inside the hearts of the singers. But it is worth noting that the song uses nature symbols in depicting Mary's sacred: forest, hill, berry, apple, rapids. In Finnish-Karelian pre-Christian religion nature, especially the forest, was sacralized in many ways, including its eroticization.[140] The indigenous ways of interpreting nature as sacred seem to be breathing through the song. In nature symbols the singers comprehended the notion of the Christian sacred as well, although mixed with their former forms of sacredness. Singing of St Mary and the berry, they and their listeners experienced something of St Mary's sacred experience, everyone in his/her way, and they enlarged St Mary's experience with analogies from their own lives. They did not explain their symbols; they lived with them.[141]

---

[139] Bynum, 'Introduction: The Complexity of Symbols'.

[140] Tarkka, *Rajarahvaan laulu*, pp. 258–60.

[141] For living with symbols, compare Bynum, 'Introduction: The Complexity of Symbols'; compare also Vuola, '*La Morenita* on Skis', citing Robert A. Orsi, for 'lived religion', meaning 'religious practice and imagination in ongoing, dynamic relation with the realities and structures of everyday life in particular times and places' (p. 496).

The Story of the Song of the Berry

As was seen above, almost every passage in the conception song seems to have resonance or equivalents in other Kalevala-metre songs: in heroic and mythical epics, in charms and incantations, in women's narrative songs, in lyrics and wedding songs. This means that the song had been composed and later continually recomposed using Kalevala-metre language, which incorporates not only metre but also poetic lines, formulae, images, passages, motifs, and themes current in this tradition. The song may also have given material to other songs. From another angle we could say that nothing was borrowed or given — these traits do not 'belong' to any song or even genre; they are simply elements of poetic language and could be used freely in the processes of oral creation.[142]

All the ideas and images of the conception song do not, of course, represent the indigenous Kalevala tradition alone. The core of the song is Christian: the virginal conception of Christ, the image and the name of St Mary, the image of Eve and the apple tree. Above I have presented corresponding textual and pictorial materials from Eastern and Western Christianity. I do not mean that the ideas were adopted exactly from these. But the singers were in contact with these kinds of ecclesiastical materials in their homes and local chapels and churches, and they must have assigned meanings to their texts also in these contexts.[143] Nevertheless, the Christian core was so profoundly incorporated within the Kalevala-metre expression and its mythical and poetic images that the distance of the Song of the Berry from ecclesiastical Christianity seems to be greater than is the case in other North European legend songs. There is no Gabriel, no Josef, no temple. Christ's name is usually not mentioned; he is merely her son, the 'golden apple'. The centre of the song is St Mary and her encounter with the berry or an apple — with the sacred.

Thus the Karelians and Izhors created Christian poetics of their own, as oral communities tend to do. The Song of the Berry expresses this. When the song was initially created, and what it then contained (possibly only a short account of how Mary ate the apple and became pregnant), is impossible to say, but it seems to have occurred before the Karelians migrated from the shores of Ladoga to the more northern districts where the song was found. The core

---

[142] Compare the intertextual analysis of Kalevala poetry by Lotte Tarkka (Tarkka, *Rajarahvaan laulu*); especially in this frame of research the idea of something 'belonging' to something is unnecessary.

[143] Compare Knuuttila and Timonen, 'If the One I Know Came Now', pp. 262–64.

idea, a variant of the miraculous conception model, was possibly, but not at all certainly, received from South Slavic areas.

The song developed differently in different Finnic traditions. In Ingria it was kept short, telling simply but emphatically the facts of seeing and eating the apple. In Archangel Karelia the apple was changed to the berry and the act of its eating was recomposed into a lengthy, dramatic narrative. In northern Olonets Karelia the rejection of St Mary as a whore and her relations to her family became the second centre of the song, extending its scope. In Ladoga and southern Olonets Karelia the Christian connection of the song began to disappear and the berry-eating motif merged more or less into other, non-religious songs.

The first learned interpreters of the whole song cycle in the seventeenth century appreciated the folk religiosity expressed in it. The unknown author of the song is 'well acquainted with sacred matters', said Erik Cajanus in 1697.[144] Later the opinions of the literati changed. Elias Lönnrot, who recorded many variants of the song in the 1830s, did not approve the singers' religion. He wrote:

> This song is sung in Russian Karelia, and maybe it represents the only knowledge they have of Christianity there. The authorities send to them teachers as to other places, but they stubbornly depend on their old magic, i.e. on their so called 'old belief', and do not care for teachers. This Song of Mary proves how they have fallen into miserable darkness because of their stubbornness and contempt. Almost everything in this song is empty gossip, which has not the slightest foundation in the Bible. Mary did not become pregnant from a lingonberry or any other berry, but from the Holy Spirit [...]. But as foolish and false as this song is, on the other hand its verbal expression is beautiful; so we see that the subject matter and the verbal expression are separate things, although it is not always easy to distinguish one from the other.[145]

Nevertheless, Lönnrot so greatly appreciated 'the verbal expression', that is, the poetics of the song, that he published his versions of it in the *Kalevala* (1835, 1849) and in the *Kanteletar* (1840). He ended the *Kalevala* with the story of Marjatta (not Mary!), who eats the berry and gives birth to a new king and a new era. Thus this folk song, once inspired by a religious canon, having lived through centuries in a state of oral freedom and transformation, in the end became fixed in the canon of national literature.

---

[144] Cited in Sarajas, *Suomen kansanrunouden tuntemus*, p. 93.

[145] Lönnrot, *Valitut teokset*, ed. by Majamaa, v, 358.

Works Cited

Primary Sources

Apuleius, *Cupid & Psyche*, ed. by E. J. Kenney (Cambridge: Cambridge University Press, 1990)

Danmarks gamle folkeviser, ed. by Svend Grundtvig and others, 12 vols (København: Samfundet til den danske literaturs fremme, 1853–1976)

Eesti rahvalaulud: antoloogia, ed. by Ülo Tedre, 5 vols (Tallinn: Eesti raamat, 1969–74)

Finnish Folk Poetry: Epic. An Anthology in Finnish and English, ed. by Matti Kuusi, Keith Bosley, and Michael Branch (Helsinki: Suomalaisen Kirjallisuuden Seura, 1977)

Folkloren erotikon, ed. by Florentina Badalanova, 7 vols (Sofia: Rod, 1993–99)

Hennecke, Edgar, *New Testament Apocrypha*, ed. by Wilhelm Schneewelcher, trans. by R. McL. Wilson, 2 vols (Philadelphia: Westminster, 1963–64), I: *Gospels and Related Writings*

The Kalevala, trans. with intro. and notes by Keith Bosley (Oxford: Oxford University Press, 1989)

Karjalan kansan runot, ed. by V. Jevsejev, 2 vols (Tallinn: Eesti Raamat, 1976–80)

Legendat: kansankertomuksia Suomesta ja Karjalasta, ed. by Irma-Riitta Järvinen (Helsinki: Suomalaisen Kirjallisuuden Seura, 1981)

Lönnrot, Elias, *Valitut teokset*, ed. by Raija Majamaa, 5 vols (Helsinki: Suomalaisen Kirjallisuuden Seura, 1990–93)

Oláfr Thordarson Hvítaskáld, *Dritte grammatische Abhandlung: der isländische Text nach den Handschriften AM 784 1,4 und Codex Wormianus*, ed. by Björn Magnus Olsen, with translation and commentary by Thomas Krömmelbein, Studia Nordica, 3 (Oslo: Novus, 1998)

Slovenske narodne pesmi iztiskanih in pisanih virov, ed. by Karel Štrekelj, 5 vols (Ljubljana: Natisnila Zadružna Tiskarnica, 1904–07)

Suomen kansan vanhat runot, ed. by Aukusti Robert Niemi and others, 34 vols (Helsinki: Suomalaisen Kirjallisuuden Seura, 1908–48, 1997)

Sveriges medeltida ballader, ed. by Bengt R. Jonsson, Svenskt visarkiv, 5 vols (Stockholm: Almqvist & Wiksell, 1983–2001), I: *Legendvisor, Historiska visor*

Secondary Works

Alexiou, Margaret, *The Ritual Lament in Greek Tradition* (Cambridge: Cambridge University Press, 1974)

Annunciation (London: Phaidon, 2004)

Anttonen, Veikko, 'Pihlaja, naisen kiima ja kasvuvoiman pyhä locus', in *Amor, locus & familia: kirjoituksia kansanperinteestä*, ed. by Jyrki Pöysä and Anna-Leena Siikala, Tietolipas, 158 (Helsinki: Suomalaisen Kirjallisuuden Seura, 1998), pp. 136–47

Asplund, Anneli, 'Legendenlieder', in *Atlas der Finnischen Volkskultur*, ed. by Matti Sarmela, trans. by Tuuli Mahringer and others (Münster: Waxmann, 2000), pp. 263–74

Badalanova, Florentina, 'Notes on the Cult of the Virgin Mary in Slavia Orthodoxa: The Interpenetration of Folk and Christian Themes', in *Slavianskoe i Balkanskoe Iazykoznanie 14: Chelovek v Prostranstve Balkan. Podevencheskie Stsenarii i Kul'turnye Roli*, ed. by I. A. Sedakova and T. V. Tsiv'ian (Moskva: Indrik, 2003), pp. 159–203

——, '"Zavetnii fol'klor" kak etnokul'turnaja paradigma ponjatii "BLAGO" i "BLAZHENSTVO"', in *Folkloren erotikon*, ed. by Florentina Badalanova, 7 vols (Sofia: Rod, 1993–99), I, 71–83

Badalanova Geller, Florentina, 'The Spinning Mary: Towards the Iconology of the Annunciation', *Cosmos*, 20 (2004), 211–60

Batho, Edith C., 'The Life of Christ in the Ballads', in *Essays and Studies by Members of the English Association*, X, collected by W. P. Ker (Oxford: Oxford University Press, 1924), pp. 70–97

Beškow, Per, 'Runor och liturgi', in *Nordens kristnande i europeiskt perspektiv: tre uppsatser*, ed. by Per Beškow and Reinhart Staats, Occasional Papers on Medieval Topics, 7 (Skara: Viktoria, 1994), pp. 16–36

Bezsonov, P., *Kaleki perekhozhie: sbornik stikhov i izsledovanie*, with a new intro. by Sergei Hackel (Westmead: Gregg, 1970)

Borenius, A. A., 'Suomen keskiaikaista runoutta I: Luojan virsi', *Virittäjä*, 2 (1886), 58–82

Bringéus, Nils-Arvid, 'The Rest on the Flight into Egypt: A Motif in Scandinavian Folk Art', *Folklore*, 114 (2003), 323–33

Bynum, Caroline Walker, 'Introduction: The Complexity of Symbols', in *Gender and Religion: On the Complexity of Symbols*, ed. by Caroline Walker Bynum, Stevan Harrell, and Paula Richman (Boston: Beacon, 1986), pp. 1–20

Danckert, Werner, *Symbol, Metapher, Allegorie im Lied der Völker*, 3 vols (Bonn: Verlag für systematische Musikwissenschaft, 1976–78), III: *Pflanzen* (1978)

Davidson, Hilda Ellis, *Roles of the Northern Goddess* (London: Routledge, 1998)

DuBois, Thomas A., 'An Ethnopoetic Approach to Finnish Folk Poetry: Arhippa Perttunen's Nativity', in *Songs Beyond the Kalevala: Transformations of Oral Poetry*, ed. by Anna-Leena Siikala and Sinikka Vakimo, Studia Fennica folkloristica, 2 (Helsinki: Suomalaisen Kirjallisuuden Seura, 1994), pp. 138–79

——, 'From Maria to Marjatta: The Transformation of an Oral Poem in Elias Lönnrot's *Kalevala*', *Oral Tradition*, 8 (1993), 247–88

Dundes, Alan, 'The Hero Pattern and the Life of Jesus', in *Interpreting Folklore* (Bloomington: Indiana University Press, 1980), pp. 223–61

Foskett, Mary F., *A Virgin Conceived: Mary and Classical Representations of Virginity* (Bloomington: Indiana University Press, 2002)

Gaster, Moses, 'Rumanian Popular Legends of the Lady', in *Studies and Texts in Folklore, Magic, Medieval Romance, Hebrew Apocrypha and Samaritan Archaeology*, 3 vols (London: Maggs, 1925–28), II (1928), 1090–1130

Geertz, Clifford, 'Religion as a Cultural System', in Clifford Geertz, *The Interpretation of Cultures: Selected Essays* (New York: Basic Books, 1973), pp. 87–125

Guldan, Ernst, *Eva und Maria: eine Antithese als Bildmotiv* (Graz: Böhlaus, 1966)

Haavio, Martti, 'Jeesus-lapsi ja hänen ahdistajansa: Kylvöihme', in Martti Haavio, *Kansanrunojen maailmanselitys* (Helsinki: Werner Söderström, 1955), pp. 76–120

——, 'Jumala-kuningas ja hänen vastustajansa: Hiiden sepän kahlinta', in Martti Haavio, *Kansanrunojen maailmanselitys* (Helsinki: Werner Söderström, 1955), pp. 7–75
——, *Kirjokansi: Suomen kansan kertomarunoutta* (Helsinki: Werner Söderström, 1952)
——, *Suomalaisen muinaisrunouden maailma* (Helsinki: Werner Söderström, 1935)
Hiekkanen, Markus, *Suomen keskiajan kivikirkot*, Suomalaisen Kirjallisuuden Seuran toimituksia, 1117 (Helsinki: Suomalaisen Kirjallisuuden Seura, 2007)
Hirn, Yrjö, *The Sacred Shrine: A Study of the Poetry and Art of the Catholic Church* (London: Macmillan, 1912)
Honko, Lauri, 'Rethinking Tradition Ecology', *Temenos*, 21 (1985), 55–82
Janson, Henrik, ed., *Från Bysans till Norden: Östliga kyrkinfluenser under vikingatid och tidig medeltid* (Skellefteå: Artos, 2005)
Järvinen, Irma-Riitta, *Karjalan pyhät kertomukset: tutkimus liivinkielisen alueen legendaperinteestä ja kansanuskon muutoksista* (Helsinki: Suomalaisen Kirjallisuuden Seura, 2004)
Keinänen, Marja-Liisa, *Creating Bodies: Childbirth Practices in Pre-Modern Karelia* (Stockholm: Stockholm University, 2003)
Kirkinen, Heikki, 'Inkerin keskiaika ja uuden ajan alku vuoteen 1616', in *Inkeri: historia, kansa, kulttuuri*, ed. by Pekka Nevalainen and Hannes Sihvo (Helsinki: Suomalaisen Kirjallisuuden Seura, 1991), pp. 35–66
——, *Karjala idän kulttuuripiirissä: Bysantin ja Venäjän yhteyksistä keskiajan Karjalaan* (Helsinki: Kirjayhtymä, 1963)
——, *Karjala idän ja lännen välissä*, 2 vols (Helsinki: Kirjayhtymä, 1970–76), II: *Karjala taistelukenttänä* (1976)
——, *Pohjois-Karjalan kalevalaisen perinteen juuret* (Helsinki: Suomalaisen Kirjallisuuden Seura, 1988)
Knuuttila, Seppo, and Senni Timonen, 'If the One I Know Came Now', in *Myth and Mentality: Studies in Folklore and Popular Thought*, ed. by Anna-Leena Siikala, Studia Fennica folkloristica, 8 (Helsinki: Suomalaisen Kirjallisuuden Seura, 2002), pp. 247–71
Korpela, Jukka, *Viipurin linnaläänin synty*, Viipurin historia, 2 (Helsinki: Karjalan Kirjapaino, 2004)
Kriza, Ildiko, 'The Survival of Medieval Tradition in Contemporary Hungarian Folklore', *Acta ethnographica Academiae Scientiarum Hungaricae*, 25 (1976), 91–106
Krohn, Julius, and Kaarle Krohn, *Kantelettaren tutkimuksia*, 2 vols (Helsinki: Suomalaisen Kirjallisuuden Seura, 1900–01)
Krohn, Kaarle, *Suomalaisten runojen uskonto*, Suomalaisen Kirjallisuuden Seuran toimituksia, 137 (Porvoo: Werner Söderström, 1915)
Kupiainen, Tarja, *Kertovan kansanrunon nuori nainen ja nuori mies*, Suomalaisen Kirjallisuuden Seuran toimituksia, 996 (Helsinki: Suomalaisen Kirjallisuuden Seura, 2004)
Kuujo, Erkki, 'Ruotsi vai Venäjä Antikristuksen valtakunta? Vanhauskoisuuden leviämisestä 1600-luvulla Ruotsin alaisiin Karjalaan ja Inkeriin', in *Karjala: idän ja lännen silta*, ed. by Hannes Sihvo, Kalevalaseuran vuosikirja, 53 (Helsinki: Werner Söderström, 1973), pp. 23–34

Kuusi, Matti, 'Keskiajan kalevalainen runous', in *Suomen kirjallisuus*, ed. by Matti Kuusi and others, 8 vols (Helsinki: Suomalaisen Kirjallisuuden Seura, 1963-70), I: *Kirjoittamaton kirjallisuus* (1963), ed. by Matti Kuusi, pp. 273-397

——, 'Pakanuuden ja kristinuskon murros suomalaisen kansanrunouden kuvastimessa', in *Novella plantatio: Suomen kirkkohistoriallisen seuran juhlakirja Suomen kirkon juhlavuotena 1955*, ed. by Aarno Maliniemi, Mikko Juva, and Kauko Pirinen, Suomen Kirkkohistoriallisen Seuran toimituksia, 56 (Helsinki: Suomen kirkkohistoriallinen seura, 1955), pp. 146-64

——, 'Questions of Kalevala Metre', in *Songs Beyond the Kalevala: Transformations of Oral Poetry*, ed. by Anna-Leena Siikala and Sinikka Vakimo, Studia Fennica folkloristica, 2 (Helsinki: Suomalaisen Kirjallisuuden Seura, 1994), pp. 41-55

——, 'Salamnius, Matthias (1640-1691)', in *Kansallisbiografia* (Helsinki: Suomalaisen Kirjallisuuden Seura, 2006), <http://www.kansallisbiografia.fi/kb/artikkeli/2340> [accessed 2 August 2012]

Laitila, Teuvo, 'Vienan kansanomainen ja kirkollinen uskonnollisuus ennen Suomen itsenäistymistä', in *Minun Bysanttini: kaukana ja lähellä*, ed. by Aune Jääskinen and others (Helsinki: Suomen Bysanttikomitea, 2005), pp. 149-73

Laitinen, Heikki, 'Anni Tenisovan Marian virsi', in *Kalevala ja laulettu runo*, ed. by Anna-Leena Siikala, Lauri Harvilahti, and Senni Timonen (Helsinki: Suomalaisen Kirjallisuuden Seura, 2004), pp. 157-93

Leeming, David Adam, 'Virgin Birth', in *The Encyclopedia of Religion*, ed. by Lindsay Jones, 2nd edn, 14 vols (Detroit: Macmillan, 2005), XIV: *Transcendental meditation–Zwingli, Huldrych*, pp. 272-81

Leino, Pentti, 'The Kalevala Metre and its Development', in *Songs Beyond the Kalevala: Transformations of Oral Poetry*, ed. by Anna-Leena Siikala and Sinikka Vakimo, Studia Fennica folkloristica, 2 (Helsinki: Suomalaisen Kirjallisuuden Seura, 1994), pp. 56-74

——, *Language and Metre: Metrics and the Metrical System of Finnish*, Studia Fennica, 31 (Helsinki: Suomalaisen Kirjallisuuden Seura, 1986)

Leskinen, Juha, 'Karjalaisten kielimuotojen alkuperän arvoitus', in *Viipurin läänin historia*, ed. by Matti Saarnisto and others, 6 vols (Lappeenranta: Karjalan kirjapaino, 2003-10), I: *Karjalan synty* (2003), ed. by Matti Saarnisto, pp. 448-49

Lindgren, Mereth, 'Gideons fäll och Arons grönskande stav: om Maria-typologi i svensk medeltidskonst', in *Maria i Sverige under tusen år: föredrag vid symposiet i Vadstena 6-10 oktober 1994*, ed. by Sven-Erik Brodd and Alf Härdelin (Skellefteå: Artos, 1996), pp. 373-406

Mansikka, V. J., 'Legendat ihmeellisestä synnyttämisestä', *Kaukomieli*, 4 (1910), 1-11

Oinas, Felix J., 'The Search for the Lost Child', in *Studies in Finnic-Slavic Folklore Relations: Selected Papers*, ed. by Felix J. Oinas, Folklore Fellows Communications, 105 (Helsinki: Suomalainen Tiedeakatemia, 1969), pp. 86-92

Peltomaa, Leena Mari, *The Image of the Virgin Mary in the Akathistos Hymn*, The Medieval Mediterranean: Peoples, Economies and Cultures, 400-1453, 35 (Leiden: Brill, 2001)

Pentikäinen, Juha, *Oral Repertoire and World View: An Anthropological Study of Marina Takalo's Life History*, Folklore Fellows Communications, 219 (Helsinki: Suomalainen Tiedeakatemia, 1978)

Purhonen, Paula, *Kristinuskon saapumisesta Suomeen — uskontoarkeologinen tutkimus*, Suomen Muinaismuistoyhdistyksen aikakauskirja, 106 (Helsinki: Suomen Muinaismuistoyhdistys, 1998)

Royston, Pamela L., '"The Cherry-tree Carol": Its Sources and Analogues', *Folklore Forum*, 15 (1982), 1–16

Sarajas, Annamari, *Suomen kansanrunouden tuntemus 1500–1700-lukujen kirjallisuudessa* (Helsinki: Werner Söderström, 1956)

Sarmela, Matti, *Volksüberlieferung*, trans. by Tuuli Mahringer and others, Atlas der Finnischen Volkskultur, 2 (Münster: Waxmann, 2000)

Shikalov, Yuri, 'Old Believers in the Kemi Jurisdictional District: Old Believers in Dvina Karelia and White Sea Coast in the Late 19th and Early 20th Centuries', in *My Byzantium, Far and Near*, ed. by Aune Jääskinen (Helsinki: Finnish National Committee for Byzantine Studies, 2008), pp. 67–76

Siikala, Anna-Leena, *Mythic Images and Shamanism: A Perspective on Kalevala Poetry*, Folklore Fellows Communications, 280 (Helsinki: Suomalainen Tiedeakatemia, 2002)

Stark, Laura, *Peasants, Pilgrims, and Sacred Promises: Ritual and the Supernatural in Orthodox Karelian Folk Religion*, Studia Fennica folkloristica, 11 (Helsinki: Finnish Literature Society, 2002)

Tarkiainen, Viljo, 'Suomalainen messiadi', in *Piirteitä suomalaisesta kirjallisuudesta* (Helsinki: Werner Söderström, 1922), pp. 60–77

Tarkka, Lotte, *Rajarahvaan laulu: Tutkimus Vuokkiniemen kalevalamittaisesta runokulttuurista 1821–1921*, Suomalaisen Kirjallisuuden Seuran toimituksia, 1033 (Helsinki: Suomalaisen Kirjallisuuden Seura, 2005)

Timonen, Senni, 'The Mary of Women's Epic', in *Songs Beyond the Kalevala: Transformations of Oral Poetry*, ed. by Anna-Leena Siikala and Sinikka Vakimo, Studia Fennica folkloristica, 2 (Helsinki: Suomalaisen Kirjallisuuden Seura, 1994), pp. 301–29

Tshernjakova, Irina, 'Repolan seurakunta 1800-luvulla', in *Aunuksen Repola*, ed. by Heikki Tarma (Joensuu: Repola-seura, 2001), pp. 28–65

Tuominen, Marja, 'The Mother of God Image in the Chora Church: A Hymnographic Aspect of the Iconographical Approach', *Byzantium and the North: Acta Byzantina Fennica VIII (1995–1996)* (1997), 134–84

Uino, Pirjo, 'Viikinkiaika n. 800–1100 jKr.', in *Viipurin läänin historia*, ed. by Matti Saarnisto and others, 6 vols (Lappeenranta: Karjalan kirjapaino, 2003–10), I: *Karjalan synty* (2003), pp. 291–380

Vilkuna, Kustaa, 'Maria i folketraditionen. Finland', in *Kulturhistoriskt lexikon för nordisk medeltid: från vikingatid till reformationstid*, ed. by Helge Pohjolan-Pirhonen and others (Helsinki: Örnförlaget, 1966), XI: *Luft–Motståndsrätt*, pp. 373–74

Virtaranta, Pertti, and others, eds, *Karjalan kielen sanakirja*, Lexica Societatis Fenno-Ugricae, 16, 6 vols (Helsinki: Suomalais-ugrilainen seura, 1968–2005)

Vranska, Tsvetana, *Apokrifite za Bogoroditsa i Blgarskata narodna pesen*, Sbornik na Bolgarskata akademija na naukite, 34 (Sofia: Derzhavna Petshatnitsa, 1940)

Vuola, Elina, '*La Morenita* on Skis: Women's Popular Marian Piety and Feminist Research on Religion', in *Oxford Handbook of Feminist Theology*, ed. by Mary McClintock Fulkerson and Sheila Briggs (Oxford: Oxford University Press, 2012), pp. 494–524

Weigle, Marta, *Creation and Procreation: Feminist Reflections on Mythologies of Cosmogony and Parturition*, Publications of the American Folklore Society (Philadelphia: University of Pennsylvania Press, 1989)

Index

Åbo: *see Turku*
Aarhus: 112
Åland *alias* Ahvenanmaa: 70, 118, 203–04, 355 n. 50
Abrahams, Roger: 357
Achilles: 147–48
Adam: 155, 161–62, 183, 186, 349, 361
Adam of Bremen: 6, 190 n. 55, 368, 379–80, 383–85
   Historia Hammaburgensis Ecclesiae: 368
Aeneas: 154
Ælfric: 164 n. 75, 229 n. 20
   De falsis diis: 164 n. 75
   Pastoral Letter to Wulfsige: 229 n. 20
Ælnoth: 13
   Legend of St Canute: 13
Aeneid: 154
Æsir: *see Asia*
Africa: 157, 161
Ahvenanmaa: *see Åland*
Aino: 407
Akathistos hymn: 413, 419
Albert, Jean-Pierre: 356
Albert, bishop of Riga: 297 n. 8, 299 n. 21, 302, 308–09, 311, 315 n. 80, 316, 321–22, 328–29, 330 n. 133
Alexandria: 284, 360
Alfǫðr *alias* All-father: 153
All-father: *see Alfǫðr*
Alps: 50
Althoff, Gerd: 296, 333
Altuna stone, the: 181–82
America (Americans): 3, 124, 296, 298, 313, 357

Amor: 412
Amorites: 332
Anders *alias* Andreas Sunesen: 21, 308, 328
   Hexaëmeron: 21
Andersson, Theodore M.: 214
Andreas Sunesen: *see Anders Sunesen*
Annan: *see Athra*
Annunciation Day: 400–02, 404, 409, 413–14, 418–19
Anselm of Laon: 22
Anton Koberger: 100
Anttonen, Pertti: 3, 35
Apocrypha: *see Bible*
Apuleius: 412
   Eros and Psyche: 412
Arbusow, Leonid: 300, 302, 304 n. 37
Archangel *alias* White Sea Karelia: 10, 12 n. 19, 129, 277 n. 18, 287, 390, 392, 397–398, 406, 411, 423 n. 136, 426
Ari: 12
   Book of Icelanders: 12–13
Arnkell goði: 266
Asdís: 264 n. 51
Asgard: 180
Asia (Asians *alias* Æsir): 144, 146–48, 152, 154–57, 160–63, 180–81, 186, 188–91
Asmundr: 264–65
Assyrians: 159
Athra *alias* Annan: 162
Atli: 253, 264–65
Auðr, wife of Ankell goði: 266
Augustine: 158–59, 161
   De civitate Dei: 158
   De Genesi ad litteram: 161

Augustinians: 7, 299
Augustin Ferber: 109
Ave Maris Stella: 309

Baal *alias* Baalim *alias* Bel *alias* Beel *alias* Beelphegor *alias* Beelzebub *alias* Belus: 158–59, 162–66
Baalim: *see Baal*
Babel *alias* Babylon: 156–58, 161–66, 301
  Tower of: 157–58, 161, 167
Babylon: *see Babel*
Badalanova, Florentina: 417 nn. 107–08, 418–19
Baldrs draumar: 378 n. 29
Balkan: 417
Ballad: 1–2, 11–13, 35, 114–16, 132, 214, 341–63, 372, 384, 394, 409, 414 n. 91
  English: 35, 346n, 349, 358, 361
  European: 414 n. 91
  Ingrian: 409
  Scandinavian: 1, 394
  Wendish: 350
Bällsta stone/inscription: 368–69, 372, 376–77, 379 n. 30
Baetke, Walter: 173–75
Bagge, Sverre: 47, 202
Baktrians: 159
Bálagarðssíða: 201–02
"Ballad of the Death of Bishop Henry" *alias* "Piispa Henrikin surmavirsi" *alias* "The Song of the Slaying of Bishop Henry"*: 114–16, 132, 342, 352
Balthasar Russow: 213
  Chronica der Provintz Lyfflandt: 213
Baltic (Balts): 2, 6–7, 9, 18, 21, 26–27, 34, 78, 102, 130, 200–215, 298, 300, 309, 394 n. 22
  Sea: 4, 6, 8–9, 27, 130, 419
  Language: *see Languages*
Barthes, Roland: 257 n. 27, 269 n. 60
Bartholomaeus Ghotan: 100
Bartlett, Robert: 298, 327
  The Making of Europe: 298
Baum, Paull Franklin: 361
Bavaria: 80 n. 31
Beel: *see Baal*
Beelphegor: *see Baal*
Bekker-Nielsen, Hans: 226
Bel: *see Baal*

Belgrad (the white town Beelzebub: *See Baal*): 202
Belus: *see Baal*
Benedictines: 7, 31, 150
Benedictus, bishop: 91 n. 61
Ben-Hadad, Syrian king: 304
Beowulf: 6, 251, 371 n. 13
Bergen: 5, 8, 224
Bergr: 251–53
Berthold, bishop of Üxküll: 299, 310, 321–22, 326
Beškow, Per: 403 n. 50
Bible: 9, 81 n. 32, 88, 121–22, 144, 157, 231, 238, 278, 309, 347–48, 360–61, 389 n. 3, 391, 393, 411, 323, 326
  Genesis: 157, 161–62, 310 n. 61, 319 n. 94
  Exodus: 306 n. 48, 325, 331 n. 134
  1 Maccabees: 306 n. 47, 307 n. 47, 311 n. 68
  Job: 185, 189, 310 n. 61
  Psalms: 62, 237, 301, 303 nn. 36-37, 306 n. 48, 308 n. 51, 309 n. 57, 315 n. 79
  Ecclesiastes: 238
  Wisdom: 63, 152–53, 155, 164–65
  Ecclesiasticus: 122
  Ezechiel: 311 nn. 64-65
  Matthew: 63, 122, 302–04, 311 n. 64
  Luke: 117, 122 n. 42, 309 n. 60
  John: 121–22, 297 n. 9, 299 n. 23
  Philippians: 310
  2 Peter: 121
  Apocrypha
  Book of James: 278, 402, 411–12
  Gospel of Judas: 342, 360–61
  Gospel of Mary Magdalene: 360
  Gospel of Nicodemus: 183
  Gospel of Thomas: 360
Bing, Kristen: 209
Birgisson, Bergsveinn: 215
Bogatyrev, Petr: 251 n. 8
Bohemia: 68, 80 n. 31, 87–88, 112, 275
Bohlin, Folke: 112 n. 12
Boklund-Lagopoulou, Karin: 343, 438–48, 362
Bolli: 260–61
Bologna: 21
Bolton, Brenda: 305

Borg: 254
Borgund: 224 n. 5
Bǫrkr: 267 n. 56
Borst, Arno: 157
   Der Turmbau von Babel: 157
Bothnia: 115
   Gulf of: 101
Brennu-Njáls Saga: 202, 214, 260–61, 266, 371
Bridgettines: 7, 30, 71, 90–94, 101, 132–33, 275
Britain: 295, 298, 300, 346
Bruges: *see Brugge*
Brugge: 8
Brøndsted, Mogens: 11
Brøndsted, Karl Gustav: 183, 190–91
Bugge, Sophus: 177
Bulgaria: 400, 405, 417–19, 423 n. 136
Burke, Peter: 295, 300, 333
   Historical Anthropology of Early Modern Italy: 300
Bury St Edmunds: 22
Bygdøy: 224 n. 5
Bynum, Caroline Walker: 421–22
Byzantium: 13, 392, 413

Caianus: 207
Caupo, Livish chieftain: 316 n. 84
Cedercreutz family: 352
Cerquiglini, Bernard: 148–49
Child, Francis James: 343, 359
   English and Scottish Popular Ballads: 343
Chrétien de Troyes: 6
Christ *alias* Jesus *alias* the Saviour: 36, 60–61, 63–64, 116, 119–27, 152, 184, 186, 189, 227, 241, 275–79, 284–85, 288, 297, 302, 308, 310, 312, 315, 319 n. 94, 325 n. 115, 331, 341–49, 356–58, 360–61, 389–426
Christfried Ganander: 285
   Mythologia Fennica: 285
Chronicle of the Bishops of Åbo: 71
Cistercians: 7, 21, 77–78
Clanchy, Michael: 175
   From Memory to Written Record: 175
Clemet Henrikinpoika Krook: 209
Cleophas: 279
Clover, Carol: 371–72, 377–78
Codices descriptorum: 149 n. 12

Coen Brothers: 256, 258
Cologne: *see Köln*
Congaudentes Exultemus: 53–55
Constantinople: 279, 288 n. 79, 392, 419
Conti, Aidan: 3, 33
Copenhagen: *see København*
Creator: *see God*
Crete (Cretans): 159, 161, 163–64, 166
Crucifixion: 423
Curonians: 313 n. 74
Cush: 157

Dahl, J.C.: 224–25
Dain, Alphonse: 239
Daniel, priest: 318–19
Danish: *see languages*
Dante Alighieri: 256, 273
   Divine Comedy, the: 256, 273
David: 209, 238, 305, 307
Degnbol, Helle: 149 n. 11, 166 n. 81, 225 n. 7
Denmark (Danes): 5–8, 11–15, 18 n. 35, 19, 21, 26, 34, 46, 88, 112, 203–04, 280, 308 n. 52, 309, 311, 320, 328, 357
Derrida, Jacques: 257 n. 27
Devil: 126, 133, 183–86, 189 n. 53, 288–89, 320, 326, 351, 391, 398–99
Dijderijk Pehrsson Ruutha: *see Theodoricus Petri*
Diodorus Siculus: 163 n. 72
Dollinger, Phillipe: 205
Dorpat *alias* Tartu: 328, 394
Douglas, Mary: 313 n. 73, 314, 331
Drangey Island: 263
Draumkvæde (draumkvedet): 214
Dronke, Peter: 173, 348
Dronke, Ursula: 173
DuBois, Thomas: 214, 407, 423
Dünamunde (Daugaugriva): 320 n. 99
Dumézil, Georges: 175, 178–79
Dvina: 315, 322, 323
Dynna stone: 375

Edda:
   Poetic *Edda*: 1, 143 n. 1, 172, 178, 193
      Hymiskviða: 178, 189 n. 53
   Prose *Edda*: *see Snorri Sturluson*
Eggen, Erik: 61, 63
Egils saga: 252n, 255, 258, 266

Egilsson, Sveinbjörn: 202
Egypt: 342, 360–61, 415
Einarr Þorbjarnarson: 266
Eiríkr Bloodaxe, king: 376
Eiríksmál: 377
Elisha: 307
England (Englishmen): 7, 13, 22, 35, 49, 67, 69, 73, 75–77, 79, 81, 83, 85, 88, 98, 101, 120, 125–26, 163, 181, 203, 229, 280–81, 341–49, 356–58, 361, 372
English: *see Languages*
Ennius: 163 n. 72
Erik Axelsson Tott: 205
Erik Cajanus: 392, 426
Espoo: 275 n. 15
Estonia (Estonians): 2, 6–8, 20–21, 27, 32, 202, 208, 211–13, 297, 299, 302, 308–14, 319–330, 355n, 391, 393–94, 413
Estonian: *see Languages*
Euhemeros: 163 n. 72
Eurasia: 391
Europe: 7, 9, 15, 32, 45, 52–3, 55, 67–9, 72, 74, 76, 84, 87, 100, 103, 159, 172–73, 213, 223–24, 226, 274, 275 n. 13, 281–82, 325, 332–33, 348, 359 n. 59, 392, 394, 414–415
  Central: 281
  East Central: 8, 68–9, 86, 102
  Northern: 15, 34, 74, 154, 161, 171, 178–79, 191, 425
  Western: 67, 71, 171, 275 n. 13, 279, 421
Eusebius: 159
Eve: 361, 418–20, 425
Exeter, Cathedral of: 203 n. 20
Eyrbyggja saga: 214, 266
Eysýslu: *see Ösel*

Fagrskinna: 376
Fantoft: 224 n. 5
Faroes: 8, 14
Faulkes, Anthony: 148 n. 8, 149, 150 n. 13, 150 n. 15
Finland (Finns): 2, 6, 8–14, 18, 20, 22, 26–7, 30–32, 34–5, 67–102, 109–34, 145, 200–12, 213, 273–90, 341–42, 348, 350–57, 358–60, 362, 389, 391–96, 400, 403, 414, 418, 420, 426
  Grand Duchy of: 12 n. 19
  Gulf of: 10, 27, 32, 283, 396

Finnish Literature Society: 115, 207 n. 39, 277–78, 352 n. 36, 394, 396 n. 28
  Folklore Archives: 115, 277, 352 n. 36, 396 n. 28
  National Library of: 72, 84
Finnboga saga ramma: 251
Finnbogi the Mighty: 251
Finngálkn: 202
Finnish: *see languages*
Finström: 275 n. 15
Fish, Stanley: 257 n. 27
Flanders: 275
Flateyjarbók: 380–81
  Vǫlsa Þáttr: 380–82, 384, 386
Flosi: 266
Folklore Archives: *see Finland*
Foley, John Miles: 33, 124, 199, 250
Fornaldarsǫgur: 248
Fortun: 224 n. 5
Foucault, Michel: 257 n. 27
Fourth Lateran Council (1215): 21, 299 n. 21, 303, 311
France: 6–7, 21–22, 67, 73, 76–78, 81, 83, 85, 98, 101, 175, 281, 326, 347, 357
Franciscans: 85, 90–91, 132, 229, 275 n. 15
French: *see Languages*
Freyr: 213
Frigg: *see Frigiða*
Frigiða *alias* Frigg: 162, 417
Fulgentius: 164 n. 77

Gabriel: 402, 413, 419, 425
Gaute, archbishop of Nidaros: 205
Geary, Patrick J.: 298, 334
Geatisc meowle: 371 n. 13
Geertz, Clifford: 295, 393 n. 19
  The Interpretation of Cultures: 295
Geirríðr: 266
Geisli: 60–61
Germany (Germans): 6–9, 12, 27, 30, 34, 67, 69, 73, 76, 78–79, 81, 83, 85, 88, 98, 100–01, 110, 127, 130, 172–77, 179, 183, 190, 192–93, 205, 223 n. 3, 224 n. 5, 275, 281, 296, 300, 309, 323, 328–29, 379
German: *see languages*
Gideon: 305
Gimle *alias* Vingólf: 153

INDEX 437

Ginzburg, Carlo: 274, 289, 296
Gísla saga: 214
Gísli, Swedish priest: 230–32, 266
Gísli Jónsson, bishop of Iceland: 112–13, 130–32
Gjúki: 373
Glauser, Jürg: 14–15
  Skandinavische Literaturgeschichte: 14
Glora: *see Lora*
God *alias* Creator: 33, 45, 47, 62–63, 83, 87, 120–22, 126, 128, 144, 152–53, 155, 158, 161–62, 183–85, 190, 193, 206, 227, 231–32, 234–36, 240, 278, 280, 284 n. 53, 285, 303, 306–07, 309–10, 314, 316, 319, 321, 349, 353, 355, 410–12, 414, 418, 422, 424
God of Thunder, *see Thor*
Gol: 224 n. 5
Gordeinen, Okuli (Okki): 398–400, 403–04, 406, 409–12
Gosforth: 181
  stone: 181–82
Gotland (Gothland): 22, 79, 90, 205, 308 n. 52, 323
Great Schism, the: 98
Greece: 9–10, 12, 23–25, 163, 247, 250, 280–86, 356, 360, 413
Greenblatt, Stephen: 313
Greenland: 8, 14
Gregory the Great: 183–85, 240–41
  Homilia 34 (De sancto Michaele et omnium angelorum): 240
Greifswald: 109
Grettir the Strong: 253–54, 262–65, 267 n. 56, 382–83, 386 n. 46
Grettisfærsla: 382–83
Grettis saga: 214, 253–54, 263, 264, 382–83, 386 n. 46
Grimkell, bishop of Nidaros: 203
Grimm brothers: 172, 175, 177, 192–93
Grimm, Jacob: 172
  Deutsche Mytologie: 172
Grundtvig, N.F.S.: 172 n. 2
Grusia: 417–18
Gschwantler, Otto: 179, 183, 187
Guðmundr Arason: 230
Guðrún: 372–76
Guðrúnarhvǫt: 371, 374
Guðrúnarkviða I: 371–72, 375, 378 n. 29

Guðrúnarkviða II: 373
Guðrún Ósvífrsdóttir: 259–61
Gunnhildr: 259–61, 376–77
Gunnarr: 260
Gunnars saga Keldugnúpsfífls: 252
Gustaf Vasa, king of Sweden: 210
Gylfi, king of Sweden: 145, 147–48, 153–54, 180–81, 186–88, 192–93
Gýríðr: 369, 376–78

Haavio, Martti: 203–04, 206–07, 209, 213, 285, 251–52, 354, 415
Hadeland: 376
Häme: 205, 352
Halldórsson, Ólafur: 383
Halliwell, James Orchard: 343
Hákon Hakonarson, king of Norway: 144–45
Halberstadt: 100
Hallberg, Peter: 11–13
Ham: 157, 165
Hamburg-Bremen: 6, 78–79, 203
Hamðismál: 371, 375
Hamites: 157, 160, 163
Hammarstedt, N.E.: 208–210
Hanseatic League: 8, 27, 100, 205
Harðar saga: 371
Harris, Joseph: 369, 377, 379 n. 30
Harva, Uno: 208–09
Harvilahti, Lauri: 3, 32, 35
Hattula: 205, 275 n. 15
Hauho: 205, 275 n. 15
Hauksbók: 148, 153, 164, 166
Havelock, Eric: 23–24, 28
Hebrews: 158, 163–64, 304
Hector: 147–48
Heiðarvíga saga: 371
Heikkilä, Markku: 357
Heikkilä, Tuomas: 2–3, 29–30
Heininen, Simo: 357
Helgakviða Hundingsbana II: 370, 372–73
Helgason, Jón: 368–71, 378
Helgi: 370, 373–74
Hell: 160–61, 183–84, 189, 285, 391
Helsinki: 81n, 202, 295
Hemmingius de Marco *alias* Hemmingius Henrici: 31, 110, 112 n. 12, 113–14, 124, 127–30, 132–34
Hemmingius Henrici: *see Hemmingius de Marco*

Henry of Livonia: 21, 34, 295–334
    Chronicon Livoniae: 21, 34, 295–334
Henten, Jan Willem van: 356
Herdalar: 201–02
Herod *alias* Ruotus: 305, 390
Herodotus: 23
Hesiod: 24
Heusler, Andreas: 173, 188 n. 50, 372, 382
Hevaa: 398
High *alias* Just-as-high *alias* Third, king of the Æsir: 180, 186–80
Hildebrand, Heinrich: 304 n. 37
Hildigunnr: 378 n. 29
Hill, Thomas D.: 346 n. 8
Himinhrjótr: 188–90
Hirdal: 202
    Battle of: 202
Höfler, Otto: 179
Hólar: 230
Holland: 275
Hollola: 275 n. 15
Holm: 315n, 320n, 322, 326
Holtsmark, Anne: 153, 173
Holy Ghost: *see Holy Spirit*
Holy Land: 308
Holy Spirit: 123, 128, 302, 411, 414, 426
Homer: 23–24, 256
    Iliad, the: 250
    Odyssey, the: 256
Homiliae in evangelia: 240
Hómilíubók: 184
Hongas: 295
Honko, Lauri: 215, 288
Honorius Augustodunensis: 166
    Elucidarius: 153, 166
Hopperstad: 224 n. 5
Hrabanus Maurus: 229 n. 21
Hrafnkell: 266
Hrafnkels saga: 214, 266
Hrolleifr: 267–68
Hrútr: 259–61
Hugh of St Cher: 22
Hundred Years War: 7 n. 11
Hungary: 46, 68, 80, 78–88, 204
Huotari, Lukkańi: 273
Hus: *see Jan Hus*
Hymes, Dell: 200
Hymir *alias* Ymir: 144, 178, 186–87

Ialgsama: 329
Iceland (Icelanders): 1, 5–6, 8, 13–16, 19, 21, 26–27, 31–33, 51, 112, 143, 145, 150, 155, 171–72, 175–77, 179–81, 183–85, 187, 192, 194, 224, 226, 230, 242, 247–48, 259–61, 268, 270, 371, 382–84
Icelandic: *see Languages*
Iku-Turso: 284 n. 54
Ilia, Vestal virgin: 413 n. 89
Iljan virsi: 210
Ilmarinen: 415
Ilomantsi: 286
In dedicatione temple sermo (Kirkjodagsmal): 224, 233, 235, 238
Ingå *alias* Inkoo: 202
Ingibjǫrg: 259–61
Ingimundr: 267–69
Ingria (Ingrians *alias* Izhors): 10, 12 n. 19, 36, 210, 392–98, 400, 404–06, 408, 411, 414, 417–19, 423, 425–26
Inkoo: *see Ingå*
Innocent III, pope: 303, 305 n. 42, 316 n. 84
In regali fastigio: 59–62, 64
Iro (Irina): 411 n. 82, 415
Isidore of Seville: 159
    Etymologiae: 159
Islendingasǫgur: 248–270
Ismaroinen: 211
Israel (Israelites): 278, 302–05, 307, 314, 325
Italy: 7, 67, 160–61, 164, 274, 281

Jackson, Tatjana: 206
Jacob, apostle: 189 n. 53
Jacobus de Voragine: 279, 348
    Legenda aurea: 279, 348
Jacobus Petri Finno: 112–13, 127, 132 n. 63, 133
Jakobson, Roman: 200
James, disciple (the Greater): 279
James, disciple (the Less): 279
Janakkala: 275 n. 15
Jan Hus: 112
Janson, Henrik: 3, 28, 30
Japheth (Japhetide): 159, 161
Järvinen, Irma-Riita: 3, 33–34
Jerusalem: 122, 184, 226, 345, 347
Jesus: *see Christ*

Jews: 345, 347, 361, 390
Joachim: 278–80
Job: 185
Jochumsson, Matthías: 263
Johannes Messenius: 353
Johannes Schefferus: 112 n. 12-113 n. 12
    Svecia Litterata: 112 n. 12
Johansson, Karl G.: 149 n. 11, 150 n. 15, 151
John, apostle: 189 n. 53, 279, 349
John, priest of Holm: 321–22
John the Deacon: 55
    St Nicholas' *vita*: 55–57
Jǫkull Ingimundarsson: 251–53, 262, 267
Jǫkull Bárðarsson: 252–53
Jǫkull Búason: 252–53
Jǫkull Hólmkelsson: 252–53
Jǫkull the Viking: 252–53
Jǫkull Þorgrímsson: 252–53
Jǫkuls þáttr Búasonar: 252
Jomala: 204, 275 n. 15
Jón Ögmundarson: *see St Jón of Hólar*
Jöns Budde: 94, 133
Jónsson, Eiríkur: 166
Jónsson, Finnur: 149 n. 13, 150–51, 166
Josef: *see Joseph*
Joseph *alias* Josef: 279, 411–13, 425
Joseph the Just, disciple: 279
Joyce, James: 256, 258
Jupiter: 159–61, 164
Judas (Iscariot), apostle: 35, 304, 332, 341–362
Judašowa pšerada (Der Verrath des Juden): 349
Jude, disciple: 279
Judgment Day: 349
Just-as-high: *see High*
Justikkala, Eino: 354
Justinian: 279

Kabell, Aage: 188
Kalanti: 275n, 355
Kalevala: *see Lönnrot, Elias*
Kaljundi, Linda: 2–3, 21, 34
Kalvola: 205
Kambsnes: 254
Kanteletar: *see Lönnrot, Elias*
Karadžić, Vuk: 211 n. 57, 257 n. 22
    Srpske narodne pjesme: 211 n. 57
Karelia: 10, 12, 27, 34, 36, 129 n. 54, 130, 273–290, 371 n. 14, 389–426
    Border Karelia: 277 n. 18
    Isthmus: 10, 109, 277 n. 18
    Ladoga Karelia: 10, 277 n. 18, 285, 397, 407, 415, 426
    Lake Ladoga: 394, 396
    Olonets Karelia: 397–398, 400, 410
    Russian Karelia: 129 n. 54, 426
    White Sea Karelia: *see Archangel*
Karelian: *see languages*
Karis *alias* Karjaa: 202
Kári Sǫlmundarson: 266
Karjaa: *see Karis*
Katajala, Kimmo: 354
Katla: 266
Kaukamoinen (Kaukamely): 351 n. 29
Keminmaa: 275 n. 15
Kengála: 263–64
Kerttu, Lalli's wife: 353
Kiev: 392, 419
King's Mirror: 1, 12
Kirkinen, Heikki: 389, 391
Kirkioda(g)smal: 235–37, 239
Kisko: 275 n. 15
Kjalnesinga saga: 252
Kjartan: 259–61
Klinge, Matti: 355
Klingenberg, Heinz: 154
Knivsta: 350
Knuutila, Jyrki: 203 n. 20, 205
Korhonen, Arvi: 213
Kronos: 163n
Krötzl, Christian: 203
København: 7, 224, 241
Köln: 8, 78
Köyliö (Kiulo): 351, 353, 359
    Lake: 342, 351, 352
Kokenhusen (Koknese): 321
Koroinen: 355 n. 50
Korpela, Jukki: 398 n. 30
Krohn, Kaarle: 415, 418 n. 19
Krohn, Julius: 415, 418 n. 19
Kuhn, Hans: 173, 175
Kuituva: 285
Kumlinge: 275 n. 15
Kuopio: 207
Kupiainen, Tarja: 409
Kurkijoki: 210
Kurs: 321, 326

Kuusi, Matti: 352, 391, 418
Kuusisto: 118
Kveld-Úlfr: 265
Kyrian: 321

Lactantius: 163
  Divinae institutiones: 163
Ladoga: *see Karelia*
Lalli, supposed murderer of Bishop Henry of Finland: 35, 124–25, 350–58
Languages: 5–10, 17, 25, 28, 30, 47, 57, 68, 96, 123, 131–32, 143, 154–57, 160–62, 165, 234, 269, 287, 343, 376, 385, 413, 422
  Asian (Oðinnic): 154–55
  Baltic: 34
  Baltic Finnic: 9, 130, 212
  Danish: 5
  Estonian: 9
  Faroese: 9
  Finnish: 10, 31–32, 111, 113, 116, 127–28, 130–34, 206, 278, 287, 342, 350, 352 n. 32, 354, 354–58, 362, 389 n. 3, 394, 403, 414
  Finnic: 130–31, 394 n. 21
  French: 25
  German: 6, 15, 25, 95, 97, 101
    High: 8
    Low: 8–9, 131–32
  Germanic: 9
  Icelandic: 9, 185
  Indo-European: 9
  Izhor: 9
  Karelian: 9–10, 12 n. 19
  Latin: 13, 15–17, 20-21, 25, 29–31, 33–34, 45–46, 50, 52, 55, 57, 64, 80, 85, 88, 96–97, 102, 109–16, 123, 127, 129–34, 144, 176, 225–26, 229, 233–34, 341, 403
  Latvian: 9, 32, 213–13
  Livvian: 9
  Nordic *alias* Scandinavian: 8–9, 11, 15, 20, 47, 113, 225, 230, 298 n. 15, 367 n. 1, 369
  Old English: 164 n. 75, 229, 371 n. 13, 372
  Old Icelandic: 183, 259 n. 30
  Old Nordic: 370
  Old Norse: 2–3, 5, 11, 13–16, 19, 25, 27, 33, 35, 143–45, 147, 148 n. 9, 150, 156 n. 40, 158–60, 164, 166, 171, 179, 192, 202, 224–26, 240, 259 n. 30, 367 n. 1, 369–72, 377, 379, 382, 384–85, 417, 422
  Old Russian: 389 n. 3
  Scandinavian: *see Nordic*
  Slavonic: 9–10
  Swedish: 5, 9–10, 71, 85, 94–97, 101, 109–10, 131, 132–33
  Votic: 394
Last Supper: 347
Latvajärvi: 398
Latvia (Latvians/Letts): 6, 32, 211–12, 311
Latvian: *see languages*
Laudes crucis: 63–64
Lausitz: 349
Lauwers, Michel: 326
Laxdæla saga: 255, 258–61
Layan: 321
Legenda nova: 71
Legenda St Henrici: 70–71, 86–88, 116, 341, 350, 353
Lehtinen, Anja-Inkeri: 22, 73 n. 14
Lehtonen, Tuomas M. S.: 3, 31
Lemland: 275 n. 15
Lemminkäinen: 415
Lenttisi: 398
Leo XIII, pope: 203
Leofric Collectar: 59 n. 27, 203 n. 20
  Red Book of Darley: 59 n. 27, 203 n. 20
Leopold Bloom: 256
Letabundus exultet: 61
Lettgallians: 299, 311–12, 314, 330
Leviathan: 183, 185, 187
Lindanise: 328
Linköping: 30, 79, 93
Literacy: 12, 14, 20 n. 42, 23, 45, 47, 64, 67–103, 130–34, 175, 192, 250, 256 n. 20
Liturgy: 3, 5, 17, 20–22, 25–26, 30, 32, 45–65, 73–74, 77–80, 88, 91, 119, 122, 144 n. 2, 298, 302, 305, 325
  Åbo: 91
  Dominican: 78, 91 n. 61
  English: 77
  Latin: 3, 5, 30, 45–46
  Norwegian: 79
Livonia: 7–8, 20, 27, 297, 299, 301–04, 308–12, 315, 318, 320–22, 326,

328–29, 331, 391
Livs: 299, 301, 304, 311 n. 68, 312-19, 322–24, 326, 329–30
Ljósvetninga saga: 214
Lönnrot, Elias: 12n, 352 n. 32, 398, 423, 426
   Kalevala: 11–12, 352 n. 32, 355 n. 50, 398, 407, 423, 426
   Kanteletar: 426
Lönnroth, Lars: 13
Lofoten: 5
Lohja: 275 n. 15
Lokalahti: 277
London: 77
Lora *alias* Glora: 162
Lord, Albert B.: 248 n. 2, 249–50, 257
Lord Sabaoth: 401
Loviatar: 416
Lübeck: 8, 100, 308, 350
Lüthi, Max: 347
Lund: 5–6, 19, 21, 308, 328
Luther, Martin: 289
Lux illuxit: 58–64
Lux illuxit dominica: 60
Lux iucunda, lux insignis: 60

Maaria: 355 n. 50
Maccabees: 303, 306–07
Macedonia (Macedonians): 159, 163
Madonna: 289
Mälaren, Lake: 355 n. 50
Magdeburg: 297 n. 8
Magnus Eriksson, king of Norway and Sweden: 95
Magnus Olai: 119, 207
Manuscripts:
   Åbo, Maakuntamuseo
      Uncatalogued fragment: 94 n. 65
   Cambridge, Corpus Christi College, MS 422: 59 n. 27
   Cambridge, Trinity College Library,
      MS B.14.39: 343
      MS 323: 343
   Helsinki, Folklore archives of the Finnish literature Society, Tytärsaari 1936,
      Aili Laanti 1699: 283 n. 49
      Aili Laanti 1807: 283 n. 49
      Lauri Laiho 3815: 283 n. 49
   Helsinki, Folklore archives of the Swedish literature Society,

Card index of Calendar Customs: 283 n. 51
Helsinki, Kansalliskirjasto,
   F.m. I.9: 76 n. 16
   F.m. I.21: 75, 76 n. 16
   F.m. I.24: 76 n. 16
   F.m. I.30: 76 n. 16
   F.m. I.115: 91 n. 62
   F.m. I.131: 82 n. 35
   F.m. I.199: 82 n. 35, 91 n. 62
   F.m. I.278: 91 nn. 62–63
   F.m. I.283: 91 nn. 62–63
   F.m. I.285: 91 n. 62
   F.m. I.288: 91 nn. 62-63
   F.m. I.291: 91 nn. 62-63
   F.m. I.308: 91 n. 62
   F.m. I.329: 91 n. 62
   F.m. II.10: 76 n. 16
   F.m. II.40: 82 n. 35
   F.m. II. 90: 94 n. 65
   F.m. II.117: 94 n. 65
   F.m. II.118: 92, 94 n. 65
   F.m. II.120: 92, 94 n. 65
   F.m. II.121: 94 n. 65
   F.m. III.2: 76 n. 16, 78 n. 28
   F.m. III.12: 76 n. 16
   F.m. III.13: 76 n. 16, 78 n. 28
   F.m. III.14: 76 n. 16, 78 n. 28
   F.m. III.18: 76 n. 16, 78 n. 28
   F.m. III.29: 76 n. 16
   F.m. III.33: 76 n. 16, 78 n. 28
   F.m. III.54: 76 n. 16
   F.m. III.68: 82 n. 35
   F.m. III.113: 91 n. 62
   F.m. III.150: 91 n. 62
   F.m. III.186: 91 n. 62
   Fm. IV.1: 76 n. 16, 74 n. 19
   F.m. IV.2: 76 n. 16
   F.m. IV.5: 76 n. 16
   F.m. IV.10: 76 n. 16
   F.m. IV.27: 91 n. 62
   F.m. IV.31: 91 n. 62
   F.m. IV.32: 91 n. 62
   F.m. IV.35: 91 n. 62
   F.m. IV.45: 91 n. 62
   F.m. IV.46: 91 n. 62
   F.m. IV.51: 91 n. 62
   F.m. IV.138: 94 n. 65
   F.m. IV.156: 94 n. 65

F.m. IV.157: 94 n. 65
F.m. IV.160: 94 n. 65
F.m. IV.170: 94 n. 65
F.m. IV.173: 94 n. 65
F.m. VII.1: 91 n. 62
F.m. VII.5: 82 n. 35
F.m. VII.6: 76 n. 16
F.m. VII.21: 82 n. 35
F.m. VII.24: 76 n. 16, 78 n. 26, 81 n. 32
F.m. VII.33: 76 n. 16
F.m. VII.86: 76 n. 16
F.m. VII.132 (=180?): 94 n. 65
F.m. VII.136: 76 n. 16
MS A° II 55: 94 n. 65
MS C IV 10: 76 n. 16, 77 n. 24
MS F.m. V.Var26: 99
Pergamentti-kokoelma 6: 96
København, Den arnamagnæanske håndskriftssamling,
　AM 242 ("Codex Wormianus"): 145 n. 4, 146 n. 5, 147 n. 7, 149–52, 153 n. 31, 154 nn. 33-34, 154 n. 36, 155–66
　AM 619 4to: 224–25, 233, 236–37, 240–41
　AM 674a, 4to: 166 n. 81
　AM 677 4to: 240
　AM 756 4to: 149 n. 12
London, British Library,
　Harley 2961: 59 n. 27
Oslo, Riksarkivet,
　In situ 4A 121 23:119, 6C: 58
　Lat. fragm. 471: 54
　Lat. fragm. 479: 58
　Lat. fragm. 537: 58
　Lat. fragm. 714: 55 n. 19, 56 n. 22
　Lat. fragm. 930: 55 n. 19
　Lat. fragm. 932: 61
　Lat. fragm. 1023: 49, 55 n. 19, 56 n. 22
Reykjavík, Stofnun Árna Magnússonar í íslenskum fræðum,
　AM 217 a folio: 233, 234 n. 34
　AM 237 a folio: 225, 240–41
　AM 556a 4to: 382–83
　AM 624 4to: 225, 233–34, 237 n. 48
　GKS 2367 4°: 149–50, 152
Stockholm, Kungliga Biblioteket,
　15 4to ("Icelandic Homily Book"): 224–25, 233, 236–38, 240

A57: 85 n. 39
A942: 85 n. 39
Stockholm, Riksarkivet,
　Fr. 112: 81 n. 32
　Fr. 116–21: 81 n. 32
　Fr. 124: 81 n. 32
　Fr. 130–33: 81 n. 32
　Fr. 152–55: 81 n. 32
　Fr. 184: 81 n. 32
　Fr. 686: 81 n. 32
　Fr. 711: 81 n. 32
　Fr. 726: 81 n. 32
　Fr. 1385: 94 n. 65
　Fr. 2070: 76 n. 19
　Fr. 2859: 94 n. 65
　Fr. 7762: 81 n. 32
　Fr. 7856: 94 n. 65
　Fr. 7971: 91 n. 63
　Fr. 8187: 91 n. 63
　Fr. 8322: 91 n. 63
　Fr. 8342: 91 n. 63
　Fr. 8639: 91 n. 63
　Fr. 8691: 91 n. 63
　Fr. 8994: 94 n. 65
　Fr. 9034: 81 n. 32
　Fr. 9101: 91 n. 63
　Fr. 9303: 81 n. 32
　Fr. 10113: 81 n. 32
　Fr. 10367: 94 n. 65
　Fr. 10370: 94 n. 65
　Fr. 10406: 94 n. 65
　Fr. 10407: 94 n. 65
　Fr. 10437: 94 n. 65
　Fr. 10771: 81 n. 32
　Fr. 10897: 91 n. 63
　Fr. 20274: 94 n. 65
　Fr. 20275: 94 n. 65
　Fr. 20340: 94 n. 65
　Fr. 28359: 94 n. 65
Uppsala, Universitetsbibliotek,
　C 292: 71 n. 13
　C 134: 77 n. 22, 98 n. 76
　C 199: 98 n. 75
　C 272: 98 n. 75
　C 453: 98 n. 75
　DG 11: 144, 149–51
　K 12a: 71n, 98 n. 75
　Palmskiöldiana 312, Åbo och Åland, 369–73: 71 n. 11

Utrecht, Bibliotheek der Rijksuniversiteit, 1374: 149–50, 152
Mariúgrátr: 369–70
Marjatta: 426
Marketta: see St Margaret
Mars: 413 n. 89
Mary (Virgin): see Saint Mary, Song of Mary
Mary Cleophas: 279
Mary Magdalene: 360
Mary Salome: 279
Marschand, James W.: 183
Matthew, apostle: 63
Matthias Salamnius, priest: 392
   Ilo-laulu Jesuxesta (Joy Song of Christ): 392
McCullough, Peter: 229 n. 17
Meinhard, bishop of Üxküll: 299, 304, 310, 314–15, 316 n. 84, 320–21, 326 n. 120
Mennon: *see Munon*
Metsola: 285
Miðfjarðarreyjar: 254
Midgard: 32, 147, 148 n. 8, 178, 184–87, 189
Midgard serpent: 32, 147–49, 178, 184–87, 189–90
Mikael Agricola: 113, 127, 209, 285
   Dauidin Psalteri: 209
Mogk, Eugen: 174–75–191
Mohn: *see Moon*
Moon (Muhu) *alias* Mohn: 299, 325
Mǫrðr Valgarðsson: 260
Morten Børup, headmaster from Aarhus: 112
Mortensen, Lars Boje: 46, 200, 204, 298
Moscow, Grand Duchy of: 10
Moses: 284, 307
Muhu: *see Moon*
Mundal, Else: 3, 35, 214, 261 n. 36
Munon *alias* Mennon: 162
Murray, Alan V.: 321
Murray, Alexander: 20
   Reason and Society in the Middle Ages: 20
Muslims: 177, 250
Nådendal: *see Naantali*
Naantali *alias* Nådendal: 71, 92–94, 101, 275
National Geographic: 342
Nativity: 116, 423
Nazareth: 341
Neptunus: 159–61
New Cambridge History of Scandinavia: 13
Nicolaysen, Nicolay: 224
Nidaros: *see Trondheim*

Niðrstigningarsaga: 183
Nimrod: 157, 165
Ninus, king: 158–59, 165–66
Njáll: 254, 260
Njáls saga: see Brennu-Njáls saga
Njǫrðr: 160
Noah: 120–121, 123, 125, 128, 157, 159
Nokia: 295
Nordal, Gudrun: 151, 180 n. 29
Nordic Union: 7
North Sea: 6–8, 187
Norway (Norwegians): 6–8, 11, 16, 18–9, 22, 26, 30, 32, 35, 45–48, 51, 53, 55, 58–59, 61–62, 64, 79, 88–89, 145–47, 203–04, 209, 223–26, 242, 251–61, 266, 351, 357, 367 n. 1, 375
Notker Labeo: 6
Notre Dame: 112
Nousiainen: 84n, 350, 352–53, 355
Novgorod: 27, 84, 118, 205–06, 330 n. 133, 352, 355 n. 50, 396, 419
Nuremberg: 100
Nyland *alias* Uusimaa: 109

Oddr, son of Katla: 266
Oddrún: 370
Oddrúnargrátr: 369–70
Odenpäh (Otepää): 330 n. 133
Odense: 357
Óðinn *alias* Odin: 143, 145–48, 154, 156, 160–63, 166–67, 180–81, 187–91, 193, 213, 262, 375, 417
Odin: *see Óðinn*
Odysseus: *see Ulysses*
Øresund: 6
Ösel *alias* Saaremaa *alias* Eysýslu: 202, 299, 308, 319, 325, 328
Øystein Erlendsson: 22–23, 46 n. 2, 203
Okulina: 410–12
Olason, Véstein: 13
Olavinlinna (St Olaf's Castle): 205, 209–10
Old Belief sect: 398
Oldman, Gary: 295
Olof Laurinpoika Tolloin: 207
Ommundsen, Åslaug: 3, 29–30
Ong, Walter J.: 175
   Orality and Literacy: 175
On the Origin of Disbelief: 153, 164 n. 75
Orality: 12, 24, 80, 130–34, 175, 192, 214,

250, 256 n. 20
Orkney: 8, 51
Oslo: 224 n. 5
    National Archives of: 45
Ovid: 413 n. 89

Pälkäne: 205
Päntty: 398
Pál Jónsson, bishop of Skálholt: 228, 230
Páls saga byskups: 230
Panchaea: 163 n. 72
Paradise: 348, 418 n. 119, 419
Paris: 21–22, 58, 60, 77–78, 112
    University of: 21, 98
Passion of Christ: 116, 189, 346 n. 8, 392
Passio (et miracula) Olavi: 46, 58–59, 61–62, 87–88, 204
Paulaharju, Samuli: 210
Paul the Deacon: 164 n. 76
    Historia Romana: 164 n. 76
Paulus Juusten, bishop: 116, 118
    Catalogus et successio ordinaria episcoporum Finlandensium: 116, 118
Pērkons: 212
Perttunen, Arhippa: 398–400, 402, 404–07, 409–10, 414, 421, 423
Petrozavodsk: 394
Petrus Cantor: 22
Petrus Comestor: 22, 165
    Historia scholastica: 22, 165
Pharaoh: 325
Philippus Cancellarius: 112
Philistines: 304–05, 332
Phrygia: 162 n. 69
Piispa Henrikin surmavirsi:
    see Ballad of the Death of Bishop Henry
Pilate: 345, 347
Piltz, Anders: 13
Pirinen, Kauko: 351, 354
Plato: 23–24, 28, 144, 174, 260
Pliny: 158
    Naturalis historia: 158
Plutus: 159–61
Pöytyä: 275 n. 15
Pohjola: 207, 285, 355 n. 50, 416
Poland: 7, 68, 88, 275
Polypoetes: 148
Pompey: 160
Poole, Russell: 163–64

Popol Vuh: 420
Postola sögur: 189 n. 53
Prague: 98 n. 75
Priam, king of Troy: 147–48, 154, 162
Priamos: *see Priam*
Propyläen Geschichte der Literatur: 12–13
Pseudo-Clemens: 157
    Homiliae: 157
Pseudo-Matthaeus: 415
Pskov: 314
Psyche: 412, 413 n. 89
Puritans: 228
Pyhtää: 275 n. 15

Quiché Maya Indians: 420

Raab: 301
Räsänen, Elina: 275
Ragnarok: 147
Ragvaldus, bishop of Turku: 31, 117–18
    Ramus virens oliuarum (The Green Branch of the Olive Tree): 31, 110, 113, 116–27, 130, 132
Ranković, Slavica: 3, 33
Rappaport, Roy: 46, 48
Rauma: 275 n. 15
Rautalampi: 210
Redfield, Robert: 3, 22
Red Sea: 325
Reinius, Th.: 115
Reiss, Georg: 60, 63
Reliquiae antiquae: 343
Remus: 413 n. 89
Renfrew, Colin: 176 n. 16
Repola: 398, 412
Rerir, king: 417
Revillout, E.: 361
    Patrologia orientalis: 361
Reykholt: 174
Reykjavik: 5, 175 n. 15, 224–25, 233, 382
    Árni Magnússon Institute: 175 n. 15
Rhineland: 80n, 281
Rhyme Chronicles: 11
    Danish: 1
    Swedish: 1, 32, 206
Ribe: 5
Riga: 21, 34, 298–330
    Lake: 324 n. 112
Romance (genre): 20, 25, 413 n. 89

Romania: 391, 412, 417
Rome: 12, 19, 39, 36, 47, 68, 72, 154,
    163, 166, 281, 286, 299 n. 21, 301,
    315 n. 80, 316 n. 84, 352, 357, 382,
    389, 392, 403
Romulus: 166, 413 n. 89
Rostock: 109
Rothmar, abbot: 297 n. 8
Rühs, Friedrich: 172, 174, 177
Ruotus: *see Herod*
Russia (Russians): 7, 10, 12 n. 19, 32, 34,
    70, 72, 205–06, 210, 314, 321, 328–31,
    391–92, 394, 396–97, 413, 417, 426
Rymättylä: 275 n. 15

Saaremaa: *see Ösel*
Saari (Kirkkosaari): 351
Säästöpankki Savings Bank: 359
Sæmundr Fróði: 177
Saga of the Trojans, the: *see Trojumanna saga β*
Saints:
    Adalbert: 88
    Andrew: 284
    Anne (Ann/Anna/Anni/Annikki/annikka/Annatar): 33–34, 273–290, 417
        Guild of: 280
    Bernard of Clairvaux: 88
    Birgitta: 1, 11, 13, 15, 275
        Visions: 1, 11
    Canute: *see Knut*
    Catherine: 282 n. 47, 284
    Elijah *alias* Ilja: 32, 199–215, 307
    Elizabeth: 274
    Emeric: 88
    Eric/Erik Jedvardsson, king of Sweden:
        31, 70, 86–88, 113, 118–22, 125–26,
        205–06, 208, 342, 351–52, 355, 357
    Eskil: 77
    George: 351
    Hallvard: 51, 58
    Henry of Finland, bishop of Uppsala:
        31, 35, 70–71, 77, 86–88, 113–17,
        121–23, 126–29, 132, 203, 213,
        341–42, 350–62
    Ilja: *see Elijah*
    Jón of Hólar *alias* Jón Ögmundarson: 51,
        230, 384, 386
    Knut *alias* Canute: 13, 357
    Ladislaus: 88
    Lawrence: 26
    Lucy: 282
    Ludmila: 88
    Magnus of the Orkneys: 51
    Margaret *alias* Marketta: 351, 411 n. 82
    Mary *alias* Virgin Mary (Maria, Marja):
        13, 27, 33–34, 36, 114, 128,
        189 n. 53, 212, 274–290, 309, 318,
        320, 369, 389–426
    Michael: 213, 241
    Nicholas: 26, 30, 46, 53–57, 64
    Nicolaus: 211 n. 57
    Olaf: 22, 32, 35, 46, 48, 50–1, 58–64, 91,
        93, 101, 111, 191, 199–215, 352,
        357, 380
    Paul, apostle: 122, 236–37
    Peter, apostle: 26, 113, 121, 210, 273,
        284, 344–45, 349
    Sigfrid: 77
    Stephen: 88, 390–91, 398
    Victor: 58, 60, 63–64
    Vincentius: 60
    Wenceslas *alias* Václav: 88
Salmelainen, E.: 210
Salo, Unto: 202
Salome: 279
Saracens: 288 n. 79
Sastamala: 275 n. 15
Satakunta: 205, 342, 355
Satan: 183–84, 347
Saturn *alias* Saturnus: 143, 156, 159–64, 167
Saturnus: *see Saturn*
Saviour, the: *see Christ*
Savo: 205, 210, 284, 400 n. 37
Savonlinna: 205
Saxo Grammaticus: 1, 13–15, 29, 171
    Gesta Danorum: 171
Saxony: 19, 22, 297, 299, 309, 322–23
Scandinavia: 1, 4, 8–9, 11, 13–16, 26–27,
    35, 46–47, 51, 68–69, 73–74, 77, 81,
    86–88, 98, 113, 148, 155, 171–175,
    179–183, 190, 192, 200–215,
    223–225, 230, 262, 275, 367 n. 1, 368,
    378, 391, 394, 413, 417
Scandinavian (language): *see Languages*
Scania: 21
Scior, Volker: 332
Schmitt, Jean Claude: 296

Schröder, Franz Rolf: 178–79
Sebastian Münster: 133 n. 65
　Cosmographey: 133 n. 65
Second Grammatical Treatise: 150
See, Klaus von: 173, 370 n. 10
Segeberg: 297 n. 8, 299
Selch Jensen, Carsten: 318–19
Selonians: 320
Semigallians: 313 n. 73
Semites: 157, 161
Sennaar Plain: 157
Serbia: 211 n. 56, 250, 257 n. 22, 349, 423 n. 136
Sermon: 2, 28, 33, 71, 88, 133, 153, 184, 185, 187, 225–45, 307, 308, 319, 350, 353
Shakespeare, William: 295
　As you like it: 295
Shetland: 8
Síðu-Hallr: 266, 269
Siegfried, monk: 326
Sigfrid Aronus Forsius: 109, 129
Sigtún alias Sigtuna: 22, 90, 154, 160–61, 169
Sigurðr: 372–73, 375
Sigurðsson, Gisli: 175–76, 179–80, 183, 191
　The Medieval Icelandic Saga and Oral Tradition: A Discourse on Method: 175
Siikala, Anna-Leena: 416, 419, 421
Simon, disciple: 279
Sjögren, A.J.: 392
Skálholt: 228, 230
Skalla-Grímr: 254, 265
Skara: 77
Skarpheðinn: 266
Skúli, Norwegian Earl: 144–45
Slovenia: 417
Snorri: 254, 266 n. 56, 267 n. 56
Snorri Sturluson: 31–32, 143–46, 150–52, 155, 171–93, 200, 202, 254
　Edda (prose Edda): 1, 3, 31–32, 143–52, 162, 166, 171–93
　　Gylfaginning: 145–51, 153, 163, 178, 180, 188–91
　　Prologue: 31, 145–46, 149–67, 173, 188 n. 50
　　Skáldskaparmál: 144–45, 149, 151
　　Háttatál: 144–45
　Heimskringla: 32, 146, 200–02
　　Óláfs saga Helga: 200, 202

Ynglinga saga: 146–47, 174
Society for the Preservation of Ancient Monuments (Fortidsminneforeningen): 224
Sogn: 225
Solomon: 152, 226, 235
Solovki: 397
Sonatorrek: 371, 377
Song of Iro: 415
Song of Marketta: 411 n. 82, 415
Song of Mary, the (song cycle) : 284, 389–93, 296, 400, 401–03, 407, 409–10, 414, 420, 423–24, 426
　Song of the Berry: 390, 393, 396, 398, 407, 419, 415, 421, 425–26
　Song of the Search for a Bathhouse: 390, 398, 412 n. 88
　Song of St Stephen: 390–91, 398
　Song of the Sowing Miracle: 390
　Song of the Search for the Lost Child: 390, 398–99
　Song of the Resurrection: 391, 399
　Song of the Shackling of the Devil (Hiisi): 391, 398–99
Song of the Slaying of Bishop Henry: see Ballad of the Death of Bishop Henry
Songs: 2–3, 23, 29, 25–36, 46, 48, 51–53, 55, 63, 109–10, 112–19, 121–23, 127, 132 n. 63, 133–34, 211 n. 57, 212, 257 n. 22, 342, 346–47, 349–54, 357–58, 362, 367–86, 389–426
　Bulgarian: 405
　Danish: 413 n. 90
　Epic: 257n, 389, 395
　European: 414–15, 425
　Finnish: 362
　Folk songs (folksongs): 132 n. 63, 211 n. 57, 354, 389, 392–93, 407, 411, 413–14, 417, 426
　Izhor: 392 n. 14
　Karelian: 400, 411–12
　Latin: 29, 109–10
　Mourning songs: 35, 367–86
　Romanian: 412 n. 88
　Russian: 413
　Serbian: 211 n. 57, 423 n. 136
　Slavic: 417
Spjótsmýrr: 254
Stafaholt: 174
Sten Sture the Elder: 206

Stephen Langton: 22
Stiklestad, Battle of: 203, 357
Still, Judith, 257
Stjórn I: 158–59, 164–66
Stockholm: 71, 111, 224, 348, 355 n. 50
　Riksarkivet in: 72
St Pére de Chartres Homiliary: 229
St Petersburg: 10, 12 n. 19, 392
Strängnäs: 77, 79
Strerath-Bols, Ulrike: 163
Sturla: 254
Suistamo: 285
Suulaansaari: 398
Svanhildr: 379
Sveinn, farmer: 264
Svendborg: 280
Sven Estridsen, king of Denmark: 6
Sweden (Swedes): 5, 7–11, 13–15, 18 n. 35, 19–20, 22, 26–27, 30–31, 34, 62, 69–73, 76–90, 94–96, 100–01, 109–10, 113, 115, 118, 120, 126–27, 129–30, 145, 147, 154, 161, 180–81, 186–88, 203, 205, 208–09, 230, 232, 275, 282–83, 328, 342, 352, 354–55, 357, 368, 380
Swedish: *see Languages*
Switzerland: 275
Sword Brethren: 303, 306 n. 48, 307 n. 48, 310–11, 321 n. 103
Syria: 304
Sysmä: 275 n. 15
Sørensen, Preben Meulengracht: 5–6, 12–13, 15, 179

Tacitus: 379
　Germania: 379
Taivassalo: 351, 355
Tallinn: 8
Tapani: 390
Tapio: 273, 284–88
Tarkka, Lotte: 124, 284, 408, 410, 416
Taroi: 398, 405, 409
Tartu: *see Dorpat*
Tavastia: 27
Tennyson, Alfred: 256
Tharapita: 319, 325
Theoderic of Treiden: 312, 315 n. 80
Theodoricus Petri: 109, 112, 117
　Piae Cantiones: 109, 11–13, 116–17, 127, 129
Þingeyrar: 230
Þingvellir: 254
Third: *see High*
Third Vatican Mythographer: 164 n. 77
　De diis gentium et illorum allegoriis: 164 n. 77
Tholowa (Tālava): 329
Thomas, apostle: 113, 360
Thomas, Keith: 296
Thomas of Finland, bishop: 22, 77, 90, 98 n. 76
Thor *alias* God of Thunder *alias* Tror: 32, 247–48, 154, 160–62, 166, 178–81, 186–93, 199, 208–11, 213, 262
Þorbjǫrn Noise: 264
Þorbjǫrn ox-might: 254
Þorgeirr Skoargeirr: 266
Þorgerðr: 255–56, 258–61
Þorgerðr Egilsdóttir: 255–56, 258–61
Þorgímr: 266
Þorkell: 202
Thórlakr Thórhallsson, bishop of Skálholt: 230
Þorolfr: 252n, 259, 265
Þorsteinn: 252n, 267–68
Þráinn Sigfússon: 266
Þrúðheim: *see Tracia*
Timonen, Senni: 3, 36
Tinkle, Theresa: 164 n. 75
Toholampi: 115
Törnerus Andreae: 98 n. 75
Tracia *alias* Þrúðheim: 154, 162
Triumphalis lux illuxit: 60
"Trojumanna saga β" *alias* "The Saga of the Trojans": 148, 160–61
Trondheim *alias* Nidaros: 6, 22–23, 45–64, 203–05, 357
　Cathedral of: 22
Tror: *see Thor*
Troy (Trojans): 146–49, 152–56, 160, 167, 188 n. 50
　Trojan war: 147–48
Troyes: 99
Turks: 146–47
Turku *alias* Åbo: 10, 30–31, 68–102, 112–13, 117–19, 204, 275, 280, 342, 350–52, 355 n. 50
　Cathedral of: 98, 117–18, 275, 355 n. 50

Missale Aboense: 100, 208, 350
Tyerman, Christopher: 300
Tyrvää: 205
Tytärsaari: 283

Üxküll (Ikškile): 299, 310, 314 n. 79, 320 n. 99, 321, 326
Ukko: 32, 208–214
Ukraine: 391, 418
Ulfr: 368–69, 379 n. 30
Ultima Thule: 68, 76
Ulvila: 205, 275 n. 15
Ulysses *alias* Odysseus: 256, 258
Ulysses Everett McGill: 256
Undset, Sigrid: 45
Ungannians: 330 n. 133
Unnr, wife of Hrútr: 260
Unnr (Auðr the Deep-minded): 254
Uppland: 181
Uppsala: 5–7, 22, 30, 70, 77, 80, 110, 113, 118, 120, 126, 144, 350, 355 n. 50, 357, 379–80
Uranos: 163 n. 72
Urjala: 275 n. 15, 276
Urne: 223 n. 2, 225
Uusimaa: *see Nyland*

Vadstena: 89, 93–94
Väinämöinen: 211, 403, 415
Väinölä: 355 n. 50
Valla-Ljótr: 259 n. 30, 267 n. 56
Valla-Ljótr saga: 259 n. 30
Vang: 223 n. 3, 224 n. 5
Västerås: 79
Valamo: 397, 401
Valk, Ülo: 323–24
Vargyas, Lajos: 346
Vatnsdæla saga: 251–53, 267
Vatnsdalr: 251
Vesilahti: 275 n. 15
Vezirskaja, Ana: 418
Viborg *alias* Wiborg *alias* Viipuri: 96, 109
Víglundar saga: 252
Viipuri: *see Viborg*
Vincent of Beauvais: 99, 158–59, 165
  Speculum historiale: 99, 158, 165
Vingólf: *see Gimle*
Virgin Mary: *see Saint Mary*
Vironia (Virumaa): 319

"*Viron orja ja isäntä*" *alias* "*The Slave of Estonia and his master*": 129 n. 54
Visby: 22, 308
Vita:
  St Eric's: 88
  St Nicholas': *see John the Deacon*
Vladimir, king: 330 n. 133
Vladimir, prince of Polotsk: 330
Vladimir Propp: 361
Völsunga saga: 417
Vöyri: 275 n. 15
Volsungs: 417
Volucrontes: 147–48
Votes: 393, 398
Votic: *see Languages*
Vries, Jan de: 202
Vulgata: 122n, 123
Vuokkiniemi: 398
Vuola, Elina: 420

Waldia (Valjala): 319 n. 94, 325 n. 115
Ward, Donald: 347
Warner, David A.: 296, 333–34
Weber, Gerd Wolfgang: 154, 173
Wellendorf, Jonas: 3, 31, 214, 252 n. 12
Wends: 202, 309, 349–50
White Russia: 391
Wiborg: *see Viborg*
William of Modena: 299 n. 21, 308 n. 52, 312
Wolaitar: 207
Wolfram von Eschenbach: 6
Worton, Michael: 257
Wright, Thomas: 343

Ymir: *see Hymir*

Zaccheus: 117
Zarathustra: *see Zoroaster*
Zenidba mjesečeva (The wedding of the moon): 211 n. 57
Zeus: 163 n. 72
Zoroaster *alias* Zoroastres *alias* Zarathustra: 143, 156–67
Zoroastres: *see Zoroaster*

MEDIEVAL IDENTITIES: SOCIO-CULTURAL SPACES

All volumes in this series are evaluated by an Editorial Board, strictly on academic grounds, based on reports prepared by referees who have been commissioned by virtue of their specialism in the appropriate field. The Board ensures that the screening is done independently and without conflicts of interest. The definitive texts supplied by authors are also subject to review by the Board before being approved for publication. Further, the volumes are copyedited to conform to the publisher's stylebook and to the best international academic standards in the field.

Titles in Series

Robin Hood in Greenwood Stood: Alterity and Context in the English Outlaw Tradition, ed. by Stephen Knight (2011)

In Preparation

Speaking to the Eye: Sight and Insight through Text and Image (1150–1650), ed. by Thérèse de Hemptinne, Veerle Fraeters, and María Eugenia Góngora